TECHNIQUES OF
CRIME SCENE INVESTIGATION

Techniques of Crime Scene Investigation

by **ARNE SVENSSON**
Chief Superintendent, Director of Laboratory,
Criminal Investigation Department, Stockholm, Sweden

and **OTTO WENDEL**
Superintendent (Ret.), Criminal Investigation Department,
Stockholm, Sweden

SECOND, REVISED AND EXPANDED AMERICAN EDITION, EDITED BY
JOSEPH D. NICOL
Superintendent, Bureau of Criminal Identification and Investigation
Springfield, Illinois

with a Foreword by
O. W. WILSON
Superintendent of Police, Chicago, Illinois

AMERICAN ELSEVIER PUBLISHING COMPANY, INC.
NEW YORK

AMERICAN ELSEVIER PUBLISHING COMPANY, INC.
52 Vanderbilt Avenue, New York, N.Y. 10017

ELSEVIER PUBLISHING COMPANY, LTD.
Barking, Essex, England

ELSEVIER PUBLISHING COMPANY
335 Jan Van Galenstraat, P.O. Box 211
Amsterdam, The Netherlands

Original Swedish Title
Handbok I Brottsplatsundersökning

First edition in English entitled Crime Detection, *published 1955*
Translated by G. MIDDLETON, B.SC., F.R.I.C., LONDON

First printing, 1965
Second printing, 1969
Third printing, 1970
Fourth printing, 1971

The material contained in the second, revised and expanded
American edition was translated by JAN BECK.

International Standard Book Number 0-444-00035-6

Library of Congress Card Number 65-13894

Printed in the United States of America

Preface

Criminal attacks on persons and property occur everywhere, and police in all countries are charged with the detection of the offender and with finding evidence to connect him with the crime. To this end the proper examination of the scene of the crime can play an extraordinarily important role. It is at the scene of the crime that conclusive evidence is to be found and reconstructions are made to establish the nature and severity of the crime; it is also the central point from which all threads will emanate to eventually connect with the criminal. A thorough crime scene investigation is therefore in many cases a condition for the ultimate solution of the crime.

This handbook is devoted solely to the examination of the crime scene and the traces which can be found there. We have intended to establish guidelines for those policemen who are responsible for this difficult and demanding task.

While the technical methods of crime scene investigation are generally the same all over the world, there are still certain variations due to different laws of evidence and criminal procedure. These variations must be considered in order to make the recommended procedures applicable in the country where the manual is to be used. As American readers had shown great interest in the first edition of the book, we asked two American specialists, Joseph D. NICOL and Jan BECK, to prepare a revised edition for use in the United States. Their revision has included the addition of certain sections and the enlargement of others, as well as a consideration of new methods which have been adopted in this special field during the past few years. We are greatly indebted to the American editors for their work and for the enthusiasm which they have shown in the preparation of this new edition.

In turning this book over to its readers we hope that it will be a useful guide in the field of scientific crime detection.

Stockholm, September 1964

Arne SVENSSON
Otto WENDEL

Foreword

Techniques of Crime Scene Investigation is an excellent treatise for introducing police officers, detectives and criminal investigators to scientific crime detection. It is not intended to train lay personnel in the technical aspects of the physical sciences or to make forensic scientists of them but rather to develop an appreciation on the part of the average law enforcement officer of the potentialities of scientific crime detection and to suggest how he can exploit these potentialities to the fullest in his investigation of a crime.

The first two chapters set forth specific rules for the first officer on the crime scene – rules that the investigator should follow in order that the search of the crime scene will be thorough, methodical and revealing. Not every officer appreciates the importance of protecting the crime scene. In Chicago we have created the position of evidence technician and have carefully selected and trained about fifty officers in this specialty so that we will always have enough of them on patrol in every area of the city, round the clock, to respond to any important crime scene within a few minutes. Their cars are equipped with cameras for photographing crime and accident scenes and physical evidence in location at the scene as well as with kits to be used in the search for, collection and preservation of physical evidence and its transportation to the laboratory in an unchanged, uncontaminated form. The evidence technicians are also trained in the use of breathalyzers and carry this equipment with them in their patrol cars to test motorists suspected of driving while under the influence of intoxicating liquor. *Techniques of Crime Scene Investigation* will doubtless become their bible.

The material in the book is logically presented; it is simply stated, understandable and highly readable. It is obvious that the authors have had much in the way of personal experience with their subject matter. Practical field applications of scientific crime detection, such as the search for and preservation of fingerprints, toolmarks, weapons and biological evidence, are fully and interestingly covered and illustrated by anecdotes and pictures.

I commend it as a textbook for law enforcement officers and as reference material for the civil service examiner.

O. W. WILSON
Superintendent of Police,
Chicago, Illinois.

Editorial Introduction

Police investigations are constantly becoming more difficult. The development of new tools of crime detection are matched by the adaptation of new devices for criminal ends. Increased communication between police agencies is equalled by the growing mobility of criminals. New interpretations of the laws pertaining to arrest, search and seizure are making the officer's and the prosecutor's task more complicated. These factors place new demands on the investigator who is now, more than ever, challenged to increased efforts and a more sophisticated approach to crime detection. Crimes can no longer be investigated and prepared for court by the vanishing breed of policeman who is armed only with his wits, his perseverance and a knowledge of local criminals. Crime investigation must be in the hands of policemen with an adequate knowledge of the law, police science, and the art of crime scene investigation. This handbook is specifically directed to the latter effort.

The task of editing this book has been enjoyable and rewarding. The editors have been users and admirers of this manual for some time, and working with this text has only strengthened our regard for the valuable contribution made to police literature by Arne SVENSSON and Otto WENDEL. Based on the latest Swedish edition and the English edition we have endeavored to bring suggested procedures up to date and in closer conformity with American police practice. Some suggested procedures may seem idealized, but a careful analysis will show that they are based on sound practice from which local modifications can be made.

Since this text is intended as a manual for police investigators in the field, we have not attempted to include all the recent developments in the field of instrumental analysis. However, a great number of references to the periodic literature of recent years have been added for the benefit of readers who want to study further the specialized topics.

For their valuable support and assistance in providing new illustrative material we thank Mr. Joseph E. RAGEN, Director, Department of Public

Safety, State of Illinois, and Mr. Charles W. ZMUDA, Chief of Technical Services Division, Metropolitan Dade County Sheriff's Office, Miami, Florida.

J. D. N.

J. B.

Contents

Chapter 1 **Rules for the first officer at the scene**

It is of the utmost importance to the success of the investigation that the officer who first arrives at the scene makes no errors, whether by commission or omission. The actual scene of the crime is the place from which all leads will emanate. It provides the investigating officer with a starting point of the search for the offender and yields important clues for specialists who may arrive later. The first officer on the scene must therefore avoid diminishing or destroying potential clues which may eventually lead to the apprehension of the criminal.

Any officer, regardless of rank or assignment, may happen to be the first officer to arrive at a crime scene. However, the rules for that officer's conduct at the scene are always the same. In this regard, the seriousness of the crime is of minor importance. If he is, in fact, confronted with a location where a criminal can be assumed to have left clues, it is his duty not to destroy or change anything which may serve to reconstruct the crime or which may be useful as evidence against the offender. Nor must the officer inadvertently add material which may be misleading to the investigators.

Obviously, this general rule cannot be applied to cases of petty theft or other misdemeanors. The extent of the preliminary measures must, of course, be in proportion to the type of crime, the location of the crime scene, the availability of personnel, etc. It can happen that a comparatively serious crime is committed in a location where effective safeguarding of the scene is impossible, as for example on a street in heavy traffic. Or, it may not be possible to rope off the scene early enough to prevent evidence from being destroyed. The deciding factor in safeguarding a crime scene under such conditions will be the likelihood that the criminal has left clues and the likelihood that these clues can be recovered. Each case must be decided on individually.

At first glance, the measures to be taken by the first officer on the scene may seem simple and not outside the scope of routine police duties. Some further examination of these duties will show that this is not the case.

First of all, the officer must not approach the scene hastily. Rather, his moves should be calm and deliberate. He should always suspect the worst, and thus take what may seem to be precautions too extensive for the conditions. He should not approach his task with a mind already made up about the crime because this may lead him to carelessness and false moves which may prove disastrous.

Errors committed during interrogation and other aspects of the preliminary investigation can perhaps be corrected, *but errors committed in the safeguarding and examination of the crime scene can never be rectified.* The eventual success of the investigation can thus be completely dependent on the preventive and preliminary measures taken by the officer who first arrived at the scene. Many examples could be given of how an omission or a false move on the part of the first officer proved fatal and resulted in a crime not being cleared up.

In difficult conditions the officer is often faced with problems which put to a severe test his ability to analyze quickly a situation and to take the appropriate steps. But if he follows the basic rule of always anticipating the worst and takes extensive rather than minimum precautions, he should be able to avoid the most serious errors.

As the conditions on crime scenes can vary infinitely, it is not possible to lay down hard and fast rules. However, certain guidelines can be formulated. These are mainly applicable to homicides and other serious crimes because it is in just these cases that the officer is faced with the most difficult tasks and his actions have the most far-reaching consequences. These rules are also basically pertinent to less serious crimes.

Recording the time

Precise notations of time are of great value to the detective officers. They are most important in checking a suspect's story of his actions but can often be quite important in other connections. Therefore, the officer who first arrives at the scene should write down the times which may turn out to be important, for example the time when the crime was committed, when the police officer was first called, when he arrived at the scene, etc. Such notations also lend precision and reliability to the officer's testimony, should he later be called on to testify about his part in the investigation.

Entering the scene proper

When entering the scene the officer should as quickly as possible try to form an estimate of the situation. This estimate is the basis for any appropriate action. When entering the scene proper, or the focal point of events, he must proceed with extreme caution and concentrate his attention upon possible clues which may be found on doors, doorknobs, light switches, floors, etc.

He must make an effort to observe details, particularly those that are transient, and make written notes on such points as:

1. *Doors.* Open, closed or locked? On which side was the key?
2. *Windows.* Open or closed. Were latches closed?
3. *Electric lights.* Were they on or off? Which lights were on?
4. *Blinds.* Open or closed?
5. *Odors.* Was there a smell of cigar or cigarette smoke, gas, powder, explosives, perfume, oil, etc.

Nothing on the scene may be moved unless absolutely necessary for one reason or other because the crime scene must, as far as possible, be intact when the investigating officers arrive. If it should be necessary to recover or to move an object in a public area because it may be disturbed by onlookers, the officer must think of the possibility that it may bear finger prints. Before any object is moved its location must be noted. The exact position of an object may turn out to be of vital importance to the case. Its position can be marked with chalk or noted on a rough sketch. On no condition should the officer walk around the scene and satisfy his curiosity by touching things. There are actual cases recorded where the first officer to arrive toured the scene, leaving his fingerprints on a variety of objects. Such carelessness cannot be tolerated.

Nor should the officer use the toilet, turn on water, smoke, or use towels at the scene of the crime. The criminal may have used the bathroom and used towels to wipe himself or weapons which may have been bloodstained. There is also a possibility that blood may be caught in the sink trap.

The first officer should clearly understand that he may be called on later to account for every move he made on the crime scene. This is necessary for the investigating officers to get a clear picture of the original condition of the scene.

It sometimes happens that complainants or the deceased's relatives attempt to clean up the premises. Such persons would like everything to be in proper order when the police arrive, or they may be trying to conceal the true situation. If such rearranging is in progress at the officer's arrival he should ask that it be stopped. If it has already been accomplished, or if the officer suspects that such is the case, he should make detailed inquiries in order to establish the original conditions at the scene. It is often possible to recover undamaged objects which may have been thrown in the trash.

Murder. A store owner was robbed and badly beaten in his store. He died during transport to the hospital. Immediately after the victim had been removed, and before the scene could be roped off, the owner's wife began cleaning up the store. A considerable amount of blood, including spattered stains, were washed off, and other valuable clues were destroyed. This made the subsequent examination of the scene so difficult that the attack could not be reliably reconstructed. The assailant was caught and confessed, but he was seriously ill and died before the investigation was completed. If the crime scene had been left intact, the detailed events of the murder could certainly have been reconstructed and the investigation speeded up considerably.

Protecting the scene

As soon as possible after arriving at the scene, the officer should take steps to protect the scene from curiosity seekers and family members. He will sometimes have to use some ingenuity because sufficient personnel to block unauthorized entry may not be immediately available. If the crime scene can be closed off by simply locking a door, the solution is given. But usually or generally curious onlookers must be kept outside an area which cannot be restricted by a closed door. In such situations the officer can use ropes, boards or pieces of furniture gathered from some place away from the scene. These arrangements must, of course, not be left unguarded, in which case they would be no protection at all.

The extent of the protective measures must be decided on in each case. A general rule is that if the scene is indoors the barricade should include the central scene and, where possible, the criminal's entry and exit paths. In this connection it is important to focus attention on potential clues on the ground outside a window, in rooms through which the criminal had to pass, in stairways, entrances, etc. If the location is outdoors, an ample area should be roped off to include the path taken by the criminal to and from the central scene. Some of the most valuable evidence is often found on or near this path because the actual crime scene may be so trampled by onlookers prior to the arrival of the police that a search for clues is impossible. In open spaces the barricading can practically only be accomplished if the officer positions himself outside the perimeter or walks around it, seeing to it that no bystanders gain entry. The protection of the scene in this instance merely means that the officer should not walk around aimlessly inside or immediately outside the roped off area. He should limit his movements so that he later will be able to account for his own tracks.

The officer should remain at the scene whenever possible, and should send other persons to call headquarters or investigative personnel. He may leave the supervision of the crime scene to a non-policeman only in exceptional circumstances.

The protective measures at the scene should be taken as early as possible, thus preventing valuable or even vital evidence from being destroyed. It is further essential that the barricades are made extensive enough from the start, because experience has shown that a sufficient area often is not protected soon enough.

When large areas are to be protected outdoors the officer should take the initiative in enlisting the aid of reliable local citizens such as auxiliary police, civil defense or other persons who can be relied on to assume responsibility for protecting the scene.

Injured person on the scene

If an injured person is on the scene he shall, of course, be given first aid immediately even though valuable clues may be unavoidably destroyed. All other considerations must yield when a human life can be saved. If first aid to the injured is not immediately essential, the officer should note the victim's position on a simple sketch or by marking the floor or by forming a mental picture of the position. He should note how the victim is lying or sitting, how he is holding his hands, arms and legs, the condition of his clothes, etc. It is also important to notice if the victim has anything in his hands such as hairs, fibers and the like.

When a doctor or ambulance personnel arrive the officer should – without in any way interfering in their work – instruct them how to enter the scene so as not to disturb it needlessly. He should further observe the actions of the medical personnel and note what objects they moved, where they walked, etc.

If the injured person is moved in an ambulance with non-police attendants, a police officer should accompany the victim. An alert investigator may hear an important word or accusation or what might be equivalent to a *res gestae* utterance that might be the key to the entire case. Some years ago, in a large American city, a dying woman was supposed to have said something – possibly named her assailant – only to have this fall on the untrained, inattentive ears of the civilian ambulance attendants. No amount of interviewing could sharpen their recall.

The officer should arrange for the correct removal and custody of the clothing of the victim. All too often, when the hospital or mortuary is contacted for the purpose of obtaining the victim's garments, they may be incinerated or at best wadded into an almost hopeless mess after being cut or ripped from the body. It would be to the advantage of all investigative agencies to make periodic visits to their local hospitals in order to instruct medical personnel in the proper handling of evidence. The medical profession's prevalent lack of interest in and knowledge of evidence is surprising, considering the otherwise broad scope of their training.

Dead person on the scene

If the first officer on the scene is able to establish certain signs of death, i.e. marked rigor mortis, odor, lividity, beginning decomposition, etc. (see 'Establishing the time of death') the rule is not to touch or remove the body until a detailed examination can be made. In such situations reverence for the dead should not be allowed to interfere with the investigation. Although a homicide investigation is always aided by knowledge of the victim's identity, a search for wallets, calling cards, money belts, 'suicide notes', and the like, prior to an examination and recording of the physical scene by technical personnel can only result in a continuation of the low rate of clear-up of cases involving 'ride' victims and other victims found in outdoor locations.

Summoning of a doctor

Whether a doctor should be called at this point depends somewhat on local ground rules and customs. Actually, it is pointless and may hinder further expert medical examinations to summon a local physician at this stage of the investigation. Occasionally a coroner who is not trained in medicine may have a selected group of doctors who assist him in such matters. Over a period of time, sadly too often by trial and some considerable error, they may develop a certain degree of skill in medico-legal matters. In any case, a cooperative effort on the part of the investigator and the medical group will produce far better results than can be derived from a negative approach.

Where trained medical examiners are available, and where a Medical Examiner's Office is legally established, the medical examiner has prime jurisdiction. He is all the more aware of the benefits to be had from mutual cooperation and understanding and, together with a knowledgable investigator, will form an effective homicide investigation team.

On the other end of the scale the situation will occur where no medical person, of any degree of training, can be induced to take an interest in legal cases. Under these conditions, State or Federal aid might be enlisted. This may require a delay but the result will be worth waiting for in most cases. Each investigative agency should survey its situation in this respect and formulate a plan of procedure and persons to be notified. After notification, the requesting agency should have the courtesy and patience to keep the crime scene intact. Needless to say, it is discouraging and frustrating for an expert to travel some distance in the early hours of the morning only to learn on his arrival that the body has already been moved, cleaned up and embalmed and all that awaits him is a 'cold' crime scene and a bundle of bloody clothing to be transported to the laboratory.

On rare occasions it will happen that the first officer must take immediate steps for the removal of the body. In such situations the officer must see to it that the deceased is placed on the stretcher *in the same position* in which he was dicovered, provided that circumstances permit. Limbs which are fixed in a certain position must not be straightened out. If the victim is found face down, he should not be removed on his back or in another position because the lividity may change position and appearance, trickles of blood may change direction, etc. If the rigidity must be broken in order to transport the body properly, the officer should make notes thereof and preferably make a sketch showing the original position. Before the body is moved its position must be marked on the floor or on a sketch. It is important in this connection that the position of the head, arms, hands, knees and feet be indicated on the sketch. The officer should also note the condition of the clothes and tracks of blood that may be present. The latter can become extremely important in answering the question as to whether the body had been moved. Blood may also run as the body is being removed, and the question may later arise as to how and where this secondary flow of blood occurred.

Suspicious Death. A woman was found dead on the floor in her room. The officer who was called made a superficial examination of the scene. Some of the deceased's relatives stated that the woman had been very ill. The officer had the body removed from the scene without examining the body. He had erroneously been led to believe that the woman had died from natural causes. As the deceased was removed it was discovered that she had died of strangulation. A scarf was tightly wound around the neck three times and was knotted at the throat. A trickle of blood had run over one cheek from the mouth in an upward direction in relation to the position of the head at the time of the brief examination. The continued investigation of this case became very complicated and in some respects impossible due to the officer's premature move in allowing the body to be removed. It was never established whether the blood had flowed during the transportation or before.

In cases of strangulation or hanging where unmistakable signs of death can be observed the officer should do nothing about the deceased. If there is a danger that the rope might break, the officer should attempt to support the body but he should not cut it down. If obvious signs of death are not present the officer shall, of course, take immediate measures to save the person's life. In doing this he should not loosen the knot if it can be avoided. The knot may be of a special kind typical of a certain occupation or the like. Instead, the noose should be cut and the loose ends labeled so as not to be mixed up. Instead of labeling, the ends may be tied together with string or thread. If such materials are not available the noose or rope should be placed so that the officer can later remember which ends belong together. In emergencies the knot may be loosened somewhat and the noose pulled over the victim's head. It is also important to remember which end of the rope had been anchored to a fixed object or pulled over a branch, beam, etc. The direction of distorted surface fibers on the rope may indicate whether the victim was pulled up. It is always possible that a hanging had been arranged to cover up a murder.

Firearms and ammunition on the scene

The general rule is that such objects should be left untouched until the investigating personnel arrives. It can happen, however, that their recovery is essential, for example when they may be inadvertently moved or lost during the removal of an injured person, or where conditions are such that the officer cannot effectively protect the scene alone and bystanders may be expected to disturb the evidence. In the recovery of weapons the officer should also concentrate on the possibility that valuable clues may be found on cartridge cases as well as on weapons. If there is reason to believe that plastic finger prints may be present in oil or grease on the weapon found on a crime scene outdoors in cold weather, it should not be moved to a heated room. The heat may destroy this valuable evidence. In picking up pistols and revolvers *a pencil or a stick should not be inserted in the bore* in order to lift the weapon. Dust, blood, particles of tissue, etc. which may be present in the barrel could thereby be destroyed. Instead, the weapon should be lifted by grasping with two fingers the checkered surface of the grips on which finger prints cannot be deposited. If the butt is provided with a lanyard ring the weapon may be lifted by it. Before the weapon is recovered its position should, of course, be marked on a sketch or on the floor. This marking is of the utmost importance. There may also be a mark in the floor under the weapon indicating that the gun fell from the hand of a suicide; the position of bullets and cartridge cases may reveal the direction of the shot and many times the position of the assailant. The position of hammer and safeties should be noted.

Suspicious death. A dying man with a bullet wound in his head was found in his apartment. A police officer and ambulance personnel arrived and brought the man to a hospital where he was dead on arrival. The officer accompanied the injured person to the hospital, a move that lengthened and complicated the investigation. Detectives immediately began an investigation of the apartment. In the room where the victim had been found and where he apparently was shot, a bullet and a cartridge case were found but no weapon. An automatic pistol was, however, found on a shelf in the hallway. It appeared to have been recently fired. Since the injured man could not have placed it there himself, a suspicion of murder arose immediately. A thorough and time-consuming examination of the apartment was begun. After the officer who had first arrived at the scene had been questioned and the rest of the investigation was completed, the case could be reduced to an ordinary suicide. The officer had found the gun by the victim and without thinking of the consequences he had examined the gun and then placed it on the shelf before he left the apartment. Had the investigators ascertained facts from the first witness – the first officer – before engaging in speculation, much time could have been saved.

Never pull the slide back on a pistol or turn the cylinder of a revolver. Do not touch the trigger or the safety catch. The weapon must be turned over for examination by a specialist in the exact condition it was at the time of recovery, or in certain cases accompanied by a detailed description of what was done to the weapon. Limited alterations on the weapon, such as removing a cartridge from the chamber, marking the position of the cylinder, etc. should only be done by the crime scene investigators.

What to do when a suspect is found at the scene

The first officer to arrive at a crime scene is sometimes faced with the necessity of apprehending a suspect. In such situations he must follow the rule of doing the most important duties first. The officer must use his own judgment in taking whatever measures he can in order to protect the scene. He should charge some reliable person with safeguarding the scene until reinforcements arrive. He must, however, remember to give such persons detailed instructions on how to guard the premises since this is likely to be a strange task for them. While not forgetting to search the suspect's person, the officer should remove the suspect from the scene as soon as possible. This is to prevent the suspect from creating new clues and from observing detailed conditions at the scene.

What to do until the investigating personnel arrives

While waiting for the investigators to arrive the officer need not remain idle. The following general rules should guide his conduct during this time:

1. *Write down names of witnesses and other persons who are known to have entered the scene*. This is important for the subsequent sorting of fingerprints and other clues found at the scene.
2. *Who was at the scene when the officer arrived?* This information can become particularly important if the crime has just occurred.
3. *Establish the basic facts*. A factual account of what happened is of great assistance to the investigators when they arrive because it helps them decide on the next move. However, the officer should *under no circumstances* undertake lengthy and detailed interrogations which may damage later questioning or give rise to suggestions in the statements of witnesses. Furthermore, the officer cannot properly guard the scene if he is occupied with interrogations.
4. *Keep suspect and witnesses separated wherever possible*. If suspect and witnesses are allowed to talk, it may interfere with later questioning. *Family members* may be left in the care of neighbors when necessary, taking care that no alcoholic drinks or sedatives are administered. Remember that the dramatically grieving relative may be your prime suspect.
5. *Instruct witnesses not to discuss the events* so as to prevent distortion by suggestion. If possible, the principal witnesses should be separated. In re-

lating events to each other, the witnesses may distort each other's impressions to the point where they believe that they saw things which they really did not see or which never happened.

6. *Do not discuss the crime with witnesses or bystanders.* This is also intended to prevent suggestion and distortion. Further, broadcasting the details of the crime may hinder the investigation.

7. *Listen attentively but unobtrusively.* An alert officer can often pick up information of vital importance to the investigation.

8. *Protect evidence which is in danger of being destroyed.* During rain or snow, divert water and cover tracks with boxes, cardboard, etc. If the crowd of onlookers becomes large it may become necessary to expand the protective measures at a given location in order to prevent the trampling of evidence.

When the investigating officers arrive, the first officer should report all that he has learned and observed and the action he has taken. This is of great importance to the estimation and planning of the crime scene investigation. It is particularly important that he report the extent to which the scene has been altered, objects have been disturbed or moved, etc.

The continued protection of the scene

In protecting the scene after the investigators have arrived, the officers detailed to guarding the scene should act only on order from the investigator in charge. During the technical examination of the scene it is the crime scene investigator who is in charge of the officers on guard duty as well as the scene proper.

No one is allowed access to the crime scene without the investigator's permission, not even other investigators or superior officers. Command officers would render a fine service to their investigators if they would preserve the integrity of the crime scene with a passion and set an example for other officers. Those officers permitted on the scene must move with their *hands in their pockets.* Through carelessness or without being aware of it, they may touch objects on the scene. Police officers on sight-seeing tours through the crime scene sometimes destroy more good evidence than any body of laymen could possibly accomplish. In one celebrated crime scene, the presence of one more police official would have threatened the collapse of the building. These instructions should apply also to the doctor who is called in cases where death is established. It is a known fact that even experienced investigators are guilty in this respect, especially in cases of murder of other serious crimes. The explanation might be that a desire to do something prompts them to touch objects which should not be touched before they have been examined. The wearing of gloves should not be permitted on the crime scene. There is always a risk that the wearer becomes careless and touches objects which bear the criminal's finger prints, thereby destroying or wiping them out.

Newspaper reporters sometimes arrive at the scene before the officers who are to examine it. They are usually called by persons in the neighborhood or even by ambulance personnel, or they may have heard a call on the police radio. Officers at the scene should under no circumstances give information to reporters. To inform the press is the responsibility of the police chief or officers designated by him. All officers should remember not to favor a certain reporter or newspaper by giving out information which may not be available to his competitors through prescribed channels. This should also be the officer's stated reason for declining to give information. Merely referring to standing orders which prohibit the officer from talking to reporters may be interpreted as misguided zeal or unwillingness to cooperate. In dealing with reporters the officer should be firm but not curt or nonchalant, even when the newspapermen are persistent. He should remember that newspapers often give invaluable help in the investigation of major crimes. However, *press passes should be disregarded during the protection of a crime scene.*

Chapter 2 Rules for the crime scene investigator

The purpose of a crime scene investigation is *partly* to effect a complete reconstruction of events with respect to the sequence of events, method of operation, motive, property stolen, and whatever else the criminal may have done, and *partly* to recover the clues which will serve as evidence against the criminal. In fortunate cases the investigation will yield results which point directly to the offender and provide convicting evidence against him, even before he becomes a suspect. Generally this happens when the criminal's finger prints are found at the scene and his prints are already on file. Such cases are relatively rare, however. The task of the crime scene investigator is particularly thankless because laymen and far too many police officers think that, like Sherlock Holmes, he should be able to magically produce complete information as to the identity of the criminal. If he does not succeed in doing just that, he is considered to have failed. This attitude is, of course, erroneous. It is the duty of investigators and detectives to track and apprehend the criminal. The duty of the crime scene investigator is to gather all evidence available at the scene. Both must give each other the utmost cooperation.

The crime scene investigator must understand that the criminal always leaves some kind of trace and that it is his duty to find these traces and to preserve them so that they may be used in the reconstruction of the crime or as evidence against the criminal. He should not overlook the value of a given item to the reconstruction even though it has no value as direct evidence. He must also understand that an apparently unimportant object or fact may turn out to be extremely important after some time has elapsed. Nothing, however small, must be overlooked. Nothing should be left to chance.

The rules of conduct for the first officer on the scene are also largely applicable to the crime scene investigator. He should proceed with calm and deliberation. He should not approach his task with preconceived ideas, nor should he draw hasty conclusions. He should have his eyes open for details.

Fig. 1 Two investigators at work on a homicide scene. One investigator is measuring while the other is making notes.

He should always suspect the worst and rather do too much than too little, and realize that it is better, at the completion of an investigation, to have done too much than to have overlooked something. A complete investigation may produce information corroborating a confession or refuting a defense contention raised at the time of the trial. He must clearly understand that *mistakes during the investigation can never be rectified*.

The crime scene investigator should not allow a nervous superior or a doctor who has been called in a death case to influence his calm deliberation on the case before he undertakes the actual examination. Nor should he speed up the investigation on their account. They will have to wait, *because the investigator is personally responsible for the mistakes, and therefore he has the right to determine his own actions at the scene.*

If an experienced crime scene investigator is asked to give an account of how he proceeds at the scene he may be hard put to formulate a general rule. This is to be expected since one crime scene is different from any other crime scene. The basic qualities of a good crime scene investigator, however, are *intuition* and an *eye for what needs to be done* in each individual case – in addition to a thorough knowledge of the methods of locating and preserving evidence.

It is therefore not possible to lay down specific rules for the conducting of the investigation. Only a rough outline of the procedure can be drawn in order to suit the infinitely varying conditions. No matter how experienced the investigator is, he will always be faced with new situations and be forced to master completely unfamiliar problems.

Before any actual physical investigation takes place, the investigator should stand at a suitable vantage point on the periphery of the scene and formulate a systematic plan: geometry of search, location of photographs, possible sources of clues, and so forth. After this, he can proceed in the investigation of the crime scene.

The investigation of the scene can be broken down into the following parts:

1. Photography (overall views).
2. The investigation proper (when needed, combined with photography – detail views).
3. Sketching (combined with 1. and 2. – detailed sketches may be required during the investigation).
4. Writing notes. (to be done all during the investigation – constant interruptions for notes are the rule).

Note taking at a crime scene is all too rare in major as well as in minor cases. (For some reason or other there are investigators who seem to hate being caught writing notes. At the office, these officers will amplify a few brief notes scribbled on the back of an envelope into a two- or three-page report). Good, freshly written notes are invaluable at the time of trial. And how frustrating for the officer who receives the assignment of an old open case if there is no record of initial observations by the original team of investigators. There is no substitute for good notes at all phases of the investigation.

It may, of course, happen that the investigator is forced to examine a detail part of the scene or to make a sketch of some object which has to be moved – immediately on arriving at the scene. *Consequently, the order of the various phases must be decided from case to case.*

Another general rule for the investigator is to be *extremely curious* of everything, even the smallest object. The criminal may have forgotten or dropped something. A seemingly innocuous item may later turn out to be the decisive evidence. The investigator should further take a critical attitude and not accept conditions or appearances without first questioning them. The crime may be simulated.

THE ACTUAL EXAMINATION OF THE SCENE

During the entire examination, the investigator should attempt to think through and reconstruct the actions of the criminal. If his reconstruction does not make sense, or if he finds gaps in it, he should go back to the starting point and retrace the process. It is a good idea to proceed by elimination while reasoning: 'He could not have done it this way, nor that way' and so on, until perhaps only one or two possibilities remain.

Always bring a few pieces of chalk in the equipment kit and keep a piece in your pocket at the very start of the investigation. If some object has to be moved, for example to make room for the camera tripod, mark the original position of the object on the floor. If no chalk is available, a pencil or crayon will do.

Unless it is unavoidably necessary, *do not examine a crime scene outdoors until good daylight prevails*. If for some reason the investigation must be done outdoors under artificial illumination, the scene should be kept intact as far as possible for a final survey in daylight. For, no matter how powerful his lighting equipment, the investigator's best assistant is daylight. Experience has shown that *certain evidence which cannot be discerned in artificial light shows up quite clearly in daylight.*

Do not start a crime scene investigation if it is clear from the beginning that specialized personnel will take over the job. The crime scene specialist's task is a difficult one which should not be made more difficult by letting him finish what someone else has begun. He should be permitted to take charge of the crime scene intact. This will guarantee the best possible results.

How many men should work on the scene? The answer is *two, but not more.* One man could carry out the investigation but two men is best, partly because their later testimony will be more reliable. There are cases when the strict rule must be abandoned, however. The crime scene investigator may call on an officer who is an experienced photographer and let him photograph the scene. He should then take on full responsibility for the photographic job. Similarly, the investigator may use temporary assistance in the developing and preservation of fingerprints, sketching, packaging of evidence, etc. This assistance should only be employed on the condition that the helpers are given detailed instructions and are closely supervised.

The two crime scene investigators should preferably be accustomed to working on crime scenes together. In any case they should be able to cooperate. While at the scene *they should not work on separate tasks but as a team*. One way of dividing the work is for one investigator to do the actual examination while the other keeps notes and assists by making his own observations and by helping to examine a particular area. Two persons working together are able to observe not twice as much as a single person but many times more. What one of the investigators discovers he should immediately report to his partner. They also do well to discuss the different possibilities of how a certain clue might have been caused, how the criminal proceeded, etc. What might not occur to one person might well occur to the other.

In cases of homicide and other serious crimes it is important that *the crime scene specialists have no other investigative duties*. They can thus devote their full attention to the scene and get the most out of it. If crime scene work and investigative tasks are combined one of the tasks, usually the crime scene duties will inevitably be neglected. Specialized personnel assigned to crime scene duties should, of course, cooperate closely with the investigating officers. This division of tasks between specialized personnel may not always be possible due to a lack of sufficient manpower. However, the two types of work should be separated wherever feasible.

On arriving at the scene, the crime scene investigator should first of all obtain the basic facts from the officers already at the scene. It is important that the investigator be as well informed as possible about the case before he undertakes to examine the scene. When required he should also make adjustments in the protective measures and instruct the guarding personnel accordingly. He should also note the time of arrival and the weather conditions. Another detail which requires immediate attention is to find out which persons have had access to the scene and whether they have caused any changes in the original conditions there.

When entering the actual scene the investigator should proceed with great caution, keeping in mind potential clues on floors, doorknobs, light switch-es, etc. Even though he has been told that evidence could probably no longer be found on, for example, a doorknob, the investigator should not exclude this possibility at this stage. The investigator should not walk around the crime scene aimlessly. He would do well to exercise the same caution which he himself would expect of inexperienced personnel. He should watch where he puts his feet even if a great many persons have already trampled the scene. While it might be excusable for untrained officers to destroy a clue by inadvertently handling it or stepping on it, it is never excusable for the crime scene investigator.

Before he begins his examination the investigator should stop *to think thoroughly over the case*. This is very important because he may overlook some very significant circumstance if he starts without first having evaluated the situation thoroughly. The investigator should make a complete and systematic survey of the actual scene as well as of the immediate surround-ings, indoors and outdoors. He should attempt to reconstruct the actions of the criminal and constantly ask himself: 'why'? Why did the criminal do this, how did he manage to enter the building, how did he make this mark, etc. Nothing should be allowed to interfere with the investigator's initial reconstruction of the case which is essential if he is to plan his investigation intelligently and get the most out of the scene.

Everything the investigator learns during the investigation should be taken down in writing. Notes should be taken all during the progress of the examination, and constant interruptions should be made for this purpose. The position of an object should be measured and recorded in the notes along with a description of the object, before it is moved or examined in detail. In some cases it might be necessary to make a detailed sketch or a close-up photograph of the object before moving it. The record of the ex-amination should not be edited at the crime scene, but the notes should be made in the order of the various phases of the work. The editing and report writing must be left for completion later. The extent of the notes must, of course, be somewhat proportionate to the seriousness of the crime. A burg-lary will not require as detailed notes as a murder. In the latter case, how-ever, *the notes must be complete enough so that a complete reconstruction of the case could be made even 15–20 years hence*. All objects and details pertinent to a description of the scene must be described. The report of the investigation of a major crime can never be too detailed. The completeness of the report is especially important in those crimes which are not solved within a reasonable time. Rough notes and sketches made at the scene must not be discarded. They should properly be placed in a separate envelope which is included with the case file.

With respect to newspaper reporters, the same rules apply to the crime scene investigator as to the first officer at the scene. In major or sensational crimes the reporters often try to photograph the crime scene, preferably including the officers working there. Do not pose for such pictures unless ordered by a superior officer, or when it cannot be reasonably avoided. A police officer who poses for photographs at a crime scene usually looks ridiculous and only serves the doubtful purpose of satisfying the readers' desire for sensation. Newspaper photographers should not be permitted to photograph the actual crime scene without express permission from the officer in charge.

The investigator should also see to it that the newspaper reporters do not learn of specific clues or conditions at the crime scene which may be essential to the solution of the crime. As a rule, it is only the criminal who profits from reading detailed accounts of discoveries made by the police. Such information should be given to the press only if it would assist the investigation, and only the investigating officer in charge can give permission for its release.

If a doctor has been called, he should be allowed to enter the crime scene whenever an injured person is present or when death has not been established with certainty. The crime scene investigator should nevertheless see to it that the physician does not needlessly destroy clues.

When unmistakable signs of death (rigidity, lividity, odor, beginning decomposition, etc.) are present, the doctor should not be called until the first phase of the investigation has been completed. The physician should, in all cases, be asked to wait until this phase is completed. The investigator should cultivate a good cooperation with the doctor. A smooth cooperation between the two is a requirement for successful completion of the investigation.

A crime scene investigation is characterized by *organization, thoroughness* and *caution,* three essential conditions for success.

After the 'mental reconstruction' of the case, the investigator's first task should normally be to take overall photographs of the central crime scene. (See 'Photographing the crime scene'). When this is finished, the actual investigation should as a rule begin with the central scene, unless the initial survey showed that traces are likely to be found along *the criminal's route* and these traces cannot effectively be protected. If such is the case, these clues should be examined and recovered first. The search of the criminal's route should, however, always start from the central scene.

The central crime scene should be searched beginning, for example, with the floor or a certain area of the floor and then the rest of the room with the door as starting point. The investigator should attempt to work according to a system which will vary from case to case. He thereby runs the least risk of overlooking something. No trace or object, no matter how insignificant it may seem, must be overlooked. The perpetrator may have forgotten or dropped something. The image of Sherlock Holmes at work need not seem strange to the crime scene investigator, although he may employ different methods than this fictional character.

A number of cases will be related in the text in order to illustrate how a curious and alert crime scene investigator found evidence vital to the conviction of the perpetrator or to the exoneration of the innocent.

When a dead person is still on the crime scene, the investigator should not begin with a detailed examination of the body. In doing so he might set aside other aspects of the scene which require earlier attention. Also, the examination of the body might not be as thorough as it would be if the investigator had formed a clear picture of what happened by first examining the whole scene. *Let the detailed examination of the body wait until the basic examination of the scene has been completed*. Important clues may be destroyed if the body is moved before this phase has been completed. If the rest of the scene is examined before the body, the body might yield more valuable information than if the order is reversed. During the initial examination of the scene the investigator may be able to discover facts which were not previously known and which may be of great value in relation to findings on the body. This does not mean, however, that an examination of the body sufficient to suggest mode of death should not precede the crime scene search. Obviously, knowing that the deceased has a gunshot wound would indicate that bullets or cartridges should be sought. Likewise, if considerable time will be consumed in the crime scene search, it would be important to determine body temperature and other factors indicative of time of death.

In many cases it can be of significant value to leave at least the most important objects in their original positions during the investigation. This is most valuable to the reconstruction of the crime because it sometimes happens that a question is raised about a certain item during the reconstruction of events, or the logical steps of the reconstruction do not mesh. When this happens it is of great help to be able to start all over and retrace one's steps. If it seems necessary to the reconstruction of the crime, the body should not be removed in haste but should be left in the original position until a satisfactory record and study has been made. In some instances it would be ideal to leave the deceased even overnight. However, consideration should be given to the availability of a pathologist. If an autopsy can be performed immediately this should take place as soon as possible after the deceased's position has been recorded. However, if the only purpose for moving the body is to place it in storage in a mortuary, this would be a serious error. *Mere consideration of the dead should not influence this decision.* The initial examination by a doctor can be superficial with a later time for closer examination.

The investigator should at the very start select a place as a 'trash pile' where he may put things which should not be lying about the scene. A certain amount of waste normally accumulates during the use of film packs, flash bulbs, blood testing materials, etc. A place is also needed for sharpening pencils, developing finger prints on small objects, handling casting material and dropping cigarette ashes and butts. While it is not proper to smoke at a crime scene, the rule is not inflexible, particularly where the investigator is forced to work for a long period of time. Such a trash collecting point should be located as far as possible from the central crime scene. It might be started by spreading a newspaper, placing a dinner plate on the paper and marking the location.

As to the special methods of detecting, preserving and evaluating evidence found at the crime scene, the reader is referred to subsequent chapters which deal with methods used at different kinds of crime scenes.

Chapter 3 The doctor's participation in the investigation

In the preceding chapter the first officer to arrive at the scene was advised not to summon a doctor if unmistakable signs of death are present; further, the crime scene investigator should not call the doctor until the preliminary phase of his investigation is completed.

These principles, as explained below, are intended as an ideal and are subject to local practice and ground rules. Obviously, any other scheme that has been found successful in many cases over a long period can be pursued. However, if years of practice do not support a different method, it cannot be defended against the logic of the following procedure.

Application of these rules will insure that nothing is disturbed on the scene before the investigators arrive and that they will be able to preserve those clues most likely to be destroyed. There seems to have developed a rule among some officers, whenever a body is found in suspicious circumstances, to call a doctor to confirm that the victim died as a result of homicide. This is an erroneous procedure. As soon as there is reason to suspect homicide, the place where the body was found should be sealed off and examined as if the death was due to criminal action.

If, at the outset of the investigation, a physician is called who is not familiar with the requirements of criminal investigation, irreparable damage can be caused by his movements on the crime scene. If, instead a medical examiner or a medico-legal pathologist is called, no harm is done from the investigator's point of view. A medico-legal pathologist is fully aware of the importance of clues on the crime scene and will avoid entering if he can determine from a distance that death has occurred. By calling the pathologist too soon, however, he is forced to wait unnecessarily, perhaps for hours, while the initial phase of the investigation is completed. This should be avoided since the pathologist is usually a very busy professional. If there is any doubt that death has occurred, a physician should be called immediately and given access to the crime scene.

In such cases all other considerations must be set aside. Duties of the police officers during the doctor's presence at the scene have been outlined above.

From what has been said, the rule should be for the first officers to *let the investigators call the physician*. This tends to eliminate the inconvenience to both parties.

Through medical examiners and some coroner's offices assistance is provided to the law enforcement agencies by pathologists specially trained in investigating crimes of violence. Unfortunately, such specialists are not available to the extent which is desirable. Ideally, the pathologist who is later to perform the autopsy of the body should be present during the investigation of the crime scene. He should be informed of the findings which have come from the technical investigation. This is important not only because the pathologist will be able to give an early opinion as to the time of death, as to what could have served as murder weapon, etc. The investigator's observations, moreover, help the pathologist in forming a complete picture of the case.

The desire to have the pathologist partake of the findings at the crime scene does not negate the rule of not calling the doctor before the first phase of the investigation. This phase consists of a time-consuming evaluation, photography, sketching, and preservation of evidence which might be destroyed. All these findings are reported to the pathologist upon his arrival. Further, the investigating officers are thereby not rushed, which is essential to insure that they do their best work.

Whenever the pathologist is unable to be present until perhaps the following day, the investigation of the scene should of course not be postponed in order to give the pathologist an opportunity to take part. In such cases, and wherever emergency measures are required which will alter the conditions, such as in traffic, the pathologist should be given a detailed account of the findings at the scene. He should also be given an opportunity to view the scene accompanied by one of the officers.

The investigating officers and the pathologist should not work independently of each other. Their tasks complement one another, and together make up a complete reconstruction of the crime. They should be expected to understand each other's methods of examination and to exchange their observations. *Investigators should therefore, on their part, be present at the autopsy to learn of the findings on the body*. The pathologist and the crime scene investigator should establish a close working relationship and discuss the case in terms of their own separate observations. This may bring out significant details which might otherwise have escaped their attention.

The question naturally arises as to who should direct the crime scene investigation. *Direction and responsibility for this task must be assumed by the police officer*. This is as it should be if one considers the highly specialized crime detection techniques which are required for successful results. This rule should not, however, be interpreted so strictly as to prevent cooperation. If both parties consider the duties and methods of the other, misunderstandings can be eliminated.

Professor Einar SJÖVALL of Lund, Sweden, has devoted two chapters of his book 'Legal Medicine' (1946) to the topic of crime scene investigation. In the opinion of the authors, this authority has very succinctly stated the guidelines for cooperation between the medical examiner and the police officer. His opinions are based on many years of experience, and the authors take the liberty of quoting some of these:

'Even the physician who is familiar with this kind of work can, in many instances, contribute observations and conclusions from his own field of work. He should therefore take part in the investigation whenever his knowledge might further it, but the work should be clearly delineated between the medical officer and the policeman. This division guarantees that no essential examination is overlooked because one expected the other to take care of it. It is also clear that they should understand each other's working methods and share their observations.'

'The first rule of crime scene investigation is that nothing must be moved or disturbed. This also applies to the body, except in those instances where its removal is necessitated by special conditions, for example, traffic.'

'It sometimes happens that the physician is called for purely medical purposes by the persons first to arrive. He is called on to confirm the death, or when this is not clearly established, to take the necessary steps to keep the victim alive. In the latter case the physician obviously has the right to enter the scene. But when one can determine that death has occurred (observable signs of post-mortem changes), from some distance away, even the physician should not enter the premises before the investigating officers'.

'Identification of the person and establishing the time of death could be considered as preliminaries to the main phase of the examination, the purpose of which is to reveal the circumstances under which the death took place. Also, in this respect the physician is able to cooperate, although the investigation is a principal task of the police officers and should be directed by them.'

'When criminal action is suspected, the tracing of the criminal's actions on the scene becomes a very important part of the investigation. The person who examines these traces must always be a policeman. In view of the professional skill which he must possess for this investigation it is solely his responsibility to observe marks which could have been caused by the offender; finger prints and prints of feet and shoes. It is likewise his responsibility to preserve and to analyze these personal clues. The participating physician can only be expected to be aware of the value of these observations, to know where marks of this type are likely to be found, and to meticulously avoid disturbing or destroying such clues.'

It is not only at the crime scene that the police officers can get valuable help from the pathologist. During the examination of a suspect's person, or of an assault or a murder weapon, the pathologist can make important observations which may even be decisive in clearing up the crime. It is essential, however, that the pathologist be given a detailed description of the case on which to base his conclusion – whenever he has not personally been present during the crime scene investigation. During the autopsy the pathologist can also in many cases determine how certain injuries were caused on the body by means of a particular weapon or object. He can also give his opinion on whether an object used during an assault can be considered a dangerous weapon. As concerns the examination of suspects, the physician should be asked to assist in taking samples of blood, hair, saliva, urine, excreta, and to search for hair, blood or sperm on the suspect's body or objects which he may have swallowed or otherwise hidden on his person.

Chapter 4 **General Instructions**

DESCRIPTION OF THE CRIME SCENE

As previously mentioned, the notes which are made at the crime scene should be made in the order of the various phases of the examination. These notes should be as complete and legible as possible so that there will be no doubt as to what was meant. Even negative conditions should be noted, such as the absence of bloodstains at a given location or the fact that the light was not turned on, etc. Vague expressions such as 'near' or 'to the left of' should not be used. The investigator should instead select fixed points from which compass directions and exact measurements are given. Sometimes two measurements are required in order to fix the location of an object, e.g. 'on the north wall, 18″ east of the window and 55″ from the floor.'

Notes made at the crime scene should never be discarded but placed in the case file after the final report has been written.

After the crime scene investigation is completed, the notes are rewritten into a report. This report should be clearly written and detailed. The narrative sequence should describe the scene to the reader from the outside inward. The exterior is described first, followed by the central scene and the detailed descriptions. Sketches and photographs should be referred to where necessary.

A suitable outline of the report of a homicide investigation might be:
1. When was the discovery first reported to the police?
2. Who ordered the investigation of the scene?
3. A brief description of the crime or event which led to the investigation.
4. Who conducted the investigation of the scene? Who took the photographs and made the sketches?
5. When did the investigation begin and end?
6. What persons or how many persons were present at the scene at the start of the investigation?
7. Weather conditions (rain, snow, freezing, etc.) at the time of the offense and at the time of the investigation, as it affected the investigation.

8. The location of the scene and the community, in relation to larger communites, roads, rivers, forests, etc.
9. The location of the scene; distance to nearest house.
10. Conditions at the scene.

    A. *Inside:* description of the house (number of entrances, rooms, windows, etc.) See 'Detailed examination of the scene', Ch. 12.

    B. *Outside:* detailed description of the terrain (vegetation, type of soil, etc.).
11. Description of the body and the detailed findings at the scene.
12. The conclusions of the investigator, stating specific clues and conditions as reasons.

    It is actually debatable whether the investigator should put his conclusions in the report. An old rule states that the investigator may draw his own conclusions but should not put them in writing. There is, however, little doubt that the conclusions of the officer will be of great help to the readers of the report. There is always a risk that a person who reads a lengthy report containing a lot of details will overlook significant points. The officer in charge should decide whether the crime scene investigator's conclusions should be included in the report.
13. The results of search for finger prints (number of prints recovered, whether glove prints were found, etc.); an account of all other evidence and objects recovered; which objects were submitted to the laboratory for further examination, and where the remaining evidence is kept.
14. An account of measures taken regarding the body (finger prints, finger nail scrapings, examination of the clothes, etc.).

The crime scene report should be signed by the officers who conducted the investigation.

SKETCHING THE CRIME SCENE

By sketch is meant a drawing which represents the scene of the crime. The commonly accepted meaning of sketch is a rough outline, but this does not describe a police sketch. It should be drawn to scale and be so accurate that exact measurements can be made on it. In exceptional cases the sketch may be based on estimated or paced off measurements, in which case the basis for measuring should be clearly indicated. The great importance which is attached to the crime scene sketch can be appreciated in major criminal trials.

The police type of sketch, or drawing, can fall in the following categories: projection, perspective, schematic and detailed drawings.

The *projection* drawing is the type most frequently used. It is so commonly used that the designation 'projection drawing' need not be entered on the drawing. The projection drawing is a picture wherein all places and objects are drawn in one plane, as seen from above. It can also be done in the form of a *cross-projection* drawing wherein the walls of a room are seen as folded out into the same plane as the floor. This type of drawing is employed to illustrate the interrelation between objects in different planes.

The *perspective drawing* may be used when no camera is available. It can also be used when a demonstrative photograph cannot be made, such as a house which is hidden behind trees and shrubbery.

The *schematic drawing* is used to illustrate an event, for example the various phases of a traffic accident or the path of a bullet through a wall or through an article of furniture.

The *detail drawing* is usually an enlarged area of a portion of the projection drawing and is made when the scale of the main drawing does not permit showing small details in a great number.

The most suitable scale for a drawing is $1:50$ (or $^1/_4''$ equals $1'$). Other scales may be used, but they should not be so small that details become cramped and too close together for clarity. Drawings of larger areas, for example showing the criminal's path to and from the scene, may be drawn to a scale of perhaps $1:1,000$.

The measurements should be made very carefully at the crime scene. The usual method is to make a rough sketch on which the dimensions are noted. These measurements are later transferred to the final drawing. The rough sketch should not be discarded but should be kept in the case file.

The rough sketch from the crime scene is drawn in finished form in pencil on white drawing paper of the same size as the written report. If there is not room on one sheet of paper, it should be drawn on a larger sheet which is then folded for inclusion in the report. The drawing should be oriented so that the arrow indicating north should point generally upward. The drawing is then finished in black drawing ink. The legend is lettered in or typewritten.

In the drawing proper there need be no other text than the designation of the rooms or the street names. All other markings are in the form of numbers which refers to a legend. In a drawing of a single room, the identification of the various objects may be written along the margins with lines drawn to the respective objects. These lines must, however, be drawn in a different color so as not to confuse the actual details.

Photographs taken at the scene may be identified on the drawing by means of small circles with arrows pointing in the camera direction. The designation of the photographs, 'A', 'B', etc., are drawn in the circles.

The drawing should be identified by a heading and a scale. It should be dated on the day the measurements were made and signed by the officer who made the drawing.

Although the crime scene rough sketch may contain the location of evidence such as the body, bloodstains, etc., there are valid reasons for not including these in scaled drawings which are to be used as courtroom exhibits. The rough sketch should include all pertinent physical items; furniture, windows, doors, location of evidence, each item measured as found. When a scaled drawing is presented in court, it is advantageous for this to be one of the first acts of the prosecution. Witnesses can then place themselves at the crime scene by referring to the scaled drawing. If only the necessary furniture is included, prosecution and defense can speedily accept the drawing. However, if items of evidence are included, i.e. items that must be connected by later testimony, or items which may be excluded, the early acceptance of the scaled diagram may be in jeopardy.

The execution of a scale drawing requires a minimum of engineering or drafting skill but does not require the services of an architect. Like any other testimony, the investigator must be prepared to be cross-examined on his qualifications and the accuracy of his work. If necessary skills are lacking, a draftsman can prepare a drawing from the investigator's rough sketch and the scaled drawing can sometimes be presented by the investigator as having been prepared under his supervision.

PHOTOGRAPHING THE CRIME SCENE

Before any detailed examination is undertaken of the scene, it should be photographed. The photographs should illustrate the appearance of the scene and, when required, the path of the criminal to and from the scene. Detail pictures should as a rule also be taken, for example of injuries on a

Fig. 2 A good example of a crime scene photograph showing important objects: the gun, the overturned ash tray and the bullet on the mat.

(Metropolitan Dade County Public Safety Department)

body, bloodstains, a weapon, etc. Insofar as possible the pictures should be taken so that they can be arranged in a series which illustrate the events of a crime in logical sequence. In a homicide, the following series of photographs might be appropriate: 1. overall view of a village (showing the murderer's way to the house); 2. exterior view of the house at the edge of the village (the scene of the crime and the criminal's path); 3. a room photographed from different directions including pictures of the body; 4. close-up views of the body; 5. detail views of injuries on the body; 6. detail picture of blood stains; 7. detail view showing an axe; 8. a view of another room in the house; 9. close-up of a desk in that room; 10. detail view of tool marks in this desk; 11. overall view of the house and a portion of the surrounding area (showing the fleeing murderer's path and the place where he was stopped), and 12. exterior view of the house as seen from the point of view of an eyewitness.

The photographs cannot, however, be taken in the proper sequence. Usually the pictures of the central scene are taken first and the exterior pictures last. The officers responsible for the investigation of the scene

Fig. 3 Same scene as shown in Fig. 2: close-up of bullet on mat.
(*Metropolitan Dade County Public Safety Department*)

should take the photographs themselves. When this is not practical, a specialist officer or a professional photographer may be employed who should work under direction from the investigators.

Most crime scene photographs are taken in black and white. However, in view of the technical advances made in color film, color photographs are being used increasingly for crime scene illustrations. There is little doubt that color photographs in many instances depict a scene or an object more realistically and 'as it appeared to the officer' than black and white photographs. The investigator should therefore familiarize himself with the techniques of color photography and apply it wherever it would serve the purpose of accurately illustrating conditions at the scene.

Another valuable aid to crime scene illustration is aerial photography. In major crimes, one or more aerial photographs will often depict a large area in a way which ground-level photographs combined with drawings could not. In the series of pictures outlined above in a homicide case, the overall views showing the assailant's way through the village could very well have been demonstrated in aerial photographs. Although none but the largest police departments have aircraft or helicopters, the services of aerial photographers are available in most communities. The investigators should therefore not hesitate to request aerial photographs whenever they would be useful.

Photographs of the crime scene should illustrate details which are pertinent to the case. The photographs need not be beautiful as long as they serve their purpose. Each view should preferably be exposed twice. One exposure could be faulty without the photographer noticing, and it is therefore useful to have another exposure as reserve. *It is a good rule to make an excess of photographs rather than too few.* Unimportant exposures can be sorted out later.

Notes should be made concerning the different exposures so that each photograph can later be identified as to time and place and exact location of the camera. The camera location should be marked on the rough sketch of the scene.

Either photoflood or flash illumination may be used for indoor photographs. Photoflood illumination is, however, safer in that the picture may be previewed on the ground glass before exposure. A tripod or other steady support is absolutely necessary if accurate, sharp pictures are to be taken. Focus, depth of field, area included, probable distortion, and unwanted shadows and glaring highlights can be studied on the ground glass and appropriate steps taken to insure correct results. Although genius and artistic ability are not necessary, careful technique is essential. No amount of apologies will recover a missed or poor picture. Since the conditions at the scene should not be altered, it may be necessary to take pictures of obstructed subjects in two parts: first with the obstruction in place and then with

Fig. 4 Photograph of a crime scene outdoors from ground level.
(*Metropolitan Dade County Public Safety Department*)

Fig. 5 Aerial photograph of the same crime scene as shown in Fig. 4. Orientation of the car to roads and canals is now readily apparent.
(*Metropolitan Dade County Public Safety Department*)

the obstruction lifted or removed. If an object is known to have been moved, it should be photographed as found. It should then be replaced in its original location and photographed again.

It is sometimes necessary to mark the location of an object which is too indistinct to be noticed in the photograph. This is usually the case with crime scenes outdoors, particularly in wooded areas. Special markers, consisting of cardboard or metal discs bearing numbers, should be used for this purpose. They should be affixed to stakes which are set in the ground at the required locations. The stakes should preferably be painted so that they will show up in the photograph in order that the marker not be seen as hovering over some indeterminate spot. The markers should not be used in indoor photographs where they may confuse the appearance of the scene. If necessary, such markings can be made directly on the finished print. Minute details may also be marked by drawing on the object with chalk or by placing cardboard arrows to indicate the detail. The area should, however, be photographed both without and with markings.

A dead body should be photographed from several different directions. One exposure should also be made directly from above. If conditions do not permit such a photograph, two or more pictures may be taken from above showing the head and chest in one picture and the trunk and legs in another.

Close-up photographs of details should as a rule *include a small scale which is placed next to the object, especially in pictures of injuries, tool marks and bullet holes.* Because of limited depth of field in close-up pictures, a tripod and a camera with ground glass focusing will insure good results.

In photographing tire tracks, photographs should first be taken of the tracks as found. The impressions are then dusted with a suitable powder (red lead on snow, ice or very light soil, otherwise dry plaster) and photographed again. Tracks of rolling wheels, braking marks and skid marks may be marked in different ways, for example by dots, dashes or solid lines. The pictures should be taken with the camera at eye level and from different directions and, where possible, from a position as high as possible to include the whole area.

All crime scene photographs should be printed in a size no smaller than 4×5 inches. It was mentioned above that an excess of pictures should be taken. This advice was intended as a safety precaution. The photographs which are attached to the crime scene report should not be too many in number, since they may have a confusing effect. Instead, a sufficient number of views should be selected which clearly illustrate conditions at the scene. They should be arranged in a logical sequence and be given letter designations. They should be mounted (pasted) on to paper of the same kind as the report. If a clarifying caption is required, it should be written under the photograph. Details which are difficult to see should be marked by writing a clarification in the margin and drawing a line to the detail in red ink. The lines should not interfere with other details in the picture.

PACKAGING AND SHIPPING OF EVIDENCE TO THE LABORATORY

Evidence which is to be sent to a laboratory for further examination should be packaged in such a way that it does not run the risk of breaking, spoiling or contamination which might destroy its value as evidence.

Containers should be *tight* and, depending on the nature of the material, *strong* enough that they will not break in transit.

If the evidence consists of several objects they should be packaged in separate containers or wrapped individually in paper. Each item should be clearly marked as to contents and then packed in a shipping container. Loose evidence is thereby kept from contaminating other evidence. In some cases it may be necessary to fix articles to the container separately so as not to come in contact with each other. *Bottles and other* glass vessels which contain liquids should not be packaged with other evidence, since they may break and contaminate the other material.

If *excelsior or other wadding is used* as cushioning material, all objects which would be altered by contact with this material should be separately and tightly wrapped.

Even though objects may have individually identifying markings, such as serial numbers, they *should be marked with the recovering officer's initials and date so that the identity of a given object cannot be questioned*. The markings may be placed either directly on the object, on a tag attached to the object or, when this is not practical, on the sealed container of the object. It is also useful to place a seal on the final package so that the shipment will reach the laboratory expert intact. The latter should always be done with evidence from serious crimes.

A complete inventory of the items submitted and *a request for examinations to be performed* should be included with each shipment. The inventory enables the expert to check the contents so that a small object among many items is not lost or overlooked. The request for specific examinations enables the laboratory to begin examinations, even though the written request has not yet arrived.

The written request to the laboratory should always contain as complete information as possible about the case (sequence of events, statements of the suspect, the victim, witnesses, etc.). This facilitates the expert's evaluation of the extent of necessary examinations and of the techniques required. This information may also provide answers to questions which come up as a result of the laboratory's findings or provide confirmation of findings which necessarily went beyond those specifically requested. It is helpful to include copies of pertinent police reports or interrogations.

In the following paragraphs are given instructions for the packaging of selected types of evidence. (See also individual headings for various types of material found at crime scenes).

Objects bearing *finger prints or glove prints* should be packed so that they do not come in contact with each other or the package sides.

Original tool marks should be protected from contamination and moisture. Marks may be protected from rust by a light film of oil, if transfer of trace material is not indicated.

Fig. 6 An evidence bullet carelessly marked in the region of the rifling impression. Valuable evidence was thereby destroyed. Bullets should be marked for identification on the base and cartridge cases on the side, near the mouth.

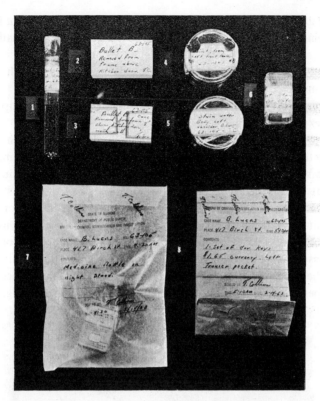

Fig. 7 Suggested methods for sealing and labeling evidence containers. Sealing wax, gummed labels or transparent tape may be used to insure containers against tampering. Small objects to be processed for finger prints are best enclosed in a glassine bag (7). Fine evidence such as paint and soil should be placed in tight containers (1, 4, 5 and 6).

Clothing containing dry stains of blood, seminal fluid, etc. should be wrapped separately and in such a way that the stains are not broken or rubbed off. The part of the garment which is stained may be attached to a piece of cardboard which is then fixed to the bottom of a cardboard container. If several garments are submitted, they may be fixed separately in compartments built inside the container.

In cases of sexual attack the victim's clothing must not come in contact with that of the suspect.

Garments bearing hair should not be allowed to come in contact with other garments which may contain hair.

Firearms should be rigidly fixed inside a wooden container without further wrapping. Postal regulations should be consulted before mailing firearms.

Cartridge cases and bullets should be packed separately and with soft cushioning material.

Loaded cartridges should be packed to protect finger prints and shipped by railway express.

Stomach contents or other organs for toxicological examination should be placed in tightly sealed glass jars which are packed in cushioning material. The containers should be of a size proportionate to the amount of fluid, so that volatile agents do not evaporate.

Sleeping tablets and the like should be tightly cushioned in vials or pill boxes so that they will not break. Sterile absorbent cotton should be used.

Charred paper should be packed in strong boxes and supported on all sides with absorbent cotton. The container should preferably not be shipped but should be hand-carried to the laboratory. It is also possible to place the charred paper in a large plastic bag which is blown up and sealed tightly.

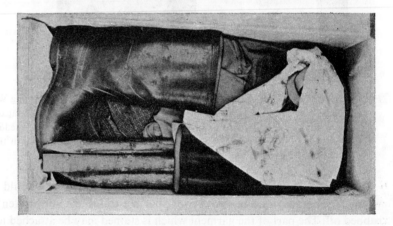

Fig. 8 Faulty packaging of evidence for transmission to the laboratory. Hair, blood and fibers could easily be transferred from one object to another, all of which should have been wrapped separately.

Chapter 5 Finger prints and foot prints, impressions of clothes, teeth, etc.

Among the most valuable clues at the scene of a crime are finger and palm prints. Such prints are strong evidence. The report made by the expert after his examination either contains the decision that the print *was* or *was not* made by the suspect, or the statement that the print is *not identifiable*. The value of finger prints is greatly increased by the possibility of tracing a criminal by searching through the single finger print file.

In the continuation of this section the term 'finger prints' includes all types of prints of friction ridges. Prints of the palm of the hand and of the sole of the foot are made under the same conditions as finger prints, and are preserved in the same manner as the latter. It is often difficult to decide whether a print has been left by a finger, the palm of a hand or the sole of a foot. For this reason, in ordinary speech the term finger print has come to include also prints of the palms or feet.

How do finger prints occur?

When the criminal works he cannot avoid leaving clues in the form of finger prints, unless his hands are covered with gloves or some other form of protection. Prints may be produced when he takes hold of some object, or supports himself with his hands. Generally prints are formed from the friction ridges, which deposit grease and sweat on the object touched. It may also happen that the fingers are contaminated with foreign matter, e.g., dust, blood, etc., or they may press against some plastic material and produce a negative impression of the pattern of the friction ridges.

Where should finger prints be looked for?

In a case of burglary, the investigation should commence at the place where the criminal made his entry. Generally it is possible at that point to determine whether he worked with protected hands or not. In the case of a door which has been broken open, prints are looked for on the lock or its immediate surroundings, or at any place where entry was forced. With regard to windows, special attention should be given to searching for pieces of broken glass. The method of breaking in through a window is generally by knocking a small hole in a pane of glass so that it cracks, after which the criminal breaks away pieces of glass with his fingers until he has succeeded in making an opening large enough to enable him to reach the window latch. Almost always there are, on the broken pieces of glass, prints either of fingers or of gloves or other protection. The broken pieces do not always lie just inside the window – the criminal often throws them away or conceals them. When climbing in through the window finger prints are left on the inside of the window sill, the frame and jamb, from a firm grip on those parts.

A good rule is that the police officer searches for finger prints as quickly as possible at places where the burglar may have taken food or drink. Finger prints on glass or china are generally good ones. If the criminal has discovered and drunk liquor, a satisfactory result may be expected from the search. There have been cases of breaking-in where the burglar had his hands protected at the start, but gradually became intoxicated, forgot all caution, and took off his hand coverings. If bottles of liquor have been taken away from the place, prints may be found on glass or china which has been moved out of the way or on bottles which have been examined by the thief.

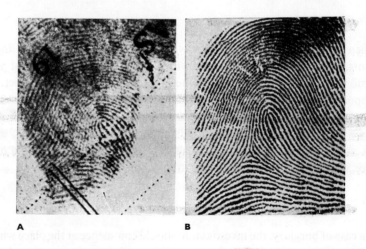

A   B

Fig. 9 The left-hand photograph shows the enlargement of a finger print found on paper used by a burglar. Photograph B shows the finger print taken from file.

Where there is electric light the switch and fuses should always be examined, and also any lamps which have been loosened or removed.

If it is possible, at an early stage, to decide that the criminal worked with his hands protected, special care should be taken at places where his activity was of such a type that a hand covering would be a hindrance, for example, when opening a case or drawers with stiff locks, searching in the drawers of a bureau, etc. It is a common weakness of thieves that they generally remove their hand coverings too early after leaving the scene of the crime, and leave finger prints for example on the banisters. If the thief has relieved himself (as often happens) he may have removed the inconvenient hand coverings. Finger prints should therefore be looked for on the handle of the toilet, the lock of the door, on paper used, etc. On objects which the criminal has brought and forgotten there are good prospects of finding finger prints: paper used for wrapping tools, flashlights (including the battery), etc.

All smooth surfaces on which prints could be left should be examined. The best prints are found on glass or china, on objects with polished, painted or otherwise smooth surfaces, and on smooth cartons and paper. Under favorable conditions a print may be found on rough surfaces, on starched collars, cuffs, newspapers, etc. When examining furniture one should not omit places which the criminal may have touched when pulling out drawers, moving furniture, etc. Even if the thief worked with protected hands he may have left prints when, for example, he moved a heavy piece of furniture. The gloves may have slipped, or they may have been so open at the wrist that a small part of the palm left a print.

In looking for finger prints a flashlight is generally used, as they can be seen best in obliquely falling light. If it is expected that prints should be found at a certain place, but they cannot actually be discovered, the place must be examined by special methods which are described under the heading 'Latent finger prints'.

During the investigation the police officer should not wear gloves, but must accustom himself to work in such a way that he does not leave his own prints. If he wears gloves there is always the risk that he may become careless and destroy prints left by the criminal. Further, it may happen that the scene has to be re-examined by a police officer who is more familiar with such matters, and if the latter finds glove prints which were made in the first investigation he may easily be misled.

Should an officer accidentally deposit finger prints, this fact should be recorded so that they may later be eliminated from the relevant prints.

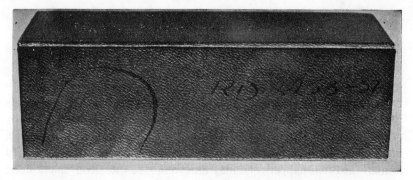

Fig. 10 Finger print on rough carton taken in ordinary light.

Fig. 11 The same carton photographed in 'specular' light shining against the observer or camera lens.

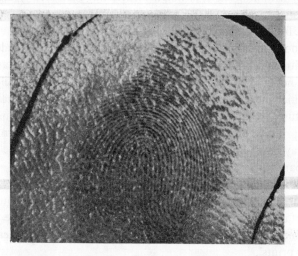

All prints at the scene of a crime should be preserved, even if they can be assumed to belong to the people of the house.

Different types of finger prints

Finger prints can be divided into three main groups: 1. plastic finger prints; 2. prints of fingers contaminated with some foreign matter; and 3. latent finger prints.

1. *Plastic finger prints* occur when the finger touches or presses against a plastic material in such a way that a negative impression of the friction ridge pattern is produced, Such a print may be found in paint on a newly painted object, in the gum on envelopes and stamps, on substances which melt easily or soften when they are held in the hand (for example chocolate), on adhesive tape, in thick layers of dust, plastic explosives, putty which has not hardened, wax which has run from a candle, sealing wax; in edible fats, flour, soap, thick and sticky oil films, grease, pitch, tar, resin, clay, etc.

Fig. 12 Finger impression in putty.

2. *Prints of fingers contaminated with foreign matter*. The commonest type is the dust print. When a finger is pressed in a thin layer of dust, some of the dust sticks on the friction ridges. When the finger is subsequently placed against a clean surface, a finger print results which in a favorable case is fully identifiable and may even be so clear that it may be searched in a single-finger print file. Similarly, a print can be left when the finger is contaminated with other substances, for example pigments, ink, soot, flour, face powder, oils, certain types of safe insulation, etc. Finger prints in blood are generally indistinct and less usable for identification purposes.

In general, the prints first made are completely filled up, but if the same finger makes several prints in succession the last one may be identifiable.

Fig. 13 Finger prints on broken pane of glass, developed with aluminum powder and photographed against black background.

3. *Latent finger prints.* This type results from small amounts of grease, sweat and dirt being deposited on the object touched from every detail in the friction ridge pattern on the tip of the finger. The skin inside the hands and soles of the feet have no oil glands. The grease which is found on the inside of the fingers comes mostly from other parts of the body which are continually touched with the hands. The secretion from the friction skin contains 98.5–99.5% water and .5–1.5% organic and inorganic components. If the hands are cold practically no liquid is secreted; when they become warm this secretion returns to normal.

'Latent prints' thus include not only those invisible to the naked eye but also all which are in any way visible or distinguishable but which can only be examined properly after development.

Latent prints are usually found on objects with polished or smooth surfaces, and on paper, but under favorable conditions they also appear on rough surfaces, starched fabric, etc.

Development of latent finger prints

A. Development with powders is done by brushing a finely divided pigment over a latent print. The substances which form the print are shown up and the print becomes fully visible. The choice of pigment depends partly on the kind of surface on which the print is found, and partly also on how it is intended to preserve the print. If the latent print is good the choice of material for development is relatively unimportant. Every self-respecting finger print expert has his own special powder mixture and he is generally convinced that this is the best. Commercially available powders of good quality can also be recommended.

Some of the most commonly used powders are aluminum powder, lamp black, mercury and chalk (Hydrarg. cum creta), and white lead (basic lead carbonate).

In development with powder a soft, round camel's hair, feather or fiber-glass brush, which must be absolutely dry, is used. If the brush is damp or oily it is quite useless. The brush is first dipped lightly in the powder and then tapped with the finger so that only a small amount of powder is left on the brush. The object is then brushed lightly, the brushing being done in curved strokes, and the particles of powder stick to all places where there is grease or dirt. If there are fingerprints on the object they show up more or less clearly.

When brushing, the powder should not be sprinkled over or tapped on to the object, as in this way it is easy to destroy any prints made with very sweaty or dirty fingers or which have been produced by such a firm grip on the object that the friction ridges have spread out and almost filled up the spaces between them. If too much powder has been put on a print, so that it becomes blurred, it can be 'washed' by pressing a finger print lifter against it (see below). If the lifter is then drawn off, generally the spaces between the friction ridges are almost free from powder. If necessary the procedure can be repeated to get a favorable result.

Aluminum powder is generally used on hard surfaces such as glass or china, painted, polished or varnished objects, patent leather, cellophane, etc. An indispensable requirement is that the object shall be absolutely dry. The aluminium powder is often mixed with lycopodium (about 1:25 by volume). This mixture is used in place of pure aluminum powder in examining objects which are or are suspected of being covered with a thin oily layer, such as polished furniture, lacquered surfaces of cars, plastic objects, etc. It can be used freely without danger of the print being destroyed. If a print shows up sufficiently clearly, it can then be intensified with unmixed aluminum.

Lampblack is used at times as a universal developer, as it gives a good contrast with most surfaces. The lampblack should be as pure as possible and not contain too much oil, in which case the adhesion between the particles of powder and the surface under examination is so great that the whole of the surface is blackened. Lampblack is used also as a developer for paper. If the kind used has a tendency to blacken the paper too much on brushing, the powder can be poured on to the object under examination and, by moving the paper, can be made to slip to and fro so that it sticks in the finger print. Another method of avoiding this difficulty is to mix the powder with other substances. A common mixture consists of one part by weight of lamp black, 3 parts by weight of finely-powdered quartz and 4 parts by weight of lycopodium. This mixture has been found to be a very good developer for finger prints on paper. The powder is applied profusely with a brush and the surface is worked energetically, after which the excess is brushed away.

Sweat and grease which form a finger print on paper soon disappear from

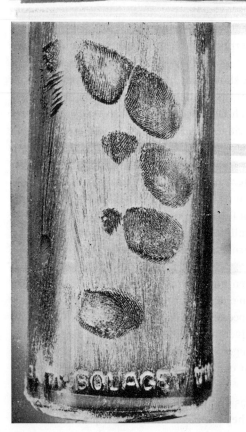

Fig. 14 Finger print on oily bottle, developed with white lead.

the surface and penetrate into the paper after which they will not react to the mechanical powder method. If the print which is being sought is supposed to have been made a long time before the examination, it is of little use to treat it with powder. In such a case some other method should be used, such as iodine, ninhydrin or silver nitrate treatment (see below).

If the powder mixture mentioned above is used on a smooth surface (glass or china), great care must be used in the brushing, since the sand in the powder is a powerful abrasive and may easily cause the print to disappear. *White lead* can be used for developing finger prints on practically all kinds of surface except paper and white objects. A special advantage is that it clings to oils and fats, and can therefore be used on sticky and fatty surfaces where other powders would not be able to bring up any prints. For development pure white lead is used, poured on to the object under examination, for example with a spoon. If the surface is dry the excess powder is then brushed away by light and cautious strokes of the brush in *one* direction. If the surface is sticky and the powder has formed a coherent layer, the brushing must be done more energetically until the finger print shows up. In this case it is recommended that the brushing be done a few hours after the powder has been applied.

White lead is used with advantage in developing prints on parts of machines, tools, objects of bakelite or other plastics, bottles which have stood in a cellar, etc. It should be noted that the powder is a powerful poison, and if administered even in small amounts over a long period it can cause chronic poisoning.

As mentioned above, the choice of a development powder depends to a large extent on the color of the surface on which the finger prints are. For a dark surface aluminum powder, mercury and chalk, or white lead is used: for a light one, lampblack. If the prints are on a multi-colored surface, for example a cigarette packet or colored picture, then the problem is how to photograph the finger print without part of it disappearing. One way is to use a development powder which fluoresces on irradiation with ultraviolet light.

Examples of such fluorescent powders are:
1. anthracene $(C_4H_6)_2 \cdot (CH)_2$
2. zinc sulphide ZnS
3. zinc orthosilicate $2ZnO \cdot SiO_2$
4. powdered rhizome of hydrastis (Hydrastis canadensis).

The development of aerosol sprays for finger print powders in various

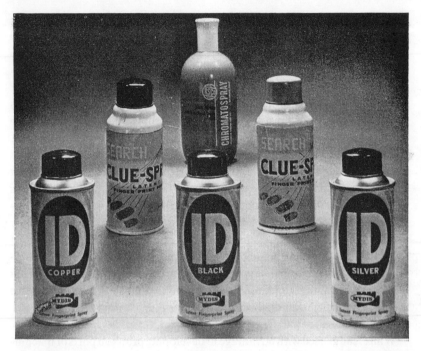

Fig. 15 Several commercial aerosol sprays for finger print development. The first and
second rows are powders; the last bottle is silver nitrate in solution.

colors permits the investigator to cover large areas with ease. After shaking
the can and clearing the nozzle, powder is sprayed from a distance of eighteen or more inches. Development with light brushing produces sharp, clear
prints. Not all available products give reliable results, however, and the
technician should test the different brands before using the spray at a crime
scene.

Another recent aid to finger print development, the Magna-brush, uti-
lizes magnetic powders and a magnetic applicator. Streamers of magnet-
ized powder, as shown in figure 16, are brought in contact with the suspected surface. Powder adheres to the latent print while the excess is removed by
the magnet. This method has the advantage of not leaving excess powder
on the object and the surrounding area. Due to the nature of the process,
it can only be used effectively on non-magnetic surfaces.

B. Development with iodine. This method is based on the fact that iodine
attacks and discolors objects exposed to it. The organic substances which

are found on the skin, and which are deposited in the form of finger prints, discolor especially strongly. The iodine method is generally used for the development of finger prints on paper and raw wood. As a rule the development is not done at the scene of the crime, since the equipment required is too bulky. On the bottom of a flat-bottomed glass dish are placed some tacks of glass or plastic, on which the paper is to be laid. Between the tacks there is placed a thin layer of iodine crystals, after which the paper under investigation is placed on the tacks so that it does not come into contact with the crystals, and the dish is covered to prevent the escape of iodine vapor. The iodine vaporizes even at ordinary temperature, and the gas form-ed attacks the paper, producing a brown color. At places where the paper surface is contaminated, by e.g. a finger print, or where the surface is uneven from folding, a stronger brown coloration appears. Under favorable con-ditions finger prints show up quite clearly. Development should be stopped before the surface of the paper becomes too dark, since otherwise the con-trast between the background and the print is reduced. The print should be photographed as soon as possible, since it fades quickly and disappears owing to the iodine going off as gas.

A more permanent arrangement for iodine development is a cabinet con-

Fig. 16 Developing latent finger prints on a carton by the Magna Brush method. Only the 'rays' of magnetic powder touch the surface.

structed of wood or plastic with glass sides which allows several pieces to be processed at one time and allows the development to be observed.

For processing objects at the crime scene, iodine fumers can be constructed from a glass tube containing calcium chloride (as drying agent), glass wool (as a separator) and iodine. The fumer is used by blowing through the tube, the opening being held close to the surface under examination. Note that this type of fumer and any other apparatus using iodine should be sealed tightly when not in use since iodine vapors are highly corrosive.

Development with iodine can be used both with fresh finger prints and also in cases where the powder method would fail owing to the substances which form the print having disappeared from the surface of the paper. In the latter case the developed print is usually rather vague and pale, although often quite usable for identification. It is hardly possible to give time limits, since many factors affect the possibility of developing and bringing up a print. There are examples where a five-week old finger print on paper has been developed with iodine vapor, and this print has been used for the search in the finger print file with positive results.

C. Development with silver nitrate solution. As mentioned above, the secretion from the skin of the inside of the hands (sweat) consists mainly of water, but there is a proportion of salts, urea, etc., dissolved in it. Among the dissolved salts is sodium chloride (NaCl). If a finger print is made with a sweaty finger on a porous surface the sweat penetrates the surface, and when the water evaporates sodium chloride remains behind, while the other chemical compounds gradually decompose. Thus the finger print is represented by a deposit of sodium chloride. If an aqueous solution of silver nitrate ($AgNO_3$) is allowed to act on the latent print, a chemical reaction occurs between the sodium chloride and the silver nitrate so that in their place two other chemicals appear – sodium nitrate ($NaNO_3$) and silver chloride (AgCl), of which the last mentioned is light sensitive. By means of ultraviolet radiation, the silver chloride is reduced to metallic silver which brings out the print in a brown to black color. Originally, only water was used to make the silver nitrate solution. Water does, however, bring the risk that the sodium chloride dissolves and spreads into the paper fibers before the chloride ions have reacted with the silver to form the insoluble silver chloride. The developed prints may thereby become indistinct. Furthermore, the unnecessary amount of water has a certain adverse effect on the paper. The original method has now been modified so that the solution consists of only a small amount of water, the rest being made up of acetone.

The developing solution is prepared by dissolving 5 grams of $AgNO_3$ in 10 milliliters of distilled water. To this is added 115 milliliters of acetone. The solution is distributed over the object in the form of a fine spray from a compressed-air sprayer or atomizer until the surface is completely covered. The solution can also be spread over the surface with a clean brush. The object is then subjected to ultraviolet radiation or direct sunlight whereby the silver is reduced. Developed finger prints should be photographed as soon as possible as the paper surface retains a certain amount of silver nitrate. While this silver salt also decomposes under the effect of light, it reacts more slowly than silver chloride. The background also gradually becomes blackened and the print contrast will be lost if they are not immediately photographed or protected against light.

Fig. 17 Finger print on lottery ticket, developed with silver nitrate solution.

The silver nitrate method is useful for developing finger prints which are no more than six months to a year old.

D. Development with Ninhydrin solution. Among the organic components of sweat are the amino acids. Latent prints deposited by sweaty fingers can therefore be developed if the amino acids are made visible by ninhydrin (triketohydrindenhydrate). Like the chlorides the amino acids penetrate into the paper fibers and delineate the friction ridge pattern. Unlike the chloride ions, however, they do not migrate very rapidly into the paper but remain unchanged for a very long time. For this reason it has been possible to develop finger prints over thirty years old by means of ninhydrin. One condition is that the paper must have been stored under dry conditions from the time of deposit to the time of development. Amino acids are water soluble and under moist conditions they spread into the paper fibers. The developing technique was introduced by ODÉN and VON HOFSTEN in 1953.

The developer consists of ninhydrin dissolved in acetone. Ninhydrin is a yellowish powder which dissolves rather slowly in the acetone and must be thoroughly stirred. A suitable concentration is .2 grams of ninhydrin in 120 milliliters of acetone. When the solution is ready, 4 milliliters of glacial acetic acid are added. It is not recommended to prepare more solution than can be used in one day as the activity of the solution deteriorates with time and eventually becomes useless.

In the developing process the solution is sprayed over the surface of the object in the form of a fine mist by means of an atomizer. In emergencies the solution can be brushed on with a clean brush, but this method entails the risk of discoloring the paper by dissolved ink if the paper bears ink writing. The spraying must be done with care so that the paper is not soaked, while still insuring complete coverage of the surface.

After the spraying the paper is allowed to dry to the point where the acetone has evaporated. The paper is then heated to about 80–90° C for three to four minutes. The print will appear in a purple color during this time. Heating is best done in an oven or drying cabinet equipped with a thermostat. Other heat sources may, of course, be used if the heat can be controlled.

Developed finger prints usually increase in intensity during the following two days, provided that they are not exposed to direct sunlight. Recording of the prints can thus be postponed for a few days. This is accomplished by photography on panchromatic film material with a yellowish-green filter.

If the developed prints are sufficiently intense, they can also be preserved by a 2% solution of cupric chloride in alcohol. This has the effect of chang-

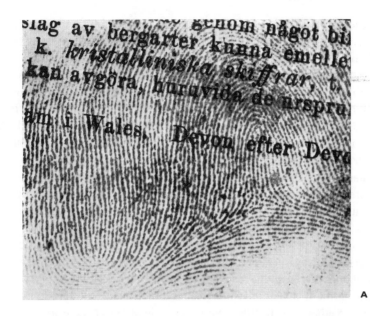

A

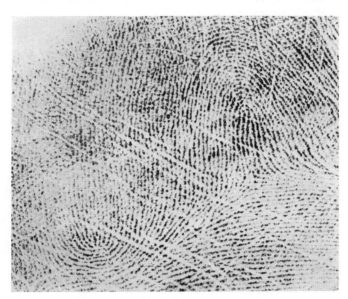

B

Fig. 18 A: palm print developed with ninhydrin on a schoolbook page after about 30 years; B: inked comparison print taken 30 years later.

ing the purple color to red which does not subsequently change in color or intensity. As this method of preservation is somewhat delicate it should only be used in exceptional cases.

E. Development of blood prints. In cases of murder, manslaughter, assault and rape it often happens that the criminal gets blood on his fingers from the wounds of the victim. Or the criminal himself may be wounded as in the above cases, or from broken glass in housebreaking or the theft of vehicles. A print formed with bloodstained fingers sometimes shows fully identifiable patterns, but more often appears as spots of blood which run together Actually liquid blood dries quickly, and on a subsequent grip with the fingers there is formed a finger print with a very clear pattern, although it is difficult to distinguish without development. Some experts advise the use of the usual blood test media such as benzidine or leuco-malachite green solution, but these tend to dissolve the blood so that the friction ridges in the print run together. There is described below an easily volatile solution which does not have this tendency (*ad modum* Arne Hanson).

One gram of leuco-malachite green is dissolved in 50 grams (or 70 milliliters) of ether, and to this solution are added about 10 drops of glacial

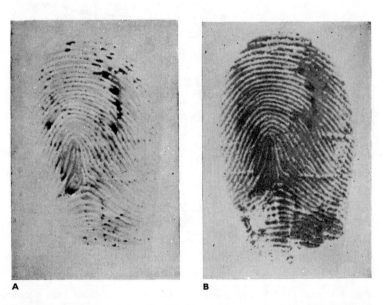

A   B

Fig. 19 Photograph A shows print made with blood serum.; B: same print developed with solution as described.

acetic acid. A portion of the solution is placed in a test tube and a few drops of fresh hydrogen peroxide (25–30%) are added. The mixture is sucked up in a pipette, the upper end of which is closed by a finger. The point of the pipette is placed against the surface on which the finger print is, and the liquid is allowed to run out by removing the finger from the upper end of the pipette. By touching with the pipette the liquid is caused to spread out over the print. At the same time the investigator blows against the surface to assist evaporation, which is so rapid that the solution is unable to dissolve the blood and blur the print appreciably, even though it may be on a smooth surface such as glass. The finger print shows up in a green color, and should be recorded by photographing immediately after development. The method can be used on all surfaces, including human skin.

Preservation of finger prints

A. Photographing. Prints found at the scene of a crime should preferably be preserved by photographing. This procedure has many advantages, including among others:

   1. the object is left intact and further photographs can be taken if the first are unsuccessful,

   2. it is easier to produce the evidence before a court of law if the print has been recorded, since parts of the object which carries the print will be seen in the picture.

The photography of finger prints and other clues differs considerably from ordinary pictorial photography. The photographer must be a master of photographic technique and understand the optical and chemical relations involved in order to be able to obtain a reproduction of a finger print as accurate and true to reality as possible. At the same time he must have a good knowledge of the principles of finger print analysis in order to be able to take into consideration what the finger print expert requires for his working material. The completed photograph should either be white on a black background or black on a white background. It should also be in natural size, in view of the measurements required subsequently for classification. Further, the investigator should know, and should inform the expert, whether the print is direct or a mirror image.

If the print is visible without development it should be photographed as found, in view of the possibility of any measures taken for development destroying it. This can generally be done by a suitable arrangement of lighting. An attempt can then be made to make the print clearer, for example by treatment with powders, after which more photographs are taken.

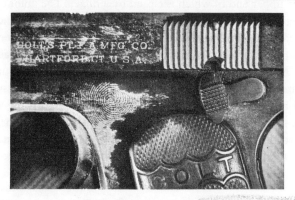

Fig. 20 Print on automatic pistol developed with white powder.

The camera should be a bellows camera with double extension, and provided with a ground glass. With such a camera it is possible to work without being tied to special illumination, and without the print having to be on a flat and easily accessible surface. Focussing with a ground glass screen is preferable to using a view finder. In addition to sharp focussing there is the possibility of controlling the arrangement of the lighting. Such control is often decisive in obtaining a satisfactory photograph of a finger print. It should be remembered that the prints may often be found on surfaces of the most different types, so that standard equipment and standard lighting may play tricks with the photography.

Suitable camera types are Linhof Technika, Speed Graphic and similar equipment.

The illumination can be arranged with one or more lamps. Its strength is not decisive so long as the camera and the object are steady and vibration does not make a short exposure essential. Exposure by flash is normally not used with photography of this sort, since the advantage of control of the reflection of light from the surface which is to be photographed is lost.

A number of firms have brought out special so-called finger print cameras. These consist of a camera housing with openings arranged so that they are at twice the focal distance of the objective. The camera, which has built-in lighting and batteries, is placed with the opening over the finger print. This type of camera is intended for one particular standard case where the print is clear and distinct, but it does not fulfil all the requirements of an all-round camera for all the situations which may occur at the scene of a crime.

However, there has recently been devised a special fixed-focus attachment for use on view cameras by means of which finger print photographs can be made in actual size using photolamps or flash. It consists of a metal guide which is affixed to the lens barrel and is open on two sides to admit light.

Regarding the choice of negative material the most suitable type is cut film (or film pack) because the sheets can be individually exposed and developed and because it is available in a wide variety of emulsion types.

Finger prints occur on the most varied types of surface. Often they cannot be photographed without first making them clearer by treatment with a powder, which should be chosen so that it forms the best possible contrast with the background. Table I shows most usual combinations of developed finger print and variously colored backgrounds, with a statement of the most suitable negatives and filters in the different cases.

TABLE I Combinations of finger prints and backgrounds

Print	Background	Filter	Type of negative	Negative	Positive
white-silver	black	—	hard process	black on clear	white on black
white-silver	blue-green	red	hard panchromatic	black on clear	white on black
white-silver	yellow-green	violet	hard orthochromatic	black on clear	white on black
white-silver	orange	blue	hard process	black on clear	white on black
white-silver	red	blue-green	hard orthochromatic	black on clear	white on black
white-silver	yellow	blue	hard process	black on clear	white on black
black	white	—	hard process	clear on black	black on white
black	green	green	panchromatic	clear on black	black on white
black	orange	orange	panchromatic	clear on black	black on white
black	red	red	panchromatic	clear on black	black on white
black	yellow	yellow	panchromatic	clear on black	black on white

Sometimes there are found visible identifiable prints which have been made with bloody fingers. The prints are then in a red-brown color and the negative should be chosen with reference to the color of the background, a suitable filter being used:

a. Print on white, light blue, light grey, very light yellow or light green ground – blue sensitive negative without filter.

b. Print on dark grey or dark blue ground – blue sensitive negative and blue filter,

c. Print on red, dark yellow or dark green ground – orthochromatic negative and yellow filter.

In dealing with methods of development mention was made of the difficulties which arise when a finger print is on a multi-colored background. Parts of the print may disappear completely when photographing with ordinary light, owing to the strong reflection of certain colors. As a means of overcoming this difficulty it is recommended to use a developing powder which fluoresces strongly when irradiated with ultraviolet light, e.g. anthracene or zinc sulphide. The print, treated in this way, is photographed in a dark room by exposure to the rays from e.g. a mercury lamp provided with a filter which excludes visible light. When the ultraviolet light falls on the finger print the latter fluoresces, that is, the rays are changed partially to visible light, which is recorded by the camera. As a protection from stray ultraviolet light the camera should be provided with a filter which excludes these rays. The time of exposure is relatively long depending on the kind of negative used.

 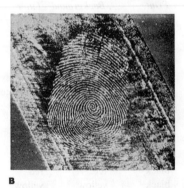

A   B

Fig. 21 A: thumb print on the label of a whisky bottle, developed with powdered Hydrastis canadensis root. The background is dark brownish-red and the text is in gold, photographed in ordinary light; B: fluorescence photograph of the same print.

B. *Preservation of plastic finger prints*. When a finger print has been left in material which has hardened or is able to stand transport, and when it is on an object which, being small, is easily transportable, it may be sent direct to the expert.

The preservation of plastic finger prints poses some special problems. As a rule they should be preserved by casting, but the casting medium must be suited to the material on which the print is found. In order not to risk destroying the print by selecting the wrong medium, it should first be photographed in oblique light. Such a photo can sometimes suffice for further examination of the print. This is not always the case, however, as impressions often are so deep that it is very difficult to record the whole ridge pattern on film.

Most fingerprints of this kind can be cast in latex or some of the modern plastic materials. The goal should be a cast in the form of a film which can be flattened so as to facilitate further processing. One material suitable for this purpose is liquid latex which is similar to thick cream in consistency. The thick liquid is dropped on to the surface of the impression and blown out to a thin layer which is allowed to dry to an elastic film. Another, similar, casting material is Castoflex which consists of about 60% pure latex. It is applied in the same manner.

Solutions and emulsions of plastics are available which have some properties superior to latex. The cast usually dries quicker and the finished film is tougher. One of these materials is an emulsion of polyvinyl acetate which is widely used in the form of a white glue (Elmer's, Dupage's, etc.). A film of the required thickness normally sets in 20–30 minutes. The drying can be accelerated by means of a hair dryer or a heat lamp, but care must be taken that the carrier of the print does not melt.

The finished plastic cast is transparent so that it can be used as a photographic negative in a contact printer or enlarger. It can also be inked with printer's ink and reproduced on paper. In the latter process the final print will be reversed with respect to color and side.

Plastic finger prints in greasy substances may, in emergencies, be cast with a very thin plaster mixture.

Impressions in dust, flour, safe insulation and similar substances should be preserved by photography. Any other method usually leads to destruction of the print.

In cases of the murder of new-born children there is the possibility of finding prints on the body of the infant. After delivery the skin of the baby is covered with a sticky semi-solid greasy substance, the so-called vernix caseosa. Plastic finger prints or portions of them may appear in this film, for example from a throttling grip on the neck of the baby. It may be important that such a print should be preserved, since it may considerably facilitate any subsequent legal proceedings even if the print itself is not identifiable. Preservation is best done by casting with negocoll, which is allowed to cool for about an hour after casting. The cast is then removed and placed be- tween moist absorbent cotton in a strong container for submission to the laboratory.

C. Preservation with finger print lifters. This method of preserving finger prints was described in 1899 by DuBois, a Brazilian. It requires the print to be first developed with powder, after which a lifter with a sticky surface is pressed against the print and then pulled away. Part of the powder sticks to the surface of the lifter and gives a mirror image of the original print. After removal, the surface carrying the print is protected by a thin sheet of transparent celluloid which is laid on the surface of the lifter. Originally, the sticky layer of the lifter consisted of a mixture of gelatine and glucose, but rubber is now more commonly used. Black lifters are used for prints which have been developed with aluminum or light-colored powder and white lifters for prints developed with lampblack or dark-colored powder. If the print has been developed with white lead and is to be preserved with lifter, it should be remembered that this powder gradually alters under the action of the constituents of the sticky layer and becomes invisible. White lead prints preserved with gelatine lifters are thus not permanent and must be photographed as soon as possible. Rubber lifters do not have this dis- advantage.

The lifting method is simple and easily mastered. It needs no knowledge of photography and no photographic equipment. Its use, however, neces- sitates great accuracy in specifying the position of the print. Carelessness in this respect can have catastrophic results. Further, one cannot rely on obtaining a result which is technically as good as that obtained by expert photography of the print. In spite of this, the method has been largely used in different parts of the world, especially in proceedings connected with minor crimes.

D. Preservation with strips of tape. Recently strips of transparent tape have been used as a substitute for lifters. This material is supplied in rolls, and for use in finger print work must be at least 1 inch wide. When used, the end of the tape is fixed at the side of the developed print, after which the tape is brought over the print with the aid of a finger and smoothed down so that there are no air bubbles. The tape is then drawn off. The particles of powder adhere to the sticky surface of the tape and thus transfer the pattern of the finger print. The tape is finally fixed on a card of a suitable color

Fig. 22 Finger prints on glass developed with aluminium powder and transferred to black lifter. The prints are reversed.

contrasting with the powder used. Alternatively a transparent, not too thin, piece of celluloid can be used as underlayer.

E. *Preservation of iodine-treated prints* is best done by photographing the developed print. It is not the only possible method. Often it may be impossible to obtain a satisfactory result in this way, as for example when photographing *developed prints on multi-colored paper or paper with a printed text*, which is not possible by the use of a color filter. If a finger print has been developed with iodine on such paper or cardboard there is another method of preservation which can give a very good result. After the print has been developed, the paper is aired for a little while, after which a well-cleaned silver or silvered plate is pressed against the print. If the latter is a clear one, the plate need only be laid on for a few seconds. When the plate is removed the transferred pattern shows weakly on the silver surface, and it is then developed photo-chemically by exposure to light. In the development metallic silver is formed by reduction and shows the pattern of the finger print in black on the white plate. When the print has been developed to the desired degree of clarity the plate is dipped for a moment in fixing solution (diluted about 1:20), after which it is rinsed. The finger print now shows even those details which previously were more or less invisible on account of being situated above the text or colored part of the paper. The print on the silver plate may be kept for up to two months (McMorris, 1937).

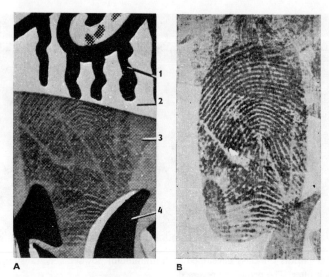

Fig.23 A: finger print, developed with iodine vapor on paper showing green, white, black and red colors. Photographed with panchromatic plate and red filter. 1: green; 2: white; 3: red; 4: black. B: same print as in A, transferred to silver plate and then photographed.

WAGENAAR (1935–1936) has described a method of preserving a print which has been developed with iodine. He uses paper which has been sprinkled with starch solution and then laid over the print. The iodine in the latter reacts with the starch and the finger print is transferred to the starch layer on the paper, where it shows as a mirror image in a blue-violet color. In practice this method has been found to be difficult.

Another method which is also based on the color reaction between iodine and starch has, on the other hand, fulfilled practical requirements. In place of Wagenaar's starch paper, dextrin paste (library paste) is used. The print is developed for a short time in iodine vapor so that it shows up only weakly. It is important that iodine shall not attach itself too much to the surface of the paper around and between the papillary lines. The operator then takes a dab of dextrin paste on his right index finger and runs the finger over the print from the top down, so that a thin layer of paste sticks on the surface. The print appears in a strong blue-violet or violet color, depending on the composition of the paste. This print is stable, but the picture is in the paste layer and care must therefore be taken that the paper is not wiped or exposed to any other injurious action after the paste has dried.

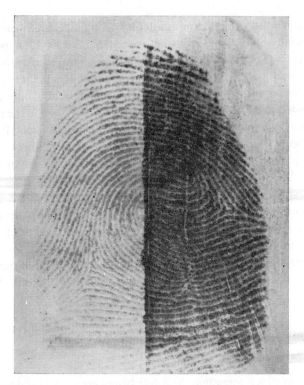

Fig. 24 Print on paper developed with iodine. The righthand part of the print has been preserved with dextrin paste.

How long does a finger print remain on an object?

Plastic prints remain for any length of time provided that the object on which they are left or the substance in which they are formed is itself stable. In investigations it sometimes happens that police officers find finger prints which give the impression of having been made in dust, but which on closer examination are found to be dust-filled plastic prints in oil paint, made years earlier.

Prints which have resulted from contamination of the fingers with soot, flour, face powder or safe filling are soon destroyed. Prints of fingers contaminated with blood pigments, ink and oil are more resistant and under favorable conditions can be kept for a long time.

Latent prints on glass, china and other smooth objects can remain for years if they are in a well-protected location. On objects in the open air a print can be developed several months after it was made. Finger prints on paper are generally blurred and indistinct even after a few days. On paper of a loose texture, for example newspaper, the print is destroyed after merely a matter of hours. If paper found during an investigation is thought to carry finger prints, development must be carried out immediately, for if only a few hours are allowed to elapse it may be too late; the oil and sweat in the print may have diffused so that the print becomes merely a blurred stain. Prints which have been deposited several years previously can, however, be developed with ninhydrin solution, provided that the paper has not been exposed to a humid atmosphere. Finger prints disappear very quickly when the air is warm and dry, or when they are exposed to direct sunlight. In investigations outdoors it ist herefore necessary to develop prints as quickly as possible, or to protect them in some way from direct sunlight.

In searching for finger prints at the scene of a crime the investigator must never consider the time elapsed since the crime was committed but should, *in all circumstances*, work with the goal in mind of finding all prints of the perpetrator.

The effect of temperature conditions on the possibility of developing finger prints

When objects on which there may be finger prints are found outdoors in ice or snow, they must be thawed slowly – placed so that dirty thaw water does not run over and destroy the prints. A suitable method of treatment is to scrape away as much snow and ice as possible, with the greatest possible care, before the object is brought into a warm place. Only when the object is quite dry should the print be developed.

When plastic finger prints are present in oil or grease the thawing must proceed slowly and under close scrutiny since the print may easily be destroyed by heat. Such prints should preferrably be photographed when they appear.

Damp objects are air-dried in a room at ordinary room temperature.

Regarding the examination of automobiles which are found outdoors in cold weather or in direct sunlight, see Chapter 11, 'Motor Vehicles'.

It should be taken as a general rule never to examine cold objects, especially of metal, until they have been kept for at least some hours in a place at room temperature.

In indoor investigations in a cold house, the rooms should first be heated.

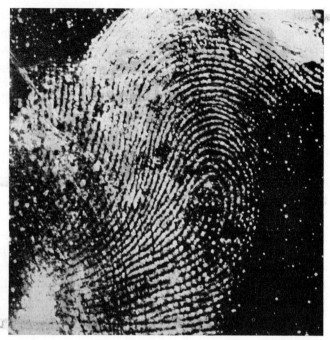

Fig. 25 The size of the crime scene finger print does not determine its evidential value. The small print on the left is suitable both for classification and identification, the print on the right only for identification.

The heating should not be so rapid that thaw water runs off frosted objects or places.

Examination of developed finger prints

The officer who investigates the crime scene should only search for, develop and preserve the finger prints. Unless he is specially qualified by training and experience in the identification of finger prints, he cannot be expected to carry out the continued examination of the developed prints.

A detailed account of finger print identification is omitted here, partly because it lies outside the scope of crime scene investigation, and partly because it is a vast and specialized subject. Several comprehensive works on this subject are listed in the literature references.

The officer examining the scene should preserve *all* developed finger prints. Even small, fragmentary prints which might seem insignificant to a non-specialist may turn out to be very valuable when examined by an expert. Large finger prints are not necessarily more valuable than small ones. It happens frequently, as in the illustrated instance (see fig.25), that the larger print is usable only for comparison with a suspect's finger prints. It is useless for searching in a single-finger print file. The smaller print, however, is usable for both purposes.

Palm prints

On the inside of the hand there are patterns of friction skin just as there are on the fingers, and they are of equal value as evidence. When parts of a palm print are found, the area involved can often be deduced from the position of the print or from other parts of the hand and possibly fingers having left marks in the form of 'smears' or portions of prints. If the position of the hand represented by the fragment can be estimated, a simple sketch of the inside of a hand will greatly facilitate the work of the expert.

Prints of friction ridge patterns from the sole of the foot

On the soles of the feet there are friction ridges with the same evidential value as finger prints; they are developed and preserved in the same way. There have been cases where a housebreaker, lacking gloves or other protection for his hands, has taken off his socks and put them on his hands, not thinking that his unprotected soles would leave a print!

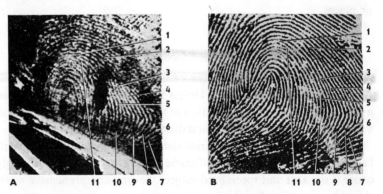

Fig. 26 A: finger print found at scene of murder. B: print of the person suspected. Note the similarities where numbers correspond.

Packing of objects on which prints are found

For the transport of objects to be examined for finger prints the police officer must decide on the most suitable method of packing for each particular case. Under no circumstance should the object be wrapped directly in paper or cloth, since this would destroy the print. If possible the object should be wedged firmly in a strong box in such a way that the surface is not touched by the packing. Since a rigid suspension can cause breakage or other damage to an object in transit, the box must be wrapped in a sufficient quantity of soft material, such as excelsior, corrugated paper, crumpled newspapers, etc. If nails are used to fix the object in the box or for the lid, they should not be hammered right in: the heads should be left free so that they can be pulled out without using much force.

Taking finger prints for elimination

As a rule, it can be expected that the majority of finger prints found and developed at the crime scene have been deposited by persons who have had legitimate access to the premises. It is of great importance that these finger prints be eliminated, so that the continued examination may be concentrated upon the remaining prints – presumably those of the perpetrator. The investigating officer should therefore always take so-called elimination prints of all persons on the premises. These should be submitted to the finger print examiner together with the crime scene prints.

As the identification of legitimate finger prints is as critical as the identification of the criminal's prints, the elimination prints should be as clear as those recorded of criminals for filing purposes. Elimination prints should therefore be taken by printer's ink or by specially prepared ink pads. It is not required, however, that they are recorded on standard finger print forms, nor that the person's name is indicated as long as they are clearly marked as being for elimination purposes.

A large proportion of the latent prints developed at a crime scene are palm prints. *Elimination palm prints* should therefore also be taken, in addition to the elimination finger prints. Inked palm prints require special care in order to be useful for comparison purposes. The palm should be inked with a roller to insure that all parts of the palm are inked. The prints should be made on sheets of white paper laid over a bottle or a length of dowel, the palm being rolled over this cylinder. The hollow in the center of the palm usually does not reproduce if the palm is simply laid flat on the paper.

PRINTS OF GLOVES

The general knowledge of the great value of finger prints as evidence has resulted in criminals using gloves as the most usual protective measure. In many cases, when looking for finger prints 'glove smears' are found, and possibly in most cases little attention is paid to them, search being concentrated at places where it may be expected that the individual would have been compelled to work with bare hands or to use a good deal of force, whereby the hand coverings would slip so that the wrist or a part of the palm near the wrist would be exposed and leave an imprint. Prints of gloves may be just as valuable as finger prints, so that it is advisable always to examine them and to preserve them for closer investigation, so long as they are not typical 'smears', that is, are formed by the glove-covered hand slipping against a surface.

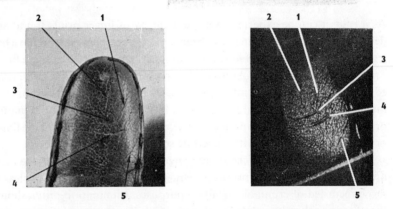

Fig.27 On left, index finger of kidskin glove: on right, a print on glass made with that finger, developed with aluminum powder (print reversed). Cracks in the surface of the leather show clearly on the print.

The leather of a glove shows a surface pattern which is often of a very characteristic appearance. It may show furrows in a more or less definite pattern, or be perforated in a fairly regular manner. It is much the same with fabric gloves, the surface pattern of which varies according to the method of manufacture and the yarn of material used. It is only the wrinkled or perforated surface pattern of leather gloves which can make identification possible, as in this case there is often great irregularity. The surface pattern of fabric gloves is on the other hand regular for each type, so that in general identification cannot be based merely on this. Characteristic and, from the point of view of identification, very valuable formations in the seams may be present, especially at the tips of the fingers.

After they have been worn for some time both leather and fabric gloves become shaped to the hands, and there are often produced typical wrinkle formations in the leather of the fingers, at the seams or at places where the gloves do not fit the fingers properly. These wrinkle formations and injuries in the form of tears or holes or, in the case of leather gloves, in the form of cracks in the surface of the skin, generally show in the print and are most valuable. In rare cases it is even possible to find fragments of a finger print within a glove print. This can occur when the gloves have such large holes that some part of a finger is exposed and leaves a print at the same time as the print of the glove. If prints of gloves and of friction ridges appear together it may be difficult to distinguish the difference without closer examination, and at first glance the print gives the impression of being blurred or of being composed of two glove prints within one another. On a closer examination however the glove print is distinguished by its regular lines which lack the detailed pattern of the friction ridges.

Glove prints are always formed best on smooth surfaces. Their development requires great care, since the prints are not as strong as finger prints and therefore are easily destroyed if too much powder is used. In order to be sure of not destroying any such prints which may be present at the scene of the crime, the area should not be 'painted' vaguely, but a systematic search should be made with a lamp, and then brushing should be done cautiously. On the other hand there is a prospect of finding glove prints at conspicuous and easily accessible places, since in most cases the criminal throws away all caution and believes that he is fully protected by his gloves, and he therefore uses his hands freely.

In developing prints aluminum powder, white or black powder may be used. The developed print can be taken off on a finger print lifter but it is better to take possession of the object on which the print is found so that it can be compared directly with prints from the gloves of a suspect.

That a print can be produced by leather or fabric gloves is due to the fact that, with the former, the leather itself contains some fat, while both leather and fabric gloves become contaminated with dirt, skin grease and the like after being in use for some time. In addition, at least with fabric gloves, the warm and moist secretion from the skin of the hands plays an important part.

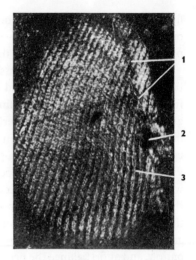

Fig. 28 Left above: print of thumb covered with wool glove, found on pane of glass and developed with aluminum powder. Right above: comparison print on glass made by suspect's glove and also developed with aluminum powder. Below: photograph of thumb of glove of suspect. Note the similarities.

Comparison prints from the gloves of a suspect are best made on glass, which is generally the most convenient even when the original prints are on furniture. In certain special cases, however, it may be necessary to form a print on the same kind of material as that at the scene of the crime, so that where possible such material should always be enclosed when a print and gloves from a suspect are sent for examination. Comparison prints should be made in a manner similar to the original ones. Thus if it is possible, in view of the placing of the latter, to decide for example how the hand of the suspect gripped when making the grip, this information should be communicated to the expert so that the same grip can be used for the comparison print. Consideration must also be given to the degree of pressure which may have been used in forming the original print, and statements forming a guide for judging the pressure should also be submitted. It is of great importance that neither too great nor too small a pressure should be used in making the comparison prints, since their appearance is greatly affected thereby.

It is often difficult to make clear prints with a glove, but the operation may be assisted by breathing slightly on the finger of the glove. Under no conditions should it be treated with powder, fat or the like, since there would be a risk of destroying any characteristic details.

PRINTS OF OTHER COVERINGS

In place of gloves, socks, towels, handkerchiefs, etc., are sometimes used as protection for the hands, and it has also happened that an individual has protected the inside of his hand with adhesive tape to prevent the formation of finger prints.

In most cases, when using the first-mentioned objects, prints are left only if the material is thin, dirty or somewhat damp. If however it is thick, dry or relatively clean it leaves no prints.

Prints of such hand coverings rarely have any value from the point of view of identification. Only in cases where the material used has a characteristic surface pattern, shows typical injuries, unusual seams or characteristic crease formations, which are reproduced in the print, identification is possible. In such a case the investigation is tedious on account of the fact that the extent or the edges of the protective medium are not definitely fixed as it would be in the case of a glove, and therefore it must be searched for before a direct comparison can be undertaken.

Although the possibility of identification of hand coverings in such cases is not great, the print should still be given some attention, since the method of operation may be typical for a particular individual or for a gang, who have perhaps carried out other crimes in the same or another district.

FOOT PRINTS

Foot prints made by a criminal at or near the scene of a crime are generally of great value as investigative leads; under favorable conditions they may also become positive evidence. A detailed examination of foot prints is tedious work, and such evidence is often overlooked – possibly because the police officer thinks that he does not have sufficient time to deal with them, or perhaps he merely lacks experience in this subject. In serious crimes, however, all foot prints must be investigated very carefully, especially when the crime scene is outdoors, as these foot prints may be the only evidence of any value.

When a cast is made of a foot print left in soft ground, one expects to obtain a faithful reproduction of the heel and sole of the shoe which made the print. As a rule, however, the result of casting is actually quite different – the cast has an arched form. The back of the heel and the point of the toe are considerably lower than the other parts of the cast. This is due to the fact that, in normal walking, the back of the heel is placed on the ground first, after which each part of the heel and sole is pressed down on the ground in succession until the foot is lifted with a final strong pressure of the point of the toe against the earth. The pressure which regulates the depth of the impression is the greatest at the back of the heel and at the point of the toe. When running the foot prints are less distinct, partly owing to slipping of the foot and partly to sand and earth being thrown into the print. The form of the print depends on the individual's style of running; many people run on their toes, others set both heel and toe hard in the ground, and others again set the whole foot down in the earth at once. In deciding whether an individual walked or ran there is only one certain guide – that is the length of the step.

Gait pattern

The series of foot prints made by a person walking or running is called a gait pattern. There may be a great difference in the gait patterns of different people, and thus it has great value in the search for the criminal. The description of a gait pattern comprises the *direction line, gait line, foot line, foot angle, principal angle, length of step and width of step* (Fig.29).

The direction line (A) expresses the path taken by the individual.

The *gait line* (B) in normal progress coincides with the direction line. It is often more or less zigzag, owing to the individual proceeding with the legs wide apart. Heavy persons, seamen, elderly people, and those employed on railway trains, often walk in this way in order to keep their balance, and therefore they may have a very broken gait line. Sometimes the gait line may be broken 'inward', i.e. the right heel print is on the left side of the direction line and the left heel print on the right of it. If the gait line at the same time is irregular, the walk is probably that of a person who is intoxicated or otherwise unable to keep his balance.

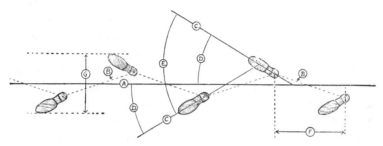

Fig.29 Gait pattern. A: direction line; B: gait line; C: foot line; D: foot angle; E: principal angle; F: length of step; G: width of step.

The *foot line* (C) goes through the longitudinal axis of the foot marks and may be different for the right and the left foot.

The *foot angle* (D) is the angle formed between the foot line and direction line. It may vary considerably in different individuals, and therefore forms a valuable detail in the gait pattern. In normal walking foot angles are very characteristic and do not change much, but they may alter if the individual runs, carries a heavy load, or moves over broken ground.

The *principal angle* (E) is the angle between the foot lines of the two feet and is thus the sum of the two foot angles.

The *length of step* (F) is the distance between the center points in two successive heel prints of the two feet. As the gait line is broken (zigzag), the length of step is reckoned between the points on the direction line opposite the centers of the heel prints. The step length depends on the speed of progress and also on the size of the individual and, in some cases, occupation. Generally, a tall person takes a longer step than a short one when they both proceed at the same speed. Varying lengths of step in the same gait pattern are due to the individual having walked with a limp.

The length of step varies between 20 and 40 in. When walking slowly the normal length of a man's step is 28 in,. when walking quickly 36 in. If the length of step exceeds 40 in., it may be assumed that the individual was running. The *width of step* (G) is calculated between the outer contours of the two feet in the gait pattern.

It is easy to detect if a criminal goes backwards with the object of misleading. The length of step is appreciably less and the foot angles are irregular, while the points of the feet press down more deeply than with normal progress. When walking backwards in soft ground, e.g. snow, the slip marks (i.e. marks made when the foot is lifted out of the foot mark and at the same time moved back) show clearly the true direction of progress. If a person, moving backwards on hard ground, treads in, for example, blood then the decreasing and finally disappearing blood prints show the actual direction of movement. Furthermore, a person walking backwards will put his feet down in places where he would not step when walking normally.

The gait pattern is best preserved by accurate measurement and sketching, and the sketches must be supplemented by photographs taken with the camera placed as high as possible, It is desirable to place a measuring scale in the track and, if necessary, to paint the track with aluminum powder or pigment.

The value of foot prints

The individual foot prints are generally only preserved if they contain details of value for identification. The most valuable details are signs of wear, characteristic fittings or marks of fittings which have come off, injuries, marks of nails and pegs, especially when these are irregularly placed, and repair marks. If they are particularly characteristic or occur in sufficient numbers, such details may form decisive evidence. In serious crimes foot prints are preserved even they do not show any details, in the interest of thoroughness.

While the size and shape of the shoe or a pattern in the heel or sole are of lesser evidential value, a representative print should nonetheless be preserved for its value as an investigative lead.

If foot prints are found in snow which has a frozen crust it is a waste of time to attempt to take a cast of them. When the foot breaks through the hard surface of the snow, the surface snow goes with it and forms a hard bottom to the mark. The coarse grains of ice in the surface layer do not reproduce any details of the shoe, not even such large defects as a hole through the sole, and it is not possible to obtain any useful information of the size by measuring the foot print since the hard snow is broken and pressed down at points a considerable distance outside the outer contour of the shoe.

A foot print may be a *foot impression or a foot print (dust print)*.

Foot impressions occur when the foot treads in some mouldable material such as earth, sand, clay, snow, etc.

Foot prints are formed on a hard base when the foot or the sole and heel of a shoe are contaminated with some foreign matter such as road dirt, dust, flour, blood, moisture or the like. Foot prints may also be latent when they have been formed by naked or stocking-covered feet on a smooth surface.

Preservation of foot impressions

Foot impressions are generally found outdoors, and the first precautionary measure is therefore to protect the impression from alteration or destruction, preferably by covering it with a box. Impressions in snow are especially troublesome when it is thawing, so that they should be protected by a box which is covered with snow. If a foot impression is in such a position that there is a risk that it will gradually get filled up or damaged by running water, it must be surrounded by a wall of earth, sand or snow, or alternatively a hole may be dug close to the impression and the water led away to the hole, the latter being emptied when necessary. However, these protective measures are only stopgaps and the actual preservation should be undertaken as soon as possible.

Preservation should be done either by *photographing* or *casting*; in important cases by both methods.

Photographing foot impressions is done with the camera placed *vertically* above the impression, a foot rule being placed at the side of the latter. If the bottom of the impression is appreciably deeper than the surface of the ground or snow, the scale should be brought down to the same level. Before photographing, any material which may have fallen into the impression after it was formed should be cleaned away, and for this purpose it is convenient to use tweezers, or a piece of paper on to which are rolled lumps of earth, etc., which cannot be picked up by the tweezers. If it is not possible to carry out this cleaning without injuring details of the impression, it should be omitted. Materials which are trampled into the impression, such as for example leaves, grass, etc., should not be removed, as they actually form part of the impression and no details will be found under them. Careless removal of a trampled blade of grass can destroy large parts of the impression. Any water which may be present should be led away to a small pit dug for the purpose, the run-off being made at a place in the impression where there is no detail. If a foot impression has been made in snow there is difficulty is getting a clear picture of it. Hard snow may be dusted with aluminum powder, which gives a clearer picture: with loose snow aluminum powder can be dusted into the mark by tapping the brush.

As the details in foot impressions are three-dimensional in nature the photograph should be made under illumination which will bring out those details to best advantage. Direct sunlight will enhance the details by creating highlights and shadows. When the sky is cloudy and the daylight diffuse and practically shadowless, artificial light must be used; either photoflood or flash illumination is suitable. These considerations, of course, also apply to situations when it is imperative that the pictures be taken at night. The important point to remember about the illumination is that the light must not be held at too low an angle, since too much shadow will obscure details rather than emphasize them.

Casting of foot impressions is generally done with plaster of Paris; in certain cases paraffin, sulphur or silicone rubber may be used.

Casting with plaster of Paris

This method can be used for all casting of foot impressions, whatever material they are in, but for impressions in sand paraffin wax is better. Casting of foot impressions in snow by means of plaster can give very good results, but the method requires a great deal of experience. Even those familiar with the technique will sometimes fail, and the impression will be destroyed. For casting impressions in snow, sulphur is therefore to be preferred.

In some cases the foot impression must be *prepared* before making a plaster cast, but this should be avoided as far as possible since it involves covering the impression with a surface layer which, although extremely thin, is liable to alter or damage the small details in the impression. Preparation is sometimes unavoidable, as without it casting could not be done at all.

Fig. 30 Casting a foot print with plaster of Paris.

In place of coating it is sometimes useful to moisten the surface with water. The water is distributed over the impression by means of an atomizer or an insecticide gun until the surface is thoroughly moistened. It is always advisable, however, to test the spray on the ground near the impression as the water may not penetrate but collect in droplets at the bottom of the impression. In this event the water should not be applied.

Foot impressions in loose, dry sand and earth are prepared with clear lacquer or shellac solution which is sprayed in the surface of the mark with a sprayer, which is held at a distance of not less than 18 inches from the mark, and the solution should fall as a fine mist into it. When the mark has been dampened uniformly and has assumed a brownish color, it should be allowed to dry and harden for a few minutes, after which the spraying is repeated a few times. When the shellac film has dried – which requires less than half an hour – talc is blown into the impression so that an extremely thin layer is formed.

Foot impressions in dust, flour, ash, powdered safe insulation, and other finely divided material cannot be cast without previous preparation with shellac solution. Before commencing to spray, a test should be made at another area to decide how near the spray should be held. Instead of

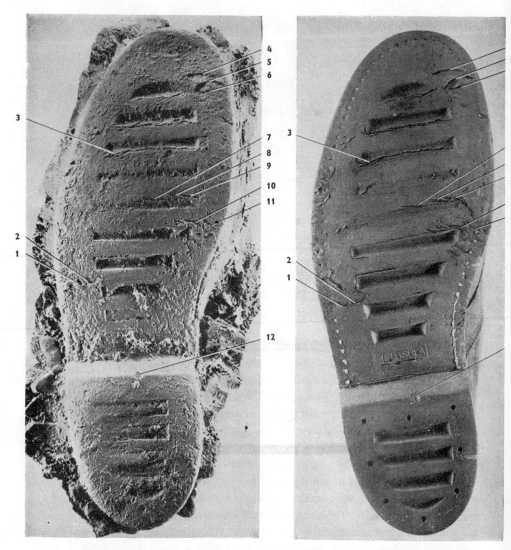

Fig. 31 A comparion between the cast, in plaster of Paris, of a foot print in damp earth at the scene of a crime, and shoe of suspect.

dusting with talc, a thin oil such as sewing machine oil is sprayed on the shellac film in the impression, using an atomizer.

Foot impressions which have hardened from drying or cold can be prepared with thin oil which is brushed or sprayed into the impression. Preparation is not absolutely necessary in this case, but should be done where there is risk of the casting sticking in the impression.

Foot impressions in damp or wet material are not usually prepared.

It may be reckoned that about 1 quart of plaster and 1 quart of water are required for casting a foot print. The plaster must be dry, free from lumps, and not granular. The mixing can be done in any sort of container, but preferably in a rubber bowl, which is easily cleaned afterwards. Before commencing to mix, a few small sticks of green wood should be placed at hand for strengthening the cast. Dry wood should not be used since it absorbs the water, swells and cracks the casting.

Strips of metal screening, about 2 in. by 8 in., are also suitable as reinforcement. They may be prepared in advance and made part of a separate kit of casting materials.

The plaster is prepared by sifting or strewing the powdered plaster over the surface of the water, allowing each portion to sink before more plaster is added. Plaster is added until finally a little top of dry plaster is raised above the liquid. Only then is the mixture stirred with a spoon so that all lumps are broken down. The stirring should not be too vigorous, otherwise air bubbles might be stirred into the plaster. No fresh plaster is added after stirring commences, but water may be added provided that it is done before the mass becomes too thick. When the mixture is as thick as heavy cream, it is ladled out in spoonfuls: not thrown directly into the impression but caused to ooze out over it with the aid of the spoon. It is important to see that the bottom and edge of the impression are covered as quickly as possible and that the plaster does not harden anywhere, since lap marks would be formed at such points. When the bottom and edges have been covered by the mass, the sticks of green wood are laid in both directions on the plaster, pressed in only slightly since otherwise the bottom of the casting might be damaged. When the impression has been covered with a layer of plaster the remainder can be poured in directly without any risk of destroying details. When complete the casting should have a thickness of at least $1^1/_2$ inches, as it cracks easily if it is thinner.

If the foot impression is comparatively shallow, an edging of thin sheet metal or cardboard strips is placed round it so that the plaster does not flow out at the sides. The strip should not be pressed down too hard, or it may displace the outer contour.

After about half an hour the plaster has hardened sufficiently and the cast can be lifted out. In loose sand or earth this is most easily done by

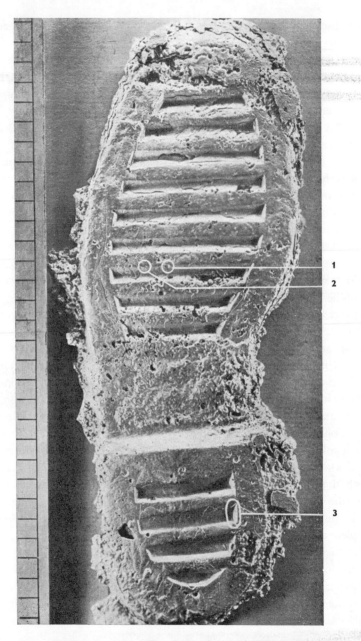

Fig. 32 Establishment of identity between casting, in melted sulphur, with foot print at scene of crime

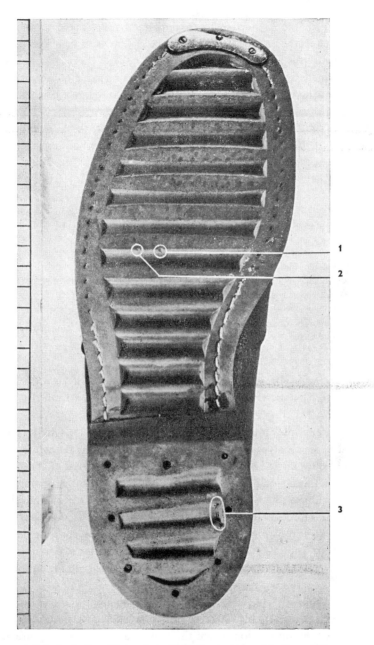

d shoe of suspect. Injuries in the rubber sole and heel are reproduced in the casting.

spreading out the extended fingers of both hands along one edge and raising up the cast. If the impression is a deep one or the cast is firmly seated in the impression, it is advisable to excavate around it so that it finally lies on a pillar, which is then cut off. When lifting, the underside of the cast should not be touched, since details may be destroyed at places where the plaster has not hardened fully. Earth or sand sticking to the cast is not removed until after some hours, when the cast is cleaned by careful washing, *but no brushing or rubbing should be employed.* Firmly attached objects, such as small stones, sticks, blades of grass, leaves, etc., should be allowed to remain: if they are removed, misleading details may be formed in the cast.

Murder. The body of a man carrying multiple stab wounds was found in a river. The police found clear tire tread impressions in the soft clay and gravel surface of a narrow road where it approached the high bank of the river. Impressions of the soles and heels of a certain type of shoe were also discovered. Plaster of Paris casts were made of the tire treads, the soles and heels.

A son of the victim and another boy were suspected. Both were missing from their homes. One of the fugitives was arrested and among his personal effects was a pair of shoes similar to those used by U.S. Army paratroopers. Plaster casts were made of the heels and upon examination it was found that the right heel of one of the shoes belonging to the fugitive corresponded with the casts made of the heel impressions at the scene of the crime (MOORE, 1950).

Casting of marks in snow is best done with sulphur. If this is not available, plaster must be used, but it is advisable first to make a trial cast.

When casting impressions in *compact wet snow*, the impression need not be prepared. Snow is placed in the mixing water to cool it, and the powdered plaster is spread out on paper so that it also is cold. When the water is cold the snow sludge is removed and the plaster is stirred in. The mixture should be thicker than when casting an impression in other material, as if it is thin it filters down between the grains of snow and ice and into the bottom of the impression, so that the underside of the cast becomes porous and mossy. The cast can be considered useless if even the coarsest details do not appear. The cast should not be taken up until after two hours.

When casting in *loose snow* a different method is used. The impression may be prepared with lacquer or shellac solution and talc and the plaster mixture spooned into the impression. However, the following method is considered more reliable: A layer of dry powdered plaster, $1/4''$ thick, is sifted into the impression, when the plaster absorbs the moisture in it. If the surface of the plaster remains dry there is not enough water, so that some must be added by sprinkling. Then a fresh layer of dry plaster is strewn on, up to $^1/_2''$ to $^3/_4''$ thick. This layer is reinforced with green sticks. Then a folded cloth is laid on the plaster and water is poured on so that the plaster becomes soaked. Instead of the last layer of dry plaster, plaster mix can be spread over the layer applied first. The cast should be allowed to stand two hours before it is removed.

When casting foot impressions in mud and sludge one of the two previously mentioned methods should be adopted.

With all casting of plaster in snow, the freshly removed cast should be handled carefully. In general there will be snow and ice on it, and when that melts the movement of the thawing water can damage details in the cast, which is not yet very hard. It should therefore be placed aside with the underside horizontally down. The surface of a fresh plaster cast is loose and slimy, so that it must be allowed to dry for at least a day before it is examined.

Casting of water-filled impressions. When a foot impression in the bottom of a puddle, in marshy ground or in melting snow cannot be freed from water, other methods of casting must be used, and often give very good results. Dry plaster is simply sprinkled on the surface of the water over the impression. The plaster gradually sinks to the bottom of the mark, and the sprinkling is continued until the cast is sufficiently thick. It should remain *in situ* for at least two hours before being removed.

Casting with paraffin wax

For casting *foot impressions in sand* paraffin wax is the best medium, giving a reproduction which is definitely better than any that can be produced with plaster. The impression is well sprinkled with water so that the sand becomes thoroughly soaked. At the side of the impression a casting pit is built up, the bottom of which should be a few inches higher than the highest part of the impression, and from the pit a small channel is made leading down to the impression. The place where the channel enters should be chosen carefully so that it does not come against important details or outlines. The pit and channel are also soaked with water, and if necessary a wall is built round the impression so that the wax cannot run out at the sides. The wax is melted in a pan and allowed to cool, with gentle stirring, until it is not too hot for a finger to be held in it. Immediately before wax is poured into the impression, the whole of the latter together with the pit and channel is soaked afresh with water by sprinkling, and the melt is then poured into the casting pit so that it runs over into the impression in a uniform stream. The finished cast should be about $^1/_2''$ thick. Reinforcing is not necessary.

Casting with sulphur

For *foot impressions in snow* sulphur is the most reliable medium. The procedure is always the same and follows definite rules. Sulphur can also be used for casting foot impressions in other materials, but has the disadvantage that it sticks too much to the base layer; it may be used with advantage, however, for foot impressions in moist hard clay or loam. Like paraffin, sulphur is not poured directly into an impression in snow, as it might go right through the bottom. A casting pit is made and connected to the impression. The impression is not prepared. Sulphur granules are melted in an enamel or aluminum pan with gentle stirring – the heating should not be done too quickly since the sulphur would then assume a viscous syrupy consistency and be unusable. It actually melts at about $115°$ C and then becomes a thin liquid similar to water. During the melting care should be taken that the sulphur does not catch fire. Although it is difficult to see the flame of burning sulphur, firing may be detected by the suffocating fumes which are produced. When all the lumps have dissolved, the melt is allowed to cool, during which time it should be stirred at intervals. In cold weather, stirring should be continuous as the sulphur has a tendency to solidify on the sides of the vessel. It is most important that cooling should be continued until small crystals, which have the same appearance as ice forming on water, form on the surface of the molten sulphur. The melt is then given a final stir and poured in an even stream into the casting pit. The part of the melt which comes into contact with the snow solidifies almost immediately, so that it is possible to pour the last part of the melted sulphur directly into the impression without much risk, once the surface has been covered. The cast should have a thickness of at least $^3/_4''$. If it is too thin, more sulphur can be melted and poured directly on to the cast, which cools rapidly, in a few minutes. This must be done with great care since the molten sulphur may run over the edges and underneath the cast where the snow is now melted. The cast should be lifted before it becomes completely cold and freezes hard to the bottom of the impression. At first the cast is brittle but it hardens quickly.

Casting in moist hard clay or earth is done in the same manner as in snow. When the cast has cooled it must be dug free, since it holds fast in the clay and is easily broken if an attempt is made to lift it.

Casting with silicone rubber

Silicone rubber, such as Dow Corning 'RC 900' or General Electric 'RTV 60', is a useful material for casting foot prints in a variety of soil conditions. As it is more expensive than the materials described above, it should be used in cases where importance justifies the cost.

The success of the procedure depends upon uniform mixing of silicone rubber and catalyst (setting agent). Mixing must not be so vigorous as to trap air and cause voids in the surface of the cast. The mixture should be free-flowing so that it will flow into fine details in the impression. Lower viscosity silicone rubber can be mixed with higher viscosity material to produce a thinner mixture. The flow property can be controlled by the amount of catalyst added, as prescribed in the manufacturer's instructions. Setting time varies with the amount of catalyst added, and it is desirable to pour a small amount of the mixture next to the print in order to determine when the cast can safely be removed. When hard, the cast has an opaque white color and is quite durable.

Preservation of foot prints (dust prints)

Foot prints are *always* preserved by photographing (see 'Preservation of foot impressions'). After this is done, one of the following methods should be applied:

1. recovering the object on which the foot print is made;
2. lifting by a special rubber lifter; or,
3. lifting on photographic paper.

1. Foot prints are often found on objects stepped on by the criminal who entered in the dark through a window, for example. If the window is broken all fragments of glass are examined. This type of print is usually best detected by low-angle illumination from one side. Rubber heels and soles leave exceptionally good prints on glass. Detailed prints are often also found on paper or cardboard which may be strewn about the room during a safe burglary. All such loose objects bearing prints should be carefully preserved for transport to the laboratory. When the seriousness of the crime warrants it, and when the print consists of a dried liquid such as blood or ink, it may be advisable to remove a portion of linoleum or floor tile which bears a clear impression.

2. *Lifting by a special lifter* is preferred whenever the print is made by

Fig. 33 When a burglar was surprised at the scene he fled by jumping from a window onto a tin roof. The foot prints shown were left because the burglar's shoes were coated with dust.

dust or a dust-like substance from the shoe. The lifter ('Lift-print') is a sheet of black rubber with a slightly sticky surface which is pressed against the print, picking up a faithful replica of the whole print. Oblique light photography under laboratory conditions will bring out this dust print to a contrast which is often better than that observed in the original print. The lifter is re-usable after cleaning.

If a sufficiently large *finger print lifter* is available it may be used instead of the special lifter. Care must be taken not to stretch the rubber lifter whereby the dust image may become distorted.

If the dust is dark, silicone rubber (see above) may be poured over the print, allowed to set and then peeled off. The hardened sheet of silicone rubber acts in much the same way as the rubber lifters.

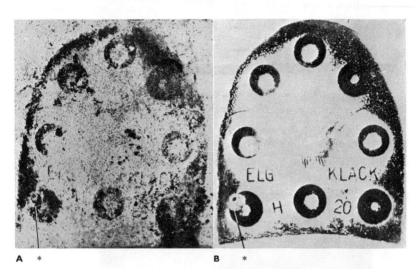

A   *   B   *

Fig. 34 Rubber heel print from the crime scene lifted with finger print lifter (A). B: comparison print made with suspect's shoe in printer's ink; *C:* the actual heel.

C   *

3. *Lifting by photographic paper* may be employed when special lifters are not available. Photographic paper, either black (exposed, developed, fixed and washed) or white (fixed, and washed) is used, as determined by the color of the material in the print. The paper is dampened with water or dilute ammonia, laid – emulsion side down – over the print and beaten against the print with a stiff brush or clapped with the palm. When the whole surface has been thoroughly beaten the paper is removed and laid out to dry.

Taking comparison foot prints from a suspect

When taking *gait pictures* the suspect will not necessarily have the same foot covering as he wore at the scene of the crime, but he must wear something similar. When it is a question of foot prints the feet or shoes should be blackened with finger print ink. A good method is to cause the suspect to walk some yards on a spread-out piece of white wrapping paper about eighteen inches wide. If it is a case of a gait pattern in snow, then the comparison should also be made in snow.

Fig. 35 Bloody foot prints on linoleum at a homicide scene.

When the original prints are from covered feet (socks, shoes, galoshes) these should be worn when making the comparison prints. Comparison prints from soft foot coverings (socks, rubber shoes, etc.) must be made by the suspect himself, but with hard floor coverings (shoes with leather soles, boots, etc.) the police officer can make the prints himself with his hands, using the actual foot coverings, as it is not necessary that they be worn.

When taking comparison *prints* the shoes may be coated with the same material which caused the crime scene prints or with the normal dust from the floor. Test prints are then made on white paper. The soles and heels may also be inked with a roller and printer's ink, especially when comparison is to be made with prints made by a liquid. In most cases the latter method will suffice.

In taking prints of naked feet, the feet are blackened by being pressed against a thin layer of printing ink. In order to get a true picture of the formation of the sole of the foot in different positions, four different prints are taken; in normal standing position, in the standing position with pressure against the outside of the foot and with pressure against the inside, and finally when walking. This also applies to stockinged feet.

Comparison of foot prints

Comparison between foot prints found at the scene of a crime and those of a suspect should be made by an expert, but this does not prevent a police officer from undertaking a preliminary examination.

Prints or impressions of shoe-covered feet are seldom of the same size as the shoes themselves; even when they are being made, slipping and the movement of walking can damage the print. The mark of a naked foot in movement can be as much as $1''$ longer than the mark of the same foot in the standing position. A foot impression in wet earth can become appreciably smaller when the earth dries: in clay the length can decrease by up to $3/4''$. Thus in establishing identity too much significance should not be attached to the dimensions. When examining the mark of a shoe-covered foot a check of the circumference characteristics should be carried out. If the marks from the scene of the crime and from the suspect are similar in form, it is less important that they may differ somewhat in size.

Identification is based mainly on characteristic marks on the sole or heel. The examination is best done by direct comparison of the preserved foot mark from the scene of the crime with the foot covering of the suspect.

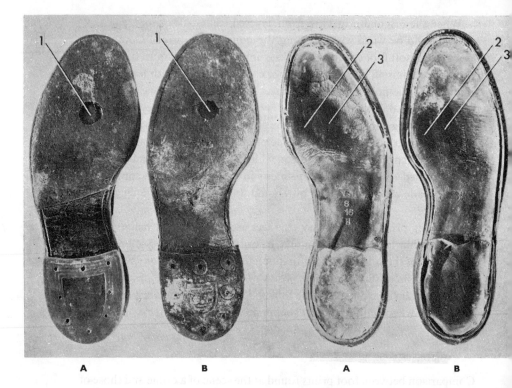

A   B   A   B

Fig. 36 An unknown body was identified as a man missing for several years partly by
the shoes found on the body. The right foot was somewhat deformed, leaving a
characteristic mark on the inside of the sole (2 and 3) which corresponded to
a worn area on the outside (1). A: shoe from the body; B: shoe from the missing
person's home.

These are photographed side by side, and characteristic points are marked.
With foot prints, however, it is generally convenient to take a print of the
foot covering of the suspect, comparison being made between the prints.
When it is a question of prints of naked feet, an examination is made first
to see if there are any identifiable friction skin patterns, and if this is the case
then the investigation is carried out as for finger and palm prints.

In examining the foot covering of a suspect, dust, dirt, earth, etc. should
be kept and if necessary compared with similar materials at the scene of the
crime.

If the perpetrator has left overshoes or galoshes at the scene they may be compared with a suspect's shoes. Characteristic marks on the shoes, particularly on the soles, may be reproduced inside the overshoes. For this examination the overshoes must be cut open. If a shoe is found on the crime scene it may contain characteristic marks of wear from the owner's foot. Such marks can then be compared with the markings inside shoes which can be proven to have been worn by the suspect.

MARKS OF CLOTHES AND OF PARTS OF THE BODY

If clothing is pressed against a smooth surface, a latent print may be produced. Such a print is developed in the same way as a finger print or glove print. Clothing which is contaminated with a foreign body, such as blood, can also form a print. When clothing comes into contact with a plastic substance, for example clay, an identifiable plastic impression may be formed in it.

When a mark from clothing is to be recorded, it must be photographed with the camera placed vertically above or centrally in front of the mark, a foot rule being placed at the side of the mark in a direction corresponding with the structure of the fabric: if the mark is sufficiently large, the scale may be placed in the center of it. In such cases a number of pictures should

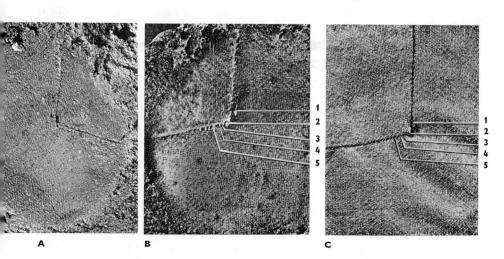

Fig. 37 The three photographs show A: mark of clothing in damp soil; B: casting made from it; C: trousers of the suspect showing repair near the knee.

be exposed and the scale should be moved to either side for each exposure so that details are not concealed.

Marks of clothes are identified with the aid of the structure of the fabric, faults in the latter, seams, patches and other repairs, damage, etc.

It sometimes happens that a whole section of the body forms a print or impression. In one case a burglar fell from a water spout on to the damp earth below, making an impression which showed clearly his face with a characteristic nose and both hands, one holding a crowbar and the other a pistol. When a hand has made a print or impression on a plastic medium, identifiable friction skin patterns should be looked for. Other marks may also be found, such as those of rings, injuries, characteristic skin wrinkles, hand coverings, etc. The preservation of marks of parts of the body is done in the same way as for foot prints.

TOOTH MARKS

Tooth marks occur in the form of bite marks in butter, cheese, fruit, chocolate, etc. Bite marks may also occur on the skin of victims of rape or sexual murder, or on a criminal. Cases have occurred moreover in which the criminal has become involved in a hand-to-hand fight with some person and a tooth has been knocked out, or a dental plate broken, and parts of the tooth or the dental plate may be found.

Bite marks can at times be so characteristic that they make possible definite identification of a suspect. The relative positions of the teeth, their width and the distance between them, together with ridges on the edges of the teeth and grooves on the back or front, vary for different individuals and may show in the bite mark. Deformations resulting from caries or illness, injury in the form of portions broken, away, characteristic wear of the teeth, fillings, and other dental work, the loss of certain teeth, etc., are all noted in the bite.

Generally tooth marks come from front teeth in the upper and lower jaws. With children and young people the edges of the front teeth usually have three ridges (sometimes more) which are distinguished by shallow incisions, sometimes in the form of furrows continued on the front and back sides of the teeth. With increasing age these ridges and furrows generally disappear so that at the age of 30 the front teeth are generally smooth. As a result of congenital syphilis, rickets, etc., the teeth may undergo characteristic changes which are also shown in the bite.

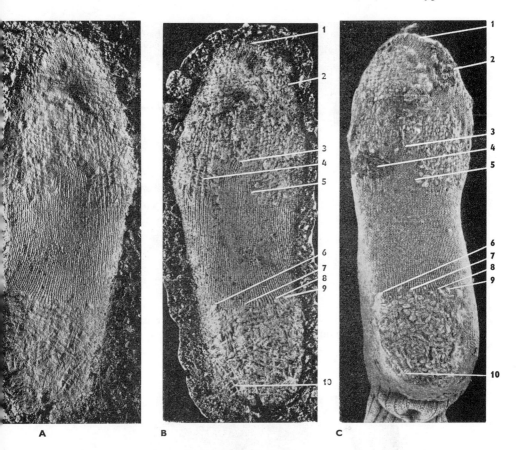

Fig. 38 Three comparison photographs of a sock belonging to the suspect. A: impression in earth. B: casting. C: the actual sock itself.

Bite marks should be carefully preserved by photographing and casting. They are generally formed in material which cannot be sent away or kept for a long time without the bite mark changing in appearance on account of drying or decomposition of the material. Marks made in fruit can be preserved in 0.5 percent formalin solution, which prevents changes resulting from drying, decay, etc. It is, however, not convenient to leave the fruit in the solution for sending away to an expert by mail as the fruit may be broken up and mixed with the solution as the result of shaking. An apple, showing a bite mark, which is to be sent away for examination, should instead be fixed by keeping in the solution for some hours, then wrapped in tissue paper

Fig. 39 Comparison between a cast of a bite in a piece of candy (A) and a cast of a suspect's teeth (B).

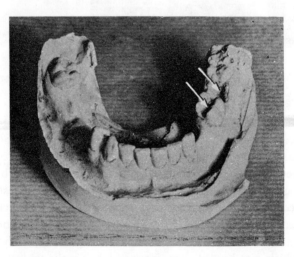

Fig. 40 A dentist's plaster cast of a lower jaw. Several teeth are missing, and those indicated by arrows are badly decayed.

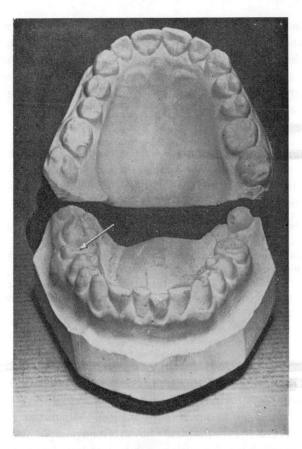

Fig.41 An ordinary plaster casting of the teeth of the upper and lower jaw made by a
dentist. The irregular placing of the teeth in the lower jaw will be noted. The
arrow shows a tooth with badly decayed cavities.

which has been moistened with formalin solution: the whole is then packed
in a carton or box.

For *photography*, oblique lighting is used so that details appear most
clearly. It should be noted that there is a risk that, e.g. butter or soft cheese
might melt under the heat from a photographic lamp. All bite marks should
be photographed before casting, since the casting may go wrong and bite
marks generally alter during casting in such a way that a fresh cast cannot
be taken.

The casting material must be chosen with regard to the proporties of the material in which the bite has been made. If the material contains water-soluble substances, e.g., chocolate and certain types of cheese, then the casting mass should not contain water; or the bite mark must be isolated from the casting mass by spraying with a thin layer of collodion or the like. The most suitable casting media for different materials are given below:

Human skin

Casting according to Poller's method (which is discussed later). In the case of a body sometimes the piece of skin containing the bite mark can be kept and preserved in alcohol or formalin solution. The specimen should be taken during the post mortem.

Murder. On the breast of a dead woman there were found three bite marks. The skin with the marks was removed, without previous casting, and kept in such a way that it shrunk to $1/3$ of its original size, whereby the subsequent investigation was made much more difficult. An attempt to restore the bites to their original size was unsuccessful. The bite marks were very characteristic. With the aid of the position of, and damage to, the teeth of a suspect, from whom a tooth impression was taken, full proof against the latter was possible (LOOCK).

Cheese

Casting with good ordinary plaster, dental plaster (Coecal, Moldano, Whip-Mix, etc.), Kerr dental material, molten sulphur or Woods metal. Plaster should only be employed for cheeses which have a dry and hard consistency. The plaster mix must not be made too thin, since the moisture from it would loosen the cheese before the plaster has set. Good results are obtained only with plaster which is quick setting, such as dental plaster or ordinary plaster with salt added ($1/2$ teaspoonful per pint of plaster mix).

Butter

Casting with a thin mix of good ordinary plaster. Before casting, the butter, and also the water used for the plaster, is cooled.

Sausages, sandwiches, etc.

Bite marks in such materials are especially difficult to cast with satisfactory results. Possibly a thin mix of Kerr Permlastic might be used. In any case the mark should first be photographed in oblique light.

Apples

Casting with dental plaster.

At the scene of a crime there was found an apple which showed clear tooth impressions. At one point in the impression there were found marks of three front teeth in a row, of which two were comparatively large and the third smaller and with an irregular contour. A dentist who examined the bite stated that the latter tooth must have been strongly attacked by caries. A person suspected of the crime was found to have very defective teeth. Two of his front teeth were found to agree with two of the marks in the apple, but the tooth which corresponded to the one which left the irregular impression was actually missing. With the aid of the remains of teeth still in the jaw it could be established that the missing tooth and the one next to it were at the same angle, with respect to one another, as the corresponding teeth in the impression. The suspect finally admitted the murder and stated that the tooth in question had been knocked out in a struggle with the victim (PAULICH, 1940).

Chocolate

Casting with dental plaster. Before casting the surface must be covered with a thin layer of collodion, clear lacquer, or similar material, since the moisture of the plaster would otherwise soften the sugar and destroy the mark.

Where possible, comparison bites from a suspect should be taken by a dentist, but if necessary they can be taken by the police officer himself in which case he should cause the suspect to bite in plasticine. Marks in plasticine can be subsequently cast with good ordinary plaster or dental plaster. The best material for taking tooth impressions, however, are the special purpose dental impression materials.

Chapter 6 Tool marks

Marks of tools or of objects which have been used as tools are often found at the scene of a crime, especially in cases of burglary. Marks may have been left in wood, metal, putty, paint, etc., and among the tools which leave identifiable marks are axes, knives, screwdrivers, chisels, crowbars, pliers, cutters and drill bits. Some of these tools may be home-made.

These marks are essentially of two types, those in which only the general form and size of the tool are apparent, and those in which injuries, irregularities and other peculiar characteristics of the tool are reproduced in the form of striations or indentations.

Marks of the first type do not make a definite identification of the tool possible but only serve as a guide when it is necessary to decide whether the tool of a suspect *could* have produced the marks or not.

Tool marks which show striations, indentations or similar details resulting from damage or other irregularities in the tool are the most valuable as evidence.

Tool marks should, whenever possible, be kept in the originals. This may be done by recovering the whole object or part of the object on which the marks appear. Sometimes it can be arranged that the marks remain untouched at the scene of the crime to be recovered later if this is required. This is only permissible, however, when the marks are in such a position that they are completely protected, for example, a small mark on the inside of a door or window frame. If a mark in metal is not immediately recovered, it should be covered with a thin film of oil to prevent oxidation.

In recovering the mark it is important that it be protected against dirt and moisture during the transport. Tissue or other soft paper is preferably placed next to the tool mark in packaging.

Casting or other methods of taking impressions of a tool mark should only be used as a last resort. However good a cast, it can never be equal to the original and this applies especially to tool marks made in soft materials such as wood, putty, paint and the like, since many of the casting media most

A   B

Fig. 42 Identification of axe mark in timber. A: the disputed mark; B: test mark made
with the tool of the suspect.

suited for these materials are unable to reproduce the finer details which are
decisive for identification. Experiments have shown, for example, that
scratches in paint caused by extremely small irregularities in the edge of a
tool cannot be reproduced by an impression or a cast. Consequently, a
microscopic comparison of the cast with a mark made with the suspected
tool does not lead to any positive results. If, however, the original mark is
compared with one made directly by the tool, then full proof against the
criminal may be obtained.

In the casting of tool marks very satisfactory results may, however, be

A   B

Fig. 43 Comparison of marks in wood. A: the mark left in wood at the scene of the crime;
B: marks made in a test by the knife belonging to the suspect.

obtained with dental impression materials or silicone rubber, and the completed cast will show even the finest markings (see further below).

It is admitted that difficulties and some expense may be involved in
taking possession of the original tool mark, and it should therefore always
be subjected to a close examination with the aid of a magnifier in order to
make sure that it shows typical details from the tool, before any further
steps are taken. In each particular case consideration must also be given to
the type of crime, value of the object, whether a tool from a suspect is available, or the probability that such a tool may be found, etc.

Whether the actual mark is recovered or a cast is made, the tool mark
should be photographed whenever practical. The picture should show clearly the location of the mark in relation to the rest of the object. Close-up
photographs are generally taken in cases where there is risk of the mark

being destroyed in the casting process or during removal. The photographs must be made carefully, with the film plane parallel with the mark and should include a scale. Oblique lighting is used to show up details in the mark. Close-up photographs should, if possible, be in actual size, or in the case of smaller marks, enlarged. It is generally not possible to identify the tool used from photographs.

In connection with all tool marks and suspected tools it should be remembered that the tool may also have deposited traces in the form of paint, oil or other contamination, while clues in the form of wood fragments, paint or the like from the object may, in turn, be found on the tool. These traces are sometimes just as valuable as the tool mark itself. Samples of paint, wood, etc. should therefore always be taken from the area of the tool mark whenever the actual mark is not recovered. It should also be remembered that valuable tool marks are sometimes found on splinters of wood, loosened flakes of paint, chunks of safe insulation, etc.

During the examination of the crime scene the possibility should always be kept in mind that any tool mark found may be compared with marks from previous crimes. It happens frequently that identity is established among tool marks from different burglaries long before the criminal is apprehended or the actual tool is found.

The investigating officer should always endeavor to imagine himself in the position of the criminal when making the tool marks, and to consider how the criminal held the tool, how he stood or supported himself when breaking in or prying open, etc. A housebreaking may be faked with the object of concealing an embezzlement, or of defrauding an insurance company. One should therefore always remember to examine the opposite part of a mark (e.g. in a door frame). The faker often overlooks the fact that this other part of the mark must be present. It is moreover essential for the expert who is to carry out the comparative examination of the tool and the tool marks to understand how the criminal held the tool when making the marks. In most cases, if the examination is to have any prospect of leading to the identification of the tool, the expert has to make a comparison mark in exactly the same way as the criminal has done. This applies especially to those tool marks which show scratches resulting from damage or other irregularities in the tool. The distance between the scratches varies according to whether a knife, for example, is held at right angles to its direction of movement or is held askew (Fig.50), and the appearance of the scratches will depend on the angle taken by the knife in relation to the plane of the cut.

A   B

A   B

Fig.44 Identification of a scraping tool mark on the inside of a lock. A: the questioned mark; B: comparison mark made in lead using the suspect's screwdriver.

Fig.45 Identification of marks of bolt cutter on shackle of a padlock. A: the disputed mark. B: test mark in lead wire produced by tool of suspect.

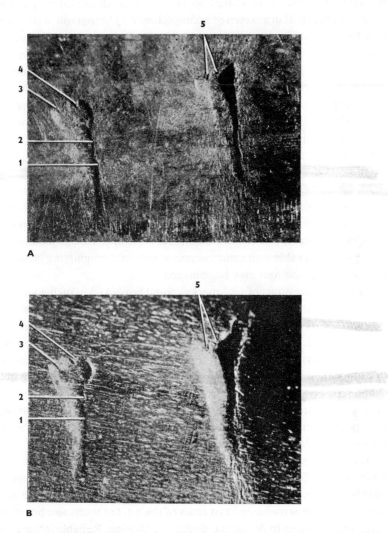

Fig. 46 Comparison of marks made by a pipe wrench. These marks were made on locks at two different burglaries and show the same wrench was used at both places.

It is best if the position of a 'fixed' mark and the conditions at the place are shown to the expert in a sketch or a comprehensive photograph; a statement that the suspect is right or left-handed should also be added. It is moreover essential that the comparison mark should be made in the same material (with the same paint or surface treatment, of the same degree of moisture etc.) as the mark at the scene of the crime, as the clarity of definition of the microscopic scratches varies with different materials. A quantity of material for use in producing comparison marks should therefore be sent with the tool and tool mark – it may be necessary to make ten or more such marks with the suspected tool.

The police officer should not himself attempt to make a comparison mark with a suspected tool. In most cases he has not access to an instrument which is suitable for the closer examination of the character of a tool mark, and this may be necessary in order to decide how the comparison mark is to be made: there is also the risk that traces of paint or foreign metal on the tool, only observable with a microscope or powerful magnifying glass, may be lost, or that the tool may be damaged.

Casts or impressions of tool marks should be packed in such a way that there is no risk of their being altered or destroyed during transport. *Positive casts should never be made*, since this may cause fine details to become obscured. If there is any risk of the negative cast of the mark being destroyed in transmission, it is best to make two and to keep one in reserve. *Regarding boring marks*, identifiable marks are generally left only by *wood bits* and *certain spiral bits*. Both the bottom of the boring, if there is one, and boring chips, are important. Regarding *other types of bits*, identification is only possible in the most favorable cases and then as a rule only when the bottom of the boring is present.

At times the police officer comes up against the problem of deciding from which side of, for example, a window frame (outside or inside) a hole has been bored. In most cases this can be seen from the more or less loose wood fibers round the entrance and exit holes of the bit, but with some bits it may actually be difficult to decide the direction of boring. Reliable information is obtained by cutting through the surrounding wood in the longitudinal direction of the hole – by first sawing through the wood around the hole from each side up to about half an inch from the hole, and then breaking the wood apart. It will then be found that the wood fibers are directed upwards from the hole in one edge of each half, and downwards in the other edges. The wood fibers around the boring are displaced in the direction of rota-

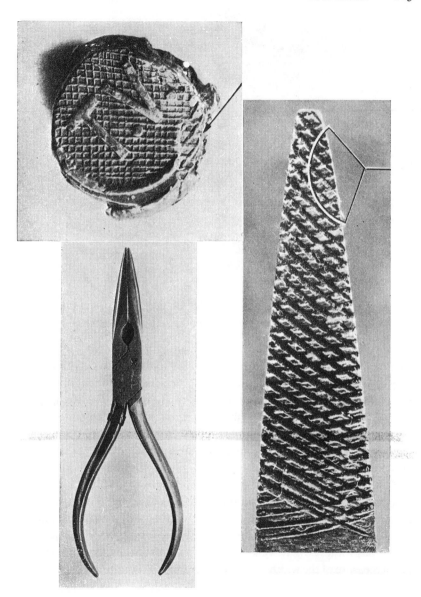

Fig.47 Plier marks (*A*) on a lead seal identified as coming from the inner surface of pliers shown at the right.

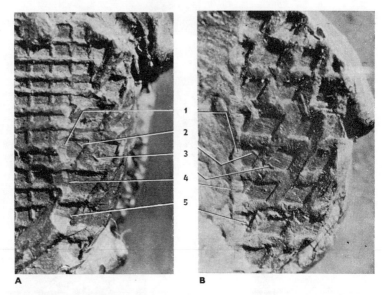

Fig. 48 Identifying characteristics in the lead seal shown in *Fig. 47*. A: The lead seal which had been opened and resealed; B: test mark made with the suspect's pliers in another seal.

tion of the drill, so that on cutting the boring into two parts in this manner they reveal clearly the direction of boring. The degree of orientation of the wood fibers varies for different types of bits and it is possible to obtain an idea of the type of bit used by carrying out test borings with different bits.

Saw marks do not offer any possibility of definite identification of the saw used. In a favorable case, however, a certain degree of guidance may be obtained by noting the degree of set and possibly also the number of teeth per inch of the saw used, but this can be done only if the sawing was stopped before the piece of wood had been sawn right through. Under favorable conditions it is possible to find, in the base of the saw cut, impressions of the teeth of the saw, made when the saw was at rest for an instant before it was withdrawn. It is also possible to obtain, from the base of the saw cut, a measure of the width of cut and therefore of the approximate amount of set.

In the case of marks from *hack saws* there is no possibility of identification. However, the blades are made with different numbers of teeth per inch, and if the saw blade has not gone right through the piece of metal, so that there is a possibility of examining the bottom of the cut, it may be

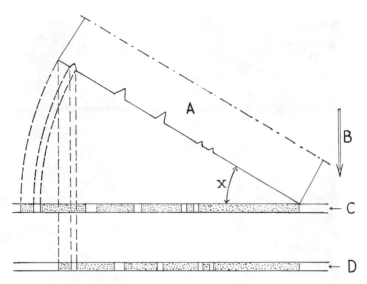

Fig. 49 The distance between details (scores) in an axe mark depends on the angle assumed by the tool in relation to its direction of movement; A: tool with damaged edge; B: direction of cutting; C: marks on cut surface at incidence of 0°; D: marks on cut surface at incidence of X°.

possible to observe the impression of the teeth and thereby to obtain an idea of the number of teeth per inch. This may also be observed at places, at the sides of the actual cut, where the saw, especially when first started, jumped and left shallow marks of the teeth in the surface of the metal.

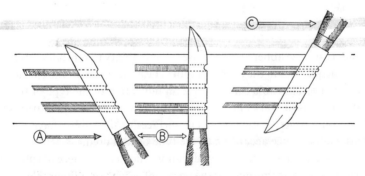

Fig. 50 If a knife is held at right angles to the direction of movement the distance between details (scores) is greater than if it is held at an angle. The appearance of the also differs if the knife is held by a left-handed person. A: direction of cutting; B: right-handed; C: left-handed.

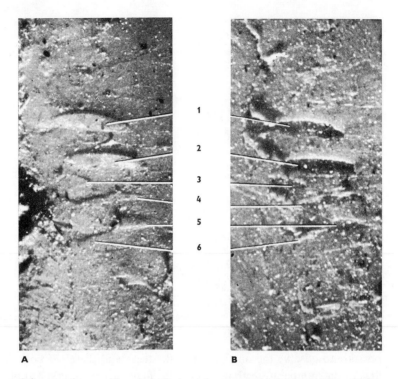

Fig.51 Scissor marks on rubber cloth. Such marks are valuable in determining whether or not a piece of cloth has been cut from a certain larger piece.

Rubber cables or other rubber objects which have been snipped or cut through only show identifiable marks in exceptional cases, owing to the elasticity of the rubber and its consequent inability to reproduce damage or other inequalities in the edge of a tool. The appearance of the cut surface of a snipped or cut cable can still give an indication of the type of tool used, and comparison marks may be made on similar cable with various tools. On account of its elasticity, the cut surfaces of the rubber have a characteristic appearance according to the type of tool used.

If, however, it is a question of deciding whether one piece of rubber sheet or cable was cut from another, the possibilities are more favorable, since the cut or clipped rubber surface often assumes a very characteristic appearance. Fig.51 shows such a case, where a small piece of rubber sheet was proved to have been cut from a larger piece by the cut surfaces showing characteristic details which corresponded completely with one another.

Impression or casting media must be chosen for each particular case, taking into consideration the material in which the mark is formed, its character, details in the appearance of the mark, the desire for reproduction of detail, etc. The most suitable media are described below.

Kerr Permlastic

Kerr Permlastic is a dental impression material in paste form which is prepared by mixing the contents of two tubes, one of which is the catalyst, or setting agent. Strips of equal length are squeezed out on a glass plate or a piece of cardboard where they are mixed with a spatula. The mixing should not take longer than one half minute. The material is then carefully worked into the mark by means of the spatula or a brush. In room temperature the cast hardens in 3–5 minutes and can be removed from the mark. This material is suitable for casting marks in wood or metal, and the marks need no preparation with a release agent. The finished cast is elastic and durable and does not shrink. It reproduces even the finest details in wood.

At temperatures lower than room temperature the material hardens more slowly. Under cold conditions the setting can suitably be accelerated by the heat from a photolamp or a portable hair dryer.

If the casting should prove difficult to hold in the mark, as on a door or a wall, it can be reinforced with a piece of gauze. A small piece of cardboard could also be used as a 'tray', the casting material being applied both to the tray and the mark. The tray is then pressed into the mark and held until the material sets.

If some of the casting material should stick to the mark after removal of the cast, it can be removed with a solvent such as paint thinner or acetone.

Silicone Rubber

Dow Corning Silicone Rubber 'RC 900' is another casting medium which is suitable for reproducing coarse as well as fine details in a tool mark. It is a thick paste to which is added catalyst in the form of drops from a tube. The proportion of catalyst to silicone rubber is important for proper setting, and the manufacturer's recommendations should be followed closely. The mixing is done in a bowl with a spatula and must be thorough so that no soft spots will occur in the finished cast. The setting time varies from 5 to 10

Fig. 52 Comparison photomicrograph of an original tool mark (left) and a positive silicone rubber cast (right). This is an example of the ability of this material to reproduce fine details in tool marks.

minutes, after which a tough, flexible casting can be removed. The finished cast has an opaque white color which may be made metallic by dusting the surface with fine aluminum powder. Aluminum, or other metallic powder, may also be mixed into the silicone rubber before the catalyst is added.

Kerr Perfection Impression Compound

Kerr Perfection Impression Compound is a material used to fashion trays for dental impressions. It is brownish in color and comes in small, hard cakes which are softened by the heat from a flame or in hot water. When soft, this material can be used to reproduce very fine details in tool marks in metal or wood which are not too large nor too deep. A corner of the softened cake is simply pressed against the mark until it cools and hardens. The finished cast is hard and permanent.

While this material is more convenient to use and faster to apply it does not reproduce as fine details as the dental casting materials such as Kerr Permlastic.

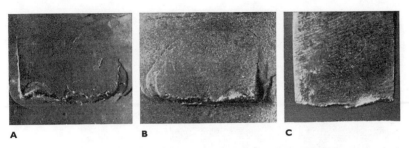

A   B   C

Fig. 53 Crowbar marks on painted wood A: shows the mark; B: shows the mark cast in plasticine; C: shows the edge of the crowbar used.

Castoflex

Castoflex is a green, plastic material which consists of 60% pure latex. It cures merely from the action of oxygen in the air and can therefore be used in very cold weather as well as in hot weather. The setting time at room temperature is several hours and in cold weather the setting takes even longer. At a temperature of about 60° C, which can be generated from a photolamp or a hair dryer, the material hardens in about 15 minutes.

Castoflex can be used for casting tool marks in wood and metal. Its ability to reproduce even microscopic details is very good.

When necessary, the material can be thinned with a 2% ammonia solution. The finished cast is very elastic and can easily be removed from the most irregular mark. Large casts can suitably be reinforced with strips of gauze.

Plasticine

A suitably large piece of plasticine is kneaded until it is soft. It is then formed into a blunt-ended point which is dipped in lycopodium powder and then pressed steadily, but not too heavily, against the mark, which is thereby reproduced in the mass. The lycopodium prevents the mass from sticking in the mark.

This method of making an impression is most suitable for marks in wood, and can only be used when the material of the mark is more resistant than the mass. Plasticine does not take any impression of the finer scratches or other microscopic details, so that it should only be used for those marks in which merely the form and size of the tool and larger imperfections and inequalities appear.

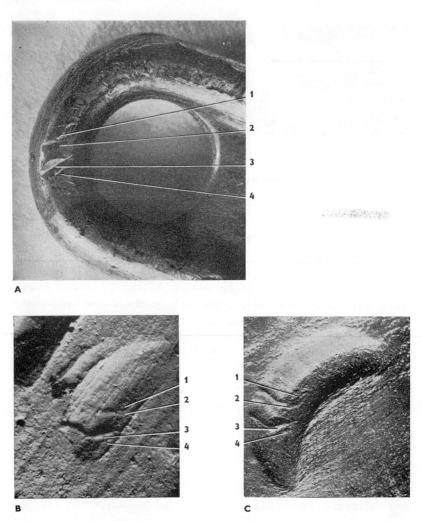

Fig. 54 A comparison between marks found on a broken door and the surface of an adjustable wrench. A: shows marks on the wrench handle; B: shows casting in plasticine of mark on the door; C: shows casting in plasticine of test mark produced in wood with the handle of the wrench (A).

Poller's casting method *(Negocoll, Hominit and Celerit)*

This method has a large sphere of application and can be used for casting marks in many different materials. It has a high reproducing power. The Negocoll negative is somewhat elastic and can be removed from the mark even if the mass has penetrated into small hollows and the like. In the case of deep marks in, for example, wood, the method cannot be used since the the cast sticks in the mark.

The method is, however, rather too troublesome for ordinary field work, and it requires practice and experience to obtain the best results. (For method of casting refer to taking of death masks.)

Plaster of Paris

Occasionally it may be necessary to cast a tool mark directly in plaster of Paris, e.g. in the case of large marks which are lacking in fine detail but of which the size and form may be significant.

The material used for casting is an ordinary good plaster of Paris or dental plaster (see 'Foot prints' and 'Tooth marks'). The mark is first painted over with thin oil, preferably sperm oil.

FRAGMENTS OF TOOLS

At crime scenes where doors, windows, or locked drawers show signs of forcible entry the investigating officer must remember to examine carefully the floor immediately adjacent to the point of entry before examining the actual tool marks. It is not uncommon for burglary tools to break during forced entry. Large or small fragments of the tool may therefore be found on the scene and may prove to be very valuable as evidence. Broken pieces of a tool might also be found inside a lock on which picking or prying has been attempted.

In many cases it is possible to establish that such broken fragments originally were parts of tools found in the possession of a suspect. The physical matching of two or more pieces which originally were one – a so-called 'fracture match' – is a most convincing and easily demonstrable type of proof against an offender.

The converse situation should also be kept in mind: a broken tool left by the burglar at the scene can be matched with fragments of that tool which

Fig. 55 A 'fracture match' between one jaw of a pair of cutters from the suspect's home and a fragment found at a burglary scene.

may be found in the suspect's home or workshop or in his clothing. Pieces may also have been left at the scene of another burglary.

The search for such tool fragments is best done with a flashlight the beam of which is directed over the search area at a very low angle. When the light strikes a metallic fragment it will give off bright reflections which make the

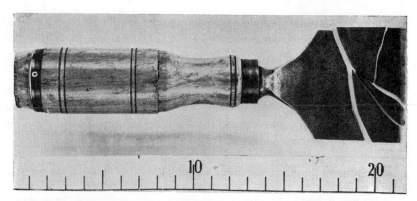

Fig. 56 Metal fragments found at a crime scene are shown matching a chisel found in the suspect's possession.

Fig. 57 A small fragment of metal was found inside the lock of a desk at a burglary scene. It could be shown to have been broken from the tip of the suspect's knife.

particles easy to find. Any suspected fragment should be recovered and placed in a vial, envelope or pill box which can be labeled as to the time and place of recovery.

A magnet can also be used in searching for tool fragments.

If the officer does not make a deliberate effort to look for such pieces of broken tools he runs the risk of trampling them into the ground, imbedding them in his own shoe, or kicking them aside while engaging in the other routine of crime scene search.

Burglary. During a burglary the door of a cabinet had been forced open by means of a wood chisel and four pieces of the chisel blade were found near the cabinet.

A few months later a safe burglary with explosives was committed in the same town by two men. After the burglary they had hidden a brief case containing detonators and some dynamite. The brief case was also found to contain a broken chisel. The fragments from the other burglary could be fitted perfectly to this chisel, thereby clearing up also the first offense. (Fig. 56).

Burglary. A man was caught in the act of attempting entry into an office. Among his possessions was a pocketknife with one broken blade. A burglary had been committed in the same building two days previously, and during that investigation a piece of metal had been found on the basement floor. This fragment could positively be shown to have come from the broken blade of the suspect's knife. By a thorough examination of the littered basement floor it could thus be proven that the suspect had also committed the earlier burglary.

Chapter 7 Blood and other biological evidence

Bloodstains found at the scene of a crime, on objects or on a suspect are very important clues, and even the mere confirmation of the presence of blood may often be of decisive significance. Stains can also be valuable information in reconstructing the events at the scene. A detective is required to have a good knowledge of the methods of searching for, and preserving, stains which are suspected of being blood, and also to draw the correct conclusions from the formation and position of the stains. Identification and further investigation, however, are a matter for the expert. The results of these latter investigations are in fact dependent on the way in which the police officer acts when he finds the bloodstains, and he must therefore have some knowledge of the purely scientific methods of investigation and of the results which can be obtained from them.

What is blood?

In the living body blood consists mainly of blood liquid (blood plasma), together with red and white blood corpuscles (blood cells). In a healthy man the blood makes up about $1/_{13}$ part of the body weight, which means that a full-grown man has more than 9 pints of blood.

The red corpuscles which give the blood its red color contain the blood pigment haemoglobin, and are present to the number of about 5 million per cubic millimeter. In the lungs the haemoglobin of the blood corpuscles is saturated with oxygen and is then carried by the arteries into the body, where the oxygen is used up in combustion. When the blood returns from the capillaries of the body it is poor in oxygen. This is the reason why the color of blood is brighter in the arteries than in the veins.

The white blood corpuscles are fewer in number than the red ones: for every 1000 red there are only one or two white.

Blood plasma contains a few percent of salts and also 8–9 percent of albuminoids of various kinds, including fibrinogen, which is the cause of the coagulation of the blood.

When blood coagulates it divides into two parts – blood clot, which consists of fibrinogen converted to fibrin, together with red and white corpuscles; and blood serum, which has a pale straw color and contains other constituents from the original blood.

In the further investigation of bloodstains or of stains which resemble blood, the following questions are liable to arise:

Is it blood or not?

In nearly all cases this question can be answered with certainty, but it is essential that the quantity available should not be too small. The examination is carried out microscopically, microchemically and spectrographically.

Is the blood human or animal?

This can be determined by the precipitin reaction, if a sufficient quantity of the sample is available. The test is, however, interfered with or made impossible if the blood has putrefied, been heated, or changed by the action of hydrogen peroxide, soap, shoe polish and other interfering agents.

From what kind of animal did the blood come?

This can also be determined by the precipitin reaction. To distinguish nearly related species of animals is difficult, although possible in some cases. Here also the quantity available must not be too small.

A blue serge jacket was found to have on the sleeves some stains which gave the chemical test for blood, the microscopic test for mammalian blood, and the precipitin test for horse blood. Inside the jacket pocket was a handkerchief with stains upon it of mammalian blood, and the application of the precipitin test showed these stains to be human blood. On examining the coat with a lens, several short bay hairs were discovered, and also two or three long black hairs. These hairs had the characteristics of horses' hair. The coat belonged to a man who was accused of horse maiming, his victim being a bay mare with black points. At the time of arrest the accused had a recently cut finger. The scientific findings entirely confirmed the charge against the accused (WILLCOX, 1928).

Does the blood come from a certain individual?

This question can be answered partially by a blood group examination, but it is essential that a sufficient quantity should be available. A blood group determination can, however, never result in a definite statement that the blood comes from a certain individual, even if the blood groups are identical; there are a large number of persons with the same blood group. Any difference of blood group in the samples examined excludes their having the same source.

In all cases where a blood group determination may become important, the police officer should arrange, as early as possible, for the necessary blood sample to be taken. This applies not only to taking a sample from the body of a person who has been killed, but also to taking one from a criminal or from a victim of assault, rape, as thus unnecessary delay in the investigation is avoided.

It is a useful practice to take a sample of blood from each assault victim if there is any suspicion that blood has been shed, however slightly. Only medical personnel should take blood specimens from living persons. In some states there are legal problems associated with the removal of blood from a deceased person unless it is done as part of an autopsy. In any case, blood must be obtained prior to embalming of the body.

Medical records should not be relied on for information on the victim's blood type.

From what part of the body does the blood come?

This can be determined in rare cases when the blood contains typical impurities, as for example, with blood from the nose (secretions and hairs) and menstrual blood (epithelial cells from the vagina, and hairs).

Methods are available by which fetal blood can be differentiated from the normal blood of the mother.

Does the blood contain alcohol?

This can be determined chemically, but it is essential that the blood should not be contaminated, that the sample is obtained either from the body or a short time after being shed so that drying or evaporation cannot occur, and that it is taken in a clean and well-sealed container (preferably a capillary tube).

Does the blood contain carbon monoxide?

If a sufficient quantity is available this can be determined, assuming that the blood has not dried out and that it has not undergone any considerable amount of decomposition or contamination. The examination is done chemically or spectrographically.

How old are the bloodstains?

To determine the age of a bloodstain is generally very difficult. The determination depends on how far the change in the blood pigments has proceeded. If, for example, the haemoglobin has been changed to haematin then the bloodstain cannot be fresh. How quickly this change occurs depends however on a number of factors such as the character of the material on which the stain is deposited, the strength and color of the light acting on it, the degree of moisture, etc. The expert therefore needs accurate statements of these factors, preferably together with a clean sample of the underlying material for comparative examination. Tests, which must be done chemically and spectrographically, and must be based on a comprehensive comparison with blood on the same or a similar underlayer and under similar conditions, can sometimes result in the age of a bloodstain being estimated with accuracy. It is essential that fairly large stains be available for these tests.

Some useful information may be obtained from studying the degree of drying of a bloodstain. If the blood is fluid the stain is very fresh; an hour old, more or less, depending on the size and thickness. If the blood is gelatinous, fibrin has been formed. The line made by a pencil drawn through the blood will remain visible due to the lack of fluidity. On further drying the stain contracts and finally puckers and cracks around the edges. The speed with which this series of changes occurs will depend on atmospheric conditions, such as humidity and temperature. However, the investigator may form some judgment as to the time elapsed.

Preliminary blood tests

By means of preliminary blood test reagents crime investigators can determine, even at the scene of a crime, whether a stain *may be or is not* blood. No preliminary test can prove definitely that a stain is blood, as certain other substances also give a positive reaction. *The test gives the same result with animal blood as with human blood*.

Bloodstains on which the reagent has been used are destroyed as far as any further examination is concerned, and therefore reagents are *not used except in the cases mentioned below*, and then only in such a way that the smallest possible quantity of blood is used.

1. In extremely urgent cases;

2. When a considerable number of stains are available;

3. In cases where the test is applied to a large stain or merely to marks of a dried or washed-away large stain, and the reagent can be used without requiring so large a proportion of the stain that any further examination is rendered impossible. In such a case the reagent may show that the stain in question is not blood, so that the exhaustive and tedious work of preservation can be avoided.

4. When it is simply a matter of confirming the position and extent of the bloodstains in, for example, a large area or on a stairway, where blood is certainly present.

The most convenient reagents for use at the scene of a crime are *benzidine* and *leuco-malachite green*. With both of these the positive reaction arises

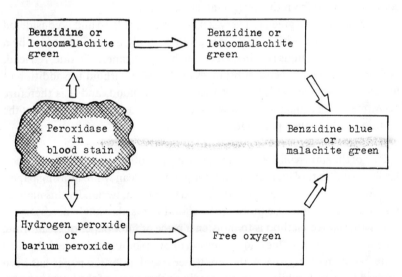

Fig. 58 Diagram showing what happens when a positive reaction is given by a reagent. Oxygen, combined in the reagent, is set free on contact with a peroxidase and acts on the reagent to produce a color.

from an oxidation process which is brought about by oxygen, combined in the solution, being released on contact with an enzyme (peroxidase), which occurs in blood, and elsewhere, and the oxygen set free acts in its turn on the reagent so that a color is produced (Fig.58).

Benzidine. One tablet of benzidine is dissolved in 20–25 ml. of glacial acetic acid, after which the solution is ready for use. The benzidine tablets contain combined oxygen in the form of barium peroxide, so that the addition of hydrogen peroxide is unnecessary. If however the solution is prepared from benzidine itself (5% solution in glacial acetic acid), hydrogen peroxide must be added before use – 5 or 6 drops of concentrated hydrogen peroxide (25–30%) to about 5 ml. of solution.

In the oxidation process the benzidine is acted on with the production of benzidine blue. Peroxidases occur not only in blood but also in fresh fruit juices, fresh milk, urine, and other substances.

Leuco-malachite green. One gram of leuco-malachite green is dissolved in 100 ml. of glacial acetic acid and to this solution is added 150 ml. of distilled water. Before use 5–6 drops of concentrated hydrogen peroxide (25–30%) are added to about 5 ml. of the solution.

In the oxidation process malachite green, which has an intense blue-green color, is formed from the leuco-malachite green.

Leuco-malachite green is a very sensitive test for blood and is considered to be reliable. A positive reaction is given not only by blood but also by a number of compounds rich in oxygen, such as manganese dioxide, red lead, and permanganates. These substances give a color without the addition of hydrogen peroxide, which is not the case with blood, and it is therefore desirable, when using this test, always to carry out a control test without the addition of hydrogen peroxide.

The *preliminary test* is conveniently done as follows:

Part of the stain which is to be tested is scraped off with a razor blade, clean knife or similar tool on to piece of filter paper or clean white blotting paper, and some drops of the reagent are poured over the material. By this method it is not necessary to use more of the stain than is absolutely necessary.

An alternative method is to moisten a piece of filter paper or clean white blotting paper with saline (0.9% solution of pure sodium chloride in distilled water) – in an emergency with pure water – and, after the paper has been pressed for a little while against the stain so that some of the latter is transferred to the paper, to put some drops of the test reagent on the transferred stain.

If the stain is on fabric, a thread soaked with the stain is pulled out and extracted with saline on a watch glass. After the extraction a few drops of the reagent are added. On 'shaggy' material blood often does not penetrate into the fibers but remains as crusts on the hairs. In this case some of the stain is scraped off on to filter paper with a razor blade or a clean knife, and covered with the reagent.

Under no circumstances should filter or blotting paper, soaked in the reagent, be pressed against the stain which is to be tested, since the latter would be rendered useless for any further investigation.

When using the preliminary test it should always be remembered that such methods never prove the stain is composed of blood. A positive reaction shows that the material tested *may be* blood, and a negative one that it *is not* blood.

Searching for bloodstains

A dried but relatively fresh bloodstain generally has a reddish-brown color, and is glossy in contrast to, for example, rust stains. In a very thin layer the color may be greyish-green. The gloss disappears slowly under the action of sunlight and heat, wind and weather, or as the result of an attempt to wash it away; and the color finally becomes grey. Bloodstains can, however, assume other colors from red to brown or black, or they may appear green, blue or greyish-white. The color, and also the time required for the change, depends on the underlying material: the change is quicker on metal surfaces and slower on textiles. With some types of cloth the blood soaks into the threads, with others it lies on the pile. The surface gloss is often less marked on fabric. Bloodstains on wallpaper may show surprising colors on account of the blood taking up color from the paper. Certain other stains, composed of pigment, rust, tobacco, snuff, urine, feces, coffee, etc., can easily be confused with bloodstains. In searching for bloodstains, marks should not be classified according to color and character, since a stain which appears to deviate from the normal character of a bloodstain may be composed of blood, whereas one which resembles blood may be composed of some other substance.

When searching for stains it is convenient to allow the light from a flash light to fall obliquely against the surface under examination. Sometimes a stain shows up better against a surface when it is illuminated with colored light. Red, green and ordinary light are used successively.

Fig. 59 Typical blood marks at the scene of a crime. 1: dropping blood: 2: pool of clotted blood; 3: mark of hand drawn though blood; 4: mark of blood-stained hand; 5: mark of blood-stained clothing.

Often the search for bloodstains may be aided through the use of the Luminol test. This reagent reacts to blood by luminescing. The test is therefore limited to areas which can be made totally dark. Since the reagent also reacts to copper and its alloys it is not specific for blood. Its use does not interfere with confirmatory and typing tests.

The reagent is prepared by mixing sodium perborate with a mixture of 3-aminophthalhydrazide and sodium carbonate in a ratio of 0.14:0.02:1. The dry ingredients are dissolved in water and sprayed on the suspected surfaces immediately, using glass or plastic sprayers. Strong luminescence indicates the presence of blood or copper compounds.

Occasionally the assailant will clean up the premises. Furniture is straightened, damage is concealed and blood is washed off – all for the purpose of concealing the crime, delaying its discovery or destroying evidence. The search of the scene should therefore also be extended to places which are not in direct view. A criminal with bloody fingers may, for example, have opened a drawer, fingered through papers, grasped a doorknob, etc. Wash basins, garbage pails and the like should be given close attention. The drain traps should also be examined since there may be blood in the trap if the criminal washed his hands. Towels, draperies and other fabrics which may have served to wipe off blood should also be examined. If a floor has been washed in order to remove bloodstains, blood may possibly be found in the cracks of the floor, joints between tiles, under the edges of linoleum, etc.

The search for blood on *clothes* must be carried out carefully and systematically. Even if blood has been washed off the more conspicuous parts, stains may still be found on the seams, lining, inside the sleeves, in pockets, etc.

Stains which have been diffused by washing may be concentrated in the laboratory, and in some cases typing has been successful.

A suspected person may also have bloodstains, not merely on his clothes, but also on his body.

In the open air, the search for bloodstains is often especially difficult. Rain, snow, sun and wind may have obliterated the marks more or less completely. The blood mark may have changed its color in a very short time on account of the character of the ground. If the ground gives the impression of dampness in certain parts, these parts should be given special attention, as also blades of grass, leaves, branches of trees, and the like.

Objects on which the presence of bloodstains is suspected should be examined very carefully in cracks, joints and seams, since bloodstains can sometimes be found in such places even after the object has been washed or cleaned. It should also be remembered that it does not follow that blood *must* be found on a knife or similar object which has been used in a murder or assault. The edges of the wound may wipe the blood off the blade as it is drawn out.

If *blood has run through bedclothes in a bed* it is necessary to consider whether it has run through all the bedclothes or has remained in, for example, the mattress. This is of the greatest importance in estimating the total quantity of blood and sometimes in enabling the doctor to decide on the time which has elapsed since death.

Fig. 60 Bloody prints of bare feet and a tuft of blood-stained hair (see arrow) at a homicide scene.

When a quantity of blood is found at the scene of a crime, the amount should *always be estimated*; it should bear a reasonable relation to the injuries of the victim. If the quantity is too large or too small in comparison with the latter, an explanation must be found. In the first case part of the blood may have come from some other individual, possibly the criminal; and in the second case it may be that the missing quantity of blood is to be found at some other place where the crime was actually committed.

In this connection there is always a risk of estimating the amount of blood as more than is actually present. Most people tend to place the estimate too high, and the investigator should therefore obtain a second person's estimate. Bodies in advanced stages of decomposition are often found in a large pool of dark, blood-colored fluid which is often referred to as blood in the report of the investigation. This fluid should more properly be called 'blood-like fluids due to decomposition'.

Drops and splashes of blood

The form and position of bloodstains can often give valuable information regarding the course of events.

If drops of blood fall vertically on to a hard surface they assume various forms according to the height of fall. The character of the underlying surface (stone flooring, linoleum, wood flooring) also has some effect, but not to such an extent that there is any considerable change in the form of the drops.

The following summary forms a guide in estimating the height of fall:

Up to about 20 in. – round and sharply delineated spots (Fig.61).

20 in. to 4 ft. 6 in. – spots with prickly edges: the projections are at first thick and sparse, but as the height of fall increases they become finer and closer together (spiked club form) (Figs.62 and 63).

Over 4 ft. 6 in. – fine and close projections and also ray-like splashes which may extend even to as much as a foot from the center of the drop. Small droplets are set free on striking and thrown out of the drop itself (Fig.64). Drops and splashes of blood which fall in an oblique direction against a surface assume a drawn-out form which varies, according to the speed of the splash, from the shape of a pear to that of an exclamation mark. Sometimes a small drop is set free and thrown a somewhat longer distance, forming the dot under the exclamation mark. This dot or the pointed end of the splash shows the direction of travel of the drops or splashes (Fig.65).

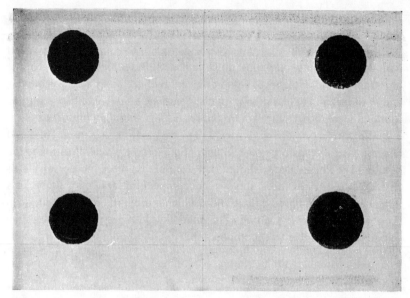

Fig.61 Drops of blood on a plain surface falling from a height up to 20 in.

Fig.62 Drops from a height of 20–40 in. The spines are large and sparse.

Fig.63 The same from a height of 40–60 in. The spines are fine and close.

By studying the appearance of such drops or splashes, with their direction and placing, it is sometimes possible to determine where an assault occurred, the position of the injured part of the body during the assault, where the criminal was at that moment, whether the victim attempted to evade the criminal, the number of blows given, etc. In general blood splashes come only from a blow against an already bleeding part of the body, but there are exceptions, which appear to depend on the filling of the blood vessels and the fragility of their walls.

Murder. A business man, while sitting at a table in his office, was killed by a number of blows on the head with an axe. The investigation showed that blood had been sprayed in all directions over the floor, but that there was none in an area behind the chair on which the man was sitting. In view of this, it was evident that the murderer must have stood at that place when he wielded the axe, and it could be assumed that the blood which must inevitably have been thrown out in that direction had gone on to the clothes of the murderer. The injuries in the head of the victim showed that he had sat with his back turned to the murderer. Local conditions were such that one could hardly imagine that a client or person unknown to the business man would have had an opportunity of standing behind his chair, since, for reasons of caution or of politeness, the man would have turned to face him. It could therefore be assumed that some person, known to the victim, had stood behind the chair and struck treacherously with the axe. This theory was found to be correct. The murderer was a person who had previously been employed in the business.

Splashes of blood are sometimes found at a distance of several yards from the place of the assault. In the case of blood splashes it is necessary to consider the possibility that they might have been produced by swinging a blood-covered weapon, from the movement of an injured limb, e.g. an arm, from the victim swinging the latter in order to throw off blood, or from the victim having spat blood. Such accumulations of blood splashes show only one or two directions and therefore should not be confused with the shower which results from, e.g., a blow, when the blood spreads out in all directions. Blood splashes of the first-mentioned type are sometimes found under furniture and similar places, and bear no relation to other groups of bloodstains. Sometimes they have the form of showers of fine spray.

Murder. Two sacks were found floating in the sea. The sacks were found to contain portions of a female body and, on examination at the mortuary, these were proved to have come from the same body.

The police investigation resulted in the arrest of a man, suspected of having murdered the woman, and an examination of his house was undertaken by the laboratory. A

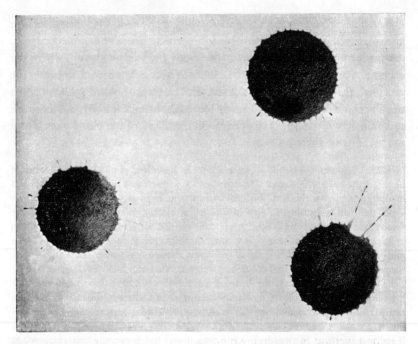

Fig. 64 The same from 60–80 in. The spines are fine and close and splash out in a sun
     ray design.

brownish stain, looking suspiciously like blood, was found on the front door which led
into a hall, and an examination showed that it was blood. Closer inspection of the door
showed four blood-stained areas grouped on the surface of the door; two on the jamb
and two on the panes. Of the two on the jamb the upper one showed a blood mark on
the edge, splashing to one side, that is into the jamb and forward towards the panel, indicating that some blood covered object had struck with a fair degree of force against
the edge of the door when the door was open, at a height of about 40 in. above ground
level. Immediately below there was a line of blood which had run down the
edge of the door from the above-mentioned splash. The two stains on the panels of the
door were lightly streaked and about 5 in. long. The streaks had evidently been caused
by a blood-stained object having been drawn or brushed along the door from left to right.
The stains were all due to human blood which had recently been shed. They could have
been produced only by some object, heavily stained with human blood, striking against
the door and brushing along it when it was open; the moving object passing from within
the house outwards. The stains could have been produced by a blood-stained object,
such as a sack, carried over the left shoulder of an average-sized man, and it might be
assumed, that it had been caused by some person carrying out on his shoulder something
heavily stained with human blood.

    This reconstruction contributed considerably to the solution of the crime (SMITH, 1941).

If blood is thrown against a wall in drops or large coherent masses, small splashes are scattered round the main stain, which afterwards runs down. The character of such stains can therefore be determined without difficulty.

Description and recording of bloodstains

In the case of bloodstains, a description should be made of their form, color, size, position, direction of splash, estimated height of fall, etc. They should be photographed as well as sketched, a scale being included in the close-up views. If the dynamics of the deposition of the blood must be determined, such scaled close-up photographs are absolutely essential. For photographing bloodstains it is best to use orthochromatic film and to carry out the photography in such a way that the orientation is shown (e.g. a door post visible on the photograph). It is also possible to lay a piece of tracing paper over the dried stains and to draw their contours which may be useful when there is some doubt regarding the height of fall.

Preservation of bloodstains

The best method of preserving bloodstains is, of course, to *take possession of the object on which they are found*. It should be remembered that blood holds firmly on to cloth, paper and wood, but poorly on to painted or

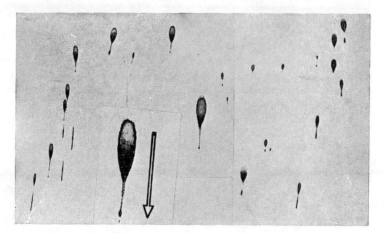

Fig. 65 Blood splashes which have hit a wall at an angle. The pointed ends indicate the direction of movement (see arrow).

polished surfaces, polished metals, etc.; and in the latter case it becomes loose when it dries and may fall off at the slightest touch. If there is any risk of this a piece of thin transparent paper may be moistened with a solution of gum arabic and placed over the mark before moving the object. If necessary the bloodstain may be covered with a piece of pure white paper dampened with water. The gum solution or water does not interfere appreciably with any future investigations.

If the case is important the officer should not hesitate to ask permission to remove pieces of tile, linoleum, flooring, wallpaper, etc.

Dried stains on objects which cannot be detached or taken away can be preserved in various ways according to circumstances.

The blood can be scraped off with a clean razor blade or knife on to clean white paper, and the material removed placed in a clean sample tube.

If bloodstains are found on an object which is not permeable or absorbent to water, the stain may be moistened with saline or with a little water and allowed to stand for a while, after which the blood and water are stirred with a clean glass rod or piece of wood. When the blood has dissolved in the liquid, the solution is sucked up in a capillary tube, which is then sealed. A 4–8 day old stain dissolves in about half an hour; a 2–4 week old one in two hours; and a very old stain needs several hours to dissolve in water or saline.

Fig. 66 Bloodstains on wall fanning out from the head of the person killed by axe. They clearly show the position of the head when struck.

It is also possible to moisten a piece of clean white blotting paper or filter paper with saline and to lay this over the bloodstain, which is thus softened and sucked up into the paper. After drying, the paper should then be preserved in a closed test tube.

Bloodstains on walls, stones and the like are sometimes difficult to deal with. Flakes of blood may be loosened with a clean knife and allowed to fall on to clean white paper and then enclosed in a test tube. If the stains are attached so firmly that it is difficult to loosen any flakes, a clean white linen cloth is washed over with gum solution, pressed against the stain, and kept there under pressure until the gum solution has dried completely, which may take a whole day. The cloth is then drawn off cautiously, and the stain comes with it.

Bloodstains on the ground are preserved simply by taking up the blood-soaked earth with a trowel or knife, and then placed in a glass (mason) jar. Worms and insects must be removed as far as possible, since they eat blood. When taking the sample one should remember to measure the depth to which the blood has penetrated the soil.

Bloodstains on grass and plants are collected, in the case of grass, by tying a string around the tufts of grass and then cutting the latter with a knife. The tuft is placed in a carton, glass jar or the like. Blood *on twigs and leaves of shrubs and trees* is collected by cutting off the twigs or leaves and placing them in cartons, glass jars or the like. In the case of marks of *still liquid or undried blood* it should be noted that the object should not be placed in a tightly closed container, since the blood would putrefy instead of drying and this would interfere with any further investigation, or make it impossible.

Blood which has not yet coagulated can be taken up with a capillary pipette or eye dropper and diluted with saline solution. This procedure gives a cell suspension from which major blood groups and sub-groups may be determined. A special type of pipette for this purpose, Unipettes, may be used for this operation, and with a little practice even small wet stains can be collected. If saline solution is not available it can be made by dissolving two heaped teaspoonfulls of table salt in a quart of water. In the absence of saline solution, moist blood will putrefy at room temperature. Therefore it becomes necessary to absorb the blood on filter paper or clean white blotting paper and permit the specimen to dry before packaging.

In the case of bloodstains on *clothes, draperies, etc.* the articles themselves should be recovered. It is less suitable to cut out the stained area. If for any reason this becomes necessary, as with upholstery, unstained portions of the fabric should also be cut out because it is of the greatest importance that such material be available for control tests. In preserving a garment or piece of material bearing bloodstains it is advisable to spread it out on a piece of tissue paper and then place another piece of tissue paper over the garment and then to roll the three layers up so that the paper isolates the different layers from one another. If tissue paper is not available, clean unused wrapping paper may be substituted. If the stains are still damp they should *first be dried*, preferably in a dust free, dark room. Recovered blood stains should be sent to the expert as soon as possible. Delay in doing so can result in the stain being changed to such an extent that later examinations are complicated or even made impossible.

When submitting the material a statement should be made to the expert as to whether the bloodstains are known to be *contaminated* in any way, or to have been *exposed to heat* (e.g. by pressing of the clothes) together with a statement of the method of preservation used, whenever pertinent.

It is of the utmost importance that not only the blood or stains be submitted to the expert but also *samples of blood* from the victim or the suspect be sent along for comparison. This detail should never be overlooked. Such blood samples are taken by a physician or a nurse, and the officer should make arrangements for taking such samples. In order to prevent clotting, a small amount of sodium citrate should be added to the blood sample.

HUMAN SECRETA AND EXCRETA

Stains from the excretion and secretion products of the human organism can appear at the scene of a crime, on the victim of a rape, and also on clothing or other objects which are connected in some way with the crime. Excretion and secretion products have their greatest value in connection with the possibility of determining the blood group of an individual. Actually this is only possible if the individual is a secretor, by which is meant a person who has group-specific substances, not only in his blood but also in other body fluids, so that a blood group determination on the latter is possible. About three persons out of four are secretors. A blood group determination is sometimes possible even when only minimal quantities of secretion products are available, since the concentration of the group-specific substances in many of these products is appreciably greater than in blood. The result of the group determination is not appreciably affected by thorough drying of the material. Moreover, impurities do not affect this determination to the same extent with secretion products as with blood stains.

When an expert is asked for a determination of the blood group of a secretion product, he should be given a statement of the blood group of the individual in question together with a sample of his blood, and if possible a sample of the particular secretion product from that individual. This is a simple matter in the case of urine, saliva and the like, samples of which should be taken by a physician or a nurse or, in emergencies, by the police officer himself. In the case of sweat, nasal secretion and the like, samples can be obtained from the sweatband of a hat, some article of clothing, a handkerchief, etc.

The mere identification of a secretion product is in fact often sufficient to give the required proof or to make possible a reconstruction of the course of events.

Stains on clothing or other objects can often be located with advantage by using an ultraviolet lamp, before packing for sending away. This is especially the case with stains of semen, which generally show a very strong fluorescence, but stains of other secretory products may also show up very clearly under ultraviolet light. Too great importance should not be attached to a negative result of such an examination, since the stains may have lost their fluorescence owing to their age or being contaminated with impurities. A slight admixture of blood, for example, will completely extinguish the fluorescence of semen. Clothing or the like which is suspected of carrying stains of such a kind should therefore be sent to an expert for examination, even if visual inspection or a preliminary examination under ultraviolet light gives a negative result.

Both dried and moist stains should if possible be kept on the underlying material. Only in an emergency should they be scraped off. If the part carrying the stain has to be cut out, one should always remember to keep an unstained part of the underlying material, as it is of the greatest importance that the expert should have such material available for a control test.

It is sometimes important to determine the presence of a particular microorganism in secretion. This is usually very difficult, especially in dried stains, and requires a complicated and time-consuming laboratory analysis.

Semen

Semen stains have a characteristic greyish-white appearance and feel stiff on cloth, but if the stains have been exposed to rubbing for some time they lose their stiffness. When contaminated with blood, feces or urine they may not be visible to the naked eye.

The investigation of semen is based largely on finding undamaged sperm cells (spermatozoa). In addition a preliminary test, using Florence's and Puranen's micro reactions, is done. It is therefore of the greatest importance that the stains should not be exposed to friction or rubbing, which would disrupt the sperm cells. The packing of objects carrying semen stains should preferably be done in such a way that the contaminated surface is fixed on a sheet of cardboard which is then placed in a package so that the latter does not come into contact with the stains.

The stain may consist of semen even though sperm cells cannot be found, since they may be absent on account of age or sickness, or because the stain represents the last of a series of successive ejaculations; this is also the case with the so-called secondary stains which result from the semen having penetrated one layer of material on to another so that the spermatozoa are filtered out. In such cases the enzyme method for the detection of acid phosphatase in the liquid fraction of semen is of the greatest value. Acid phosphatase is an enzyme which, in high concentration, is characteristic of semen. This method also has a special significance in cases of sterility, since spermatozoa may not be present in semen even though it contains acid phosphatase.

Semen stains on a solid material, e.g. a wooden floor, should not be collected by scraping off, since this would destroy the sperm cells. It is best to cut them out with a scalpel or razor blade together with a portion of the support, or to dissolve the stain with glycerin or clear water and then draw it up on filter paper.

Semen stains on the body are collected by the doctor. If on the skin they are softened with distilled water or glycerin and soaked up with clean filter paper, which is then packed in a test tube. Hair with attached semen is cut off and packed in a tube similarly.

If clothes from a victim of rape or indecent assault are to be recovered for examination it is not sufficient merely to take the panties, as they do not always make a good subject for investigation since they are usually pulled down and are therefore rarely exposed to direct contamination with semen.

Moreover, panties are liable to be contaminated with other stains of vaginal secretion, urine, feces, etc., which interfere with the examination. In searching for stains of semen, attention should rather be directed towards the underclothes, girdle, garters, stockings, and the back of the slip, dress or coat, where there is more likelihood of finding stains of value for the investigation. The examination of the victim should, when possible, be done by the nearest doctor who, in looking for semen, should examine not only the vagina but also the pubic hairs, thighs, abdomen or other parts of the body which may be supposed to have been exposed to contamination. The police officer should also request the doctor to take a natural (that is, not cathetered) *sample of urine* from the victim, since an examination of this may give good results. Cases have occurred in which spermatozoa have been detected in female urine passed 18 hours after intercourse.

During the post-mortem examination of a body in connection with any case in which the victim is a woman, the police officer should, if necessary, remind the pathologist to take several samples of the vaginal secretion. Spermatozoa may actually be detected in this even a comparatively long time after death.

In sex offenses against children the child's *clothing should be recovered immediately* because there is always a risk that the parents will wash or soak the garments. There have been cases where parents destroyed valuable evidence by burning the child's clothes.

Urine

The determination of whether a stain consists of urine or not is done microchemically and is possible even when only small stains are available. (HANSON, 1945).

A determination of alcohol concentration can also be done on a sample of urine.

To determine whether urine is human or animal is very difficult, but in favorable cases it may be possible, provided that a fairly large amount is available.

Feces

Feces are occasionally found at the scene of a crime and can sometimes be explained as the result of nerve strain of the criminal; at other times they have either been left as an impudent gesture, from superstition, or of necessity. With the exception of the possibility of a blood group determination, feces merely offer clues of possible value in tracing the criminal, except in very special cases.

Various undigested food residues, such as fruit pits, beans, peas, etc., can certainly give an indication of a particular meal, but the value of such a confirmation is generally slight, not least because of the relatively long time which elapses between the consumption of food and its excretion in the form of feces. Intestinal parasites, if found, may give a direct indication in tracing the criminal.

Much more valuable clues can be obtained from paper or the like used by the criminal to wipe himself. Finger prints may be found and the paper itself may give a direct indication of the criminal.

Burglary. For superstitious reasons, a criminal left his feces at the scene of a crime. By the side of it there lay a release ticket from a prison, which the criminal had used to wipe himself. The ticket gave all the information required about the criminal.

Fecal matter should be collected in clean glass (mason) jars.

Stomach contents (vomit)

Material which has been vomited at the scene of a crime may sometimes show the composition of the last meal and other significant matters.

Death from attempted abortion. A woman was found dead in her home. On a floor mat, and elsewhere, there were indications of vomit, among which was found a small piece of a gelatine-like material on which was a small quantity of white powder.

Closer examination showed that this was the remains of a gelatine capsule containing quinine sulphate. There was therefore a suspicion that the woman had taken quinine capsules with the object of procuring an abortion. Further investigation showed that she had died as the result of an attempted abortion.

The determination of the blood group from stomach contents is possible even after a very long time. Thus a Danish investigator (ANDRESEN, 1952) states that such a determination can be done on a six months old residue of vomited stomach contents.

Murder. At a homicide scene a certain amount of vomit was collected. Examination indicated that the stomach contents originated from a person with blood group O or from a non-secretor. Blood group determination on the victim showed that he was of group B and a secretor and could therefore not have left the vomit.

A few days later a suspect was arrested for the murder. He was found to have group

A but was a non-secretor. Therefore the vomit could have come from this individual. He later confessed to the crime. (ANDRESEN, 1944).

Saliva

An investigation of saliva or of marks of saliva may be important in several connections. A piece of cloth which is suspected of having been used as a gag or to obstruct the external air passages in a case of suffocation may show stains of saliva, and detection of the latter may be significant. A determination of the group may possibly indicate a particular person from whom the traces of saliva are derived. A handkerchief left behind at the scene of a crime may also carry stains of saliva, while saliva itself may be found at the scene of a crime in the form of expectorations. By a determination of blood group, these materials may give a lead in tracing the criminal.

Saliva may also be identified when in the form of dried stains, using microscopic or microchemical methods.

A blood group determination is also possible on toothpicks, cigarette or cigar butts, postage stamps, envelopes, bottles, glasses, cups and any other drinking utensil which has come in contact with the lips. Tobacco juice, lipstick, cigarette paper, cork and other materials do not appreciably interfere with this determination.

The determination can be done even on very small quantities of dried material. Thus it is stated in the technical literature that it is possible to determine the blood group from only 1/16 part of a postage stamp.

Murder. An old man was found murdered in his apartment. The presence of drinking glasses and cigarette ends indicated that he had had a visit shortly before his death. An analysis of the situation showed that 5 persons could be considered as suspects. The cigarette ends from the scene of the crime, bloodstains from the clothes of the dead man, and cigarette ends which were known to have been smoked by the suspects were sent to an expert for determination of blood groups. His examination, done more than one month after the murder, showed that all the cigarette ends found at the scene had been smoked by one man belonging to group B, and therefore could not have been smoked by the dead man who belonged to group O. Of the 5 suspects only one belonged to group B (HARLEY, 1944).

A determination of alcohol is also possible on a sample of saliva. A number of investigators have shown that there is a definite relation between the concentration of alcohol in the saliva and in the blood. The method does not appear to have been used much in forensic medicine, no doubt mainly because saliva is much more liable to contamination than blood, and this interferes with a micro-analysis of this type.

Sweat

The detection of sweat, and a blood group determination on it, is often of great value from the point of view of tracing the criminal. This is especially the case with handkerchiefs, headgear and other articles of clothing left at the scene of a crime. Sweat from any part of the body offers equal possibilities for investigation.

Nasal secretion, vaginal secretion, etc.

In the case of such secretions the possibilities of blood group determination are the same as with other secretory products.

The identification of the secretion is done biochemically or microscopically. Nasal secretion is often very characteristic in its composition, and in vaginal secretion there are sometimes found epithelial cells. Both of these materials may contain hairs – from the nose or pubic region – which can be identified.

HAIR

Hair may be found at the scene of a crime, on the criminal, on weapons or instruments, or on the victim of a crime of violence. They may be very difficult to find, and searching is very tedious and requires a great deal of patience and care. At times the result of an examination of hairs may not appear to justify the work involved in the search, but this should not induce the investigator to neglect clues of this kind. In certain cases hair is of the greatest importance, not merely for reconstruction but also as evidence of the guilt or innocence of a suspect, or for elucidating important particulars. Hair may be pulled out from a criminal in a struggle, attach itself to him during the execution of a crime, or attach itself to the victim of an act of violence; it may also fall out under such conditions that the criminal is probably unaware of the fact and therefore has no possibility of guarding against it. For these reasons, together with the difficulty of eliminating such clues, hair has an important place in forensic science, in spite of the fact that frequently an investigation results merely in a statement of probability.

When hair is found at the scene of a crime, on the victim of a crime, or on a person suspected of crime, various questions may arise.

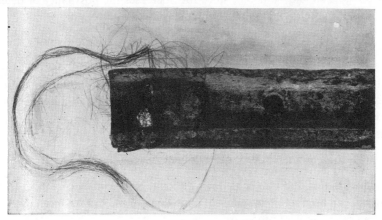

Fig.67 Human scalp hair adhering to iron rail used to batter a victim to death.

Is the material actually hair or merely some hair-like material?

This question can always be given a definite answer, since hair has a very characteristic microscopic structure and can be identified without difficulty.

Does the hair come from human beings or from animals?

This question can also be answered definitely. Human hair differs from the hair of animals, in particular in the diameter of the medulla which amounts at most to one half that of the whole hair, and in the form of the cells of the cuticle. Certain difficulties arise in the case of hair from anthropoid apes, but in most cases a definite answer can be given.

From what species of animal is the hair derived?

This is sometimes a very difficult question, but an answer is possible in most cases. It is easiest to distinguish hair from beasts of prey and from deer and rabbits. On the other hand it is very difficult to distinguish horse hair from cow hair, or for instance elk hair from reindeer.

Hairs from the same region of one animal may vary greatly in character, and hairs from different parts of the body may show many points of difference. It is therefore important, in collecting a sample of hair, that as much as possible should be taken, since this increases the possibility of determining the species of animal.

Does the hair come from a particular animal?

This question can never be answered with certainty. Actually there are no hair structures which are characteristic for a particular individual and not found in others of the same species.

Does the hair come from furs or from an animal?

To answer this question is at times difficult, but in many cases a definite answer can be given. The task is of course easy if the hair has been dyed or shows other signs of preparation.

Does a human hair come from a man or woman, and from what part of the body?

To determine if a hair comes from a man or woman is sometimes possible. The problem is intimately related to that of determining *what part of the body a hair comes from*. This is deduced from the length, thickness, form and type of cross section of the hair. It is also of importance whether the hair has been cut or not. If the hair has been cut the appearance of the cut surface (curved or sharp-edged) shows whether it has been cut recently or a long while ago. If the roots are present, it is possible to decide from their appearance (whether dried up or not) whether the hair has been torn out or has fallen out by itself. Any *contamination* may also indicate the part of the body (armpits or pubes).

How old is the person from whom the hair has come?

This question can be answered with a certain degree of probability only in special cases and under favorable conditions.

The hair of young people differs from that of adults merely by its smaller diameter and weaker pigmentation, but in practice no exact determination of age can be based on these factor. With elderly persons the hair has a tendency to become narrower, and pigment is often absent.

Does the hair come from a particular person?

This question can never be answered with certainty. The examination will only result in a statement that the hair in question, with a greater or lesser probability, *could* have come from the suspect. Hairs from different individuals are often very similar and, conversely, hairs from one individual may be quite dissimilar. The examination is carried out with reference to the length, thickness and form of cross section of the hair, the appearance of the ends, content of pigment, occurrence and amount of medulla, any contamination (occupational contamination, hair parasites, etc.), artificial coloring, and indications of injuries (singeing, burning, crushing). Hairs found at the scene of a crime, or on an instrument, weapon or the like, can sometimes be of the greatest value for reconstruction especially if they show signs of injuries such as cutting, crushing or the like, and if it can be determined from what part of the body they come. In certain cases they may give an indication of the type of instrument with which the injuries were made.

A conclusion about the identity of hairs is sometimes more significant if the laboratory findings can be related to the circumstances at the scene of the crime.

Assault. The weapon used in a certain assault was a large piece of granite, which was found split into two halves. At the edge of the broken surface of the larger part there was observed a fragment of a strand of coarse grey hair. The spectacles of the victim were also found, damaged and blood-stained. They showed that the victim had been struck above and outside the left eye, and at the post-mortem examination a corresponding injury to the cranium was found. The scraps of hair were found to be from the eyebrows, and to be identical with the hair of the victim.

The French investigators PIÉDELIÈVRE and ZÉBOUNI (1933) have carried out thorough investigations with the object of determining the characteristic changes undergone by hair when exposed to the action of gradually increasing heat. The results show that, from the appearance of the individual hairs on, for example, a burnt body it is possible to determine the degree of heat to which the hair has been exposed. The method appears to be suitable for practical police work only in very special cases.

When it is necessary to decide whether a gunshot wound in a hair-covered part of the body has or has not been produced by a near shot, changes in the structure of the hair resulting from the temperature of the muzzle flash may form a good guide.

GREENWELL, WILLMER and KIRK (1940–41) have devoted special attention to the question of human hair and have shown the possibility of determining the race, sex and age of an individual by the aid of the refractive index of the hair.

Hair at the crime scene

The search for hair at the scene of a crime can only be done by subjecting the floor, furniture and other objects on which hairs might be found to an especially thorough examination. For this work a flashlight and a pair of tweezers are recommended. Hair which is found on an object or in a certain location is folded into a clean sheet of paper and then placed in an envelope labeled clearly with the place where it was found, which can if desired also be marked on a sketch. Test tubes are not desirable as containers because the hairs may, after a period of time in the tube, take on a curly appearance which may be misleading. It is not desirable to attempt any sorting out of material which is not hair – everything which is found should be sent to the expert for examination. Great care should be taken that the hair is not injured or contaminated or lost in a sudden draft. If a hair is dropped it may be extremely difficult to retrieve. The investigator must also see that there is no admixture of foreign hairs, for example his own.

In collecting hair during the investigation of a crime scene it is of the greatest importance, as mentioned above, that *all* hair should be kept in order to obtain a possible 'hair picture', i.e. a characteristic combination of different hairs.

Assault. Two old women were attacked, severely assaulted and robbed at night in their house, an isolated café. The criminal had broken into the house, struck the women unconscious, and ransacked the premises, and in doing so had torn open a mattress so that the stuffing had fallen out and was scattered around in the room. The detective who investigated the scene got his clothes thoroughly covered with hair-like fibers from the stuffing, and drew the conclusion that the clothes of the criminal would have been covered with similar material. After some days a suspect was brought in. Examination of his clothes showed, in the cuffs of his trousers, a considerable quantity of similar fibers.

On examination of the stuffing of the mattress, part of which had been kept, it was found to consist of animal hairs, cow hair, dyed sheep's wool and vegetable fibers. The material taken from the cuffs of the suspect showed remarkably good correspondence with the stuffing of the mattress, so that there was no doubt that they were both of the same origin.

Torn-out strands of hair may be found in the hands or under the nails of a victim of murder; and on a victim of rape or sexual murder there are often found hairs from the sexual parts of the criminal (pubic hairs) on or near the sexual organs of the victim, on the bed, floor or the like on which the victim lay, etc.

In rape cases the victim's pubic area and clothing from the lower half of the body should immediately be examined, and any hairs which may be from the attacker should be recovered. This should be done by a physician, nurse or police woman. The investigating officer should arrange for this examination as soon as possible.

Clothes which belong to a person suspected of murder, rape or assault should be examined immediately for hairs, etc. Hairs may become entangled among the threads of fabric and accumulate in wrinkles and folds in such a way that they are only noticed in an extremely thorough examination. This also applies to the clothing of a person suspected of illegal deer hunting and the like.

A person suspected of rape or sexual murder should be subjected to a very thorough bodily examination by the doctor, who must be very alert and vigilant, so that the suspect has no opportunity of interfering with the investigation and possibly causing the loss of valuable clues in the form of hair.

Murder. While examining the body of the suspect the doctor discovered, under the foreskin of the suspect, a hair. He turned around in order to take from a table a pair of tweezers with which to pick up the hair. At the same moment the suspect made a hasty movement with one hand and succeeded in brushing away the hair, which was lost (HESSELINK, 1934).

Rape. Strands of hair from the clothes of a suspect were found to correspond with those of the victim, as also a loose pubic hair which was found on the penis of the suspect. Under the foreskin the doctor found a small clump of mucus which on investigation was found to consist of small tangled scraps of wool, most being dyed in bright colors. These colors showed complete correspondence with the wool in a sheepskin bed cover which was lying on the bed at the time of the crime.

How a sample of hair is taken

When a sample of hair is to be taken it must always be remembered that the sample must be *representative*. Human hair should not be taken merely from the crown of the head, but also from the temples and neck. Moreover the sample should contain hair which has been pulled out, hair which has been cut off as near the roots as possible, and hair which has been collected by combing. Combing gives an idea of how easily the hair comes out, which may be important. Each type of hair (pulled out, cut off, combed) is placed in a separate envelope or test tube labelled clearly with the type and place from which it has been taken. In writing to the expert it should also be stated whether the individual in question has a strong growth of hair, is partially bald, etc., and the firmness of attachment of the hair. Samples of hair from other parts of the body are collected in the same way.

Hair samples from living persons should preferably be taken a physician or nurse; by the officer only in emergencies. Samples from women, other than head hair, should be taken by a doctor, nurse or police woman. The police officer should see that the samples are representative and properly packed. Samples from dead bodies may be taken by the officer if a physician or pathologist is not available.

In collecting samples of hair from animals, *all* parts of the coat are pulled with the fingers so that the hair which is ready to fall out is obtained. If necessary the hair is pulled out. It is placed in an envelope or test tube labelled clearly with the part of the body from which it comes.

Samples of hair should be taken from *all* victims of murder and fatal traffic accidents. It is the job of the pathologist to take the samples, but the police officer should see that is it done before the body is buried.

It may also be necessary at times to take samples of hair from victims of rape or other assault when hair, which is suspected of having come from the victim, has been found on a suspect. Samples of hair should also always be taken when hair has been found which is suspected to have come from the criminal. The object is to be able to distinguish the different hairs from one another.

OTHER BIOLOGICAL SUBSTANCES

Under this heading are discussed additional types of evidence which may be left on the scene as a result of violence, either from the assailant's or from the victim's body. (See also the section 'Traces on the suspect'.)

Skin fragments

Fragments of skin from the crime scene can easily be recognized microscopically. They should be preserved in a test tube. In order to keep the fragment from drying and possibly lose its evidential value, alcohol should be poured over the fragment in the test tube.

The value of skin fragments is greatest if the suspect is apprehended soon enough after the injury that the wound is not completely healed. The fragment is fitted into the injury and photographed so as to demonstrate the physical match of the two parts.

Burglary. A jewelry store window had been smashed, and a fragment of skin about one inch square was found among the broken glass in the display window. A suspect who was subsequently arrested wore a bandage on his right hand. A closer examination revealed that the bandage concealed a wound of approximately the same size and shape as the recovered fragment. The fragment was fitted into the wound by a physician. As the fragment had shrunk and the hand had swollen somewhat the fragment did not fill the wound completely but the shape and edge details corresponded perfectly. Confronted with these findings the suspect confessed.

If the skin fragment is bloodstained and is to be used for blood group determination, it should be brought to the laboratory for examination immediately and without preparation. Should it run the risk of drying, the fragment in the test tube should be immersed in saline solution. However, decomposition may set in if too much time is allowed to elapse before the fragment is turned over to an expert.

Brain substance

Even minute amounts of brain substance can be identified microscopically. In some cases it is also possible to establish from which part of the brain the sample originated.

Brain substance is recovered in a test tube. It should not be allowed to dry since this interferes with the examination. Alcohol or 10% formalin is used to cover the sample. If blood group is to be determined, saline solution should be used and the sample turned over to the expert as soon as possible.

Vaginal epithelial cells

Epithelial cells from the vagina are easily identified under the microscope. They are most valuable as evidence in cases of sadistic murder, rape and child molestation when they may be found under the assailant's fingernails, on or near his sexual parts.

By dust is meant airborne particles which are macroscopic, microscopic or sub-microscopic in size. In forensic science, however, dust also includes minute particles which cannot be handled by ordinary means or are only detected during the collection of other dust. Dust may be very characteristic of a particular place. This applies especially to places such as flour mills, building sites, workshops, coal cellars and the like. A person who has worked at or visited such a place carries on his clothes dust characteristic of that place, and a close examination of the dust will reveal his occupation or his visit. He may also leave traces in the form of dust from shoes or clothes, which are characteristic of him and which can be a guide in tracing a criminal. In dust there can moreover be found particles the occurrence of which can be connected directly with a crime. Thus a burglar may have on his clothes small particles of glass, fragments of paint, splinters of wood, etc., which became attached when he was breaking in; and a safebreaker may carry particles of dynamite, safe insulation and the like. Particles characteristic of the dust on the clothes of the criminal (also specific textile fibers from the clothes) may be found on an object (e.g. a weapon or tool) which a criminal has carried in his pocket. The possibilities offered by a detailed examination of dust should therefore be utilized, even though the work may appear difficult and tedious.

Dust at the scene of a crime or on clothes should be collected by a vacuum cleaner fitted with a special filter whereby the dust is collected on filter paper. It is important that the dust from different parts of the scene or from different parts of the garment should not be mixed together because the exact place where the dust was recovered may be of decisive importance.

At the scene of a crime

The area, for example, of a floor which is to be swept is marked off and each section is treated separately, and the dust taken from each section is packed suitably, preferably so that the filter paper with the dust is placed in a large test tube, glass jar or the like, which is labelled clearly. Articles of furniture are each treated separately. It is best to mark the different sections and objects on a sketch.

If a vacuum cleaner is not available and the surface involved is small and smooth, such as a window sill, the dust may be collected by sweeping it up on a filter or blotting paper. The paper should then be placed in a test tube or in a jar.

Clothes

Clothes are spread out on a large piece of clean white paper and examined with a magnifying glass, larger particles being collected with tweezers and placed in a test tube. The garment is divided into a number of smaller sections, each of which is vacuumed separately, and each filter paper with the dust from each section is packed in a separate test tube or other suitable container. It is convenient to make a sketch of the garment and to mark on it the different sections, each being numbered and corresponding numbers being placed on the containers.

Each trouser cuff and each pocket should be treated as a separate item and the dust should not be mixed from other parts of the garment.

Murder. A man was found murdered, with a knife stab in the heart. The persons who found the body were so anxious to help him, in spite of the fact that he was already dead, that the surrounding area had been trampled down everywhere. The investigation of the scene therefore gave no clue as to the murderer. In a routine campaign against vagrants in the district, some days later, there was found a man with a number of small blood stains on his clothes. It was therefore suspected that this man might have had something to do with the murder, and his clothes were sent for investigation to a laboratory expert who found that the stains were of blood. On one sleeve of the coat were also some seeds from a rare species of plant (Compositae) found in the district. A fresh investigation at the place where the body had been found showed that this species grew in the neighborhood of that place, and that the plants were in the seeding stage. The murderer had presumably come into contact with the plants during a struggle, and the seeds had clung to him. He could therefore be connected with the place. After persistently denying the murder he finally admitted it when the result of the investigation was communicated to him (LOCARD, 1934).

If no special cleaner is available for collecting the dust, it is best to send the clothes to the expert for examination; each garment being packed individually in a separate wrapper. In an emergency an ordinary tank-type vacuum

Fig. 68 Special attachment for vacuuming traces from clothing. With this device there is no danger of contaminants from a previous examination. With careful handling, large particles of soil can be collected intact.

cleaner can be used for collecting dust at the scene of a crime. This should first be cleaned thoroughly (including the tube) and the filter bag washed. A large filter paper should then be shaped into the form of the bag and placed inside it; the bag being changed so that one filter paper is used for each section of the scene or for each piece of furniture.

Shoes

Dust adhering to shoes may be very valuable evidence in placing a suspect at a specific location. Shoes and other footwear should preferably be brought to the expert as they are. They should be wrapped separately and thoroughly. Samples of dust and soil taken at the location in question should be submitted along with the shoes. (See 'Traces of soil, etc.')

If the shoes cannot be submitted for examination the dust should be scraped off and collected on clean paper. The removal process should be selective, beginning with the material which reasonably could originate at the critical place and time. This material should be placed in one container – one for each shoe – and the remaining material from the shoes in another, separate container.

Dust and other foreign substances inside the shoes may also be of value as evidence.

Other objects

Dust and foreign substances on tools and weapons should be left in place and protected for transport to the laboratory. This is best done by placing cellophane or plastic bags over the suspected end and taping the bags tight so as to prevent loss of particles.

If the instrument bears larger particles which are in danger of being lost, the particles should be carefully removed and placed in appropriately labeled containers.

Laboratory examination of the dust, which is sometimes very thorough and comprehensive, is done first under the microscope, any characteristic particles being separated and examined more closely by suitable methods. In connection with *cobwebs*, marks of which can sometimes be found on clothing, it should be noted that a specialist, with the aid of a single thread of a web, can sometimes decide from what species of spider it came. It may therefore be possible to decide whether a person has visited a certain place, e.g. an attic, wood, etc, where webs of the same kind are to be found.

TRACES OF SOIL, PAINT, RUST, etc.

Traces of this kind can occur at the scene of a crime, on the criminal, on the victim of an act of violence, and on various objects and they may be of the greatest importance.

If such material is sent to an expert for examination, any comparison material which is sent with it should always be taken in a sufficiently large amount. Thus, in the case of soil, the sample should be sufficiently representative of the soil at the actual place; and in the case of other materials or substances the sample should be sufficient for any detailed analysis which may be required for the comparison. If the mark is a stain, then if possible this should not be scraped off but left on the supporting material, a sample of which should always be sent in with the stain to be used in control tests. (See 'Traces on the suspect').

Soil

Soil is easily identified under the microscope. Sometimes the type can be determined geologically and comparison can be made with soil from a particular place. The possibilities of the examination are, of course, increased when it is possible to detect in the soil remains of partially decomposed leaves, pine needles, pollen grains or other plant fragments which can be identified.

Soil samples should be taken at all crime scenes where the criminal's body or clothing are believed to have been soiled. It is very important that the samples be *representative* of the area's soil characteristics. The soil should not be dug too deeply, nor should the various samples be mixed since this complicates the expert's examination. About one cubic inch of the surface soil, collected from different parts of the scene, is sufficient. Each sample should be placed in a test tube, jar or other sealed container. If the foot impressions in soil are deep, samples should be taken from different levels at the edges of the print. Samples of ground cover (plant material, etc.) should be similarly collected and packed separately.

In serious crimes the expert who is to make the soil comparison should be consulted for advice or be allowed to collect the samples himself.

Rape. On one trouser leg of a man suspected of rape there were large marks of dried soil, which agreed in detail with soil from the place where the crime occurred. The suspect stated that he got the soil on his trousers when he fell over near a hedge at another place. Samples of the soil at that place were also taken, but did not in the least agree with the soil on his trousers.

Paint

Important factors in identification are shades of color, chemical composition and the number of coats of paint. The examination is carried out chemically, spectrographically and microscopically. Paints which contain no metallic constituents (e.g. synthetic lacquers) are difficult to identify, but under favorable conditions chemical examination can be successful.

Burglary. Safes had been broken open in a series of burglaries.

Four persons, suspected of the burglaries, were detained and their clothes were investigated, traces of paint, kieselguhr and powdered cork being found in their trouser cuffs. One of the suspects had a pair of lined pigskin gloves, and a seam of the right hand one had split open for a short length. Between the lining and the leather of that finger of the glove there were found some small flakes of paint, which were examined microscopically

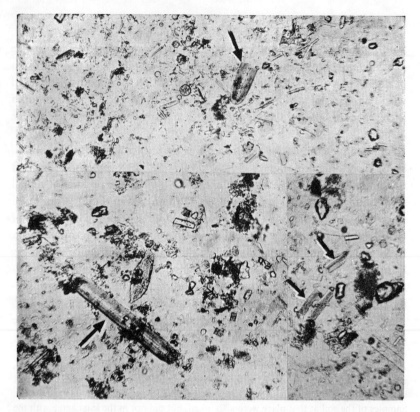

Fig. 69 Photomicrograph of safe insulation. Arrows show the skeletons of diatoms.

and found to consist of three layers, a white, grey and green one. These flakes of paint corresponded exactly with the paint on one of the opened safes. The suspect admitted the crime.

Samples of paint should always be taken whenever a painted surface has been damaged at points of forcible entry or at points of impact by a motor vehicle. These may later become important evidence when compared with paint from suspected clothing, tools or automobiles. Such samples should always be removed so as to include *all the paint layers* down to the bare wood or metal. Scraped-off samples of the surface paint are almost useless for comparison purposes. If samples are difficult to remove, a small portion of the underlying material should be cut out or chipped off. The damaged portion of an automobile body may require a few blows with a hammer in order to release a good sample.

Rust

Rust stains may be confused with bloodstains (see 'Blood'), but rust is easily identified chemically, as also any traces of foreign metals which may occur in it.

Metals

Filings and other metallic particles are easily identified chemically or spectrographically. A comparative examination of the components can sometimes make possible a definite identification with a particular sample of metal.

A special type of metallic trace occurs in cutting with the oxyacetylene burner. Irregular particles of slag come off from the metal, together with more or less round fused beads, the so-called welding beads. Both of these can be easily identified microscopically.

Ash

The structure and composition of different kinds of ash may be quite varied. It is identified microscopically, chemically or spectroscopically.

Asbestos

Asbestos powder occurs as heat-insulating material in safe walls. It is identified microscopically or spectrographically.

Kieselguhr

This substance is used as insulation in safe walls. It consists mainly of skeletons of diatoms, which have a very characteristic microscopic appearance and can therefore easily be identified.

Glass wool, slag wool, cork

These are used as safe insulation. Identification of the particles, which is at times somewhat difficult, is done microscopically, chemically or spectrographically. Traces of glass wool show small needle-like particles, the appearance of which may vary. In most cases the particles are solid, but sometimes they have the form of tubes with a channel in the middle.

Food residues

Food residues, in the form of dried stains on clothes, are identified micro- 'scopically and microchemically. An examination of this kind can give very useful results.

Fats and fatty oils

There is generally little difficulty in establishing that a stain is composed of fats or fatty oils, but an analysis to decide whether it is of animal, vegetable or mineral origin is generally possible only when a relatively large quantity is available.

Fat globules are sometimes found in vaginal secretions during the investigation of sex offenses because some sex offenders may use vaseline as a lubricant.

Any impurities such as particles of metal and carbon (used lubricating oil) may form a good guide to the origin.

Theft. Two juveniles were suspected of stealing tools from a garage. A large oily stain was found on the coat sleeve of one of the youths. Chemical examination showed the stain to be from lubricating oil, a fact which later became decisive evidence.

Marks of lipstick

Identification of such a mark is difficult, but in favorable cases an investigation can give a definite result. The circumstance that the mark is both fatty and red colored is very important, also the nature of the pigment, if that can be determined. For this, however, a comparatively large quantity is required. The colors commonly used for lipstick are eosin, phloxin, fluorescein compounds, erythrosin, etc.

Face powder

Face powder contains components which can easily be identified microscopically. Among other materials used are starch (often of rice, wheat or arrowroot), kaolin, talc, titanium dioxide, zinc oxide, magnesium stearate, organic and inorganic pigments, and perfumes.

Brick dust

Brick dust may be found on a person's clothes, shoes or hands after coming in contact with bricks. It is very difficult to identify but the shade of color and the presence of small characteristic particles will facilitate the examination which is done microscopically.

Mortar

The presence of cement or lime and sand will often result in a positive finding. The examination is done chemically, microscopically or possibly by spectrography.

Pipe oil

Stains from pipe oil are revealed by their odor and color. The may be identified microchemically, demonstrating the presence of nicotine.

FRAGMENTS OF TEXTILES, TEXTILE FIBERS, SEWING THREAD AND BUTTONS

This type of evidence is usually found at crime scenes where the criminal happened to tear his clothes by crawling through a broken window and leaving fibers on the jagged edges of the glass or on a brick ledge. Fabric and fibers may also have been torn from the criminal's clothes by the victim of an assault. Conversely, the material may originate from the victim's clothing or from a garment, rug or sack, etc. which the criminal used or at least came in contact with. Textile fibers may therefore also be found on the criminal's person.

Evidence of this type is usually very difficult to detect and the investigator must exercise great care in his search.

Fragments of cloth

These are of the greatest value, since they can be fitted directly to the clothes of a victim or suspect, and therefore form strong evidence. Color, pattern of weave, thickness of thread, nature of material, etc. should be noted.

Hit and run. A man who was under the influence of alcohol drove his car up on the sidewalk of a bridge, striking a boy and girl. The boy was thrown over the railing into the river and drowned. The driver who proceeded without stopping was later arrested in a nearby town. During the examination of the car a small piece of fabric was discovered on the right front fender. The fragment turned out to match a tear in the victim's coat. Complete agreement was observed with respect to pattern, color, thread thickness and fiber type and to the type of white thread used in the lining of the coat.

Fig. 70 Fragments of cloth on the right came from the right front fender of a car and were found to fit an injury in the overcoat worn by a youth who had been knocked down and killed. 1: white threads from the lining of the coat.

Textile fibers

Textile fibers are compared with respect to thickness, type of textile material and color with fibers from the clothes of the suspect or victim. The nature of the textile material is determined microscopically or chemically. Fibers which are especially characteristic in any of the respects mentioned are significant. If a number together form a fiber picture characteristic of the garment, a more positive statement of identity may result.

The fibers used in textiles can be of many different types. The commonest ones are mentioned below, with the properties characteristic of them.

Cotton

Cotton is the most common fiber material. A fiber of cotton has the form of a flat, spirally twisted or corkscrew-like band: cotton fibers are soft and short.

Linen

The fibers are similar to those of cotton but, unlike the latter, are smooth and straight and show numerous cross bands. They are derived from the stalk of a plant. Linen occurs both in the bleached and unbleached state.

Hemp

The fibers come from the stalk of a plant. Hemp is similar to unbleached linen, but is lighter in color. Ordinary hemp is used mostly for tarpaulins, sacks, ropes and cords.

Jute

Jute is also composed of stalk fibers which may have lengths of up to several yards. The fibers are coarse and stiff and have a yellow to brown color. Jute differs considerably in appearance from linen and hemp. It is used for making sacks, linoleum and cheap woven mats.

Manila hemp

The fibers come from the leaf of a plant and are used mostly in the twine and rope-making industries. It has a greyish-brown color.

Sisal

Sisal is also composed of leaf fibers. It is used for making string, rope and coarse mats. The fibers are yellowish-white in color and have a fine gloss.

Animal fibers

The animal fibers used for textiles include sheep's wool, camel hair, hare or rabbit hair, cow hair and horse hair. These differ from vegetable fibers in the medullae which are characteristic of them and in the presence of cuticular cells. Generally it is possible to decide from what species of animal the hairs come.

Natural silk

The original so-called cocoon threads are formed of two single threads stuck together: chemically they are composed of two proteins. The natural silk threads used as textile fibers are spun from 3 to 8, usually 5, cocoon threads.

Synthetic Fibers

Synthetic fibers are those made from non-natural bases. They are made of synthetic raw materials and are technically called polymers. The common synthetics, nylon, Orlon, Vinyon N, Dynel, Acrilan, Dacron, are made in filaments and staple fibers of varying dimensions and cross sections. These fibers and filaments are then spun into yarn and woven into fabric either alone or blended with cotton, wool or other fibers. Identification schemes are available by which even small fibers can be identified. In addition to classification of the fiber base, the dye may be studied. The presence of matching synthetic fibers does not prove identity of source; however, if enough different fibers on the suspect match fibers from the victim or crime scene, strong suspicion can be generated.

Sewing thread

Sewing thread is nearly always of cotton, the commonest types being spun from three, four or six threads. There are also sewing threads of inferior quality which consist of a single thread of spun fibers.

Sewing thread occurs in various colors and thickness. Definite identification of a sample with the sewing thread in a particular garment would only be possible in exceptional cases.

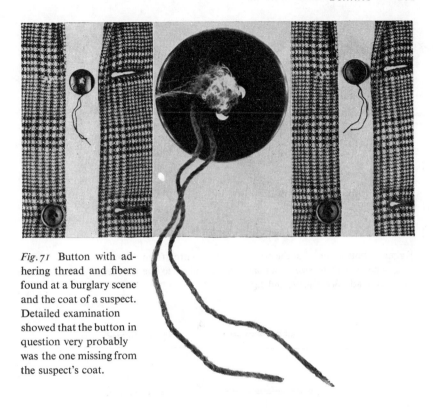

Fig. 71 Button with adhering thread and fibers found at a burglary scene and the coat of a suspect. Detailed examination showed that the button in question very probably was the one missing from the suspect's coat.

Buttons

Buttons occur in a very large range of sizes and patterns. Only in exceptional cases is it possible to identify a button definitely with the buttons of a particular garment. When a button is torn off then generally the thread, and sometimes also a piece of the fabric, comes with it. If an investigation can be extended to include both the sewing thread and the fibers of fabric then the possibility of a more definite statement of identity is increased.

If all the threads remain fixed to the button it is possible in certain cases to decide whether the button was sewn on by hand or by machine. The method of fixing the thread, together with the quantity of thread and uniformity of the threads attached to the button, varies for buttons sewn on by hand or by machine. When a four-hole button has been attached by machine, the threads run in a characteristic way on the upper side of the button.

If a fragment of a broken button is found it may turn out to be very valu-

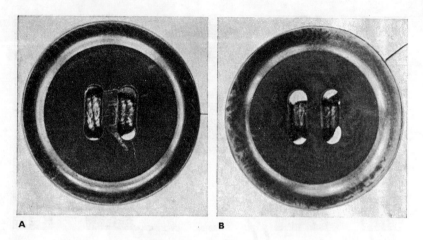

Fig.72 A: button found at the crime scene; B: button from the suspect's coat. Corresponded as to size, color and shape and as to the manner of attaching with thread. (See *Fig.71*, and *74*).

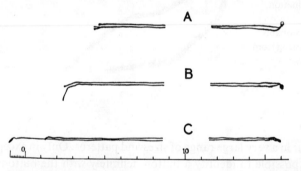

Fig.73 Thread found in the crime scene button (A) and in the buttons remaining on the suspect's coat (B and C). All were made up of three threads twisted to the right and corresponded with respect to thickness, color, fluorescence and fiber material. Only the length varied somewhat. (See *Fig.71, 72,* and *74*).

able evidence since the rest of the button may still be attached to the criminal's clothes.

Safe burglary. During a burglary a safe containing files and ledgers had been broken open. The investigator pulled out and examined the complete contents of the safe and discovered a brown snap fastener from a glove together with fragments of brown leather and fibers from the lining. A suspect who was apprehended later was found to own a

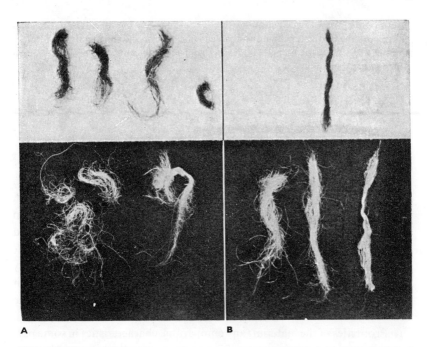

A   B

Fig. 74 The fibers which adhered to the crime scene button (A) corresponded in all respects with the fibers in the coat (B). (See *Fig. 71, 72* and *73*).

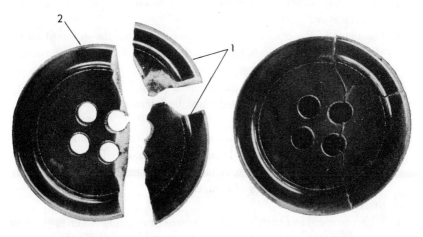

Fig. 75 Portions of a button found at a crime scene (1) matched the remainder of the button still on the suspect's coat (2).

brown lined glove with one button missing. The crime scene button corresponded completely with the button remaining on the suspect's glove, as did the fragments of leather and the fibers from the lining. The suspect confessed the burglary when he was confronted with these findings.

STRING, CORD, TWINE, ROPE, etc.

Pieces of string or rope which have been used by the criminal are sometimes found. The cord may have been used for tying up tools and material taken to the scene of the crime and unpacked there, so it is not uncommon for both string and wrapping paper to be left behind. String may also be used in wrapping up parts of a dismembered body, while thicker cord or rope, used for strangling, may be left round the neck of the victim.

If cord or rope is of the ordinary commercial kind or is made of ordinary hemp, sisal or the like, in most cases there is great difficulty in identifying it positively. In such a case the investigation is carried out according to the following scheme:

1. Properties of the material; any comparable characteristics in some particular strand; structure.
2. Number of strands.
3. The lay of the cord or rope and of its individual parts. Right or left hand.
4. Color. Any glossy material or the like which may be characteristic. Fluorescence.
5. Diameter of the cord or rope as a whole, and of the different parts. Very considerable variations may occur if one piece of the material has been exposed to strains.
6. The general appearance of the different parts.
7. The form and appearance of the smallest elements.
8. Weight per unit of length.
9. Contaminations or foreign particles derived from the manufacture or from the place where it has been kept, its use, etc. The smallest units are compared piece by piece. Attached to and between them there may be characteristic particles of dust, etc.
10. Strength.
11. Histochemical test to determine the amount of oiling which is given to the rope or cord in manufacture in order to increase its wearing properties.

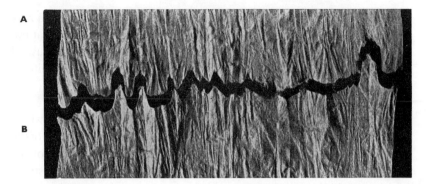

Fig. 76 Establishment of identity between paper string found at the scene of a crime (*A*) and paper string found at the home of a suspect (*B*).

12. Chemical test to determine the kind of material.
13. Expert opinion. Preferably obtained from several manufactures or dealers.

When this investigation has been completed and all points indicate identity, one is justified in concluding that the two cords or ropes under examination are of the same make and type.

To decide whether two cords or ropes come from one and the same piece is possible only in exceptional cases, and then only if characteristic and incontestable agreement is found.

Burglary. A burglar tied up a broken garden gate with string as a precaution. The string was left behind and discovered during the investigation of the scene of the crime. At the house of a suspect there was found a coil of string of similar appearance to that used on the gate. The two pieces of string were compared according to the scheme given above, and showed identity in all points. It was therefore possible to deduce that the string used at the scene of the crime was of the same make and type as that found in the house of the suspect (BECK, 1938).

Murder. In a river in France was found the dead body of a man who had been strangled with a rope, which was still round his neck. Examination of this rope by the police laboratory showed that it was contaminated with cement and plaster, and that it showed blue marks at several points. In a workshop of some plasterers, who were under suspicion, there was found a similar rope, also contaminated with cement and plaster, which showed blue marks similar to those on the rope with which the man had been strangled (BISCHOFF, 1938).

There may also be a question of cords or braids, the strands or cores of which are braided or plaited round with a number of more or less fine threads. This braiding or plaiting may have one or several colors, and may be impregnated. This naturally increases the possibility of identification, and such cords are often intended for special purposes, which is a useful lead in searching for the criminal. Such cords are examined by using suitable sections of the scheme given above.

In the case of *paper string* the possibilities of identification are greater. The various strands of paper string are composed of paper ribbons which are twisted up and then twined together to form a cord. A comparison of the width of the paper ribbon and of the color, thickness and quality of the paper naturally gives information which is of value in deciding questions of identity. If there is agreement in these respects, the investigation is completed with respect to number of strands, direction of twisting, diameter, weight, strength, contamination, etc., as with other forms of cord or rope. It is easy to decide whether two pieces of paper string came from the same length when the cut surfaces are compared. If the paper ribbons, which have been twisted to form the strands, are unwrapped, the ends show a more or less toothed or jagged from which is produced by the cutting on account of the twisting of the paper. If the pieces correspond, the toothed or uneven ends can be made to fit together perfectly. Sometimes also the creases, which result from the twisting, in the two strips of paper will be found to correspond exactly when the ends are matched.

TOBACCO VARIETIES AND MATCHES

Cigar and cigarette butts, ashes and matches are often found to have been left at the scene by the criminal. These materials usually have no great evidential value but they may provide leads to the continued investigation or assist in the reconstruction of events at the scene.

Cigar and cigarette butts

Cigar and cigarette butts should always be recovered, preferably in a test tube or other suitable container. They may show that a murder victim had a visitor and that this visitor spent some time on the premises. They may indicate the movements of the murderer or that there was more than one assailant, etc.

In favorable cases the brand or type of cigarette or cigar may be determined. This determination is, however, difficult especially when only small amounts of tobacco are available. In the case of cigarette butts it is generally possible to determine, by a miscroscopic examination of the veins of the tobacco leaf, whether they come from American (Virginia) or oriental cigarettes, but if a cigarette butt has been exposed to water, e.g. rain, the investigation becomes difficult. To identify a small particle as being a fragment of tobacco is comparatively easy under microscopic examination: tobacco shows a granular epidermal tissue, characteristic hairs (covering hairs and glandular hairs) and a mesophyll layer in which appear numerous accumulations of calcium oxalate crystals in the form of dark, almost black, points.

On cigarette butts it may be possible to observe a portion of the printing on the cigarette paper. With some brands this can also be observed on the unbroken ash of a cigarette. Certain cigarettes also carry a figure or letter which is printed on the edge of the paper and therefore comes in the seam towards one end, usually the end opposite to the printed name. This figure or letter may indicate the maker and in some cases also the particular factory at which the cigarette was made: occasionally it indicates the mechanic who was responsible for the particular machine and sometimes the date. When a certain brand of cigarette is made only by a particular factory of a tobacco firm it is possible, in exceptional cases, to determine the brand of cigarette simply from this figure or letter.

The quality, color and structure of the cigarette paper, as also the thickness and from the shape (round or oval) of the cigarette, can also give an indication of the maker. All the better cigarettes are made with linen rag paper, while inferior qualities may use wood pulp paper. With most brands the paper has a white color, but some cigarettes are produced with yellow or brownish-yellow paper.

The filter on filter-tipped cigarettes may, in certain cases, indicate the brand. Filters are manufactured in some variety with respect to filtering materials, length, color of outside wrapping, etc.

If cigarette butts have been exposed to water further examination of the paper is difficult because nitrates, etc. will have been extracted from the tobacco.

The manner of smoking cigars and cigarettes varies among smokers. Some persons will push a piece of a matchstick into the end of the cigar in order to bite on the stick; some will bite the end, while others hold the cigar with the lips. Some cigarette smokers wet the end with saliva while others leave it completely dry. Filter tips will sometimes take on a characteristic shape from the manner of smoking.

Blood group determination is possible on cigar and cigarette butts, provided that the smoker was a secretor.

The presence of lipstick on a cigarette end should always be noted. Definite identification of the lipstick may be possible.

In certain cases it may also be of significance to note how a cigar or cigarette end has been put out (pressed against an ash tray, nipped off, gone out by itself or gone completely to ash). This may reveal a habit of extinguishing the cigar or cigarette in a particular way, or indicate haste.

If a holder has been used, the cigar and cigarette butts are usually very short. The end which has been held in the holder is usually round and uniformly crimped. Such butts often burn out by themselves, or they may show an evenly burned end. Sometimes such butts are found pierced by a matchstick which has been used to remove the end from the holder.

If a person smokes only a certain, rather uncommon brand this fact has some value as an investigative lead.

Pipe tobacco

Pipe tobacco is characterized by bits of tobacco stalk, so that even small particles can sometimes be identified. In a favorable case a detailed examination may reveal the brand.

Chewing tobacco

Pieces of chewing tobacco have a characteristic form and color, and can therefore be identified.

Snuff

The characteristic form of the particles of snuff makes identification possible under the microscope, while microchemical examination can show the presence of nicotine and thereby identify small particles of tobacco. A microscopic examination for the presence of structures characteristic of tobacco is however rendered difficult by the fine degree of sub-division of the snuff and the addition of extractive substances.

Tobacco ash

The ash of tobacco can be easily identified by a microscopic examination of the ash picture. To identify the kind of tobacco from the ash is, however, not possible with the methods of analysis available at present. On the other hand it is possible to state whether the ash comes from pipe tobacco, a cigar or cigarette. In deciding between the last two the amount and appearance when found are decisive. Oriental cigarettes and cigarettes of light Virginia tobacco leave less ash than other cigarettes. The ash of a cigar is light grey in color and holds together in large clumps in which different layers of burnt tobacco leaf can sometimes be discerned. Cigarette ash has a light grey color and forms smaller clumps; it may be recognized by the traces of paper ash which can be observed under the microscope. The ash of pipe tobacco generally has quite a dark color and is mixed with unburnt or partially burnt remains of tobacco.

Cigar, cigarette and tobacco packages

On certain packages of tobacco there are small letters, which show where the package has been printed. These letters are very difficult to discern with the naked eye, and very difficult for the uninitiated to find. They can give an indication of where they were printed and therefore of the place where the goods were bought. The packages are sometimes printed at different printing works corresponding to the different tobacco factories, and the sales area may vary for different factories of the same firm. The glued seams of a tobacco package should never be opened before it has been examined by the expert, since the very small marks might be destroyed by cracking of the paper. In England many cigarette makers put secret marks on the portion of the cigarette carton which holds the cigarettes and is drawn out from the box. Through those marks it is possible to learn to what wholesalers the cigarettes were supplied and hence sometimes the retailers who received them.

Matches

Wooden matchsticks occur in different types of varying length, thickness and color, while the color of the head and also the kind of wood can vary. Some are square in section, others rectangular. There is therefore a possibility of determining the type of match from a burnt or unburnt match stick. Actually this is not of much value except in a very special case, as the various types of match are very common.

In the case, however, of a match which has been torn out of a book of matches, the possibility of identifying it with a book found on a suspect is fairly great. The matches in such a book are made of wood or cardboard, and have to be broken off, so that they can therefore be identified with the corresponding part of the book. The color of matches of this type frequently varies with different books.

Some matches, from Belgium, Italy, South America, etc. are made of waxed or paraffined cotton yarn or paper and are sometimes provided with a head at both ends.

The kind of wood in burnt matches can still be identified by microscopic examination of the carbonized material. Sometimes also manufacturing marks, in the form of small impressions in the free non-striking end of the stick, can be observed after charring.

Matchsticks are often used as toothpicks. If the individual in question is an secretor, a blood group determination can be done on the saliva on the match stick.

WRITING ON BURNED PAPER

Writing on charred or partially burned paper can sometimes be made legible by photographic or chemical methods.

If paper is found burning in a stove no attempt should be made to save it from the fire, since thereby the already burned portions would be broken up or the fire would be stimulated by a better supply of air. Instead, the air supply should be restricted by controlling the dampers and other means so that the fire slackens. When this is achieved the paper is allowed to burn completely.

The material must be collected with great care so that the burned or charred paper is not broken. The best way is to hold a piece of cardboard, a plate or a sheet of glass in front of the stove and to transfer the remains carefully to it. It may be possible to 'waft' it over with a stiff piece of paper or cardboard. Another way is to slip a piece of cardboard or a plate under the remains and then to lift them out.

If the burned material consists of a book, folded papers or currency no attempt should be made to separate the different layers of paper: the remains should be kept and sent to the expert in their original state.

The transportation of such paper residues is best accomplished in a wooden or strong cardboard box in which the charred paper is cushioned by liberal amounts of absorbent cotton. The box should preferably be hand-carried by the investigator to the laboratory and not shipped by mail or railroad. An alternate packing method is to place the residues in an air-tight plastic bag which is then carefully blown up and sealed with a rubber band or string.

A possible alternative is to spray the burned paper with a fixing medium such as shellac solution, a solution of celluloid in amyl acetate or acetone, or a 1 % solution of gelatine in water. Before commencing this operation the fixing medium should be tested on small pieces of burned paper so that the concentration of the solution can be altered if necessary. The fixing medium should not, however, be used except in cases where it is not possible to take possession of or to transport the material without it breaking up. After the preservative has been used it is *no longer possible to make any writing legible by chemical methods*, so that only a photographic method is available.

A number of methods have been worked out for making writing on burned paper legible. It is not advisable for the police officer to attempt to develop the writing himself, since this is an operation which requires experience, and the work should be left entirely to the expert.

If *writing cannot be discerned* the paper may be treated with 60% chloral hydrate solution, 5–10% silver nitrate solution, or potassium ferrocyanide solution. These methods are, however, inapplicable to typewriting.

Typewriting and printing can often be read in specular light. It may be more easily read with silver nitrate solution. In order to make the paper easier to handle it may be treated with 10–20% glycerine solution.

Chemical development media and the above-mentioned glycerine solution are mixed in a large flat-bottomed dish, in which there is placed a sheet of glass. The burnt paper is then laid in the solution and allowed to sink down to the glass plate. The latter is taken out and another sheet of glass is laid on it so that the burnt paper now lies between two sheets of glass. In this way the burnt paper is flattened and more easily handled when examining details or photographing any writing.

Photography with infrared sensitive plates can sometimes be used to make writing legible, whether previously treated with chemicals or not. In many cases very good results are obtained.

If the paper is *only partially burned* it may be cut before development so that the burnt and the unburnt paper can be treated separately. There are however a number of methods by which the paper, before treatment, is burned completely between sheets of mica, but this process has disadvantages.

WOOD

The question often arises, do pieces of wood belong together? There is perhaps occasion to suspect that a piece of timber found at the house of a person suspected of illegal cutting or possession of timber has come from a tree which has been felled on someone else's land and the stump of which has been found; or possibly it is suspected that the handle of a tool left at the scene of a crime has been made from a particular piece of wood found at the house of a suspect. It may also be of significance to know whether a chip of wood comes from an object which may have been used in the crime. Possibly sawdust or wood chips may be found at the scene of a

Fig. 77 Correspondence between log and tree stump determined by the axe cuts.

A   B

Fig.78 Correspondence between annual rings on the cut ends of a pine tree. The white
line indicates where the measurements were taken (see *Fig.77*). A: questioned
log; B: stump at the cutting site.

crime or on the clothes of a suspect (in trouser cuffs, pockets, gloves, etc.)
and it is important to decide whether this is of a particular kind. Finally
there may be a question of a small piece of carbonized wood which is suspected of being part of a burnt match or other object.

Investigations of this type generally give very good results, so that such
clues should not be neglected. Even very small particles or splinters of
wood should be kept if their examination may possibly be of value.

There is given below an account of the different types of examinations of
wood, and of the results which may be expected.

Determination of kind of tree

With large pieces of wood, whether worked or not, or chips of wood, there is no difficulty in determining the species of tree from which they are derived since the anatomical structure of wood is different for different species of tree. The structure of coniferous trees is simpler than that of hardwood ones, and the different types of cells show individual morphological characters for the different species. The investigation of the anatomical structure of wood is done microscopically, using transverse, radial and tangential sections.

Correspondence between two pieces of wood

If it is a question of deciding whether two pieces of the stem of a tree originally belonged together, the original external contour of the stem forms a good guide, if it is found in good condition. Also cracks in the bark, structures and formations on the surface of bark, the position of the sawn surface in relation to the longitudinal axis of the trunk, together with the placing and general appearance of any felling cut, all have their own significance for the task of identification ,which is simply a matter of seeing how the different pieces fit together. By matching them against one another it is frequently possible to determine the correspondence between two pieces of wood which are separated from one another in the longitudinal direction of the tree.

Both in the case of worked and of unworked timber the annual rings, which are visible on the cross section, play a very important part in identification. An annual ring is composed of a lighter part which is formed during spring and early summer and is therefore called spring wood, together with a darker part which is formed towards the end of the summer and in autumn and is called autumn wood.

The width of the annual rings varies within wide limits, depending partly on the kind of tree and partly on factors which affect its growth. Trunks of trees which are leaning or exposed to a one-sided wind pressure grow eccentrically in order to obtain the required mechanical strength. Sometimes they have an elliptical cross section, and the annual rings therefore have a different width at different parts of the transverse section. The crown of the tree develops more on the side facing the sun, which means that the transport of food materials is greatest on that side and therefore the annual rings are also broader there. Displacements in annual ring formations can

Fig. 79 Identity established between the handle of a drill and a similar piece of wood found in the possession of a suspect. The grain and fissures of the wood could be matched on both pieces. (See *Fig. 80*).

results from knots or cracks or other defects, which become covered over by a healing process in the tree. Certain species of trees show a deviation from the normal structure in that the rings becomes wavy. The breadth of a ring also to some extent reflects the climatic conditions, especially the rainfall.

From what has been said above it follows that in most cases the annual rings of a tree are very characteristic, and by making a transverse section of an object under investigation it is often possible to obtain a picture which is just as characteristic of the tree, within a limited region of the stem, as a finger print is of a man. The variation in the breadths of annual rings resulting from climatic and other conditions is also significant from the point of view of identification. It is possible to determine from it – assuming a sufficient number of characteristic variations in breadth – whether two worked or unworked pieces of wood come from the same piece of stem. The breadth of the annual rings is measured and the amount of growth shown graphically.

Bruises and decay in the wood are often characteristic in position and extent, and may assist in identification.

Fig. 80 Plasticine cast (rolled out) of the fissures in the handle of the bit (B) and in the dowel from the suspect's home (A). (See *Fig. 79*).

If an object under investigation is made of wood which has been worked in some way with tools (knife, plane, saw or the like) or which has been painted or surface treated in any other way, then the possibility of identification is increased. Injuries in the edge of the knife or plane blade (including planing machines) leave characteristic marks in the work which can possibly be found on both pieces of wood. Unplaned wood, when sawn in the direction of the grain, often shows marks of varying width and depth from the saw used. In the case of frame-sawn lumber these marks arise during the upward and downward movements of the frame saw, and variations are caused by inequalities in the setting of the teeth and by variations in the pressure on the wood under the saw. The same conditions hold for work cut with a circular saw, the marks being more or less curved depending on the diameter of the saw, and differing from the marks of a frame saw which are straight but may be more or less oblique with reference to the grain of the wood. These saw marks have special significance in the identification of pieces of wood separated from one another in the direction of the grain.

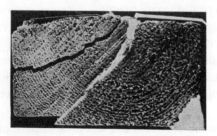

Fig. 81 Physical matching of a wood fragment (upper left) with a board.

Fig. 82 Two boards shown to have been originally one piece by matching a split and marks from a circular saw.

It can be more difficult to determine, solely with the aid of marks from the saw used, whether two cut-off pieces, originally belonged together. If the cutting was done with a handsaw identification is sometimes possible, since the marks of such a saw are often irregular and show characteristic formations. This is connected with the fact that changes in the position of the saw in relation to the piece of wood always occur on the forward and backward strokes of the sawing arm: also after a pause in the sawing the saw never takes up exactly the same position again when sawing is restarted. In cutting with a machine saw the marks are generally regular and meaningless, and therefore cannot generally be used for identification. A transverse section of wood has in fact a poorer power of reproducing marks from a saw than a longitudinal section, owing to the difference in the structure.

If pieces of wood have been painted or surface treated in any way, then shades of color may be useful for identification, and the pigment can be examined chemically and spectrographically to confirm the agreement or difference between the metallic constituents of the pigment. There may be several coats of paint, and agreement or difference in this respect may be noted.

Any knots, cracks or the like in pieces of wood, and also drill holes, nail or screw holes, are significant when it is necessary to decide whether pieces of wood previously made a unit. It is sometimes possible, from nail or screw holes or remaining nails or screws, to determine whether a certain piece of wood was previously combined with another piece, formed part of a floor or wall, etc.

If pieces of wood are separated from one another by a break running in the direction of the grain, then identity can be determined by fitting the

Fig. 83 A board matched with a post by means of nail holes. The matching position and direction of the holes has been clarified by inserting nails in the holes.

pieces to one another. In the case of a break going across the grain there are certain difficulties in doing this, since the broken surfaces are often badly splintered and a number of fibers may have fallen away and been lost.

Kidnapping, (Hauptmann case). On the ground below the room of the kidnapped baby a ladder was found which was home-made. With the aid of the species of wood and marks on part of the ladder from a planing machine with a damaged blade, it was possible to locate the lumber in a machine planing shop and a lumber yard where Hauptmann was employed. Planing marks on some of the treads were identified with a piece of wood and a hand plane in his house. One upright of the ladder had four nail holes which fitted holes in a floor beam in the attic of his house, where a board was missing (KOEHLER, 1937).

Chips and splinters of wood

Considerable quantities of chips or splinters are often found at the scene of a forced entry, and they are usually examined as a routine with a view to finding any marks from the tool used in making the entry. Chips of wood, however, can also be valuable for the direct identification of the tool in another way: among the chips from forced doors, windows and the like there may be found a chip which has broken off the handle of a chisel, hammer or other tool, so that this opportunity for identification should be borne in mind when examining the chips. There may perhaps be found later, at the house of a suspect, a tool with a damaged handle, and a small chip from the scene of the crime may be found to fit this, and form the sole and final proof. Chips of wood may be found to be painted, surface treated or contaminated in the same way as the handle of the tool.

Sawdust, wood meal or other particles of finely powdered wood

Such particles of wood can sometimes be found in the trouser cuffs, pockets, or gloves of a suspect or in his headgear, or detected in vacuuming the clothes of a suspect. Clues in the form of such particles may also be left behind at the scene owing to the clothes of the criminal being for some reason contaminated with them.

In most cases the species of tree can be determined simply by a microscopic examination, and the occurence of any foreign bodies on or together with the particles can be confirmed. If, however, it should be found that it is not possible to obtain a satisfactory result by microscopic examination, owing to the characteristic morphological structure not showing sufficiently clearly, the species can often be determined by a microscopic investigation of the ash picture (spodogram) which is obtained when the particles are burnt. After the burning, which should be complete, the mineral substances (especially calcium oxalate and silica) in the wood are left behind in a form (silica skeleton) which is characteristic for different species of trees, and

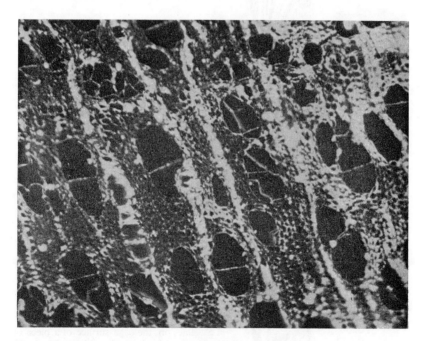

Fig. 84 The carbon picture (anthracogram) of aspen wood.

Fig. 85 The appearance of the curved
lines on the edge surface of a piece of
glass from a broken pane.

which can be observed by a microscopic examination of the ashed material. Such characteristic ash pictures are obtained, not only from wood, but also from particles derived from other parts of plants (stem, root, leaf, fruit, etc.) and preparations of these, so that this method of investigation may also be applied to such finds.

Carbonized wood

In determining the species of tree from which carbonized wood has come, the investigation of the object is done microscopically without previous treatment, as even in that state the wood retains its characteristic structure, although it may be changed to some extent. The ash picture (anthracogram) visible under the microscope is therefore characteristic for different species of tree. Owing to the fragility of the carbonized wood, sections must be made on the surface of the particles themselves. Even with herbaceous plants the carbon picture is characteristic. It should be emphasised here that *clues in the form of wholly or partially burned portions of vegetation (including wood)* should not be regarded as valueless and therefore neglected. Modern refined methods of botanical analysis make it possible to operate even with material of this kind with a good prospect of success. This holds especially for the identification of burned residues. Thus, for example, with the aid of the above-mentioned ashing method it is possible to identify with certainty many wholly or partially burned parts of plants.

BROKEN GLASS

The police officer often has the problem of having to decide whether a pane of glass has been broken from inside or outside, or whether it was struck by a bullet or by a stone. Pieces from the broken pane or the hole often show marks which are characteristic of the type of injury and the direction of the destructive force, and if correctly interpreted these indications will give positive answers.

Broken panes of glass

The surfaces of the edges of pieces of glass from a broken pane show curved lines (Fig.85) which form almost a right angle with one side of the pane and go through obliquely to the other side. These curved lines are an expression of the 'conchoidal (shell-like) fracture' which is characteristic of glass, and their direction in relation to the sides of the pane is determined by the side from which the cracks start. If they start from the side of the glass opposite to the destructive force, then the curved lines form a right angle against this side. If on the other hand the cracks start from the same side as the destructive force, then the curved lines are perpendicular to this side. When a destructive force acts in a limited area on one side of the glass, the glass first bends a little as the result of its elasticity. When the elastic limit is exceeded it cracks, forming in the first place a *radial fracture* which starts from the point of application of the force. These cracks result from the stretching of the glass on the side opposite to the destructive force. Then the portions of glass between the radial cracks are bent in the direction of the force and the glass on the same side as the force is stretched and breaks with a *concentric fracture*. These concentric cracks start as a result of stretching on the same side as the destructive force (Fig.86).

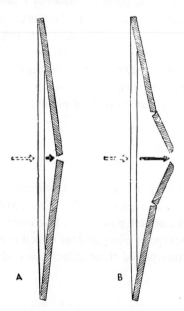

Fig. 86 Diagram showing the production of radial and concentric fracture in glass. A: radial cracks are formed first, commencing on the side of the glass opposite to the destructive force; B: concentric cracks occur afterwards, starting on the same side as the force.

Thus it follows that with *radial* fractures the curved lines meet the side of the glass opposite to the destructive force at nearly a right angle. With *concentric* fractures the lines form almost a right angle with the side on which the force acted. The distinctness of the curved lines may vary for different pieces of glass, so that it is sometimes necessary to use oblique light from a flashlight in order to observe them.

It is however most important, especially in the case of small pieces of glass, not to get the edges mixed up. It is advisable to collect all the pieces of glass and to fit them together so that a complete picture is obtained of the part of the broken pane where the force acted. In the case of windowpanes a useful indication can be obtained from the layer of dirt which is often present on the outside of the glass.

Definite conclusions should however be drawn from the curved lines of the edge surfaces only in the case of the fractures which lie nearest to the point of attack. Only with these can one be sure that they have been produced in the manner described above. Fractures at a greater distance from

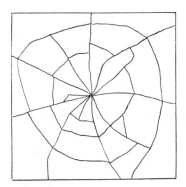

Fig. 87 Sketch illustrating the radial and concentric fractures in a sheet of glass.

the point of attack may have been produced, for example, when the object used for breaking the glass was brought back, or by projecting and interfering points of glass being broken off by hand. Further, one should not use for such an examination pieces which are near the frame or sash, since these are held too rigidly and this affects the formation of the curved lines.

When transported for laboratory examination the pieces should be wrapped separately in paper, and then packed all together in a box; or possibly the pieces, carefully fitted together, are photographed to assist in the investigation and each piece is then numbered, the numbers being also shown on the photograph. The packing should be done in such a way that there is no risk of the pieces breaking or being damaged in transit.

Panes of glass perforated by a bullet

If a pane of glass has been perforated by a bullet, the hole is expanded in a crater on the side where the bullet went out. The glass is shattered here in a conchoidal fracture.

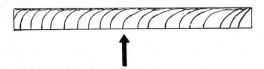

Fig. 88 Diagram showing the curved lines in the edge of the glass in a concentric fracture. They are almost perpendicular to the side from which force was applied. In radial fractures the direction is reversed.

It is thus possible to deduce the direction of the shot from the appearance of this expansion around the exit hole. If a bullet strikes perpendicularly against the glass the conchoidal fracture is distributed uniformly around the hole; but if the bullet strikes obliquely, most of the fracture is concentrated to one side of the actual hole.

The appearance of the hole is dependent on the force of the projectile, and this in turn depends on the power of the cartridge and the distance of the shot. If the projectile has a high velocity the hole is almost circular without noticeable cracking, or merely with cracks just starting. With a lower velocity there is an almost regular polygon with radial cracks running outwards in a star. The polygon is formed by the concentric cracks which are first produced: as a rule no further ones appear. If the velocity of the bullet is low there are generally radial cracks which run out for a long way, and distinctly concentric ones.

With a shot at very close range, a more or less complete shattering of the glass results from the pressure of the muzzle gases, the extent depending on the power of the cartridge and the thickness of the glass. In such cases it is impossible to obtain a clear idea of the appearance of the shot hole unless the shattered splinters of glass can be pieced together, but in most cases this is impossible because the splinters from the parts nearest the actual hole

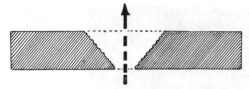

Fig. 89 Diagram showing formation of a bullet hole in a pane of glass. Note the crater form of the hole. The arrow shows the direction of the shot.

are too small. In a very favorable case indications of the metal of the bullet on the edges round the hole can be detected chemically or spectrographically.

A reliable indication that the glass was shattered by a shot at close range is the smoke deposit which is usually found on the fragments. If the cartridge was loaded with black powder the smoke deposit may be so heavy that the glass is clearly discolored.

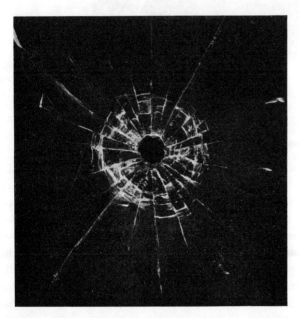

Fig. 90 Bullet hole through pane of glass. The caliber of the bullet is .22 fired from a distance of about 75 yds. Considerable degree of regularity in fractures.

Fig. 91 Regularity less marked here. Bullet from .32 automatic pistol at a distance of about 10 yds.

Shooting or stone throwing?

It is often very difficult to decide, simply from the appearance of a hole in a pane of glass, whether it has been made by a projectile from a firearm or by a stone which has been thrown or flung up by the action of a wheel of a passing car.

A small stone thrown at a comparatively high speed against a pane of glass can produce a hole which is very similar to that caused by a bullet. The crater-like expansion of a hole caused by a small stone may not actually show such a typical, uniform, conchoidal fracture in the glass as in the case of a bullet hole. Moreover, holes caused by small stones generally do not show the geometrical regularity in the radial and concentric cracks in the glass around the hole usually shown by a bullet hole.

Fig. 92 Hole in car window caused by stone. No regularity.

Fig. 93 Reconstruction of glass pane (not wholly complete) where struck by an instrument. Some regularity in 'radial' fractures.

On the other hand a large stone can shatter a pane of glass in a manner which closely resembles the result of a close range shot.

Thus the question of distinguishing between a shot and a stone cannot be answered simply by a study of the site of the fracture. In doubtful cases it is therefore necessary to look for the projectile which has caused the fracture.

Sometimes the investigation is completed by an attempt at reconstruction. This is illustrated by an interesting case, described below, of damage to a store window.

Property damage. A store owner complained that a pane of glass in his shop had been damaged. The damage consisted of 7 very small (about 1 mm) round holes on the outside of the pane, expanding to symmetrical craters on the inside. The edges and sides of the craters were uniform and smooth, with a maximum diameter of about 10 mm. They were irregularly distributed over the pane. On the floor inside the window were found seven symmetrical glass cones with smooth even sides, slightly jagged edges and somewhat truncated points; these fitted the craters in the glass, but no projectiles were found.

Experiments showed that an injury having exactly the same appearance, with glass cones forced out of the glass, could be produced when a steel ball of 4 mm. diameter was shot from an air gun against the pane at a certain distance and a certain angle.

As is seen from the above case, it may happen that a projectile does not pass through the glass but falls down outside it. This also happens with small stones thrown against the glass at a low velocity. The side of the glass which is struck by the projectile then usually shows either *a hole which is appreciably smaller than the projectile, or merely cracks*. On the other side of the pane a part of the glass generally breaks away, sometimes in the form of a crater.

Order of events in shooting, stone throwing or breakage

If there are a number of injuries in a pane of glass, the order in which these were produced can sometimes be determined. Cracks in the glass resulting from the first injury stop short either of themselves or at the edges of the glass. On the other hand cracks from subsequent injuries stop when they meet cracks already present in the glass, which are the result of earlier fractures. Even when the damage is extensive and large portions of the glass have fallen away, the order of the damage can often be established by fitting the pieces together.

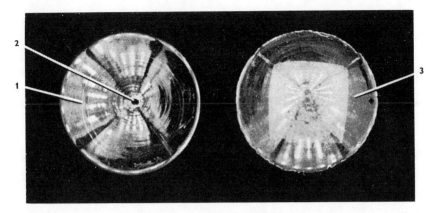

Fig. 94 Damage to a store window caused by a 4 mm pellet from an air gun. 1: crater on the inside of the glass; 2: hole about 1 mm in diameter on the outside of the glass; 3: cone of glass which fell inside.

Cracked or burst panes of glass

If a pane of glass has been *cracked or burst by the action of heat,* it shows characteristic long wavy fractures. Pieces which have fallen out are generally found in the same direction as the source of heat. If a limited area of the glass has been exposed to a direct flame, a piece of glass corresponding to that area often breaks out.

Panes of glass can, however, also break *without having been exposed to any external action.* The cause of this is that strains may be left in the glass during the manufacture, and these can cause a sudden breakage even without any external stimulus. The same result can be brought about by vibration, scratching the surface of the glass, a violent noise, etc. In this case the glass cracks in a comparatively regular pattern with a typical crackle appearance, or it may break up wholly or partially into small pieces of a regular form. Sometimes these pieces are thrown an appreciable distance from the pane of glass. Drinking glasses and other glass objects may break in a similar manner.

One variety of automobile *safety glass,* used in the side and rear windows on some cars, also breaks completely or partially into pieces or small rods of a regular form when subjected to a sufficiently violent blow or shock or when hit by a projectile of any kind. This also is due to strains in the glass, but they have been produced intentionally during the manufacture in order

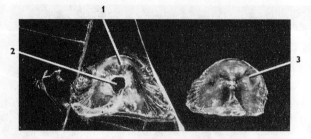

Fig.95 A small fracture caused by stone against glass of car headlamp. 1: crater produced on inside of glass; 2. small hole in glass itself; 3: cone of glass broken away and found inside lamp.

to ensure that, if the window is broken in a collision or other accident, there will be no sharp-edged points of glass to endanger the driver and passengers.

A pane of glass of this kind, shattered by a bullet or other projectile, may still remain hanging in position on the vehicle. In a typical crackle pattern the crack formation extends over the whole of the pane, but close around the point of fracture a large number of the small pieces of glass usually

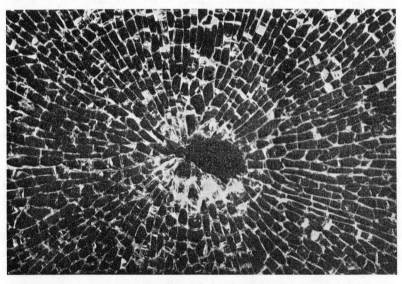

Fig.96 The appearance of pre-stressed safety glass after being shattered by a bullet. Note that only small portions near the hole have fallen out.

come loose and fall away, so that a study of the crater formation in the glass is only possible in exceptional cases. If pieces which have fallen out are found they can however, in favorable cases, be pieced together in their places near the point of impact, and the appearance of the fracture can be reconstructed.

Glass splinters

At the scene of a crime where the criminal has obtained entry by breaking a window, glazed door or the like, the investigating officer should always remember to keep any pieces of the broken glass. If the criminal is found later, a closer investigation of his clothes may show splinters of glass in his trouser cuffs or pockets, inside the lining of his gloves, or sticking in the skin of his hands. Moreover, splinters of glass may be found in the handle of a tool which was used for forcing an entry.

If splinters of glass found on a criminal or on a tool are not too small they can be compared with splinters from the scene of a crime. The refractive index, density, and chemical composition – the latter determined chemically or spectrographically – are the most important factors. Such an investigation will not result in definite identification, since glass of the same composition is widely distributed. Non-identity can however be proved and even this may be of significance in elucidating the crime.

In taking samples of a broken windowpane the sample should be selected from several parts of the pane since the thickness of the glass may vary in different parts of one pane.

TRACES ON THE SUSPECT

When committing a crime the criminal very often gets traces on his clothes cr shoes, or on his body. Clues of this kind are valuable as often the criminal does not realize their significance; therefore it is difficult for him to guard himself against them. Sometimes he has no idea that he is carrying them. It is of the greatest importance that the police officer should always consider the possibilities of proof offered by such traces, and should search for and preserve them with the greatest care. The most favorable prospects for a good result are offered by cases where a suspect is arrested shortly after the commission of the crime, but even in other cases one should never neglect

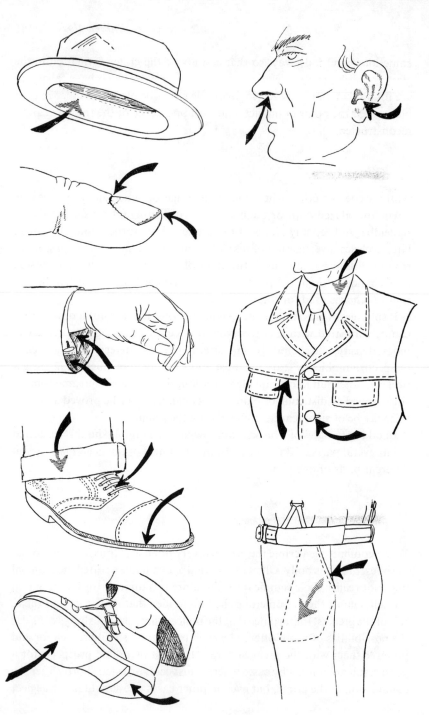

Fig. 97 Diagram showing places on person and clothing which should be examined for possible trace evidence.

the search for clues on a suspect. Many of them, for example on the clothes of a criminal or under his nails, may be found a long time after the crime occurred.

Since the character of a clue is often just as dependent on the nature of the crime scene as on the type of crime, no attempt has been made to deal with them here according to different categories of crime.

Traces on clothing and shoes

If there is reason to believe that a suspect's clothes and shoes (also on the bottoms) contain trace evidence, immediate steps should be taken to remove the clothing. This is to prevent evidence from being lost in the course of continued wearing or by intentional cleaning.

There is always a risk that small particles such as hair, paint chips, splinters of wood, etc. are lost during the removal of the clothing. The suspect should therefore undress while standing on a large sheet of clean paper. Each garment should then be placed separately on clean paper which is spread out on the examination table. If the garments are to be forwarded to a laboratory for expert examination they should be *individually wrapped* in clean paper.

Among the substances which may be found on clothes are:

Characteristic dust from the scene of the crime or its surroundings.

Portions of vegetable matter from the scene of a crime outdoors.

Splinters of glass, chips of wood, flakes of paint, etc. (burglary).

Traces of explosives or of safe insulation (safebreaking).

Particles of metallic slag, fused beads of metal or fused beads from glass wool (opening of safe by oxyacetylene burner).

Small burns in clothes from fused beads of metal (opening of safe by oxyacetylene burner).

Traces of soil, paint, grease, brick dust, plaster, lipstick, face powder, etc.

Bloodstains which may be in splashes almost invisible to the eye, also semen.

Particles of tissue, hair and feathers.

Textile fibers (also on shoes – from carpets and rugs).

Burglary. Thieves had bored out the panel of a door with a brace and bit. Holes had been bored in a continuous line – all adjoining each other – around the panel which was literally cut out. When the scene was investigated, a pile of chips was found on the floor below the door. The door was painted cream on one side and brown on the other. Later

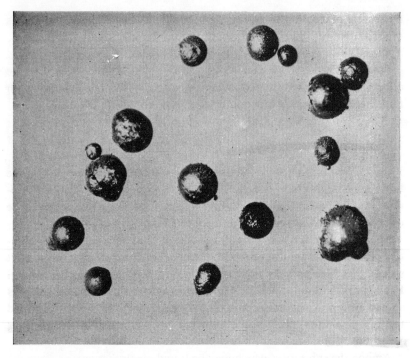

Fig. 98 Fused beads of metal found in the clothing of a person suspected of having used an oxyacetylene burner to open a safe.

two suspects were arrested and when their trouser cuffs were brushed out, a considerable quantity of very small chips and fragments of wood were found. This was sent together with a portion of the door to the Police Laboratory, which was able to show that the fragments taken from the clothing of the suspects were of Scottish pine – the same wood as the panel – and that on quite a number of chips and fragments there were minute specks of cream or brown paint. After hearing the report of the Police Laboratory the two men concerned confessed to the burglary (HATHERILL, 1952).

Murder. On one shoe of a person suspected of the crime was found a fiber of hemp which agreed in character with the fibers of a hempen mat in the murdered woman's lodging, together with a green wool fiber which agreed with a rug in her bedroom (KEITH SIMPSON, 1947).

Clues on the body of the criminal

A doctor, nurse or police woman must be employed when searching for and recovering such clues on a woman. Great care should be taken that the criminal has no opportunity of destroying clues such as bloodstains on the skin, strands of hair or the like.

Clues which may be found include the following:

Injuries resulting from a struggle with the victim or with other persons.

Injuries caused by the weapon used by the criminal. (In firing an automatic pistol the criminal may sometimes receive a graze in the region of the web of the thumb from the recoil of the slide).

Deposits from powder particles on the hand with which he fired a pistol or revolver. In order to take possession of this, melted paraffin, allowed to cool to a bearable temperature, is poured over the thumb and index finger and allowed to solidify, first covering the skin with a thin layer which is strengthened with gauze, after which more is poured on little by little until a sufficiently thick and coherent layer is obtained. The paraffin can then be loosened easily from the skin, and the powder deposit is thereby transferred to the paraffin and can be identified with diphenylamine in sulphuric acid. This test should, however, be done by an expert. Since the reagent also gives a positive reaction with, e.g. the deposit on the finger of a smoker, *a comparison test should always be taken in the same way with paraffin from the other hand.*

Hair around the penis (collected by combing) and under the foreskin – in cases of rape and sexual murder.

Bloodstains, taken by means of filter paper or blotting paper, moistened with water or saline, which is pressed against the skin.

Dust, safe insulation, and the like *in nose, ears and hair.*

Fragments of skin, vaginal epithelia, textile fibers, particles of explosives, safe insulation, etc. *under the nails.*

Nail dirt is collected over a sheet of clean white paper by means of a wooden stick (matchstick) which is shaped with a knife so that it is flat (not pointed) at one end. The nail dirt and the stick or sticks (several may be used if necessary for the same finger) are placed in a separate tube for each finger, labelled to indicate the hand and finger. Care should be taken that the dirt is not lost by spattering when collected. It is sometimes possible to dip the stick in water so that the dirt sticks better to it. *Knives, nail files or other hard objects must not be used,* as fragments of skin and epithelial cells from the skin under the nails might get mixed with the dirt.

Murder. A man was found murdered by a hammer with which the criminal had delivered a number of blows so that a large part of the top of the skull was crushed in. At the scene of the crime there were a lot of bloodstains together with pieces of bone and brain

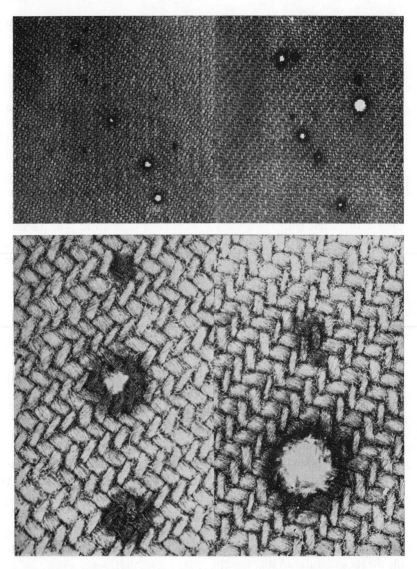

Fig. 99 Burns in cotton fabric of clothing caused by beads as in *Fig. 98*.

substance. About 5 hours after the discovery of the crime a suspect was detained. On his clothes were bloodstains which he had attempted to dry or wash away. He had washed his hands free from blood, but on the left lower arm was a distinct bloodstain which was preserved by transferring to a filter paper moistened with saline. On one shoe there was caked blood containing a small fragment of skin.

OBJECTS LEFT AT THE CRIME SCENE

It happens frequently that the criminal leaves an object behind at the crime scene because he had no further use for it and believed that it would be of no value to the police. Objects are also forgotten or lost by the criminal. He may have been surprised during the act and been forced to flee without having time to pick up his tools, articles of clothing, etc.

All such articles can be extremely valuable, both from the investigative and the evidential point of view. The most valuable objects are those which may bear finger prints. The criminal may have worn gloves while working at the scene but not while he was wrapping his tools at home.

Paper

Paper bags, wrapping paper and the like which are found at the scene of a crime may contain paint or other contamination, printing, handwriting, etc. all of which may be of value in the investigation. Such paper should always be examined for latent finger prints even when the surface of the paper is not the most suitable for prints. (See 'Finger and palm prints').

The paper may also have been torn or cut from a larger piece which may be found at the suspect's home, place of work or at an earlier crime scene. The torn or cut edges may constitute positive evidence that the two pieces were originally one piece.

Safe burglary with explosives. During the examination of a safe burglary scene a large piece of wallpaper was found. It had apparently served as wrapper for clay which had been used to muffle the explosion. Another piece of wallpaper with the same color and pattern was recovered at another safe burglary some time later. One edge of this piece was found to correspond exactly with the edge of the piece first found. A suspect in the second burglary was a house painter on whose premises was found a large number of rolls of wallpaper. One of these had the same color and pattern as the pieces found at the burglary scenes. The torn edge of this roll corresponded with the torn edge of the second piece which fact implicated the suspect in both burglaries.

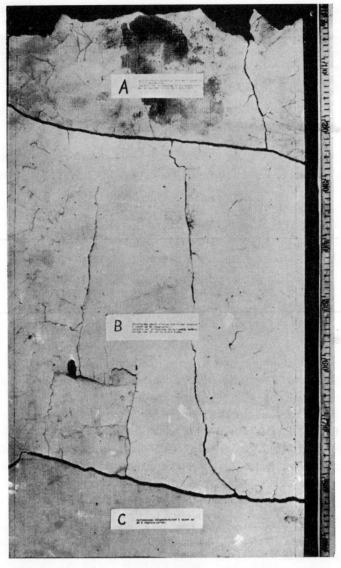

Fig. 100 Two pieces of wallpaper used for wrapping (A and B). They were found at two different crime scenes and could be shown to have come from a roll of paper (C) in the suspect's shop.

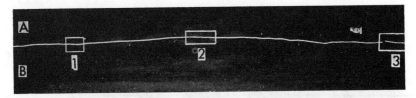

Fig. 101 Black paper from a crime scene (A) could be shown to have come from a roll of such paper (B) in a store. The areas marked 1, 2 and 3 contained certain matching irregularities on both edges (see *Fig. 102*).

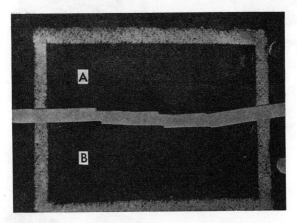

Fig. 102 Area 1 of Fig. 101 in actual size. A: paper from the scene; B: paper from the roll.

It sometimes happens that a newspaper is used as wrapper for burglary tools but it is only in exceptional cases that such paper has any investigative or evidential value. Newsprint is, however, rather fragile, and a small fragment of a newspaper may be found at a crime scene which could later be matched with a newspaper in the possession of a suspect. Pieces of a newspaper may also be found folded inside the sweatband of a hat or inside a shoe.

When a burglar takes merchandise from a store he sometimes uses wrapping paper from the premises. Cut or torn ends of rolls of paper should therefore be recovered from such crime scene for the eventuality that it may later be matched with paper in a suspect's possession.

It may also happen that paper or similar material is unusual enough to be traceable to a particular source.

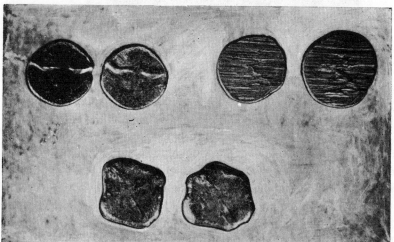

Fig. 103 Characteristic die marks on nail heads. Comparison of two nails from five packages of different types and sizes.

Safe burglary. A large piece of opaque, black paper was found at a burglary scene. It had been used to cover a window so as to allow the burglar to work undisturbed with lights on. The source of the paper was found in a nearby town where it was determined that the store in question had not sold that type of paper for some time. The cut end of the remainder of the roll was found to match the edge of the crime scene paper. The search for the burglar could thus be considerably narrowed.

Knives, tools, etc.

Some tools and weapons may carry factory markings or contaminations in the form of oil, paint, etc. which may be of value in tracing the criminal. In some cases they may tie the tools to a previous burglary where they were stolen and where the criminal may have left valuable evidence.

With respect to tools left at the scene it should be remembered that they may have left marks at previous burglary scenes. (See 'Tool marks', 'Fragments of tools', 'Chips and splinters of wood').

Pocketknives, keys and other small objects which can be carried in pockets may carry dust or fibers which are characteristic of the criminal's clothes. (See 'Dust' and 'Fragments of textiles, etc.').

A question is sometimes raised as to whether a hunting knife belongs to a certain sheath. This may be answered in favorable cases. The shape of the blade or damage and repairs to the handle may have left marks in the sheath. Rivets in the sheath may have deposited characteristic marks on the knife handle.

Homicide. After a fight where one man had been stabbed to death, a knife was found. The knife was compared with a knife sheath found in the possession of a suspect to determine if they belonged together. The contours of the blade were found outlined on the inside of the sheath and some scratches on the wooden handle corresponded to rivets which protruded on the inside of the sheath.

Nails

Nails with flat heads often show characteristic marks from the die which shaped the head. In addition, most nails show marks of the jaws of the nail-making machine, immediately below the head. It is thus possible to make comparative examinations of the die marks on two or more nails. (Fig 103.). If the marks are identical it indicates that the nails were made in the same plant with the same die and within a limited period of time, and possibly that they came from the same package. The latter determination should, of course, not be made solely on the basis of the die marks. The probability that the nails came from the same package must therefore be estimated with regard to all the circumstances in a given case.

Arson. In an arson investigation it became important to determine whether a nail used in an incendiary device was identical with two nails found at the home of a suspect. The three nails were of the wire type and of the same size. One of the two suspect nails looked very similar to the nail from the crime scene with respect to the head markings. The particular pattern of the mark lead to the manufacturer of the nails who was able to state that the two nails were made in the same machine. The machine operator could identify the die marks as well as the period of manufacture. In all probability the two nails were made within a week's time. (DAUBNEY, 1944).

Metal wire

Steel and other metallic wire of small diameter is usually made by pulling the wire through a series of holes of decreasing diameter. The die which is subjected to intense wear during the drawing process deposits a series of fine striations on the surface of the wire. The prominence and position of these striations vary with the degree of wear in the die. It is therefore possible to show, by comparison microscopy, that two pieces of such wire were originally one piece, provided that the two pieces were not separated by too great a distance. (Fig. 104).

Fig. 104 Two pieces of wire shown to have come from the same length of wire by means of marks from the manufacturing die.

Articles of clothing, etc.

Manufacturers' markings on clothing are of value only in exceptional cases. Size markings and laundry marks may, however, be quite valuable. (See 'Laundry marks, etc.'). Other marks in the form of initials or even names are, of course, extremely valuable when they are found. Hair should always be searched for on garments, as should dust which may be characteristic of the criminal. (See 'Dust'). Traces of sweat, urine, saliva or nasal secretions may in some cases indicate the criminal's blood group. (See 'Human secreta').

Pockets should be searched as a matter of course. In some cases they contain valuable evidence. Remember that objects may have fallen through a hole in a pocket which has subsequently been repaired. The lining should therefore also be searched.

Burglary. A white handkerchief was found at the scene of a store burglary; it had apparently been dropped by one of the burglars. Two suspects who were later arrested for this burglary denied any connection with the handkerchief. However, one of them had in his pocket a handkerchief which was similar to the one from the crime scene. Ultraviolet light revealed identical fluorescent laundry marks on both handkerchiefs. Both suspects confessed to the burglary when confronted with this finding.

Homicide. A man and a woman, owners of a clothing store, were found murdered with wounds from a hammer and a knife. In the store was also found a package containing two used men's suits, presumably left by the assailant after taking new clothing from the racks. In one of the coat pockets was found a number of small fragments of a torn-up letter. When the fragments of the letter were pieced together, a name could be read. This individual was arrested with an accomplice and both confessed to the double murder. They had intended to take along the package containing the old suits but when leaving the store they had inadvertently tripped the latch on the door so that they could not get back in to retrieve the old suits and a bundle of new clothes they had stolen.

Shoes may contain impressions of the soles and toes, and their size can usually be determined. (See 'Foot prints' and 'Identification of the dead'). Shoes may also show wear and deformations which are characteristic of the wearer.

Galoshes and rubbers sometimes contain a clear impression of the soles and heels of the wearer's shoes.

A shoe tongue left at the scene became important evidence in the case related below.

Burglary. A worn shoe tongue was found at the scene of a burglary. The suspect's shoes were found to be missing one tongue. A closer examination revealed that the holes from the seam on the shoe matched the holes in the tongue. Markings from the laces and the lace holes also matched the shoe. The suspect confessed to the burglary.

Traceable markings

A number of commercial products are marked, on labels and containers, with designations for date, lot number, plant, etc. These markings are intended to help the manufacturer check on the distribution and sales of his product but they can also be of help to investigators in tracing the origin of articles left at a crime scene. Conversely, they may also help in establishing the origin of stolen property.

The markings usually take the form of printed or rubber stamped letters and numbers. A special variety is the notched code found on some bottle labels, the so-called 'Codedge'. Since the markings are usually in code, the manufacturer or distributor of the product should always be consulted for the meaning of the symbols.

In some areas the labels on liquor bottles are marked in code to assist in the tracing of stolen liquor.

Chapter 9 Weapons and Explosives

In such crimes as murder, attempted murder, assaults and in suicides, weapons or different kinds of objects are often used to produce injuries or trauma, as the medical profession calls it. These weapons are of the greatest importance to the reconstruction of the crime and as proof of guilt. A weapon brought to the scene of the crime may have been recently purchased or stolen by the criminal. Or he may have had the weapon in his possession for a long time. He may have picked it up at the scene, or he may have left it there to create an impression of suicide or accident. He may have forgotten it at the scene, thrown it away in fleeing, or he may have kept it in his possession. In some cases it is, therefore, necessary to extend the search for weapons beyond the crime scene proper. The exact position of the weapon is very important for the differentiation of homicide, suicide or accident. Weapons may have traces of the victim, of the assailant or of the place where it had been stored. Sharp or blunt weapons may have a characteristic form which is revealed in the victim's injuries. The type of firearm may often be determined from recovered cartridge cases and bullets.

Depending on the particular circumstances, it is thus possible for the weapon to be used as an aid to the reconstruction of events, in tracing the criminal and in connecting him with the scene of the crime.

Weapons of different kinds, cartridge cases and bullets should, therefore, be given the closest attention by the investigating officer in order that all their potential value as evidence be realized. From the viewpoint of crime scenes indoors, the following pages will discuss the recovery of such evidence and the information which may be drawn from it. The principles are, however, to a large extent, also applicable to outdoor crime scenes and to cases of illegal hunting.

Fixing the position of a weapon

The most important rule is that a weapon at the scene of a crime must not be moved or touched until its position has been photographed, sketched and indicated in a report, and marked. If there is reason to suspect that it has been removed by any person or the doctor before the arrival of the police an effort should be made to get this question cleared up as quickly as possible, so that a reconstruction can be made before the appearance of the scene of the crime is altered. The position of a weapon is of decisive significance for the reconstruction and for deciding, for example, whether a case is, or is not, one of suicide.

If a weapon is found on the floor a depression or other marks may be found in the floor under or in the vicinity of the weapon, showing that it fell from, e.g. the hand of a person who killed himself. There may also be marks on the weapon in the form of wood fibers, paint, cement, or the like from the floor.

If the dead person is holding the weapon it is important to note the exact grip and position of the weapon in his hand. It may have been placed there by the murderer. In such a case the way in which a weapon is held in relation to the injuries on the body are decisive in deciding whether the dead person could have produced the injuries himself. In the case of an automatic pistol the recoil of the slide may have caused a surface graze in the region of the thumb or the web of the hand, and the presence of such an injury is strong proof that the dead person fired a shot with an automatic pistol. A closer examination of the hand of the dead person may show marks of powder, especially if a revolver has been used. From these marks, the investigator may deduce that both hands were in the vicinity of the muzzle blast or the gap of the revolver. One hand may have been used as a guide while the other pressed the trigger, or both hands may have been held up in defense.

In the case of long barrelled guns, rifles and shotguns, special attention should be given to the possibility of the dead person having fired a shot at himself with the weapon. Special arrangements such as string, belts, sticks, etc. may have been used, and these in their turn may have left marks in the form of fibers, dirt, soot or the like on the trigger or trigger guard. One shoe may be removed in order that the trigger may be pressed with a toe.

Suicide. A young woman was shot by a rifle and her fiancé was suspected. On the trigger and trigger guard of the weapon there was found ash of brown coal, which was identified microscopically and microchemically. It was established that the woman had committed suicide by holding the muzzle of the weapon against her chest and pressing the trigger with a poker.

The positions of cartridges, cartridge cases and bullets is just as important as that of weapons. From their position it is possible to deduce the position of firing, direction of the shot and in certain cases also the path of the bullet. If a bullet has penetrated a tree, a piece of furniture or a wooden wall, the shot track gives information regarding the direction of the shot and often also the path of the bullet. There is a much better opportunity of determining the exact course of a bullet when it has passed through a fixed object such as a windowpane, and then struck a wall. With the aid of the path of the bullet and of shot wounds on the dead person it is possible to determine his attitude and position when shot. In calculating the distance of the shot, the depth to which a bullet has penetrated, e.g. a wooden wall, is significant. The penetrating power is dependent on the distance of the shot, but allowance must also be made for the loss of energy in passing through an object, such as a body. A more accurate determination of distance can be made with the aid of gunshot injuries on the clothes and body of the dead person.

The position of a bullet found at the scene of a crime should be recorded in the same way as for weapons, and bullets should be collected separately and packed so that there can be no confusion. If two or more weapons have been used it is important that the bullets should not get mixed up, so that at a later date the place where each one was found can be fixed exactly. Great care should also be taken in collecting and packing them, so that the microscopic marks from the barrel of the weapon are not injured or destroyed. For this reason a bullet which has penetrated or lodged in a wall should not be probed for and dug out by means of a knife, ice pick or chisel. Instead a portion of the wall surrounding the bullet should be carefully removed in one piece and the bullet recovered by breaking away the the supporting material. Since it may become important to ascertain other objects that came in contact with the projectile, it must not be handled by persons who have touched blood, nor should adhering dirt be removed until a microscopic study is possible. Care should be exercised that marking of the bullet does not destroy this trace evidence.

The same considerations with respect to fixing the position and taking possession of weapons and bullets apply to cartridges and cartridge cases found at the scene of a crime. The position of a cartridge which has misfired or of a case which has been ejected from an automatic pistol can give an indication of the type of automatic pistol and form a valuable supplement to the determination of the make of pistol from the marks left by the weapon on the bullet and case. Many automatic pistols differ in respect to the ejection of the cases; some throw them out to the left, some to the right, and others again straight up. The case is thrown out with a force which varies for different types of pistol but is generally considerable, so that it may rebound against furniture, walls, wall coverings etc. and change direction. The position can nevertheless give some indication of the type of weapon. If a cartridge case has not bounced off any object and has moreover fallen on to an underlayer which prevents it from rolling (carpet, lawn, etc.) then its position gives a direct indication of the type of weapon and place or direction of firing. If three of these factors (position of cartridge case, type of automatic pistol, place of firing, direction of shooting) are known, then the fourth can be determined. Outdoors, however, it is necessary to take into account the direction and strength of the wind, and in all cases the inclination of the weapon must be considered.

Homicide. The police were called to an incident where a woman, according to the statement of her husband, happened to shoot herself in the chest while handling his automatic pistol (Walther, Caliber 6.35 mm). The incident was supposed to have occurred in the hall of their residence. The investigating police officer could not actually find any cartridge cases in the hall, but after a careful search he found one on the plate rack in the kitchen. It was found to be impossible for a case from a shot fired in the hall to have been thrown through the open door into the kitchen and up on to the plate rack, so that the man's statement was proved to be incorrect.

The position of wads and over-shot wads, which often remain relatively undamaged, from shotgun cartridges and muzzle-loading weapons also gives information regarding the direction of shooting. These can generally be found about 5 to 8 yards from the place of firing in the approximate direction of fire, but it is necessary to take into consideration the direction and strength of the wind. The over-shot card placed in front of the charge of shot shows, in most factory-loaded cartridges, a manufacturing mark and also the size of shot given by a number or letters.

As mentioned previously, weapons and also cartridge cases, bullets, shot and wads may carry marks from the victim or the criminal, with the aid of which the crime can be unravelled.

Cutting, stabbing and striking weapons

It should always be remembered that both latent finger prints and finger prints in blood, grease or the like may be found on weapons or instruments, and that these must be protected.

On an instrument which has been used in a case of murder, suicide, assault, marks are always found from the victim in the form of blood, hair, fragments or textiles, cloth fibers, etc. Such clues may appear to be of little value, but it must not be forgotten that it may be necessary to prove that the weapon was actually used in the particular case, and these clues are then of the greatest value. Loose hairs, dried blood, fibers and the like must be placed in a test tube, and the weapon taken and packed in such a way that finger prints or other clues are not destroyed but are kept for investigation. A container that suspends the weapon with the minimum of bearing surfaces is preferred. These can be constructed from peg board, heavy cardboard, Erector sets or similar material. Wrapping an object in cotton, gauze, tissue, will more than likely dislodge trace evidence.

If both finger prints and bloodstains are found on a weapon it should be remembered that the latter may be destroyed if the whole of the weapon is painted with finger print powder. It is therefore convenient, first, to make sure of such clues of blood, hair and the like as are not on or near finger prints. The presence of latent finger prints on metal surfaces can be confirmed by breathing lightly on the object. Finger impressions can be observed easily under proper lighting.

Contamination in the form of oil, cement, paint or similar material may also be significant in elucidating the way in which a criminal acquired an object or tool used as a weapon, or it may give an indication of where it was kept previously. It may possibly have been taken from the criminal's place of work or been taken in an earlier burglary where the criminal was less careful and left finger prints or other clues which can be used as evidence against him. If a tool used as a weapon comes from a large factory it may have a works number stamped on it, making definite identification possible.

If the weapon is new a manufacturer's mark or name of a firm may lead to the place where it was bought.

If the weapon has been concealed either at the scene of the crime or in the vicinity, or taken away by the criminal, it is of the greatest importance to know the sort of weapon one is searching for. The only means of determining this is from a study of the injuries on the victim, in which the form of the weapon will have revealed itself in some way or other. In practice it is often difficult to draw the correct conclusions from the appearance of the wounds, since it is effected by the elasticity of the skin, by the underlying bones and muscles, the angle of application, etc. In such cases, however, the pathologist can give valuable assistance. A study of contact areas on bone may show significant characteristics by which a specific tool, such as a hatchet, may be identified as having made the injury.

Frequently, especially in cases of assault, there arises a question of whether an object, used as a weapon, shall be considered as dangerous to life or not.

Firearms

The firearms employed in cases of murder, attempted murder and suicide are usually pistols and revolvers, occasionally rifles and shotguns.

It is usual to distinguish between hand and shoulder weapons, depending on whether they require the use of one or two hands.

Firearms may also be classified according to their construction as single-shot weapons, weapons with rotating cylindrical magazines, repeater weapons, semi-automatic and automatic firearms.

Firearms may further be designed for muzzle-loading (muzzle-loaders) or breech-loading, and provided with smooth or rifled barrels. Smoothbore guns are usually intended for small shot or for both shot and bullets, while rifled ones are in most cases only intended for bullets.

Firearms may also have a visible hammer, built-in hammer (hammerless), or a striker or similar arrangement.

Revolvers usually have only one barrel (multiple barrelled construction is known) and they always have a rotating magazine holding 5 to 12 (usually 5 or 6) cartridges. The oldest types of revolver were arranged for muzzle loading, that is, the chambers were loaded from the front. Later, following the production of unit cartridges, they were designed for pin fire and finally for the present cartridges which are arranged for rim or central fire.

In a revolver the fired cartridge cases are not ejected automatically after each shot, but the empty cases must be removed before the weapon can be reloaded. With many forms of construction this is done with the aid of an extractor which is common to all the cartridges, while with others they must be extracted by hand one at a time.

At the present time, pistols usually have one barrel. Older types, intended for muzzle-loading, sometimes had two or more barrels. Television Western stories have brought back into popularity weapons used in pioneer days. Today, the Frontier model revolver and the Derringer are in production. Pistols may be constructed for loading with one cartridge placed directly in the chamber (single-shot weapons) or for loading with several cartridges in

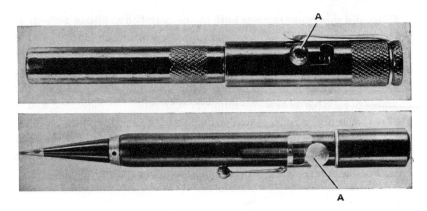

Fig. 105 'Fountain pen pistols' for rim fire cartridges. The top weapon has a relatively long rifled barrel and simulates a fountain pen. The lower version has no actual barrel and is intended for blank cartridges. A: the striker release.

a special magazine, the latter type usually being semi-automatic or automatic. The magazines hold a number of cartridges varying with different makes and calibers. With both of these types of pistol the gas pressure is used to eject, with the aid of the slide, the fired cartridge case and to bring a new cartridge up into the chamber from the magazine. With semi-automatic pistols each shot is fired individually, while with automatic ones the shots are fired in succession as long as the trigger is pressed. Most modern pistols are semi-automatic, apart from machine pistols (sub-machine guns), which are shoulder weapons. There are only a few types of automatic pistols. Most semi-automatic pistols are capable of malfunctioning and not firing fully automatic for two or more cycles. An inspection of the weapon will usually disclose the underlying cause of the malfunction.

Of the pistols constructed for loading with one shot only, most are made for rim fire cartridges.

Nearly all semi-automatic pistols are intended for central fire. There are only a few types of semi-automatic pistols for rim fire, and all are of .22 caliber (5.6 mm) and intended for the ordinary .22 Long Rifle cartridge with lead bullet. The commonest pistols of this type are the German Walther Mod.PP, Walther Olympia pistol and Walther duel pistol, together with the Erma (Parabellum-Luger), the American Colt, Ruger and High Standard, the Spanish Star, the Italian Beretta and the Swiss Hämmerli.

Rifles and shotguns are made both in one-barrelled as also in 2-, 3- or 4-barrelled forms, and may be arranged for muzzle or breech-loading, and in the latter case for cartridges for pin, rim or central fire. Rim fire cartridges are used only in guns of small caliber (.22 or 5.6 mm).

Rifles and shotguns may be constructed for loading with one shot in the chamber of each barrel or with a number of cartridges in a magazine, and in the latter case may be of repeater, semi-automatic or automatic type. With repeater weapons a movement of the hand is required to eject the fired cartridge case and to bring a new cartridge into the chamber from the magazine (bolt, lever, slide and pump or trombone action).

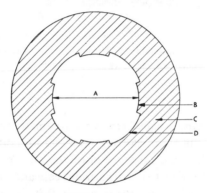

Fig. 106 The caliber of a rifled weapon is generally reckoned from the diameter of the bore, measured between two opposite lands. There are, however, exceptions to this rule. A: *Caliber*; B: land; C: *barrel*; D: groove.

The bore of weapons intended to fire bullets is now always spirally rifled so that the bullet is caused to rotate when fired. The direction of the twist is usually right-handed, but left-handed twist also occurs. The depressions in the bore are termed the grooves, and the raised parts are lands. The number and width of the lands varies for different calibers and makes; the depth is moreover often greater in a weapon intended exclusively for lead bullets than one for jacketed bullets. The number of lands is usually 4 or 6, but there are weapons with 5 or 7. The caliber of a rifled weapon is nearly always reckoned from the diameter of the bore measured between two opposite lands. (Fig. 106). There are, however, weapons whose caliber designation is based on the diameter of the bore measured between the bottom of two opposite grooves or on the diameter of the bullet in the cartridge intended for the weapon, but these represent only rare exceptions from the

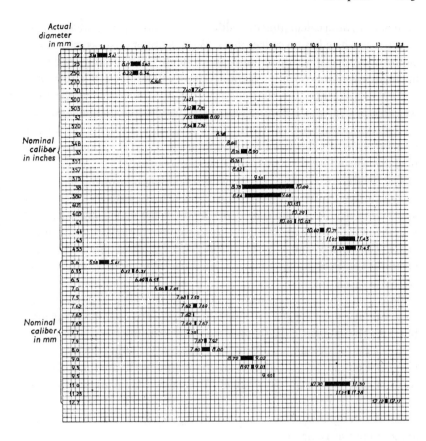

general rule. With weapons from Europe caliber are generally given in mm; those of American manufacture in hundredths of an inch and British fire-arms in thousandths of an inch.

A bullet is generally somewhat larger than the diameter of the bore measured between the lands, so that the latter can grip the metal of the bullet and cause it to rotate. (Expansion bullets and bullets intended for muzzle-loaders form an exception to this rule – they are of lead and have a diameter which is less than the bore). Jacketed bullets are therefore com-pressed during their passage through the barrel.

Although the caliber of a weapon is based on the diameter of the bore between lands, the caliber designation does not always correspond exactly with the actual diameter of the bore, and there is often some difficulty in determining the nominal caliber of a weapon which does not have a caliber designation, or in calculating the caliber of a weapon from a fired bullet or a cartridge which has no caliber mark. When a doubt exists as to the exact caliber of a projectile, submission of the evidence to a laboratory having an adequate reference collection of ammunition will usually result in the correct answer. Furthermore, the laboratory can determine whether the bullet was fired in a gun of the bore size for which the cartridge and bullet was intended. An attempt by the investigator to determine caliber or other accurate dimensions in the field may result in frustrating misinformation, particularly where severely mutilated bullets are involved.

The diagram on page 213 represents a combination of the statements of caliber designations of weapons with the actual diameters of the bores, and makes clear both the limits within which the actual diameters can vary in one caliber group, and the relation between the caliber designations expressed in inches and in mm. (*If it is desired to change fractional parts of an inch to mm, multiply by 25.4: to change mm to fractions of an inch divide by 25.4*).

With small caliber shotguns in which cartridges with lead bullets can also be fired, caliber are given in mm, hundredths or thousandths of an inch, but with shotguns of larger caliber the older British system is used; this being based on the number of spherical lead bullets, fitting the bore, which weigh one pound (British). If there are 12 such bullets to a pound, then the weapon has a caliber of 12 (12-gauge). This caliber designation is the same over the whole world.

Caliber designations for shotgun barrels, reckoned in inches and mm, are given in the Table 11.

TABLE II   Caliber designations for shotgun barrels

Caliber	in.	mm	Caliber	in.	mm
12-bore	.729	18.52	24-bore	.579	14.71
16-bore	.662	16.81	28-bore	.550	13.97
20-bore	.615	15.62	32-bore	.526	13.36

In measuring the bore of a shotgun barrel any choking must be allowed for. Choke boring means that the barrel is contracted at the muzzle end for a length of up to $2^1/_2$ in., in order to produce a denser distribution of the shot. With double-barrelled guns one barrel is often choked more than the other. Single barrel shotguns may have a device on the muzzle by which the choke may be varied. The setting of this device must be noted at the time the weapon is recovered, in order that accurate shot patterns can be produced for comparison with case patterns.

Handling of Weapons

In lifting weapons great care must be taken not to destroy clues.

When lifting a pistol or revolver the best way is to hold it with two fingers on the checkered part of the butt, or possibly by the ring on the butt. Shot guns may conveniently be held by the sling or sling buckles; otherwise around the checkered part of the neck of the butt; or if necessary the weapon can be lifted by a steady grip with the fingers on the trigger guard. It is undesirable to lift a weapon by placing a stick or similar object in the trigger guard, even with a light weapon such as a revolver or pistol, as the weapon may be cocked and a shot might be fired if the trigger happens to be touched. It should be taken as a general rule never to lift a weapon found at the scene of a crime before first making sure that no one is in the direction in which the muzzle is pointing, and of course one should not expose oneself to the risk of being hit when lifting the weapon, if it should happen to go off. The weapon may actually have got caught in some way so that even the slightest movement would cause a shot to be fired.

It is *absolutely wrong* to lift a weapon by putting a lead pencil, stick or the like in the barrel. This might destroy valuable clues in the barrel which might possibly have been of use in elucidating the case. In a contact shot i.e. when the muzzle is in contact with a body, which is common with suicide, it often happens that blood, grease, fragments of fabric and textile fibers are blown into the barrel of the gun due to the violence of gas pressure and the splash of tissue and blood in all directions in this type of shot. With a contact shot it has sometimes happened that such particles have been recovered in the magazine of an automatic pistol.

There may also be found in the bore a layer of dust, spider webs, or loose rust particles, showing that no shot has been fired from the weapon for some time. The absence of a powder deposit or the presence of grease in the bore may also indicate that the weapon has not been used, while an examination of the powder layer in the bore may show that the fired cartridge was loaded with black powder or with smokeless powder. To decide, from the appearance of the powder deposit, how long has elapsed since the last shot was fired from the weapon, is difficult. It can therefore be appreciated that if the bore of a weapon is to be examined for any such clues, the introduction of

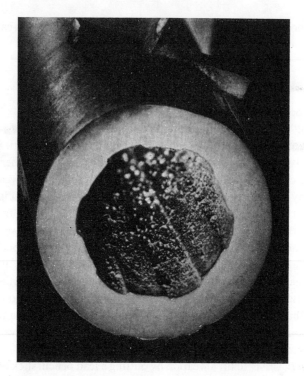

Fig. 107 Dust deposit in barrel of rifle. A most valuable clue.

any object into the bore will interfere with its examination or make it impossible. For the same reason cotton or the like must not be put in the muzzle during transport of the weapon or when it is sent to the expert. In order to protect any deposit in the bore, a twist of paper, rubber cap or muzzle protector can be placed over the muzzle. The layer of dust in the bore is always thickest near the muzzle and decreases in thickness progressively towards the breech, assuming that it has resulted from a long period of storage. The confirmation of such a distribution of the deposit nearest the muzzle is therefore of great importance. Under no circumstances should the investigating officer put the weapon into his own pocket for safekeeping. After only a brief contact with pocket dust, the gun will appear to have been unfired for some time.

Homicide. A man was found in his house, dead, with two shot wounds in his head. A little to the right of the body lay a revolver, which belonged to him. The revolver was not loaded and did not contain any empty cartridge cases. An investigation of the barrel showed that the latter was contaminated with dust to such an extent that it could hardly have accumulated during the two days which were supposed to have elapsed after the shooting. Further investigation revealed that the man had been shot with a revolver of the same caliber and type as his own, and that the murderer had placed the latter near the body to give the appearance of suicide.

After the weapon has been picked up, any loose objects or particles such as hair, fibers, dried blood, brain substance, etc., which might fall off in transport, are removed and kept. With a near shot against a hair-covered part of the body, sometimes strands of hair can be found, held fast between the slide and barrel of an automatic pistol. Any clues on the weapon in the form of fibers of wood, paint, cement, or the like, which might indicate that the weapon had fallen on the floor, should also be secured while at the scene of the crime.

When taking possession of a weapon, it should be subjected to a preliminary examination for finger prints. Finger print impressions in grease or blood can easily be seen. Latent finger prints on metal surfaces can, as mentioned above, be made evident by lightly breathing on the object. If both finger prints and bloodstains, fibers, etc., are found on the weapon, and all have to be preserved, it is convenient first to make sure of the marks which are not in the immediate neighborhood of the finger prints, as otherwise they could easily be destroyed by the finger print powder. Here a warning should be given: if the weapon is found outdoors or in an unheated room in cold weather, and there are finger print impressions in grease on it, then the weapon should not be brought into a warm room, since the grease would be softened or melted and the prints would be lost. If latent finger prints are to be developed by powder, care must be taken to keep the powder from entering the barrel. Likewise, when a revolver is processed by powder dusting, the front of the cylinder must be protected so that the mouth of each chamber can be examined for flares.

Everything which is found in the first examination of the weapon should be noted down accurately, and any objects or particles which are removed from it should be placed in a test tube or envelope labelled accurately with the exact place of finding. For the sake of identification any maker's or type markings should also be indicated, as also the caliber marking and serial number. The investigator's initials should be inscribed on some major part of the weapon, such as, the barrel or frame.

It is most important to note down whether the weapon is at safety or not, which can be seen from the position of the safety catch (on revolvers there is generally no visible safety device), and whether the weapon is cocked and loaded. With some automatic pistols the latter cannot be observed by a superficial glance, but where it is shown by, e.g., an indicating pin, it should be noted. On the most common types of weapon this condition can easily be confirmed from the position of the rear part of the bolt. It should also be noted whether the bolt (breechblock or slide) is closed, partly open or fully open. If a cartridge case is jammed in the ejection port, this should be noted, together with a statement of the exact position of the cartridge, whether the base or neck of the case is turned outwards, etc., and also whether the magazine is firm or loose (not pushed right home).

After the exterior of the weapon has been processed for finger prints, the gun may be unloaded and rendered safe before shipping to a laboratory. With an automatic pistol the magazine is loosened, after which the slide is moved to remove any cartridge in the chamber. In doing this it should be remembered that finger prints may be found in grease on the cartridge in the chamber and on the sides of the magazine, which should therefore be examined first before any further handling. The weapon should not be considered unloaded until an inspection is made by looking into the chamber through the port of the gun. A broken extractor, jammed cartridge or other factor may cause a cartridge to remain in the chamber. It is a poor practice to assume that a weapon is unloaded simply because a cartridge was not ejected. The cartridge is initialed and placed in an envelope or test tube with a label attached, and a label can also be tied on by a thread around the groove of the cartridge. Any cartridges in the magazine should not be 'stripped' if the weapon is to be sent to an expert for examination. Cartridges may carry finger prints and also marks from the guiding surfaces of the magazine, and it may be of significance to confirm them (e.g. whether the cartridges have been charged into the magazine several times). Further, the order of the cartridges in a magazine may be of importance in certain cases and should always be noted.

In the case of a revolver nothing should be done with the cartridges in the cylinder, if the weapon is to be examined further. The exact position of the cylinder at the moment when the weapon is found is significant from many points of view and should be noted, e.g. what is the position of the fired cartridge in relation to the hammer? The position of the cylinder can be marked if desired with a lead pencil or chalk mark, provided that this does not destroy other clues. The cylinder should not be 'rolled', since in that case irrelevant marks from the recoil plate or firing pin could then be formed on the base of the fired cases and the cartridges.

In the case of weapons of single-shot or repeating types, nothing should be done with the bolt unless the weapon is cocked, or with the empty case in the chamber. If however the spring to hammer is cocked there is reason to suspect that an unfired cartridge is in the chamber, and this should be removed to prevent any accident. The cartridge is taken out and labelled as described above. Semi or fully automatic weapons generally have a cartridge in the chamber unless the bolt is in the backward position, so that the slide should be moved while making sure that no fresh cartridge is introduced into the chamber. In order to prevent this a detachable magazine is freed; in the case of a fixed magazine the uppermost cartridges are held back with a piece of wood or some other object which will not injure the cartridges or deposit any fresh marks on them.

Fig. 108 Print of base marking of cartridge case in grease and dirt on breechblock of a .22 caliber rifle (reversed), with base marking on a cartridge of the type which was last fired from the weapon.

All precautions which are taken with a weapon must be put down accurately in the report. *Later, possibly, the investigating police officer may be required to describe the precautions taken, in connection with legal proceedings. What may appear to be of subordinate importance during the investigation of the crime may later be found to be especially significant.*

In connection with all firearms, when a weapon is to be sent to an expert for examination the only clues which need to be preserved are those which might be destroyed in transit, and the only measures taken are those which cannot be omitted without risk of accident, or which are essential in assisting the search for the criminal. Many traces on the weapon or significant facts in connection with the mechanism can be of such a character that special instruments or specially trained personnel are necessary to deal with them properly.

On the breech face or recoil plate there may perhaps be marks of colored lacquer from the sealing around the primer, and a chemical examination may be required to confirm whether this could have come from a particular fired cartridge. Even in the bore there may be found lacquer pigments from the sealing between the bullet and case, or metallic particles from the jacket of the bullet. In grease and dirt on the breech face there may also be an impression of the markings on the base of the cartridge case, and special arrangements will be required for photographing this impression.

As mentioned earlier, from the point of view of identification any marks indicating the maker, type and caliber should be recorded, together with the serial number. With many weapons, in particular with certain pistols and revolvers, such markings are often lacking. The butt plates are however usually marked with the maker's or seller's initials, which can be a good guide.

Many weapons also carry *proof marks.* In many countries all firearms are tested under government control before they are allowed to be sold, and they are given special marks which are stamped on the barrels or on other metal parts. Even imported weapons must be proved and stamped. Such proof marks can be a guide in determining the maker when other indications are lacking. The countries which have such official control institutions include Great Britain, France, Germany, Belgium, Italy, Spain, Austria, Hungary and Czechoslovakia. In the U.S.A. some makers put on their weapons stamps which show that they have been subjected to a proof firing; this is the case especially with weapons intended for export. There is, however, no national inspection in the U.S.A.

On weapons which were made in Germany and in a number of occupied countries during the last war there are also *code marks* for the different factories. There marks are composed of 1, 2, or 3 small letters. These letters must be included as a part of the serial number. Although the probability of a second weapon, bearing the same serial numbers, being deliberately or accidently substituted for the evidence weapon is remote, this possibility should be prevented by marking the weapon with the investigator's initials.

Cartridge cases

If no cartridge cases are found at the scene of a shooting, it may be suspected that a revolver, single-shot pistol, automatic pistol with cartridge case collector, rifle, or shotgun was used. Theoretically one might expect that a criminal would attempt to guard himself by picking up the cartridge cases thrown out by an autoloading weapon but in practice it is hardly ever done, since it would often waste time and the criminal would run more risk of being discovered, especially if the shooting was heard by persons in the vicinity.

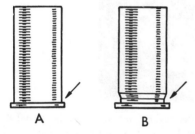

Fig. 109 The difference between a revolver cartridge case (A) and a cartridge case intended for an automatic pistol (B). The former has no extractor groove.

In taking possession of cartridge cases one should not forget the possibility that on them there may be found significant clues in the form of loose particles or finger prints. They may be picked up by means of a clean match stick, or the like, introduced into the case, and then placed in an envelope marked with the place of finding. The internal diameter of a cartridge case corresponds, at the neck with the diameter of the bullet. From the size, form and appearance of a cartridge case it is possible to obtain an indication of the type of weapon used.

Cartridge cases fired in a rifle can generally be distinguished without difficulty from pistol and revolver cartridge cases, with the exception of .22 caliber (5.6 mm) cartridges, which can also be fired from pistols and revolvers.

Revolver cartridge cases are almost always fully cylindrical with a rim but no extractor groove (a groove for the extractor running round the case with the rim). They may be made for pin fire (the base of the case being quite smooth with a pin near the base at right angles to the cylindrical surface), rim fire (smooth base) or central fire (with primer cap).

Many manufacturers make revolvers to take automatic pistol cartridges.

Fig. 110 Rear of the cylinder of a loaded revolver recovered in a homicidal shooting. From the sequence of shots and the location of the corresponding bullets, it could be shown that the suspect's statement of the events was not true.

Thus both Colt and Smith Wesson make revolvers of .45 caliber so that automatic pistol cartridges of .45 caliber can be used in them. Similarly, automatic pistol cartridges of 7.65 mm can be fired in .32 caliber revolvers and automatic pistol cartridges of 6.35 mm can be fired in .25 caliber revolvers. Automatic pistol cartridges (with the exception of .45 rimless cartridges, 9 mm Parabellum cartridges and bottle-neck cartridges) have a rim which, although not much larger than the cylindrical surface of the cartridge, is quite sufficient to hold the cartridge fast in the chamber of a revolver cylinder when the internal diameter of the latter corresponds with the diameter of the cartridge. In many revolvers which are provided with one common extractor for all the cartridges, this also functions quite satisfactorily when pistol cartridges are used.

When firing .45 rimless pistol cartridges in .45 caliber revolvers however, conditions are different. The rim of these cartridges does not project beyond the cylindrical surface, so that they cannot be held fast in the chamber of the cylinder of the revolver, unless specially constructed clips are used. These clips (two are required), which are provided with cut-out parts fitting the extractor grooves of the pistol cartridges, also give a good hold for the extractor which can then push all the cartridges out of the cylinder at once, after which reloading can be done quickly. If such clips are used, typical marks of scraping from the recoil plate of the revolver are produced on the base of the case owing to the smaller clearance when the cylinder rotates. A special type of pistol cartridge of .45 caliber with projecting rim, called 'auto-rim', also occurs, and these can be fired in a revolver without using special clips.

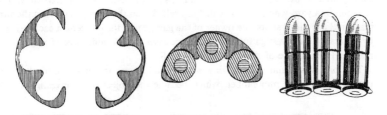

Fig. 111 Clips for use when firing pistol cartridges (.45 rimless) in .45 caliber revolver.

Pistol cartridges of 7.65 mm caliber should not, however, be used in revolvers of .320 caliber. In revolvers which are constructed so that automatic pistol cartridges can also be used in them the lands are lower than with revolvers intended only for cartridges with lead bullets.

Modern pistols of single-shot type are generally intended for rim fire cartridges of .22 caliber (5.6 mm), while automatic pistols are generally made for center fire cartridges, the latter being provided with both rim and extractor grooves in contrast with the former, which have only a rim. There is an exception however in the previously mentioned automatic pistols, Walther, Erma (Parabellum-Luger), Colt, Ruger, High Standard, Star, Beretta and Hämmerli, which are constructed for rim fire cartridges of .22 caliber. Pistol cartridges have a cylindrical or bottle-shaped case.

Revolver cartridges of .320 caliber can also be fired in certain automatic pistols of 7.65 mm caliber, and cases occur where such pistols have also repeated normally and even ejected revolver cartridge cases, but these ejected cases are often ruptured and sometimes jam the pistol.

Smaller caliber projectiles can be fired in larger bore weapons with serious effect. An example of this is the ability of a .38 Special revolver to fire a .32–20 cartridge. Desperate persons, in need of ammunition, will wrap cartridges in paper to accomodate a larger chamber, reduce the diameter by filing, even perform the dangerous act of driving a cartridge into a chamber by means of a hammer. Only an expert can determine with reasonable certainty the type of gun that might have been used in a shooting by an examination of the fired bullets or cartridges. An investigator must be careful not to pass up a weapon because it does not *seem* to correspond to the ammunition at hand.

Assault. Two drivers surprised a man who was about to take a car out of a garage which he had broken into. The man fled from the scene. The owner of the garage, who arrived shortly afterwards, followed the man and was later assisted by a policeman who trailed the man to a yard where he concealed himself. When the pursuers entered the yard the man fired five pistol shots, the owner of the garage and the policeman each being hit by two shots. In the investigation four cartridge cases were found, three of 7.65 mm caliber marked FN and one of .320 caliber marked RWS.

The man was found the next day, and he had an automatic pistol marked 'Ortgies patent' and of 7.65 mm caliber, which became the object of an investigation. In the

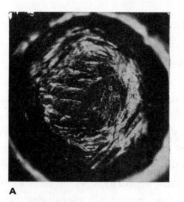 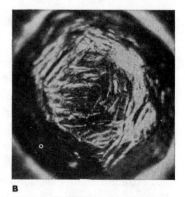

A   B

Fig. 112 Identification of a cartridge case of 9.3 mm caliber (A) with a cartridge case fired in a repeating rifle of 9.3 mm caliber (bolt action) owned by a suspect (B). The microscopic details in the marks of the firing pin on the primer agree completely in the two cartridge cases.

chamber of the pistol there was a fired revolver cartridge case of .320 caliber, which was only removed with difficulty. The magazine was charged with a number of pistol cartridges and a revolver cartridge of .320 caliber.

Before the shooting the pistol had been loaded with a mixture of pistol cartridges of 7.65 mm caliber and revolver cartridges of .320 caliber. The case of the first revolver cartridge fired was ejected and the weapon repeated, while the other revolver cartridge stuck in the breech.

On the base of the cartridge case there are generally both manufacturer's and caliber marks, and sometimes also the year of manufacture is given. Sometimes the maker's marks are in code, consisting of letters and figures or of letters or figures only. Swedish military rifle ammunition which is made in state or private ammunition factories bear a code mark for the different factories. A similar coding of wartime ammunition was in practice in the United States.

The material in the case and primer together with the size of the flash hole of the latter can also be a guide in determining the factory and year of manufacture.

Fired cartridge cases are especially valuable from the point of view of identification, since they show marks from the weapon which in most cases make it possible to decide with certainty whether they were fired from a particular weapon or not. It is therefore of special importance in a case of shooting in the open air that all possible efforts should be made to deter-

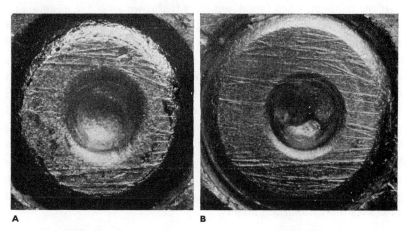

A   B

Fig. 113 Identification of two cartridge cases from marks of breech face on the primer. Scratches on the breech face are reproduced and form a characteristic pattern. (Repeating rifle) A: cartridge case from scene of crime; B: comparison cartridge case.

A   B

Fig. 114 A: mark of extractor on front of rim of a pistol cartridge case; B: identification
of cartridge case from scene of crime (1) and comparison cartridge case (2) from
the extractor mark.

mine the scene of the shooting with the aid of indications of different types,
so that any cartridge cases left behind can be sought for. The most valuable
marks on cartridge cases are those made by the firing pin on the primer
and by the breech face on the primer and base of the case, but the marks
produced by the extractor, ejector and the edge of the breech may also be
important. Flaws or damage in the chamber may also show on the metal
case and make identification of the weapon possible.

If the criminal, when found, has already thrown away the weapon at a
place where it cannot be recovered (e.g. in water) it is important to attempt
to find out whether he or some other person (e.g. the previous or legal owner)
ever fired a test shot, and if so where. It is possible that both the cartridge
case and bullet may be found there. With cartridge cases it is not of great
importance whether the test shot was fired a long time before or not. The
part of the weapon which leaves marks on the case may not have altered
even though there was a long interval of time between the test shot and the
crime. It is different in the case of bullets, since sometimes the bore of a
weapon may undergo such changes in a comparatively short time that comparison with a test shot fired previously is useless. The nature of the place
where the weapon has been kept and the number of shots which have been
fired with it are important factors.

Murder. A woman was found dead, shot in the neck from behind with a pistol bullet of
7.65 mm caliber.

After passing through the body of the woman the bullet had struck a wall and was
found, slightly damaged, on the floor, where there was also a pistol cartridge case of Eley

manufacture and of the same caliber. Suspicion was directed towards a man B, who had committed bigamy by marrying the woman. B had previously lived with a man R who owned an automatic pistol of 7.65 mm caliber. Earlier this pistol had been stolen from a bag which was kept in the men's lodging, and R suspected B of the theft. At the time the pistol had been loaded with 5 or 6 cartridges, mostly of Eley manufacture. R had previously fired a trial shot and had kept a fired case, which he used for rolling insulating tape on. This case was recovered and comparison with the cartridge case found at the scene of the crime showed that both had been fired from the same weapon.

On the basis of this investigation and some other evidence B was convicted of murder. The pistol used was never found (SIMPSON, 1948).

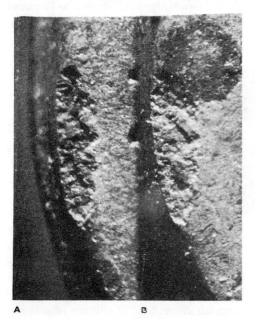

A   B

Fig. 115 Two cartridge cases identified as fired from the same weapon by means of the marks produced by the ejector on the base of the cartridge cases. A: case from scene of crime; B: comparison case.

From the marks made by the extractor, ejector and edge of the breech of an automatic pistol on a cartridge case it is also possible to determine the make of automatic pistol from which the case was fired. Automatic pistols of different types and makes are often constructed differently with respect to the position of the extractor and ejector and this in its turn affects the formation of the breech. The combination of these factors forms what is known as a system, that is, the characters mentioned give classification of the type of construction of the pistol. MEZGER, HEESS and HASSLACHER

(1931) have made a thorough study of the construction of different types of automatic pistols and have compiled a pistol atlas for the determination of the make.

If both cartridge case and bullet are available for the determination of the make, the possibilities are of course increased, since the number of land marks on the bullet, their width, and the angle of twist can also be characteristic of a type of weapon and in any case form a valuable contribution to the investigation.

Under no conditions should a cartridge case which is to be examined be tried in the chamber of a weapon, since any marks made by the weapon on the cases may be destroyed and other marks be formed.

A   B

Fig. 116 Identification in comparison microscope of two cartridge cases, by means of marks of scraping produced by the ejector. (Semi-automatic weapon). A: cartridge case from scene of crime; B: comparison case.

With cartridge cases from cartridges fired in military rifles the question sometimes arises as to whether the cartridge was loaded with ball or blank (i.e. with a bullet of wood or other soft material). It sometimes happens that accidents occur during military exercises owing to blank and ball ammunition being mixed. With a fired case from a blank cartridge the inner diameter of the neck of the case is appreciably less than that of one from a ball cartridge. The neck of a blank cartridge case differs from that of a ball case by being strongly 'upset', the edge of the neck of the case being bent inwards. Moreover the primer of a case from ball cartridge becomes more flattened against the breech face than that of a blank cartridge. Such differences between cases from ball and blank cartridges can also be observed with cases fired from other weapons (e.g. pistols).

It happens sometimes that at the scene of a crime where a firearm has been used, there is found a cartridge which has misfired and has been thrown out by movement of the slide or bolt, or which has jammed between the breechblock and the edge of the breech and has been removed by hand. Even such an unfired cartridge may carry valuable marks which can make possible an identification or determination of the make of the weapon used.

Homicide. A currency exchange operator was fatally shot in a hold-up, by a man carrying a 9 mm Luger automatic pistol. Several days later a suspect was apprehended. A search of his room failed to recover a suitable weapon. However, in the search, a small box containing nine unfired 9 mm Parabellum cartridges was uncovered. One of these cartridges had a prominent ejector mark on the head. This mark matched, in many details, the mark on the head of the cartridge case ejected at the shooting. This match served, in the absence of the weapon, to connect the suspect with the crime.

Bullets

Bullets that penetrate hard objects are often severely mutilated, sometimes to the degree that the weapons from which they were fired cannot be identified. Therefore, every effort must be made to preserve what little remains of the rifling impression when a bullet is lodged in a wall, a tree or a bone. In the latter case, the method of removal, if at all, will depend on whether the shooting victim is dead. If the victim is dead, the principles for bone, tree or wall are alike. *No projectile should be pried from its postion*. Instead the supporting material and the bullet should be cut out as one piece. Then the surrounding bone, plaster or wood can be broken away carefully, leaving the projectile in the best possible condition, considering all circumstances. If the investigator wishes, the bullet as imbedded in supporting material, can be sent to the laboratory. Bullets removed by probing will show ample evidence of the destructive effect of improper technique.

Prior to removal, some careful testing will indicate the direction of the bullet's track.

After removal, the bullet should be initialled on the base. No mark should be placed on the rifling impression nor on areas of ricochet. If in doubt as to the proper area to mark, the investigator should place the bullet in an envelope, a plastic vial or a small box, seal and mark the container.

Bullets may be of different sizes and shapes and made in different ways. Commonest types are either entirely of lead or semi or fully jacketed; but there are also bullets with a hole in the point (hollow point), with the point

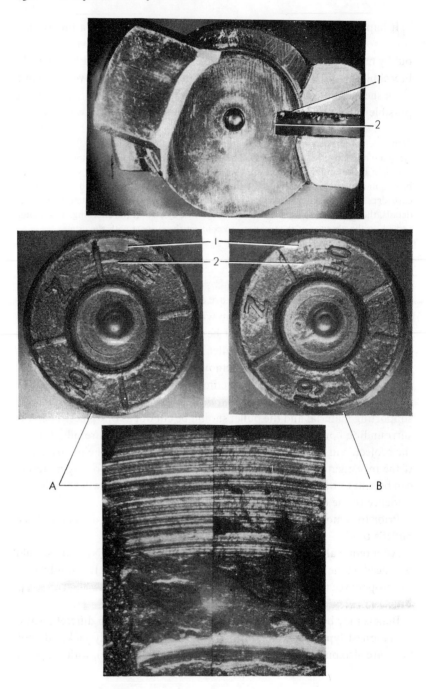

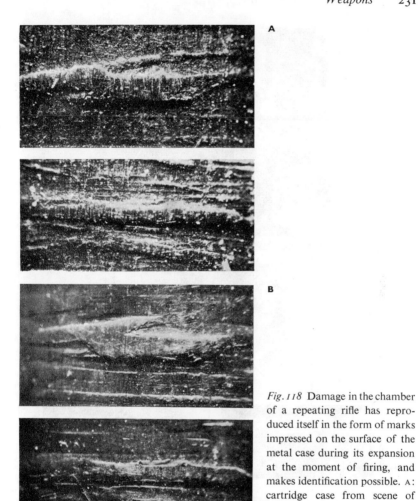

A

B

Fig. 118 Damage in the chamber of a repeating rifle has reproduced itself in the form of marks impressed on the surface of the metal case during its expansion at the moment of firing, and makes identification possible. A: cartridge case from scene of crime; B: comparison cartridge case.

←

Fig. 117 Two cartridge cases identified as having been fired in the same rifle by means of machining marks on the face of the bolt near the extractor recess (1 and 2). A: cartridge case from the crime scene; B: comparison case.

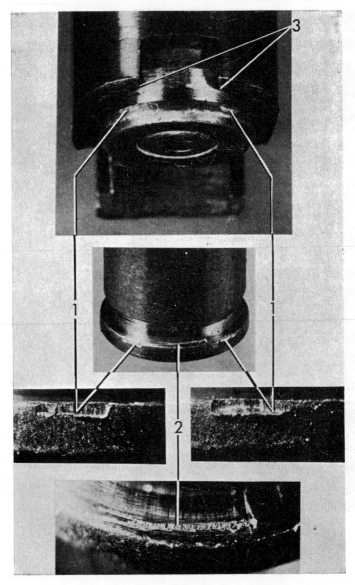

Fig. 119 The type and make of an automatic pistol could be determined from marks on the cartridge case. 1: marks from the breech end of the barrel around the extractor recess (3); 2: mark of the extractor. (Beretta, 7.65 mm).

covered with softer metal, lead bullets with a copper cone pressed into the point, etc.

With fully jacketed (solid nose) bullets the jacket encloses entirely the point of the bullet but is open at the rear end of the bullet, exposing the lead core. With a semi-jacketed (soft nose) bullet on the other hand the jacket encloses the whole of the rear end of the bullet while the core is free at the point to a larger or smaller extent. The semi-jacketed bullet breaks up

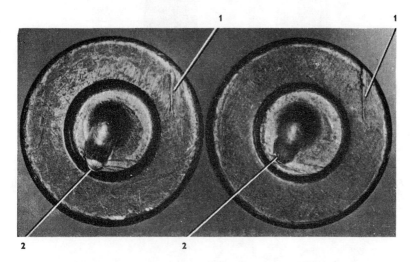

Fig. 120 Determination of the make of pistol. Cartridge case fired in the Russian Tokarev pistol of 7.62 mm caliber. Marks of scraping of the firing pin (1) and the form and position of the ejector mark (2) are typical of this weapon.

when it meets a bone or other hard part of the body, but if it passes merely through soft parts it may remain relatively undamaged. If it strikes against the branch of a tree in its flight it may actually be split or deformed before reaching its objective. On the other hand a fully jacketed bullet often remains undamaged or only slightly deformed on striking, for example, a body. Less scrupulous marksmen sometimes file the point of a fully jacketed bullet in order to produce the same effect as that of a semi-jacketed one. This result is obtained if the bullet leaves the barrel whole, but on account of the jacket being open at both ends there is a risk of the lead core only being driven out and the jacket remaining behind in the barrel. If this is not noticed, then when the next shot is fired the result will be that the weapon bursts or a bulge is produced in the barrel.

Lead bullets may be of different degrees of hardness. Bullets of soft lead are often greatly deformed and sometimes break up when they strike a body, while those of hard lead may retain their regular shape to the same extent as a fully jacketed bullet.

Fig. 121 Automatic pistol cartridges (9 mm Luger) which have been damaged by mal-functioning; The cases were jammed in the ejection port.

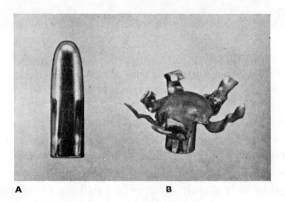

A   B

Fig. 122 A fully jacketed bullet is rarely deformed to any extent on striking, e.g., a body (A), but a semi-jacketed one breaks up (B).

Ammunition intended for automatic pistols usually has fully jacketed bullets, while revolver ammunition usually has lead bullets. There are however also automatic pistol cartridges with lead or semi-jacketed bullets and revolver cartridges with fully jacketed bullets. An intermediate position

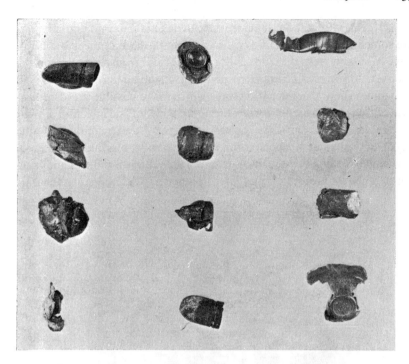

Fig. 123 Examples of severely mutilated projectiles from which the weapons could be
positively identified.

is taken by the previously mentioned cartridges of .22 caliber with lead bullets, which can be fired in certain automatic pistols, in single-shot pistols,
in revolvers and in rifles. Also, as mentioned previously, revolver cartridges
of .320 caliber, which are provided with lead bullets, can be fired in
pistols of 7.65 mm caliber.

Thus if a lead bullet is found at the scene of a crime or in a body it is not
possible to conclude immediately that it was fired from a revolver or rifle.
Some guidance can however be obtained in such a case from the depth of
any land impressions visible on the bullet. A weapon which is intended
exclusively for lead bullets has in most cases somewhat higher lands than a
weapon which is intended exclusively for jacketed bullets. Lead bullets
fired in a weapon intended for such ammunition generally show comparatively deep land marks.

The material of the jacket of a jacketed bullet may give an indication of
the maker of the cartridge, and the composition of certain lead bullets can

also give this information. In American cartridges, for example, lead bullets are sometimes copperplated. On a fired bullet the bore of the weapon will have left marks from the lands and sometimes also from the bottom of the grooves. A microscopic examination of these land and groove marks will sometimes show characteristic details which make possible an identification of the weapon used. Further, the number, width and direction of twist of the lands and grooves makes possible a determination of the make or makes of weapons from which the bullet may have been fired. The angle or rate of twist can be determined, but this is difficult and inaccurate when the projectile is mutilated. It is easier to determine class charac-

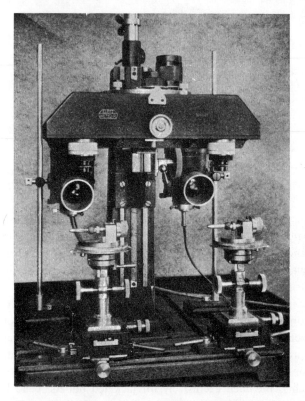

Fig. 124 Comparison microscope for examining fired bullets and cartridge cases, also tool marks, etc. The microscope is constructed so that it shows a double image, on one side the object under examination and on the other comparison material, whereby direct comparison of the microscopic marks is made possible. In the picture the microscope stages are provided with special holders for bullets.

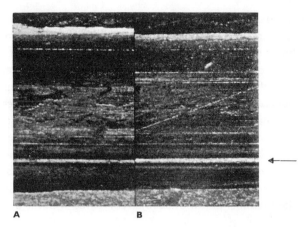

A   B

Fig. 125 Determination in the comparison microscope of identity between two jacketed rifle bullets of 9.3 mm caliber, from the microscopic marks in the engravings of the lands. A: bullet from scene of crime; B: comparison from weapon of suspect. Note the well-defined score in the mark of the land (see arrow), caused by one serious injury to the actual land in the bore of the weapon.

teristics on bullets fired from automatic pistols than on bullets fired from revolvers.

The number and width of the land marks together with the direction and angle of the twist vary for different manufacturers and types of weapons. Under no conditions should a bullet be tested in the bore of a weapon

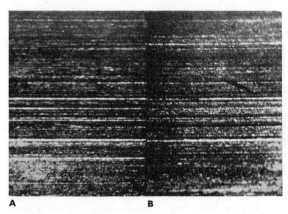

A   B

Fig. 126 Identification in comparison microscope of jacketed rifle bullets from a large number of microscopic details in the marks of the lands. A: bullet from scene of crime; B: comparison bullet from weapon of suspect.

by pushing it into the muzzle, if the bullet and weapon are to be subjected to further investigation with the object of identification. The microscopic marks on the bullet might be completely destroyed in this way. If it is necessary to *search for a weapon* in connection with a bullet which has been found, the police officer can obtain a useful guide from a study of the land marks on the bullet. The number of marks, their width and the direction of the twist can be compared with a suspected weapon. If it is such a long time after the actual shooting that any deposit of dust or powder in the barrel would no longer be significant, or if the barrel has evidently been cleaned or oiled, then a suitable piece of plasticine, which has been moulded to a point, is introduced into the muzzle of the weapon to obtain an impression of the lands so that their number and width can be compared with the marks on

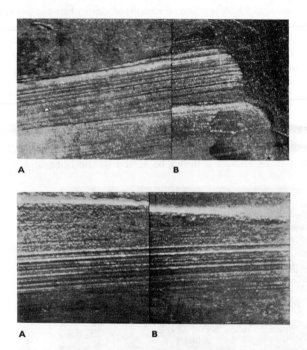

A   B

A   B

Fig. 127 Identification in comparison microscope of jacketed rifle bullets, from the 'primary' land marks which are produced by the lands during the first stage of the passage of the bullet through the barrel and before it commences to rotate. They are therefore parallel with the long axis of the bullet and at the side of the actual land marks A: bullet from scene of crime; B: comparison bullet from weapon of suspect.

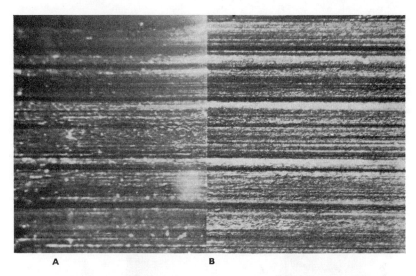

Fig. 128 Microscopic comparison between two jacketed rifle bullets. The striations are in the groove impressions (between the land impressions). A: bullet from the scene; B: bullet fired from the suspect's rifle.

the bullet. Otherwise this information must be obtained from inspection of the muzzle of the weapon, possibly with the aid of a flashlight.

As a rule, the number of 'suspect' guns in any investigation is not large. Therefore, it is better to let the laboratory sort these weapons by firing test shots. A number of factors effect the width of land impressions so that an

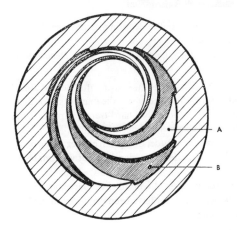

Fig. 129 The appearance of the barrel of a weapon with right-hand twist. A: land; B: groove.

exact comparison between a cast of the barrel and the bullet cannot be made. Anything within a reasonable range of tolerance should be submitted for laboratory tests.

If there is reason to suspect that a bullet which has been found has *rico-chetted*, and it is important to confirm this, it must be remembered that small grains of sand or other foreign matter may have stuck in flaws in the bullet, which should therefore be treated with care so that such particles do not fall off. Damage resulting from a ricochet can often be identified micro-scopically.

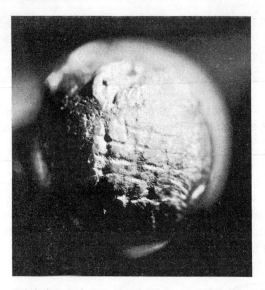

Fig. 130 Fabric impression on the nose of a lead bullet denoting its passage through fabric supported by the victim's chest.

(*Metropolitan Dade County Public Safety Department*)

Accident. A man was shot dead by a sentry who stated at the hearing that he had aimed to one side of the man. A couple of yards from the place where the man was shot there had been noticed a score in the ground, which was actually a hard-trampled path. It was assumed that the score represented the point where the bullet had struck.

The autopsy showed that there was a Mauser rifle bullet of 6.5 mm caliber in the body, and that the fatal injury could well have been caused by a ricochet, but was unable to prove anything more definite.

Further investigation of the bullet showed damage at a number of places both in the point and on the surface of the jacket, which could not have been produced in the bore of the weapon or by passing through a human body.

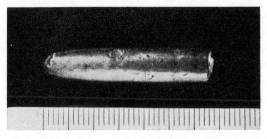

A

Fig. 131 Ricochetted bullet with a grain of silica (A), about 0.5 × 0.3 mm in size, stuck
in the point.

In the point of the bullet there was also observed a semi-transparent particle of about
0.5 × 0.3 mm, stuck in the metal. This was removed and examined microscopically, and
found to be a grain of silica.

Thus the investigation of the bullet showed that it had ricochetted against a hard
surface covered with stone, gravel, sand, or the like, and that the statement of the sentry
was correct.

If a *muzzle-loading weapon* has been used it is possible that the bullet may
show marks from the ramrod used, so that these should be looked for.
Home-made bullets can possibly be identified with the mold used.

In the case of muzzle-loaders it is also necessary to search at the scene of
the crime for any paper wads or the like which might have been used in
loading the gun. These often remain uninjured, and the paper can perhaps
be identified as torn from a newspaper or from a piece of paper in the possession of a suspect.

The *rifled slugs and single balls* of lead sometimes used in shotguns do not
give any opportunity for identification of the weapon used: they can only
give information as to the caliber. Home-made balls can possibly be identified with the molds in which were made. Rifled slugs and single balls
cannot be fired in shotguns which have any appreciable amount of choke.

Small shot

At close range the charge of shot, which has not yet dispersed, makes a large
wound in a body, but at longer range the shot spreads out, more or less
on the degree of choking of the gun. The amount of spread gives an opportunity of estimating the distance of the shot. If scaled photographs of the
wound or shot pattern are available, comparison shots can be fired using
the suspect weapon and ammunition of the same make and vintage. These

are usually fired at heavy poster board or blotting paper. Without scaled photographs or comparison tests, only very broad estimates are possible, since the patterns produced by various combinations of gun and ammunition will vary over a considerable range.

Table 13 gives an example of the influence of the degree of choke on shot patterns. These figures will not apply to all shotguns and all ammunition.

TABLE III   Diameter in inches of the spread at various ranges of a shotgun charge

	Range in yards						
Boring of gun	10	15	20	25	30	35	40
True cylinder	19	26	32	38	44	51	57
Improved cylinder	15	20	26	32	38	44	51
Half choke	12	16	20	26	32	38	46
Full choke	9	12	16	21	26	32	40

The depth of penetration of shot in, for example, wood gives an indication of the range.

As mentioned above, at a distance of 5 to 8 yards from the place of firing in the approximate direction of fire one can sometimes find wads, and, in the case of factory loaded cartridges, also the over-shot card wads placed in front of the shot, which in most cases carry a manufacturer's mark and the size of shot. The size of shot is sometimes given by a number, and sometimes shown by letters. There is no internationally uniform method of designation of shot: the procedure varies in different countries.

By measuring the diameter of any shot found it is thus possible to find the size of shot which would be marked on the cartridge. In this connection it should be noted that there may be certain minor variations in size of shot in one and the same cartridge. It is therefore important to collect as many pellets as possible, so that the determination is more reliable. Often the shot is deformed to such an extent that it is impossible to measure its diameter with the desired accuracy. In this case it is convenient to weigh as large a number of shot as possible and to calculate the mean weight, and then to weigh the same number of shot from cartridges with the different sizes of shot which may be supposed to come into question and to calculate their mean weight for comparison.

In different countries shot is made with different degrees of hardness, this

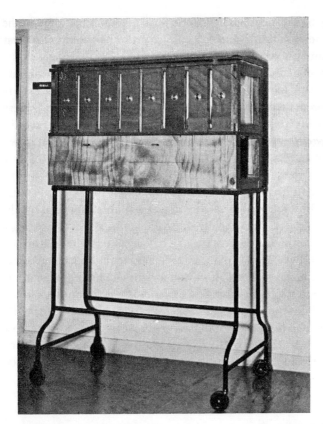

Fig. 132 Arrangement for test firing of revolvers and pistols. The bullet is braked by the
wadding with which the sections are filled. The wadding is held in position by
thin cardboard placed on each side.

being regulated by the antimony content. By a determination of the latter
there is the possibility of distinguishing between shot made in different
countries. The difference in antimony content, however, is often so small
that it is not possible to distinguish shot from different makers.

If a *weapon is sent to an expert* to determine whether a bullet or a cartridge case has been fired from it, a sufficient number of cartridges (5,6 or
more) of the same type as that used in the actual incident should be sent with
it. This is particularly necessary if powder or shot patterns are to be fired.
All ammunition in the weapon and any partial boxes of unfired ammunition associated with victim or suspect should be submitted with the weapon.

There may be sufficient differences between ammunition found in the gun and other ammunition available to the expert so that comparison tests are difficult, doubtful or impossible.

If a number of tests must be fired for transmission to various laboratories for comparison, inquiries should be made as to the nature and make of test ammunition desired in each investigation. For best results, these test specimens should be obtained by a laboratory and not by the field investigator. *Test firings* of a weapon must be done in such a way that the bullet can be recovered undamaged. For all jacketed bullets and most types of lead bullets cotton waste is used to stop the bullet. As a consequence of its rotation the bullet twists itself up in the waste which finally forms a ball around the bullet, and the velocity progressively decreases until the bullet is finally held in the cotton waste. Occasionally, long staple surgical cotton is placed in front of the cotton waste. This forms a ball around the bullet, further protecting the surface. Because of the mild damage to the bullet's surface due to the abrasive action of the cotton, water is becoming more common as a collecting medium. Five to six feet of water is ample for the collection of projectiles fired from hand guns. Generally, it is undesirable for the police officer himself to carry out test shots with the weapon since the microscopic imperfections in the bore of the weapon may be destroyed in the process. It is particularly important that the expert have an opportunity to examine the weapon before any tests are fired.

EXPLOSIVES

Explosives are a useful tool by which man has accomplished remarkable engineering feats. However, like many other things, explosives are used for criminal ends as well. Suicides, murder, intimidation, burglary and sabotage as well as industrial accidents will require the attention of investigators. Because of the inherent danger and the occassional loss of life when handled by inexperienced policemen, bombs and explosives are usually treated as specialties within a department, often associated with the investigation of arson.

In broad terms, an explosive is a material capable of rapid conversion from solid or liquid form to gaseous form with a resultant heat and pressure. Many chemicals, alone, or in mixtures, possess necessary properties for an explosion. Except for compounds classified as explosives, the rest

Fig. 133 Radiation pattern from the site of a high explosion. Note pulverized concrete. (*Metropolitan Dade County Public Safety Department*)

will come to the investigator's attention as the result of some accident. Usually, in such a case, consultation with chemists will provide a satisfactory explanation for the explosion. The reaction rates of all explosives are not alike. This permits a division into *high* and *low* explosives. High explosives have detonation rates of 15,000 feet per second, whereas low explosives have a detonation rate of the order of 3,000 feet per second. For example, low explosives might include black powder, smokeless powder, high pressure boilers, dust and gaseous mixtures. Black powder has a low speed of burning, and on exploding it forms poisonous gases and a large amount of greyish-white smoke which contains some unburnt carbon and causes a heavy bluish-grey to greyish-black deposit. Black powder is exploded by a jet of flame from ordinary safety fuse, by a bare flame or by sparks. High explosives may be divided into *plastic*, *powder* and *mass* explosives and include those described below.

The chief *plastic explosives* are the different types of dynamite, which are the most commonly used of all explosives.

Blasting gelatine (Nitroglycerine gelatine, Torpedo Explosive No. 1, Gummidynamit, Sprenggelatine) is most powerful in the fresh state, its power being reduced after long storage. It contains only water-insoluble substances and is therefore used especially for underwater explosions, for charging swampy bore holes and, on account of its power, for breaking up hard rocks. Blasting gelatine is amber yellow in color when fresh and has a leathery, gelatine-like, consistency. If the fresh material is held against the light a large number of extremely small air bubbles can be seen, looking like sparkling crystals. These disappear after a long period of storage and the color becomes a mahogany brown. In the fresh state it is not sticky but readily separates from paper. On the other hand old blasting gelatine is sticky and sticks to the paper. Blasting gelatine itself *does not give any smoke* on detonating. The 'smoke' which can often be seen when blasting with blasting gelatine comes from the site of the explosion and is composed of

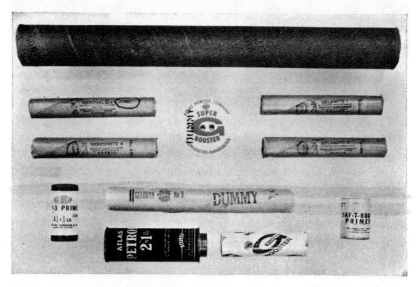

Fig. 134 Several forms of commercial explosives.

sand, dust, powdered stone, etc. Blasting gelatine has a *slight aromatic odor* which is very difficult to detect.

Gelatine dynamite is less powerful than fresh blasting gelatine but is used for most kinds of blasting with good results. Like blasting gelatine, modern gelatine dynamite is very insensitive to cold. In color it is flesh pink, and on detonation it gives a grey smoke with a tendency to yellow. Most of the 'smoke' which can be seen after an explosion consists of sand, dust, powdered stone, etc.

Various types of gelatine dynamite are made, with different contents of nitroglycerine (Straight Dynamite, Low-Freezing Dynamite, Gelignite, Ajax Powder, Polar Ajax, Polar Saxonite, Polar Samsonite, Grisoutine, Forcites etc.).

All gelatine dynamite has a characteristic bitter almond odor which can be identified without difficulty and can even be recognised among the fragments at the center of the explosion.

All dynamite has a high speed of detonation. For initiation a detonator No. 4 can be used but generally No. 8 is employed since the full explosive power is only obtained with a powerful detonator. Dynamite *does not give any poisonous gases on complete combustion*. All dynamite, and in particular blasting gelatine, is toxic to the human organism, especially by contact, and also by inhalation. On direct contact the toxic constituents pass through the skin of the hands, so that rubber gloves should be worn if it is necessary to handle the material for any length of time. The poisonous action is characterized by headache, vomiting and distorted vision. If, after handling, the hands are contaminated with dynamite, care should be taken that they are not allowed to touch the eyes, nose, mouth or sexual parts, since the mucous membrane is especially sensitive to the material.

Other plastic or semi-plastic explosives include Borenit, Territ, Permonit, Coronite, Percoronite, Imatrex, Rock-A-Rock, etc. These are to be considered as substitutes for dynamite and are used when a less powerful disruptive action is required.

They are generally very slow and not sensitive to initiation, and an unconfined charge cannot be made to detonate completely even with the most powerful detonator. Only when strongly confined, as in a bore hole, can they be made to detonate completely.

For military use there are also *special plastic explosives*, which are characterized by ease of molding, high speed of detonation and great insensitivity to shot, shock, moisture and frost. They are not poisonous on contact.

One type of plastic explosive is made of *hexogen* (RDX, T4, Cyclonite, Onit) *and vaseline*. This has a yellow-brown color and is quite stiff at − 20 °C. On detonation hexogen develops a dense black smoke with a suffocating odor and causes a lot of blackening. The odor of ammonia can be observed at the site of an explosion after exposure to rain.

Another type of plastic explosive is made of *PETN and mineral oils*. This has a dark canary yellow color, smells like used lubricating oil, and only stiffens at − 30° C, when it can be softened by kneading. This is considerably more powerful than gelatine dynamite. On detonation it gives a black smoke but leaves no smell at the site of the explosion.

These plastic explosives can be initiated by a detonator No. 8, and also with ordinary detonating fuse, which should preferably be tied in a knot which is placed in the middle of the explosive.

Among *explosives in powder* a very large number may be mentioned, including Trojan Explosive, Trojan Coal Powder, Antracite, Apcol, Apache Coal Powder, Austin Red Diamond, Big Coal D, Big Red, Bitumite, Black Diamond, Columbia, Cheddite, Carlsonit, Donarit, Nitrolit, etc. These are characterized by relatively high speeds of detonation which are fairly constant whether the explosive is confined or not. They are however very sensitive to water and damp. For initiation a detonator No. 6 can be used, but generally No. 8 is employed.

Among *mass explosives* are included TNT (trotyl, triton, trilite, trinol, tritolo) and PETN (pentyl, pentrit) in the form of cast and pressed, or only pressed, charges. PETN as powder goes into detonating fuse. TNT and PETN are both used very largely for military purposes. They are both very powerful explosives with high speeds of detonation.

TNT is yellow in color and on detonation gives a black smoke with a slight suffocating odor. When pressed it is initiated with detonator No. 8, but cast TNT cannot be initiated except by a primer of pressed TNT or plastic explosive in which is placed a detonator or detonating fuse.

PETN is white in the pure state and on detonation gives a greyish-black smoke with a slight 'gunpowder' smell. It is very sensitive to shock and moisture and can be initiated with a detonator No. 4 or detonating fuse. In the pressed form PETN is usually *phlegmatised*, that is, it is made less sensitive than pure PETN by the addition of some substance such as paraffin. PETN, phlegmatised in this way, has a rose color, can be broken, cut or bored, and is insensitive to shot. PETN can be initiated with detonator No. 8, detonating fuse or plastic explosive.

Gunpowder and other commercial explosives are supplied packed in paper: gunpowder in tubes or boxes often of multi-colored paper; and explosives in tubes, of different sizes, of paraffined paper with a characteristic form and color varying for the different explosives. The tubes of explosives are packed in cartons of paraffined cardboard with a wrapping of paraffined paper. On the tubes, as also on the wrapping, there is generally the name and year of manufacture of the explosive and in many cases the name of the maker is also given. This is not always the case with military explosives, but it is the rule with explosives for civil use. If a larger or smaller portion of a packing of gunpowder or explosive is found there is therefore a good possibility of identifying the nature of the explosive or powder used.

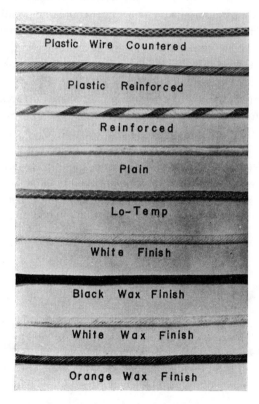

Plastic   Wire   Countered

Plastic   Reinforced

Reinforced

Plain

Lo–Temp

White   Finish

Black   Wax   Finish

White   Wax   Finish

Orange   Wax   Finish

Fig. 135 The top five specimens are examples of detonating cord, the lower four are examples of safety fuse. (All are manufactured by the Ensign-Bickford Company).

Initiating medium

The task of the initiating medium is to cause the explosive to detonate at a certain time. As already mentioned, black powder can be exploded by the jet of flame from a safety fuse. On the other hand other explosives can only be detonated by a much more powerful initiating stimulus which is produced by a detonator or detonating fuse.

Safety fuse

Safety fuse is composed of a train of black powder spun around with jute or cotton yarn. Generally the wrapping is composed of three layers (outer, middle and inner threads), but safety fuse with a smaller or larger number of layers is also found. The number of threads in the layers varies with different makers. In recent years some manufacturers have commenced to use tape in place of jute or cotton yarn, so that now safety fuse with one or more layers of tape is found in certain countries.

Next to the core there are generally one or more identification threads of a color which varies for different products. These threads are burnt away in the burning of the fuse.

The color of safety fuse is usually black or white, although other colors are found. The white fuse is intended to be used mostly in mines, tunnels and similar dark places.

Safety fuse is impregnated to protect it against moisture and mechanical

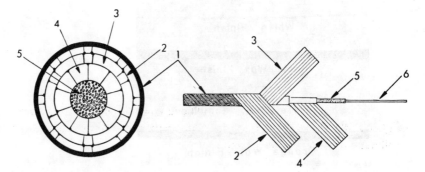

Fig. 136 Diagrammatic illustration of safety fuse with three layers of threads. 1: outer insulation; 2: outer threads; 3: middle threads; 4: inner threads; 5: black powder; 6: identification threads.

action, tar or gutta-percha being generally used as insulating material. With the same object, certain types of safety fuse are covered with an outer layer of rubber or plastic.

Safety fuse should normally burn with a certain definite speed, but it may burn quicker or slower as the result of damage or faults resulting from the storage or handling of the fuse. After a period of storage the speed is always reduced somewhat. More rarely it happens that there is a fault in the manufacture. Many shotfirers and blasters still hold the erroneous view that in the manufacture of safety fuse there may be a deficiency of powder over a longer or shorter stretch, and that the flame in the train of powder can 'jump over' this part and shorten the time of burning. If the supply of powder ceases during the spinning, the inner threads become twisted up to a compact braid and the fuse is considerably narrower at this point. This results in the fuse definitely going out. If the fuse is pinched by a stone being placed on it or standing on it, or is exposed to corresponding pressure in any other way, then there is a 'puff' and a rush at the pinched part, shortening the time of burning considerably. For every such pinching the fuse 'rushes' about 4 inches, but then burns normally. If the fuse is pinched at several places this is repeated and a dangerous reduction of the burning time will result.

Detonating fuse (detonating cord)

At one time there was a type of detonating fuse on sale which was imported from France and was made of a lead tube of about 7 mm diameter, filled with fine-grained TNT or the like, which detonated at a speed of about 18,000 feet per second. Such detonating fuse can still be found but is mostly used only for measuring the velocity of detonation.

Nowadays there is only one type of detonating fuse, which has found a comprehensive sphere of application for both military and civil use. This fuse has a train of PETN covered with cotton braid and on the outside is an isolating layer of varying composition. The fuse, which detonates at a speed of 15,000–18,000 feet per second, is very insensitive to shock and blows and to all handling with ordinary hand tools. It is moreover proof against shot from service rifles unless it is right against, for example, an iron girder.

Detonating fuse, with a No. 8 detonator, is often used instead of electrical detonation to cause a large number of charges to detonate simultaneously. The fuse leaves a mark on the underlayer on detonation, so that it is easy to see where it has been. On wood it produces a deep groove, and even on stone a distinct mark is left.

Detonators

Detonators are composed of copper or aluminum cases filled with lead azide as initiating charge and TNT or PETN as detonating charge.

There are two types of detonators, for ignition with safety fuse and for electrical detonation.

When fitting a detonator to a fuse, special detonator pliers are generally used for crimping the detonator on the fuse. The different types of pliers all leave characteristic marks on the detonator. In safebreaking, sabotage and the like, pliers of many different types are used, and these can be identified easily from the marks on the detonator. Ordinary cutting pliers make impressions which approach one another or meet on one side: nippers give impressions which lie at the same distance from one another on both sides. The marks of both of these are generally at an angle with reference to the edge of the detonator. Sometimes the back of a sheath knife is used to nip up the detonator, or the neck of the detonator is hammered on the fuse with the back of a sheath knife or with a stone. Moreover, old shotfirers sometimes fix the detonator by biting with their teeth.

In mines and other undertakings where detonators are used to a great extent special apparatus is used, and this may be of different forms. Some produce longitudinal grooves (rectangular and sharply defined) in the neck of the detonator, while others make 'notched' depressions (grooves) around it.

In most cases the detonator is completely destroyed in the explosion, but at times it may happen that at or in the neighborhood of the explosion there is found the burnt fuse on which a portion of the detonator still remains. The marks formed on the detonator when it was pinched onto the fuse can then be a guide in tracking the criminal by indicating the type of pliers used or showing that the detonator was bitten or hammered up. *Detonators for electrical ignition* are divided into *instantaneous detonators* which explode at the moment when the current passes, and *interval detonators* and *time detonators* which explode after a shorter or longer period following the passing of the current.

Instantaneous detonators, like other electrical detonators, are provided with two insulated wires, the 'pole leads', of a length which varies for differ-

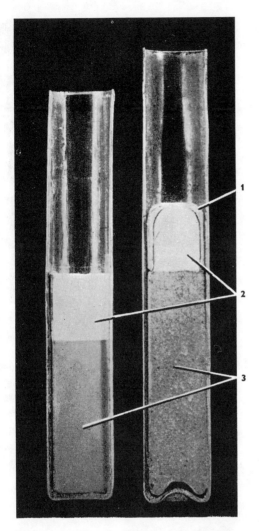

Fig. 137 Detonators with and without covering hood, in cross section.
1: covering hood; 2; initiating charge; 3: detonating charge.

ent types. Inside the detonator the wires are connected with a thin glowing wire of chrome nickel or tungsten, which in its turn is enclosed in a 'detonating pill' (which will explode easily) above the exploding charge of the detonator. With *interval* and *time detonators* the detonation is delayed by a

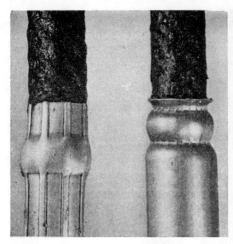

Fig. 138 Two examples of detonators crimped by machinery.

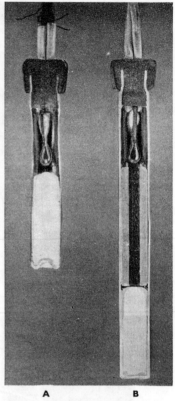

A   B

Fig. 140 Electrical detonators in cross section. A: instantaneous detonator; B: time detonator.

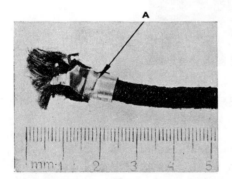

Fig. 139 The detonating end of a piece of safety fuse with detonator fragments attached. Marks from the crimping tool are visible on the fragment (A).

slow train of powder or fuse between the glowing wire and the charge. As mentioned, detonators for electrical ignition are always provided with two pole leads fixed in the detonator in a way which varies for different types. In most cases the pole leads and also their fixing arrangement remain at or in the vicinity of the explosion.

Investigation of explosions

The first step is a general assessment of the nature of the damage. If the premises appears to have been demolished by a big push from within, moving the walls outward, permitting the roof and floors to fall into the interior, a low explosion is suggested. More than likely, the source is a gas leak. Witnesses will report having smelled the odor of commercial gas and report the

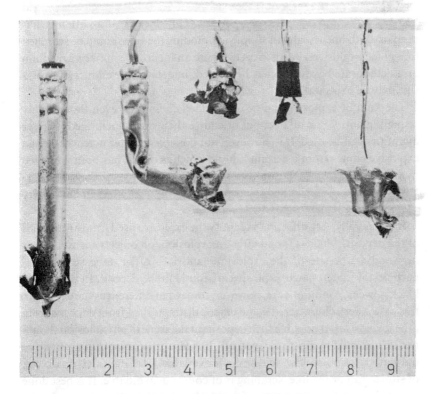

Fig. 141 Remnants of electric detonators found at safe burglary scenes.

sound as a low 'boom' in contrast to a sharp 'crack'. Furthermore, there will be an absence of definite localized point of origin of the force.

On the other hand, if localized shattering is seen, with flying debris radiating from this point, a high explosive is indicated. Although, this classification provides a starting point for the investigation, it would be erroneous to state that low explosions are accidental and non-criminal, whereas high explosions are criminal. Either case must be thoroughly investigated as to the nature of the explosive, manner of initiation and, if criminal, motive behind the act.

When investigating the scene of an explosion where the explosive used is unknown, one should always attempt to determine whether there is any residual smell from the explosion by smelling among the debris at the center of the explosion; the smell is often more pronounced after digging. At the site of explosions where one might expect to find undetonated residues of explosive, a special search should be made. If an attempt has been made to open a safe, the floor surrounding the safe should be searched for spilled explosives. Also, in cases where an ineffective initiating medium or a deteriorated explosive has been used, undetonated residues of explosive may be expected.

The kind of explosive can be determined chemically even though only a small quantity is available, but of course the work is facilitated if larger quantities can be used. It is, however, not possible to determine whether an explosive comes from a certain sample which is old or has been damaged by frost. Definite identification is only possible in cases where typical impurities can be detected and recovered both in the material under enquiry and in the other material to be compared.

It is generally very difficult to identify the explosive used from an analysis of the deposit, which is found after an explosion, on objects such as stones or wood at the site of the explosion: and it is often impossible unless particles of undetonated explosive are found in the deposit. In the case of black powder, conditions are, however, somewhat different as the deposit in this case is very characteristic and can be distinguished from deposits from other explosives. If possible such deposits at the scene of an explosion should not be collected by being scraped off. It is also important that as much of the material as possible should be made available. If the deposit is on a block of stone, wall or the like, scraping is of course unavoidable. It is best done with a clean knife, the scraped-off deposit being collected on a piece of white paper held underneath and subsequently packed in a sample tube.

With safebreaking it sometimes happens that the criminal is alarmed and flees before finishing the job. If in such a case the explosive has been packed into the keyhole it should not be poked out, neither should a key be used in the lock. In safebreaking, nitroglycerine, dynamite, or detonating cord may be used. If dynamite or nitroglycerine remains undetonated, it must be removed before the locking mechanism can be manipulated with safety. Plastic explosives should be rinsed away with water followed by acetone. It must be remembered that the latter is inflammable and that the room should therefore be well aired. After using acetone a rinse is given with 20% caustic soda. The caustic alkali should not be used before first rinsing with water and acetone, since if the alkali comes into direct contact with large quantities of pure explosive it may cause a rise of temperature followed by detonation. The above rinsing procedure should be repeated several times before attempting to unlock the door of the safe. Powder explosives, which are used occasionally for safebreaking, are simply rinsed away with water.

When the mechanism has been washed as clean as possible, some arrangement must be made to work the locking mechanism from a distance, since residual explosive can cause injury on detonation.

Due to technical advancements in safe construction as well as the development of other mechanical means of safebreaking, explosives are now rarely encountered in safe burglaries.

Bomb mechanisms

Because of the variety of mechanical and electrical triggering devices available for initiating the explosion of a bomb or infernal machine, an exhaustive list cannot be given here. A bomb may be designed to detonate at a certain time, actuated by a mechanical or chemical clock; it may be intended for detonation if displaced, triggered by a lanyard, inertia switch, levelling device, etc. If the package was delivered, it is not likely that these factors prevail. In all probability, a delivered parcel is designed to explode when it is opened in the normal fashion. It is rare that bombs are constructed in an ingenious manner, defying any means of detection or inactivation.

Certain standard procedures are necessary whenever a package is suspected to contain a bomb. The primary concern is for the preservation of life; therefore, a generous area, 100–300 feet, surrounding the suspect package should be evacuated. Step two involves containing the explosion and minimizing property damage by barricading with heavy furniture, sand bags or similar material. Depending on circumstances, detection devices such as microphones, portable X-ray units may help to determine the nature of the contents of the package. Although most bomb scares are brought about by an unknown, but innocent package, sufficient real bombs have detonated when improperly handled to cause police agencies to exercise every caution in their study and handling of a suspect bomb. Due to the inherent unknown initiating mechanism and the possibility of an explosion, all possible information visible on the outside should be recorded before the 'bomb' is moved. Photographs and sketches of labels, writing, knots, etc. should preserve some investigative leads if the package should detonate when moved.

After all preliminary precautions have been made and even with the best protective devices, one, or at most two, officers must risk approaching and handling the 'bomb'. Every care should be exercised to keep it in the same position, to check it for attached wires or strings, and finally, to move it to a remote site by the least populated route.

Although some police departments feel inclined to destroy the object by explosives, such procedure does not enable the department to prevent a similar and perhaps more tragic occurrence. It is a better practice to 'age' the package in an explosion-proof shelter, such as described by MUEHLBERGER, and cautiously and remotely, open it in a manner that will preserve evidence. The construction of the bomb may permit tracing of components, identifying finger prints, tool marks or handwriting. The dismantling of the bomb is to be attempted only by experienced experts. If no such person is locally available, help should be sought from military experts.

If a bomb has detonated, all of the circumstances leading to the explosion must be determined. A bomb delivered by mail must be constructed in a different fashion from one 'planted'. The scene must be searched for burnt fuse, fragments of blasting caps, wires, metal, etc. All of these may permit the reconstruction of the device and may lead to the maker.

Chapter 10 **Burglary**

The type of crime scene most frequently investigated is the burglary scene. Burglary scenes are so varied in nature that it is not possible to formulate definite guidelines for their investigation. Techniques for the recovery of various types of evidence are found described in detail in Chapters 5 through 8. However, some of the conditions commonly found at burglary scenes will be treated in some detail on the following pages. Particularly the subject of safe burglary with explosives will be thoroughly described with a minimum of references to preceding chapters. This has resulted in a number of repetitions, but these are intentional because such investigations are so complicated that both the criminal's and the investigator's methods must be described as a whole.

Officers charged with investigating the scene of a burglary must keep in mind that even the most experienced burglar usually does not consider the multitude of trace evidence which he may have picked up at the scene. Such material may be found on his person or in his clothing a long time after the burglary. The investigator should therefore take specimens of any and all material at the scene which may have been carried away by the burglar. Waiting until he is apprehended may be too late. The contaminating material may be altered or lost in the interval.

One type of material which repeatedly is used as evidence against burglars is paint. Chips of paint have great evidential value, especially when they originate from an object which has been painted a number of times. When a burglar forcibly opens a door or a window, pries open drawers, or breaks the lid of a cashbox, chips of paint may fly in all directions and stick to clothes, particularly the trouser cuffs. If the burglar climbed over a painted fence, up a drainpipe, or through a window, his hands or clothing may pick up rather large amounts of paint.

Another type of evidence often found in the clothing of burglars is particles of glass from broken windows. When someone breaks a windowpane it is almost unavoidable that some of the flying fragments adhere to the person's clothes. The investigator should therefore also take samples of all broken windows. He should, of course, keep the various samples separate and take the samples from glass remaining in the frames. Splinters on the ground below the window usually are less valuable as evidence because they can easily be explained as not pertinent. The crime scene investigator should further take samples of various types of dust at the scene and of any other material which could possibly have adhered to the criminal's body or clothes. See also Chapter 8 'Miscellaneous Material'.

ENTRY THROUGH WINDOWS, DOORS, ETC.

In preparing a burglary, the thief always keeps in mind the possibility of entering through windows. He knows that a windowpane will offer the least resistance to entering the premises. He also knows that most people try to protect themselves against burglary by installing complex and substantial locks but forget that anyone can enter simply by breaking a fairly thin sheet of glass in a window or a door. Experienced burglary investigators are often puzzled by the fact that even public buildings are equipped with heavy doors and burglary-resistant locks but at the same time have panes of glass unprotected. By breaking such glass a burglar can sometimes open the door faster than a person using the appropriate key.

Entry through windows

Entry through windows is usually effected by breaking a hole in the pane and then removing the broken glass to the point where the latch can be reached. In order to avoid the noise from falling glass the burglar may press a rag coated with grease or tar against the window. Fly paper and adhesive tape have also been used. Less experienced burglars may attempt to cut out a piece of the glass by means of a glass cutter. Such attempts usually fail because glass which has been scored with a cutter requires a blow from the opposite side, namely the inside of the pane. It has happened that the burglar has completely removed the pane by cleaning out the putty and removing the retaining tacks. It has even happened that the burglar replaced the glass intact and put in new putty. Cases have also been recorded where the burglar heated the glass to the bursting point with a blowtorch.

Where a window is covered by a screen, a careful examination of the edges of any cuts may show fibers from the suspect's sleeve as he inserted his arm to open or break the window.

The investigation should include the search for finger prints. Samples should be taken of glass, putty, paint, dust or soil. It should be determined whether or not the burglar actually entered through the particular window and whether he left the premises through this opening.

Entry can also be made by pushing back a latch which has not been completely locked. This is usually accomplished by means of a knife which is inserted between the two parts of the window. In such cases the tool marks may be very indistinct, and there is a risk that the investigator does not notice them. The marks should be examined with the possibility in mind that fragments of a broken tool may be found.

Forcing of windows by using a prybar, screwdriver or other suitable tool is quite common. The force is usually sufficient to pull the screws holding the latch completely out. Tool marks should be searched for both on the sash and the bottom of the window.

When forcing a window, the burglar usually tries several windows until he finds one which is suitable or yields most easily. The investigator should therefore consider tool marks and other evidence which may be present on other windows.

Entry through doors

A burglar usually opens a door by using a prybar to attack the door and jamb around the lock until either the bolt can be pushed back or the bolt is actually freed from the striker plate. A door jamb may sometimes be so weak that it may be spread apart far enough to free the bolt. This can be done by mere pressure from the body or by inserting a jack horizontally across the door frame. The lock might also be made accessible through a hole which is drilled, sawed or broken in a door panel. Far too many doors are fitted with glass which is simply broken so that the lock may be reached.

Other weak points which may be attacked are mail slots, the frame of which may be removed, and transoms, which may have been left open.

A common method of entry is to push back spring-loaded bolts by means of a knife. The knife is inserted between the door and the jamb and the bolt is gradually worked back. The bolt is kept from springing back by outward pressure on the door. This method is easily detected by the series of scratches which run lengthwise along the bolt. Burglary by this method is prevented by safety catches and deadlocks.

Snap-lock bolts can also be opened by inserting a knife, spatula or a piece of celluloid which is pressed against the beveled face of the bolt, pushing it back. The instrument can be inserted either between the door and the jamb or behind the molding on the jamb. This method of entry is generally difficult to detect because a piece of celluloid can be used without leaving any marks. It is, however, possible that pieces of celluloid are broken off and may be found in or near the lock. On locks where the beveled face of the bolt faces inward, the bolt may be pushed back by a suitable tool or a piece of wire which forces the bolt back by a pulling movement. It is usually discovered by the scratch marks on the face of the bolt.

Special attention should be given the opening for the bolt in the striker plate for the possibility that it may contain wadded paper or other material. It has happened that a burglar surreptitiously stuffed something in the opening in the door jamb during an earlier visit to the premises. The effect of the wadding is to prevent the bolt from locking, so that the burglar may later return and push the bolt back.

If there is reason to suspect that the lock has been picked, the lock should be disassembled with great care. The investigator should avoid making new scratch marks inside the lock. If a pick has been used, it may have left marks in the coating of dust and oil usually found inside locks. Broken knife points, metal fragments from lock picks, etc. may also be found inside the lock.

Cases have been recorded wherein mechanics who installed the lock made certain alterations in order to facilitate a later burglary.

Entry can also be effected by cutting the hinge pins off by means of a bolt cutter. More commonly, however, the pins are simply knocked out with hammer and chisel or screwdriver. With the pins out, the door can be lifted off the hinges. The door may then be replaced and the pins reinserted. The method of entry is readily revealed by the damage to the hinges and the chips of paint or metal on the floor below the hinges.

Cylinder (pin-tumbler) locks may be picked by special picks, but usually the whole door is forced or the cylinder is removed. The cylinder may be pulled out by means of a special puller shaped from a pair of large nippers. To avoid detection of the removal, the lock cylinder is sometimes replaced or a similar cylinder put in its place. Sometimes the retaining screw is removed surreptitiously during an earlier visit to the premises which facilitates the removal of the cylinder.

Entry through basement windows and skylights

These windows are forced in the same manner as ordinary windows, but the investigator should pay special attention to the possibility that the burglar may have torn his clothes and left cloth fragments or fibers behind. (See 'Fragments of textiles, textile fibers, etc.'.) He should also take samples of the dust and dirt which is usually found in such places.

Entry through roofs

The presence of convenient utility poles, ladders and other aids, plus the concealment of the edge parapet, makes entry through flat roofs a favorite modus operandi. Many otherwise well-protected stores have 'tissue paper' roofs.

Building material may contaminate the clothing of any burglar using this technique. A careful search will also show signs of ropes for entry and exit.

Most stores are equipped with roof ventilators and exhaust fans. Entry through the ventilating system may result in tool marks, finger prints and dust contamination of clothing.

Entry through walls

Walls are broken either by tools or by explosives. A brick wall is easily broken by a hammer and chisel or a sledge hammer. Since the burglar can be expected to become covered with dust during such an operation, samples of mortar and brick should always be collected in such cases. In blasting, a hole is usually chiseled between two bricks and the charge is inserted. Several small charges are normally used in order to avoid severe detonations and the possibility of the whole wall collapsing.

Small hydraulic jacks may be used to force holes into a wall. In this operation, a narrow passageway is usually chosen where the base force can be distributed over a wide area by padding. After the initial hole is made, repeated thrusts are used to enlarge the hole sufficient to effect an entry.

Where an empty or infrequently occupied store is adjacent to the target, plaster walls may be cut to a thin supporting layer and the entire section removed at once.

Entry into vaults is usually accomplished through the walls which are

Fig. 142 Entry through a brick wall by blasting and hammering. Through this hole the
burglars entered a vault.

easier to force than the door. The walls are often constructed of reinforced
concrete which can be broken by repeated blasting or by hammer and chisel
and oxyacetylene burner.

Entry through floors

This method of entry is often preferred in the case of warehouses or other
buildings which have a crawl space underneath. The burglar usually drills
or saws a hole in the floorboards large enough to crawl through. Entry

through walls and floors are also made when the criminal suspects or knows that the premises are protected by burglar alarms on doors and windows.

Simulated burglaries

Simulated burglaries are most often attempts at insurance fraud. But they may also be the result of mentally disturbed persons who call the police to investigate a burglary which he himself arranged. An employee may be using this mode of providing a substantial increase in salary. To create a successful imitation of a burglary which will deceive the police officers, the simulator must strive to carry it out as naturally as possible. Otherwise there will be gaps in the sequence of events.

When windows are entered, the officer should therefore always check whether the windowpanes were in fact broken from the outside, whether there are foot prints outside the window, whether broken glass has been trampled in these prints, whether the burglar really could have reached the window, whether there are traces of actual entry (sand, dirt, etc.), whether objects inside the window are so placed that the window could be opened to permit entry, and so on. Regarding damage to windows, see 'Broken panes of glass'. If the outside of the window glass is very dirty, there should be marks from the object used to break it. If the glass is relatively clean, the side on which the force was applied might be revealed by dusting with aluminum powder.

In cases of forced doors, the damage should be examined to see whether it is only on the outside portions. Marks of prying should be present on the door as well as on the door jamb. If the tool marks are located so high up that the burglar must have stood on a box or a ladder, the support should be examined.

Whenever a burglary is suspected to be simulated, all tools belonging to the victim should be compared with the tool marks present and, if necessary, recovered for further examination.

Holes in floors, walls and ceilings should be examined to determine the side from which the attack was started. The holes should also be examined to determine if there is evidence of a person having crawled through.

The officer should further make an estimate of how long a time the burglar spent on the premises. He should follow the burglar's actions in searching for valuables; whether he has opened doors and emptied drawers or went directly to the right place and made the theft.

THE DETAILED EXAMINATION OF THE SCENE

As a rule, the detailed examination of the scene must begin at some place other than the central scene in order to prevent destruction of evidence which cannot be protected. The path of the burglar to and from the scene is established by means of foot prints, traces of climbing, obstacles removed (barbed wire and the like), and objects thrown away (tools, opened cash boxes). The number of thieves involved should be estimated from the foot prints when possible. Places where someone has crawled or climbed should primarily be examined for such evidence as fibers from clothing. If there was more than one burglar, one of them might have been a look-out. At the place where the lookout has been standing the investigator might find, aside from foot prints, cigarette butts, scraps of paper, etc.

Safe Burglary. One man who had been placed as lookout during a safe burglary occupied himself by picking up and hiding pieces of glass from a broken window. In doing so he accidentally cut his finger and then removed his glove. During the few moments when the glove was off his hand, the thief had time to deposit a finger print in blood on one of the glass fragments. This finger print was sufficient to convict the burglars.

The point of entry to the scene should immediately be examined for pieces of broken tools. It happens all too often that such evidence is not noticed but becomes trampled into the ground or imbedded in someone's shoe. The search for, and recovery of, evidence at doors and windows should be undertaken as soon as possible since it might be destroyed by the effects of weather. The officer should try to determine if the burglar took steps to put out street lights or outside lights. He should also search for tire tracks or other marks of a vehicle, and for paper or boxes which may have been used as wrappers for tools.

The examination of the central crime scene must often be carried out while taking into consideration the wishes of the owner of the premises. The business activities of a store or large office cannot be completely stopped, and the loss from a work stoppage may in fact be greater than the loss from the burglary. The best solution is to allow the owner or manager to specify which portions of the premises he needs first. If a safe has been forced open it will normally be the most valuable area, from the point of view of evidence, and should therefore be examined last. However, this should not keep the officer from carefully sorting out selected documents which the proprietor might need immediately.

After planning the examination of the scene, the examination proper should be carried out while keeping in mind all the types of evidence described in the earlier chapters on 'Finger prints', 'Tool Marks', 'Blood' and 'Miscellaneous Materials'. As the examination of the various portions of the premises is completed, the proprietor should be notified. If evidence is found which requires time-consuming recovery, the owner and other personnel should be notified of this fact and asked to stay away from the area.

The investigator should attempt to form a picture of the whole crime scene in order to estimate whether the burglar was familiar with the premises or not. He should make this estimate without the help of the owner, because burglary victims almost always claim that the burglar must have had an intimate knowledge of the premises. It would be impossible to list all the features which could point to the burglar's familiarity with the premises. The circumstances in each individual case will determine this. However, a few good indicators are: whether the burglar had used keys kept in a hiding place and whether he had taken valuables from a rather unlikely place without first going over the rest of the room.

The investigator should also attempt to make an estimate of the professional ability of the burglar. As a rule, experienced burglars cause less damage than beginners.

It sometimes happens that the criminal defecates on the premises. This may be an act of vandalism, but in most cases it is probably just the result of acute anxiety. On such crime scenes the investigator may expect the burglar to have been nervous enough to have left finger prints, even on paper which he might have used.

SAFE BURGLARY

Although most people, businessmen and policemen alike, refer to any piece of furniture designed to protect valuables as a 'safe', these devices can be classified according to whether the hazard is fire or burglary. Obviously, a box designed to protect papers against fire may offer little resistance to a burglar. In spite of manufacturers' warnings, amazingly large sums of money and valuables are stored against burglary loss under only fire protection. The safe manufacturers are constantly and ingeneously improving

Fig. 143 Peeled safe. The front was struck with a sledge hammer until sufficient buckling of the door permitted insertion of a ripping bar.

(*Metropolitan Dade County Public Safety Department*)

protective chests in order to provide the protection of time. Increased protection gains time for alarms and patrols to intercede. Needless to say, inventiveness is not confined to the lawful side. As new tools of potential use for burglary are developed for industry, criminals will adopt them for illegal ends. Therefore, the following suggestions are subject to day-to-day changes to keep abreast of new technology. All burglary investigators should familiarize themselves, and keep up-to-date on safe and lock construction as well as new cutting, drilling, sawing, burning, and pushing devices.

The opening of safes is accomplished by pounding, ripping, drilling, cutting with special devices, cutting with oxyacetylene burner or by explosives. The latter method is described in a separate section.

Pounding and ripping is usually only done on safes of weaker construction and where the local conditions will allow the burglar a considerable amount of noise without being detected. Sometimes the burglar attacks a weak point, the back side or bottom of the safe where he can break through or remove an outside plate. The edge of the door of such safes is usually also vulnerable when the upper left corner is attacked. One or more chisels or wedges can be driven into the crack to the point where the frame gives way and the locking bolts are freed. Sometimes the door frame is so weak that it can be knocked away directly by using a sledge hammer. A fairly common method is to use a large chisel or prybar to break open the door plate beginning at the dial hole and then enlarging the hole by means of a suitable wrench or bolt cutters until the bolts are accessible. Sometimes a pipe wrench is used to enlarge the hole which results in a characteristic appearance of the hole. It has also happened that burglars have peeled back the plate by using an axe.

Drilling is usually effective but it is a time-consuming method and is therefore only rarely used in safe burglaries. It is commonly done by perforating the door plate around the keyhole by a series of holes close together. A large portion of the lock mechanism is thereby bared so that the bolts can be manipulated. The front plate of some safes can also be peeled back if some of the screws or rivets in the edge are first removed. The paint covering the rivets is first scraped off so that the rivets are bared. The rivets are then drilled deeply enough for the plate to be separated. After a few rivets have been removed, the front plate is then forced up sufficiently to insert a chisel which is used to break the remaining rivets without drilling. On some safes

Fig. 144 Safe tipped on its back and the bottom ripped open.
(*Metropolitan Dade County Public Safety Department*)

the locking bolts can be reached by drilling through the side of the safe, directly against the face of the bolt. The bolt can then be driven back with a punch. The exact location of the bolts can be determined by the marks in the door frame which occur when the safe door is shut while the bolts are protruding in daily use.

In cases of drilling the burglar can be expected to have used some kind of lubricating oil for the bit. Samples of such oil and samples of metal shavings should be collected because the burglar may have gotten these materials on his body or clothing.

The door plate can also be opened with a special type of tool shaped like a can opener. If a sufficiently large hole is drilled or chopped in the plate, the 'can opener' may be inserted and the plate peeled back far enough to make the locking bars accessible.

Simpler types of safes with combination locks may be opened by means of a thick, square steel plate which is provided with an opening at the center to be slipped over the dial knob. The corners of the plate are equipped with threaded bolts, the points of which touch the safe door. By tightening the bolts with a wrench the knob and spindle are torn out.

It also happens that safes are opened by a special bridge device which is screwed to the safe with bolts. The portion of the bridge which is over the door frame contains a threaded hole. A strong bolt is fitted into this hole and tightened far enough to force the door open.

Another method employs a circular cutter. Such devices are made in several different forms. Some are affixed to one or more holes which have been drilled into the safe, while others are strapped to the safe by long bolts and nuts or steel cable. Common to all types, however, is one or more hardened steel cutters which are held against the safe under tension and are turned by means of a handle. The result is a round hole in the safe wall. These devices are normally not used on the safe door since the locking bars would interfere, but rather on the side or back of the safe.

Cutting by oxyacetylene burner is a very effective method against which only the specially designed steel chests are completely resistant. A considerable disadvantage of this method lies in the fact that the apparatus required is heavy and difficult to transport. For this reason the burning method is usually only used where complete welding equipment is available on the premises. Some burglars have used compact equipment which is large enough to do the job but light enough to be carried easily.

The burning is usually started around the dial hole. A sufficiently large

Fig. 145 A typical 'safe job'. Althought the outer door was successfully peeled, the inner
round door prevented access to the money.

(Metropolitan Dade County Public Safety Department)

hole is cut in the front plate of the door so that the lock mechanism is
accessible. The operator may cut this hole in the form of a tongue which is
folded back. Where the cutting is done on the sides or back of the safe, the
inside plate must also be cut through. This method often ignites the contents of the safe, whereupon the burglar may use a soda pop bottle as a fire
extinguisher. Sometimes the burglar will cut off the safe door hinges which
reveals his ignorance of the construction of the safe.

The manner of opening the safe by burning reveals the skill of the burglar.
When the investigator is himself unable to estimate this skill, he should
consult a specialist. Samples to be collected at the scene are molten particles
of metal (beads), slag, molten safe insulation etc. Such particles may be
found in the clothing of a suspect. The investigator should also keep in
mind the possibility that there might be minor burns in the burglar's clothes
from flying particles. When the contents of the safe have caught fire, the

Fig. 146 Rear view of a steel safe entered by burning away a corner by means of an oxyacetylene torch.

(*Metropolitan Dade County Public Safety Department*)

burglar may have been able to recover paper currency, some of which may be charred.

Safe burglaries are often carried out by transporting the safe to an isolated location where it is opened by tools or explosives. In such cases the burglars are usually less careful in their movements at the place of opening. Valuable foot prints or tire tracks may be found at such places. The investigation should be carried out as soon as possible since inclement weather conditions may destroy the most valuable evidence.

Safe burglary. A safe was hauled out during a burglary and transported in a car to a wooded area where it was opened with explosives. During the examination of the outdoor scene a door handle from an automobile was recovered. The car of a suspect who was later arrested for the burglary was found to have a broken handle. The handle from the scene matched the remains of the handle in the car. It had apparently been broken off while the safe was taken out of the car. The suspect confessed.

Fig. 147 Exterior of a safe door, the locking mechanism of which had been cut out with an oxyacetylene torch.

(*Metropolitan Dade County Public Safety Department*)

SAFE BURGLARY WITH EXPLOSIVES

It is often very difficult to gather physical evidence which will convict a safe burglar specializing in explosives. As a rule he is not a novice at the game. He takes pride in sweeping the crime scene clean of all traces which may be used as evidence against him. When examining such burglary scenes the investigator should therefore proceed very thoroughly and take advantage of the mistakes which are sometimes made even by this type of burglar. Experience has shown that the explosives expert usually makes his mistakes when he is disturbed or has to flee the premises. He may then leave behind or drop objects which have potential value as evidence.

One weakness of this specialist is that he usually sticks to one method in all his burglaries. The investigator thereby gets an opportunity to tie certain burglaries to a given criminal or to others who have been trained by him. This fact may be valuable even when the burglars are not known.

The explosives operator usually does not pick locks or make his way into the premises by other light-fingered methods. Since his work is carried out with a great deal of noise, this is also characteristic of his method of entry. He generally uses great force on doors and windows and may even use a charge on a door which could much more easily have been opened the usual way. On the other hand, he is very careful to protect himself from surprise. He very rarely works alone and may have several helpers whose only duty is to act as lookouts.

Regarding the placing of the safe for the 'blowing', three methods are normally found: it is left in place, it is pulled out from the wall, or it is laid on the floor. The first method is the most common. The second method is used by burglars who do not want to have the safe blown against the wall and create vibrations in the buildings which may be more noticeable than the detonation. It has happened that a safe was thrown so violently against the wall that it broke the wall and started cracks which ran into an apartment above. The third method is more seldom used. Its advantage is that it facilitates the placing of the charge.

In examining safes which have been moved or laid down the investigator should be very careful in searching for latent finger and palm prints. While the explosives specialist will be sure to use gloves or other covering, it is still possible that he may leave identifiable fragments of palm prints on a safe which he has moved. The glove may slip during the heavy work, exposing a small piece of the palm – enough to produce a valuable print. In developing prints which have been deposited under such conditions great care must be exercised because the prints easily become smeared or even completely filled in due to the great pressure. The most suitable developing media are black powder and aluminum powder which should be used sparingly. See also 'Finger prints and palm prints', and 'Prints of gloves'.

The charge is usually placed in the dial spindle hole after the dial is knocked off. The charge may be dynamite in powder or paste, Primacord or other solid explosive. The hazard and the refined technique associated with the use of nitroglycerine usually limits its use to only the elite of the safe burglars. The advent of the round door chest has discouraged the use of explosives, however.

Wrappers from explosives should be searched for and recovered, even though latent finger prints are never found on waxed wrappers. In a favorable case the wrapper may still be valuable as evidence (see 'Objects left at the crime scene').

Concerning detonators found at the scene, see 'Detonators'. In general, the adhesive material used to affix the detonator and which is found on the scene, such as clay, putty, plasticine, or soap is brought in by the burglar. These substances must be soft and well-kneaded in order to serve the purpose. As the burglar may have kneaded these materials before going to the scene without wearing gloves, there is a possibility that plastic finger prints are present. Such prints should be searched for not only on the surface but also on inside layers of the kneaded material. Plastic prints may also be found on strips of tape but these are usually hard to detect.

The length of safety fuse – when it is used – may vary from 3–4 inches to 5 yards. Since explosives specialists usually cut these lengths before going to the scene and since they have widely varying ideas of the proper length, this fact may be of some value. Those using the longer fuses usually are the ones who prefer to light the fuse and then retire to a safe place from which they can observe the effect of the explosion and whether it was noticed.

Safe burglars vary as to whether they use a dam or sound-absorbing blanket to contain the explosion. Those who do use a dam probably do so to muffle the detonation and to keep windows from bursting. Since the charge is mostly inside the door, the effect of the explosion will not be enhanced by the use of a dam. When the burglar intends to demolish the door completely, the dam does have some effect but it is usually an effect which the burglar wants to avoid. He runs the risk that the inside door plate is blown into the safe with such force that he has to place new charges to dislodge it. Many explosives men make a habit of not using a dam at all. Instead they will open windows in the room where the safe is located so that the shock wave will dissipate without breaking windows or attracting unwanted attention. Some burglars will soak the dam with water, partly to make it denser and heavier and partly to prevent the possibility of fire.

The material used in dams are either brought to the scene or collected at the scene. The damage to the material will give an indication of how many separate charges were used. Material which has been brought to the scene may sometimes give good leads for the investigation and the search for the criminal.

The ideal explosion occurs when the charge is so well-balanced that the locking bolts are pulled back and the door flies open. In such cases the external damage to the safe may be limited to a slight bulge in the front plate.

around the dial hole. It does happen, however, that the locking bolts remain more or less closed, so that new charges must be set off. In order to avoid this snag, some burglars will put weight on the door handle in the direction of opening of the handle. A heavy cord is commonly tied to the handle and a heavy object, such as an adding machine or a typewriter is attached to the other end. Another method is to tie a heavy metal bar to the handle to act as a lever. At the detonation the handle is turned by the weight of the heavy object so that the locking bolts are turned back.

Safe burglary. A safe burglar who used explosives had developed the above-described method to perfection. He always worked with the safe laid on its back. After igniting the charge he would lie alongside the safe grasping the handle which turned at the detonation. He always worked with small, well-calculated charges so that he was never injured.

Locked drawers and compartments inside the safe are either forced open or blown. The investigator should keep in mind the possibility of finding parts of broken tools as well as tool marks at these places. Fragments of tools should be searched with a magnet since they are very difficult to find in the powdered insulation which usually pours from the broken safe.

The search for finger prints at scenes of safeblowing is usually complicated by the layer of finely-divided safe insulation which settles on everything in the room. This dust should be removed before developing with powder. It is preferably done by careful blowing. To brush off the dust is wrong because the dust usually consists of gritty particles which will destroy the finger print. Visible prints which have been deposited by a dusty finger must be treated very carefully. See 'Finger prints and palm prints'.

Whenever an unexploded charge is found in the safe it should be neutralized with great care. See 'Explosives' and 'Detonators'.

When a suspect is apprehended his clothes should be thoroughly searched for the presence of safe insulation or paint. Anyone who has been present in a room where a safe has been blown can hardly avoid getting dust and safe insulation on his clothes. The dust may also adhere to the burglar's skin or in his hair, ears and nostrils and under the fingernails. Such dust may be found on any part of the clothing, but particularly in the trouser cuffs and on the shoes, mainly in the seams and lace holes and on the soles. Paint chips are usually loosened in the explosion, and the burglar runs the risk of picking up such chips on his clothing when examining the safe after the detonation.

In searching the scene, the investigator should therefore collect samples of the safe insulation and paint on the outside and inside of the safe for use in possible comparisons. He should also evaluate the possibility of wall paint, loosened by the explosion, falling on the burglar. He should note the manufacturer of the safe, so that he may later be contacted for information on the composition of insulation and paint.

If safe insulation or paint are not found on the suspect's clothes, the investigator should remember that the suspect may have done everything possible to eliminate such traces.

Safe burglary. A suspect was arrested in connection with a safe burglary using explosives. It was learned that the suspect, immediately after the job, had turned his clothes into a dry cleaner. He obviously knew the risk of being caught with dust from the crime scene in his clothing.

The suspect's hands and clothing should also be examined for the presence of traces of explosives. If the hands are not immediately washed, there may be traces of explosives under the fingernails. In the clothing, such traces should primarily be searched for in the pockets. Even the gloves may contain traces. If the burglar carried safety fuses in his pockets, there may be characteristic stains on the pocket lining.

When a safe is blown it sometimes happens that the burglar is injured on sharp metal edges. It may also happen that his nose starts bleeding from the shock of the detonation. This is more common when electric detonators are used since the burglar is forced to stay rather close to the safe. If blood is found on the scene it should be recovered for later examination. It may even happen that the burglar is so severely injured that he must seek immediate aid.

Safe burglary. Two burglars were in the process of laying down a safe in preparation for blowing. The safe slipped and fell on one of the men, breaking his leg. The accomplice saw no other way out than to call the police.

In writing the report of an explosives scene, it should be stated whether human lives were endangered by the explosion. If residential quarters are nearby, their location should be shown on a sketch.

Chapter 11 Motor vehicles

EXAMINATION OF MOTOR VEHICLES

The examination of motor vehicles is primarily a traffic or accident investigation function, and is therefore not directly related to the responsibilities of a crime scene investigator. This chapter will therefore only deal with those instances where the automobile itself is the object of the crime (automobile theft) and where the driver is the victim or the offender (assaults on taxicab drivers, 'lovers lane murders' and hit-and-run). The methods described here could, of course, also be applied to the relatively minor offenses such as malicious damage to vehicles, traffic accidents, etc.

For practical reasons the chapter has been divided into sections headed 'Automobile theft', 'Homicide in an automobile' and 'Hit-and-run'. The investigator who is to examine automobiles might, however, find that all the requirements for examination are not listed under a particular heading but are to be found under one of the other subjects. In the investigation of homicide in an automobile, for example, he should apply all the methods described under 'Automobile theft'.

AUTOMOBILE THEFT

The investigation of stolen or 'borrowed' motor vehicles is usually limited to the taking of finger or palm prints. Unfortunately, this step is not performed until it is a last resort. Although the existence of an isolated or abandoned car should give rise to the suspicion of theft, all too often the officer finding the vehicle throws caution to the winds and rummages through the glove compartment searching for the owner's identity. On the other hand, the frequency of auto thefts and limited police personnel does not permit an idealized preservation and investigation. Some compromise must be established that will preserve the maximum possibility of apprehension and conviction.

Usually, a car is repeatedly observed by a patrolling officer, or the license and description corresponds to that contained in a police bulletin. What ever the case may be, a short preliminary investigation of the car and contents will suggest the need of further technical investigation. Before any technical examination is conducted, however, it may be necessary to remove the vehicle to a dry, sheltered location. If trace evidence such as hairs, fibers and dirt seems to be a possibility, all persons must refrain from entering the car and it must be towed to the examination site. If trace clues are absent or seem unlikely, the car may be driven using an auxiliary clamp-on wheel in order to preserve prints. The absolute minimum contact necessary for safe operation should be observed. It is particularly important to advise all garage personnel that no one is to have contact with the car until it has been processed for finger prints.

The best medium for the development of finger prints on or in a car is aluminum-lycopodium mixture. On the painted surfaces and metal parts of a car there is generally a thin and almost invisible layer of oil or grease, and if the usual developer – aluminum powder – is used there is a danger of the print becoming smeary and indistinct or being quite filled up. On the other hand aluminum-lycopodium mixture gives a much better result. If single prints remain indistinct they can be strengthened with undiluted aluminum powder. White lead is a very good development medium, but there are certain disadvantages in its use. On the one hand it is difficult to localize on a vertical surface and on the other the preservation of prints is much more difficult than when using the first mentioned development medium. In investigating unpainted metal surfaces and very oily parts of the car, white lead is the only really suitable medium, so that it should always be kept at hand.

The investigation should in the first place be concentrated on certain parts on which the criminal is likely to have left finger prints. A criminal who drives or rides in a car in connection with the execution of a serious crime rarely uses gloves or other hand protection. When he is attempting to escape it can be assumed that he will too apprehensive to remember the danger of leaving finger prints, and should he drive the car himself he will feel hampered by wearing gloves. In the investigation of stolen or 'borrowed' cars it has been found that the largest number of identifications of finger prints are made on the rear view mirror. It is quite natural for the criminal to adjust the mirror to see if anyone is following him, and prints should be looked for both on the glass and on the back of the mirror. On the outside of the doors there are often prints which have been made when the door was slammed on getting out of the car. Prints of the criminal are often found on the side windows, the instrument panel and glove compartments. To break into a locked car he usually forces open a movable side window an inch or two with a screwdriver, after which he pushes it down with his hands so that he can put his arm in and open the door from inside. Generally his finger prints show up clearly on the inside of the window.

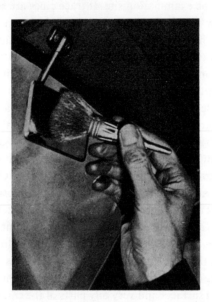

Fig. 148 On stolen cars the thief's finger prints are very often found on the rear view mirror which should be examined on both sides.

On the steering wheel and on all parts which have to be handled when driving the prints are usually blurred and indistinct owing to their being contaminated with oil and skin grease.

A car which is damp must not be examined before it is completely dry. When developing finger prints only a fraction of a drop of water on the brush is sufficient to make it quite unusable for its purpose, and it must be dried before it can be used again.

Regarding cars which are cold or have been standing outside in winter, the rule is that no attempt at development should be made until the car has stood in a warm garage for some time, preferably not less than one day. There is no possibility of developing a print on or in a car which is standing outdoors in cold weather. At low temperatures, there are great difficulties. Allowance must be made for the moisture in the breath of persons in a car depositing itself on any latent prints and then freezing to a thin layer of ice, making development impossible. Even if it is not freezing, moisture is deposited everywhere in the car and destroys all possibility of development. Thus before an investigation in wintertime the car must first be stored in a warmed garage, and before it is driven in, all snow and ice must be carefully scraped away so that running or dripping thaw water does not destroy any prints. When the car is put in the garage it is advisable to leave the doors open, with the windows almost closed. In summer there is a risk of the prints being destroyed by direct sunlight. A finger print can be completely destroyed by this means a few hours after having been made, although it was at first visible without development. The car should therefore be placed in a shady place, preferably under cover.

In securing developed finger prints in and on a car with finger print lifters, the back of the lift should be marked with indications which must in general be more detailed than on lifters used in, for example, the scene of a burglary. In many cases it has happened that a criminal has admitted that he might have left his prints in or on a car, but stated that this happened when he put his head in over the top of a window from curiosity and grasped the upper edge of the window, or when he passed by or stood near the car and unconsciously touched it. The police officer must therefore, by labelling each lift make clear not only the position of the print but also under what conditions it was made, for example 'left front door, outside, grip from inside over upper edge of partially lowered window.' The best method of securing the prints is by photography.

ABANDONED CARS

Every policeman who finds or investigates an ownerless car which has not been reported as stolen should *not* drive it away or subject it to more detailed examination until he has been informed by the driver or owner of the reason why the car was standing at that place. If he knows that a serious crime has been committed, he must remember that the investigation of the car has to be done with the utmost care and thoroughness. It may be difficult for an experienced investigator to complete such an investigation in less than a day.

The investigation must be planned carefully. The basic search for clues in and on the car should be carried out in a well-sheltered place, preferably in a garage or other suitable building, because rain or snow or even strong sunlight can destroy certain clues. The car should therefore be driven or towed from the place of finding as soon as possible, but only after certain preliminary investigations have been carried out.

The place where the car is found should be photographed and sketched in the usual way. Photography is done while the car is still on the spot, but sketching can wait till later. In sketches the distance to the nearest occupied dwelling and to the nearest village or city should be given. If necessary, a sketch plan may be made of the immediate surroundings, and another of neighboring districts, but the latter may be replaced by suitable maps. The recording of the speedometer or taximeter should be noted: it is best to inquire of an expert whether there is anything of special significance to be observed. The supply of gasoline is checked. An attempt is made to determine whether the car stopped at that point for some reason unforeseen by the criminal, for example engine trouble, failure of gasoline supply, inability to drive it further, etc. The floor in front of the driving seat is examined carefully. Preferably all dust and dirt at this place should be kept. The exterior is examined for the presence of any clues which might fall off when the car is driven or towed away. Further, a preliminary examination of the whole of the car should be made for clues which are easy to secure or which for any reason might be damaged or destroyed when the car is driven away.

The detailed investigation of a car should not be carried out at the place where it is found, but the site chosen should be as near the place of finding as possible. A long drive or tow can cause a deposit of dust or dirt which may completely destroy any possibilities of finding clues in the form of finger prints. Only the man who is to drive the vehicle away should sit in it, and he should wear gloves and understand that he must not touch any object in the car other than what is necessary for driving. If he touches any finger-printed object with a gloved hand the print may be destroyed.

After the car has been taken to a sheltered place, a thorough investigation is made of the place where it was found and of its surroundings. It must be borne in mind that the criminal, after the deed was commited, may have unconciously dropped or thrown away objects which either show the route which he took or give a direct clue to him. The investigation must be done as quickly as possible, especially if a fall of snow is anticipated. If larger areas or stretches of road have to be searched it may be advisable to call in the help of local people but they must first be instructed in how they are to act if they find any clues.

The detailed investigation of the car is done only after it is completely dry. In general the floor of the car, running boards and seats are examined first, and only after this is done are any finger prints developed. It may be convenient first to examine the outside of the car in order to avoid the risk of anyone unthinkingly destroying a clue or making a fresh one. The contents of ash trays are examined and kept, the various objects being noted in *the order in which they occur from the top.* The contents of the glove compartments and any other storage spaces are examined and noted in a similar way. In and under the seats there are often found objects which the criminal has dropped. Any bloodstains in and on the car are examined for direction of splash and fall, height of fall, direction of movement, etc., after which they are preserved. Marks of the swinging of a weapon, damage from gunshot, and the like are preserved. The engine and baggage space is examined.

In the investigation of a car in which a crime of violence has been committed it is advisable, after securing the evidence, to make measurements of the amount of room in the car. There may arise a question of the possibility of a criminal swinging an instrument, handling a firearm, etc. Any evidence of the vehicle being used in any crime should be noted; safe paint and insulation in the trunk, outlines of boxes or tools, even bullet holes, should be sought.

All normal serial numbers should be checked in order to detect alterations in the identity of the car.

Any damage to the car may indicate its abandonment and reported 'theft' in order to hide an accident. The exact condition of damage should be carefully noted and photographed. Under suspicious circumstances the temperature of the water in the radiator and the surrounding air temperature should be recorded. From this data, it may be possible to establish the duration of time since abandonment.

HOMICIDE IN AN AUTOMOBILE

Taxicab drivers are very frequently the victims of robberies, often in combination with assault which may be fatal. As is well known, they usually carry large sums of money in order to be able to make change for large bills. For a criminal who is desperate enough, it is a relatively simple matter to order the driver to a desolate area, assault him from behind without too great a danger to himself, and then rob him. Since it would be dangerous to attack the driver while the cab is moving, the driver is asked to stop under some pretext or other. After the robbery is completed it is not uncommon for the attacker to hide the victim and then drive the car as far as he can away from the scene.

In those cases where the robbery victim dies one can expect to find the car and the victim in different locations; sometimes the car is found first. There is a great risk, therefore, that the examination of the car is made difficult or impossible because curiosity seekers cannot leave the car un-molested, or because an over-zealous officer has the car removed, thinking that he is only dealing with a case of 'joy-riding'. For this reason, every officer who finds an abandoned car should suspect the worst and exercise extreme care. After a license check has revealed the fact that the car may have been the scene of a crime, the procedure suggested for 'Abandoned Cars' should be followed, as well as the procedure for the specific type of crime.

HIT-AND-RUN CASES

In a certain proportion of traffic accidents the driver of the car makes no attempt to assist the victim, but drives on in order to conceal his identity and to avoid the consequences. The usual course of events is that, immediately after the accident, the driver drives on with the greatest possible speed and does everything he can to avoid recognition, for example switches off the lights, drives the car to a remote place where it is left and then declared to be stolen, etc. A more elaborate precaution, carried out with the object of avoiding an investigation, is to arrange matters so that the death has the appearance of an accident in which only the victim is involved.

In a large percentage of hit-and-run cases, the driver is either under the influence of alcohol or drugs or is driving under license revocation.

An old man was found dead in a mortar mixing box by the side of a public road. The circumstances at first gave the impression of an accident in which the man, while cycling, had run into the box and fallen off his cycle on to his face in it. However it was noticed that there was a crease in his coat near the neck, which gave a distinct impression that it had resulted from someone gripping his clothes and dragging the body. This led to a thorough investigation of the case which resulted in the conclusion that the man, while

Fig. 149 The body of a man found in a mortar mixing box. He was the victim of hit-and-run and was dragged to the place where he was found.

cycling, had been hit in the back and killed, presumably by a car. The post-mortem examination showed that the man had lain on his back at the scene of the accident long enough for livid stains to be produced on the back, after which the body had been conveyed to the mortar box.

When the body of a victim is found on or near a roadway, it becomes necessary to establish whether a fatal automobile accident has occurred or whether such an impression is intended in order to conceal another form of homicide. It is unfortunate that such bodies are usually found by laymen who do much to destroy clues. The exact position of the body, as found, should be checked against signs of post-mortem lividity. The body may have been placed as found after death occurred elsewhere. Before the victim is taken to a hospital or mortuary, the immediate area should be checked for foot prints, tire prints, drag marks and so forth. All necessary precautions should be taken to insure that loosely adhering paint, glass, dirt and the like will not be lost in moving the body. Clean sheets or plastic bags will provide maximum preservation.

Some preliminary and cautious examination of the body at the scene may assist in correlating marks observed at the scene.

The marks of the car which are found at the scene of the accident itself usually consist of wheel tracks, braking marks, glass from broken lamps and windows, parts which have come loose, flakes of paint, etc. All glass is collected and packaged in a manner that will prevent abrasion and chipping. In the laboratory, the glass of a broken headlight is fitted together, since the pattern of the glass is sometimes characteristic of a certain make of car. Furthermore, when a suspect car is found, glass from the scene may be matched with glass remaining in the frames of the suspect vehicle. An attempt is made to determine whether the car went on without stopping or whether it stopped for a time. Dripping oil, water or other fluids can indicate stopping points and direction of travel. The driver may have taken precautions to conceal the body or to move it off the road, and in doing this he may have dropped something or left clues in some other way.

The marks of a car which does not stop, and which may be found on the victim, consist of dirt, glass broken from headlamps and windows, flakes of paint, impressions from the bumpers and headlamps, patterns of tire treads and radiator grill, etc. At the site of a collision, dirt may be dislodged from the underside of the car in layered chunks. Every effort should be made to collect and preserve the layered specimen intact since these layers may serve to strengthen an identification of a suspect car.

Occasionally, parts of the car are driven into the body and broken off, leaving a clue as to the make of vehicle and an excellent means of positive identity of a suspect car. Dirt on the body may also take the form of impression marks from some part of the car. Impression marks are generally more distinct on the body than on the clothes, especially in cases where the victim was killed so quickly that no bruises have formed around the injuries. From these injuries, an opinion can be rendered as to a collision contact or a running over of the victim. Further, it may be possible to see evidence denoting a truck or a passenger car as well as the postion of the victim when struck.

If the victim of the accident was himself on a vehicle, for example a cycle, there may be marks which are more easily interpreted than the injuries on the body. In such a case where there is reason to suspect that the driver of the car carried or lifted the cycle out of the way after the accident, finger prints should be looked for upon it. Marks of the car causing the accident are generally represented by paint and collision damage. Paint is kept for possible future investigation. In America, such paint should be submitted to the laboratory of the Federal Bureau of Investigation for comparison with the National Automobile Paint File from which the make of car may be deduced.

Fig. 150 In the examination of a car, which was suspected of having struck and severely injured a woman cyclist from the rear and then gone on without giving assistance, the following clues were detected and formed valuable evidence against the driver. 1 = headlamp glass broken; 2, 6 and 7 = dents; 3–5 = woollen fibers of grey color; 8 and 9 = marks of scraping. Cf. Fig. 151.

Collision damage may consist of those caused directly by the collision together with subsequent damage resulting from falling, sliding along the road, crushing or being run over. A superficial inspection of the damage may be confusing, but by a detailed investigation and comparison with damage on a suspected vehicle it can generally be fitted into the different phases of the accident.

The clothing and cycle of a victim should not be disposed of until it can be assumed that the car in question will not be found within a reasonable time, and before doing so all marks should be preserved, photographed and described. Samples of different kinds of fibers, and preferably also whole

Fig. 151 Reconstruction of the accident of Fig. 150 from clues on the car and cycle. 1 = marks of scraping; 2 = damaged luggage carrier; 3 = front bumper, on the left of which were marks of scraping corresponding with the damage to the wheel of the cycle; 4 = in this position (the second stage of the impact), the saddle of the cycle, on the back of which were marks of scraping, fits well in the one dent in the left fender of the car and the damage to the luggage carrier is explained, as also the occurrence of scraping marks on the lower part of the fender (5).

pieces of cloth, should be taken from the clothing. If the cloth is rough, specimens of the scraping marks of the weave are taken in plasticine. Samples of paint and scraping marks in plasticine are taken from a cycle at points which may be supposed to have been scraped along the car. If considered necessary, samples are also taken of the rubber of the tires of the cycle.

The doctor should be reminded to take samples of blood and hair from the body.

If a suspected car is found, it should immediately be taken off the road and driven to a nearby place for investigation, although it is better to examine it at the place where it is found, so avoiding any risk of more dust and dirt being deposited on top of any marks. If the car is found immediately after the accident and the owner tries to show that it had been stolen at the time of the accident, then this statement should be investigated through finger prints.

The clues which may be found on a suspected car may include blood, small fragments of skin, hair or other matter from the body of the victim, together with damage arising from the collision with the body of the victim. There have been cases where the victim has put his hands on the car and left identifiable finger or palm prints. Marks of scraping may be found in the dirt on the car. If dirt is found on the victim, a comparative examination may be made. Marks from the clothes of the victim consist of marks of scraping and fibers or torn-off pieces of fabric. Scraping marks from clothing are usually indistinct and are best examined by oblique lighting. Marks from the victim's cycle may consist of enamel paint, rubber scrapings from the tires, and collision damage. The pattern of the cycle tire may have left prints on, for example, the bumper. The pattern of the car tires is compared with tracks at the scene of the accident and marks on the victim. Any glass found on the victim or at the scene is compared with glass in the suspected car. Damage to the paintwork of the car is compared with paint flakes. In a favorable case flakes of paint can be fitted to corresponding damage in the paintwork of the car. With regard to bumpers, headlamps and radiator grills, as also other places where collision damage is found, their form and height above the ground are compared with injuries on the body and on the cycle. In a case of running over marks should also be sought on the under part of the car.

In order to do an effective investigation, adequate lighting is necessary, and a hoist or grease rack greatly facilitates the examination of the underside of the car. Standards of grease and dirt should be collected from various parts of the car for later comparison with contamination on the victim's clothing. Standards of paint should be removed from the damaged area, preserving all layers intact. It is not suitable to scrape fine shavings of paint, mixing the layers in a heterogeneous sample.

The suspect car and a 'stand-in' of the same bodily size as the victim should be photographed in the estimated position of collision. If the victim was on a bicycle or motorcycle, this should be shown in the situation picture.

Due recognition must be given to the fact that the suspect will try to minimize his responsibility by stating that he thought he had passed over a bump or hole in the road and failed completely to have any knowledge of the accident. Photographs of the scene will record any possible or impossible excuses for failing to note the presence and striking of the victim. Furthermore, the suspect may deliberately have a collision with an object such as a barricade in order to cover up previous damage, made when the victim was struck. From a careful examination of the suspect car, a series of contacts with objects may be reconstructed in their proper sequence.

MARKS OF VEHICLES

Vehicle marks are composed of tracks of wheels or of runners. In a particular case there may also be an indication of a particular type of load, for example, slipping branches in a load of wood, or ends of logs in a load of lumber, the smell of fuel oil or lubricating oil, etc.

With the aid of *wheel marks*, direction of movement can be determined. When the ground is damp the underlayer on which the wheel rolls forward is compressed, and the bottom of the mark is formed as a series of steps. The compressed clods of earth in the mark are lifted in the same direction as the wheel is rolling. To assist the memory in this respect it is easy to remember the rule: for the mark to become level again the wheel must roll in the opposite direction.

A vehicle which travels in a straight line actually leaves only the track of the rear wheels, and to observe marks of the front wheels it is necessary to

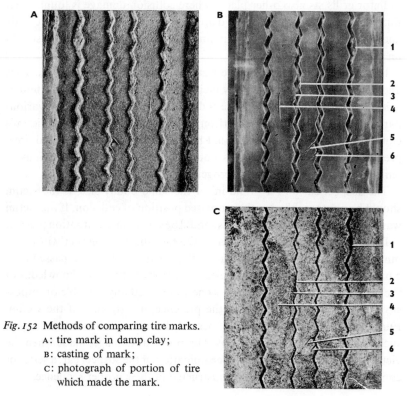

Fig. 152 Methods of comparing tire marks.
A: tire mark in damp clay;
B: casting of mark;
C: photograph of portion of tire which made the mark.

find some place where the vehicle has turned sharply or has reversed.

In examining wheel marks, places showing defects or repairs in the tires are looked for. With the aid of successive marks of this type the circumference of the tire can be determined. The track is measured between the center points of the two wheel marks.

Preservation is by photography and casting, selecting points showing characteristic marks or wear. When photographing, a foot rule is placed across the track and another along one side of it. Casting is done in the same way as for foot marks.

In examining vehicle marks, it should be noted whether wheels which follow one another go in the same track or whether there is any deviation. If dual wheels are found, both tread marks should be recorded simultaneously, since the relationship of one tread pattern to the other will provide additional characteristics for the identification of the vehicle.

Burglary. Early one morning a police constable, patrolling his beat on the outskirts of Edinburgh discovered that the front of a branch shop of a large dairy produce company had been forced open. The investigating officers found that the premises had been ransacked and that a large and heavy safe had been carried away by the intruders.

That a motor vehicle had been used to carry the safe away seemed probable and this theory was supported by the presence, on the footway outside the shop, of tire tracks which had been made by a motor car driven across the footway to the door of the shop. As the footway was of cinder ash covered with sand, the tire impressions were fairly clear. Measurements taken of the distance between the near and off-side tire tracks of the front and rear wheels showed that the width of the wheel base was 4 ft. 9 in. in each case. A cast of each tire impression was made in finest art plaster of Paris.

On examination of the casts of the tire tracks, it was found that the near-side front tire impression was that of a Dunlop Fort tire, the degree of wear being greater on the outside of the impression than on the inside. The casts of the tracks of the off-side front and rear tires showed that the tires were worn smooth in the middle, the edge pattern in each case corresponding with that of a Dunlop Fort tire. The cast of the track of the off-side rear tire was that of a Pirelli Wayfarer tire in good condition.

In the course of the investigation a certain convicted thief, who was known by the police to own a Hillman saloon car, became suspected of the crime. A rough inspection of his car showed that it was shod with tires of the same make as those of the car which had been used to commit the crime. The car was later driven over a stretch of firm sand and a plaster cast was made of each tire track. For comparative purposes, and to allow a more detailed examination being made, these casts were photographed along with those made at the scene of the crime.

The sequence of coincident detail which became apparent on comparison of the photographs of the casts of the four tires proved beyond doubt that the tire tracks found at the scene of the crime had been made by the Hillman car (MORREN, 1942).

Chapter 12   Death Investigation

General instructions for officers at the scene of a crime were outlined in the first two chapters, especially as they pertain to cases of homicide and suspicious deaths. To establish a definite procedure applicable to all crime scenes is impossible since no two cases are identical. However, the following sections will describe different procedures which are applicable to all types of death investigations, including suicide and sudden, unexpected death.

The general rule in investigating a death scene is that the investigator should show appropriate respect without allowing the effectiveness of his work to suffer. This rule applies especially when members of the victim's family are nearby and can observe and overhear the officers. Even ordinary police terminology or normal police practices may be interpreted as cynicism by a sensitive family member.

After the officer has begun the investigation and realized that a crime has been committed, he should attempt to find and recover *all* clues which may be used as evidence against the criminal. This includes items which at first sight might appear to be of no value. In cases of murder there is usually an abundance of clues, even when the murderer did his best in trying to obliterate them. Even when the murderer has carefully planned the crime and taken all imaginable precautions to avoid leaving traces, they are still found. As a rule, the murderer comes to a sudden realization of the terrible results of his deed after the killing. He may then lose his head completely and try to obliterate the evidence of his act, but in his confused state of mind only works against himself by leaving new clues.

The perfect murder, i.e. a premeditated killing where the murderer makes such arrangements as to make all aspects of the death look like an accident, is only possible in theory. Someone may object that many murders have been judged to be suicides or accidents, and murderers have gone free. However, such crimes cannot be considered perfect crimes; they are simply failures in bringing out evidence of deliberate killing.

In most cases it is not difficult to determine that a suspicious death is in fact a homicide. What is more difficult in many cases is to determine if the death is due to suicide or accident. The officer who is charged with the preliminary investigation of a suspicious death is therefore required to be thoroughly familiar with all aspects of homicide investigation. The initial analysis of the situation and the evaluation of the case requires at least as much knowledge as the subsequent investigation of the crime scene.

It is therefore not advisable to read the section on suicide investigation as a separate subject because it is closely related to the whole subject of death investigation.

The officer should further keep in mind that *if he judges a suicide to be murder, he has not committed a serious error*, even though the investigation becomes more extensive than is necessary. *However, if he has judged a murder to be suicide, he has not only failed in the investigation but may also have made the solution of the crime and the apprehension of the criminal more difficult, if not impossible.*

MURDER, SUICIDE OR ACCIDENT?

In evaluating whether a person died from accident or suicide, or if the death was caused by another person, it is always best to suspect the worst, namely murder. Even if the circumstances give an overwhelming impression of suicide or accident, they should be investigated in as much detail as possible. A clever muderer may very well arrange an accident, or make the death appear to be due to suicide. Such a murderer has every opportunity of arranging matters to deceive those who treat their task of investigating the circumstances too lightly. But a systematic and accurate investigation will reveal the homicidal intent.

When investigating cases of sudden death, the officer should as quickly as possible attempt to evaluate the circumstances revealed at the crime scene. The following questions must be answered immediately:
1. What are the causes of death? 2. Could the person himself have produced the injuries or brought about the effect which caused death? 3. Are there any signs of a struggle? 4. Where is the weapon, instrument or object which caused the injuries, or traces of the medium which caused death?

There are innumerable other questions which should be answered, but these are the most important ones for guiding the continued investigation.

The first two questions are treated later in the sections dealing with different causes of death.

Signs of struggle

If, at the scene of a death, there are found distinct signs of a struggle having taken place, the case may be put down right from the start as one of death by violence by the action of another person. In a room the signs of a struggle generally consist of bloodstains, torn-off hair, overturned or displaced articles of furniture, rumpled rugs, marks of weapons and injuries caused by the deceased defending himself.

Signs of a struggle show most clearly when an injured victim has retreated, or when he has attempted to avoid the attack of the criminal. From the visible signs, the course of events can usually be reconstructed accurately. Bloodstains can be considered the best clues for the reconstruction of the course of events in a case of murder. Generally no bloodstains are produced during the first stage of the attack, before bleeding has commenced. If the victim does not immediately become unconscious at the first blow, stab, cut or shot, it can nearly always be reckoned that his hands will become covered with blood from touching the injured parts of his body. If the victim tries to escape or to put up a resistance, his blood-covered hands leave marks which often indicate his position in certain situations. After a struggle in a furnished room a surprisingly large number of marks of blood-stained hands may be found on the legs of tables and chairs. A frequently occurring bloodstain is the typical one which comes from bloody hair. Such hair imprints in blood are often found on the *underside* of tables and chairs. Those who examine the scene of a crime should look very carefully for bloody imprints on doors (and especially keys, door handles and knobs), telephone, hung-up clothes, draperies, curtains, etc. If blood has spattered on a door, it is not sufficient to state on which side it is, but it is necessary to consider what the position of the door was when the blood was spattered against it, and from what direction it came.

Drops of spattered blood can give an indication of how far the drawer of a piece of furniture was pulled out, or whether the door of a closet, kitchen cupboard or other piece of furniture was open during a struggle. A specially important clue is a foot print in blood. Usually such a print is blurred and hardly suitable for identification, but it may be possible to decide whether it was made by the victim or by the criminal. One should not forget to draw down any roller blinds and to look for marks on them. The parts of the legs of tables and chairs which touch the floor should also be examined.

Torn-out hair which is found in a case of death from violence is a certain indication that a struggle has occurred. When found it should be recovered immediately, as it can easily disappear or alter its position, e.g. from a draft.

Overturned and displaced furniture gives a good idea of the direction in which a struggle proceeded, or the route by which the victim attempted to escape. Chairs, pedestals and other light pieces of furniture fall in the direction in which the struggling persons are moving. If there is reason to suspect that a criminal has righted overturned furniture, the articles should be examined for possible finger prints. A murderer is usually in such a state of mind after the deed that he does not consider the risk of leaving finger prints. When a print is found on a light piece of furniture its position should be examined carefully: a firm grip on a chair may give rise to the suspicion that the chair was used as a weapon. When heavy furniture has been displaced, the amount of force required to move it and the way in which this force must act, should be determined. Furniture placed irregularly often gives the impression that it has been displaced from its position. Marks of scraping indicate displacement, and the floor generally shows clearly whether furniture has stood in the same place previously.

Rumpled rugs often provide signs of a struggle, while marks of sliding on the floor sometimes form a useful guide. The victim of a murder who defends himself in a lying position may kick against a wall, the floor or furniture, and the shoes then leave marks of shoe polish, dirt and rubber scrapings. Such marks should also be looked for on the undersides of the furniture.

Marks of weapons may occur, e.g. when an axe is swung and scrapes a ceiling or slips along a piece of furniture, or when the victim avoids the blow and the weapon hits the wall, floor or furniture instead. In the case of a murder with an axe or similar weapon a frequently-occurring mark is one which is formed on walls when the criminal swung the weapon back and up before striking. A bloodstained weapon may leave a bloodstain at a place where it was laid down or dropped. If it is wiped on, for example, a handkerchief, the edge or head may leave a print in blood. Among the indications of weapons are also included the presence of cartridges, cartridge cases, bullets and bullet holes.

Defense injuries are a fairly certain indication that there has been a fight. In cases of suicide and accidental death marks are often found which at first sight appear to be marks of a struggle. A person weary of life may have taken a number of measures at various places to shorten his life. In a state of confusion he may overturn or move furniture and also leave blood and other marks which at first cause suspicion. A careful investigation of the scene, however, always gives a clear picture of the true course of events.

In cases of death by violence outdoors, signs of a struggle are in general not so distinct as indoors. If a fight preceded the murder, the ground will be trampled. When foot marks made with shoes of different size and appearance are found, this must be considered as evidence of a fight, and similarly if the marks have the form which results from the feet being set down obliquely against the ground. At the scene of a suicide, especially in a case of hanging, the ground may be trampled, but as a rule the marks have a normal appearance as of a person walking. Other signs of a struggle out of doors may be bloodstains, torn-off tufts of hair, marks of weapons and resistance injuries. Broken-off twigs, trampled leaves, torn-up moss and grass, foot prints at places which a person would normally avoid, etc., can also be considered as signs of a struggle.

In cases of death by violence the cause of death must be decided as soon as possible, so that the weapon, tool, instrument or other lethal object may be searched for. The absence of a weapon or instrument at the scene indicates murder. If the weapon or instrument has been found then the analysis of the situation must give a preliminary decision as to whether it is a case of murder or suicide. In searching for a weapon, nothing should be moved or altered at the scene of the incident, and if there is danger that clues may be destroyed in the search then the search must be postponed. If the weapon is found it should be photographed and described in the position in which it lies. A pathologist should always be consulted when it is required to determine of an object can be considered a dangerous weapon.

EXAMINATION OF A DEAD BODY

Before examining a dead body the police officer should consider all the precautions which he should take during the course of the work. A careless move – even one so slight as undoing a button or lifting a flap of a garment – may subsequently prove a great mistake. An example is on record of a police officer, in misdirected zeal, proceeding so far with the examination of a dead body that he attempted to determine the track of a bullet and depth it had penetrated into a body by probing the wound with a pencil. Such measures are entirely misguided. When clothes are found on the body they must be examined at the same time as the body, but if no pathologist is present the examination should only include the visible parts. Their position and state should be described in the report, including, among other matters, how they are buttoned or attached, creases and wrinkles, injuries, stains, etc.

The position of the clothes, for example how far the trousers are pulled up, whether garments are twisted sideways or pulled down or even inside out, may be of great importance. Any displacement from the normal position is measured. Buttoning and other fastenings, e.g. zippers, safety pins, cases, etc., are described. Unbuttoned or torn-out buttons are indicated, as also buttonholes.

Folds in the clothes should be examined, especially on the lower parts of the body. The report should indicate whether the folds go horizontally or vertically, or if they have resulted from crumpling of the garment. When a body is dragged along horizontal creases occur which are dirty on the outside but clean in the folds. When a body is lifted or moved by a grip on the clothing characteristic formations are produced. If the raised part of a fold is bloodstained but the inner part is free from blood, then the position of a part of the body when violence was exerted can be determined with certainty. If a garment is bloodstained and on the inside of the bloodstain there are sharply limited clean areas, then the fold formation can be reconstructed.

Injuries to the clothes occur from tearing, crushing, cutting or penetration by edged weapons, axe blows, etc. The damage is measured, and the report should contain statements of the kind, position, size and manner of occurrence of the damage. In pertinent cases the damage to the clothes should, during the autopsy, be compared with the position of corresponding wounds on the body. In this way important information can be obtained regarding a particular body position when the injury was inflicted.

Stains may consist of blood, semen, saliva, phlegm, vomit, feces, urine or other liquid or also of dust, dirt or other contamination. They are described with reference to type, location, size and, in pertinent cases, direction of flow. If liquid stains go through clothing material it is necessary to determine from which side the liquid has penetrated.

In describing blood marks on a dead body the terms generally used are bloodstain, blood smear, blood spatter and stains from dropping blood. Bloodstain means marks containing a lot of blood, which occur either from direct bleeding or when, for example, a garment is soaked in an accumulation of blood. Blood smear means a mark with a smaller amount of blood, and can occur when a bloodstained object brushes against or touches something. A special form of blood mark is a finger print in blood. (See 'Finger prints and palm prints').

From stains of blood, saliva, phlegm, vomit, urine or other liquid on a dead body, important information can be obtained if the direction of flow is observed. Especially streams of blood can contribute to the reconstruction of events in a case of death by violence. All marks of blood flowing 'in the wrong direction' are examined and photographed.

Mauslaughter. Seaman A was shot dead by seaman B on a naval ship. B stated that at the time A was lying in a hammock. B had intended to hand a pistol over to A but dropped it: he had caught it in its fall, but for some reason a shot had been fired and hit A. The injured man was taken to the sick bay but died on the way. On investigation it was found that B's statement could not be true and that the fatal shot had been fired under quite different conditions. An autopsy showed that the flow of blood was in such a direction that A could be supposed to have received the shot in a standing or sitting position. When this was pointed out to B, he realized that his position was so untenable and dangerous that he admitted the actual course of events. In the belief that, in accordance with regulations, there was no cartridge in the chamber, he had jokingly fired against A lying in his hammock. Unfortunately there was a cartridge in the chamber, and a shot was fired. Regarding the flow of blood, it was confirmed that the injured man had been carried to the deck of the vessel in a vertical position, so that blood flowed down the body from the wound.

A special form of blood mark is the appearance of blood froth. When a person continues to breathe after blood has penetrated the air passages, a thick froth is formed which can become so extensive that if the face is turned upwards it comes out of the mouth and nasal passages in the form of billowing foam which can be several inches thick. Frothing can also occur on putrefied bodies when gases create foam in the decomposition fluids.

Occasionally there occurs a case of murder in which the criminal wipes or washes the blood away from his victim. Such cleaning is generally easy to detect, especially when the skin is clean and white around the wound.

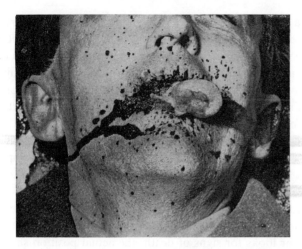

Fig. 153 Blood froth caused by breathing after blood has penetrated the lungs. Owing to its viscosity the blood has formed a mass of froth.

Washing or wiping the hands generally leaves a thin rim of blood on the nails near the cuticles. When the blood has coagulated, small rolls of blood and dirt are often formed and penetrate cracks and hollows of the skin. If blood has been washed from the head, this fact is often easily detected by the traces of blood which remain in ears, nostrils and hair. Moisture around the body may also reveal washing with water.

In connection with the occurrence of blood at the scene of a crime, some attempt should always be made to estimate the amount. If blood has flowed out on to an absorbing layer the depth of penetration should be determined. Floorboards should be lifted.

Murder. A woman was found lying dead outdoors, with her head partly shattered by a number of axe blows, from which it could be assumed that most of the blood had been lost from the body. Under the head of the dead woman there was actually found only a small amount of blood, possibly a half a pint. From this it appeared that the woman had not been murdered at the place where she lay. On further investigation the lost blood was found at a place about a quarter of a mile from the body. It was found that the woman had been murdered here and that the body had then been transported to the place where it was found. If the small amount of blood at the place where the body was found had not been noticed it is possible that that place would have been considered the scene of the crime and investigated as such, while the actual scene of the crime would never have been known. Investigation of the latter produced evidence against a local suspect who later confessed the crime.

In examining a dead body it is generally possible to take the necessary steps in a certain order, which is a guarantee that nothing will be forgotten or neglected. The various steps in an investigation, when a pathologist is present, are described below. When the pathologist does not arrive in time, the investigation is carried out in the same way, but the investigator must reconsider his moves so that the clues which only a medical expert is capable of judging and investigating are protected as much as possible.

The first measure which should be taken without delay is to confirm the appearance of signs of certain death, of which the type and development, and the time of their confirmation, should be noted in the report.

The body is then photographed. Preferably all photographing should be completed before the position of the body is altered. If for some reason a change has been made after it was discovered, e.g. when relatives cover it up or the doctor looks for signs of death, the actual position should be photographed first, and then the original position is reconstructed and photographed. The camera should thereafter be held in readiness for additional pictures during the course of the examination.

A preliminary investigation of the pockets of the dead person may precede the more detailed investigation only when it is considered absolutely necessary. This is to be avoided if possible, but it may be necessary to confirm quickly whether there are in the pockets any identification documents, wallet, purse, watch or other valuable articles. This examination must be done so carefully that the original position of the clothes can easily be restored later. *It should be noted whether the pockets are turned inside out* – this may show that they have been examined earlier.

A preliminary sketch of the position of the body is made. In view of the fact that the position will have to be altered by degrees, marks are made at certain places on the floor, e.g. at the top point of the head, ears, elbows, hands, crotch, knees, heels and points of the toes, and these points are measured on sketches. The whole of the outer contour of the body may be marked with a continuous chalk line. If the body lies on some loose base, its position should be marked in a similar manner. If later, when the body has been removed, it is found that the original position has to be reconstructed, then it can be done easily with the aid of the chalk outline.

Manslaughter. An apartment which had been the scene of a killing had been routinely examined at the time of the crime. Three weeks later it became necessary to reconstruct the crime, but the apartment was already cleaned and vacated. The furniture was then moved back into the apartment. The linoleum floor had been washed but traces of the original chalk outlines could still be discerned. A reliable reconstruction was eventually effected, partly by using the chalk marks and partly by the measurements which had been made on a rough sketch at the time of the original investigation.

The position of the body is next described briefly, without any details. The position of the body in relation to the nearest article of furniture, object or fixed point is measured and noted. Then the visible clothing is described, without details.

The next step is the detailed examination. Only visible details are examined and described. The original position must not be changed. It is preferable to describe the head, then the trunk, arms and finally the legs.

The head is described and examined in relation to its position with respect to the body, whether the eyes and mouth are open, color of the skin, injuries, presence of blood, state of the hair, presence of saliva, phlegm and vomit and foreign bodies (soil, sand, vegetable matter, hair, etc.). The direction of flow of liquids is easily determined on the skin of the face and should therefore be noted.

In examining the trunk, note should be made of its position, any bending or twisting, the position of visible clothing and its condition, folds, injuries to the body and clothes, presence of blood, saliva, semen, phlegm, vomit and foreign bodies (especially hair).

Then the arms, and finally the legs, are examined in the same way as the trunk. The hands should be given special attention. The presence of rings, jewelry or wrist watch or marks left by these objects should be noted. Foreign objects are examined, especially fragments of hair or skin under the nails. The dirt from the nails should be collected. If a detailed examination of the hands cannot be made on the spot, the hands should be enclosed in clean paper bags which are tied securely at the wrists. When examining the legs, the distance between the knees and between the heels should be measured. Special attention should be given to the soles of the feet or shoes with respect to the presence of blood or other material in which the person may have stepped.

After the examination of the visible parts of the body the police officer should attempt to visualize the course of events as deduced from his observations. He should not rely merely on his own judgment but also listen to the opinions of others, especially the pathologist. From a number of opinions it is often possible to get a good reconstruction of the events.

The underside of the body and those portions which are covered by clothes should *not* be examined at the scene, unless it is done in the presence of the pathologist and at his request. Normally the body will not be turned over or undressed until the time of the autopsy. However, after the body has been photographed and described in all pertinent detail and has been lifted onto a stretcher, the area under the body should be examined. A critical piece of evidence may have been hidden under the body, perhaps in a large pool of blood. Bullets, or fragments of bullets, sometimes penetrate a body completely but are stopped by clothing. The projectile may thus roll out of the clothing of the victim and may even be overlooked, unless great care is exercised in lifting and transportation. The relationship between the location of injuries and bloodstains on the floor should also be established.

The body should be transported in the position in which it was found, if possible. If necessary, the clothing can be fixed in its original position by means of pins. In appropriate cases the body should be moved on a clean sheet of cotton or plastic or on an undertaker's impregnated paper sheet. This is partly to protect the body from contamination and partly to prevent minute evidence from being lost.

An officer should accompany the body to the hospital, morgue, or other place where the autopsy is to take place.

THE AUTOPSY

The investigator who examined the body at the scene should also be present at the autopsy. His presence is usually desired by the pathologist so that he can assist in the removal of clothing and inform the pathologist of pertinent findings at the crime scene and other circumstances which may be of value to the examination.

At the autopsy it is the pathologist who is responsible for the final examination of the clothes. However, the officer should take every opportunity of making tactful suggestions as to the proper preservation of evidence in those cases where the autopsy surgeon is not an experienced medicolegal pathologist.

In those cases where the body was removed from the scene before arrival of the investigators, the body should be photographed, both clothed and unclothed, as described in the preceding section. In many instances it is necessary for the police investigators to make the complete pictorial record of the body and its injuries. It is generally only the large and well equipped medical examiners and coroner's offices which routinely take the required photographs. The crime scene investigator should further take advantage of the opportunity to photograph the body under conditions far superior to those at the crime scene. The body is elevated on the examination table, and the photographer can make precise arrangements of camera and lighting for close-up photographs. All pertinent injuries should be photographed close up, with a scale included in the field. Internal or external injuries which are considered pertinent by the pathologist should also be photographed.

Suggestions made in Chapter 4 regarding color photography apply especially to injuries on a body. The nature of abrasions, bullet wounds, etc. is more faithfully reproduced in color than in black and white.

The actual recovery of evidence from the body is normally done by the pathologist with the assistance of the investigator. Local conditions, mainly the medico-legal skill and experience of the pathologist will determine the specific procedure to be followed. On the one hand, an experienced medical examiner's pathologist knows the requirements of the investigators and the crime laboratory and can be relied on to recover the pertinent evidence properly; on the other hand, a hospital pathologist in another locality may be performing his first autopsy in a police case and needs considerable guidance in evidence recovery.

Clothing should be removed from the body in the usual way, if possible, and *should not be cut*. When garments have to be cut, great care should be taken not to cut near stains, tears, knife cuts and bullet holes. Each garment should be placed in individual paper bags which should be marked for identification. A convenient way to mark clothing for identification is to affix tags which have a wire and a lead seal.

Garments which bear wet bloodstains should be hung up to dry before wrapping.

It is the investigator's responsibility to take inked finger and palm prints of the body whenever the morgue technicians do not perform this task as a matter of routine. He should also search the skin of the body for possible bloody finger prints of the assailant. The investigator should also take fingernail scrapings from all homicide victims. Before undertaking any manipulation on the body, the investigator should ask the pathologist if it is convenient so as not to interfere with the performance of the autopsy.

The taking of hair and blood samples is the task of the pathologist, but the officer may need to remind him of this requirement, particularly if the doctor is not experienced in police matters. *Hair and blood samples should be taken of all homicide victims.* There have been instances where this important point was overlooked, and the body had been buried before someone realized that the samples would be necessary.

DETAILED EXAMINATION OF THE SCENE OF THE CRIME

After the preliminary investigation has shown that death was caused by the intent or agency of some other person, or by suicide or accident, the detailed investigation can begin. How thoroughly this is to be done must be decided for each particular case. In suicide or accidental death, the detailed examination can be limited simply to those matters which appear to be directly related to events. If the death is caused by the intent or action of another person everything should be investigated, even in cases where the criminal has been arrested immediately after the crime and has confessed. In such cases the investigation should decide whether the statements of the criminal are consistent. In his first statement a criminal often makes consciously incorrect statements about his actions in order to create extenuating circumstances. Those who investigate the scene of a crime have an opportunity of producing such an accurate reconstruction of the actual course of events that such an attempt by the criminal cannot succeed. When the examination of the body has been concluded, the body can generally be removed for the autopsy. Photographing the scene of the crime should have been completed before this. Before the body is taken away, the places at the scene where ambulance personnel have to walk should be examined for such clues as might be destroyed, including the presence of blood. Even if the body is well wrapped up, drops of blood may fall from it as the result of unforeseen circumstances. Such marks can cause much unnecessary work for the investigators later. Those who carry away the body should be warned not to step in any blood.

As a rule the investigation can then be continued, with attention to such details or places where anything of significance might be expected. Then follows a methodically planned examination of the scene of the crime as a whole; this being the basis for the report of the investigation. It is started at a suitable point, and everything is inspected in such a way and in such an order that nothing is forgotten. It may be convenient first to examine and describe the entrance, doors, and lock arrangements. Then follows a description of the room as a whole without going into details. The length, width, height to ceiling, windows, doors, floor covering, paint of walls and ceiling, color of wallpaper, lighting conditions, etc. should be described. Following this the room is described in detail and investigated in a certain order commencing from the entrance or from the place of death. Everything must be examined and described as a coherent whole. If, for example, a writing desk is examined then there follows a description of the nearby parts of the floor and walls and also of the surface of the floor under the piece of furniture. As a rule it is best for the ceiling to be described and examined last and as a whole. If for some reason a place has been examined in detail and described earlier, then a reference to it is put in the notes to facilitate the writing of the final report.

In the investigation everything is noted, even if it appears to have no significance in the case. Such unessential details are sorted out when the report is written up, as also similar details which appeared to be important at first but were later found to be immaterial. The notes made at the scene of a crime must not under any circumstances be thrown away but should be placed in the file and kept with the records. Experience shows that such rough notes may be of great importance at some future date if the investigator is required to prove that he has not omitted to examine certain details.

It is convenient to develop and preserve finger and palm prints at the same time as the final detailed investigations. As far as possible everything should be put back into its original position. When furniture is moved, it should be replaced with the greatest accuracy because the scene must be in its original state in case of any hearings in the presence of witnesses or suspect at the scene of the crime. Before any furniture is moved, a chalk mark should be made around the legs or other suitable parts. Objects placed on furniture can be treated similarly.

A final important step is measurement, prior to sketching the scene of the crime. It is desirable that this should have been done earlier, but this may not have been possible, for there is a risk that those who do the measuring may destroy clues which have not yet been discovered, or that they may produce fresh and misleading clues. One method which can be used is to have a preliminary sketch made as early as possible. Gradually, as the investigation proceeds, and before each object is moved, measurements are made and the results are put down on the sketch. This method is, however, somewhat inconvenient, since the measuring cannot be done as systematically as is desirable. Under such conditions even experienced sketchers can easily forget important measurements.

When there has been a shooting at the scene of the crime, weapons, cartridges, cartridge cases and bullets are looked for. If a weapon is found, it is photographed at that spot, and a chalk line is drawn around it before it is moved. Finger prints are recorded before the weapon is examined. In cases of presumed suicide it is necessary to check whether the weapon lies in a place to which it might have either dropped or slid. The base on which the weapon lies should always be examined. A dropped or thrown weapon generally leaves a mark, e.g. a scratch or dent in the furniture or floor, and the absence of such marks should be considered as suspicious.

When cartridge cases are found, their position should be noted in the report and on the sketch, and they are then placed in an envelope which is marked as to the place of finding. Bullets and bullet holes are examined. The place from which the shot was fired can be determined quite accurately from the direction of the bullet penetration – a string being stretched along the calculated path of the bullet. The reconstruction is then photographed. A bullet which has buried itself in a wall is cut out, but great care must be used so that *the bullet is not touched by the tool used*. In cases of suicide it can happen that the suicide may fire one or more trial shots before he directs the weapon against himself.

Below is an enumeration of certain details which should be examined where appropriate. It consists partly of those of such a changeable nature that the examination must be done immediately or as soon as possible, and partly of those which have been found to be easily forgotten or passed over even by an experienced investigator.

On stairs, passages and entries to the scene, together with streets, passages and yards in the immediate vicinity: bloodstains; finger prints on railings; objects which the criminal has dropped or thrown away; illumination; if there is an elevator, the elevator shaft should be examined; clues in wastepaper basket or trash cans.

Outer doors: bolted; locked; marks of breaking in; does the doorbell work.

Windows: bolted; position of window catch; marks of breaking in, possibility of seeing in; position of curtains and blinds; are there indications of marks outside the windows.

Mailbox: date on mail or papers; are they in the right order of time. *Other papers and mail, daily milk supplies, etc. at the scene of the crime;* date marks; have the letters been opened; do the papers give the impression of having been read. Number of milk bottles.

Inside doors: bolted; locked; on which side was the key.

Hall, entrance: presence of clothing and objects which do not belong to the place and to residents there, especially outer garments, headgear, scarves, gloves, galoshes, umbrellas.

Lighting: which lamps were on when the crime was discovered; gas burners, gas meter and electricity meter readings.

Heating conditions: is there any fire or embers in stove or fireplace; any remaining heat in them; is there still heat in the gas oven, gas burner, or food and drink in preparation.

Fireplaces: do not forget to examine ash and burned residues.

Smell: gas; gunpowder; strong tobacco fumes; alcohol; perfume.

Clocks and watches: are they running and showing the right time; when did they stop; time set on alarm clock.

Signs of a party: how many bottles; labels on them; contents (not always as label); are seals or corks on or in the bottles; how many glasses or cups of different kinds; contents, residue or odor in them; spilled liquor; overturned objects; have cigarette butts and matchsticks been thrown on table or floor; how many persons were set for; what dishes; are there any finger prints.

Contents of ash trays: remains of smoked tobacco; brand marks on cigarette butts; way in which they have been extinguished; marks of lipstick; burned matches.

Drawers and compartments in writing desks, cabinets or other furniture: shut; locked; in which drawer is the key; drawers pulled out or taken away; objects taken out; are there signs of disorder such as might result from a hurried search; are cash, bank books and objects of value exposed in a conspicuous or easily detected place.

Paper baskets, trash cans: any object thrown there by the criminal; torn letters.

Kitchen, bathroom, toilet: are towels, rags, etc. damp or do they show bloodstains; are there bloodstains on draining board, bath, washstand, toilet or buckets; are there objects or suspicious liquids in watertrap or toilet.

Privies: is there, in the outer layer of excrement, any object pushed in or concealed in some other way (knowing the disinclination of police officers to examine such places, the criminal may have concealed a weapon or other there); remember that finger prints may be found on the paper used.

Compost heaps, manure heaps: these are very convenient for concealing objects without leaving distinct signs of digging.

General disorder: is this typical of violent happenings or a struggle; can it result from lack of cleaning up over a long period, or incidentally, for example, in carrying out ordinary household operations, etc.

Damage to ceiling, walls and furniture: investigate how it could have occurred in connection with the crime: marks of plaster or paint soon disappear from the floor due to trampling.

Shooting: the investigating officer should either be able to account for the actual number of bullets fired together with a corresponding number of cartridge cases, or give a good explanation of why they are not found or cannot be found in the correct number (consider the possibility of a cartridge case getting caught up in the clothes of the dead man and not being found before the autopsy).

Hanging and strangling: quick confirmation of whether the cord used was taken from the scene or locality.

Hiding places for weapons or objects which the criminal wished to conceal quickly: some of the places which are most often forgotten by the investigating police officer are locations above a stove and high furniture or between these and the wall, behind books in a bookcase, in the coal or wood bin, amongst bedclothes in a bed, behind heating elements and on high shelves in wardrobe, pantry and kitchen cupboard.

Garments taken off: at what places; in what order reckoned from top; turned right side out or inside out; properly hung up or in disorder.

Suicide note: is it in the handwriting of the suicide; has the pen been found; has indented writing come through onto other paper underneath; is there more than one note; are there finger prints of persons other than the deceased.

When the investigation has been concluded, the scene of the crime, in every case of serious crime, should be kept intact until the final report has been written and read through by the superior officer concerned and by the prosecutor, recovered evidence has been examined, and the post-mortem examination has been completed. When material which is recovered for examination has value as evidence, it should be preserved even after the criminal has been tried. There may be a review of the case perhaps several years later, and the evidence may then have to be produced.

EXAMINATION OF OUTDOOR SCENES

The examination of a crime scene located outdoors must be planned quickly and be carried out as soon as possible. Changes in weather conditions may completely jeopardize the chances of finding the evidence which is there. A number of different clues which are easily detected at first may disappear in a very short time, for example by precipitation, drying, vegetation, flood conditions, etc. It is even more difficult to examine such a scene at night.

Bloodstains on grass change their color rapidly so that they are difficult to detect. A brief shower may completely wash away smaller stains. Other biological evidence, such as hair, seminal fluid, urine, feces, vomit, saliva, nasal secretions, skin fragments, brain substance, etc. are quickly changed by drying or being washed away. During the time of year when insects are particularly plentiful, biological evidence may be destroyed by their action. The path of a person through dewy grass may be discernible to the naked eye, but even after an hour or so of direct sunlight the dew is dry and the grass has recovered its original shape. It may subsequently take hours be-

Fig. 154 The central crime scene roped off and a single access path marked by stakes and rope.

Fig. 155 Systematic division of crime scene search area into convenient plots. Plots may be searched in succession or assigned to members of the search team. After completion of search, absence as well as presence of evidence may have significance.

fore this track can be followed. Foot prints and tire marks should therefore be protected and recorded as soon as possible.

When a shooting has taken place outdoors, the direction of firing must be determined quickly. A bullet's path through foliage, bushes or hedges is usually marked by fresh twigs and leaves which have fallen to the ground. Already after a few hours these traces may have taken on the appearance of the surroundings. It may thus take hours to establish the direction of firing from these clues. Evidence of a bullet striking the ground is usually found in the form of dirt or sand thrown over the surrounding vegetation. A quick shower may wash off these traces and make the location of the impact impossible to find. Cartridge cases run the risk of being trampled into the ground.

The crime scene must be effectively roped off, and the investigating officer must follow a definite plan of action. Experience has shown that most of the evidence found at crime scenes outdoors was put there by officers who carelessly and aimlessly wandered around the area.

In cases of suspicious death the officers can expect that the person, or persons, who discovered the body did not enter the scene with caution – which is to be expected. One of the first duties of the crime scene investigator is therefore to find out where those persons walked. The record of many cases has shown that clues created by these citizens have caused a tremendous amount of unnecessary work which could have been avoided if the persons had been properly interviewed.

In making up a plan of action, the officers should decide on a path to be used in going to and from the body. Since this path will be used frequently it may suitably be marked with stakes. The examination of the body then follows according to the outline given earlier in this chapter. Before too much attention is given the body, the ground around the body should be carefully examined. A second chance will hardly be available after a number of persons have looked at the body and trampled the area.

The area surrounding the central scene should then be examined. The investigator must try to remember his own tracks so that he can distinguish them from others which he may discover. On snow-covered ground this is easily accomplished by the investigator dragging his feet so that his own tracks become distinctive.

Insofar as possible, one should avoid examining outdoor crime scenes at night. This rule should be followed even where suitable illumination is available. Most clues at outdoor scenes consist of minor changes in the ground cover, such as matted grass, torn moss, broken twigs, indistinct foot prints, etc. Such tracks may be visible from several yards away in daylight, but are almost impossible to detect at night, even with powerful illumination. If a scene is viewed at night and an estimate made of the topography, one might find in daylight that the picture is quite different from that seen at night. Since it is difficult to survey the scene and to correctly interpret even gross evidence it follows that it is even more difficult to find clues as small as bloodstains, fragments of cloth, fibers, etc. Such clues may be overlooked or destroyed if a thorough examination is attempted in darkness.

Prevailing weather conditions or expected weather changes play an important role in deciding whether to postpone the examination until daylight. If there is a chance of snow, the examination must be started – even though important evidence may be destroyed. Other weather conditions may, depending on the type of crime involved, also have a certain influence. If snow should fall before the examination is completed, some evidence may be covered and not retrieved until the snow has melted.

Whenever the examination must be done immediately, it is better to refrain from recovering the evidence and instead cover it with tarpaulins, boxes, etc. and then wait for daylight for the completion of the examination.

Before the arrival of daylight certain precautions should be taken. Some flash exposures should be taken of the body. The body should then be covered with a clean sheet over which is laid a tarpaulin in order to keep out dust, leaves, etc. If the body is suspended, the noose may break, and it is advisable to secure the body with a rope tied loosely around the chest. If the body is on the shore line, it should be lifted far enough onto the beach so that swells will not make changes on the body.

In taking the photographs and the precautionary measures the officers should not walk around aimlessly. As described above, a path should be selected and marked with stakes.

The investigator should, of course, make note of changes which may take place on the body, such as signs of death, moisture of the clothing and under the body, and so on.

EXAMINATION OF A LOCATION WHERE A BODY HAS BEEN FOUND

When a homicide victim has been moved from the actual crime scene and hidden at another location, conditions are somewhat different. Although the examination of such places is generally carried out in the same way as crime scenes, a reliable reconstruction of the crime is usually not possible. Such places normally do not yield as many clues to the criminal as the place of attack.

The question often arises as to how long the body has been lying at the place where it was found. The vegetation and other conditions surrounding the body may give some indications. (See 'Signs and time of death').

The path over which the body was transported should be established at the outset. This detail should be attended to immediately, especially when there is risk of precipitation. If the criminal's foot prints are not clear enough, his path should be estimated as that most easily traversed if someone were carrying a body. Even when there are no foot prints, there may be other signs, such as trampled grass, stains of dripping blood, marks from dragging, broken twigs, etc. If the criminal left the scene by another route, this path should also be examined in due time.

The body should be examined as described under 'Examination of a dead body'. Dust, dirt and other traces on the skin and clothing which might point to the scene of the crime should be recovered. A preliminary evaluation of such traces may suggest leads for the search for the actual scene. In removing the dead body from the place where found, it should be placed on a clean plastic sheet or bed sheet which is wrapped around the body. Plastic bags used by morticians are useful for this purpose. Blankets and tarpaulins should not be used because one can never be sure that they are absolutely clean. Since it is almost impossible to examine properly and recover traces on the body it should be transported intact to the place for the autopsy where the detailed examination can take place.

After the body has been removed, the area underneath the body should be examined. The amount of blood and body fluids should be estimated. It should also be determined how deeply into the ground such fluids have penetrated. If the murder weapon could reasonably be expected to be found in the area, a search for it should be started. If the body was covered with branches, straw, etc. it should be examined for the possibility that the criminal may have dropped something while engaged in covering the body.

SIGNS AND TIME OF DEATH

In cases of murder, suicide or suspicious death, determination of the time of occurrence of death is of the greatest importance. The most reliable information of the time usually comes from the police investigation, but the result obtained from this must be completed or supplemented by the evidence of time obtained from the pathological examination and the observations made at the scene of the death. It often happens, however, that the time must be based solely on the results of the pathological examination and investigation of the scene.

As a rule it is reckoned that death occurs when the breathing ceases, the heart no longer beats and the pulse cannot be detected. These changes in vital functions cannot, however, be considered as certain signs of death, but the following are unquestionable signs of death: 1. changes in the eyes, 2. coldness of the body, 3. rigidity of the body, 4. livid stains on the body, and 5. signs of putrefaction.

Where there is some delay through a doctor not being able to attend at once, the police officer himself can establish that the person is dead without the risk of making a serious mistake. Livid stains on the body and indications of putrefaction are certain signs which can hardly be mistaken. Regarding mere stiffness of the limbs, there is a possibility of doubt. A police officer who has had sufficient experience in investigating cases of death should himself be able to decide whether full rigidity should be regarded as a certain sign of death or not. Where the only signs are coldness of the body and changes in the eyes, the police officer should not judge these as certain signs of death, and the supposed dead person should then be treated in the same way as a sick or injured person. It should be mentioned that in many cases of electrocution and shock (vagal) deaths, life is in fact still present. Under all conditions the police officer who is confronted with a dead body should remember that the investigation of the matter can be completely ruined if he allows the body to be moved, if in fact death has not supervened.

Changes in the eyes

After death a decrease in the liquid in the body occurs which becomes noticeable in the eyes, among other parts; the cornea becomes turbid and dull, while the eyeballs become less firm and sink in their sockets. If a doctor does not arrive within a reasonable time, and it is necessary for the police officer himself to investigate whether the vital functions have ceased in a supposedly dead person, he can determine this with the aid of the corneal reflexes. If the cornea is touched and there is no reaction, it can be stated with a high degree of probability that death has occurred.

Coldness of the body

This is shown by a drop in the body temperature, and the body feels cold after 8 to 12 hours. The temperature of the surrounding air, water or other material may be attained after 18 to 20 hours. The speed of cooling also depends on the amount of flesh and covering on the body. In cases of death from strokes, brain injury, strangulation and heatstroke a brief rise of temperature may precede death and affect the cooling of the body. The temperature of a body is best estimated by the police officer in the armpits. Of great value is of course a measurement of the temperature (but not with a climatical thermometer). At autopsy this is to be done within the abdomen. In cases where a sexual assault is suspected the vagina and perhaps the rectum must be avoided. When measuring the temperature of a body at the scene the clothing should be disturbed as little as possible.

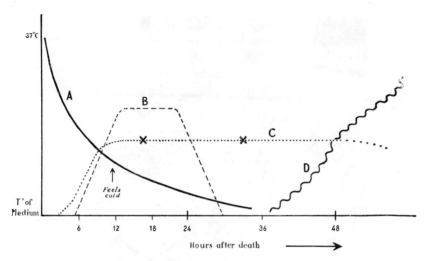

Fig. 156 Diagram showing changes undergone by body relative to time elapsed from death. A: body temperature; B: rigidity of body. It falls away after 24 hours; C: the appearance of lividity; D: decomposition (*Keith Simpson*).

Rigidity of the body

This is caused by a process of coagulation in the muscles, which contract and stiffen, so that the body becomes rigid, and the limbs can be moved only by the application of force. Generally rigidity is noticed first in the muscles of the neck and jaw, where it appears one to one and a half hours after death, after which it proceeds downwards in the body, generally appearing earlier in the legs than in the arms. It may be assumed that rigidity is complete in 6 to 7 hours after death, and usually it remains for two to three days and then disappears.

If the time which has elapsed since death is not too long and the doctor has an opportunity of observing the onset of rigidity, important information may be obtained regarding the time of death. If, after the doctor breaks the rigidity in a limb, it reappears, this may be taken as proof that not more than seven hours have elapsed since death occurred. In cases where a doctor cannot arrive within a reasonable time, the police officer can perform the test himself, but the result must later be confirmed by a pathologist.

In certain cases of death by violence rigidity may appear very early and

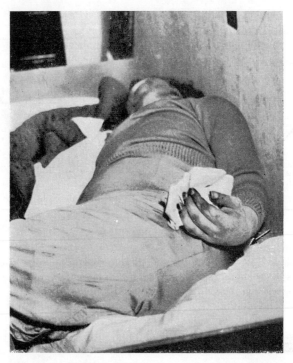

Fig. 157 Changes in the original position of a body may be detected by observing the rigidity. The woman was sitting supported on her left hand at the time of death. After the onset of rigidity, the position of the body was changed, and the left hand became raised above the bed in an unnatural position.

can be specially intense. This may be the case with death from injury to the spinal cord, heatstroke, lightning, carbon monoxide and strychnine poisoning, and also after burning. When a person has died under such conditions, the body appears curiously hunched up, which is generally called 'pugilistic attitude'. In cases of death during muscular strain, e.g. in states of cramp, rigidity of the body may appear very quickly and be very pronounced. With children and well-rested persons rigidity comes on quite slowly and is not so intense.

Livid stains on the body

In cases where it is not possible for a medical expert to examine a body, the police officer can give the doctor important, and possibly decisive, indications from his own observations of the occurrence of livid stains (lividity), which are the earliest indication that the action of the heart has stopped. After death the blood sinks to the lowest parts of the body, where it forms blue or reddish-violet marks on the skin; in cases of poisoning by carbon monoxide and cyanide the marks are light red; and in poisoning by potassium chlorate light brown. Before the onset of putrefaction the livid stains acquire a brownish color. The black and blue marks of bruising can easily be confused with livid stains, and only autopsy can identify such discolorations of the skin. The first indication of lividity may appear half an hour after death; after 3 to 4 hours they are fully developed and from then on become progressively more conspicuous. Under certain conditions the livid stains can move or change if the body is moved or its position is changed, but not if the body rolls in water. They are not formed on the parts of the body which are exposed to greater pressure, for example those parts which lie against the floor. If the position of a body, or the position of articles of clothing pressing on it, is changed within a period of about 3 hours after the occurrence of death the original livid stains may

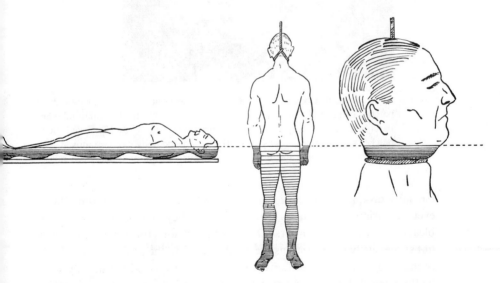

Fig. 158 The distribution of lividity in different positions. After death the blood settles in the lowest parts of the body and appears as reddish or bluish-purple discoloration. If the flow of the blood is restricted, e.g. by a noose, the livid stains will appear immediately above the ligature.

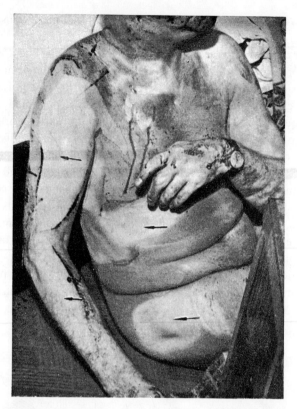

Fig. 159 Appearance of a body which has lain on the right side – the arrows show patches of normal skin color which have resisted the livid staining of other parts of body due to pressure on the flesh where the body has rested. Such patches are valuable clues as to whether or not the body has been moved. The left arm is still rigid and has not straightened as the body has been raised.

partially disappear and new ones may be formed. After this time, however, the original livid stains remain, though they may become somewhat bleached. Even 9 to 12 hours after death, and sometimes even later, new but successively weaker stains are produced when the position of the body is changed, although the stains which were first formed are usually fixed by this time and do not decrease in intensity. After one day the livid stains do not change any more. If a lot of blood has been lost from the body the livid stains are generally weak. As a rule fresh livid stains are not produced by a change in position 12 hours after death.

Signs of putrefaction

The most certain sign of death, and one which cannot be misinterpreted by anyone, is the beginning of putrefaction. When death occurs the tissues begin to decompose, and this change is assisted by putrefying and other bacteria from the intestines and centers of disease in the body, which multiply without meeting any resistance. Putrefaction proceeds most rapidly, with normal access of moisture and oxygen, at a temperature of 20–30° C. Under some conditions the bacteria are less active, while at a temperature of about +2° C their activity ceases, although it recommences when the temperature rises again. As a rule the bacteria are killed at temperatures below −15° C. The activity of putrefying bacteria is dependent to a large extent on access to water and oxygen, and in a body which is buried or under water the action of the bacteria is largely prevented by lack of oxygen.

The first visible sign of putrefaction is a greenish-red discoloration on

Fig. 160 Another good example showing that the woman had lain on her left side—arrow shows left side of face uncolored by livid stains.

the skin of the abdomen and in the groin. The action of the bacteria produces gas which causes the body to swell up, while an unpleasant odor begins to become noticeable. Blisters filled with water and gas appear on the skin, which gradually becomes almost black. The contents of the stomach may be forced up through the mouth, nose and anus, and the pregnant uterus may blow out its fetal sac.

Bodies in water normally show certain changes which, in a favorable case, can lead to an estimate of the time of death. If the water is (slightly) warm the skin of the fingers and toes becomes nearly white and tightly puckered already after about two hours. After 1 or 2 days this change has spread to the whole of the hands and the soles of the feet. After a week the outer shell of skin begins to come off and after two to three weeks may come away like the fingers of a glove with the finger and toe nails attached. These changes are the result of the loosening of the skin in water – so-called maceration. In cold water this is considerably delayed, and in winter it commences after 4 to 5 days and may not reach its full development before a full week.

A body in water generally decomposes slowly on account of both the cold and a deficiency of oxygen. It usually sinks to the bottom, and remains there until the formation of gas brings it to the surface. After some time the skin and tissues burst, so that the gases escape and the body sinks to the bottom again. Fresh gas formation can then raise it again to the surface. In some cases a body may lie on the bottom for a period of up to a couple of months before it rises (2 days in summer, 4 to 5 days in spring or autumn, 8 to 10 days in cold, weeks or months in icy water). It will have changed considerably when it is taken out of the water. On bodies taken out of the water there is often a slimy layer of lower organisms, such as algae and molds, which accelerate the changes.

When a body is buried shallow in loose earth it is destroyed fairly quickly, and after one to three years all soft parts have usually disappeared. The skeleton remains very much longer, but the most of it is generally destroyed after ten years. In peat bogs, parts of the bones may be preserved for thousands of years. Bodies which have been buried in close-textured clayey earth generally change only slowly.

In certain cases a body may be relatively well-preserved through mummification or the formation of adipocere. Under extreme drying conditions the putrefaction is retarded and mummification may begin; and it can become complete in warm dry air or when a body is buried in dry porous earth with a small bacterial content. Under conditions of low temperature mummification is only partial, so that portions of the softer parts are destroyed by putrefaction, while other parts dry out. Formation of adipocere can occur in bodies which are buried or sunk in boggy or swampy ground. Bodies in water are also subject to the formation of adipocere, and when this process is complete it is characterized by the external contours of the body being remarkably well-preserved. If the soil contains lime, the appearance of the dead person may be recognizable. The formation of adipocere begins after 6 to 8 weeks. The process is considerably delayed in winter, to the extent of 3 months or more. Complete formation of adipocere can have occurred after one and a half to two years.

When a body lies in a cellar or other damp place it may be completely overgrown with a thick layer of mold, which leaves black marks on the body. Buried bodies may also be attacked by mold.

The stage of development of the eggs, larvae and pupae of insects found in a dead body can give a good indication of the time of death. (See 'Action of insects and other animals on a dead body').

Estimating the time of death

In favorable cases the pathologist can draw certain conclusions, during the autopsy, from the character of the contents of the stomach and intestines, regarding the time of the last meal, its quantity and composition. The degree of filling of the bladder can give information as to whether the death occurred a longer or shorter time after the individual in question went to bed, or whether the death occurred after a longer or shorter period of unconsciousness. It is therefore important that the investigator, when investigating the place of death, should confirm whether fresh urine stains are found under or close to the dead person.

The investigator can also assist the pathologist by informing him of any clues found as to the composition of the last meal.

Watches and clocks may be a valuable guide in determining the time of death. A clock may stop when it receives a blow during a struggle or is moved from its position, as may happen with an explosion or shot. When investigating a suspicious death the police officer should therefore give careful attention to the clocks which are found at the scene, and in the report of the investigation he should give indications regarding the position of the hands of the clock, and see if it has stopped from external action. If clocks or watches are running, it should be noted if they are showing the right time, and the time at which they finally stop should be determined. In the case of alarm clocks the report should state the time for which the alarm was set and whether the ringing mechanism has run down or the alarm has been shut off. When a more detailed investigation is required a watchmaker should be consulted.

Pocket watches of older construction generally stop immediately if they come into contact with water, but a watch provided with a tight-fitting case and glass can run for a little while before stopping, while modern watertight watches go for a long time under water. If a pocket or wrist watch is found on a body, the police officer should not himself carry out any further examination of it or do any tests – a watchmaker should be consulted.

In investigating cases of suspicious death certain conditions can give a good indication for an approximate determination of the time of death. This may be obtained from daily milk, papers and letters in a mailbox, dated receipts, the state of decomposition of food materials, the dampness of washing which has been hung up, dust on furniture, cobwebs, the evaporation of liquid in a glass, cup or other vessel, the withering of flowers, drying in flowerpots, date on a calendar or diary, etc.

When a dead body is found outdoors the growth of vegetation under and around the body can be a good guide in deciding the time when it came there. Flowering plants may be buried and thus may indicate closely the time of burial. The coloring matter of plant leaves under the body undergoes certain changes: thus chlorophyll generally disappears after a week. A good indication can also be obtained from a comparison between the stage of growth of plants under the body and of similar plants in the vicinity. When a body has lain in one place for a considerable time, in favorable cases, the decaying vegetation under it can indicate the time of the year when the body was placed there. When the weather had been changeable, the amount of moisture under the body, compared with that in the surrounding area, may give some information. When a dead body is found in snow, its position in relation to the layers of snow produced by successive falls should be determined accurately.

Some guidance may also be obtained from the extent of decay of clothing. Cotton fabrics decompose after 4 to 5 years; wool after 8 to 10 years; leather and silk only after 20 years or even longer.

ACTION OF INSECTS AND OTHER ANIMALS ON A DEAD BODY

When a dead body lies above ground it is generally destroyed quickly by the action of insects and their larvae. Different kinds of insects lay their eggs in the body and these rapidly develop into larvae (maggots) which, when the weather conditions are favorable, can appear in such numbers that the dead body positively 'teems with life'. The body of a full-grown man can be completely destroyed in less than two months, only the skeleton remaining; that of a child in less than a month. It has been found that the insects which appear on a body, either to feed on it or to lay their eggs in it, always come in a certain definite order, depending on the state of decomposition of the body. This question has attained great importance in medico-legal practice, since by examining the insects which are found on a body at a particular time, it is possible to obtain a good idea of how long it has lain at a particular place.

The insects which as a rule first attack the body are flies. Even when a person is lying in the death agony the flies may begin to lay their eggs in the body, preferably in the mucous membrane – e.g. in the eyes, nose, and mouth – but also in wounds and bloody parts of the body. The eggs are white and about 1/16 in. long, and are laid in clumps. On a body lying indoors they come especially from common houseflies (*Musca domestica*). This may be a significant point in the investigation, since if eggs, larvae or pupae of houseflies are found in a body lying outdoors or buried, it must be concluded that it has previously lain indoors. On bodies lying outdoors it is chiefly common bluebottles (*Calliphora erythrocephala*), greenbottles (*Lucilia caesar*) and sheep maggot flies (*Lucilia sericata*) which lay their eggs. Flies can also lay their eggs in bodies buried in shallow graves. After only one to two days the larvae of the fly come out of the eggs and immediately commence their work of destruction, changing into pupae after 10 to 14 days, and after a further 12–14 days the flies come out, to multiply again in their turn after a couple of weeks.

Among the beetles which live or multiply on a body should be noted first the burial beetles and other kinds of carrion beetles, which may appear in enormous numbers on a dead body. Ants also attack bodies and produce brownish withered areas and skin damage which, when found in the face, may be mistaken for the effects of sulphuric acid poisoning. When a body is buried immediately after death the insects are not able to lay their eggs in it, but the process of decomposition is accelerated in that case by certain types of worms which bore into the body. A species of fly can live and multiply for years in a buried body.

When larvae, pupae or insect eggs are found on a body or in its clothing there is a possiblity of calculating the shortest time during which it has lain at the scene. This applies also to fully developed insects which, in their natural course, must have gone through all their stages of development in the body. The examination should, of course, be done by an entomologist.

If insects are to be sent for expert examination, they are first killed by being placed in gasoline or some commercial insecticide. They are then preserved and dispatched in 85 % alcohol. Insect eggs, larvae and pupae are killed and preserved by placing in 70–80 % alcohol.

Unburied bodies are often attacked by animals. Rats and moles have a great liking for projecting parts of bodies, e.g. nose, ears and fingers. When they attack the hands the injuries may produce the impression of being defense injuries. When such injuries are discovered the pathologist should examine them immediately, since they dry comparatively quickly and there is difficulty in deciding on their origin. Cats, pigs and foxes also produce injuries on a body, and sometimes eat it. Dogs do not eat bodies but they may produce injuries on them. Gulls, ravens, crows and tits eat the loose tissues, e.g. in the eye sockets. Bodies in water are exposed to injury from lampreys, crabs, lobsters, water beetles and mackerels. Eels use the hollows of the body as hiding places, but do not eat it to any extent. Starfish cause injuries by attaching themselves firmly, the injury taking the same pattern as the animal itself.

EVALUATING INJURIES AND ESTIMATING THE CAUSE OF DEATH

It is very valuable for crime scene investigators to have a thorough knowledge of the evaluation of injuries and the estimation of causes of death by violence. The pathologist might not consider a police officer capable of making such determinations, even when he has considerable experience in the investigation of deaths. This opinion must be considered justified, but it is also true that the officer must sometimes take immediate steps in order to launch an investigation without the benefit of a medical opinion or the results of an autopsy. The officer's estimate of the cause will also determine the course of action in examining the death scene and in the search for the criminal. An erroneous estimate may direct the investigation into wrong channels and may even jeopardize the solution of the crime. If, for example, an inexperienced officer judges a gunshot injury to be a stab wound, the whole investigation may become sidetracked. The characteristic injuries from gunshot which may be found during a timely inspection of the body may have been altered by the time the pathologist reports on the actual cause of death.

These comments should not lead the investigator to confuse 'experience' with 'expertise', for it is the medicolegal pathologist's province to determine cause of death, no matter how experienced the investigator. On the other hand, the officer should consider his primary duty and keep in mind the success which usually results from teamwork between pathologist and investigator.

INJURIES FROM EXTERNAL MECHANICAL VIOLENCE AND GUNSHOT INJURIES

Injuries by external mechanical violence are made either by blunt or sharp instruments.

Injuries from blunt external violence can be divided into the following types: abrasions, contusions, crushing injuries and bone injuries.

Abrasions

This generally results from violence applied obliquely, but can occur sometimes from violence directed straight against the body, and may reproduce the shape of say the radiator of a car or the details of a weapon's surface. As a rule there is no bleeding. In a favorable case there is a possibility of deciding in which direction the body received the violence and, with some degree of certainty, what caused the injury. In general it is very difficult to determine whether scraping of the epidermis was produced before or after death, and removal or unclothing of the body must therefore be carried out with care, so that no injuries are produced. The body of a new-born baby is very easily injured.

Included in abrasions are fingernail marks which are narrow and usually somewhat curved. If the fingers slip, the nails produce scratches or tears.

Contusions or bruises

These are injuries to the tissues and organs produced by blunt external violence and result from compression, usually against the parts of the skeleton lying underneath. The most usual type of contusion is an extravasation of blood, and when this is close to the skin it is commonly called a bruise or blue mark. In extravasation the blood comes out into the surrounding tissues and remains there without being able to get away either to the outside or to the body cavities. A bruise or 'black and blue mark' shows initially a swelling, and has at first a reddish color; it then assumes a blackish-blue to bluish-red color, changing gradually to brownish with strong shades of green and yellow. In rare cases a bruise resulting from a blow with a weapon will have the same form as the striking surface of the weapon used. If a bruise is found on a dead body, it may be concluded

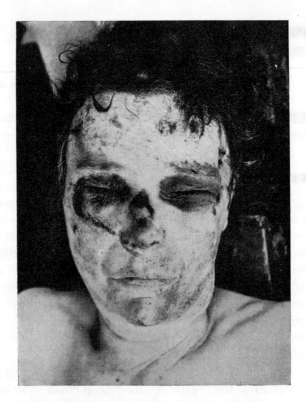

Fig. 161 Black eyes caused by severe blows to back of head.

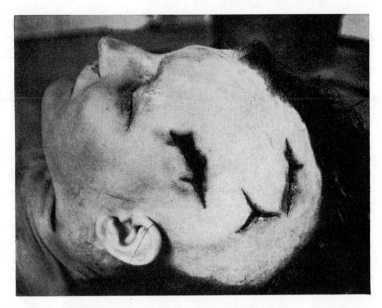

Fig. 162 Injuries to skull caused by repeated attacks with electric iron.

with certainty that the injury was produced when living. At the autopsy it is usually possible to determine whether a contusion has been produced some time before, or in direct connection with, the death. Only a pathologist can distinguish the livid stains found on a dead body from bruises.

Contusions may occur at places other than those where violence was applied. A blow against, for example, the back of the head produces bruises around the eyes. Similarly, with an abnormal accumulation of blood in the blood vessels, as in cases of hanging or other forms of suffocation, bruises appear in the face. Diffusion of blood may also appear in cases of poisoning and in some diseases and infections of the blood, the diffusion resulting from injury to the walls of the blood vessels.

Crushing wounds, lacerations

These occur most readily, with blunt violence, at those places where the skin is near the bones. They are characterized by irregular form, gaping and swollen edges to the wound, and often considerable bleeding into the surrounding tissues. The wound rarely takes the form of the object producing it, but an impression of the latter may be found. Sometimes a crushing wound is remarkably straight and even at the edges, this occurring when the skin breaks over the uniform edge of a bone, or where it splits along a parallel fibered tissue structure. Such a wound may give the impression of having been produced by a sharp weapon. This type of wound can, however, be detected with certainty, since in deeper-lying parts of it the walls of the wound are uneven and connected together by bridges of elastic tissue.

A crushing wound resulting from a blow on the head with a hammer or the head of an axe sometimes has the same form as the round or angular edge which produced it. If a blow of this type is so powerful that the weapon penetrates the cranium, the injury to the latter may have the same form.

When blunt violence is used against the body, it is possible for vital organs such as the brain, heart, lungs, liver, spleen and kidneys to be damaged without any visible external injury. Bite wounds are a special form of crushing wound. The form of a bite wound may reproduce the arrangement of the teeth of the person who caused it.

Injuries to bones

These may result from blunt external violence, for example if directed against the head. If a bone injury has occurred during life, diffusion of blood is generally found near or around it. Blunt violence against the cranium may produce a fracture. The direction of the crack often makes it possible to determine the direction from which the violence came.

Injury from cutting violence may consist of cutting wounds, stab wounds or chopping wounds.

Cutting wounds

These have even, sharp edges. When the direction of cutting is across the direction of the fibers of elastic tissue the wound gapes, but when the direction of cut is parallel to the fibers, the edges of the wound generally lie against one another. Often there is great difficulty in deciding whether a cutting wound occurred during life or after death, since contusion injuries, which may form a guide in such cases, are not found around the wound. As a rule a cutting wound is deepest at the place where the cutting object was first applied. It leaves hardly any detailed information about the instrument which caused it.

In cases of suicide the cutting force is generally directed against the throat or insides of the wrists, and only exceptionally against other parts of the body. The intent of the suicide is usually to produce bleeding by cutting the arteries. In cases of suicide there may be one or several cuts, generally not of a dangerous type, which are parallel or run into one another. If it is established that such surface cuts were produced before the final fatal cut, it is quite certain that the case is one of suicide: the surface cuts being made because the suicide did not know how much force was required to produce a fatal cut, or they may be due to fear of the pain which the suicide anticipated from his act. The police officer should not, however, draw hasty conclusions from superficial cuts which give the impression of having been made before the fatal cut. There is nothing to prevent a murderer, who has knowledge of these circumstances, from adding superficial cuts after making the fatal one in order to give the impression of suicide. Only a pathologist is competent to decide in what order the cuts were made. There have been cases of suicide where the individual has made a number of trial cuts at places other than the one where he made the fatal cut. Such trial cuts, which as a rule are superficial, may be situated on the temples, arms or legs. With an active or desperate suicide the first cut may be a fatal one, but that does not prevent him from adding a number of others before losing consciousness.

A suicide generally cuts himself in the direction where the cutting hand is placed. When a right-handed person cuts his throat, the position of the cut is generally on the left side of the throat; if he is left-handed the position is reversed. In connection with cuts in the throat it should not be forgotten that a murderer may handle the weapon in exactly the same way as a suicide, if he overcomes his victim from the rear.

In cases of suicide by cutting the throat there may be incisions in the free hand, which can easily be confused with defense injuries. Such wounds may be produced when the suicide stretches the skin of the neck with the free hand, so that the weapon can penetrate more easily. Wounds may also be produced from the blade itself being held in order to be able to put more power into the cut.

In cases of death from cutting of the throat, there is reason to suspect murder when the position of the wound does not correspond with a natural hold on the weapon, or the direction of the wound does not correspond with the right or left-handedness of the victim. Murder may be suspected if the wound is very deep, as also if it is irregular. Special attention should be given to the possible occurrence of fingernail marks and scratch injuries which would be produced if the murderer held the head of the victim fast, and also to the presence of defense injuries on the hands and arms. If there are cuts on the clothing it may be murder, since suicides generally lay bare the part of the body which they intend to cut.

Stab wounds

These are generally produced by a knife, dagger or scissors, but may also result from other weapons, e.g. an ice pick, awl, pointed stick, etc. If a stab wound has been produced by a sharp knife or dagger it is not possible to determine the width of the blade from the size of the surface wound, since the wound channel is generally wider than the weapon, especially if it is two-edged. When the weapon is stuck into the body the edge has a cutting action, so that the surface wound is considerably longer than the width of the blade, and when the weapon is withdrawn, it usually assumes a different position so that the wound is enlarged still further. The weapon may also be turned when being withdrawn, so that the surface wound becomes curved or angular. A knife with a thick back produces a wedge-shaped wound.

Suicide. An almost incredible case of suicide occurred in Canada in 1944, when a 70-year old spinster hammered a blunt 4-inch spike into her head. The woman lived for three days, most of the time fully conscious and coherent and free from any sensory or motor disturbances. She received no medical attention for several hours, walked, ate and slept, then travelled 15 miles in a truck to the nearest hospital – all without any apparent suffering.

When the nail was extracted, no reflex action was stimulated; and the patient gave no hint of pain, though the operation was performed without an anaesthetic. Shortly afterwards, however, her temperature rose and her mind seemed slightly deranged. Her condition grew steadily worse until death occurred.

In spite of many medical authorities doubting the case being a suicide, the investigation of the police authorities supported this view, for apart from the patient's own declaration and other evidence of guilt, it was proved beyond doubt that the handwriting of a suicide note was that of the deceased.

At the autopsy it was disclosed that the spike had entered the head slightly to the left of the sagittal suture, at an angle of about 30° from an estimated vertical line taken from an assumed standing position. From this angle it would seem physically impossible for such an injury to be self-inflicted; but stranger still, the uppermost part of the motor gyrus was penetrated, the corpus callosum severed, and the left lateral ventricle entered, without instantaneous death or even paralysis resulting.

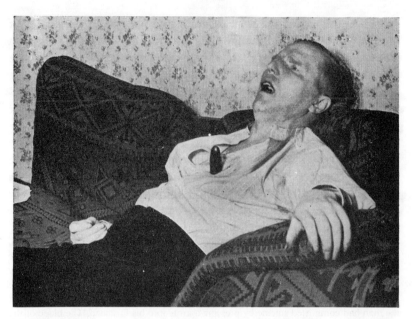

Fig. 163 Suicide by forcing knife into heart (a rare method).

Nine small circular scabbed puncture marks on the scalp had been caused by previous abortive attempts to pierce the skull. The nail had passed through the posterior fontanelle midway between the vertex and the camoda, and was so deeply embedded under the scalp that its head could not be felt.

The known circumstances of this case ruled out the possibility of homicidal violence. Had, however, the investigator come upon a corpse, instead of a living woman, with such an injury to the head, the solution would have been more difficult. Foul play naturally would have been suspected, not only because the wound itself provided a strong indication that it was other than self-inflicted, but because of an established principle that suicide should never be presumed.   (*Int. Crim. Pol. Rev.* 6, 68 (1951).

When stab wounds are produced with a weapon which has a blunted point, the outer wound is smaller than the cross-sectional width of the instrument. In such cases, when the weapon is driven into the body, the elastic skin is actually pressed inwards and stretched until it breaks; when the weapon is withdrawn the skin returns to its normal position and the external wound contracts. If the weapon is cone-shaped and rough, the skin around the wound may break in radial cracks.

With a stab wound in the heart death may not occur immediately. If the heart is full of blood death occurs instantly, but when there is only a little blood in it, it may be a while before the individual dies. There have been cases of persons surviving a wound in the heart.

When an attempt is made to commit suicide by stabbing, this is generally in the region of the heart, in exceptional cases in the stomach or other parts of the body. It is often found that a number of stab wounds are concentrated in a small limited region, i.e. around the heart. In such a case the suicide has stabbed himself several times without result, in the same way as described above under 'Cutting Wounds'. One fact which indicates suicide is that the clothes are unbuttoned or have been taken off. In suicide the stab is generally directed into the body at right angles.

Suicide. A man was found lying dead on the ground by a building site where he worked, with a knife stuck in his forehead. The left side of his chest was exposed and in the region of the heart there were three superficial knife stabs. Near the place where he lay there was a tree which showed a fresh mark in the bark at a height of about 57 in. above the ground. Near the body also lay a large flat stone. Investigation showed that the man had committed suicide by pressing a knife into his forehead. The blade of the knife was 4 in. long and it had penetrated $3^1/_2$ in. into the head. Probably the man had first pushed the knife into his forehead a little way with his hands, then pushed it further in against the tree, or possibly he had used the flat stone as a hammer. The wounds in the region of the heart, which were not fatal, had evidently occurred in a first attempt to end his life by pressing the knife into his heart, but this was in fact unsuccessful.

(LUNDEVALL, 1947).

In cases of murder the stab wounds are usually not concentrated in one place but scattered, especially when the victim has attempted to defend himself. Knife stabs are as a rule directed in an oblique direction against the body, with the exception of cases where the victim was lying down. A number of deep wounds and wounds in the back indicate murder. When the victim defended himself the wound channel may be curved due to the body being in a certain position when it received the stab. At the autopsy it may be found that a wound channel does not go right through, this being due to the fact that the position of the body was such that the muscles were displaced from their normal position when they were penetrated. In such a case the position of the dead man when he was stabbed can be reconstructed.

Chopping wounds

These are generally produced by an axe, more rarely by a blow with some other edged tool, e.g. a heavy knife, sword, broadaxe or the like. Usually the wound is similar to a cutting wound, but is easily distinguished from the latter by a ring of contusion injury around the wound, and also by the crushing effect produced when the blow meets bony parts. If the edge of the weapon is deformed tool marks may appear in these bony parts which can, in favorable cases, lead to the identification of the weapon which was used.

Murder. A 28-year old coal miner was found slain on a country road. The body lay in a pool of blood, and the head displayed numerous severe wounds apparently caused by an axe.

Another miner who was suspected of the killing was found to own an axe which was seized for examination. The chopping wounds on the victim's cranium contained a number of characteristic details in the form of scratches from the edge of the tool. Comparison marks were therefore cut in another cranium which was dealt a number of blows

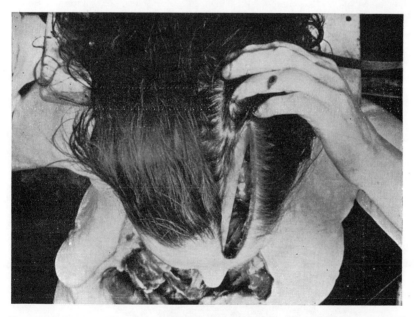

Fig. 164 Skull cut open by swinging blow from axe. Note the defense injury to the third finger of the left hand, probably caused by the instinctive raising of the hand in self-protection.

in an attempt to duplicate those of the victim. The comparison showed that there was complete agreement of the characteristic details in both skulls, forming indisputable proof that the suspect's axe had been used in the murder. (THOMAS – GALLET, 1946).

Murder. During a fight a woman received a fatal blow to the head from an axe. The assailant was arrested and admitted the act, but explained that he had thrown the axe at the woman in self-defense, from several yards away. The autopsy revealed that this statement could not be true. The skull showed an injury which could only have been caused by an instrument driven straight down into the head. The assailant had probably held the axe in a normal fashion and dealt the fatal blow from above and in close proximity.

When a person has been killed by a blow from an axe or other edged weapon it can nearly always be assumed that it is homicide. In cases of

Fig.165 Suicide by axe blows on the head. Note the typical placing of the numerous and comparatively small wounds.

murder or other violent death from an axe, the wounds are generally in the head, and are in different directions. In certain cases they may have the same direction, as for example when a sleeping person, or one who is held, is struck. Usually the criminal first delivers a few blows with the head of the weapon before completing the job with the edge.

Suicide with an axe has occurred, but is rare. Generally the suicide directs the weapon against the forehead and crown of his head. The first blow is relatively light and only produces superficial injuries which are not in themselves fatal, and he continues by putting more force in the blows and possibly using the weapon with greater accuracy, so that fatal injuries are produced. The wounds have a typical appearance which cannot be mistaken – they are directed from the forehead to the back of the head, approaching one another at the forehead.

Marks or damage on clothing in cases of external mechanical violence

These can be of great significance in the reconstruction of events. In cases of blunt violence an impression of the weapon causing the injury may be found on the clothing, while headgear may show a clear mark of a hammer or other tool. In the case of a blow against the head the tool used may even chip out a piece or corner of the headgear, this piece having the same form as the striking surface of the weapon. An impression in the corresponding part of the outer clothing may show that a bruise on the body has resulted from a kick or from trampling. Impressions in clothing may be mixed with dust, dirt or other contamination from the object producing the injury. Injuries to the clothes may be a good guide for the reconstruction of the course of events in the case of injury from cutting violence. In stabbing cases the hole in the clothing may have a position different to that of the wound. A victim who has been stabbed may lift his arms in self-defense, so that the clothing moves out of its usual position on the body; in such cases the defensive position can be reconstructed. A garment, perforated in several places by one and the same stab, indicates that there were creases in the clothes.

Defense injuries

On the hands and arms of the victim of a murder there are often injuries which are due to the individual trying to defend himself. If a knife was

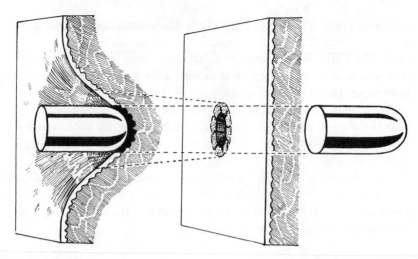

Fig. 166 Diagrammatic representation of a bullet penetrating the skin. The skin is pressed inwards, stretched and perforated in the stretched condition, after which it returns to its original position. The entry opening is smaller than the diameter of the bullet. Immediately around the opening is the contusion ring, since the bullet rubs against this part of the skin and scrapes off the external layer of epithelial cells.

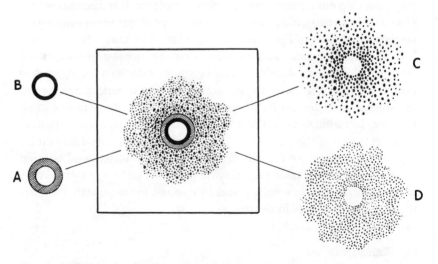

Fig. 167 A diagram showing the marks which may be found around the entry opening of a bullet in a close shot. A: contusion ring; B: ring of dirt; C: grains of powder; D: deposit of powder smoke.

used, the insides of the hands may be badly gashed from gripping the blade of the knife. Stab and cut wounds may be produced on the arms and hands when a victim attempts to parry an attack. When a crushing weapon is used in a murder, the hands of the victim may be badly injured from putting his hands on his head to reduce the violence of the blow. Among defense injuries are also included those injuries which occur when the victim attempts to defend himself by attacking, e.g. injuries to the knuckles when using his fists against the criminal, or breaks his nails when scratching.

Gunshot injuries

These must be considered as a special group of injuries, since the investigation of them differs substantially in important respects from the investigation of other injuries. One might think that, since a police officer should not touch a wound, he need not have a detailed knowledge of gunshot injuries on a body. They are, however, so frequent and so important that whenever the pathologist cannot arrive in a reasonable time the police officer himself should be prepared to make his own observations and to take whatever measures are necessary. As gunshot injuries are usually covered with blood, it is often impossible for a police officer to distinguish between a gunshot injury and one produced by other external mechanical violence. Under these circumstances it is necessary to wait patiently for the arrival of the pathologist, and this holds even when it is of the greatest importance that the type of injury should be determined at an early stage. If the police officer begins to probe in or around a gunshot wound, he may destroy or reduce the chance of the expert being able to determine the type of injury and to reconstruct the course of events, etc. Firearm injuries may be divided into bullet and shot injuries.

Bullet injuries

When a bullet strikes the body, the skin is first pushed in and then perforated while in the stretched state. After the bullet has passed, the skin partially returns to its original position, and the entry opening is drawn together and is smaller than the diameter of the bullet. The lower the speed of the bullet, the smaller the entry opening. The bullet passing through the stretched skin forms the so-called contusion ring round the entrance opening, as the bullet slips against the skin which is pressed inwards and scrapes the external epithelial layers. The skin itself, in the contusion ring, becomes conspicuous by drying after some hours. In a favorable case, rifling marks on the bullet leave such a distinct mark in the contusion ring that the number of grooves in the rifling can be counted. The combined section of the contusion ring and entrance opening corresponds to the caliber of the bullet, or exceeds it slightly. When a bullet strikes the body squarely the contusion ring is round, and when it strikes at an angle it is oval.

Together with the contusion ring there is another black-colored ring, the smudge ring, which often entirely covers the contusion ring. This does not contain any powder residues or contamination from the bore of the weapon, but consists wholly of small particles originating from the surface of the bullet. The smudge ring may be absent in the case of clean jacketed bullets or when the bullet has passed through clothing.

A bullet passing through the body forms a track which is usually straight, but can also be bent at an angle in an unpredictable manner if the bullet meets or passes through a bone. Thus it is not possible to determine with certainty the direction of the weapon when the shot was fired, from observation of the entrance and exit openings. This direction must be calculated by the pathologist from the results of the autopsy. The velocity of the bullet has a great influence on the appearance of the track; straight tracks indicate a high velocity, bent or angular ones a low one.

With gunshot injuries in soft parts of the body, especially in the brain, the bullet can produce a considerable explosive effect, which is greatest with unjacketed or soft-nosed bullets from large caliber weapons. Such a bullet may split into several parts, each of which forms its own track, and thus there may be *several exit wounds*. When such a bullet strikes the head, large parts of the cranium can be blown away and the brain is scattered around. A soft-nose bullet which, before hitting the body, is split by striking against a tree branch, can produce a number of regular entrance holes.

A shot through the head is not always fatal. To be immediately fatal the bullet must either produce a bursting effect or injure an artery of the brain or a vital brain center. A shot through the brain which is not immediately fatal does not always produce unconsciousness. Even when the heart has been perforated by a bullet, it occasionally happens that the injured person lives for several hours, retaining some capacity of movement.

Murder – Suicide. A man fired a fatal pistol shot at his girl friend, then sat on a chair and fired at his own right temple. The bullet penetrated between the skin and bone of the forehead, followed the latter and went out on the left side. He fired another shot which went through the right temple, perforated the brain and went out through the left temple. When he was found after nine hours he was sitting on the chair, living and with so much strength that he was able to answer questions. He died subsequently from his injuries.

Accident. A man stumbled on the steps of his house on his way to church, and in falling against the step, a shot was fired from a pistol which he had in his pocket. The man did not take any notice but continued on his way to the church half a mile away. After the service he was found dead in the church: the shot fired on the step had penetrated his heart.

It is often difficult to distinguish the exit wound from the entrance wound especially at long range with a metal-jacketed bullet, assuming of course that the bullet passes through the body intact. In a favorable case the exit wound may have a ragged appearance with flaps directed outwards. To determine the direction of the shot with certainty in such a case an autopsy is necessary. If the bullet has been damaged by its passage through the body, or if there has been a bursting effect, then it is generally easy to determine the exit wound, which is considerably larger than the entrance wound and shows a star-shaped, ragged character, with flaps directed outwards. Note, however, that in contact shots the entrance wound may be ragged and star-shaped. (See below). A bullet which ricochets may strike

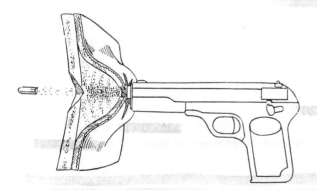

Fig. 168 Contact shot; the weapon is pressed against the head or the body. The gases from the explosion expand between the skin and the bone, producing a bursting effect and a ragged entrance wound.

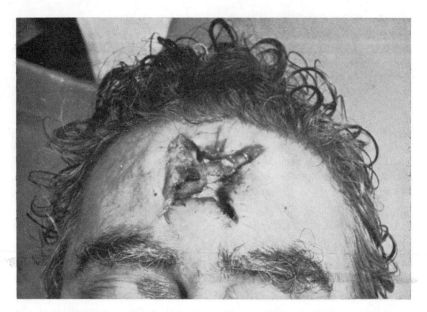

Fig. 169 Contact shot on the forehead with a 9 mm Luger pistol. Notice the star-shaped
entrance wound.

with its side or obliquely and produce a large and characteristic entrance
wound.

Close and distant shots

It is very important to be able to estimate the distance from which a shot
was fired. In many cases this fact is the only evidence available which can
distinguish between suicide and homicide, or between a self-defense killing,
manslaughter and murder.

In practice a distinction is made between contact, close and distant
shots. A *contact shot* is one where the muzzle of the weapon is pressed
against the body when the shot is fired. In a *close shot* the distance of the
muzzle is less than about 18 inches from the body, while a *distant shot* is
one fired at a distance greater than 18 inches.

In the case of a contact shot against an exposed part of the body, soot,
metallic particles and powder residues are driven into the body and can be
found there during the autopsy. Blackening, caused by soot and powder,
around the entry opening is often absent. A contact shot against a part of

the body which is protected by clothing often produces a powder zone on the skin or in the clothes, while soot, powder residues and fragments of clothing are driven into the track. With a contact discharge the entrance wound differs considerably from an entrance wound in a close shot or distant shot. When the shot is fired, the gases of the explosion are driven into the track, but they are forced out again and produce a bursting effect on the skin and clothes. The entrance wound is often star-shaped with flaps directed outwards. It is also possible, in a contact shot, for the muzzle of the weapon to mark the skin causing an impression which reproduces the shape of the muzzle of the weapon.

A close shot produces a zone of blackening around the entrance wound of the track, either on the skin or also on the clothes. Sometimes the flame from the muzzle has a singeing action round this opening, hair and textile fibers being curled up. The zone of blackening is formed of substances which are carried along with the explosion gases. When a cartridge is fired, the bullet is forced through the barrel of the weapon by the explosion gases. Only a small amount of this gas passes in front of the bullet. The combustion of the powder is never complete even with smokeless powder, still less with black powder, and the explosion gases therefore carry with them in-

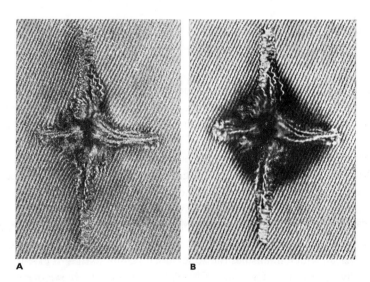

A   **B**

Fig. 170 Contact shot against loose clothing with a 9 mm automatic pistol. A damage photographed on orthochromatic film; B on infrared sensitive film, revealing the deposit of powder smoke.

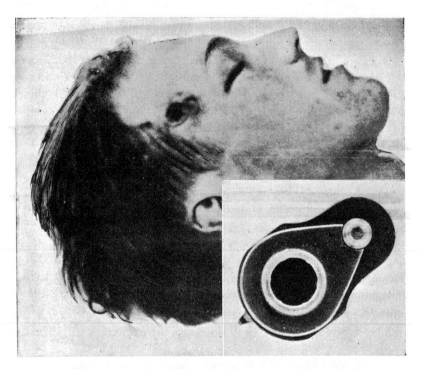

Fig. 171 A contact shot at the right temple. The outline of the muzzle is clearly reproduced on the skin of the victim.

completely burned powder residues, the amount of which decreases as the distance increases. Thus, in a close shot, a considerable amount of incompletely burned powder residue is found on the target. Together with this residue the gases also carry along impurities from the inside of the barrel consisting of rust (iron), oil, and particles rubbed off the bullet. Metallic residues from the percussion cap and cartridge case also occur in the gases of the explosion. If the shot is fired at right angles to the body the zone of blackening is practically circular; if fired obliquely the zone is oval. The extent of the zone of blackening is often difficult to determine by direct observation, and it is often better to photograph it, using infrared sensitive material, which intensifies the zone of blackening so that its extent is more easily determined. The zone of blackening gives valuable information for determining the distance from which a shot has been fired, which may be an important factor in deciding between murder and suicide. It is of decisive importance that comparative test shots can be fired with the *same weapon* and *same type of ammunition* as used in the actual crime.

Close shots with black powder show marks of burning up to a distance of 4 to 6 in., and a distinct deposit of powder smoke up to 10 to 12 in. Dispersed grains of powder imbedded in the target may be detected even at a distance of 3 ft.

A distant shot is considered to be one in which none of the characteristics of a near shot can be detected (distance over about 18 in.).

Powder residues occur on the object fired at in the form of incompletely and completely burned particles. A careful microscopic examination should precede any chemical examination, as it is often possible to establish in this way the shape and color of unburned powder particles and to distinguish many kinds of powder.

Black powder, which consists of potassium nitrate, sulphur and charcoal, is identified by the presence of potassium and nitrate in the entrance wound. Smokeless powder consists chiefly of nitrocellulose or of nitrocellulose with nitroglycerin and is identified by the presence of nitrite, which can be detected by various micro-reactions. The grains of smokeless

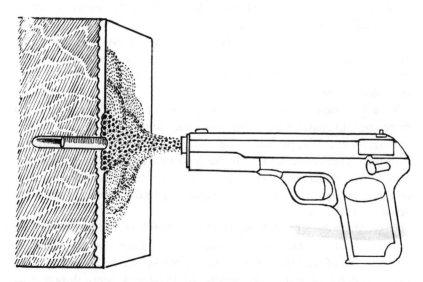

Fig. 172 Close shot – short distance. Both incompletely burned powder grains and smoke deposits in the zone of blackening. The powder grains are concentrated immediately around the entrance hole.

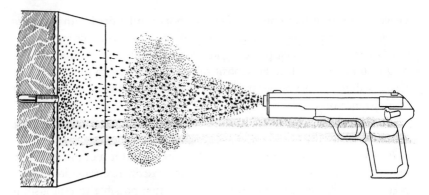

Fig. 173 Close shot – greater distance. Unburned powder grains but no smoke deposits in the zone of blackening.

powder are generally coated with graphite, and occur in many forms, e.g. round or angular discs, pellets, and cylinders.

Marks from primers. Until fairly recently a primer generally contained a percussion composition of fulminate of mercury, stibnite (antimony sulphide) and potassium chlorate with a varying amount of powdered glass. In recent years attempts have been made to eliminate the mercury and the rust-forming products from the potassium chlorate. This has resulted in the replacement of the mercury fulminate by lead compounds such as lead azide and lead styphnate (lead trinitroresorcinate), and by the potassium chlorate being replaced by barium nitrate. Stibnite is, however, still used to a limited extent.

Thus in a chemical examination of a gunshot injury the metals which first come into question are barium, lead, mercury and antimony. By determining, for example, the lead content of a bullet wound and comparing it with that obtained from a test discharge against a similar object with the same ammunition from different distances, it is possible, in favorable cases, to obtain quite reliable information regarding the distance from which the actual shot was fired.

Traces from bullets. With injuries from plain lead bullets, such as are usually used in ordinary revolver ammunition, there is always a considerable amount of lead both in the zone of blackening and in the smudge ring; and in the latter it is even possible to detect lead from a distant shot. Lead traces from the surface of the bullet can also be found frequently in the exit hole. In some types of ammunition the bullet is greased; residues from these substances may be carried along with the bullet and found around the entrance opening. Metal-jacketed bullets, which are used chiefly for automatic weapons, consist of an inner lead core with an outer shell of some hard metal or alloy – the so-called jacket – the usual materials being copper, cupro-nickel or brass. Traces of all these metals may be found in gunshot injuries.

Traces from cartridge cases. It is often possible to detect copper in the track and in perforated clothing, up to a range of 6 to 8 in. This comes from the cartridge case, from which small particles of metal are worn off by the expansion pressure. Large amounts of copper found in the dirt ring are considered as a characteristic indication of a close shot. If, however, a copper-coated bullet has been used then naturally no conclusion can be drawn regarding the possibility of a close shot, since in this case even a distant shot shows a distinct amount of copper.

Traces from the barrel of the weapon. Iron can be found in and around the entrance wound in a case of shooting with a weapon which has not been used for a long time, and the barrel of which may therefore be rusty. With automatic hand weapons traces of iron can be detected up to a distance of 8 to 12 in.

Injuries from small shot. With shotguns the shot column can have a very concentrated effect at distances up to 1 yard. With a distance of up to 4 to 8 in., the wound is practically circular. The greater the distance the more the wound is irregular. At a distance of up to 2 to 3 yards there is generally a central entrance opening, and around it are single small holes from individual scattered shot. At a greater distance the shot spreads out more into small groups: at 10 yards the scattering can amount to 12 to 16 in.

Injuries to clothes from shooting. If a shot has passed through clothes, the position of the bullet hole should be compared with the direction of the wound track in the body in the same way as described previously under the heading 'Marks or damage on clothing in cases of external mechanical violence'.

DEATH FROM SHOOTING

In suicide the weapon is usually directed against the forehead, temple or heart, while a shot fired upwards and obliquely into the mouth is quite common. In deciding if a case is one of suicide an attempt should first be made to decide to what extent the victim could have fired the shot in the approximate direction given by the track. In the case of pistol or revolver shots against the temple it is necessary to know whether the deceased was right or left-handed. It should be remembered that a person may fire a weapon with the left hand, but be otherwise right-handed.

It is an essential condition for the assumption of suicide that the victim should have been wounded by a close discharge, and that the weapon should lie in the proper position with respect to the body. If these conditions indicate suicide the question should not, however, be considered as settled, since there is nothing to prevent some other person from firing the

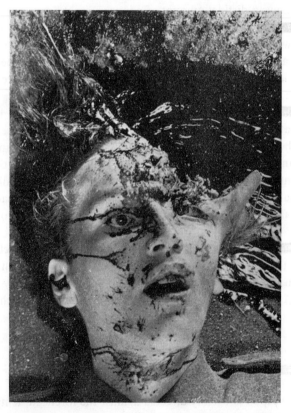

Fig. 174 The explosive effect of a close shot to the forehead – 6.5 mm Mauser rifle.

shot under the given conditions and then laying the weapon down in the proper position.

A more certain indication is available if injuries are found on the hand of the dead person which are produced when firing a shot, in the form of a mark on the thumb or forefinger or on the web of the thumb. Such marks may result from the recoil of the slide of an automatic pistol. The most certain proof of suicide is found in the form of fragments of tissue and blood spattered from the wound on to the hand of the dead person. Although, in cases of suicide, the hand of the deceased may be found to be blackened by powder, this cannot be taken as a proof since the weapon could have been pressed in the hand after the shot was fired. It is also necessary to decide whether the body is in a position which is natural under the circumstances. A fairly certain sign of suicide is when the person has taken off any hindering clothes or exposed some part of the body before firing. If the weapon is not present near the body, this is a very suspicious circumstance, but hasty conclusions should not be drawn from that fact alone. There have been cases where a fatally injured person has travelled a long way before finally expiring or thrown the weapon into a body of water. It has also happened that members of the victim's family have removed the weapon in order to deliberately create an appearance of homicide, sometimes in the hope of escaping the disgrace of a suicide in the family.

It is a certain indication that a person died through the action of some other person when the discharge was beyond arm's reach. By arm's reach is meant the length of the arm plus possible assistance from an extension in the form of a stick or some other convenient means of reaching the trigger of a long-barreled weapon. It is true that it is possible to commit suicide by means of a distant shot, but this requires arrangements of such a type (string-pulls, etc.) that there should be no difficulty in revealing the truth. When the fatal shot was fired from behind, it is safe to assume that it is not suicide. A suicide *could* fire a shot at the back of his own head, but such a possibility is very far-fetched. The fact that the shot person has more than one injury cannot always be taken as a proof that he has died from the action of some other person. Cases occur where a suicide has fired two or possibly a number of shots, each of which produced a lethal wound, before he became incapable of continuing the firing.

It is quite common for a person to be shot fatally either by accident or through his own fault: he may be out hunting and happen to slip or stum-

Fig. 175 Two bullets entered a single hole in the victim's body and then took separate
paths. The first failed to leave the barrel of the gun and was carried into the
body by the rear projectile.

ble on awkward ground, fall when climbing over a gate or other obstacle,
or drop the weapon, whereupon a fatal shot may be fired. In such cases
there are generally marks at the scene of the accident or marks on the
weapon which give a clear indication of what has happened. A fatal shot
may also be fired accidently when handling a firearm, e.g. when cleaning
it. In such cases the investigating officer should observe the greatest caution, and not assume from the start that it was an accident. The victim may
very well have committed suicide while giving the incident the appearance
of an accident, or a murderer may also simulate an accident. The police
officer who carries out the investigation of a fatal shooting must not attempt to carry out any experiment which trespasses on the sphere of activity of the doctor or chemist. But he may have to undertake precautionary measures in connection with evidence which for some reason may be
exposed to destruction. It has been stated before that, in and around a
gunshot wound, there may be found traces of incompletely burned powder residues, traces of metals from the primer, cartridge case and bullet,
grease and dirt from the bullet and from the barrel of the weapon, etc.
These marks may be of decisive significance in deciding, for example, the
distance of the shooting, and they must therefore be protected as far as

possible. In cases where the bullet has gone through the clothes there is always the risk that clues may be destroyed by rain, or when moving the dead body. The police officer should therefore protect such clues against destructive action by any suitable means, for example by covering the actual place or, in suitable cases, by fixing loose layers of clothing in a particular position by tying or pinning. If there is any risk that the bullet hole in the clothes may become soaked with blood when the body is moved, the police officer must find some method of preventing it.

It has been stated previously in this section that the hand which holds the firearm at the instant of firing can become blackened by powder in the area of the web of the thumb and on the thumb and forefinger. The deposit of powder smoke produced in this way can be identified chemically. The hand of a dead body may, if necessary, be protected by wrapping in clean paper or bags. Concerning the recovery and identification of such deposits, see 'Traces on the suspect'.

Explosion injuries are a variation of gunshot injuries. If an explosive charge contains metal parts or is enclosed in a metal container which breaks up, e.g. a hand grenade, or when it fractures metal objects, stones or the like in the immediate vicinity, the fragments thrown off have an

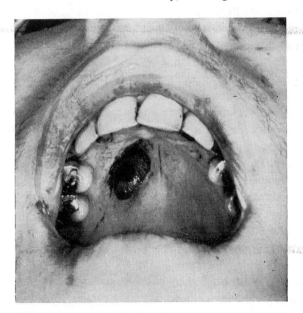

Fig. 176 Bullet entrance wound in the palate.

exceptionally great force which, however, quickly decreases. When such pieces from an explosion hit a nearby body they can produce very severe damage. A small splinter of only a few millimeters diameter can perforate the brain pan. When it penetrates the body it bores a wound channel which can easily be mistaken for a bullet track. The energy in a fragment from an explosion decreases so rapidly that generally it is not able to penetrate the body. At close quarters air pressure alone can cause fatal injury: thus the lungs may be ruptured if an individual has his mouth open during an explosion.

The fatal effect of an explosive charge is limited to the immediate vicinity; at a greater distance air pressure may cause injury from falling. Another way of committing suicide is to cause dynamite to detonate in the mouth. The effect of such an explosion is generally that the head is torn away, while the skin of the back of the neck, with adhering bone and soft parts, is left on the neck. Suicide by explosion in the mouth can be carried out with nothing more than a blasting cap. In this case the injuries are to the throat and organs of breathing. Generally no damage is visible in the face; the lips and the skin of the face remain uninjured. Suicide has also been achieved by an explosive charge placed on the chest, in which extensive lacerations are produced.

The police officer should remember that in many cases wounds have to be photographed, even when they are on a living person. He should therefore try to get into contact with the doctor who has treated an injured person in order to discuss with him the possibility of photographing. This should not be delayed too long since a wound changes its appearance as it heals. Especially in the case of bite wounds, and wounds of which the form reveals the character of the weapon or instrument, it is important that photographing should be done before a scab forms or an operation becomes necessary. Panchromatic negatives should be employed, and a scale should always be laid next to the wound.

Wounds on a dead person can be cast by the Negocoll method.

DEATH BY SUFFOCATION

The actual mode of death may be by hanging, strangulation by hand or ligature, covering the mouth or nose, blocking the larynx or windpipe, crushing to death or drowning.

Fig. 177 The devastating effect of suicide by causing dynamite to detonate in the mouth. The head has completely disintegrated. The ears can be identified, but that is all.

Hanging is a mode of death in which a cord is placed around the neck and tightened by the weight of the body. The effect of hanging is that the blood circulation to the brain ceases very quickly, which produces immediate unconsciousness, while at the same time the air passages are closed up so that respiration ceases. The action of the heart may actually continue, so that death occurs only after some minutes. With violent modes of hanging, injury may be produced to the vertebrae and spinal cord. The noose need not be very tight since only a small part of the weight of the body needs to be taken up for the hanging to be effective. The body does not therefore need to hang free: the effect is the same if the hanging occurs with the body supported in a leaning, kneeling, sitting or lying position. No one can escape from a tight-drawn noose if he once hangs in it because vagal inhibition will occur rapidly. This has been shown by a number of cases of death of persons who wished to try the effect of a hanging without any intention of completing it – they found themselves unable to recover from their situation. Thus children have been killed by hanging when, from curiosity, they wanted to test a hangman's noose. Similarly there have been cases where a hanging situation has been arranged in order to obtain a perverse sexual stimulation. The commonly-held view that death by hanging may be preceded by voluptuous sensations is, however, cer-

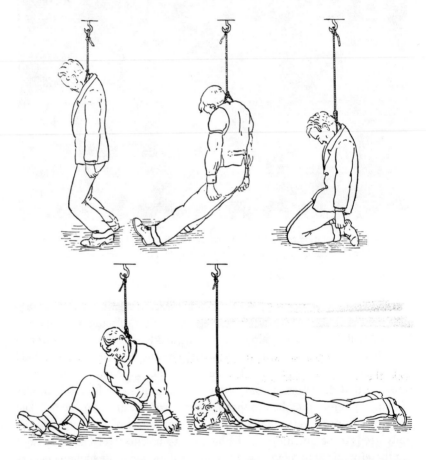

Fig. 178 Various positions in hanging with the body supported (not hanging freely).

Fig. 179 Hanging in a sitting position.

tainly incorrect. Ejaculation of semen is a usual and quite natural phenomenon in cases of death, and results from relaxation of the musculature.

In suicide by hanging it quite frequently happens that the rope breaks
and the suicide falls down, but subsequently repeats the hanging with another rope and possibly at another place. This may necessitate tedious investigations, since the suicide may have contracted bleeding injuries which
were caused either when he fell or when, after the unsuccessful attempt,
he wandered around in a daze. In such a case, wounds, marks of blood and
disorder at the scene might be incorrectly interpreted as signs of a struggle.

The rope used is generally slender cord, e.g. a clothes line, but other objects may be used, as for example belts, suspenders, towels, scarves, thick
shoelaces, etc. After hanging there is usually found a typical mark on the
neck, the so-called hanging groove. The broader and softer the noose, the
less clearly shows the hanging groove. This is also the case when some
part of the clothing comes between the noose and the neck. As a rule, however, the groove is distinct and full of detail, and it is often possible to distinguish marks of twisting, knots and irregularities, while the width of the
cord used can be calculated quite accurately.

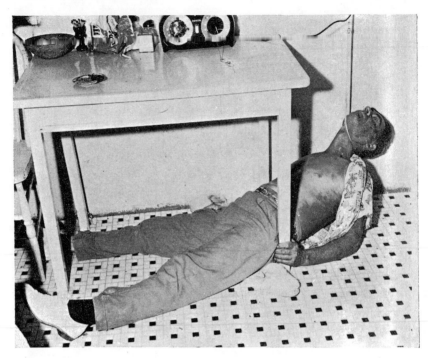

Fig. 180 Unusual position in a suicidal hanging.

(*Metropolitan Dade County Public Safety Department*)

The hanging groove generally has a typical appearance. The greatest pressure is exerted opposite the suspension point, i.e. if suspended from the back of the neck, the noose, if it is sufficiently thin or narrow, on the front side may have pressed in so deeply that it lies almost concealed by a roll of flesh. The groove then runs upwards at an angle around the side of the neck, becomes less marked, and finally fades away as it approaches the back of the neck. The edges of the groove are generally puckered in the direction in which the cord slipped when the noose tightened. When hanging occurs in a lying or inclined position the groove may be more horizontal, which gives it a certain similarity with a strangulation groove, from which it can easily be distinguished by the fact that the hanging groove is less marked and disappears at the back of the neck. In cases of strangling, where the criminal has held his hands between the loop and the neck, the groove also disappears in the direction towards the hands. In general, however, the fingernails or knuckles produce such a great pressure against

Fig. 181 Hanging in a lying position over a suitcase.

the neck that contusions appear in the skin. In rare cases the noose may be applied at an angle on the neck or right at the back of the neck, but the effect intended is still obtained since the large arteries of the neck are compressed effectively even when this method of hanging is used. Sometimes the noose may slip upwards after the first tightening, whereby two or more hanging grooves are produced. This may give rise to suspicion of a crime, but generally the pathologist will find no difficulty in elucidating the actual circumstances.

It can happen that a hanged person is found with his fingers between the noose and the neck. This is not due to his having attempted to loosen the noose, but to his fingers not having been removed when the noose tightened.

Dead persons may show, on the skin of the neck, marks which can easily be confused with hanging grooves. Such marks can be produced by articles of clothing pressing against the neck. On bodies which have been

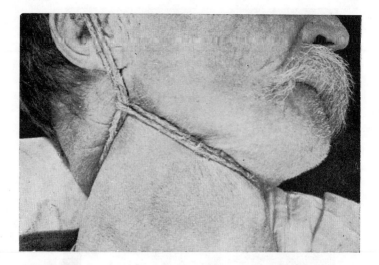

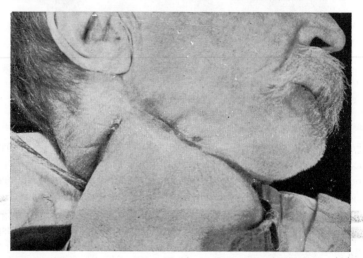

Fig. 182 Hanging with a running noose. The lower picture shows the typical appearance of the hanging groove.

in water for a long time, or which are undergoing decomposition, the hanging groove may have disappeared.

Murder by hanging must be considered as an extremely rare occurrence, and would only be used against children or persons who are unconscious or unable to defend themselves. In such cases it is to be expected that the victim will show injuries other than those which occur from hanging. A murderer may attempt to give an appearance of suicide by hanging up the body after the onset of unconsciousness or death. If this is done by hoisting up the body, distinct clues will usually be present on the supporting object and on the rope. For example, a branch of a tree may show such a clear mark of rubbing on the bark that there is no difficulty in elucidating the actual circumstances – especially when the rope has also slipped sideways. On the part of the rope which has lain on and slipped against the support, the fibers are always directed upwards against the latter.

Persons who have committed suicide by hanging sometimes show other injuries, which in themselves could be fatal. In such cases hanging has been employed after an unsuccessful attempt to kill themselves in some other way. Such cases are, however, easy to distinguish from those in which hanging is the final phase in a murder, since the local conditions generally give a clear picture of the course of events.

Suicide. In the furnace room of an apartment house the janitor was found hanging in a seated position. In one temple there was a small but deep crushing wound, and a certain amount of disorder in the surroundings could be interpreted as a sign of a struggle. A preliminary investigation of the scene gave a distinct impression of a murder in which the criminal had first rendered the man unconscious by a powerful blow and then hung him up. It was discovered however that the man suffered at times from very severe headaches, and that he was tired of life, since he knew that the headaches resulted from a serious disease of the brain. When the headache became intolerable he would rush about recklessly, holding his hands before his eyes. Careful investigation in the furnace room showed the presence of blood and hair round a bolt projecting from a heating boiler, and between this point and the site of the hanging, there were solitary stains of dropping blood. Investigation showed that the man had rushed about in the furnace room and thereby struck his head on the boiler; in desperation he had then taken his own life by hanging.

When a body is hanging free but there is no jumping-off point in the vicinity, such as a chair, table, step, stone, stump, etc., then there is every reason to suspect murder. In such cases the scene must be examined carefully in order to determine whether it was possible for anyone to have climbed up to the point of attachment. With trees it is easy to find marks of climbing, e.g. twigs broken off or leaves, bark or moss torn away, and similar traces should be found on the clothing of the dead person. An easily removable starting point, e.g. a chair, may actually have been removed by mistake before the arrival of the police.

In cases of hanging, livid stains are strongly marked on the feet, legs and hands, and also immediately above the hanging groove. If such marks should be found, for example, on the back of a freely hanging body, there is a question of the hanging having been done some time after death. The same is the case when the arms or legs are bent, as it is possible that the body may have been hung up after the onset of rigidity. After the rigidity has relaxed and the limbs have become straight, in some cases the wrinkles remaining in the clothes can indicate that the limbs were previously bent.

The presence on the clothes of dirt, e.g. leaves, parts of plants, soil, dust or other material, which is not present at the scene of the hanging, should be noted especially, as also the presence of blood, saliva or urine flowing in the wrong direction. Such observations may give rise to suspicion of a crime. If the knots and noose are formed in such a way that it is doubtful whether the dead person could have made them, this must be considered as a suspicious circumstance.

In suicide by hanging, right-handed persons usually place the knot of the noose on the right hand side of the neck, left-handed ones on the left. Reversal of these positions is suspicious.

When investigating a case of hanging the police officer should always have in mind that the autopsy can rarely decide between murder and suicide. As a rule the course of events can only be determined from examination of the scene and from police investigation.

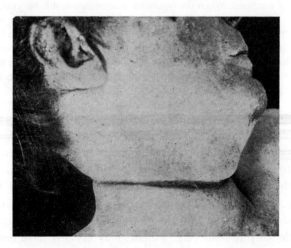

Fig. 183 Murder by strangulation with a noose. Note the position and typical appearance of the well-defined strangulation groove.

Strangling is usually done by hand or with a cord. In strangulation by hand death sometimes occurs almost immediately from shock, but usually the squeezing of the neck arteries is incomplete, so that death results from interruption of the supply of air to the lungs.

In strangulation by hand there are typical fingernail marks on both sides of the throat – from the fingernails on one side and from the thumb nail on the other. If the criminal is right-handed the mark of the thumb nail is generally on the right side of the throat, and on the left side if he is left-handed. There are often marks of several grips with the hands and abrasion of the skin where the fingers slipped. When death has occurred from shock, marks of nails may be missing. Strangulation is generally preceded by a struggle, so that other injuries may be found on the body, usually scratches or bleeding on the face, and also marks on the clothes.

Strangulation by hand has nearly always resulted from extraneous violence, i.e. by another person, although there have occurred individual cases of suicide by strangulation by hand, the suicide using a passive support for his hands so that the grip does not slip on the occurrence of unconsciousness. In strangulation by ligature death occurs in the same way as with hanging, but the strangulation groove generally has a course and appearance different to that of a hanging groove. Usually it goes around the neck in a horizontal direction, or its back part may be situated somewhat lower down on the neck than the front part on the throat. In some cases it can, like the hanging groove, be directed back and upwards. Usually the strangulation groove is located lower down on the neck than the hanging groove.

Strangulation with a cord can generally be considered as murder, and defense injuries are usually found on the victim. Such injuries may be absent if the victim was overcome from behind, or where a sleeping, unconscious or defenseless person has been strangled. In a case where the cord is left on the throat after the crime, it is generally fixed tightly by means of a number of turns and knots.

Strangulation with a cord is a rare form of suicide. In those cases in which suicide can be presumed, the strangling has been carried out with a running noose or by a scarf, rope or the like, laid round the neck and knotted with a half knot, which is drawn so tightly that the neck arteries are compressed and unconsciousness supervenes. In both cases one can expect that the hands will hold the noose fast after death, or that their position relative to it will give clear evidence of suicide.

Suicide. A man was found dead in his bed with the sleeves of his shirt wound round his throat in a strangling position. Police investigations and the post-mortem examination showed that it was a case of suicide. The man had taken off his shirt without unfastening the cuffs, so that they remained turned the wrong way. When the body was freed from the shirt the cuffs were left around the wrists. The man had then laid one sleeve of the shirt in three turns round his neck, and the other one in two, and pulled them so that death occurred from asphyxiation.

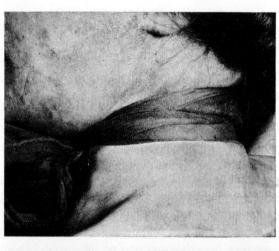

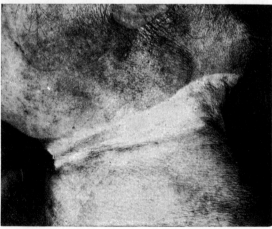

Fig. 184 Strangulation by a scarf wound around the neck three turns and tied under the chin. The lower picture shows the strangulation groove which is not very well defined due to the width and softness of the ligature.

Blocking of the mouth or nose is a rare cause of death and most commonly happens to new-born children. The stoppage may result either from a pillow or other soft object being pressed against the face or from a hand pressed against the mouth and nose, so that death occurs from suffocation. Suffocation may also result from the mouth and nose being stopped with, for example, cotton, a handkerchief or piece of cloth. When a pillow

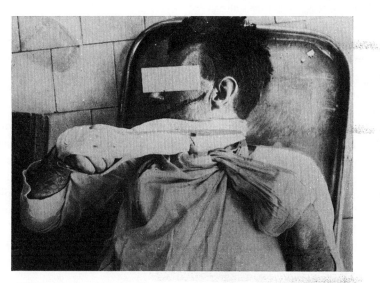

Fig. 185 Strangulation with the sleeves of a shirt turned inside out. The cuffs are still buttoned.

or other soft material is used there are no typical marks, but saliva or mucus may stick on the cushion in such quantity and in such a way that it can give some information about the course of events. It should, however, be remembered that a number of cases may be accidents when the child turns on to its face. When suffocation is done by hand, scratches may be produced on the face. If it is suspected that the mouth and nose have been stopped with, for example, cotton which was later removed, signs of it should be looked for.

In exceptional cases old persons may be killed by blocking the mouth and nose with a soft covering. It can also happen that a criminal, without intending to kill, has attempted to silence the cries of his victim, e.g. in a case of rape.

Manslaughter. The body of a woman was washed up on a beach. It was enclosed in a sack which also contained objects that came from a steamer which had passed near the place. One of the crew was suspected of murdering the woman. It was found that the woman, who was of loose character, had smuggled herself on board and hidden in the cabin of the suspected man. When he found her she made certain demands with which he would not comply. She then threatened to create a scandal and began to scream with the obvious intention of attracting the attention of the officers of the ship. With the object of silencing the cries, the man pressed a pillow against the woman's face, but held it there too long, so that she suffocated.

Blocking of the larynx and air passages. Blocking can occur, for example, when food goes the 'wrong way', or vomited stomach contents are unable to get out through the mouth. Infanticide can be committed by a finger pressed down in the throat of an infant so that death results from suffocation. In this case there will be serious injuries in the mouth and throat.

Squeezing to death can occur, for example, with a panic in a crowd, where the victim is squeezed or trampled, or where a person comes under a heavy falling object or is buried by a fall of earth. The external injuries are generally considerable and easily interpreted. Squeezing to death can generally be considered as an accident, but the possibility should also be kept in mind of, e.g. an earth slide having been arranged with the intention of murder.

Investigation of hanging and strangling

In investigating the scene of a hanging or strangling the procedure should be the same as described previously for the investigation of murder in general. It is important that the police officer should learn something about how the knots and nooses which occur in hanging and strangling are made. The formation of knots and nooses of a certain type often indicates whether or not the person hanged could have made them himself. When a knot or noose is of such a type that he could not have made it, then this must cause suspicion. This is a reason for being suspicious when, in a case of hanging or strangling, skilfully made knots and nooses have been made.

In describing knots and nooses the usual names may be used, but it is not to be expected that everyone who reads the report will be familiar with them, and their construction should therefore be reproduced by a diagrammatic sketch or sketches, and they should also be photographed.

The noose should be examined immediately, and the origin of the material used should be determined as quickly as possible. If one or both ends of the cord have been recently cut, and the corresponding pieces are not found at the scene, this circumstance must be elucidated. Cut-off portions of the material of the noose are often found at the scene, and in such a case scissors or other edged tool should be found in a likely place.

The ground under or around a hanged person must be investigated as soon as possible, so that any clues which may be present will not be destroyed. If the individual was murdered and then hanged in order to give the appearance of suicide, it is to be expected that distinct clues will be found, as considerable bodily effort is required to hang up a dead body.

It is not uncommon for a person to commit suicide by hanging or strangling, and at the same time to take measures to give it the appearance of murder. These measures may consist of binding the legs and attempts to bind the hands, but this, especially the attempt to bind the hands, is easily detected. The individual may also have provided himself with some kind of gag, for example a handkerchief, which is pushed in or bound around the mouth. See also 'Death in connection with sexual perversion'.

Knots in a hanging noose should not be undone or cut except in cases

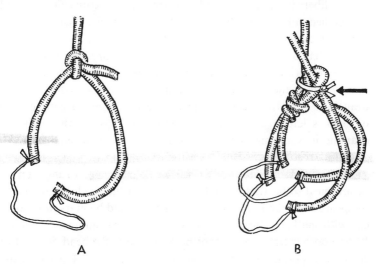

A   B

Fig. 186 When removing a noose from the neck of a body the knots should not be disturbed or loosened. A fixed noose should be cut off and the ends immediately bound together (A). With a running noose the position of the knot on the standing part (see arrow) is fixed, after which the noose is cut off. If the noose consists of a number of parts, they are cut and the ends bound together (B).

where the victim's life may still be saved. Where it is possible, cut the rope or cord some distance above the head, loosen the noose and pull it over the head.

The taking down of the body must be done so carefully that no new injuries are produced. A convenient way is to raise the body a little so that the cord slackens, and then to cut it. The body is laid down and the noose is allowed to remain on the body. After the noose has been examined and photographed in its original condition, it is up to the pathologist to remove it during the autopsy.

The part remaining on the carrying object should be cut off at such a point that the knots are not altered or damaged, after which the cut-off parts are immediately bound together with string. If, for example, a cord is wound in several turns round the carrying object, a diagrammatic sketch of the arrangement is drawn as a reminder, after which the cord is cut and immediately wound round a similar object of the same diameter. When the line is composed of several parts (double or multiple) they are cut one by one and tied together in succession with cord or thread.

In cases where it is suspected that an already dead body has been hung up, the fibers in the cord must be protected, most conveniently by placing it stretched out in a long box, so that it hangs freely. It can be held fast by loops attached by pins to the sides of the box.

What has been said about removing the hanging noose and strangling cord is the principal rule in all ordinary cases where it is to be expected that the life of the individual can be saved. If, however, the body has been dead for a long time (certain signs of death, e.g. putrefaction) the noose or cord is left in an untouched condition. It is for the pathologist to examine it when making the post-mortem examination. When for any reason the investigating officer has to remove the noose or cord from such a body, the knots must not be deranged or loosened. A running noose can be loosened so far that it can be slipped over the head, but before this the the position of the knot on the fixed part should be marked in some way, e.g. with chalk, by sticking in a piece of wire, or winding a thread round it. If the noose is tight and cannot be passed over the head, it is cut off at a convenient point, generally at one side of the neck, after which the ends are immediately tied together with string. The same method is used when conditions are such that for some reason the cord cannot be loosened and drawn over the head. In such a case the position of the knot on the fixed part is marked, after which the cutting is done.

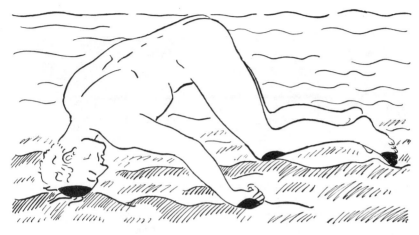

Fig.187 The portions most exposed to injury when a body scrapes against rough or stony bottom.

In cases of strangulation the ligature should be removed in the same way as a noose in the case of hanging. Special care should be taken not to cut through knots which may not be visible from the outside. In general, the ligature should be removed in such a way that the manner of application may be reliably reconstructed. This may require photography and simple sketches to illustrate the various layers and knots which may be present.

As the knots in a cord may be required as evidence, they must be sealed in a suitable manner, and the circumference of the constructive loops should be measured and recorded.

Drowning is death due to liquid entering the breathing passages so that access of air to the lungs is prevented. The liquid need not necessarily be water; it may be mud, sludge or other viscous material. Neither does the whole of the body need to be under the liquid. A person can drown when only the mouth and nose are under the surface. In a more general sense the word 'drowning' is used for every case of death in water, but this is incorrect since a death, for example while bathing, may be due to heart failure, cerebral haemorrhage or shock.

When a drowned person is drawn out of the water a white foam often comes out of the mouth and nostrils, where it forms white spongy puffs which can remain for quite a long time owing to the mucus contained in it.

When the cause of death is simply drowning, murder is comparatively

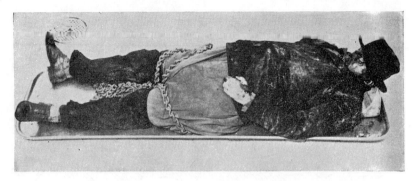

Fig. 188 The bloated appearance of a corpse when putrefaction has set in. This man
committed suicide by shooting himself in the mouth after cutting his wrists and
then falling into the sea fully clothed as shown with a chain around him. He
died of drowning. Note the discoloration of the face.

rare, and as a rule is only committed against children. If injuries are found
on a drowned person which might have been produced by some other person, the drowning can generally be considered merely as the final phase
of a course of events involving murder or manslaughter. It can also happen
that a criminal attempts to conceal the discovery of his crime by sinking
his victim under water.

In cases of drowning the question is generally whether it is suicide or
accident. If the clothes have been removed or the place is chosen with the
idea of avoiding the risk of bumping against a stony bottom, suicide is
indicated. The opposite can indicate accident, as also marks of slipping
found on stones at the edge of the water and injuries produced when the
drowning person attempted to save himself, e.g. scraping of the skin of the
hands and fingers or broken and torn nails.

The body of a drowned person may be tied in some way or heavy objects attached to it to make it sink and remain on the bottom. In such cases
the police officer must proceed very cautiously with the investigation; generally it can be reckoned as suicide, but suspicion of criminal acts should
not be excluded.

A body lying in water is exposed to damage of many kinds. Propellers
of boats may produce injuries. A body hit by a propeller can be cut right
in half. Bodies in water are also often damaged in the breakers off shore,
against rocks, or when they bump against a stony and uneven bottom.

CARBON MONOXIDE POISONING

Carbon monoxide is always produced when the combustion of carbonaceous matter is incomplete, and it is a normal constituent of smoke and explosion gases. It also occurs in mine gases, natural gas, etc. Ordinary illuminating gas contains 5–10 % of carbon monoxide, producer gas 25–35 %, and water gas up to 45 %. Exhaust gases from motor vehicles generally contain 3–6 %, but the concentration can rise at times to 10 %.

Carbon monoxide is a colorless and very poisonous gas with no odor or taste. The minimum concentration which can be injurious to man is 0.01 % by volume, while 0.2 % is dangerous to life. Continued exposure to such an atmosphere can produce death within one hour. If the concentration increases to 0.5 % by volume, or more, then unconsciousness supervenes after a couple of minutes and death follows quickly. With higher concentrations unconsciousness comes on like a blow. Chronic poisoning by carbon monoxide is quite common, and is often due to prolonged exposure in shops, garages, traffic tunnels and streets with high buildings and very heavy motor traffic, also in houses where there are faults in gas pipes, stoves or flues.

The danger from carbon monoxide is due to the fact that the senses do not give warning in time. With acute carbon monoxide poisoning there is a headache, faintness and nausea, with flickers before the eyes. This is usually regarded as a temporary indisposition, so that the individual in question may make the greatest mistake possible under the circumstances, that of lying down. Gradually he becomes sleepy and confused, and the limbs become numb. If he finally begins to realize the danger, it is usually too late, since the body is so weak that the poisoned victim cannot save himself. In a strikingly large number of cases of carbon monoxide poisoning the victim is found close to a door which he was not able to open, or by a window of which he was not able or did not think to break the glass.

It was stated in the beginning of this chapter that the so-called perfect murder is practically impossible. In cases of death due to carbon monoxide poisoning it is, however, theoretically possible to commit the perfect crime – provided that the investigating officer is not doing his job. A murderer might, for example, just open a gas valve in the apartment where his intended victim is sleeping. He can then make his exit and be assured that his victim will die as long as no help arrives in time. It would also be relatively easy to close off the ventilation in a garage where someone is working or close the dampers of a heater in a room where someone is sleeping. In cases of carbon monoxide poisoning the investigating officer should therefore not treat his job too casually. To decide on suicide or accident immediately is wrong: the case should be considered as suspicious from the start and treated accordingly. The analysis of the situation and the result of the investigation must decide whether criminal action should be taken into account. At the autopsy the pathologist can determine only the cause of death.

Murder. A woman (an epileptic) sent for a doctor and said that her child, aged two, had suddenly collapsed and died. The doctor felt instinctively that there was something wrong, suspected coal gas poisoning, and informed the police. They called in the deputy divisional police surgeon who, after examining the child, said dogmatically that death was due to natural causes. He was also asked to examine a baby aged about six months who was in a cot in the same room, and said that there was nothing wrong with it. The police, lulled into a sense of false security by the medical opinion, made no further investigation other than the routine inquiries of a sudden death, and the body was removed to a public mortuary. When it was examined by the pathologist it lay alongside a number of seasonal blue asphyxial deaths from chronic bronchitis, and its pink coloration stood out like a rising sun. Autopsy showed the characteristic signs of carbon monoxide poisoning with (as it was proved later) a saturation of over 50 %. In addition there was an area of oil staining on the left side of the mouth, which was similar to the grease on the rubber tube leading from the gas outlet to the portable gas heater. No carbon monoxide leak could be found in the flat but the woman adhered to her story. She was charged with murder and at her trial was found unfit to plead. Probably the woman disconnected the tube and placed it in the child's mouth (CAMPS, 1950).

Murder – Suicide. A woman of about 46 years, happily married, but menopausal and with some background of mental disease, was found dead, lying across the bed of her daughter aged 14. The windows were shut and a rubber tube led across the landing to the woman's bedroom where it was connected to a gas outlet. There was no evidence of violence upon the child, and it seemed that during the night the woman had brought the gas tube into the room and held it near the child, later succumbing herself. This illustrates the fact that a person can be gassed while asleep without being aroused and without any preliminary narcosis or stunning (CAMPS, 1950).

The commonest cause of carbon monoxide poisoning is illuminating gas, fumes from burning coke or exhaust gases from internal combustion motors. *Carbon monoxide poisoning from illuminating gas* is quite common in towns. The gas has a characteristic odor which cannot be mistaken. When the gas concentration is low the odor is perceived so poorly that possibly an individual does not realize that there is danger. When later the concentration gradually increases the individual may gradually come to realize the danger, but then it may already be too late. Generally, however, a warning is received from the sense of hearing, as the escaping gases usually cause a loud hissing noise.

Suicide by illuminating gas poisoning is quite common. Generally the suicide takes certain measures to seal up places where there is air circulation, generally limited to closing the window, doors, ventilators and dampers. Often the suicide allows himself time to tape over all cracks in the window and door frames, plug the keyhole with cotton and stop the ventilators and flues with rags or paper. There are many cases where the suicide has lain down with his mouth against the opened gas tap, and covered himself with a blanket, so that the high concentration of gas caused death within a few minutes, or he may simply have placed his head inside the oven. It has also happened that the suicide has closed the gas tap before unconsciousness occurred, or has taken other measures for turning it off.

Suicide. The body of a young man was found in a wooden box in a kitchen. The gas pipe of the stove had been removed from the stove and connected to the box through a hole drilled in one side of the box. Opening and pipe fitted so well that the pipe, in spite of its own weight, could not fall off the box. The lid of the box was closed, but there was no outside padlock or lock, so that it might have been possible to lift it up from inside.

The body of the young man was lying on its right side, knees folded up, the right arm under the body, the left on it. The mouth of the corpse was on a level with the opening through which the pipe passed into the box. The parents of the dead boy refused to believe in a suicide.

The autopsy showed that the cause of death was carbon monoxide poisoning. Further investigation also showed that the boy had committed suicide in this very unusual way. Due to the small air-space in the box he must have lost consciousness very rapidly. (HULST, 1949).

Suicide. A couple and their grown daughter were found in the kitchen of a house, poisoned by gas. From the investigation it appeared that all three had desired to die together. The main valve of the gas pipe had been shut off with the aid of a small lever and a cord connected the latter with the hour hand of an alarm clock.

A large number of deaths from gas poisoning are accidental. Most commonly it is a case of liquids boiling over and putting out the flame. In such cases the police officer should investigate the burner and the plate under it, and should carry out trial boilings with a test vessel of the same kind and size as the one in question. The underside of the actual vessel should be examined for signs of the liquid which has boiled over. In order that the flame shall be extinguished by the liquid boiling over, it is necessary that the liquid should run under the bottom of the vessel. If a flat-bottomed saucepan, filled to the brim with plain water, is made to boil over, it will not put out the flame. On the other hand, when the liquid foams it will run under the bottom of the pan and may extinguish the flame. Cases of gas poisoning are sometimes caused by defective or incorrectly attached gas tubing which breaks or comes loose. A sudden draft may also put out the flame. Badly cleaned, damaged or improperly constructed burners can permit the escape of considerable quantities of unburned gas when the gas is lit. This is the case when the blue cone reaches to the tip of the flame and touches the bottom of the cooking vessel.

If an explosion occurs in connection with a case of gas poisoning, this may have been caused by sparks from a doorbell, a pilot flame burning in the gas stove or heater, a glow in the fireplace, etc.

Suicide. A shattering explosion took place in an apartment. Persons who entered the scene found a man who had killed himself by opening the gas burners on a kitchen stove. The investigation revealed that the explosion might have been caused by a spark from a doorbell. A few days later a door-to-door salesman reported that he had rung the bell the moment before the explosion.

In investigating a residence or locality where coal gas poisoning has occurred, the following points, among others, should be examined and described.

Size of room or locality: cubic contents (including equipment and furniture); height to ceiling.

Odor of gas: is odor of gas noticeable in closed cupboards, drawers or closet? When the individual was in bed, the gas concentration under the bedclothes may be marked even though the room has been aired.

Doors: open or shut; sealing precautions (do not forgot keyhole).

Windows: sealing measures, drafts.

Ventilators, flues: closed or open; size and height above floor; is draft weak or strong? sealing measures; do not forget flue of kitchen stove and exhaust fans.

Gas stoves and heaters: burners; oven; valves; evidence of boiling over; pilot light functioning; smell of gas when burners are lit; condition of pipes, hoses and connections.

Carbon monoxide poisoning from coke stove. In the combustion of a coke stove there is produced about 5 c.ft. of carbon monoxide. An ordinary wood stove gives 1–3 c.ft. If the space or room is small a wood stove can produce a fatal concentration of carbon monoxide. The fumes from burning coke have a distinct suffocating smell.

In investigating a place where poisoning from coke fumes has occurred, the actual fireplace should be examined carefully. The position of the damper should be noted. The nature of the last fire in the stove is investigated. The presence of fire, glowing ash or merely of residual heat should be confirmed. The smoke passages should be examined with the idea that fumes can be generated from burning coke even though the damper is open. This may be due to a constructional fault, faulty sweeping, snow which has come down the chimney, bricks fallen down, birds, etc. A bad draft in the chimney is often due to it having been built against an outer wall and being thereby continually exposed to cooling, and the cold air in the flue stops the draft.

Carbon monoxide poisoning from exhaust gases of internal combustion motors. This can occur when the engine of a car is started up and allowed to run for a while in a garage with bad ventilation. Suicide may be committed in this way.

Fig. 189 Suicide by leading the exhaust fumes into the car through a rubber hose.

SEXUAL MURDER AND RAPE

Strictly interpreted, the terms 'sexual murder' or 'sadistic murder' denote homicide committed as a means of satisfying an abnormal sexual urge. The murderer is usually termed a 'sadist'.

Sadism is a form of sexual abnormality. Persons who have this deviation are excited by maltreating or inflicting bodily injury on another. The abuse of the victim may be the sadist's only way to achieve sexual gratification. The result is usually aggravated assault or murder. Since the sadistic act is often a substitute for the normal sex act, the usual evidence of rape or intercourse may be completely absent at the scene. The violence usually consists of biting, strangling, or cutting, stabbing or crushing injuries. Mutilation of the sexual parts, abdomen and breasts may be present.

The expression 'sexual murder' has, however, been adopted generally for all crimes where the woman has been killed in connection with a sexual crime directed against her, generally rape. In a case of sexual murder the victim may have been killed: 1. from sadistic desire; 2. in carrying out a rape (generally killing through the criminal's attempt to silence the cries of his victim by stopping her mouth with clothing, a cushion or hand, or by a throttling grip round the throat); 3. by brutality in the sexual act (generally only kills children and old people); 4. after the sexual act to prevent an accusation; and 5. from shock.

The methods used in the investigation of the scene of a sexual murder are in general the same as those used for the investigation of an ordinary case of murder or suspected death. Regarding injury on the dead person, one can usually expect to find fingernail marks from the hand of the criminal pressed against the mouth of the victim or from gripping around the throat, contusions and injuries from a blow on the head, and bruises, nail marks and other injuries resulting from a strong grip on the neck, arms and shoulders, around the back and hips, on the inside of the thighs, knees and on and around the sexual parts. Otherwise the most important clues are semen, hair from the criminal (especially pubic hairs) and fragments of skin which may get under the nails of the woman when she tried to defend herself by scratching. In investigating the clothes special significance should be placed on their position on the body (also their relative position), and any injury to them.

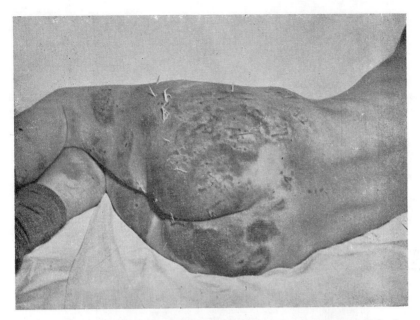

Fig. 190 A victim of sadism. The lower body of this woman was covered with bruises caused by the blows dealt her by the sadist.

Sexual Murder. A white woman had fallen victim to a sadistic murderer. A skin fragment was found under her fingernails which turned out to be from a Negro. A Negro was suspected in the case, and he was arrested. Examination of his body showed numerous scratch marks on the arms. (GONZALES – VANCE – HELPERN, 1940).

In investigating the scene it should also be remembered that violence may have been used towards a woman when she was asleep, dazed or unconscious. All indications of poisoning, the consumption of alcohol or the like should therefore be taken into account.

It is very important that the autopsy should be made as soon as possible, since marks of semen can easily be destroyed.

Where a woman alleges she has been raped or that an attempt has been made to rape her the police officer should always bear in mind the possibility that she is making a false charge. Her allegations against a man she names may be in revenge or due to mental derangement.

The accusation may also be made after the woman had voluntary intercourse with a man but later, fearing pregnancy, claims she was raped. The

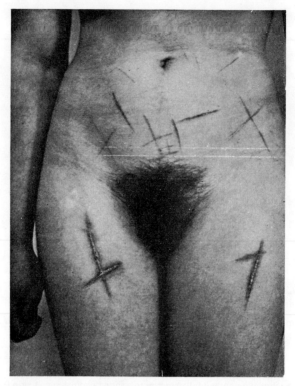

Fig. 191 The body of a victim of sadism showing cuts from a razor blade.

motivation for the accusation may be an attempt to excuse her conduct or to create grounds for a legal abortion.

Cases coming under the first two conditions have occurred where the woman, with the intention of providing evidence against the man, has made arrangements which give the impression of having been produced by the alleged rape. Such arrangements may consist of torn clothing, minor injuries on her own body, contamination of the sexual organs with blood, etc.

When a woman or girl alleges she has been taken to some building or house where she was raped or an attempt was made to rape her, it is important to have her describe fully the place or room to which she was taken, getting as much detail of the furnishings, colors, etc. as possible. Where a very young girl has been enticed by a man off the street to a room or into an automobile, such a description, found to be correct when checked, is very good evidence because the girl could not have described the room accurately if she had not been there.

In investigating the scene of a rape the ground is examined for any signs of a struggle, marks on the ground, portions of torn articles of clothing, fragments of textiles, torn-off buttons, blood, semen, etc. Samples of dust, sand, soil, vegetable matter, etc. are taken from the ground or floor covering for comparison with similar marks on the clothes of the criminal. The topography of the place should be given special attention, and a sketch made of the scene and its surroundings showing, among other things, the nearest place where people live or are to be found.

When a person suspected of sexual murder or rape is taken into custody, his clothes and body should be examined immediately. The commonest marks are scratch marks on the face, hands and arms, bite wounds, torn clothes, dirt and dust on the clothes from the place where the crime was committed, hair, blood and vaginal epithelial cells. Hairs can consist of, among other things, pubic hairs from the woman, which are attached on or around the sexual parts of the man. Blood and vaginal epithelial cells can be found on the sexual parts and their immediate surroundings, and also on the hands, especially under the nails. Regarding the occurrence of blood, the police officer should consider the possibility of a blood group determination. (See 'Blood').

DEATH IN CONNECTION WITH SEXUAL PERVERSION

An old and widespread view is that death by hanging is preceded by sexual sensations. This view is based on the fact that a hanged person often shows signs of ejaculation of semen in connection with the onset of death. This view is, however, certainly wrong, since the excretion of seminal fluid after death is a quite natural phenomenon which results from relaxation of the body. There have been many cases of death by hanging or suffocation where the individual has evidently placed himself in a dangerous position with the object of obtaining a sexual satisfaction, but has become helpless and unable to save himself from the dangerous position. Before the hanging the individual may have taken other measures which are clearly intended to heighten the sexual excitement in some way, for example, binding the legs, squeezing or binding the genitals, etc. A special variety of such preparation is the use of a plastic bag or similar covering over the head in

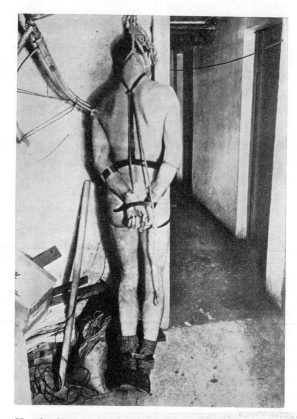

Fig. 192 Hanging in connection with sexual perversion. The victim had himself applied
the shackles but was unable to escape and died from asphyxia.

(*Courtesy of Professor Fritz Schwarz, Zurich*)

order to deliberately cut off the supply of oxygen. Sometimes the individual has also used women's clothing or pornographic pictures to heighten
the sexual stimulation.

Accidental strangulation. A man was found dead next to a bed in his apartment. He was
dressed in only an undershirt. Both legs were tied together at the ankles, and a folded
pillow was wedged between the thighs. A wide leather belt was tied around the waist.
The face was covered by a rubber bathing cap tied at the back of the neck. Inside the
bathing cap was a large piece of absorbent cotton which was apparently soaked in
ether. The investigation revealed that the man had made these arrangements in order
to receive sexual gratification but had become unconscious and died from asphyxia.
(WESTLIN, 1939).

There have been cases where persons have committed suicide under the influence of sexual disgrace from early senility or impotence. Under such conditions the suicide may first mutilate the external sexual organs and even cut them off entirely.

Attempted suicide. A man, almost bleeding to death, was found in his residence. Both arms were badly lacerated. When he was taken to the hospital it was found that his external sexual parts were completely cut away. The man stated that he had been attacked by an unknown person who committed the mutilations. Investigation of the residence showed that he had produced the injuries himself. Gradually he admitted having made them with a knife and razor blades. The external sexual parts had been cut off with a single cut and washed down the toilet.

Masochism is a form of sexual perversity which should be mentioned in this connection. Persons with this tendency want to be treated brutally and shamefully by one of the opposite sex, and find sexual satisfaction in this way.

DEATH IN CONNECTION WITH CRIMINAL ABORTION

The measures which are employed for criminal abortion can be divided into two main groups: 1. production of a toxic state in the mother, which causes the embryo to be ejected by the body, and 2. mechanical action intended to harm the embryo directly.

In recent times criminal abortion by the production of a toxic state has become rare. This method was once not unusual, due to the ease with which suitable poisons could be obtained. Phosphorus poisoning, for example, occurred most commonly during the time when phosphorus matches were in general use. Of the poisons which were employed later with the same object there may be mentioned: quinine, hormone preparations (e.g. oestrone, pituitrin), powerful laxatives (e.g. aloes, rhamnus, colocynth), ergot (ergometrine), acetum cevadillae, juniper (savin), apiol, lead pills, certain essential oils (found in furniture polishes), saffron, red lead, etc.

The method of producing a miscarriage by mechanical intervention is now the most common. Generally the intervention occurs by the sound method – the introduction of a sound, catheter, or similar object into the womb, where it is left usually for a day. The effect is generally to produce

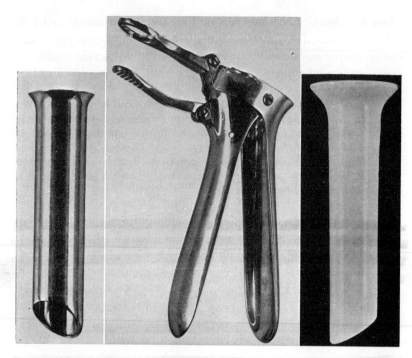

Fig. 193 Different types of vaginal speculums used by criminal abortionists.

an inflammation of the womb, whereby the embryo is destroyed and ejected from the body. The inflammation can also cause very serious sepsis
resulting in death. The probing is usually done with semi-solid sounds, but
sometimes other objects are used, for example, knitting needles, pipe cleaners, broom straws, sticks or steel wire. Often such primitive sounds are
covered with rubber. When using such instruments there is always great
risk of serious injury in the hypogastric region, often leading to death by
bleeding.

An instrument often used to produce a miscarriage is the so-called uter-
ine syringe. For this purpose it is provided with a long nozzle of metal,
which is introduced into the womb. The syringe is used for injection of
either large quantities of liquid, some chemical solution, or hot liquids.
There is great risk that there may be air in the syringe, which may get into
the large blood vessels and cause immediate death from air embolism. The
solutions which are used for injection may contain soap, sublimate, lysol,
oxalic acid, etc.

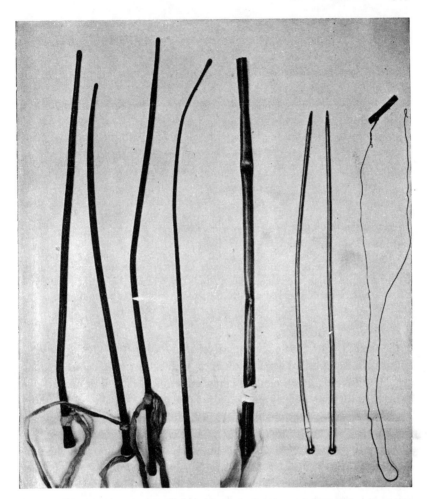

Fig. 194 Different types of sounds used for purposes of abortion. Often the sound is tied
to the thigh to keep it in place. The mishandling of sounds often couses severe
internal injuries and, not uncommonly, death. The photograph shows knitting
needles, wire and rubber tubing.

Criminal abortion can also be performed by means of a poison, for example arsenic, tincture of iodine, soap, etc., introduced into the vagina.
There are also a number of other methods which can be adopted for the
purpose of producing a miscarriage, but which are as a rule ineffective.
These may consist of a hot sitz bath and foot bath, cold bath, hot rinses

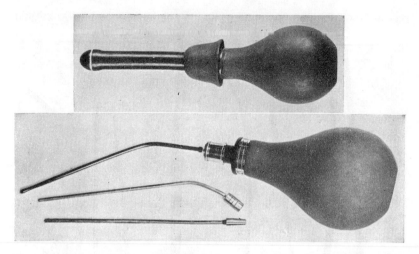

Fig. 195 Syringes used by abortionists to produce miscarriage. Above: for introduction
of liquids into the vagina. Below: with different nozzles to enter the cervix.
Liquid is then pumped up into the womb to cause the embryo to come out.

in the vagina, mistreatment of the woman by a blow or kick against the
hypogastric region, hard work, lifting heavy objects, washing clothes, danc-
ing, bicycling, etc. Such methods may sometimes result in a miscarriage,
but only with a pregnancy particularly susceptible.

In investigating a case of death where criminal abortion is suspected,
the police officer should recover everything which can be supposed to have
any connection with the case. In general the procedure should be the same
as with the investigation of death from poisoning. When there is occasion
to suspect that mechanical intervention has been employed, search should
be made for blood, surgical dressings, cotton, etc., in drains, toilet, trash
can, fireplace, compost or manure heap, etc. The possibility should also be
considered that rinsing liquids may have been poured down the drain or
toilet and may be found in the trap.

In a case of sudden death associated with criminal abortion it is not
always certain that the abortive measures have been carried out at the
place where death occurred. The operation may have been done elsewhere
and the individual may have been able to travel quite a long distance before the effect was fatal. It has happened that a woman died suddenly on
a visit to an abortionist, and the latter then removed the dead body. The

investigating police officer should therefore make an analysis of conditions at the place where the body was found as quickly as possible, in order to resolve any doubt.

At the scene of a criminal abortion the abortionist generally leaves his finger prints on instruments, vessels, bottles or other objects which have been used in connection with the case. Finger prints should therefore be looked for with the same care as with other crimes.

The investigator should recover all addresses and telephone numbers which may be found on scraps of paper, in notebooks, etc. in the victim's residence. The abortionist or middle man can often be located from this information. The victim's correspondence should be similarly searched.

INFANTICIDE

In cases where a baby is suspected of having been killed at birth and does not appear to be fully developed, the pathologist must decide whether it was viable (capable of living). A child is considered to be viable when it has attained such a state of development that it would remain alive without any special care, such as for example keeping in an incubator. Viability is considered to be reached when the child has a length exceeding 16 in. If the length is less the child is considered as not viable. Babies with a length of 10 to 16 in, can certainly be born alive, but as a rule it is considered that they have not reached such a stage of development that they can continue to live.

One condition for the slaying of an infant to be considered infanticide is that the killing occurs during the day following delivery and, in most cases, that the mother is the criminal. Investigation of the scene of the crime should be done in such a way that it will be possible to decide on the time which elapsed between the birth and the crime. If possible the investigation should also discover whether some other person, with or without the assent of the mother, committed the crime or was present or helped in it.

Infanticide can be committed by intentional neglect, killing with a weapon, suffocation with soft materials, pushing objects into the mouth, throat or nostrils, or by drowning. Investigation of the scene of the crime should be carried out in the same way as for murder with a similar procedure as described earlier in this chapter. A number of special conditions in the case of infanticide should, however, be emphasized.

Intentional neglect occurs when the mother omits to take the child under her care immediately after birth, in spite of her being able to do so. The crime may be considered as made more serious by the mother concealing the child and thus making its survival impossible. The lack of care may result in the child dying slowly from cold, which may occur even if the temperature is not abnormally low. The body of the new-born child is quite moist and its heat regulation is not properly developed, so that cold may be fatal even within half an hour after birth. It is also considered as neglect when the mother intentionally leaves the child lying where it lay after the delivery. If the child lies on its face with the face pressed against a soft surface in a bed, or in blood or amniotic fluid, death may result from suffocation. If the mother is alone the child can in fact die in a similar way because the mother is helpless during or immediately after the delivery, and for that reason is unable to take care of the new-born child. The baby may then, for example, be strangled by the umbilical cord if this is around its neck, or suffocated by the membranes.

Killing with weapons. This is usually carried out by blunt violence intended to crush the head of the baby. The killing may also be done by striking its head against some hard object. In a sudden delivery the baby can also receive severe head injuries, for example when delivery occurs in the standing position or the mother sits on the toilet. Injuries caused by a weapon are easy to distinguish from injuries from sudden delivery, since as a rule the first-mentioned are very serious owing to the mother wishing to kill the child quickly. In that case injuries from repeated violence can generally be found. If the mother states that the injuries occurred from sudden delivery, then the place of birth as given by her should be carefully examined.

Strangling with a cord. There have been cases where a new-born child has been deliberately strangled with the umbilical cord. During delivery the child may accidently be strangled in this way. Generally no strangling groove is found after strangulation. With fully developed babies a fold of skin may be found on the neck. This differs from a strangling groove by the absence of epidermal injuries. The character of the fold is shown when the head of the baby is bent. (See also 'Death by suffocation').

Strangulation by hand. In cases of strangling by hand there are usually considerable injuries on the neck. The skin of a baby is moist and slippery, so that the fingers slip easily and scratch marks occur from repeated powerful grips. It should, however, be noted that similar injuries can occur

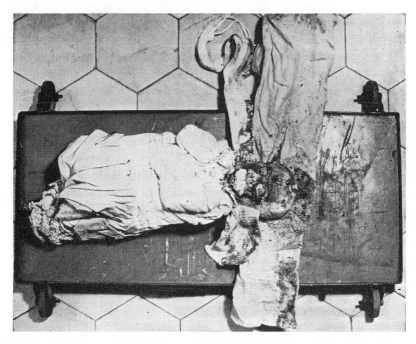

Fig. 196 The decomposed body of a baby found in a suitcase in an attic. Cotton had
    been forced into the mouth and a navel dressing and a piece of cloth had been
    wound around head several times.

when the mother attempts to hasten delivery by gripping the head and neck
of the child with no intention of harming it. The actual course of events
can only be determined by an autopsy. In strangulation by hand it is con-
ceivable that the fingers would form plastic finger impressions in the so-
called skin grease on the neck of the baby. (See 'Finger prints and palm
prints').

Suffocation by soft material. This can be caused by a pillow pressed
against the face of the baby, or a hand pressed against the nose and mouth.
In the first case the presence of mucus and skin grease on the pillow may
reveal the course of events. When suffocation is performed by hand,
scratch marks may be produced on the face. It should be remembered that
suffocation can also occur if the baby lies on its face on soft bedding, or
when pillows or covers accidently lie on it.

Pushing objects in the mouth, throat and nose. Suffocation can be caused
by cotton or the like being pressed down in the throat and plugged in the

nostrils. When it results from one or more fingers being pushed down the throat, serious injury is generally caused.

There have been cases where a mother has killed her child by dipping her finger in some poisonous substance and then putting it in the child's mouth. The presence of poison under the nails of the mother can, in such a case, explain what has happened.

Drowning can generally be considered to be deliberate. It often occurs in the particular vessel, for example bucket or chamber pot, which contains liquid from the delivery.

In cases of abandonment it often occurs that the body of the baby is found wrapped in some covering, and usually the parentage is not known when the find is made. The covering may consist of towels, sheets, portions of clothing, newspapers, wrapping paper, etc. A careful investigation of such objects can give useful information for tracing the mother.

DEATH FROM ELECTRIC CURRENT

Death from electric currents can occur from the electricity supply or from lightning.

Visible injuries may be present at the points of entry and exit of the current – the so-called current marks. If electric sparks or an arc touches the skin there is a burn which often shows the same form as the object producing it. When the direct injury is slight, there are characteristically formed fissures and figures which indicate the passage of the current. The current marks are often round, sharply delimited and light in color, or they may consist of edges or surfaces where the skin is charred. In severe cases the injury penetrates the underlying tissues of the musculature and bones. The surface of the skin may be impregnated with fine metallic dust, which emanates from the current-carrying object, and this can be so great that it appears as a discoloration, sometimes grey or black, and sometimes blue or bluish-green. The metallic dust can be determined spectrographically. Considerable changes in the skin may also be produced at the point of exit of the current. At the points of entry and exit of the current the clothing may be torn or charred; sometimes the damage consists of a number of small holes with burned edges.

Death from electric current may be either accident or homicide, but there have been cases where a trap has been set using house current, with the intention of murder.

Attempted murder. A married woman received a violent electric shock while having a bath and reaching for the soap in a metallic soap dish on the bath. This was not the first time she had experienced this and eventually she informed the police.

The police investigated this case and later charged the husband with attempted murder. At the trial evidence was given that an electric wire had been run from a bedroom closet up through the bedroom ceiling, into the attic of the house, across the attic, down through the ceiling of the lavatory, behind a wooden partition in the lavatory to the bathroom, where one end of the wire was fixed to the metallic soap dish. It was alleged that when his wife took a bath the husband connected the other end of the wire to an electric socket in the bedroom and switched on the electricity. The wife received a series of violent shocks every time she touched the soap dish. The husband was convicted of attempted murder and sentenced to ten years penal servitude (HATHERILL, 1952).

Death from lightning is rare. When injuries are present on the body of a person who can be assumed to have been killed in this way, they may consist of current marks on the neck and soles of the feet; the clothes may be badly torn; metal objects in the clothes may be fused together, burned or thrown away, even in cases where no injury is apparent on the body. So-called lightning figures on the skin are not burn injuries but result from changes in the blood vessels. These arboreal marks generally disappear very quickly after death.

VIOLENT DEATH IN FIRES

The cause of death and injuries on a person who has been burned to death can only be determined by a pathologist. Death may be due either to suffocation by smoke, carbon monoxide poisoning, or to injury from falling beams, overturned furniture, falling walls, etc. Generally the person is already dead from such causes before the fire begins to attack the body.

Burned bodies usually lie in a distorted position, the so-called 'pugilistic attitude', which is caused by the contraction of the muscles under the action of heat. The skin and soft tissues crack gradually, and the cracks sometimes have quite even edges which can easily be confused with cut and stab wounds. The bones become more or less brittle, so that breakages occur. In the inner parts of the skull the pressure may become so great that the bones of the cranium may shatter. The body is charred gradually by the

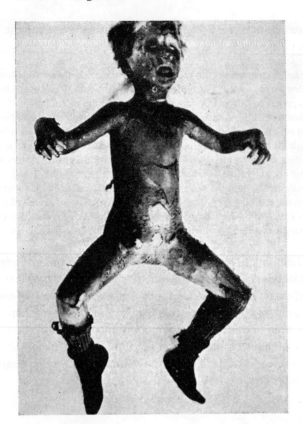

Fig. 197 The typical pugilistic attitude taken by a burned body. It is caused by the contraction of muscles due to the heat of the fire.

Fig. 198 Fissures in the skin caused by intense heat. The absence of hemorrhages indicates that the injury ocurred post-mortem. (*Dutra, 1949*)

heat, the limbs being destroyed first. A strongly charred body sometimes has the form of a torso.

For complete combustion very intense heat for a comparatively long time is required. A new-born baby can be burned away in an ordinary stove in two hours, but in order to consume an adult in the same time a temperature of 1250° C is needed, after which only certain bones remain.

Murder by burning does occur, but it can generally be assumed that the victim was subjected to other injuries before the fire was started. Disposal by fire after murder is, however, not uncommon. The criminal may in both cases have caused the fire with the object of destroying evidence. The pathologist can easily decide whether the victim of a fire was alive or dead when the fire started. If no signs of inhaled smoke or flakes of soot are found in the respiratory organs, this is a sign that he was dead. Underneath a burned body there are often found parts of the skin which have escaped burning, as also on parts of the body where tight-fitting clothing has protected the skin. In such places signs of external violence may show clearly. Traces of blood may be found on unburned portions of clothing under the body. Uninjured parts of the skin around the wrists and ankles

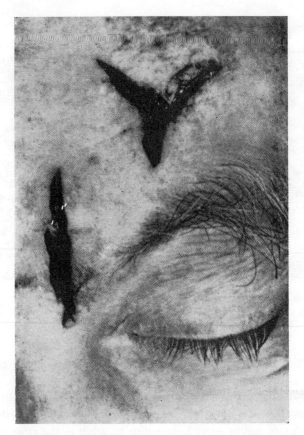

Fig. 199 Injury to the forehead simulating injury caused by heat. The wound was caused by a blow from a leather-covered lead pipe. In this case the hemorrhages
show that the injury occurred ante mortem. (*Dutra, 1949*)

may indicate that the victim was bound before the start of the fire. A noose
round the neck, destroyed in the fire, may leave a distinct strangling groove.

Murder. In a burned-down cottage an old woman was found dead and severely burned.
No injury was found on the body other than what might have been caused by the fire.
No soot particles could be found in the air passages, showing that the woman must have
been dead before the fire started. It was assumed that there had been an accident. Later
some members of a gang were suspected of having murdered the woman and then started
the fire. The investigation revealed that a hole had been bored in the wall of the cottage

at night, and exhaust gases from a car passed through a tube in the hole into the cottage, so that the woman died. After the cottage had been ransacked, the criminals had started the fire.

Suicides by burning occur, but generally the suicide, immediately after starting the fire, has employed other measures to shorten his life. There have been individual cases where the victim did not take any measures other than lighting the fire.

Suicide. A body was found in a tannery boiler. All evidence normally indicated that the case was one of murder and not suicide. However, investigation established that the deceased had attempted suicide by throwing himself into various machines in the tannery. Although these attempts were thwarted, later in the day he succeeded in crawling into the firebox of the tannery boiler and committing suicide. (NICOL, 1948).

Suicide. After a fire in a cottage had been put out, a woman was found lying, dead and badly burned, on a number of objects piled up on the floor. It was determined that the woman, in a state of mental aberration, had gathered together a pyre of inflammable objects, set fire to them and lain down in the fire. The autopsy showed that she had been

Fig. 200 Suicide of a woman by burning. She arranged a pyre, set fire to it, and lay down in the fire.

alive for some time after the fire had attained its full intensity. Thus the heart had worked even while the limbs were being burned, and had pumped up melted fat which was found at the autopsy in the form of clumps in the heart.

DEATH BY FREEZING

Freezing to death does not as a rule produce any distinguishable injuries or changes in the body. At the autopsy red spots may possibly be observed on those parts of the body where livid stains occur more rarely, e.g. the ears, tip of the nose, fingers and toes. As a rule only weak, helpless, insufficiently-clothed or drunken persons are frozen to death. The death may be the final phase of a suicide.

Freezing to death can occur as the result of criminal actions, e.g. exposure of new-born or delicate children. A person who has been rendered helpless by an assault can also freeze to death.

Persons who have died from freezing are occasionally found more or less undressed. This condition naturally gives rise to suspicions of homicide. However, in some cases it has been explained as an action by the victim who, at an advanced state of freezing, gets a sensation of heat.

DEATH BY POISONING

The confirmation of death by poisoning is usually very difficult and requires a great deal of experience on the part of the pathologist. The police officer has little opportunity of being able to state with any certainty that poisoning has occurred. He must rely entirely on his analysis of the situation. In a number of cases of poisoning, however, certain details in the appearance of the dead person or special circumstances in connection with the death give a basis for forming an opinion on the case.

When the skin around the mouth is corroded, poisoning may have been produced by, among other substances, carbolic acid, nitric acid, hydrochloric acid, sulphuric acid, oxalic acid, cresol, corrosive sublimate, ammonia, caustic potash or soda, washing soda or chloride of lime.

In poisoning by phosphorus, hydrochloric acid, sulphuric acid, acetic acid, etc. the vomit resembles coffee grounds, and has with phosphorus an 'onion' smell and is luminous in the dark due to its phosphorus content.

The feces may also contain phosphorus. Such poisons as carbolic acid, lysol, cresol, and ammonia usually have a characteristic smell.

In carbon monoxide poisoning the livid stains are light red to bright red in color. In cases of hydrocyanic acid poisoning the face including the lips are of a reddish color and the body surface very often shows pinkish irregular patches which are, however, not so pronounced as in carbon monoxide poisoning.

Opium, morphine, and nicotine cause contraction of the pupils of the eyes; alcohol, atropine (belladonna), benzedrine, cocaine and scopolamine produce dilatation.

In death from subacute and chronic arsenic poisoning there may be found a large quantity of thin stool resembling rice, and often containing blood. Considerable excretion is also usual in the later stages of poisoning from corrosive sublimate or lead salts.

Strychnine causes convulsions: the corners of the mouth are drawn up and the face is fixed in a grin, while the arms and legs are drawn together and the back is severely bent backwards due to contraction of the muscles.

Different colored material in the vomit can give clues to the type of poisoning. Brown material resembling coffee grounds indicate poisoning with strong alkalis such as sodium or potassium hydroxide; yellow indicates nitric and chromic acids; blue-green, copper sulphate; black, sulphuric acid; and brown-green, hydrochloric acid. A sharp-smelling vomit indicates poisoning with ammonia or acetic acid.

Murder by the use of a poison which must be taken internally to be effective are not numerous. Generally it can be reckoned that murder by poison is committed only within a family or close group. In such cases the criminal generally uses some poison which will not arouse suspicion from its color, odor or taste. Murder or attempted murder by the use of poisonous gas occurs occasionally. (See 'Carbon monoxide poisoning').

The police officer should know that in a case of death from poisoning only the investigation at the scene and examination of witnesses can decide whether a case is one of murder, suicide or accident. The autopsy will only decide the poison used and quantity.

It is not possible to go into a detailed description of different poisons and their action. The boundary between poisonous and non-poisonous substances is indefinite. A number of substances normally present in food can cause death by poisoning when they are taken in large amounts. Thus there is a case where the consumption of 13 oz. of table salt caused the death of a man. A number of poisons should, however, be mentioned, including those which have a powerful action and those which are responsible for most cases of poisoning.

Gaseous and liquid poisons. Arseniuretted hydrogen, benzene, benzine (gasoline), carbolic acid (phenol), carbon monoxide, carbon tetrachloride, chloroform, ether, ethyl alcohol, hydrofluoric acid, lysol, methyl alcohol (wood alcohol), nitrobenzene, prussic acid (hydrocyanic acid), sulphuretted hydrogen (hydrogen sulphide), trichlorethylene, etc.

Metallic and inorganic poisons. Compounds of antimony and arsenic; salts of barium, chromium, copper, lead, mercury (corrosive sublimate), and thallium (rat poison); phosphorus, potassium chlorate, sodium silico-fluoride (rat poison), and strong acids and bases such as hydrochloric acid (spirits of salts), nitric acid, sulphuric acid, sodium and potassium hydroxides, and ammonia.

Organic poisons. Acetylsalicylic acid (aspirin), adalin, bromural, carbromal, formalin (formaldehyde), oxalic acid, sulphonal, trional, veramon, and hypnotics of the barbituric acid group such as seconal, nembutal, veronal (barbitone), luminal, etc.

Vegetable and animal poisons. Atropine (belladonna), cocaine, digitalis, morphine, nicotine (plant spays), opium, scopolamine, strychnine, fungus poisons and snake venoms.

Bacterial poisons. Food poisoning (botulism).

The determination of poisoning as the cause of death can be made only by autopsy and chemical examination. In a number of cases of poisoning, however, certain details in the appearance of the dead person or special circumstances in connection with the death may give some indication. The police officer who investigates the scene of a fatal poisoning can greatly assist the pathologist by recovering any evidence of poisoning.

The most usual indications are, first, residual poison in the form of tablets, powder or residues in medicine bottles and secondly, powder wrappings, boxes, tubes, ampules, vials and other containers. All such clues should be recovered, and *each one should be packed separately in a tube or envelope*. When the dead person is lying in bed the bedclothes must be examined very carefully, since the poison may quite possibly have been in the form of powder, and any that was spilled would be very difficult to detect.

All medicine bottles and tubes, *including empty ones*, should be kept, even if the stated contents are considered to be harmless. Even an apparently empty bottle may contain traces of powder, which can be identified by micromethods, on the inside walls. The report of the investigation must state where such objects were found. Prescriptions can be useful guides for the pathologist.

Among the most important evidence in poisoning are cups, glasses and other containers which are found in the immediate vicinity of the deceased, or in such places and under such conditions that they can be placed in direct relation to the death. If liquids, left in a container, are found they should be transferred to an absolutely clean bottle, which is then sealed. When a container holds merely a sediment or undissolved residues, it should be wrapped in clean paper or preferably in a plastic bag. If there are finger or palm prints on it, these must be preserved. Spilled liquids are collected by means of a filter paper, which is then placed in a well-sealed clean glass jar.

When food poisoning is suspected, or it is possible that dishes may have conveyed the poison, the dishes used should be collected and packed in a suitable manner. Food dishes and remains of food are packed in a clean glass jar which is well-sealed. If such clues are not sent immediately to the laboratory, they should be kept in a refrigerator. If there is any suspicion of crime, remains of food should be looked for, also outdoors, in garbage cans, compost heaps, buried in the ground, etc.

Any hypodermic syringes which are found should be recovered and kept in such a way that they cannot become contaminated and the contents cannot run out or be pressed out. The needle of the syringe is conveniently stuck in a cork to prevent it breaking. If there are finger or palm prints on the syringe, these must be preserved. When hypodermic syringes are found, ampules and vials should be looked for in the vicinity.

Vomit, saliva and mucus on or around the dead person may contain traces of poison and must be kept. Suspected stains on clothing and bed clothes are preserved by each of the articles being spread out on clean wrapping paper and rolled separately in the paper. Stains of urine and feces can sometimes give the doctor a guide in making a decision, and should therefore be kept.

Cases of poisoning with methyl alcohol occur at times. It can usually be assumed that there are other persons involved, so that bottles and drinking vessels should be examined for possible finger and palm prints.

Chronic alcohol poisoning can give rise to sudden death, especially after bodily strain. In acute alcoholism death occurs when the concentration of alcohol in the blood reaches .4 to .5 %. The alcoholic subject can, however, provoke sudden death through various strokes of misfortune in a number of ways (drowning, falling, traffic accidents, freezing, suffocation from vomit which cannot be ejected, gagging from food in the windpipe). It has often happened that an alcoholic subject, while incapacitated, has died because he fell asleep in a position which made breathing difficult or strained the heart.

When the pathologist is present at an investigation he will decide which evidence should be collected. If he is not there the investigating police officer should keep everything which might be suspected of being a poison clue, and should subsequently hand it over to the pathologist or toxicologist.

The presence of certain poisons in the human body can sometimes be confirmed a long time after death. Metallic poisons do not disappear with putrefaction. Arsenic can be detected in hair and bony parts hundreds of years after death, while lead also remains for a long time in the bone tissues. Scopolamine, atropine, strychnine and morphine can be detected after several years; carbon monoxide poisoning up to six months after death. Potassium cyanide is decomposed during putrefaction. Hydrocyanic acid and phosphorus remain for only a short time. Hypnotics are decomposed and disappear very quickly – some even in the time which elapses between the administration and the occurrence of death. An exception is barbitone (veronal), which can be detected in the body eighteen months after death. In cases of exhuming a body of a person suspected to have died through poisoning from metallic poisons (especially arsenic), samples of the soil from the grave should always be taken. The soil itself may contain the poison.

TRUNK MURDER, DISMEMBERMENT OF THE BODY

Trunk murder is the name commonly used to describe murders in which the criminal, in order to dispose of the body of his victim, places it in a trunk, chest, large suitcase, box, etc., which he either conceals or carries away. Even more commonly the victim is placed in a sack or covered with a blanket, clothing or a tarpaulin. This crime is often associated with cutting-up of the body.

Dismemberment of a dead body may be offensive or defensive: the for-

Fig. 201 Body of a man tied in a sack and dropped in a lake. Weights had been tied to the sack by rope to prevent the body floating.

mer is usually conditioned by passion and can be regarded as a form of sadism, while the latter is employed by a criminal who wants to conceal the body or to make it unrecognizable. The method used may give information regarding occupational experience (butcher or person with anatomical knowledge), while the surfaces of the wounds can indicate the implements used (knife, axe, saw). Dust and dirt from the body can, in favorable cases, give information of local conditions where the dismemberment was carried out. The murderer may conceal parts of the body at different places over a considerable area, with the object of making identification of the victim difficult or impossible. He may also attempt to destroy the body, for example in an acid bath or by burning.

Often the place where the body was found is not the same as the scene of the crime. If the murdered person is unknown, success in the search for the scene of the crime depends largely on the possibility of being able to determine the origin of the containers or wrapping around the body, or parts of the body. The first step is to determine if labels, stamps or writing can throw any light on their origin. These examinations involve such delicate procedures that they should be entrusted to an expert from the beginning. The crime scene investigator's preliminary examination should therefore not become too extensive.

Dirt or dust present in the wrapping may give direct information regarding what had been in it before. Finger prints, hair, and other traces of the criminal should be looked for. When looking for finger prints no development media should be used until the laboratory expert has completed his examination. Bodies or parts of bodies, which are found enclosed in a

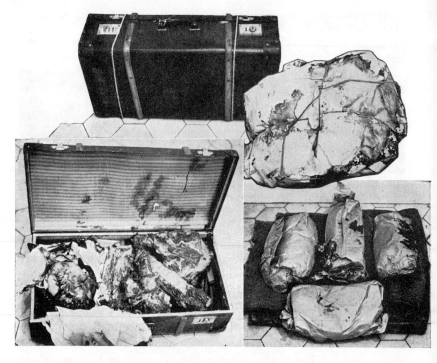

Fig. 202 Parts of the body of a woman dismembered by her murderer. The suitcase was
kept in a basement and the various parcels were planned to be dropped at
widely different places. Some of the more easily disposable parts had already
been washed down the toilet.

package, are generally wrapped in a large quantity of paper, scraps of
clothing, etc., obviously in order to prevent blood or other liquid, or odor,
from betraying the contents. The possibility that the finger prints of the
murderer, in blood or blood serum, will be found on, for example, the
paper must be borne in mind. Objects used to wrap around the body or
parts of the body can also be a useful guide in the search for the actual
scene of the crime.

Murder. An elderly woman was murdered by an intoxicated man in his apartment. Afterwards the man took a large sum of money from the victim's purse and proceeded to cut
up the body. The parts of the skeleton from which he had removed the soft tissues, the
head, hands and feet he placed in a suitcase which he hid in the basement of the building.
He then tried to flush the soft parts down the toilet but was only able to get rid of some

intestines. The other soft tissues he wrapped into packages which he hid in different parts of the apartment and basement.

SUICIDE INVESTIGATION

The most common modes of death by suicide are drowning, hanging, shooting, barbiturate poisoning, carbon monoxide poisoning and jumping from heights. It is more rare that the suicide employs such methods as cutting arteries, stabbing the heart, or burning. Occasionally, a case of strangulation occurs. Men usually choose an active method such as shooting and hanging. Women generally prefer a more passive method such as drowning or poisoning.

The preceding chapter has described how the investigator should evaluate injuries and the cause of death to determine whether he is confronted with a suicide or not.

A determination of suicide is based mainly on the results of interviews with the deceased's relatives and friends and on information from the physician who may have had the victim under his care. The scene of the suicide, the victim's home and place of work may also yield evidence to support a suicide theory. One good indication of suicide is the fact that the majority of persons who kill themselves have at one or more previous occasions either threatened or attempted suicide.

The most reliable evidence of suicide is the letter or note wherein the suicide states that he cannot go on and has decided to end it all. The majority of suicides do not, however, write notes.

When suicide notes are present, they are usually found in plain view near the body. However, the note may also have been written on a piece of paper or in a notebook which is later found in the victim's pocket. In some cases there are several notes placed around the house, or they may even have been mailed to relatives and friends. In doubtful cases the note should be examined by a handwriting expert, especially when the victim was intoxicated or otherwise impaired at the time of writing. The investigator should therefore collect known handwriting specimens of the suicide. He should consider the possibility of finger prints on the letter and the presence of indentations on other sheets of paper under the note. He should also search for the source of the paper and for the actual pen or pencil used.

In suicides using handguns, the victim usually drops the weapon or throws it – up to several feet away – when the arms are flung outwards. In such cases the floor or ground should be examined for dents or scratches resulting from the impact. Occasionally the weapon is found in the victim's hand, but this is usually due to the gun or hand having been supported in some way at the moment of discharge.

If there is no blood on the insides of the hands or on the corresponding parts of the grip of the gun – while the rest of the hand is blood-soaked – it is usually a good indication that the victim fired the shot himself. The same condition applies to knife handles when the victim has slashed himself to death. When the palm of the hand and the grip of the gun are both bloodstained it does not necessarily indicate homicide. However, there is reason to be suspicious if the blood marks on the hand and grip do not match. There have been cases where a murderer placed a gun in the victim's hand after rigidity had set in.

When someone is found dead in a room where the door is locked from the inside, it is usually considered to be a case of suicide or natural death. The crime scene investigator should not, however, be satisfied with this simple conclusion. There are methods by which doors, windows, or other openings can be 'locked' from the outside. The investigator should therefore pay particular attention to unusual traces and marks on doors, locks, latches, windows, etc. (See also Chapter 10, 'Burglary').

Suicide by jumping from buildings is not uncommon in large cities. The body may then land at some considerable distance from the perpendicular. For example, in a jump from an 80 ft. vertical cliff a body was found 42 ft. from the base. This circumstance may seem suspicious, but it is explained by the fact that the force of an outward jump continues to act on the falling body.

A fairly common motive for suicide is illness. The officer should therefore make detailed observations about the presence of doctor's certificates, prescriptions, medicines, records of treatments at hospitals and clinics, and so on.

When bad finances are the cause of the suicide it is not uncommon for bills and other business papers to be found in the immediate vicinity. The individual may have been going over his accounts when he was struck by a sudden suicide impulse. It has happened that a single bill or summons was found on the desk in front of the suicide.

A relatively less common motive for suicide is destitution. In those cases the officer should investigate the household conditions with respect to available cash, food, etc. Various evidence of unemployment may be good indicators.

Other motives for suicide are marital problems, unhappy love affairs, impending death, guilt, failures of different kinds, and senility.

Cases of suicide do happen where none of the commonly accepted motivations are apparent, even after some investigation. The investigator should not be unduly influenced by opinions of relatives and friends of the deceased who are reluctant to accept the fact of suicide. In many cases the motivations for suicide are so deeply hidden that they may remain a mystery forever.

Many suicides are committed under the influence of a mental disorder which may not have been noticed by other persons. Sometimes such suicides are preceded by the killing of family members, usually children. These cases must be investigated as thoroughly as other homicides. If the slayer in such a family drama should survive, it may become necessary to produce evidence about the mental state of the killer. The psychiatric evaluation of the slayer may be considerably influenced by the findings at the crime scene. Even if the slayer should not survive, the scene should be examined with care. It may happen that probate and insurance matters will be influenced by the order in which the victims died.

Any evidence indicating a lack of premeditation on the part of the killer should be recorded. This evidence may be found in circumstances which show that a daily routine or a long-range plan was begun but had suddenly been interrupted.

Chapter 13 **Identification of the Dead**

Personal identification is one of the most important functions of an investigation. The identity of a living person at a crime scene establishes a strong link between the suspect and the crime. Likewise, the identity, or non-identity, of a dead person sets the investigation in motion. Since the vast majority of homicide victims are killed by relatives or acquaintances, knowing the identity of the victim provides a starting point. From the identity, the character of the victim suggests possible suspects. Although not a responsibility of criminal investigations, the identity of non-criminal dead enables the deceased persons relatives to collect insurance, settle estates and provide for the welfare of dependents.

When police are called to a case of death, the identity of the body is generally established by relatives or acquaintances of the dead person or from documents or possessions found on the body. Caution should, however, always be exercised in making a decision on identity merely because documents concerning a certain person are found on a body – such documents may be stolen, or false, or 'planted'. Furthermore, the body itself may be 'planted' to permit someone to disappear. Substitute bodies have been discovered when the dead man's measurements did not agree with those of the alleged victim.

It cannot always be assumed that a relative or acquaintance is competent to identify the body. There have been instances, owing to the state of the body, where even a wife has made a mistake as to identity. It is necessary, therefore, to be careful in establishing the identity of a body even though its identity can be determined with a fair degree of probability. These precautions consist of taking the finger prints, photographing the body, its description (including the dental data), and examining and describing in detail the clothing and objects found on the body. A blood group may sometimes also prove of assistance.

Sometimes, when the body of an unknown person is found it is better to postpone a definite conclusion for a few days until the discovery has become generally known through publicity in local papers and/or the national press. Most unknown bodies are identified by relatives or acquaintances of missing persons who read or hear of the discovery and communicate with the police. The examination of the pathologist at the autopsy of the body will assist greatly in its description, particularly if the body is in an advanced state of decomposition. He will be able to give such details as the apparent age, height, build, weight, scars (including operation scars), etc.

If, however, all this information, general examination, and publicity fail to establish the identity of the dead person, the body has to be buried as that of an unknown individual but it is most important that everything, including the belongings of the deceased, which may be a guide to its identification later, is preserved for possible future use. Further samples should be taken of hair from the different parts of the body and blood group and dental data should be recorded.

In the identification of an unknown body the police officer may have to work with bodies in varying states of decomposition. The most frequent case is that of a body found in water, which can be considered as the most repugnant and difficult since at quite an early stage – in summer only a few days after death – the body swells up and the skin becomes almost black. More rarely a mummified or petrified body is under enquiry. A dead body may become mummified when it lies in a dry place exposed to sun and air, the tissues not putrefying but gradually drying up. Under certain conditions

Fig. 203 Mummified body found inside an empty railroad tank car.

a body can become petrified: the external parts become as if calcified owing to formation of adipocere, and the body resembles a marble statue. Formation of adipocere occurs chiefly in bodies which lie in a very damp place. It may also be necessary to identify a greatly changed or mutilated body or one of which only the skeleton or certain portions remain.

The deceased may be a murder victim. Therefore, before attempting identification, the work should be carefully planned. It must be decided as to how much search of pockets and other articles for identifying documents can be permitted without destroying other important evidence. It may be necessary to move the body or other form of remains to a mortuary where a careful examination can be conducted.

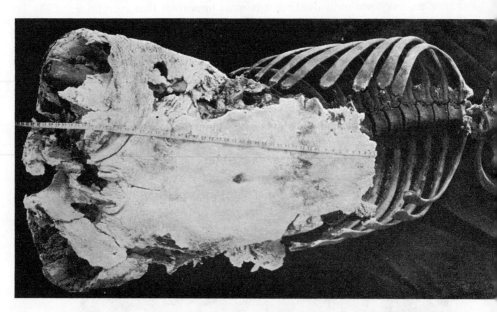

Fig. 204 A dismembered body found in water. The remaining soft tissues have developed adipocere.

Generally the first measure is a preliminary investigation of the pockets of the clothes, and if any documents or other material which can be a guide to identification are found careful note should be taken with a view to publication. If this does not lead to any result the work of identification is continued by taking photographs and finger prints, preparing an accurate description and making a detailed investigation and description of clothes and belongings, after which the discovery of the body may be published in the Police Bulletin.

A form of identification work which requires exceptionally careful organization is the identification of victims of a catastrophe, the procedure for which is described later.

IDENTIFICATION OF A BODY NOT GREATLY CHANGED

Taking of finger prints

Even if an individual is not on record in the finger print file there is a good possibility of identifying him through finger prints. There are often cases in which there is reason to assume that a body is that of a certain missing person, but even near relatives are unable to identify it as it has altered so much. Under these conditions finger prints are taken in order to compare them with latent prints in the home of the individual or at some place where he worked. Such investigation often gives a positive result.

In taking finger prints from a body rubber gloves should always be worn.

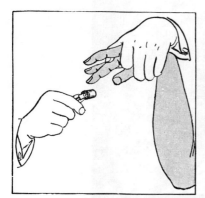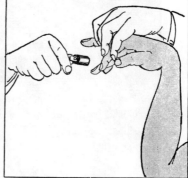

Fig. 205 In taking finger prints from a body when rigidity is fully developed, the hand of the corpse is bent at the wrist to a right angle or acute angle against the lower arm. The pictures show the grip: on left – the finger from which a print is to be taken is pressed down against the palm and is thus accessible: on right – the finger is raised somewhat while the other fingers are pressed down against the palm.

The danger of poisoning from the corpse is very small, but the wearing of gloves is a wise precaution.

There is no special difficulty in taking finger prints from a body after the rigidity has relaxed or when it has only developed to a small extent, and the body has not undergone any considerable amount of change. If there is rigidity in the fingers, the joints should be bent several times until they are sufficiently flexible. The tips of the fingers are then blackened, using a rubber roller and printing ink, and the prints are taken on small pieces of thin card. The inside of a finger is blackened and the slightly bent piece of card is pressed against the papillary pattern on the tip of the finger. The finger should not be rolled against the card because the print will inevitably suffer from slipping. With some practice the card may instead be rolled around the finger tip for satisfactory results. A number of prints of the same finger are taken so that the best results can be selected. When a sufficient number of prints have been taken from one finger, each piece of card is marked to show with which finger it corresponds. When prints have been

Fig. 206 Plastic emulsion cast of the friction skin on one finger of a decomposed and partly mummified body.

taken from all the fingers the best are selected from each and stuck on the respective sections of a finger print card. It is important to be careful not to get the fingers mixed up when sticking on the prints; if prints of two fingers do happen to get interchanged then a search in the register will probably be fruitless. It is best to make up two cards, one being sent to the state or federal file and the other filed with the records. If suitable thin card cannot be obtained, ordinary glazed writing paper can be used. In such a case the taking of the prints is facilitated by using a piece of wood or sheet metal cut to a form fitting the finger. The pieces of paper are placed on this and fixed or held fast on it when taking the prints.

When the rigidity of the body is complete it is difficult to take finger prints, as the fingers are bent towards the palm of the hand and are so stiff that they can hardly be straightened. There is no point in trying to extend such a finger. In criminological literature the police officer is often advised, in such a case, to cut certain tendons in the fingers so that they can be straightened. Certainly this method is quite effective, but it is not necessary to go so far. It is simpler to bend the hand backwards at the wrist to a right or acute angle against the forearm, whereby the fingers straighten out themselves. It is then possible to hold a finger firmly and lift it up to make the print, the bend at the wrist becoming slightly reduced. If this also should be found difficult, then the wrist is bent down again and the required finger is pressed down towards the palm and is then accessible from below.

Difficulty is often experienced when the body is considerably decomposed. The changes in the fingers consist either in their drying up and becoming horny and hard, or in the tissues becoming loose and filled with liquid and the epidermis becoming fragile and puckered ('dishpan hands'). The first occurs generally when the body has lain in a dry place; the second when it has been in water.

When the fingers have shrivelled and dried up finger prints cannot be taken by the method described above, and other methods must be employed. For example, the prints may be read directly from the fingers and classified without taking impressions. It is necessary to be very careful and if possible to do ridge counting and ridge tracing also on those fingers which are not necessary for the classification formulae. A selection is then made of the finger or fingers which are most suitable for recording with printing ink. When this has been done a proper search can be made in the finger print file. This method can, however, only be applied by persons with great experience in finger print classification and is not suitable for a police officer who

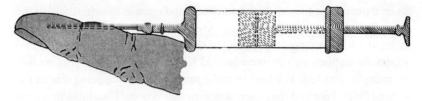

Fig. 207 Drawing showing procedure for injecting water into a finger with wrinkled or granulated skin, so that the print can be taken more easily.

seldom or never has anything to do with finger print identification. When reading a pattern direct from a finger it must be remembered that the print is seen reversed, as in a mirror.

The police officer who is unfamiliar with finger print classification can use a very simple method of casting with the aid of Kerr or other casting media which are used by dentists. The outfit consists of two tubes, and equally long strips are squeezed out of each tube on to a glass plate and mixed together, the mixture being then spread on a finger tip. After five to ten minutes the mass will have hardened and can be removed. The casting obtained shows all details of the finger print pattern, are very permanent and fully applicable for identification.

It is also possible to make a cast in plasticine, which is pressed against the tips of the fingers. As the negative casts obtained are awkward to interpret it is necessary to make a positive cast in plaster. The result can be as good as that obtained with Kerr media, but the latter is to be preferred since only one casting needs to be made.

Recently, methods using various synthetic emulsions, latex or similar material have been used. With these systems, the finger is coated uniformly with a thin layer of the solution. Additional layers can be applied by dipping or spraying the material until a coating of suitable strength is obtained. The cast is removed after setting or hardening. It may be flattened between slides and photographed or it may be flattened, inked and printed. With the latter method, the geometry and color will be reversed and care must be taken in adjusting to proper conditions for a comparison. (See also 'Preservation of plastic finger prints'.)

It is also possible to record the finger prints by photography. This method is, however, especially tedious and difficult to carry out. When the fingers are stiff and bent it is often necessary to photograph each one separately.

Frequently the finger tips are so dried up and wrinkled that the friction skin pattern cannot be read off or cast because important parts are concealed in hard folds of the skin. The pattern may be obtained by thin layer casting as described above, or the fingers may be removed by cutting, in order that the skin may be softened. The pathologist should have an opportunity to view the deceased before this step is taken. The fingers should be cut at the second or middle joint and placed in individual bottles, labelling each according to the hand and finger. This operation should be done only by a doctor or other competent person, but the police officer should be present to check that the different fingers do not get mixed up. The simplest method of softening up the finger tips is then to leave them in water for one or two days, after which they are kneaded cautiously until sufficiently soft, when a print can be taken with the aid of printing ink. Should there still be difficulties the prints must be photographed.

The taking of finger prints from a corpse which has been taken out of the water is generally very difficult on account of the effect of the alterations

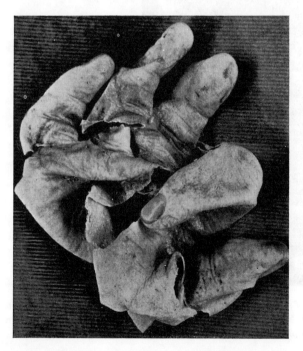

Fig. 208 Finger stalls taken from a body recovered from water. The outer skin of the hand has loosened entirely and has been removed practically as a single piece.

Fig. 209 Piece of skin taken from finger and placed between two pieces of glass to make a slide. Note that the two cuts have not destroyed the papillary pattern which is thus preserved.

in the body. In general these changes may be divided into three stages: 1. the epidermis of the finger tips becomes loose and coarsely ridged, 2. the epidermis is loose everywhere and can be removed, and, 3. the epidermis is missing entirely.

In the first stage the finger tips must first be washed and dried, preferably with cotton or a soft towel; this operation must be done with great care and without rubbing, so that none of the skin is torn off. Finger prints are then taken in the way described above for a body which has not undergone any appreciable amount of change. When the skin is wrinkled and granulated water must first be injected into the upper joint of the finger so that the creases and granulations are smoothed out. For this purpose a 10 ml hypodermic syringe with a fine needle is used. The needle is stuck in approximately at the center of the inside of the center joint and is brought close to the bone in the upper joint, after which water is injected until the skin appears hard and tense. The point must not be allowed to come too near the skin, since the pressure might be sufficient to break the skin, and the needle should not be put in the outer joint or too near it, since in such a case the return path would be so short that the water would run out again. After the needle has been removed the print is taken in the usual way. In earlier technical literature an injection of glycerin, paraffine or melted tallow is recommended. There is however no doubt that a properly performed injection with water gives better results and is easier to carry out.

In the second stage, when the epidermis has loosened, it is easier to take finger prints. The loose skin (finger stalls) of the tips is pulled or cut off from the finger tips, that from each finger being placed in a labelled test tube which is then filled up with water. The finger stalls should not be put in an envelope or other paper wrapping since after a time they will dry up and stick to the paper. When they have been removed in this way the finger stalls may be sent to the finger print bureau for examination.

The best procedure is to place the skin from each finger separately between two glass plates, when they are easier to handle and to photograph. To do this the finger print pattern is cut out of the finger stalls. Since the cut-out pieces of skin are then convex they easily split when flattened between the glass. This splitting is unavoidable, so that it is necessary to make cuts in the edges so that the splits do not occur in parts of the finger print pattern which are needed for the purpose of classification. When placing them between the glass plates a small piece of paper or card, carrying the name of the finger, is placed near the top of the sample so that it can be read only from the inside of the flap of skin, when the print is the right way round. There is not much risk of any such piece of skin being the wrong way round since the inside is lighter, smoother and more glossy than the outside. If, however, in a particular case there should be some doubt as to which is the inside, this can be determined by taking out the piece of skin and seeing which side is concave. The glass plates are bound together with tape. The finger print patterns should be photographed by transmitted light, and the lines show up very distinctly.

Prints may also be taken with the aid of printing ink. After careful cleaning and drying, the pattern area is coated with printing ink in the usual way and pressed against a piece of paper. The method is difficult to carry out, since the skin is generally so fragile that the print can be destroyed by the slightest carelessness. Occasionally the finger stalls are so strong that they can be picked up on a finger, and the print can be taken as from a living person. But it is only in rare cases that the skin on all ten digits is in such good condition that this method can be adopted.

It often happens that large portions of the epidermis become loose, but small parts remain so firmly attached that the finger stalls cannot be removed whole. Sometimes cautious scraping of the attached tissues will loosen the tips in a comparatively whole condition. If this is impossible the part of the underlying tissues to which the finger stalls are attached is cut off, and the whole is mounted on a piece of plasticine. The finger print can be then taken with printing ink, or photographed.

It is far more difficult to take a finger print from a dead person when the epidermis of the fingers has become loose and fallen away, and cannot be found. This occurs generally with bodies which have been in water for a long time. Sometimes it is possible to make out the finger print pattern in the remaining underskin. Only rarely is it possible to take these finger prints with printing ink, owing to the ridges in the pattern being so low. The only possible method is to photograph the pattern. In general, however, it can be considered that the finger prints pattern will have disappeared entirely, owing to the loosening of the skin.

It is difficult to take a palm print from a dead body, even in a case where the body has undergone little or no change. There is hardly any hope of taking a complete palm print, and it is, therefore, necessary to take portions of the print on small pieces of paper or card. To simplify the investigation of these prints each piece of paper should have outlined on it a hand, on which the part corresponding to the palm print is marked in.

In taking finger and palm prints from bodies, printing ink is the best medium since the impressions can be mounted directly on a finger print card or other suitable form. These forms can later be filed with other cards. However, an alternate method may be used which employs black finger print powder. In some cases the results of the latter method may be superior to printing ink.

The finger or palm is lightly coated with the black powder, using a brush. The impression is then obtained by lifting with transparent finger print tape. The pieces of tape are then mounted directly on a finger print card or on paper which is cut up into squares for attaching to the card. In the case of palms, overlapping pieces of tape should be laid lengthwise over the whole palm area. These pieces are then stripped from the hand together and mounted on a card or paper. This method is somewhat more difficult than the inking method but it is superior in that a full impression is obtained. A condition for successful lifting is that two persons are available: one to hold the hand and one to manipulate the tape.

Photographing

In photographing an unknown body a full-face and a right profile face are always taken. If necessary, further pictures should be taken, including a whole view, left profile – especially with a view to identification from the ears – and detail pictures of scars, injuries, teeth, tattooings, clothes, etc. It is good practice to insure that an unknown body must not be buried before it has been photographed. It is, however, important to photograph the body early before putrefaction sets in and swells or discolors the features. With regard to a body which has undergone some degree of change, it may be considered that a photograph of the face will be quite meaningless, but it should be done. It should also be remembered that the individual may be identified after burial and that the relatives may ask to see the photograph of the face. It is well known that people in general do not realize that the face generally becomes unrecognizable, but expect to be able to recognize the body from photographs taken a long time after the person died.

In taking a full-face picture the body should be laid on its back with the face turned upwards. When the body is in a mortuary there is generally a wooden rack or other structure under the head. This should be removed in the photograph. The lower jaw may sometimes show a tendency to drop

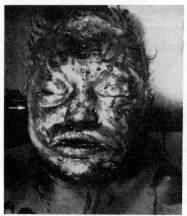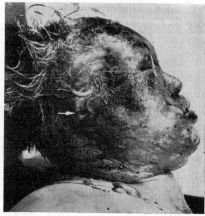

Fig. 210 A body, taken out of the water, of which the right outer ear is missing. The injury gave the impression of having resulted after the corpse had been in water
some time, but it was found that the ear had been removed by operation while
living.

and the mouth to open, so that it is best to prop it up with a peg or other
object which will not be too conspicuous in the photograph. The camera
is placed vertically above the face. The background should be chosen so
that the outer contour of the head is well-defined against it: often the simplest way is to spread a towel under the head. When profile portraits are taken,
the body should be raised so that the camera can be placed at the side of the
head. For this exposure also a suitable background is required so that the
profile shows up distinctly. The head should not be turned to one side to
make it easier to photograph, as this might cause a considerable alteration
in appearance owing to the position of the camera.

In photographing whole face the camera is placed high above the body.
If this is not possible on account of a low roof, then the body can be turned
somewhat to one side, but the procedure must be previously thought out
in view of the possibility of any blood running down or other conditions
of the body being altered. Under no conditions should the body be tied or
suspended in a leaning position. In photographing scars, injuries, tattooings
and details of clothing a *measuring tape* or ruler should always be placed on
or by the side of the object.

For photographing a dead body panchromatic film or plates are generally
the most suitable. The correct choice for photographing a scar or tattooing,

which is perhaps concealed in livid stains, is often difficult. When there is any question it is generally advisable to take photographs, using color, panchromatic and orthochromatic emulsions for the same picture thereby avoiding a possible complete failure. Flash bulbs should not be used when photographing bodies which are wet or covered with blood, since the reflections may conceal details in the picture.

Even at such an early stage that the changes in the body are limited to rigidity and livid stains, it may be difficult to distinguish scars, strawberry marks and birth marks from livid stains, discolorations of the skin and wrinkles. The further the deterioration has proceeded, the greater the difficulties. Blue tattooing is sometimes barely perceptible, since the skin becomes dark-coloured and blistery. Under such conditions the police officer must not rely on his own judgment, but must consult the pathologist.

A body was found in a lake, very much decomposed. One outer ear was missing entirely. To the layman the injury gave the distinct impression of having been produced after the body had been in water for some time. The pathologist who was called in soon found that the ear had been removed by an operation while living.

Fig. 211 Photograph of tattooing on an unknown body. This kind of photography is sometimes very difficult, since the usual blue color of the tattooing can almost entirely disappear in livid stains and other discolorations of the skin.

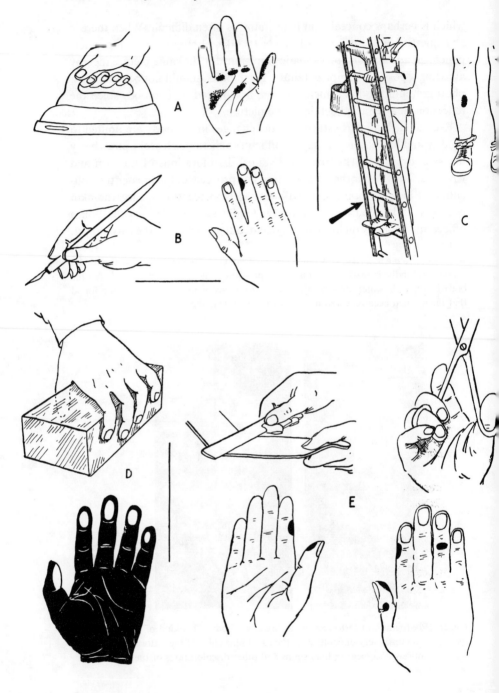

A

B

C

D

E

Any special characteristics are described in essentially the same way as for living persons, except in one respect. In the case of a description of a living person with a large number of tattooings, only those which are characteristic or unusual (names, dates, emblems, etc.) are described. With unknown bodies, however, all tattooings should be described, including those of a very common type. It is of great importance that all tattooings and other special characteristics should be described accurately in a recognized manner with respect to kind, form, size and position.

Many people are X-rayed for the purpose of diagnosing some ailment or for detecting tooth decay. These films are often retained in medical files for many years. Before an unknown body is autopsied or buried, dental and body X-rays should be taken. Not only will they provide a means for definite identification, but they might also provide information as to the cause of death.

Marks of trades or occupations

Marks of trades are nowadays less common than in the past, owing to the mechanization of work and to the use of modern machine tools, etc. There are however still found in certain trades marks which are the result of a characteristic manner of working.

Clerk, draftsman: hardening on the last joint of the right middle finger at the point where the pen rests when writing or drawing; a draftsman also has a hardening on the part or the ball of the right little finger which lies nearest the wrist.

Baker: hardenings on thumb and index fingers of both hands, resulting from handling the edges of hot pans and plates.

Engraver, jeweller: wear of nail of right thumb.

Tailor, dressmaker: marks and scars of needle punctures in the tip of left index finger.

Shoemaker, upholsterer: round hollows in front teeth from biting the thread; shoemakers also show wear on left thumb nail.

Glazier: hardening between middle and index fingers, arising from handle of diamond being held between these fingers.

←

Fig. 212 Diagram showing places on the skin where callouses may from as the result of following a certain trade or occupation. A: laundry worker; B: office worker; C: painter, etc.; D: bricklayer; E: barber.

Washerman: wear on nails of left thumb and index finger.

Dyer, photographer, chemist: nails dry, brittle and often discolored.

Butcher: callouses and hardening on inner joints of fingers and on neighboring parts of palm of the hand which holds knives.

Bricklayer, stonemason: hardening of right hand from grip round trowel or hammer; skin of left hand worn very thin from holding bricks or stone.

Carpenter, joiner: hardening in ball of the thumb of right hand from grip on plane; unusual number of injuries and scars on left index finger.

Painter: callouses and hardenings between right index and middle fingers from grip on handle of brush.

Blacksmith: small white scars on hands and forearms from flying red-hot particles of metal.

Coalworker, stoker: small particles of coal embedded in the skin.

If evidence of repeat operations are observed, these should be noted, sketched and photographed. It may take imagination, ingenuity and some practical research in order to connect these callouses to an occupation, hobby or sport.

Making a description

Making a satisfactory description of a dead body often takes a lot of time and is difficult, especially if the body has commenced to decompose. In compiling descriptions it is therefore best to avoid too definite expressions when describing details for which there is some doubt as to the most suitable choice of words, and in case of difficulty the doctor should be consulted. The body may conveniently be described in the following order: estimated age, length of body, build of body, shape of face, neck, hair, beard or moustache, forehead, eyes, eyebrows, nose, base of nose, mouth, teeth, chin, ears, hands, feet and special characteristics.

If the body has undergone a certain amount of change it is often quite impossible to decide the age, and even a trained pathologist will often avoid making any definite statement. In many cases the age can only be determined by post-mortem examination.

The length of the body is measured with the body stretched out on its back, the measurement being taken from heel to crown of head. It is often difficult to describe the build. In the case of a swollen body taken out of water there is often a temptation to write 'powerful' or 'heavy set', which may be quite wrong. The form and profile of the face can usually be described quite satisfactorily, but the fullness of the face cannot be specified in the case of a body which has undergone change. The color of the hair may change some time after death. When a body has lain in dry earth or in a dry place, the hair often becomes reddish, but in one taken from water the color of the hair does not as a rule undergo any appreciable change.

In describing the hair it should be noted whether it has been well cared for, how it is parted, etc. Samples of hair should be taken from bodies which cannot be identified. There may possibly be a question of comparison with hair which is found in the house or workplace of a missing person, e.g. on a comb or brush. In describing face hair one is often tempted to put 'unshaven', which may be quite wrong since stubble on the face often arises from the hair roots, which, lying originally at an angle to the skin, straighten up after death because of drying and shrinking of the skin. The story that hair and beard grow after death is quite erroneous.

It is often difficult to judge correctly the color of the eyes of a dead person, since at an early stage the eyes undergo considerable alteration. Special attention should be given to the presence of artificial eyes. The forehead is not liable to change much with respect to form. It is difficult to judge the form and size of the nose, since it swells up considerably. On a body which has not undergone any considerable amount of change the profile of the nose can still have altered considerably owing to the tissues in the tip of the nose having shrunk. For this reason a nose which in life was concave may become straight after death, and a straight one become convex. It is usually impossible to decide the size of the mouth, since the lips undergo great change even at a very early stage.

The ears may undergo minor changes with respect to size and form, but even in cases where the body has become completely unrecognizable, the ears may be found relatively normal. It is therefore important that both ears should be photographed, so that a comparison with a photograph of a missing person can be made at some future date.

In the case of hands the care taken of the nails should be described. If necessary the dirt under the nails should be kept, since this sometimes gives information of the trade or occupation. When an unknown body is found without shoes the foot should be measured for probable size of shoe. The pathologist concerned should be reminded to take a blood sample from the body. There may possibly be a question of a comparison with, for example, bloodstained clothing found in the home of a missing person, or a statement of the individual's blood group may be available. Although the individual cannot be identified by blood type, this material may be valuable for excluding possible identities. Typing of putrified blood is difficult and generally unreliable. However, new techniques make possible typing of blood factors in hair, fingernails and bone.

A description of an unidentified dead body should include the clothing. The visible clothes are described first, including accurate indications of the type of material, quality, color, buttons, any damage and if possible how this is thought to have been produced, stains of dust and dirt, etc. Then a preliminary examination is made of pockets and other places, e.g. between the cloth and the lining, where there may be found objects which can be a guide in identification. The garments are then taken off one by one, each being laid separately on a clean paper, in which they are to be rolled up and kept, if dry. The clothes are most easily removed by cutting, which is done if possible on the parts which face upwards. The cutting should not be done too close to seams, damaged parts of the cloth, repairs, marking tags or pockets. If there is a suspicion of a crime the garment, after cutting, is not drawn or cut loose but is left under the body until the latter has been wholly unclothed and can be lifted off. As the underlying garments are exposed exact descriptions of their condition are made. When the shoes are taken off the knots in the laces are not untied, but the laces are cut at suitable places.

When all the garments have been taken off they are investigated in more detail. In the case of pockets special attention should be given to the occurrence of fluff, dust and dirt. The lining is cut and dust and objects in it examined and kept. The buttons and their sewing are described. A good guide to identification may be obtained from any laundry marks, monograms, maker's marks, marks of firms, stamp marks, numbers, tags, sewn-on initials and marks made with marking ink on the garments. Regarding repairs to garments it is advisable to try to find out whether they have been done by a professional or other person accustomed to sewing, or by some one who is not familiar with it.

The size of the shoes, their color, make and type designation are noted. If the size is not marked it can be obtained from the length. The size of the last on which shoes are made starts at 4 in. (size 0) and increases by $1/3$ in. for each size. Thus size 8 (children's) corresponds to a length of $6^2/_3$ in. After size 13 ($8^1/_3$ in.) a fresh series of size numbers starts again from 0, so that size 8 (men's) corresponds to 11 in. in length. The external length of the shoe is greater, depending on the type of shoe.

Half solings, repairs, fittings on shoes, stamped or perforated numbers or marks, rubber heels, degree of wear and defects can be a guide in identification. Dirt in the seams, edges of the soles and arch of the foot should be examined and kept.

After a careful check for loose trace evidence, the garment may be laundered in a small washing machine. This is often necessary in order to make laundry marks visible. Furthermore, in its original condition it may not be acceptable to laymen. It is often helpful to exhibit garments to store personnel so that an assessment of cost, style and taste may be made. Occasionally, the distribution of the items can be located in a restricted area.

If articles of clothing are not be kept, sample pieces should be cut out of the different garments. Any pieces with buttons, repairs, damage, marking, etc. which might be of significance are kept. Pockets which contain dirt and dust are cut off. It is best to affix the object to cardboard and place each one separately in an envelope with a label showing its origin. If shoes are not to be kept for further investigation characteristic details such as repairs, fittings, etc., should be photographed. A sample of the upper leather with lace hole and knot on the laces should also be kept.

Laundry marks and the like

In searching for laundry marks on clothing it must be remembered that they may be invisible. Many large laundries now stamp all incoming laundry with a colorless dye which is quite invisible to the unaided eye but fluoresces strongly in filtered ultraviolet light. The mark usually comprises both the identification mark of the laundry and the number given to the customer. The identification mark sometimes consists of the first letters of the firm's name. The number of the customer is registered with the laundry. The marks are almost indelible and remain even after many washings. When the washing is marked a search is first made for old laundry marks which are crossed out with invisible ink before the new mark is put on. In this way a garment may have several laundry marks, which greatly facilitates identification. Handkerchiefs are generally washed in bundles, but in each bundle some of the articles are marked. For marking suits, trousers, coarse woollen materials and pure silk a rag marked with colourless ink is attached to the garment, and usually the laundry or dry cleaners leave this on when the garment is returned to the customer.

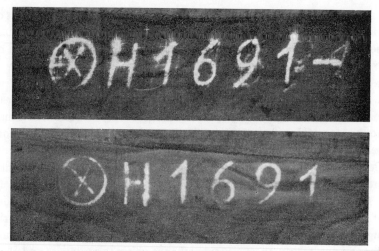

Fig. 213 Laundry marks on handkerchiefs revealed by careful searching; such marks can sometimes only be revealed by precipitation tests or in ultraviolet light.

Laundry marks may also be written or stamped with marking ink either direct on the material or on sewn-on tags. As rule these tags remain when the laundry is returned. When a laundry mark is written or stamped direct on the material, it is usually placed in a *well-concealed place*. In the case of leather gloves the mark is put inside, often right inside the thumb. A laundry mark sometimes consists of a thread which forms a letter or other mark in long stitches.

Unfortunately it is a common practice in the cleaning and laundry industry to identify garments by a paper tag clipped to the article. Unless this tag is attached in an obscure place, the customer usually removes it before wearing the garment.

A good lead for identification can be obtained from monograms, maker's marks, firm's marks, stamp numbers, sewn-on initials and markings made with marking ink. In the case of more valuable garments, such as fur coats, overcoats and suits it is important to look for marks or alterations which careful owners often place on parts turned towards the inside with the idea that the garment may be stolen and that the thief would remove the usual marks. Such identification marks may consist of seams which are sewn with a different thread, small cuts or pieces cut out of the cloth or lining, threads sewn in, etc.

Watchmaker's marks

If a watch is found on an unknown dead body, it should be examined for any marks, figures, etc. which might aid in the identification. Usually the serial number of a watch is stamped inside the case. Certain watchmakers mark watches sold by them with letters or signs which indicate their watchmakers society, together with a figure which is their membership number. When a sale is made the customer may be recommended to take out an insurance on the watch, in which case his name and the serial number on the watch is registered by the watchmaker. Some watchmakers mark the date of sale on the inside of the case.

When a watch is taken in for repair it is usual for the watchmaker to scratch on the inside of the case certain letters or marks and figures which are partly special marks of his own and partly a repair number. The latter is entered up together with the serial number of the watch, name of the owner and kind of repair. The watchmaker's own mark generally consists of one or more initials, but may also be formed of a monogram, Greek letters or other characters, shorthand signs, punctuation marks, private marks, lines,

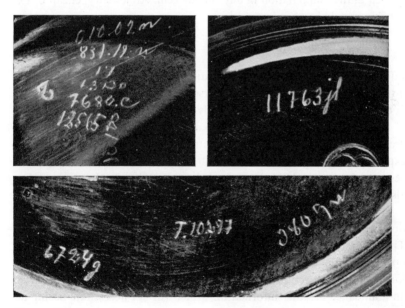

Fig. 214 Watchmaker's marks scratched on inside of watchcase.

figures or mathematical signs. In the United States, investigative agencies may send descriptions of marks, together with a description of the watch, to the United Horological Association of America, Watch Mark Identification Bureau, 1901 E. Colfax Avenue, Denver, 6, Colorado. Any matching marks will be communicated to the submitting agency. Unknown marks will be circulated in the trade journal.

Jewellry

Finger rings usually remain on a body even though it has decomposed to a considerable extent, and they can therefore be a guide for identification. Inscriptions may often be found inside engagement, wedding and other commemorative rings, while signet rings may carry initials, insignia, seals, crests or other distinctive markings. In a number of countries special rings are worn by graduates of universities etc., while orders, societies and associations may use rings as marks of membership.

Although not often used, systems have been reported for the identification of precious gems. These systems are based upon macroscopic and microscopic imperfections in any gemstone that are not likely to be found in their entire combination in any similar gem. All jewellry, cheap or expensive, should be photographed.

Teeth

Information of special value for identification can be obtained from the investigation of the teeth of a dead person, as these are often characteristic in many respects. This applies not only to a case in which the appearance of the dead person has not altered to any appreciable extent, but also to greatly decomposed corpses, badly mutilated victims of airplane accidents, explosions and catastrophes, and also to burned bodies. The teeth are in fact very resistant not only to the normal changes undergone by the body but also to fire and chemicals.

The examination of the teeth of an unknown dead person for identification is done by the pathologist, assisted if necessary by an expert in dentistry. The police officer in charge of the case will decide, according to the importance of the case, to what degree it is necessary to have detailed information in connection with a particular case. In some cases there may be an abundance of other information which will not necessitate basing an actual identity on the teeth alone.

When making an examination of the teeth attention is always directed to the changes or injuries in the face of the dead person which may possibly interfere with the subsequent post-mortem examination or identification. If a body is altered considerably the tissues of the face may be missing or may fall apart if the lower jaw is moved out of its position. In such a case photographing and examination of the body should be done first. If for any reason a police officer has to make an examination of the teeth of a body before the arrival of the pathologist, it should be done in such a way that no marks of the flow of blood or injuries in the face are aggravated or changed, and particularly that the position of any object in the mouth is not changed. If there is any danger of anything of this kind occurring the examination of the teeth must wait until the pathologist deals with the body. The first note to make in connection with the teeth is how many are present. A note should therefore be made as to which teeth are missing both in the upper and the lower jaw. This is most easily done by making a sketch of the teeth of each jaw. In a number of countries special forms are used for this purpose, and they greatly facilitate the work. On these sketches or forms are marked both the position and size of any visible damage resulting from decay (caries) and pieces broken away, cracks, missing fillings, jacket and other crowns, bridge work, root fillings, etc. The material used in crowns, fillings and the like is also noted. In this connection it may be mentioned that in the investigation of teeth of bodies which have been exposed to burning it has been observed that whole gold crowns have been amalgamated owing to an amalgam filling running out and round the mouth. Complete or partial dentures should be kept: possibly the material used in them may be a guide for identification. Dentures may have some identification inscribed or attached to them. It may be the inmate number, service serial number, doctor's identification or the patient's name. A study of the style of the identification will give some indication as to the probable source.

Further, all characteristics of the teeth should be noted carefully. The teeth can be very light (white) or dark (brown); the teeth of the upper and/or lower jaw may be directed inwards or outwards, the teeth may be widely spaced or close together or wedged in against one another; exceptionally large spaces may be found between the middle front teeth (central incisors); the central teeth in the upper jaw may be exceptionally powerful (wide) and the front teeth in the upper or lower jaw may have noticeably smooth, uneven or have inclined cutting surfaces. Attention should also be given to the bite, that is, the relation between the teeth of the upper and lower jaw when they come together. In a normal bite the lower edge of the front teeth of the upper jaw comes outside the front teeth of the lower jaw, and the outer chewing surfaces of the upper molars bite somewhat outside the corresponding teeth in the lower jaw. This is called normal occlusion. It can, however, happen that in the bite the front teeth of the upper jaw come quite appreciably outside the front teeth of the lower jaw or inside them, or that the front and canine teeth in the upper jaw come alternately in front of and behind the corresponding teeth of the lower jaw.

In examining teeth the assistance of a dentist should be obtained if possible. This is especially needed for root fillings and other work which it may be difficult for the layman to discover. A small mirror is a valuable help in the examination.

If dental work is found, there are possibilities of identification through a dentist by whom the patient was treated. Dentists generally keep a card index of their patients to record the work carried out on them. In an important case an X-ray examination should be made. Any roots, root fillings or the like remaining in the jaw bones may have a characteristic appearance, and an X-ray photograph may agree exactly with one which a dentist has kept.

Homicide. In a grave which contained a number of greatly decomposed bodies of persons who had been killed by the Germans during the occupation of Norway there was found the body of a woman. A front tooth, which had been broken earlier, had been covered with enamel in front and with a metal plate at the back. X-ray photography showed that both this tooth and another one right next to it had been root-filled. Comparison between the X-ray photograph and one which had been kept by a school clinic fully confirmed the identity. Both the formation of the root filling and shape of the metal plate agreed completely. (LINDBOE NORDTÖMME – STRÖM, 1946).

If teeth are wholly or partially missing from the body there is reason to suspect that the individual used a full or partial denture. The latter may be found at the house of a missing person or with his relatives, and it can then be fitted in the mouth of the dead person, whereby identity or non-identity can be proved.

Homicide. In the examination of a greatly decomposed body of a man killed by the Germans in Norway during the occupation, it was observed that the center front teeth in one half of the jaw were still present but that on both sides in all four teeth were missing. It was therefore suspected that the man had a partial prosthesis. One which fitted the mouth of the dead man was found in the possession of relatives of a man who had been taken by the Germans and never heard of again, whereby identity was fully proved. (LINDBOE NORDTÖMME – STRÖM, 1946).

Laying out the body

Shortly after a person has died there occur certain changes in the face of such a type that identification with the aid of photography is made difficult, and the identification may also be made difficult by the face being covered with blood or mucus and dirt. The eyes are generally closed: when open they are sunken and covered by a grey film. The lips assume the same color as the surrounding skin. Sometimes they are apart or have stiffened in an unnatural position. In this stage the face may be given a more natural appearance by 'laying out' the body, after the pathologist concerned has given his consent. Preferably the pathologist should do it himself, but when that is not possible it may be done by the police officer, at least in certain cases. The body is not laid out until the investigation has been completed, including photographing the original state.

If possible, the process of 'naturalizing' the body should be done in coordination with the mortician handling the funeral. If this is not feasible, the following procedure can be used.

The simplest measure is to wash the face clean from blood and dirt, clean and comb the hair, color the lips with a soluble color, for example carmine in alcohol, and to fill up any wounds with modelling clay or wax, followed by powdering with talc, after which the skin is rouged slightly. If there are livid stains in the face they are powdered over with talc. If any part of the face is badly disfigured, it is concealed in a suitable manner with a dressing or wrapping or, if it can be done in a natural manner, with the hat or clothing of the deceased.

In more difficult cases more advanced measures must be used. Sunken eyes are raised by a mixture of equal parts of water and glycerine injected into the eye sockets with the fine needle of a hypodermic syringe. If the eyes are completely decomposed they are replaced by artificial ones of glass. When the outer skin has fallen away, the face is powdered over with talc which is worked into the flesh. When decay has proceeded so far that large portions of flesh have disappeared, there are still certain possibilities of reconstructing the face. After checking the decay with sublimate solution, modelling clay is put on in place of the lost flesh. A mummified body is brought back to its natural form by laying it in a 3% solution of potassium hydroxide. After three to twelve hours it will have assumed its natural size, after which it is washed for a short time in water and preserved in weak alcohol or formalin solution.

Taking a death mask

When a dead person cannot be identified and is to be buried as unknown, a death mask should be taken of the face. This requires a lot of work, but in return there is obtained a picture of the dead person which can be much more true to life than a photograph of the face. Even if decay of the body has caused a certain amount of change in the face there are great possibilities, by retouching the death mask, of producing a much more natural and living picture than could have been done by laying out the body.

Moulage death masks usually are made by the Poller method. This technique uses a negative, agar base material, called Negocoll, and a positive material – Hominite – for the final cast. Various procedures are suggested in police literature; however, the one outlined below will insure satisfactory results with practice. No one should attempt to apply this technique to evidence without some practice. Although it is not difficult, it is not without pitfalls. This method of casting can also be used for casting tool marks, wounds on a dead body and parts of the body. If required a cast may also be taken from a living person, e.g. of the face, or part of it.

The negative mass, Negocoll, is a soap-like mass which contains a lot of thin fibers to hold it together. With careful and exact use it can be used repeatedly for a large number of castings without being changed to any extent. After each time it is used it should be put through a grinder.

The mass is melted in a water bath with about one-tenth of its volume of water, with gentle stirring, and can be used as soon as it is thinly fluid. It should not be heated in an aluminium vessel. If the stirring is too vigorous the mass becomes 'dead stirred' and is unusable, but must first be cooled and then heated up again. Careless stirring causes the formation of small bubbles in the mass, which can interfere with the casting. After the mass has melted it should be cooled off to a temperature suitable for casting, which is for ordinary bodies 80° C (176° F); and for bodies taken from water 70° C (158° F). When a casting is to be taken from a living person the mass should be cooled to about 60° C (140° F). When the mass has attained a temperature suitable for its purpose it should be poured or brushed over the object, but this must be done quickly since the mass solidifies very rapidly. If it starts to stiffen at some part and a fresh layer is put on afterwards, the two layers do not stick to one another. In casting the face of a dead person, the mass should have a thickness of nearly 1 inch and must also be reinforced with wires in a basket-like framework. When the mass has completely solidified, which generally occurs within twenty to thirty minutes, it is carefully loosened from the face. This can be done quite easily without any danger of breaking since it is comparatively elastic when cold. If the negative should crack it can easily be mended with pins or sticky tape. If the casting is done properly all details should show up well. Even the thinnest strand of hair shows up clearly and distinctly in the negative casting.

When the negative casting has been made, it is cast in the positive mass, Hominite. This is a hard resin-like mass which is melted in a saucepan over an open flame. The mass is heated until it runs, but is not allowed to boil, and is then brushed in a thin layer on the negative. Another method is to pour the molten mass into the negative casting and then to turn the latter about so that the Hominite runs round and covers all the surface. When casting a whole face the mass should be reinforced with gauze dressings which are laid in circles and gradually brushed over and soaked through with fresh mass. In applying the material it should be remembered that the mass should not be put on in too thick a layer all at once, since the temperature of melted Hominite is higher than the melting point of Negocoll and the Negocoll of the negative might be melted. Even with Hominite it is necessary to work quickly to avoid the formation of casting lines.

The positive casting obtained with Hominite is afterwards reinforced or filled with plaster or Celerite, which is reinforced with gauze dressings. Celerite is a mass which is melted in a saucepan over an open flame. It is better to avoid the use of simple plaster, since the Hominite would then crack easily.

Positive casting can be done directly with plaster without the use of Hominite. With large castings, e.g. in the case of a whole face, plaster should not be used direct on Negocoll since the weight of the plaster might change the form of the Negocoll negative.

When the positive is ready, the Negocoll is broken away. The Negocoll mass is carefully cleaned from plaster, Hominite and Celerite, after which it is ground up and placed in a well-sealed container. It should not be exposed to drying, and if the Negocoll negative cannot be removed within a reasonable time it should be protected by a wet towel. Any necessary retouching to the Hominite casting can be done with a warmed knife or metal spatula. Retouching of a positive casting in plaster is done with a knife and sandpaper. When the cast is finished it is painted the same color as the original object.

The dental material 'DP Elastic Impression Cream' may also be used even though it is not as suitable for the purpose as Negocoll. The material is sold in unit packages with instructions and a measuring cup. The contents of one bag is mixed with one measure of water and stirred into a paste which must be applied to the object immediately. The material sets very quickly. Positive casts should be made in plaster and without delay because the cast begins to shrink after a few hours and finally loses its elasticity and becomes hard and brittle.

Additional casting materials are available from dental and industrial sources. Although thiokol and silicone material is expensive and cannot be re-used, the fact that heat is not required may offset the disadvantage of cost. Certainly where small casts of wounds, scars and other identification details are involved, these newer methods have an advantage. Before a positive cast can be made, parting agents, such as detergent solutions or Dupenol G, must be applied to the negative cast. The same type of casting material can be used for the positive cast.

IDENTIFICATION OF A GREATLY ALTERED BODY OR SKELETON

There are often difficulties in the identification of a dead body which has undergone such a great amount of alteration that only the skeletal parts and portions of tissues and organs are left, or where the usual methods for the identification of a body can only be employed to a limited extent. Important information can be obtained from a skeleton which is found wholly or partly preserved after a very long time, or after burning or other destruction of the body, as also from any remains of tissues or organs or of clothing or other objects which belonged to the dead person or can in some other way be connected with the discovery of the remains of the body.

Such bodies or remains of bodies are most frequently discovered outdoors; occasionally indoors in a cellar, attic, heating furnace, etc. The remains may be those of a person who was murdered, who died as the result of an attempt to procure a miscarriage and whose body was then concealed, who was run over by a vehicle, who committed suicide, or who was lost and became the victim of exhaustion or exposure or was suddenly overcome by sickness and death.

From what has been said it follows that the nature of the place where the discovery is made can vary considerably. Remains may be found under the ground, or under a floor or the like; or they may be lying in the open, covered with brushwood, moss, sacks, etc. or overgrown by vegetation. If the body was originally in the open outdoors then the remains (both bones and clothing) are often dispersed over a large area owing to animals having dragged them away. It is not uncommon for remains and objects having some connection with them to be found even up to 300–400 yards away from the main site. This also applies to parts of a dismembered or burned body which have been buried or left on the ground, since different parts may have been concealed or buried at different places, often a long way apart.

Homicide. In a homicide in a Florida city, the victim's body was left on the bank of a canal. Land crabs attacked the body and carried portions of it away. Careful observations and knowledge of the habits of the crabs enabled investigators to recover the ring finger, with a wedding ring still in place, from the hole of a land crab.

If there is reason to suspect that the individual from whom the remains are derived was killed at or near the place of discovery, it is possible that the murder weapon or objects thrown away by the deceased or by the murderer (shoes, fragments of clothes, ornaments, etc.) may be found within a comparatively small area around the site. In the case of an individual who has lost his way, it may happen that in the course of his wanderings he threw off his pack, attempted to make a bed of clothing etc.; and this forms another reason why the investigation should not be restricted to the actual site of the discovery. Remains and fragments of clothing, and especially objects in pockets and the like often play an important part in the identification of the dead person; and the possibility of determination of sex from the clothes is especially important when the remains of the body are only fragmentary or inconclusive with regard to sex. Under certain conditions clothing may be in a better state of preservation than the remains of the body. Near the remains there may also be found foreign objects which are connected with the body or with the transport of the body to the site (bags, sacks, cords, etc.) and which possibly form the sole proof of a crime and may even give an indication for tracing the criminal.

A number of cases are known in which a correctly performed and accurate investigation of the place of discovery, combined with careful technical and pathological investigation of the remains of the body and other related objects, has led to the identity of the body being made.

In order that the best result shall be obtained the investigating officer needs a good knowledge of the right method of investigation and preservation of the remains and objects, and of the factors which affect the distribution of the objects within a larger area. He also needs a knowledge of the special methods used for the further investigation of the discovery and of how these can assist in the identification, determination of sex and age of the deceased, and of the time which has elapsed since the objects were first placed there. This knowledge is absolutely essential if the police officer is to pay the necessary attention to the possibly small and apparently insignificant objects which are of special significance in these respects. The precise determination of the characteristics necessary for establishing age, sex, body structure, and so forth, must be left to the anthropologist at the museum or university. Likewise, the investigator must avail himself of the services of entomologists for the life cycle of insects; the botanists for growth rates of roots, grasses and other plants; the meteorologist for weather conditions that might suggest the time of repose of the body and any other experts whose special knowledge will assist the investigation.

The investigation of the discovery of a body which is greatly altered can be divided into the following sections:

1. investigation of the place of discovery;
2. investigation of the remains of the body;
3. investigation of any remains of clothing or other objects which are found and which may be connected with the discovery.

1. Investigation of the scene of discovery means searching for and recovering the remains of the body and all the objects in the area which may be of value for identification, together with the investigation of the conditions of the ground and vegetation, the confirmation of the presence of foreign bodies which might have been scattered about with the object of accelerating the changes in the body and making its identification more difficult, the production of sketches of the scene of discovery and position of the find, together with photography of the discovery and of the surrounding scene.

2. The investigation of the remains of the body has the object of finding the time of occurrence of death, or in other words how long the individual has been dead, the mode of death, age, sex, length of body and color of hair. In addition an attempt is made to determine when (before or after

death) and in what way any injuries observed on the body were produced, to confirm the presence of any signs of disease in the bones or in any organs, and to observe what information can be obtained from the presence of insect larvae, etc.

3. The investigation of remnants of clothing and other objects has as its objective the determination of the original appearance of the garments, kind of cloth, color, etc, and the detection of any maker's or laundry marks. Shoes are examined for maker's marks, size, repairs, etc., and any object found in the clothes or at the scene is investigated, bearing in mind the possibility that it may be characteristic of a certain trade or in some other way give information about the deceased or conditions in connection with his death (murder weapon, suicide weapon, objects used in transporting the body to the place, objects thrown away or forgotten by the criminal, etc.). In these investigations special attention should be given to everything which might assist in a determination of the length of time the remains have been there, e.g. alterations resulting from weather conditions, penetration of roots and other parts of plants into clothing, etc.

Everything which arises from this investigation is combined to form, if possible, a description of the deceased and an explanation of the cause of death, time of occurrence of death, etc., which information can subsequently be used for identifying the body with some person notified as missing, for tracing the criminal, checking the statements of a suspect, etc.

Investigation of the scene of discovery

The task of investigating the scene of discovery and of searching for and keeping anything found, is one for the police officer who, as in all cases where a person is found dead under such circumstances that a crime is suspected, should consult the pathologist so that right from the start the latter has an opportunity of becoming familiar with the case. The procedure for the investigation is, of course, not always the same, but depends on whether the discovery was made indoors or outdoors, so that the two alternatives are dealt with separately.

Outdoors

A discovery outdoors may be one of three different types according to whether the remains are found buried, lying exposed on the ground, or in water.

Fig.215 Human remains found in a wooded area. 1 and 2; parts of a thighbone; 3: a shoe partly grown over with moss – only the heel is visible.

Remains which have been *buried* usually come to light in making digging operations, etc., and are generally purely historical finds from old burial sites, etc.

The police officer who is called to such a scene should first photograph it in the state in which he finds it, and then expose the body with great care. During this work, which should preferably be done with assistants, in the presence of a pathologist, detail photographs should be taken as necessary in order to show the position of the body, noteworthy details or conditions, etc.

In exposing the body special attention should be given to the occurrence, above the body, of any filling material, which differs from the surrounding earth, to any objects which are used as covering near the body, and to any foreign material or bodies in the ground or near the body. It has happened that quicklime has been placed on the body to accelerate the decomposition and make identification difficult. If anything of this kind is suspected, a sample of the earth should be taken so that it can be investigated. Attention should also be given to the properties of the earth (type of soil, dampness, etc.) as this is very important in deciding on the length of time the body has been buried.

The color of bones can vary from light greyish-white to dark brownish-black, depending on the age of the find, kind and properties of the soil, whether the parts are or were enclosed or covered in some way, or the measures which may have been taken with the body before burial, e.g. more or less complete burning. It is often difficult to distinguish between small bones and stones, twigs or other objects in the earth, and the search should

Fig. 216 The scene shown in Fig. 215 after uncovering. 1 and 2: parts of a thighbone; 3: shoe; 4: fragments of clothing, bone and other objects which had been completely obscured by the ground cover; 5: shoe.

therefore be carried out with great care and all remains, even if very small, should be kept. Certain very small bones, and also the teeth, are very important for the determination of sex and of the age of the deceased. If the skeleton is much disintegrated, the earth should be sifted through a small mesh sieve. It is also important that any remains of hair should be sought and kept.

Of great importance for investigation and identification are all remains of clothing and other objects which may be connected with the find, e.g. contents of pockets, buttons, ornaments, rings, coins, etc., and objects which may be connected directly with the crime, transport to the scene or the like, such as ropes, cords, sacks, bullets, objects pushed into the mouth of the victim. Such loose objects are looked for – if necessary by sifting the earth – and kept with great care, as the risk of falling to pieces may be great. Objects which are on or attached to the remains are not moved from their position before the discovery has been fully investigated. The position of loose objects in relation to the remains of the body should be accurately marked and sketched or preferably photographed.

In taking possession of bones and especially of remains of clothing and the like, attention should be given to their association with any vegetation. Roots of trees or shrubs which have grown through them form a valuable aid in determining the time the object has been there. A determination of the age of a root of a birch tree which has grown through clothing will give a minimum value for the time the object has lain in the ground, and this can be used as a starting point for further investigations and calculations. As far as possible such roots should be cut off and allowed to remain with the object: otherwise they must be kept and labelled with the necessary information as to their origin.

Even at the scene of the discovery attention should be given to the occurrence of insect larvae and pupae or remains of them on the body. They are placed in a test tube for examination by an expert. If, for example, remains of fly larvae are found on a buried body, that indicates that the body was above ground for a certain time before being buried, and the stage of development of the insect, larva or pupa can give further valuable information.

If only a part of a body is found, then dismemberment may have been carried out before burial. In such a case a large area of the surroundings must be investigated carefully, attention being directed especially to all changes in the surface of the ground which give the impression of having been produced by human agency. Should the find be of very old date it can be assum-

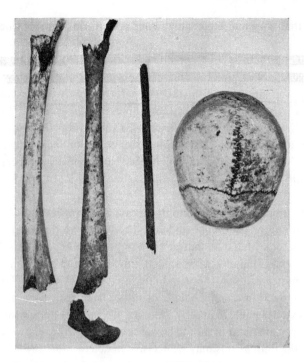

Fig. 217 Portions of a skeleton of a man missing for 11 years.

ed that any signs of disturbance of the ground will have disappeared, and the investigation becomes very difficult. The character of the ground, the possibility of burial at different places, etc. must then be used to guide the search. In some cases police dogs can be used with advantage. A sketch should be made of the terrain, giving the place where each object is found, and both total and detail photographs are taken. In photographing, each site is marked with a number or letter visible on the photograph, and these are also shown on the sketches. The objects found at the different sites are placed in cartons or boxes marked with the number or letter given to the place of discovery as above.

It is nearly always unprofitable to try to find, in the vicinity of such a a discovery, clues to the criminal, vehicle tracks or the like, on account of the long time which has generally elapsed since the assumed crime was committed. Marks on stems of trees or the like from vehicles, a bullet, etc., can, however, be found after a comparatively long time, so that a routine search should be made if the find is thought to be not too old. It should be remembered that trees and bushes may have grown considerably since the crime.

The discovery of a dead body which is found lying *free on the ground* is usually made at a lonely place in a forest, on a mountain slope, etc.

Such discoveries may be of dismembered parts of a body. In this case the investigation of the scene of the discovery must be extended to cover a large area. In the first case it is quite normal for the parts of the body to be scattered over a number of places at some distance from one another. The same applies, however, to bodies which have not been dismembered, as various animals and birds can drag the parts for a distance of up to several hundred yards from the original site.

Careful attention must be given to those cases that appear to be hiking, mountain climbing or camping accidents. These may be the result of an attempt to cover a criminal assault or robbery. Lone hikers or naturalists are easy prey to criminal attack. Special attention must be paid to absence of valuables, minor bruises from subduing blows and evidence of soil or vegetation not found in the immediate vicinity. The investigation of a discovery of this kind is made in exactly the same way as for a body which has been buried. Special attention should however be given to the relation of the vegetation to the find, as this may be decisive in determining the length of time the body has lain there. Under the remains at the original site there may perhaps be found plants which have been smothered, or possibly no vegetation at all: perhaps the plants have started to grow over the remains. If the body has lain there for several years it may happen that grass, brambles, undergrowth, moss, etc. has completely concealed part of the remains, since they have gradually become covered with a layer of soil or leaf mold from falling leaves and dead plants. It may also happen that roots of trees and bushes grow through parts of the find and especially remnants of clothing. The vegetative conditions are described carefully, stating the type of vegetation, and supplemented with photographs on which the different remains are marked in the manner described above. Any tree or other roots which have grown through the remains are kept for a determination of their age. If there is no risk of the roots falling out of the remains when moved then they should be removed with the latter. A sketch is made as described above.

The place of discovery is cleared and any remains and objects found are kept. If necessary the earth is sifted and may be preserved, for further examination or analysis. The character of the ground, i.e. type of soil, damp-

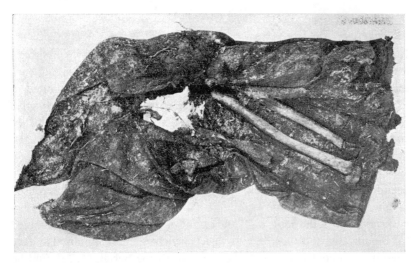

Fig. 218 Coat sleeve with the bones of the lower arm. These fragments were completely concealed by ground cover.

ness, etc., is described. If there are signs of foreign matter such as lime, samples are taken. When exposing the body attention should be given to any indications of its having been covered with stones, brushwood, sacks, etc. When necessary detail photographs are taken.

If remains of a body are found *in water* it is generally impossible to investigate the place of discovery accurately, unless it is merely a small pool which can be emptied by draining. If this is not possible the investigation must be limited to dragging and the examination of the shores. It must be remembered that currents, ice, floating timber, etc. may have carried parts of the body to places a long way from the place of discovery. Also the find may be composed of a part of a body which has been carried to the place of discovery in the same manner, possibly from a considerable distance.

If the discovery has been made in a harbor or river where there are steamers and motorboats, it should be remembered that injuries on the body may have been caused by propellers. A propeller can cut off a leg or arm in such a way that it appears as if the body has been dismembered intentionally. Injuries to tissues and organs produced in this way often show clean edges as from an edged tool.

Indoors

It is very rarely that remains of a body indoors have undergone such an extensive degree of change from decay or other causes as in the cases considered above. There have been cases where a body has been buried in a cellar or cut up and burned in the furnace of the heating system, or when remains of a dismembered and/or burned body have been placed in a suitcase in an attic.

The procedure in such a case is the same as that described above.

In the case of a body which has been buried, or of remains which have been found in a suitcase, sack, etc., then all objects which have been used to conceal the body or for wrapping are of special interest. With such discoveries indoors, the floor, walls and ceiling of the place should be examined for bloodstains and the like, and objects which might be supposed to have been used in connection with the crime, with the burial, etc., should be looked for.

If, for example, a heating furnace has been used to burn a body, it should be investigated very carefully. A skeleton is not destroyed by fire, and even in modern cremations the remains never consist of ashes but of cracked and distorted bones. After a cremation the volume of the bones of an adult amounts to $2–3^1/_2$ liters ($3^1/_2–6$ pints). In a freshly-burnt state the bones have a white to yellowish or greyish-white shade, which quickly changes under the ground to brown or brownish-black. At a certain state of the burning the bones are soft and they may then assume peculiar twisted forms which may to some extent depend on the underlayer.

The contents both of the firebox and of the ash space should be sifted and every fragment of bone must be kept. Certain very small bones have been found to be very resistant to fire and may therefore be very valuable for the determination of the age and sex of the deceased. Teeth are, of course, especially valuable. The crowns of the teeth generally break up and split under the action of heat, but the roots often remain whole. On the other hand, teeth which have not come through (e.g. with children) rarely break up and do not change in form or shrink to any appreciable extent. After burning these latter have a whitish color and a chalky consistency.

In searching for and taking possession of burnt skeletal remains great care should be observed owing to their fragile nature. If remains which are specially brittle or liable to fall to pieces are found, they should be packed separately in test tubes, glass jars or cartons according to size, with cotton, tissue paper or the like as underlayer and filling for the container.

In connection with the investigation of the remains of a dead body an account is given below of the parts of the human skeleton and organs which are specially valuable from the point of view of identification, with an indication of those which are specially resistant to decay and fire.

Packing and transport

The packing of remains of a body with any associated objects which are to be moved or sent to an expert should be done in such a way as to eliminate any danger of destruction or falling apart of associated objects as the result of shaking, etc. A skeleton, of which the long bones are still hanging together, with or without remains of soft tissues or organs, should be packed in such a way that it will remain in that state during transport. Soft paper excelsior, rags, tissue paper, etc. can be used as filling in the container and for the support of parts which do not rest on the bottom. Well-burnt remains should be transported in the charge of a police officer who keeps the package under his control all the time and sees that it is not exposed to shocks or violence. Suitable packing materials are thin soft paper, soft and flexible cloth, tissue paper, cotton wool, etc., which is packed in the container in such a way that the object has a soft support and is also supported in a definite position.

The investigation of remains of a dead body

This investigation should be done by a pathologist, possibly with the assistance of a dentist.

The discussion of the investigation below is divided into different sections according to the particular objectives, which are treated separately.

Number of individuals

This question only arises when the discovery is composed of a collection of bones which are not connected or placed in such a way that it is possible to decide whether the remains are of one or more individuals. An investigation with this objective is based on the fact that certain parts of the skeleton occur singly or in pairs in the human body. Especially significant in this respect are the tooth processes of the second neck vertebra and the wedge bone of the inner ear. In the body there is one of the former, with a characteristic form, and two of the latter, which have an obliquely directed opening for the auditory nerve. Both of these parts of the skeleton are resistant to fire. They are of small size so that great care (sifting) is required in searching for them.

Determination of sex

For the determination of sex the skeletal characters are:

Pelvis: size and form are different for men and women. The pre-auricular notch and pubic curve are especially significant, and even small fragments can make possible a determination of sex.

Cranium: the walls of the cranium are normally thinner in men than in women. The angle of the root of the nose where it comes out from the forehead (frontal nose angle) is more pronounced in a man. The curve of the eyebrows is generally more rounded in a man than in a woman.

Head of joint of upper arm: this is generally larger in a man than in a woman. The size of the head of the joint moreover shrinks only slightly under the action of fire.

Breastbone: both size and form are significant for determination of sex.

Thighbone and shinbones are also important from this point of view.

The whole of the female skeleton with the exception of the pelvis is in general more lightly constructed than that of a man.

An important point for the determination of sex, in the case of the remains of a child, is the uninjured crown of the first permanent incisor of the upper jaw. In certain cases these can show the sex according to whether their width is especially great (boy) or small (girl).

Hair is also important, and is retained for a long time unless the body has been exposed to heat.

Regarding organs, the uterus and the prostate gland respectively allow of the sex being determined. Both of these organs are also very resistant to decay. The uterus, however, if exposed to decay, can become very fragile so that great care should be observed.

Determination of age

Teeth are especially significant in the determination of age, which is possible even when only one tooth is available, but it is necessary to allow for a certain percentage of error in this case (according to some authorities, about 15–20%). If a number of teeth are found the reliability of the determination is increased. The determination of age from teeth is based on the changes which the teeth undergo with age. These changes are:

1. wearing down of chewing surfaces (abrasion);
2. loosening (paradentosis): detected from changes in the attachment of the roots;
3. formation of secondary dentine inside the pulp cavities (can also be formed as reaction to disease of the teeth);
4. deposition of cement on and around points of the roots;
5. degree of transparency of lowest parts of roots (root transparency);
6. corrosion of root points (root resorption);
7. closing of root openings. Until the teeth are completely formed the size of the root openings stands in direct relation to the age, so that this is of special importance for young individuals.

The teeth are very resistant to chemicals.

If the body has been completely burned, the crowns of grown-out teeth break up, as explained above, but the roots often remain whole. Teeth of a

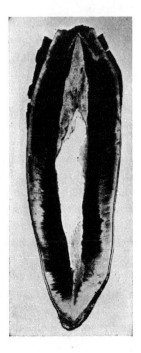

Fig. 219 Photography by transmitted light of polished section of eyetooth, for determination of age. The root opening is closed, secondary dentine has formed inside the pulp cavity and deposition of cement has occurred on the root points, while the root is partially transparent. The age of the individual was estimated from this as 62–65 years.

child or young person, if they have not come through, do not get broken up. The discovery of such teeth which have not come through or of remains of milk teeth, thus gives a direct indication of age.

In this connection it is convenient to touch on the possibility of determining whether different teeth belong together, which may be important when there is any doubt as to whether the remains come from one or more individuals. Such an investigation can often be carried out with good results. It is based on the lines in the dentine which are visible under the microscope and are characteristic of individuals, and with the aid of which it is possible to determine whether teeth come from the same individual or not.

The roof of the cranium gives information which is especially valuable for the determination of the age of an individual; the sutures (ossification lines) being specially significant. With new-born babies and children up to three years of age the sutures are straight or slightly curved. After this they commence to become saw-edged in form, passing over slowly into the forms typical of the adult. With increasing age the sutures grow together more and more, finally disappearing entirely: those of a woman, however, join up considerably later than those of a man. The appearance and degree of fusion give an opportunity of estimating the age up to fifty.

If the cranium is exposed to great heat the sutures split up, but if they have grown together completely it may happen that the cracks resulting from the heat take a new path. This circumstance to some extent makes possible an estimation of age even from small portions of the roof of a cranium.

The thickness of the roof of the cranium, and also the character of the outside and inside parts of the walls and the intermediate parts, give information which may be used as a guide for the determination of the age of an individual.

The form of the wedge bone part of the inner ear differs in children and adults. This part is already formed at the fifth month after conception.

The epiphyses at the ends of the long bones fuse with the diaphyses at rather fixed stages in the development of the skeleton. This occurs when the increase in length of the particular limb is complete. It is therefore important, for determination of age, to note whether this calcification has occurred and to what extent.

The structure of the bone tissues is also a guide in determining age, but after twenty-five years it is not possible to obtain an accurate estimation of age from this factor.

Another possibility is offered by the Haversian canals which occur in all bones. During the period of growth the diameter of these channels stands in a definite relation to the age, but when fully grown their diameter remains constant, so that the method is important mainly for the determination of the age of the skeleton of a baby or unborn child. The diameter of the Haversian canals is also different for man and for animals, so that it may become important when it is necessary to decide whether a small piece of bone comes from a man or an animal.

Finger and toe bones can also be significant. With a child these are of uniform width, becoming with increasing age wider at the ends, and the outer joints acquire a typical form at the part where the nails are attached.

Length of body

It is possible to determine approximately the body length of an individual from the skeleton or a part of it, assuming that some of the longer bones of the limbs (femur, fibula, tibia, humerus, radius and ulna) are found. The length of some of these is measured, after which the body length is calculated with the aid of formulae and tables (Pearson's formula, Roller's or Manouvrier's tables). The values given by the tables represent the length of the skeleton and should be increased by an inch or so to allow for other tissues and to give approximately correct value for the body height.

Color of hair

The hair is very resistant to change provided that it is not exposed to fire, but it may often be difficult to find at the scene of a discovery when the body has changed greatly. Generally it is only the hair of the head – more rarely hair from other parts of the body – which can be used as a basis for estimating hair color as required for a description. Great caution should, however, be exercised. There may be surprising changes in the color of hair after even a comparatively short time, depending on the character of the soil, etc.

Time of occurrence of death

To determine from the remains of the body how long the individual has been dead is very difficult, and can never be done exactly. If the remains are composed merely of portions of the skeleton the task is much more difficult than if an organ or tissues are more or less preserved. This is associated with the great resistance of the bones to change. The determination is based on how far the process of decay has proceeded; in what state the remains are found, considered against the background of the situation of the discovery (in or above ground); the character of the ground (dry, damp, chalky, etc); type of soil (sand, mold, etc.); and time of year. The presence of larvae and pupae of insects or remains of them are sometimes significant in this respect, as their time of development may assist in the estimation. The result of such an estimation is however often highly approximate and must therefore be supplemented by making use of other factors observed during the investigation of the discovery.

Mode of death

The confirmation of the cause of death generally includes making a decision on whether there has or has not been a crime. The most important factor in determining this is the presence of any injuries which can be detected on the remains. The character of lacerated wounds and gunshot injuries can be satisfactorily identified even on parts of a skeleton, but injuries caused by blunt violence, by vehicles, etc. are generally more difficult to identify. To decide whether an injury found on part of a skeleton was produced during life or not is difficult, although possible in certain cases. If an organ or fragments of tissues are so well preserved that any injuries on them can be examined, it can often be stated definitely whether the injury occurred during life or not. In judging injuries both on parts of the skeleton and on tissues and organs it is however necessary to take into account the possibility that they have been caused by animals, although in general it is possible to identify such injuries definitely, at least as far as parts of the skeleton are concerned.

Another point which is important in deciding whether there is any question of a crime is whether the body has been subjected to partial burning or dismemberment. The former can be determined in most cases from the soft tissues and even from bones, provided that the latter have been exposed sufficiently to the action of fire. It may be more difficult to decide whether a body has been subjected to dismemberment, depending on the state in which it is found. The investigation of the scene of discovery may possibly assist in forming an opinion. If there are distinct signs of dismemberment, it may also be possible to decide whether it has been done by someone with

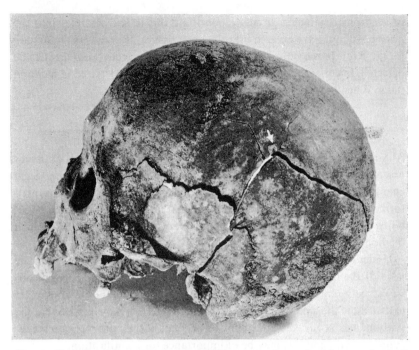

Fig. 220 Skull found 80 years after death. The arrow shows the injury to the skull probably causing death. Such evidence remains even after the passage of many years.

skill or experience in this class of work. As mentioned before, injuries closely resembling dismemberment can be caused by contact with a rotating propeller.

The removal of soft tissues, e.g. of the face, in order to make any attempt at identification difficult occurs at times, especially in the case of dismembered bodies. If the body has not changed very much then this removal will be evident.

Detection of poison in the remains

Most poisons are destroyed very quickly during the process of decay, so that it is often impossible to state whether the individual died as the result of poisoning or not. Arsenic and lead, and to some extent other metallic poisons, can however be detected a very long time after death and even when only parts of the skeleton remain, assuming that the poisoning was of a chronic character. In acute poisoning this is not possible since the poison will not have entered into the bone tissues. If organs or tissues are found in fair preservation, then sometimes even an acute poisoning can be detected. In chronic poisoning arsenic and lead can be detected in hair and nails. When burned, a proportion of these poisons is lost.

Changes in the skeleton and organs from disease or other causes

All such changes which can be confirmed in skeletal parts, organs or tissues are of great importance for the identification of the dead person. Such changes may be fractures and wounds which have healed up, fusions, malformations, tumours, indications of surgical intervention, etc. The possibility of finding such conditions depends very largely on the state in which the body is found.

Under certain conditions an interesting change may be observed in the jaws. If the deceased individual, while living, had only one or a few adjacent teeth remaining in one or the other jaw, and did not have any plate to distribute the load over a larger chewing surface, it may happen that the jawbone has acquired a thickening on account of the extra work on the remaining teeth, and this may be of importance for identification.

The presence of roots remaining in the jawbone may be confirmed by X-ray photography, and may also be a help in identification.

If bones are subjected to continuous, localized stress over a long period of the subject's life, accomodations will be made. Indians who have carried heavy loads on portages, supporting these burdens by headstraps, will show a perceptible alteration of the skull. A case is reported by MORITZ in which the ballet training of the deceased could be determined by the enlarged bones of the big toe.

Comparison between a skull and the photograph of a face

It is possible to make certain comparisons, from the point of view of identification, between the photograph of the face of a missing person and a skull which has been found, assuming that the latter is reasonably well preserved. By superimposing the face, on the photograph and the skull in the same scale (preferably natural size), and then printing the two negatives on the same piece of paper, it is possible to confirm the existence of differences which may show non-identity. The significant factors in this compari-

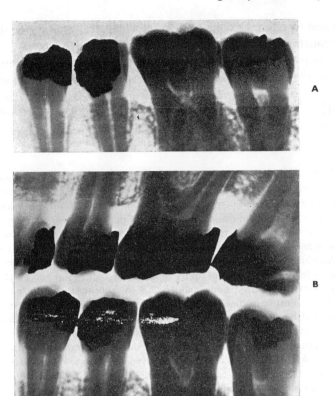

Fig. 221 The identity of a skeleton as being that of a woman who disappeared one
year before was made possible by a comparison on the fillings in her teeth as
shown in X-ray pictures. The post-mortem picture (A) shows fillings identical
in position and shape with those photographed by the deceased's dentist (B).

son are the form of the face, the width of the chin and the placing of the
cheekbones and eyesockets. It should, however, be noted that the position
of the teeth of a living person does not appear the same as on a skull, so
that the chin seems longer on the photograph of the skull than on that of
the face. It is obvious that no positive identification can be made by this
method.

A method which has also been tried is to model the face from the skull so
as to produce a picture of the face of the deceased which can be used in the
identification. This, however, requires both practice and an eye for form,

and should therefore be done by a sculptor, but the result is not always proportionate to the amount of work involved.

The relative thickness of the soft parts of the face of a normal person is used as a guide for the sculptor, although this is of no assistance in modeling the ears. If the deceased, when alive, was unusually fat or thin, then the resemblance of the model to the dead person will not be at all striking. It is moreover difficult to reproduce the lips and lineaments round the mouth which determine the appearance of a face.

Homicide. Two women, aged respectively 35 and 20, disappeared from Lancaster between September 14th and 15th, 1935. One was the wife of a Dr. Ruxton and the other her maid. Two weeks later a number of portions of a body or bodies were found in a ravine about 106 miles from that city. The parts, 68 in number, were found in an advanced state of decomposition, contained a large number of insect larvae, and had been damaged by animals. When they were investigated they were found to be derived from two different human bodies. The ages were estimated, from the sutures in the roof of the cranium, the teeth and epiphyses of the femur and humerus, as 36–45 and 18–22 (most probably 20–21) respectively. Both bodies had been dismembered in order to make impossible any identification and identification of sex. There was only one thorax and one pelvis, which had been separated from one another between the second and third lumbar vertebrae. From the position of the cut surfaces of the two parts and other anatomical characteristics it was determined that both the pelvis and thorax came from the same trunk. The older head had been removed between the fifth and sixth neck vertebrae, and fitted the reconstructed trunk. The presence of the vagina in the pelvis showed the sex of this body. Among the other separate loose parts were found portions of two different external female sexual parts and also three female breasts, which showed that the bodies of at least two women were in question.

There were found two pairs of upper and lower limbs which had been separated at the shoulders, elbows, hips and knees. One pair of arms and legs could be referred with certainty to the older woman, which made that skeleton complete with the exception of the right foot. Of the body parts there remained a head, two upper and two lower limbs, all typically feminine in appearance and all of approximately the same age. Although a trunk was missing and thus the parts could not be referred with certainty to the same individual, they were undoubtedly portions of the body of the younger woman. The length of the reconstructed body of the older woman came to 5 ft. 4$^1/_2$ in., while that of the younger, calculated with the aid of Pearson's formula, came to about 5 ft. These lengths corresponded closely to those of the two missing women. Castings from the left feet of the bodies fitted excellently in shoes belonging to Mrs. Ruxton and her maid.

Photographs of the skulls showed remarkably good agreement when they were compared with photographs in natural size of the heads of the missing women. This however did not prove identity, but merely showed that the skulls could have belonged to the missing women.

The fingernails of the young woman were scored as one would expect with a house worker, and her finger prints were identical with prints found on a number of household objects in Ruxton's home. The fingertips and toes of the older body had been removed completely. Together with the portions of the bodies there were also found newspapers of the 15th September. Certain garments could be identified, and a piece of a covering was identical with a covering found in Ruxton's house.

Dismemberment of the body had been done in such a way that it undoubtedly indicated a person with a good knowledge of anatomy. The body of Mrs. Ruxton showed signs of suffocation and also a fracture of the tongue bone. In the body which was ascribed to the maid there was a fracture in the upper part of the skull, marks of a blow on the arms and face, and a severe injury on the tongue associated with infiltration of leucocytes (white blood corpuscles), which showed that the injury had been produced one to two hours before death.

In the house of Dr. Ruxton, who was suspected of murder, there were found a number of bloodstains in the bathroom and elsewhere, fragments of human tissue in the trap of a waste pipe, and a suit belonging to the suspect, which was badly bloodstained.

Dr. Ruxton was found guilty of murder and condemned to death (GLAISTER and BRASH, 1937).

Homicide. Under the floor of a cellar was discovered the body of a woman, barely covered with earth and a yellow powdery substance which was found to be lime. The head was not attached to the body, and parts of the arms and legs were missing. Indications of burning could be observed on the body. The soft parts were almost entirely missing, but the larynx and uterus were present and relatively well-preserved.

Investigation of the remains showed that the body had been dismembered by a person with no knowledge of anatomy, and that an attempt had been made to burn the body. All tissues which could be of assistance in identification had been removed – i.e. the hair, soft parts of the face, eyes, lower jaw, hands and feet.

The length of the body was calculated from the left humerus as at least 5 ft., and at most 5 ft. $1^1/_2$ in. The age was estimated from the degree of fusion of the seams of the parietal bones and other indications as between 40 and 50. The color of the hair was determined from a number of well-preserved strands of hair found on an insignificant residue of scalp at the back of the head, as dark brown and going grey.

The uterus was partially destroyed and very dry and fragile. It was X-rayed and found to contain a tumour of 4 in. in cross section. From two hospitals there was obtained the name of a woman who had been examined with a diagnosis of tumor of the uterus; in both cases she had refused to submit to an operation.

In the upper jaw were only a few teeth, and their filling together with roots remaining in the jawbone made possible an identification by a dentist, who also indicated a thickening of the jawbone resulting from the extra work on the remaining teeth of the patient treated by him. This also agreed with the upper jaw of the remains found.

A full-face photograph of the woman who had been examined at the hospitals and been treated by the dentist was obtained. This and the skull were photographed, the negatives being printed on the same piece of photographic paper, and it was confirmed that there were no indications of non-identity.

In the investigation of the preserved larynx an internal haemorrhage was detected,

caused by the larynx having been exposed to great pressure during life. Under the contusion was found a fracture of the shield cartilage

It was considered as certain that the woman had been strangled, after which the body
had been dismembered and an attempt had been made to burn it. The remaining parts
were then buried, and lime was placed on them. The lime was actually slaked lime, so
that instead of accelerating the decomposition it had preserved certain tissues and facilitated the work of identification. The husband of the woman, who lived in the house
where the remains were found, was convicted of murder. This is known as the 'Baptist
Church Cellar' case (SIMPSON, 1943).

Homicide. Discovery of a buried corpse on a heath. One hand stuck up through the earth,
and the body was covered with a thin layer of sandy soil and turf, apparently taken from
a nearby pile of earth. The hand sticking up out of the earth and the lower arm were
dry and partially mummified, and the thumb and index finger had been completely
gnawed away by rats which had left distinct marks of their teeth. When the body was
exposed, it was found to have been attacked by fly larvae to such an extent that it
appeared probable that it had lain in the open for at least one or two days before it was
buried. Soft parts were missing from the left arm, neck and head, while the tissues of the
trunk were in a better state of preservation. A small piece of scalp with hair attached still
remained. The skull had been splintered into a number of pieces by a blow with some
blunt object. The body was that of a woman. The clothes were contaminated with blood
and earth. The heather under the body was still green and flowering had just finished.
This, with the significant presence of fly larvae, the character of the soil and a recent
warm and rainy period, allowed an estimate that death had occurred about five weeks
earlier.

Examination of the dead body showed wounds from cuts on the head, defense injuries
on the right arm and hand, contusions on the face and back of the head, and injuries
from dragging on the right lower leg and foot, the latter being produced after death and
corresponding to damage to the stockings.

On investigation of the scene of discovery there was found a right shoe 300 yards from
the body and a left shoe twenty yards further away. Near the latter there was also a
fabric bag with a string of beads and a piece of soap. About fourteen yards from the left
shoe and at practically a right angle to a line joining the two shoes there was found a
thick birch pole thirty-seven in. in length, weighing more than two lb. About six in. from
one end of the pole the bark had come loose and at this point there were a number of fine
strands of hair which had stuck in the jagged edges of the bark and in cracks in the wood.
In a heap of dead leaves about hundred yards from the bag there was found an identity
card, a life insurance policy and a letter written by a woman to a man in which she stated
that she was pregnant and hoped that the man would marry her. A little farther away
there was also a silver crucifix.

The discoveries cleared up the identity of the woman whose remains had been found,
and also gave an indication of the criminal. The age, length, color of hair and certain
deformations of the front teeth were deduced from the papers which were found, and
agreed entirely with what had been discovered in the examination of the dead body.
This was the 'wigwam' murder of 1944 (SIMPSON, 1944).

Accident. An American disappeared on a journey through the jungle in Burma. Later a greatly decomposed and mutilated body was found in a river. Examination of the remains showed the scar of an ear operation. The body was sent to New York where it arrived eight months after the man had disappeared. X-ray photography of the skull showed complete agreement with X-ray photographs of the head of the man taken seven and five years previously. At least twenty different identification marks were observed, especially with respect to operations on the nasal sinuses and the clipped bone part of the ear. The identification was thus made certain.

Homicide. During digging operations parts of the skeleton of a man were found. The skull had practically fallen apart. Remains of clothing and a belt, together with some buttons, were found with the remains, and above the latter lay a hand-forged four-pronged digging fork. On exposing the body it became evident that it had been placed in a pit which had been dug and then filled in with sand and large stones.

In the investigation of the skull typical male characters were observed. The nose bone was strongly emphasized and showed that the deceased, when living, had a large nose with a very concave end, either continued as a 'hook nose' or alternatively a definitely turned-up nose. The setting of the teeth was also characteristic, with sloping right front and canine teeth. The length of the body was estimated according to Pearson's formula from a metacarpal bone, a thighbone and a shinbone as 5 ft. $5^{1}/_{2}$ in. to 5 ft. $5^{1}/_{4}$ in. The age at the onset of death was estimated from the canine tooth as 62–65. The sutures of the cranium supported this estimate.

The cranium also showed indications of external violence. Thus the left temple and petromastoid section had been separated from the rest of the cranium by a cut or blow which has struck about 3.4 in. above the left auricular opening, from which point cracks started. Also, on the right side of the cranium a crack was noted which went about 1 in. in the right parietal bone and which could only mean that a cut or blow had struck the skull from that direction. Although the nature of the object which had been used to produce the injuries could not be stated definitely, it followed from the way in which the cranium had cracked that it must have been a pointed object which had struck with great force and at almost a right angle against the surface of the skull.

About eighty years previously a sixty-three year old man, who had lived in a house near the place where the discovery was made, had disappeared. The investigations carried out showed that it was extremely probable that the remains found came from this man and that he had been murdered and then buried.

Accident. In the early part of September 1949 the Essex County Police were informed by an inshore fisherman that he had seen what appeared to be a human skull lying on the mud on the south side of Cobmarsh Island, about two miles from the coast.

When located by the police it proved to be a human skull, and was lying face uppermost and partly covered with barnacles. It appeared to have oozed out of the mud. Further investigation revealed an almost complete skeleton lying full length as though on its back about eight inches below the surface. When examined by experts the bones were found to be those of a man about forty years of age with a height, estimated by Pearson's formula from the femurs and humerus, of between 5 ft. $7^{1}/_{2}$ in. and 5 ft. $8^{1}/_{2}$ in.

The whole of the back of the skull with the facial region, apart from an area above the left eyesocket, was heavily encrusted with barnacles. This heavy encrustation also extended along the right side of the skull. The posterior part of the right side of the skull showed a scattered and much less abundant barnacle colonization, the individual shells in this area being small and immature. Several mussels, partly embedded in the crust of barnacles, were present on the underside of the skull.

The lower two-thirds of the upper arm bone (humerus) were also heavily encrusted with barnacles, as was also the forearm (radius).

Study of the barnacles and mussels revealed several features of interest. The estimated age of the oldest barnacle was about two years, and this was also the approximate age of the largest mussel. This barnacle was the Common British Barnacle, *Balanus balanoides*, but the great majority of the remainder belonged to a species (*Elminius modestus*) which is a native of Australia. The earliest British record of this species is dated 1943, but it has since gradually spread round the coast of Britain.

The oldest specimens of *Eliminius* were about twelve months old.

From these findings it was clear that parts at least of the skull must have been denuded of flesh and exposed to colonization by mussels and barnacles not less than two years previously. The fine silt in which the bones were embedded was not of a type which causes severe scouring and abrasion, and would not therefore cause the wearing away of the skull which was present on the left side. It seemed therefore to be a reasonable inference that the initial exposure of the skull to barnacle colonization occurred at a place where coarser, presumably sandy, material was present and that the still intact body, partially denuded of flesh, had drifted inshore to the place where it was discovered. Here it became covered with fine marine silt and the partially encrusted parts of the skull and arm bones were again exposed, The part of the skull which showed a relatively light distribution of very immature barnacles had obviously been exposed only for a few weeks.

The bones were, therefore, shown to be those of an individual who had died some time prior to September 1947, since both two-year old mussels and barnacles were present on the skull. The skull bones moreover must have been denuded of flesh before either type of mollusc could have become anchored (HOLDEN and CAMPS, 1951).

Homicide. A man and his wife disappeared suddenly. They were known to have spent the night in the premises of a certain individual, who was later suspected of having murdered them. A garden adjoining the premises of this individual was dug up. At one part a distinct smell of putrefaction was observed, and in this area, at a depth of a little over a foot, a piece of skin was found, apparently the skin of a hand. Nearby there was found a dead worm similar to the round worms which infest the human intestine.

By further investigation it was discovered that the suspect had been seen digging at a certain spot on the banks of a canal about a quarter of a mile from his house a few days before the enquiry opened. On digging in this area two sacks, containing two bodies, were found.

Identification of these bodies was a simple matter, as was the cause of death and the time since death. The question however arose of whether the two bodies, or either of them, had actually been buried in the garden of the accused and subsequently removed and buried at the place where they were found.

The worm which had been found in the garden was submitted to an expert helminthologist who gave the opinion that it was a specimen of the round worm, *Ascaris lumbricoides*, which infests the human intestine. The body of the man was found to contain similar worms, and no doubt one of these had escaped from the body into the soil.

The piece of skin found in the soil of the garden was washed, hardened in formalin and photographed. The patterns on the piece of epidermis were compared with the patterns on the dermis still remaining on the fingers of the left hand of the body of the female victim, and were found to have a sufficient number of identical points to warrant a definite statement that the piece of skin had been removed from this body (SMITH, 1940).

The investigation of remains of clothing, etc.

The examination of any remains of clothing or other objects which may be found, and which can be connected with the discovery of remains of a body, is a matter for the police officer, who can call in the assistance of experts if necessary. The pathologist should always be given the opportunity of being present at or should be informed of the results of the examinations since

Fig. 222 Parts of a coat with tree and bush roots which had grown in and partially through the material. The age of the roots was determined as between 5 and 9 years.

these, like the investigation of the scene of discovery, are closely connected
with the pathological investigation.

Before the examination is commenced all objects should be laid out to
dry on a table, as this considerably facilitates the work.

Remains of clothing

Roots or other parts of plants which have penetrated portions of clothing
should be kept and provided with a label showing type of garment and of
vegetation, etc., after which the material is given to a botanist for determination of age. From tree and shrub roots which have penetrated the
remains it is possible to determine the minimum period of time that the
object has lain at the site. In the case of *unburied* remains this estimate
must be increased by one or two years since the material has first to be
'merged into' the soil before it can be penetrated by roots.

The type of cloth, color, type of garment and the question of whether
it is ready-made or tailor-made is determined, possibly with the assistance
of an expert. An expert should preferably also be called in to decide the
length of time the material has been lying there from any changes in the
garments resulting from climatic effects. Maker's mark and laundry marks
are looked for, using an ultraviolet lamp in the latter case. Buttons, together with the manner in which they are sewn on (by machine or hand)
may be significant, as also any repairs in the garments.

The remains of clothes are examined also for damage caused by edged
tools, firearms, vehicles, etc. which may possibly correspond to marks and
injuries on the body. The assistance of the pathologist is required for this.
The nature of the damage can often be determined with certainty. Damage
caused by animals may also occur on clothing, but this can generally be
distinguished from other damage.

The remains of underclothing and stockings or socks are also examined
for color, textile material, maker's marks, other marks, repairs, etc.

Boots and shoes

The original color of boots and shoes may be very difficult to determine
on account of the changes undergone by the leather under the action of
earth, damp, etc. Inside the heel, at the back of the heel or at other points
on the inside there may be the name of the maker, which is sometimes

embossed, while stamped marks may sometimes be a guide for identification. Any rubber soles or heels, their make, size and type, are also significant. The size of shoes can be determined from the length. Sometimes a distinct impression of the sole of the foot and the toes can be observed on the inner sole of a shoe, and this may be of value for comparison with shoes which may possibly be found in the house of a missing person. Any repairs may also be a guide in identification.

Other objects

Of great importance for identification are all objects which are found in the pockets of clothing or at the scene of the discovery, and which may be suspected of having belonged to the deceased. These objects are examined carefully, looking for name, initials, maker's marks, other markings, etc. The description of a missing man may mention such objects, or possibly relatives of the deceased may be able to identify them as belonging to him. It may also be important to determine the application of a particular object, which may be characteristic of a particular trade. It should also be noted that a particular collection of objects may be typical of e.g. a fisherman, hiker, tramp, etc.

Accidental death. Discovery of portions of a skeleton and of clothing of a man in a forest. Portions of the remains, which were dispersed over a limited area, were completely covered with vegetation. In the earth under the remains of the clothing and partly in them were, among other things, a pocketknife, two metal bases from fired shotgun

Fig. 223 Pocketknife found when sifting the soil where fragments of clothing were found. One blade had been reground after apparently having been broken, and the manufacturer's markings can be read on the base of the blade.

cartridges and a small brass padlock. These objects proved to be of great importance for identification.

The age of a large number of roots of spruce and birch, which grew in and partly through the remains of the clothing, was determined as between five and nine years.

The remains of two shoes showed crude and characteristic repairs.

Investigation of the portions of skeleton showed that they came from a full-grown young man and that apparently ten years had elapsed since his death, and also that they had been attacked by animals, probably mice. There were no signs of any injuries produced while living or of disease.

Eleven years earlier (in January) a thirty-four year old insane man had disappeared from his home in a neighboring parish. From the description made at the time and statements obtained from relatives it appeared that he used to carry a pocketknife, the description of which agreed with that of the knife found, and also cartridge cases and a small padlock. He had been in the habit of getting clothes and shoes from different persons, and mended them himself when necessary.

Thus it was established that the body was that of the man who had disappeared eleven years previously, and who had probably wandered in the wood and died of exhaustion and cold.

One of the most interesting criminal cases of later years in which the reconstruction and identification of a body was of importance was the famous 'Acid Bath Murder' in England. In this case the immersion of the body in a concentrated sulphuric acid bath resulted in an extensive destruction of most tissues, but body fat, gallstones and a plastic denture resisted attack, and proved of immense value in the identification. The gallstones were proved to be human by means of the precipitin reaction and the denture was compared with complete dental data available from the victim's dentist.

The presence of osteo-arthritis in certain joints could also be proved, and this showed the remains to come from a person of late adult age.

IDENTIFICATION IN CATASTROPHES

In occurrences of a catastrophic nature in which a number of people are killed, such as rail and airplane accidents, big fires and explosions, the collapse of a building, and accidents at sea, the work of identification must be organized as quickly as possible and carried out in such a way that there is no danger of faulty identification of the bodies. It is not only for sentimental considerations that accurate identification is essential: the legal requirements for proof of death must be satisfied in the case of each victim. A great deal more than mere satisfaction at having made a correct identification is involved. Questions of pension rights, the payment of insurance etc. are some of the ancillary matters which depend on a correct analysis being made.

It is essential to obtain as quickly as possible a list showing all persons who may have been killed. In air accidents this can be obtained quickly from the passenger list, but with railway trains and boats it is sometimes impossible. When the information is available the task of identification is easy, so long as the victims are not badly mutilated or burned or the bodies have not undergone any considerable amount of decomposition.

The work of identification should preferably be done by a special group, which may consist of a pathologist, a dentist and two police officers with experience in the identification of dead bodies. The group will also need assistants varying in number for each particular case. The identification group should be present when the first measures of rescue and clearance are started at the scene of the catastrophe, and as bodies are found they should take charge of them. If the group cannot be organized or does not reach the scene in time, a suitable police officer should be detailed to take the first steps in securing the bodies.

A preliminary sketch should be made of the site, and the scene as a whole should be photographed, the position of the camera and direction of the different exposures being marked on a sketch. The record is made during the course of the work. When the body of a victim is found it is given a number which may be written on a piece of card which is tied to the body. Any objects found beside the body, and which may be supposed to be personal belongings, are collected in a bag which is given a number. When possible, each victim and object should be provided with a label giving more detailed information, e.g. who found it, the time of discovery and a statement of the nature of the place, preferably in the form of a simple sketch. The numbers are entered in the record in succession and in such a way that they can easily be referred to, and the position of the object in relation to the body is recorded. Photographing should be done thoroughly. The photographing and sketching must be considered rather as a precaution which may possibly be of use in the work of identification. The numbered places of discovery are also marked on the sketches. If parts of bodies are found they are given new numbers and placed in strong bags. If a pathologist present confirms that the part belongs to a particular body, then the two are placed together, but this must be done only on his authority. As victims are found and the proper measures are taken, the bodies are wrapped in sheets or cloths so that loose objects cannot fall out and get lost, after which they are taken to a suitable place where the work of identification is to be done.

When the scene of a catastrophe is so large in extent that the bodies can neither be collected by the identification group alone nor supervised by police personnel working under the group, then the victims must first be brought to the identification point by suitable means. There each body is labelled with a number with an accurate statement of the position where it was discovered, time of handing over, and person who found and transported the body. If possible the stretcher-bearers who collect the bodies should be given instructions as to their activities, so as to avoid any mistakes.

Under all conditions the scene of the catastrophe should be cordoned off as quickly as possible, and the guards should see that unattached persons do not take part in the rescue work. Stretcher-bearer patrols should be under a specially selected head, preferably a police officer. Relatives of persons who are thought to have been killed should not be allowed to take part in this work, as there is a risk that they may pick on an unidentified body which they think they can recognize, but which is possibly an entirely different individual. The presence of the relatives at or near the scene is, however, desirable, since they can possibly give information which can help in the rescue or identification.

When the scene has been cleared or thoroughly searched and all bodies and remains have been found, and all objects which can be assumed to belong to victims have been collected, the work of identification can be commenced. The record made during the first stage should be written up in a clean copy and the photographs arranged in order as quickly as possible so that they will be available for reference together with the sketches.

During the time taken for the rescue and clearing up, and before the actual identification is started, the police authorities concerned should obtain statements of the number of persons involved with their names, occupations and dates of birth. If it is to be anticipated that the identification will offer great difficulties then the list of names must be supplemented by statements which can assist the identification. These are obtained from the relatives of the deceased or from persons who may be supposed to know them sufficiently well. In a specially difficult case the following information should be obtained:

a. description, preferably in the form normally used by the police;

b. any illnesses, operations or bone fractures (possibly X-ray photographs);

c. finger prints, if they have been taken for any reason;

d. photographs (simple amateur pictures are better than retouched studio portraits);

e. dental history or extract from it;

f. description of garments (if possible samples of cloth, statement of where bought, make, size of shoes and collar, markings, repairs, etc.), together with;

g. description of personal belongings which the deceased might be expected to have in his clothes, together with rings, jewellry and watch. In this connection there may also be needed a statement of what the deceased would have had near him, e.g. briefcase, hand or travelling case.

Thus when the work of identification is commenced all the bodies, portions of bodies and objects have been numbered in sequence. This numbering is preliminary and should only be employed as an aid to identification. In the identification a start is made with the least injured bodies or with those which offer the best possibilities of quick and satisfactory identification. One of the police officers in the identification group keeps the record. The bodies are renumbered in the order in which they are examined. In the work of identification the bodies should lie on a suitable table or bench. All loose objects in or on the clothing or on the body are recorded and then placed in a bag. If any identifying documents are found on a body, such as a pass, visiting card, identification card, etc., and this agrees with statements obtained regarding a certain person who is supposed to have been killed, then the identification may be considered as complete. There have been cases where identifying documents have been found on a body belonging to another person who was killed at the same time, owing to the bodies having been thrown against one another so that the documents were transferred from the owner to another person. If statements regarding the dead person have been obtained they must be compared with the body in order to confirm the identification. The first body examined is given the number one, after which numbers are given to the bodies in succession as the corresponding measures of identification are taken. The bags containing the belongings are given the same numbers as the bodies to which they belong, and clothes are bundled together and given corresponding numbers. Regarding injuries and assumed cause of death the report is made in the usual manner. The pathologist decides whether these statements should be made in a separate report or included in the report of the identification.

As the bodies are identified they are put to one side. Clothes and belongings are placed at the sides of the bodies. The safest way is not to allow any body to be taken away before all the others have been identified, so that any mistake can be rectified in time. When the deceased are placed in coffins, the work should be supervised and controlled by at least two members of the identification group. The coffins are marked externally with number and name.

The work of identification then proceeds to the more difficult cases, and the identification group must rely more on and refer to the statements which have been obtained. In due course it becomes easier to work on the principle of elimination, but this method cannot be employed except in cases where there is absolutely reliable information of the number of victims and their names, and the statements obtained are detailed and reliable. For the most difficult cases the group must work according to the method described in the preceding section of this chapter. It is specially important that the dentist should make a complete report of the teeth of each body.

Where there is a large number of victims the police or other authorities should not allow the body of any victim to be removed before the identification group has been organized and has arrived at the scene. Even if at an early stage a particular body can be identified with absolute certainty, its removal should not be permitted. It is the identification group which has the responsibility of identifying all the victims, and if it is to deal only with the difficult cases then it will naturally work under the suspicion that the bodies released might have been wrongly identified, and this can destroy the possibility of a certain identification of the more difficult cases.

Appendix

Equipment for crime scene investigation

The investigating officer needs special equipment to aid him in the collection and preservation of evidence, photography and sketching. These tools are necessarily extensive for the investigation of homicide scenes, while for burglary scenes they can be less complex. In any case, the equipment must be flexible and easily portable. It is therefore preferable to have a kit containing all the equipment required for homicide scenes, another for burglary and less demanding crime scenes, and separate kits for casting, photography and so on. The tools and other paraphernalia are preferably arranged in specially constructed carrying cases.

The following illustrations show the layout and composition of several types of crime scene kits used by different police agencies.

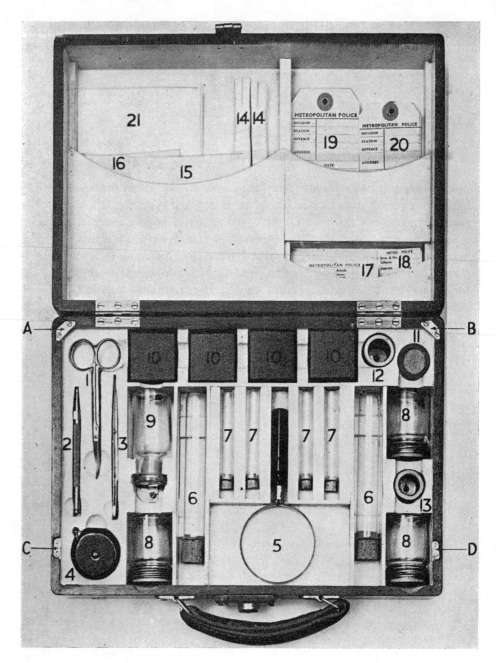

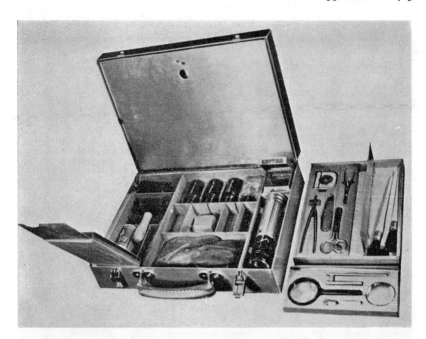

Fig. 225 Universal kit. Finger print forms and lifters are contained in the lid compartment (Switzerland).

CONTENTS: Flashlight, can of aluminum powder, three finger print brushes, scissors, inking slab, roller, printer's ink, spoon, clamps, rule, steel tape, compass, magnifier, detective dyes, talcum powder, absorbent cotton, vaseline, small brush, forceps, rubber gloves, knife, two screwdrivers, awl, pins, plasticine, soap, spare flashlight bulbs and batteries.

← *Fig. 224*

Small universal kit. (Metropolitan Police, London, England).

CONTENTS: Scissors, scriber, forceps, measuring tape, magnifier, test tubes, screw-top glass bottles, glass-stoppered bottle, cardboard boxes, rubber bands, tape, white linen bandage, absorbent cotton, glassine bags, flat paper bags, gummed labels, tags, writing paper.

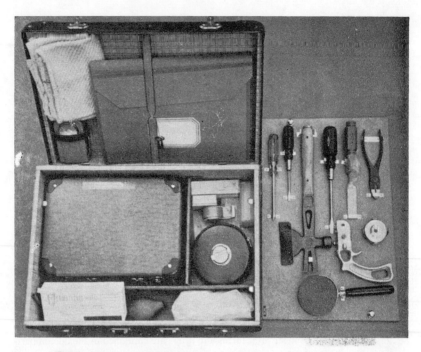

Fig. 226 Basic kit for less complicated crime scenes. (Sold by Magasin Elfo Aktiebolag, Scheelegatan 12, Stockholm K, Sweden).
CONTENTS: Folder containing clip board, pad of graph paper, paper for sketching and accident diagrams; plastic rain protector, pencils, eraser, rule, triangle, protractor, envelopes, labels, compass, measuring tape (50 ft.), steel tape (8 ft.), flashlight, magnifier, magnet, dental impression paste, mixing slab, spatula, test tubes, absorbent cotton, tape, wash cloth and soap dish; combination tool, three screwdrivers, wood chisel, combination pliers, keyhole saw with blades for wood and metal, ninhydrin sprayer and complete fingerprinting kit. (For contents of the latter, see Fig. 228, kit B).

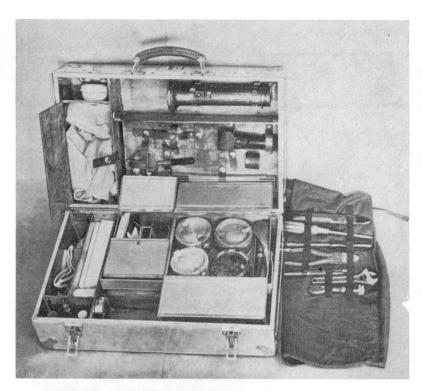

Fig. 227 Kit for burglary investigations. This kit is part of the equipment contained in the vehicle, *Fig. 236.*

CONTENTS:

1. *Fingerprinting kit* consisting of four jars of powder, two brushes, scissors, one roll of lifting tape, black and white lifters, etc.

2. *Casting materials* for tool marks consisting of one package of Kerr Permlastic two spatulas, forceps, absorbent cotton, and bottles containing oil, acetone and water.

3. *Tool kit* in a canvas folder consisting of two screwdrivers, Phillips screwdriver, lineman's pliers, adjustable wrench, knife and diamond glass cutter.

4. *Miscellaneous equipment:* large and small flashlight, pocket microscope, magnifier, compass, magnet, carpenter's rule, 8-ft. steel tape, benzidine, three test tubes, two plastic jars with lids, tape, soap dish, two wiping cloths, one plastic sheet and writing material.

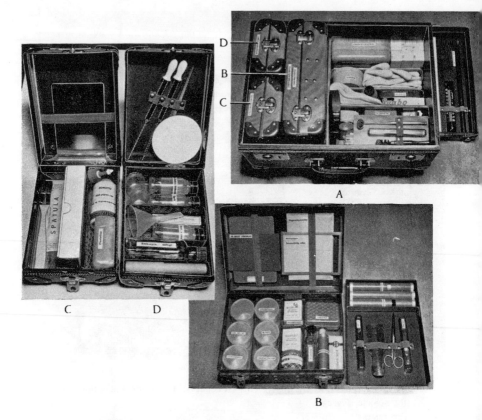

Fig. 228 Homicide investigation kit Mod. 58. (Sold by Magasin Elfo Aktiebolag, Scheelegatan 12, Stockholm K, Sweden). The large case (A) contains the three smaller kits (B, C, and D).

CONTENTS:

Kit A: Sealing materials (seal, sealing wax, burner, waterproof glue, thread, tape, labels and matches), rectal thermometer, room thermometer, magnifier, glass cutter, forceps, dental mirror, flashlight, measuring tape, magnet, six test tubes in wooden protectors, plastic gloves, first-aid kit, cleaning fluid, disinfectant, talcum powder, sponge, paper towels, crayons and plastic bags.

Kit B: Magnifier, forceps, scissors, scalpel, three surgical knives, fingerprinting spoon, inking roller, inking slab, printer's ink, ink-impregnated sheets (Neuss type), aluminum powder, lampblack powder, black powder mixture, white lead, red iron oxide powder, three finger print brushes, black and white lifters, lifting tape, glazed paper, celluloid, mineral oil, absorbent cotton.

Kit C: Mixing slab for casting materials, spatula, blow pipe, dental impression paste, plastic emulsion, and plasticine.

Kit D: Preliminary blood testing kit consisting of benzidine tablets, filter paper, glacial acetic acid, distilled water, saline, solution, methyl alcohol, two small spoons, two plastic containers, two pipettes with rubber bulbs, two glass rods, two eye droppers and a plastic funnel.

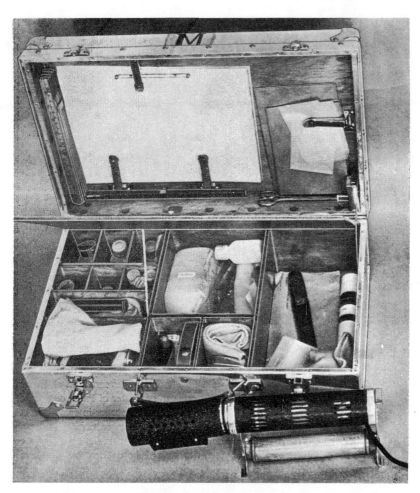

Fig. 229 Kit for homicide investigations contained in the vehicle, *Fig. 236*. This kit is used in conjunction with the burglary investigation kit, *Fig. 227*.

CONTENTS: Ultraviolet lamp, laboratory thermometer, rectal thermometer, two scalpels, two forceps, scissors, magnifier, bottle of ethyl alcohol, talcum powder, two glass bottles, six plastic containers with lids, four test tubes, six plastic bottles, two graduates, 8-ft. measuring tape, rule, diamond glass cutter, compass, inking pad for elimination prints, clip board, rubber gloves, plastic sheets, wiping cloths, soap dish, seal, sealing wax, friction tape, scotch tape, absorbent cotton, crayons, thumbtacks, paper, bags and envelopes.

Fig. 230 Casting kit. (The kit is sold by Magasin Elfo Aktiebolag, Scheelegatan 12, Stockholm K, Sweden).

CONTENTS: Butane burner with windshield and spare gas cartridge, aluminum saucepan, plastic, pitcher and stirrer, one can of plaster of Paris, one can of powdered sulphur, rubber cup, metal spoon, sifter, lacquer in spray can, oil mixture in bottle with sprayer attachment, aluminum casting frames, cans containing aluminum powder, black powder, talc and salt, flat brush, powder sprayer with nozzle, forceps, pipette, 1-liter plastic bottle for water, plasticine, carpenter's rule, plastic sheet, plastic bags, matches, twine, soap and paper towels.

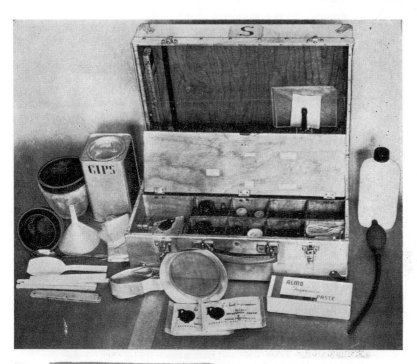

Fig. 231 Casting kit contained in the vehicle, *Fig. 236.*

CONTENTS: Can of plaster, plastic water bottle, bottle with dropping stopper, plastic funnel, rubber bulb, four rubber bowls, plastic cups, two spoons, two spatulas, two metal retaining bands, rule, laboratory thermometer, paper cups, two plastic sheets, wiping cloth, soap dish, Kerr Permlastic, DP Elastic Impression Cream, plastic emulsion, fixing spray, oil, acetone.

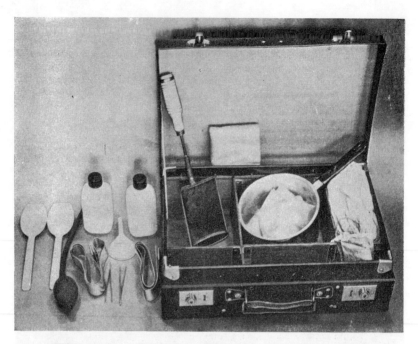

Fig. 232 Casting kit for winter conditions contained in the vehicle, *Fig. 236.*
CONTENTS: Alcohol burner, saucepan, two spoons, two casting frames of
aluminum, rubber bulb, ladle, forceps, two bags for sulphur, two plastic
bottles for alcohol, plastic funnel, wiping cloth and two plastic sheets.

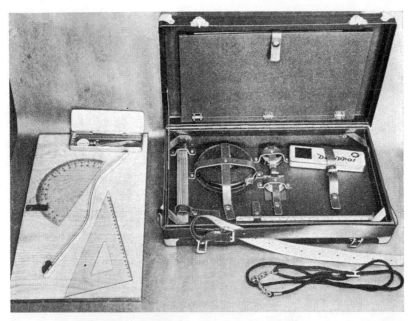

Fig. 233 Kit for crime scene sketching contained in the vehicle, *Fig. 236*.

CONTENTS: Drawing board with neck strap, protractor, triangle, drawing curves, engineers' scale, dividers, map tracer, compass, carpenter's rule, 8-ft. steel tape, 50-ft. fabric tape, tape, crayons, pencils, eraser, drawing and writing papers.

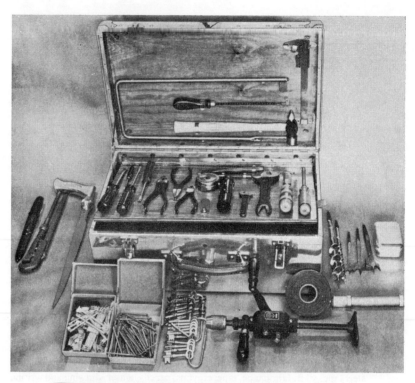

Fig. 234. Tool kit which is part of the equipment in the vehicle. *Fig. 236.*
CONTENTS: Hammer, combination pliers, pipe wrench, side cutters, flat-nose pliers, keyhole saw with two blades, knife, two wood chisels, chisel, four screwdrivers, two adjustable wrenches, hand drill, wood bits, high speed bits, vernier calipers, steel tape, special flashlight, lock picks, nails, etc.

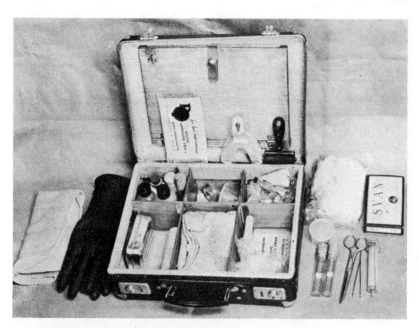

Fig. 235 Kit for the identification of bodies; contained in the vehicle, *Fig. 236.*
CONTENTS: Syringe with two needles, face mask with filters, rubber gloves, scissors, forceps, ink pad, two dental impression trays, spatula, DP Elastic Impression Cream, plastic emulsion, rubber bowl, two plastic cups, four test tubes, wiping cloth, tape, bottles with alcohol and liquid for face mask, soap dish, bags, envelopes, finger print forms and blank cards.

Fig. 236 Vehicle specially equipped for the investigation of crime and accident scenes. (Stockholm, Sweden).

EQUIPMENT IN THE VEHICLE:

1. Special kits consisting of two kits for use on burglary scenes, a homicide kit. a tool kit, one casting kit for summer conditions and one for winter, a lamp kit, an identification kit, a sketching kit and a kit containing markers.

2. Tools, consisting of prybars, shovel, handsaw, hacksaw, two axes, bit brace, wrench and bolt cutters.

3. Illuminating equipment, consisting of a generator and two floodlights with 500-foot reeled cable, extension cords, handlamps, flashlights and headlamps.

4. Darkroom equipment for developing film inside the vehicle.

5. Miscellaneous equipment, consisting of a portable heater, two fire extinguishers, two warning beacons, four traffic markers, two road markers, a ladder, lifting crane, rope, block and tackle, and a first-aid kit.

Fig. 237 Mobile unit for crime scene investigations based on a utility truck. Kits and equipment shown are contained in compartments accessible from the outside of the vehicle. Note the special cases for transporting firearms, vacuum cleaner with special collection attachment, mine sweeper and sifting screens.

(Metropolitan Dade County Public Safety Department)

Bibliography

Bibliography to Chapter 1

COLLINS, R. L., Improved Crime Scene Investigations, *J. of Crim. Law, Criminol. and Police Sci.*, 52(1961) 469.

CRUTCHETT, A., 'The detective at work' in *Crime and its Detection, Vol. I*, Editor W. TEIGNMOUTH SHORE, London, 1934, p. 247.

CUNNINGHAM, D. K., Police Duties at the Scene of the Crime, *Police*, 6(1961) 77.

DIECKMANN, SR., E. A., *Practical Homicide Investigation*, Chapter 12 (Teamwork), Springfield, 1961, p. 66.

DIENSTEIN, W., *Technics for the Crime Investigator*, Chapter 2 (The Crime Scene), Springfield, 1952.

FAHLANDER, N., *Kriminalpolistjänst*, Karlshamn, 1956, p. 16.

FINNEY, D. J., Police duties at crime scenes, *J. of Crim. Law, Criminol. and Police Sci.*, 27(1936) 321, 412.

FITZGERALD, M. J., *Handbook of Criminal Investigation*, Chapter III (General procedure in an investigation), New York, 1952, p. 34.

FRIEDEM, K., Possible ways of improving investigation of the scene of a crime, *Kriminalistik*, 13(1959) 109.

HARRIS, R. I., Accessary After the Fact – The Officer on the Scene(?), *Police*, 7(1963) 6.

NICKOLLS, L. C., *The Scientific Investigation of Crime*, Chapter 2 (Scenes of Crime), London, 1956, p. 29, 36.

O'HARA, CH. E., *Fundamentals of Criminal Investigation*, Springfield, 1956, p. 41.

SNYDER, LEM., *Homicide Investigation*, Springfield, 1950, p. 13.

STAINES, E. V., Routine Inquiries, *The Police J.*, 16(1963) 8.

SÖDERMAN, H., *Minnesbok för kriminalpolismän*, Stockholm, 1943, p. 94.

VOLLMER, A., 'Criminal Investigation' in *Elements of Police Science*, Editor R. M. PERKINS, Chicago, 1942, p. 37.

Bibliography to Chapter 2

BENNETT, J., Packing of articles at scenes of crime, *Police J.*, 19(1946) 114.

BISCHOFF, M. A., *La Police Scientifique*, Paris, 1938, p. 17.

BURGESS, W. A., Effective Homicide Investigation Aid San Diego Police, *FBI Bulletin*, 32(1963) 3.

CRUTCHETT, A., 'The detective at work' in *Crime and its Detection, Vol. I*, Editor W. TEIGNMOUTH SHORE, London, 1934, p. 247.

DIECKMANN, SR., E. A., *Practical Homicide Investigation*, Chapter 3 (The Essential Clue), Springfield, 1961, p. 14.

DIENSTEIN, W., *Technics for the Crime Investigator*, Springfield, 1952, p. 7, 16.

FAHLANDER, N., *Kriminalpolistjänst*, Karlshamn, 1954, p. 289.

FINNEY, D. J., Police duties at crime scenes, *J. of Crim. Law, Criminol. and Police Sci.*, 27(1936) 231, 412, 431.

FITZGERALD, M. J., *Handbook of Criminal Investigation*, Chapter 3 (General procedure in an investigation), New York, 1952, p. 34.

GONZALES, T. A., M. VANCE, M. HELPERN and C. J. UMBERGER, *Legal Medicine, Pathology and Toxicology*, 2nd Ed. New York, 1954, p. 8.

GROSS, H. and R. L. JACKSON, *Criminal Investigation*, London, 1962, p. 3, 76, 236.

HARRIS, R. I., *Outline of Death Investigation*, Chapter 2 (Procedure), Springfield, 1962, p. 10.

HARRIS, R. I., *Outline of Death Investigation*, Chapter 10 (Transportation of Bodies), Springfield, 1962, p. 49.

MERKELEY, D. K., *The Investigation of Death*, Chapter I (Deaths and Medico-legal Organization), Springfield, 1957, p. 3.

PARRY, L. A., 'Medical and surgical evidence' in *Crime and its Detection, Vol. I*, Editor W. TEIGNMOUTH SHORE, London, 1934, p. 113.

SNYDER, LEM., *Homicide Investigation*, Springfield, 1950, p. 3, 13.

SÖDERMAN, H., *Minnesbok för kriminalpolismän*, Stockholm, 1943, p. 95.

WILSON, R. A., *Institute on Homicide Investigation Techniques*, Springfield, 1961, p. 5.

Bibliography to Chapter 3

GONZALES, T. A., M. VANCE, M. HELPERN and C. J. UMBERGER, *Legal Medicine, Pathology and Toxicology*, 2nd Ed., New York, 1954, p. 8.

GRADWOHL, R. B. H., *Legal Medicine*, St. Louis, 1954, p. 24.

GROSS, H. and R. L. JACKSON, *Criminal Investigation*, 5th Ed., London, 1962, p. 100.

MERKELEY, D. K., *The Investigation of Death*, Springfield, 1957, p. 3.

SIMPSON, C. K., *Forensic Medicine*, London, 1951, p. 203.

SMITH, S., *Forensic Medicine*, London, 1945, p. 50.

Bibliography to Chapter 4

Sketching the crime scene

BROWN, F. A., Plan drawing, *Police J.*, 16(1943) 230.

DIENSTEIN, W., *Technics for the Crime Investigator*, Springfield, 1952, p. 26.

GRASSBERGER, R., Über das Anfertigen von Planskizzen und Situationszeichnungen insbesondere bei Brandermittlungen, *Kriminalistik*, 17(1943) 15.

GROSS, H. and R. L. JACKSON, *Criminal Investigation*, 5th Ed., London, 1962, p. 236.

KING, H. and F. J. FOWLER, About Maps, *Police J.*, 13(1940) 405.

KING, H. and F. J. FOWLER, On setting a map and fixing one's position on a map, *Police J.*, 14(1941) 67.

McGREGOR, D. C., Plan drawing – and the county policeman, *Police J.*, 22(1949) 66.

O'HARA, CH. E., *Fundamentals of Criminal Investigation*, Springfield, 1956, p. 56.
Сеᴎмɪᴅᴛ, Die Bedeutung der Tatortskizze bei der Bearbeitung von Verkehrsunfällen, *Kriminalistik*, 12(1938) 230.
SNYDER, LEM., *Homicide Investigation*, Springfield, 1950, p. 18.
SÖDERMAN, H. and J. J. O'CONNELL, *Modern Criminal Investigation*, 5th Ed., New York, 1962, p. 110.
SULLIVAN, J. W., Techniques and General Rules of Sketching, *FBI Law Enf. Bull.*, 25, no. 2(1956) 10.
TRIPP, H. A., The police and town planning, *Police J.*, 14(1941) 375.
TURNER, R. F., *Forensic Science and Laboratory Technics*, Springfield, 1949, p. 30.
ÖSTERBERG, K. E., *Polisteknisk skissering*, Göteborg, 1944.

Photographing the crime scene

BLAIR, J. S., Photographic Mapping of Accident Sites, *Police J.*, 36(1963) 307.
BREWER, E. F., Photography at Night, *Law and Order*, 11, no. 4(1963) 10.
CLAUSEN, L. S., Overhead photography in confined spaces, *Police J.*, 25(1952) 29.
DIENSTEIN, W., *Technics for the Crime Investigator*, Springfield, 1952, p. 26.
FAHLANDER, N., *Kriminalpolistjänst*, Karlshamn, 1956, p. 137.
FREI-SULZER, M., Photographie und Kriminalistik, *Kriminalistik*, 16(1962) 446.
GROSS, H. and R. L. JACKSON, *Criminal Investigation*, 5th Ed., London, p. 145.
HARRIS, R. I., *Outline of Death Investigation*, Springfield, 1962, p. 40.
HYZER, W. G., How to Measure with a Camera, *Photo Methods for Industry*, 6(1963) 34.
JONES, L. V., *Scientific Investigation and Physical Evidence*, Springfield, 1959, p. 83.
KING, D. P., Admissibility of Photographic Evidence in Prosecutions of Felonious Homicides, *Police*, 7, no. 5(1963) 17.
MURPHY, B., *Police and Crime Photography*, New York, 1960, p. 54.
O'HARA, CH. E. and J. W. OSTERBURG, *An Introduction to Criminalistics*, New York, 1949, p. 141.
O'HARA, CH. E., *Fundamentals of Criminal Investigation*, Springfield, 1956, p. 51.
RADLEY, J. A., *Photography in Crime Detection*, London, 1948, p. 46.
SCOTT, C. C., *Photographic Evidence*, Kansas City, 1942, p. 194.
SNYDER, LEM., *Homicide Investigation*, Springfield, 1950, p. 19.
SPECHT, W., Gedanken zur Tatortphotographie, *Die Neue Polizei*, 8(1954) 158.
SÖDERMAN, H. and J. J. O'CONNELL, *Modern Criminal Investigation*, 5th Ed., New York, 1962, p. 121.
TURNER, R. F., *Forensic Science and Laboratory Technics*, Springfield, 1949, p. 30.
TUTTLE, H. B., Color Photography in Police Science, *Law and Order*, 8(1960) 6.
Anon., *Photography in Law Enforcement*, Eastman Kodak, Rochester, 1959.

Packaging and shipping of the evidence

BENNETT, J., Packing of articles at scenes of crime, *Police J.*, 19(1946) 114.
DIENSTEIN, W., *Technics for the Crime Investigator*, Springfield, 1952, p. 30.
GROSS, H. and R. L. JACKSON, *Criminal Investigation*, 5th Ed., London, p. 97.
KIRK, P. L., *Crime Investigation*, New York, 1953, p. 83.
LUCAS, A., *Forensic Chemistry and Scientific Criminal Investigation*, London, 1945, p. 9.

NEPOTE, J., The transport of exhibits, *Intern. Crim. Pol. Rev.*, no. 26(1949) p. 17.

NICKOLLS, L. C., *The Scientific Investigation of Crime*, London, 1956, p. 44.

O'HARA, CH. E., *Fundamentals of Criminal Investigation*, Springfield, 1956, p. 61.

O'HARA, CH. E. and J. W. OSTERBURG, *An Introduction to Criminalistics*, New York, 1949, p. 30.

POLSON, C. J. and R. P. BRITTAIN, The protection of articles which bear fingerprints, *Police J.*, 25(1952) 31.

TURNER, R. F., *Forensic Science and Laboratory Technics*, Springfield, 1949, p. 36.

WILSON, CH. M., 'The preservation and transportation of firearms evidence' in *Homicide Investigation* by LEMOYNE SNYDER, Springfield, 1950, p. 145.

Anon., An Outline of the Rules for Handling Physical Evidence, *FBI Law Enf. Bull.*, 23, no. 7(1954) 11.

Anon., Evidence, Where's It Hidden?, *RCMP Gazette*, 26, no. 1(1964) 2; reprinted from *Spring* 3100.

Note: Most major police departments, state and local, have manuals with suggested procedures for handling various items of evidence. A request for a copy, on departmental stationary, will usually be honored.

Bibliography to Chapter 5

Finger prints and palm prints

ANGST, E., Untersuchungen zur Bestimmung des Alters von daktyloskopischen Spuren auf Papier, *Kriminalistik*, 15 (1961) I.

BATTLEY, H., *Single Finger Prints*, New Haven, 1931.

BRIDGES, B. C., *Practical Fingerprinting*, New York, 1948.

BROWNE, D. G. and A. BROCK, *Fingerprints*, London, 1954.

CAMPBELL, C., Fingerprint Powders, *Finger Print Mag.*, 31(1950) 3.

CASTELLANOS, I., *Identification Problems*, New York, 1939.

CHAPEL, CH. E., *Fingerprinting*, New York, 1941.

CHERRILL, F. R., *The Fingerprint System at Scotland Yard*, London, 1954.

CHOATE, W. L., G. R. STANGHOR and A. W. SOMERFORD, Present Status of the Ninhydrin Process for Developing Latent Fingerprints, *Identification News*, 13(1963) 9.

CONLEY, B. J., Bloody Latent Fingerpints, *Finger Print Mag.*, 40(1959) 16.

CORR, J., Flammen – Verfahren zur Sicherung latenter Fingerspuren, *Kriminalistik*, 10(1956) 429.

CORR, J., *Finger Print Mag.*, 30(1957) 16.

DAHLQVIST, S., *Fingeravtryck och signalementslära*, Karlshamn, 1952, p. 60.

DUNCAN, J. H., *An Introduction to Fingerprints*, London, 1942.

ERIKSSON, S. A. and O. RISPLING, Bloody Finger Prints, *Nord. Krim. Tids.*, 30(1960) 110.

ERIKSSON, S. A. and O. RISPLING, *Identifieringslärans grunder*, Stockholm, 1959.

FOWLER, D. C., Casting of Fingerprints, *Finger Print Mag.*, 39(1958) 6.

GRODSKY, M., Variations in Latent Print Technique, *Finger Print Mag.*, 39(1957) 16.

HARRISON, W. R., The Detection of Fingerprints on Documents, *The Criminal Law Review*, 1958, p. 591.

HEATHCOTE, A. E., If You Can See It, You Can Photograph It, *Police J.*, 36(1963) 171.

HONDA, H., Automatic Latent Print Developer Invented in Japan, *Finger Print Mag.*, 42(1960) 3.

JOLLY, R. L., Fires and Fingerprints, *Intern. Crim. Pol. Rev.*, no. 119(1958) 173.

KANDA, M., Comparison between ninhydrin and alloxan methods for detecting fingerprints, *Kagaku to Sosa*, 11(1958) 152.

KOBABE, A., The Development of Latent Fingerprints on Polished Metal, *Arch. f. Kriminol.*, 121(1958) 51.

LARSEN, J. K., The Starch Powder-Steam Method of Fixing Iodine Fumed Latent Prints, *Finger Print Mag.*, 44(1962) 3.

LOCARD, E., *Manuel de Technique Policière*, Paris, 1948, p. 22.

LUCAS, A., *Forensic Chemistry and Scientific Criminal Investigation*, London, 1946, p. 164.

MACDONELL, H. L., Iodine Fuming – New Apparatus, *Police*, 3(1959) 12.

MACDONELL, H. L., The Use of Hydrogen Fluoride in the Development of Latent Fingerprints found on Glass Surfaces, *J. of Crim. Law, Criminol. and Police Sci.*, 51(1960) 465.

MACDONELL, H. L., *BCI Bull. N.Y. State Police*, 26 (1961) 7.

MCLAUGHLIN, A. R., Developing Latent Prints on Absorbent Surfaces, *Finger Print Mag.*, 42(1961) 3.

MCLAUGHLIN, A. R., Chemicals and Their Application for Developing Latent Prints, *Finger Print Mag.*, 43(1961) 3.

MCMORRIS, J., The Iodine–Silver-Transfer Method for recording latent fingerprints, *Finger Print Mag.*, 18(1937) 6.

MIMURA, T., T. NAKASE, and A. YAMAGATA, Transfer of fingerprints impressed by oil, *Kagaku to Sosa*, 10(1957) 33.

MITCHELL, C. A., *The Scientific Detective and the Expert Witness*, Cambridge, 1931, p. 56.

MOTOSADA, K., Detection of fingerprints by use of alloxan, *Kagaku to Sosa*, 10(1957) 23.

ODÉN, S., Nya riktlinjer för framkallning av latenta fingeravtryck på papper och liknande material, *Nord. Krim. Tids.*, 24(1954) 37.

O'HARA, CH. E. and J. W. OSTERBURG, *An Introduction to Criminalistics*, New York, 1949, p. 77, 208.

RADLEY, J. A., *Photography in Crime Detection*, London, 1948, p. 37.

RAY, D. N., Nylon Spray for Lifting Latent Fingerprints, *J. of Crim. Law, Criminol. and Police Sci.*, 51(1961) 661.

RHODES, H. T. F., *Forensic Chemistry*, London, 1946, p. 3.

RISPLING, O., Avgjutning av plastiska fingeravtryck, *Nord. Krim. Tids.*, 25(1955) 144.

RISPLING, O., Säkring av fingerblommemönster från lik, *Nord. Krim. Tids.*, 26(1956) 11.

SANNIÉ, CH. and D. GUÉRIN, *Éléments de Palice Scientifique, Vol. III and IV*, Paris, 1940.

SCOTT, W. R., *Fingerprint Mechanics*, Springfield, 1951.

SÖDERMAN, H. and J. J. O'CONNELL, *Modern Criminal Investigation*, New York, 1962, p. 128.

WAGENAAR, M., Vorschlag eines Verfahrens zur Fixierung der mit Jod sichtbar gemachten latenten Fingerabdrücke, *Arch. f. Kriminol.*, 97(1935) 45.
WENTWORTH, B. and J. J. WILDER, *Personal Identification*, Chicago, 1932.

Prints of gloves
SANTAMARIA BELTRAN, J., Traces of gloves, *Intern. Crim. Pol. Rev.*, 7(1952) 79.
SVENSSON, A., Om identifierung av handsk- och vantavtryck, *Nord. Krim. Tids.*, 18 (1948) 97.
VOGELIUS ANDERSEN, C. H., Om handskeaftryck paa gerningssteder, *Nord. Krim. Tids.*, 13(1943) 113.

Foot prints
ABBOT, J. R., Reproduction of footprints, *J. of Crim. Law, Criminol. and Police Sci.*, 32(1942) 596.
ALLEN, J. W., Making plaster casts in snow, *Intern. Crim. Pol. Rev.*, 10(1955) 174.
BAUERNFEIND, X., Warum so wenig Fussspuren?, *Kriminalistik*, 4(1950) 147, 201.
BISCHOFF, M. A., *La Police Scientifique*, Paris, 1938, p. 72.
CLARKE, C. D., *Molding and Casting*, Baltimore, 1938.
ELMES, F., Footprints, *Police J.*, 10(1941) 106.
GROSS, H. and R. L. JACKSON, *Criminal Investigation*, 5th Ed., London, 1962, p. 263.
HAMILTON, D., Traces of footwear, tyres and tools, etc. in criminal investigation, *Police J.*, 22(1949) 42.
HARRISON, W. R., Reproduction of Marks on surfaces which cannot conveniently be photographed, *FBI Law Enf. Bull.*, 7(1938) no. 6, p. 11.
HICKS, S., Tracking – A Vanishing Heritage, *Police*, 4(1950) 43.
JAQUILLARD, R., The lessons of a crime, *Intern. Crim. Pol. Rev.*, 38(1950) 137.
KARLMARK, E., The taking of casts in the snow, *FBI Law Enf. Bull.*, 8(1939) no. 4, p. 3.
LOCARD, E., *Manuel de Technique Policière*, Paris, 1948, p. 70.
LUCAS, A., *Forensic Chemistry and Scientific Criminal Investigation*, London, 1945, p. 167.
LUFF, K. and B. HESS, Alginate and Silicone Impression Materials, *Arch. f. Kriminol.*, 123(1959) 146.
MARTIN, F. W., A simple method of taking footprints, *Police J.*, 9(1936) 450.
MEZGER, O. and HEESS, W., Überführung durch Knieabdrücke, *Arch. f. Kriminol.*, 87(1930) 249.
MOORE, R. E., Heel prints prove nemesis of slayers, *Finger Print Mag.*, 32(1950) 15.
MORREN, W. B. R., Tyre tracks, *Police J.*, 15(1942) 276.
NICKENIG, A., Fussspuren im Schnee, Richtig gesichert, *Arch. f. Kriminol*, 120(1957) 37.
NICKOLLS, L. C., Footprints and Tyre Impressions, Chapter 7, *The Scientific Investigation of Crime*, London, 1956, p. 136.
O'HARA, CH. E. and J. W. OSTERBURG, *An Introduction to Criminalistics*, New York, 1949, p. 103.
OWEN, F., A latent heel impression, *Police J.*, 27(1954) 221.
REYNARD, J. N., Footprints – The practical side of the subject, *Police J.*, 21(1948) 30.
SOULE, R. L., Reproduction of Foot and Tire Track by Plaster of Paris Casting, *J. of Crim. Law, Criminol. and Police Sci.*, 50(1959) 198.

SPELLER, H. C., The identification of crepe-rubber sole impressions, *Police J.*, 22(1949) 260.

SVENSSON, A., Några mindre vanliga spårtyper, *Nord. Krim. Tids.*, 28(1958) 113.

STEDRY, W., Einfluss der Bodenbeschaffenheit auf die Grösse von Fusspuren, *Kriminalistik*, 11(1957) 465.

SÖDERMAN, H., Minnesbok för kriminalpolismän, Stockholm, 1943, p. 43, 57 and 84.

SÖDERMAN, H. and J. J. O'CONNELL, *Modern Criminal Investigation*, 5th Ed., New York, 1962, p. 156.

TILLER, C. D., Examination of Footprints at Crime Scenes, *RCMP Gazette*, 24(1962) 12.

TRYHORN, F. G., Scientific aids in criminal investigation, Part V, Marks and impressions, *Police J.*, 10(1937) 19.

WATSON, J., A Method of Lifting and Photographing for Evidence, *J. of Crim. Law, Criminol. and Police Sci.*, 49(1958) 49.

WILD, E., The murder at Diamond street, *Police J.*, 27(1954) 181.

ZMUDA, CH. W., Identification of Crepe-Sole Shoes, *J. of Crim. Law, Criminol, and Police Sci.*, 44(1953) 374.

Anon., Pick up the trail with plaster casts, *FBI Law Enf. Bull.*, 20(1951) no, 5, p. 6.

Anon., Pick up the trail from impressions found on firm surfaces, *FBI Law Enf. Bull.*, 20(1951) no. 6, p. 12.

Anon., Preserving Prints of Shoes and Tires on Hard Surfaces, *FBI Law Enf. Bull.*, 30(1961) no. 6, p. 7.

Anon., Shoe Print on Rug Links Hold-up Man to House Robbery, *FBI Law Enf. Bull.*, 30 (1961) no. 6, p. 18.

Anon., Tips on Making casts of Shoe and Tire Prints, *FBI Law Enf. Bull.*, 32(1963) no. 10, p. 18.

Anon., Silicone Casting, *Finger Print Mag.*, 41(1960) 7.

Tooth marks

BUHTZ – EHRHARDT, Die Identifikation von Bisswunden, *Dtsch. Z. ger. Med.*, 29(1938) 453.

GROSS, H. and R. L. JACKSON, *Criminal Investigation*, 5th Ed., London, 1962, p. 289.

KARLMARK, E. and E. TORNBERG, Aufnahme und Aufbewahrung gerichtsmedizinisch und kriminalistisch wichtiger Einzelheiten von Spuren mit einer praktischen Kautschukmasse, *Kriminalistik*, 13(1939) 78.

KORKHAUS, G., Identifizierung von Haut-Bisspuren durch den Zahnarzt, *Arch. f. Kriminol.*, 116(1955) 171.

DE LAET, M., L'Identification par empreintes dentaires. Un cas démonstratif. *Rev. Droit pénal*, 15(1935) 502.

LOOCK, *Chemie und Photographie bei Kriminalforschungen*, Düsseldorf, p. 24.

NICKOLLS, L. C., Identification by tooth-marks, *Police J.*, 23(1950) 263.

OHLSSON, K. H., Tandavtryck som bevismedel, *Nord. Krim. Tids.*, 8(1938) 92.

PAULICH, J. J., Bisspur in einem Apfel überführt Mörderin, *Arch. f. Kriminol.*, 107 (1940) 45.

SCHAIDT, G., Untersuchung zur Auswertung von Bisspuren in Lebensmitteln, *Kriminalwissenschaft*, 1(1954) 53.

SVEEN, R., Politiet og Tannlaegen, *Nord. Krim. Tids.*, 3(1933) 156.
SÖDERMAN, H., *Minnesbok för kriminalpolismän*, Stockholm, 1943, p. 62.
VON HENTIG, H., Der Biss, *Arch. f. Kriminol.*, 131(1963) 121.
Anon., Identification by tooth marks, *Police J.*, 27(1954) 131.

Bibliography to Chapter 6

ANDERSEN, A. C., Om spor etter inbrudstyverier, *Nord. Krim. Tids.*, 21(1951) 61.
BELLAVIC, H., Identifikation von Sägespuren, *Arch. f. Kriminol.*, 94(1934) 139.
BELLAVIC, H., Spuren an Bohrspänen, *Kriminalistik*, 16(1942) 82.
BELLAVIC, H., Identifikation von Bohrspuren, *Arch. f. Kriminol.*, 102(1938) 97.
BESSEMANS, A., Die Identifizierung der Spuren von Schneide- und Hackwerkzeugen, *Arch. f. Kriminol*, 116(1955) 61.
BESSEMANS, A., Identification au moyen du microscope de comparaison, d'une cisaille ayant servi à la section d'un fil de fer barbelé, *Acta Med. Leg. et Soc.*, 1(1948) 406.
BESSEMANS, A. and A. CUELENAIRE, Sur les traces des instruments coupants ou tranchants et en particulier de leur fil., *Acta Med. Leg. et Soc.*, 1(1948) 398.
BIASOTTI, A. A., A Comparison of Hatchet Cuts on Wire, *J. of Crim. Law, Criminol. and Police Sci.*, 47(1957) 497.
BIASOTTI, A. A., Plastic Replicas in Firearms and Tool Mark Identification, *J. of Crim. Law, Criminol. and Police Sci.*, 47(1956) 110.
BURD, D. Q. and P. L. KIRK, Tool marks, factors involved in their comparison and use as evidence, *J. of Crim. Law, Criminol. and Police Sci.*, 32(1942) 679.
BURD, D. Q. and R. S. GREENE, Tool mark comparisons in criminal investigation, *J. of Crim. Law, Criminol. and Police Sci.*, 39(1948) 379.
BURD, D. Q. and R. S. GREENE, Tool Mark Examination Technique, *J. of For. Sci.*, 2(1957) 297.
CHURCHMAN, J. A., Engravings and impressions, *RCMP Quart.*, 14 (1949) 136.
DAVIS, J. E., *An Introduction to Tool Marks, Firearms and the Striagraph*, Springfield, 1958.
EHRHARDT, W., Überführung eines Forstdiebes durch Werkzeugspuren trotz Fehlens eines Tatwerkzeuges, *Krim. Rundschau*, 2(1948) 85.
ENKLAAR, F., A New Burglary Tool And Proof by the Metal Chips, *Kriminalistik*, 10 (1956) 452.
FLYNN, E. M., Toolmark Identification, *J. of For. Sci.*, 2(1957) 95.
GROSS, H. and R. L. JACKSON, *Criminal Investigation*, 5th Ed., London, 1962.
HART, A. B., Ramification, Tool Marks in Firearms Identification, *BCI Bull.* N.Y. State Police, 25 (1960) 10.
KOEHLER, J. A., Technique used in tracing the Lindbergh kidnaping ladder, *J. of Crim. Law, Criminol. and Police Sci.*, 27(1937) 712.
LINDÉN, B., Säkring av verktygsspår i metall, *Nord. Krim. Tids.*, 21(1951) 140.
LOCARD, E., *Traité de Criminalistique, Vol. II*, Lyon, 1931, p. 733.
LUCAS, A., *Forensic Chemistry and Scientific Criminal Investigation*, London, 1945, p. 140.

MAY, L. S., The identification of knives, tools and instruments as a positive science, *Am. J. Police Sci.*, 1(1930) 246.

MAYER, R. M., Kann man Säger aus der Sägespur wiedererkennen? *Arch. f. Kriminol.*, 92 (1933) 157.

MEZGER, O., F. HASSLACHER and P. FRANKLE, Identification of marks (axe) made on trees, *Am. J. Police Sci.*, 1(1930) 358.

NEWMANN, F. H., The examination of tools and toolmarks, *Police J.*, 11(1938) 214.

NICKENIG, A., Untersuchungen zur Altersbestimmung von Werkzeugspuren, *Kriminalistik*, 16 (1961) 397.

NICKOLLS, L. C., Instrument Marks, Chapter 6, *The Scientific Investigation of Crime*, London, 1956, p. 109.

NOUSIAINEN, H., Om spår efter rörtänger, *Nord. Krim. Tids.*, 17(1947) 140.

O'HARA, CH. E. and J. W. OSTERBURG, *An Introduction to Criminalistics*, New York, 1949, p. 121, 131.

PELZ. R., Sägespuren, *Kriminalistik*, 10(1956) 171.

POLKE, J., Schartenspuren durch Werkzeugen veranlasst, *Kriminalistik*, 17 (1943) 23.

PROUTY, R. W., A Survey of Tool Mark Techniques, *Finger Print Mag.*, 40(1958) 3.

PURTELL, D. J., The Identification of Paper Cutting Knives and Paper Cutters, *J. of Crim. Law, Criminol. and Police Sci.*, 44(1956) 262.

ROSCHEK, K., Schraubenköpfe als Spurenträger, *Arch. f. Kriminol.*, 130(1962) 17.

SEELIG, E., Spuren an Bohrspänen, *Kriminalistik*, 16(1942) 82.

SELINGER, A., Identification of toolmarks on a skull, *Intern. Crim. Pol. Rev.*, 11(1956) 48.

SPECHT, W., Welche Arten von Werkzeugspuren gibt es und wie erfolgt die Sicherung, *Krim. Monatsh.*, 9(1935) 148.

SPECHT, W., Schartenspuren, *Krim. Monatsh.*, 10(1936) 223.

SVENSSON, A., Några mindre vanliga spårtyper, *Nord. Krim. Tids.*, 28(1958) 113.

SÖDERMAN, H., *Minnesbok för kriminalpolismän*, Stockholm, 1943, p. 72.

THOMAS, F. and G. GALLET, Homicide by blows dealt to the head by means of an axe. Identification of the weapon, *J. Belge Neurol. et Psychiatrie*, 7(1947) 417; *Intern. Crim. Pol. Rev.*, 1947, no. 10, p. 13.

TRYHORN, F. G., Scientific aids in criminal investigation, Part VI, Marks and impressions, *Police J.*, 10(1937) 139.

Bibliography to Chapter 7

Blood

ANDRESEN, P. H., *The Human Blood Groups*, Springfield, 1952.

BERG, S. P., Diaminoxydasebestimmung bei Spurenuntersuchungen, *Dtsch. Z. ger. Med.*, 39(1948) 89.

BERG, S. P., Der Nachweis von Geburts- und Abortusblut bei der Untersuchung von Spuren, *Dtsch. Z. ger. Med.*, 39(1948) 199.

BOYD, W. C. and L. G. BOYD, Blood grouping in forensic medicine, *J. of Immun.*, 33 (1937) 159.

COIMBRA, F., Determination of blood-group on the scene of the crime, *Intern. Crim. Pol. Rev.*, no. 43(1950) 330.

DADLEZ, J., Das Verbleiben der Blutflecke auf im Wasser eingetauchten Gegenständen und einige Bemerkungen über den Einfluss des Blutes auf die Rostbildung, *Dtsch. Z. ger. Med.*, 28 (1937) 384.

DAVIDSOHN, I., Blood grouping tests described simply, *Police J.*, 14 (1941) 271.

DAVIDSOHN, I., The medicolegal application of blood grouping tests, *J. of Crim. Law, Criminol. and Police Sci.*, 31(1941) 643.

FAHLANDER, N., *Kriminalpolistjänst*, Karlshamn, 1956, p. 200.

GLAISTER, J., *Medical Jurisprudence and Toxicology*, Edinburgh, 1950, p. 324.

GONZALES, T. A., M. VANCE, M. HELPERN and C. J. UMBERGER, *Legal Medicine, Pathology and Toxicology*, 2nd Ed., New York, 1954, p. 622.

GRADWOHL, R. B. H., Identification of blood by the precipitin test, *The Laboratory Digest*, 15(1952) no. 9, p. 4.

GRADWOHL, R. B. H., Ed., *Legal Medicine*, St. Louis, 1954, p. 500.

GRANT, J., *Science for the Prosecution*, London, 1941, p. 235.

GRODSKY, M., K. WRIGHT and P. L. KIRK, Simplified preliminary blood testing. An improved technique and a comparative study of methods, *J. of Crim. Law, Criminol. and Police Sci.*, 42(1951) 95.

GROSS, H. and R. L. JACKSON, *Criminal Investigation*, 5th Ed., London, 1962, p. 103.

HARLEY, D., *Medico-Legal Blood Group Determination*, London, 1944.

HARRIS, R. I., Blood, Chapter 14, *Outline of Death Investigation*, Springfield, 1962, p.75.

HINDEN, J., Die Verwendung der Blutgruppenbestimmung bei Sexualverbrechen, *Arch. f. Kriminol.*, 114(1944) 53.

KERR, D. J. A., *Forensic Medicine*, London, 1946, p. 84.

KIRK, P. L., H. L. ROTH and W. R. CLAYTON, Separation of blood stains and other soluble materials by capillary action, *J. of Crim. Law, Criminol. and Police Sci.*, 42(1951) 392.

KIRK, P. L., C. BROWN and A. B. CONNERS, Some Problems in Blood Testing and Grouping, *J. of Crim. Law, Criminol. and Police Sci.*, 45(1954) 80.

LOCARD, E., *Manuel de Technique Policière*, Paris, 1948, p. 96.

LUCAS, A., *Forensic Chemistry and Scientific Criminal Investigation*, London, 1945, p. 23.

MARTIN, O., Zum Nachweis winzigster Blutspritzer, ausgebürsteter und ausgewaschener Blutspuren, *Kriminalistik*, 9(1955) 144.

MELONI, J. F., Beitrag zum Blutnachweis durch die Acetonhäminprobe, *Arch. f. Kriminol.*, 114(1944) 105.

MERKELEY, D. K., Blood Stains, Chapter XI, *The Investigation of Death*, Springfield, 1957, p. 115.

MOUREAU, P., Blood groups and scientific police, *Intern. Crim. Pol. Rev.*, no. 17(1948) 9.

MUEHLBERGER, C. W. and F. E. INBAU, The scientific and legal application of blood grouping tests, *J. of Crim. Law, Criminol. and Police Sci.*, 27(1936) 578.

NEUREITER, PIETRUSKY and SCHÜTT, *Handwörterbuch der gerichtlichen Medizin und naturwissenschaftlichen Kriminalistik*, Berlin, 1940, p. 99, 220.

NICKOLLS, L. C., Blood Stains, Chapter 9, *The Scientific Investigation of Crime*, London, 1956, p. 165.

O'Hara, Ch. E. and J. W. Osterburg, *An Introduction to Criminalistics*, New York, 1949, p. 34, 339.

Olbrycht, J., On the reliability of the tests used in investigating blood-stains, *Acta Med. Leg. et Soc.*, 3(1950) 113.

Ponsold, A., *Lehrbuch der gerichtlichen Medizin*, Stuttgart, 1950, p. 366, 375, 473, 483, 494, 517.

Rauschke, J., Beitrag zur Frage der Alterbestimmung von Blutspuren, *Dtsch. Z. ger. Med.*, 40(1951) 578.

Rhodes, H. T. F., *Forensic Chemistry*, London, 1946, p. 43, 49.

Rizer, C., Blood Drop Patterns, *Police*, 4(1960) 18.

Sannié, Ch., Les taches et les traces d'origine biologique, *Ann. Méd. Lég. etc.*, 26(1946) 251.

Scheibe, E. and E. Ulrich, Eine einfache Methode zum Nachweis von blutgruppen-aktiven Substanzen im menschlichen Zahngewebe, *Arch. f. Kriminol.*, 128(1961) 155.

Schiff, F. and Boyd, W. E., *Blood Grouping Technic*, New York, 1942.

Simonin, C., *Médecine Légale Judiciaire*, Paris, 1947, p. 764.

Simpson, C. K., *Forensic Medicine*, London, 1951, p. 38.

Simpson, C. K., *Modern Trends in Forensic Medicine*, London, 1953, p. 98.

Sjövall, E., *Rättsmedicin*, Stockholm, 1946, p. 39.

Smith, S., Studies in identification and reconstruction, *Police J.*, 14 (1941) 21.

Smith, S. and J. Glaister, *Recent Advances in Forensic Medicine*, London, 1939, p. 125, 156.

Snyder, LeM., *Homicide Investigation*, Springfield, 1950, p. 43.

Söderman, H., *Minnesbok för kriminalpolismän*, Stockholm, 1943, p. 65.

Söderman, H. and J. J. O'Connell, *Modern Criminal Investigation*, 5th Ed., New York, 1962, p. 236.

Szollosy, E. and B. Rengei, Identification of human blood on the basis of a proteo-lytic enzyme system and its application, *J. of For. Sci.*, 5(1960) 331.

Thieme, F. P. and C. M. Otten, The unreliability of blood typing aged bone, *Am. J. Phys. Anthrop.*, 15(1957).

Thomas, J. C., The examination of blood and seminal stains, *Police J.*, 10(1937) 490.

Tryhorn, F. G., The examination of blood and blood-stains, *Police J.*, 10(1937) 394.

Turner, R. F., *Forensic Science and Laboratory Technics*, Springfield, 1949, p. 48, 173.

Vogel, G., Untersuchung von Blutspurenmaterial, *Kriminalistik*, 16(1962) 439.

Walcher, K., *Gerichtlich-medizinische und kriminalistische Blutuntersuchung*, Berlin, 1939.

Weinig, E., Eine Methode zur Alterbestimmung von Blut- und Spermaflecken, *Dtsch. Z. ger. Med.*, 43(1954) 1.

Widy, W., Spektroskopischer Feststellung minimalster Blutspuren mit Hilfe eines ein-faches Reagenses, *Arch. f. Kriminol.*, 129(1962) 13.

Wiener, A. S., *Blood Groups and Transfusion*, Springfield, 1945.

Wiener, A. S. and E. B. Gordon, Examination of Blood Stains in Forensic Medicine, *J. of For. Sci.*, 1(1956) 89.

Anon., 'Blutstrassen', die sich kreuzen; Über die kriminalistische Deutung von Blut-Rinnspuren, *Arch. f. Kriminol.*, 110(1942) 144.

Anon., Practical applications of the examination of blood stained evidence, *FBI Law Enf. Bull.*, 7, no. 6(1938) 18.

Anon., Collection and submission of blood evidence, *FBI Law Enf. Bull.*, 20, no. 4(1951) 8.

Anon., Examinations of blood stains by the FBI laboratory, *FBI Law Enf. Bull.*, 21, no. 3(1952) 10.

Anon., 'Corpus Delicti' is Established by Blood Evidence, *FBI Law Enf. Bull.*, 26, no. 8(1957) 17.

Anon., Blood, Fibers and Hair Evidence in Crimes vs. Person, *FBI Law Enf. Bull.*, 27, no. 6(1958) 13.

Human secreta and excreta

ANDRESEN, P. H., *The Human Blood Groups*, Springfield, 1952.

ANDRESEN, P. H., Blodtypebestemmelse av spyt og maveindhold i krimanalsager, *Nord. Krim. Tids.*, 14(1944) 73.

BALTHAZARD, V., *Précis de Médecine Légale*, Paris, 1935, p. 523.

BERG, S. P., Diaminoxydasebestimmung bei Spurenuntersuchungen, *Dtsch. Z. ger. Med.*, 39(1948) 89.

BERG, S. P., Der Spermanachweis nach Puranen und seine forensische Bedeutung, *Dtsch. Z. ger. Med.*, 39(1949) 283.

BERG, S. P., Die Blutgruppendiagnose aus Speichelspuren und anderen Körpersekreten in der kriminalistischen Praxis, *Arch. f. Kriminol.*, 116(1955) 81.

DÉROBERT, L. and A. HADENGUE, Étude comparée des méthodes d'examen microscopique du sperme en médecine légale, *Ann. Méd. Lég. etc.*, 29(1948) 215.

DÉROBERT, L., A. HADENGUE and R. LE BRETON, Nouvelle technique pour la recherche des spermatozoide dans les taches, *Ann. Méd. Lég. etc.*, 30(1950) 386.

FORBES, G., The scope and fallacies of the Florence reaction for seminal stains, *Police J.*, 13(1940) 162.

FREI, M., Mikrospuren bei Sittlichkeitsdelikten, *Kriminalistik*, 11(1957) 428.

FROM HANSEN, P., En ny metode for den retsmedicinske spermapletpaavisning, *Nord. Krim. Tids.*, 15(1945) 121.

FROM HANSEN, P., Determination of the acid prostatic phosphatase as a new method for medico-legal demonstration of sperm spots, *Acta Pathologica*, 23(1934) 187.

GLAISTER, J., *Medical Jurisprudence and Toxicology*, Edinburgh, 1950, p. 350, 436.

GONZALES, T. A., M. VANCE, M. HELPERN and C. J. UMBERGER, *Legal Medicine, Pathology and Toxicology*, 2nd Ed., New York, 1954, p. 611.

GRADWOHL, R. B. H., Tests for seminal stains with description of a new test by Walker, *The Laboratory Digest*, 14(1951) 4.

GRADWOHL, R. B. H., Ed., *Legal Medicine*, St. Louis, 1954, p. 593.

GREENE, R. S. and D. Q. BURD, Seminal stain examination: A reagent for destruction of supporting fabric, *J. of Crim. Law, Criminol. and Police Sci.*, 37(1946) 325.

GROSS, H. and R. L. JACKSON, *Criminal Investigation*, 5th Ed., London, 1962, p. 121.

HANSON, A., Kriminalteknisk undersökning av saliv och salivfläckar, *Nord. Krim. Tids.*, 19(1949) 3.

HANSON, A., L'Examen microchimique des taches d'urine en criminalistique, *Sv. Kem. Tids.*, 57(1945) 235.

HARAGUCHI, I., Type determination with used tooth picks and cigarette stubs, *Am. J. Police Sci.*, 1(1936) 423.

HARBITZ, F., *Laerebok i Rettsmedisin*, Oslo, 1950, p. 188.

HARLEY, D., *Medico-Legal Blood Group Determination*, London, 1944, p. 102.

HAZIM ASADA and M. KOMINAMI, Die Untersuchung von Schmutzflecken, die von Fäzes stammen, *Arch. f. Kriminol.*, 76(1924) 145.

HEPNER, W., Utilisation d'excréments humain dans le cadre de la recherche d'indices en criminologie, *Rev. Criminol. Pol. Techn.*, 6(1952) 176.

JOHNSON, D. L., Analysis of fecal matter as evidence of guilt, *J. of Crim. Law, Criminol. and Police Sci.*, 39(1948) 129.

JONSSON, B., Några praktiska rättskemiska synpunkter på undersökningar av sperma-fläckar, *Nord. Krim. Tids.*, 14(1944) 37.

KAYE, S., Identification of seminal stains, *J. of Crim. Law, Criminol. and Police Sci.* 38(1947) 79.

KAYE, S., The acid phosphatase test for seminal stains, *J. of Crim. Law, Criminol. and Police Sci.*, 41(1951) 834.

LAGUNA, St. and J. MAKOWIEC, Feststellung der Blutgruppe des Täters aus Speichel-spuren an Zigarettenstummeln, die am Tatort gefunden wurden, *Arch. f. Kriminol.*, 116(1955) 90.

LOCARD, E., *Traité de Criminalistique, Vol VII*, Lyon, 1940, p. 313.

LOCARD, E., *Manuel de Technique Policière*, Paris, 1948, p. 109.

LUNDQUIST, F., Expérience sur la réaction de la phosphatase pour le diagnostic des taches de sperme, *Acta Med. Leg. et Soc.*, 1(1948) 393.

LUNDQUIST, F., Medicolegal identification of seminal stains using the acid phosphatase test, *Arch. of Path.*, 50(1950) 395.

MARTIN, O., Search, Collection, Examination and Evaluation of Traces in Morals Cases, *Kriminalistik*, 13(1959) 281.

MOUREAU, P., Facteurs d'individualisation de la sueur en médecine légale, *Ann. Méd. Lég. etc.*, 29(1948) 262.

NAKAI, R., Über die Blutgruppenuntersuchung von Speichelflecken auf Papier, *Arch. f. Kriminol.*, 107(1938) 43, 116(1955) 89.

NELSON, D. F. and P. L. KIRK, The Identification of Saliva, *J. For. Med.*, 10(1963) 14.

NICKOLLS, L. C., Seminal Stains and Stains of other Body Fluids, Chapter 10, *The Scientific Investigation of Crime*, London, 1956, p. 196.

O'HARA, CH. E. and J. W. OSTERBURG, *An Introduction to Criminalistics*, New York, 1949, p. 34, 426.

PALMIERI, V. M., Considérations sur la microcristallographie des taches de sperme, *Ann. Méd. Lég. etc.*, 29(1949) 328.

POLLAK, O. J., Postmortem examination in cases of suspected rape, *Am. J. Clin. Path.*, 13(1943) 309.

POLLAK, O. J., Semen and seminal stains; Review of method used in medico-legal in-vestigation, *Arch. of Path.*, 35(1943) 140.

PONSOLD, A., *Lehrbuch der gerichtlichen Medizin*, Stuttgart, 1950, p. 497.

RHODES, H. T. F., *Forensic Chemistry*, London, 1946, p. 45, 53.

SAND, K., Blood typing in criminal cases, *Intern. Crim. Pol. Rev.*, no. 19, (1948) p. 9.

SANDOVAL SMART, L., Bioquimica de las substancias grupo-especificas, *Rev. Crim. Pol. Cie.*, VIII, no. 107(1948) p. 9.

SANDOVAL SMART, L., Semen, *Rev. Crim. Pol. Cie.*, VIII, no. 110(1948) 35.

SANNIÉ, CH., Les taches et les traces d'origine biologique, *Ann. Méd. Lég. etc.*, 26(1946) 251.

SIMONIN, C., *Médecine Légale Judiciaire*, Paris, 1947, p. 779.

SIMPSON, C. K., *Forensic Medicine*, London, 1951, p. 186.

SMITH, S., *Forensic Medicine*, London, 1945, p. 308.

SMITH, S. and J. GLAISTER, *Recent Advances in Forensic Medicine*, London, 1939, p. 151.

STROIER RASMUSSEN, M. P., Un nouveau principe pour le diagnostic des taches de sperme sur les étoffes, *Ann. Méd. Lég. etc.*, 25(1945) 110.

SÖDERMAN, H., *Minnesbok för kriminalpolismän*, Stockholm, 1943, p. 69.

SÖDERMAN, H. and J. J. O'CONNELL, *Modern Criminal Investigation*, 5th Ed., New York, 1962, p. 249.

THOMAS, J. C., The examination of blood and seminal stains, *Police J.*, 10(1937) 490.

TURNER, R. F., *Forensic Science and Laboratory Technics*, Springfield, 1949, p. 199.

VANNI, V., A New Method of personal identification through the microscopical examination of fecal matter, *Finger Print Mag.*, 31(1949) 3.

WEIL, A. J., Immunological Test for Semen on Female Genitalia as Evidence of Intercourse, *J. of For. Sci.*, 4(1959) 372.

WEINIG, E., Eine Methode zur Alterbestimmung von Blut- und Spermaflecken, *Dtsch. Z. ger. Med.*, 43(1954) 1.

Hair

CLAVELIN, P. and L. DÉROBERT, L'Expertise médico-légale des cheveux et des poils, *Ann. Méd. Lég. etc.*, 31(1951), 195.

CLAVELIN, P. and L. DÉROBERT, Sur la valeur de l'expertise en matière de cheveux au point de vue médico-légale, *Acta. Med. Leg. et Soc.*, 3(1950) 206.

DAVIDSON, J. and W. D. TAYLOR, The staining of the cuticular scales of hair, *J. of the Quekett Microscopical Club*, 4, vol. 1, no. 6, p. 289(1943).

DESOILLE, H. and GRINFEDER, Sur l'identification des poils provenant de sujets de race noire, *Ann. Méd. Lég. etc.*, 18(1938) 306.

FOURCADE, J. and C. SIMONIN, Cheveux arrachés, cheveux spontanément. Caractères morphologiques, *Ann. Méd. Lég. etc.*, 24(1944) 151.

GAMBLE, L. H. and P. L. KIRK, Human hair studies. II. Scale counts, *J. of Crim. Law, Criminol. and Police Sci.*, 31(1940) 627.

GLAISTER, J., *Medical Jurisprudence and Toxicology*, Edinburgh, 1950, p. 110.

GLAISTER, J., *Hairs of Mammalia from the Medico-legal Aspect*, Cairo, 1931.

GONZALES, T. A., M. VANCE, M. HELPERN and C. J. UMBERGER, Microscopy of Hair and other Material, Chapter 28, *Legal Medicine, Pathology and Toxicology*, 2nd Ed., New York, 1954, p. 674.

GREENWELL, M. D., A. WILLMER and P. L. KIRK, Human hair studies. III. Refractive index of crown hair, *J. of Crim. Law, Criminol. and Police Sci.*, 31(1940) 746.

GROSS, H. and R. L. JACKSON, *Criminal Investigation*, London, 5th Ed., 1962, p. 109.

HARRIS, R. I., Hair, Chapter 15, *Outline of Death Investigation*, Springfield, 1962, p. 84.

HARVEY, L. A., The examination of hairs, *Police J.*, 10(1938) 61.

KERR, D. J. A., *Forensic Medicine*, London, 1949, p. 100.

KIRK, P. L., Human hair studies, I, General considerations of hair individualization and its forensic importance, *J. of Crim. Law, Criminol. and Police Sci.*, 31(1940) 486.

KIRK, P. L., S. MAGAGNOSE and D. SALISBURY, Casting of hairs – Its technique and application to species and personal identification, *J. of Crim. Law, Criminol. and Police Sci.*, 40(1949) 236.

LOCARD, E., *Manuel de Technique Policière*, Paris, 1948, p. 88.

LOCHTE, TH., *Grundriss der Entwicklung des menschlichen Haares*, Frankfurt, 1951.

LOCHTE, TH. and H. BRAUCKHOFF, Über erhitzte Haare in gerichtsmedizinischer Beziehung, *Dtsch. Z. ger. Med.*, 39(1948) 1.

LOCHTE, TH. and H. BRAUCKHOFF, Über mikroskopisch sichtbare Bewegungserscheinungen an menschlichen und tierischen gedehnten, superkontrahierten und erhitzten Haaren, *Dtsch. Z. ger. Med.*, 39(1949) 566.

LOCHTE, TH., *Atlas der Menschlichen und Tierischen Haare*, Leipzig, 1938.

MITCHELL, C. A., Circumstantial evidence from hairs and fibres, *Am. J. Police Sci.*, 1(1930) 594.

MUELLER, B. and H. BARTH, Nachweis kosmetischer Haarveränderunger, *Dtsch. Z. ger. Med.*, 40(1951) 553.

PALMGREN, A., Något om hårundersökningar och deras betydelse, *Nord. Krim. Tids.*, 19(1949) 1.

PONSOLD, A., *Lehrbuch der gerichtlichen Medizin*, Stuttgart, 1950, p. 532.

SANNIÉ, CH., Les taches et les traces d'origine biologique, *Ann. Méd. Lég. etc.*, 26(1946) 251.

SCHWARZACHER, W., Über die Grundlagen der vergleichenden Haaruntersuchung, *Arch. f. Kriminol.*, 113(1943) 11.

SIMONIN, C., *Médecine Légale Judiciaire*, Paris, 1947, p. 782.

SJÖVALL, E., *Rättsmedicin*, Stockholm, 1946, p. 42.

SMITH, S., *Forensic Medicine*, London. 1945, p. 98.

SMITH, S., Conviction by fibres, hair and soil, *Police J.*, 12(1939) 369.

SMITH, A. and J. GLAISTER, *Recent Advances in Forensic Medicine*, London, 1939, p. 86.

SÖDERMAN, H. and J. J. O'CONNELL, *Modern Criminal Investigation*, 5th Ed., New York, 1962, p. 188.

SÖDERMAN, H., *Minnesbok för kriminalpolismän*, Stockholm, 1943, p. 63.

TURNER, R. F., *Forensic Science and Laboratory Technics*, Springfield, 1949, p. 48, 107.

Anon., Hair and fibres help to solve sex crimes, *FBI Law Enf. Bull.*, 19, no. 5, (1950) p. 7.

Anon., Blood, hair and fibre analyses, *FBI Law Enf. Bull.*, 19, no. 3 (1950)2.

Anon., Blood Fibers and Hair Evidence in Crimes vs. Person, *FBI Law Enf. Bull.*, no. 6(1958) 13.

Other biological substances

FRAZIER, L. D., Skin fragments dooms attacker to the chair, *Finger Print Mag.*, 33, no. 3(1951) 7.

GONZALES, T. A., M. VANCE, M. HELPERN and C. J. UMBERGER, *Legal Medicine, Pathology and Toxicology*, 2nd Ed., New York, 1954, p. 685.

JONES, L. V., *Scientific Investigation and Physical Evidence*, Springfield, 1962, p. 32.
MULLER, M., G. FONTAINE, P. H. MULLER, A. GOURGUECHOV and F. M. OLIVEIRA DE
SAL, Medicolegal considerations of immunoelectrophoretic study of human and
animal skin, *Pathol. Biol. Semaine Hop.*, 10(1962) 249.
SANNIÉ, CH., Les taches et les traces d'origine biologique, *Ann. Méd. Lég. etc.*, 26(1946)
251.
SMITH, S., Studies in identification, no. 6, *Police J.*, 13(1940) 148.
Anon., Prowler tips hand at crime scene, *FBI Law Enf. Bull.*, 25, no. 6(1956) 20.

Bibliography to Chapter 8

Dust

BERG, S., Sicherung von Mikro-Spuren am Tatort, *Die Neue Polizei*, 12(1958) 158.
BRITTON, H. T. S., Dusts and their importance in crime detection, *Police J.*, 12(1939)
352.
GERDAU, W., Staubsicherungsgerät mit regulierbarem Vakuum und Luminiszenzfilter,
Kriminalistik, 9(1955) 473.
GROSS, H. and R. L. JACKSON, *Criminal Investigation*, London, 5th Ed., 1962, p. 114.
KIRK, P. L., Microscopic evidence – Its use in the investigation of crime, *J. of Crim.
Law, Criminol. and Police Sci.*, 40(1949) 362.
LOCARD, E., *Manuel de Technique Policière*, Paris, 1948, p. 91.
LOCARD, E., Dust and its analysis; an aid to criminal investigation, *Police J.*, 1(1928)
177.
LOCARD, E., The analysis of dust traces, *Am. J. Police Sci.*, 1(1930) 276, 401, 496.
LOCARD, E., L'analyse des poussières en criminalistique, *Rev. Criminol. Pol. Techn.*,
1(1947) 69.
LUCAS, A., *Forensic Chemistry and Scientific Criminal Investigation*, London, 1945, p.
56, 135.
MACLEAN, G., Petrology in criminal investigation, *Acta Med. Leg. et Soc.*, 1(1948) 739.
MARTIN, E., Unsichtbare Spuren am Tatort, *Arch. f. Kriminol.*, 131(1963) 177.
MATHEWS, J. H., Metallographic analysis in crime detection, *Am. J. Police Sci.*, 1(1930)
439.
NICKOLLS, L. C., Dirt, Dust and Debris, Chapter 3, *The Scientific Investigation of Crime*,
London, 1956, p. 38.
O'HARA, CH. E. and J. W. OSTERBURG, *An Introduction to Criminalistics*, New York,
1949, p. 32.
PIRK, G. W., Metallurgical examinations in criminal cases, *Police J.*, 13(1940) 435;
14(1941) 84.
POPP, G., Botanische Spuren und Mikroorganismen in Kriminalverfahren, *Arch. f.
Kriminol.*, 104(1939) 231.
RHODES, H. T. F., *Forensic Chemistry*, London, 1946, p. 14.
SÖDERMAN, H., *Minnesbok för kriminalpolismän*, Stockholm, 1943, p. 71.
SÖDERMAN, H., Zur Frage des kriminaltechnischen Staubsaugeverfahrens, *Arch. f.
Kriminol.*, 93(1933) 156.
TÜRKEL, S., Über Pollenanalyse, *Arch. f. Kriminol.*, 88(1931) 69.

WARD, T. J. and C. A. MITCHELL, Identification of demolition dust, *The Analyst*, 69(1944) 121.

WYNDHAM, J. L. P., A Method of Sampling Micro – Amounts of Dusts, Powders and Fibers for Examination, *Med. Sci. and Law*, 3(1963) 141.

Traces of soil, paint, rust, etc.

BREVER, J. G. and D. Q. BURD, Paint comparison – A method for the preparation of cross sections of paint chips, *J. of Crim. Law, Criminol. and Police Sci.*, 40(1949) 230.

ELGOOD, M. R., Identification of Microsamples, *Paint J. Australia, New Zealand*, 2(1957) 7.

FAHLANDER, N., *Kriminalpolistjänst*, Karlshamn, 1956, p. 208.

FOURNIER, F., S. POUGHEON and P. F. CECCALDI, Review of identification of paint, color in lacquers, in criminalistic, *Rev. Criminal. Pol. Techn.*, 16(1962) 66.

GOIN, L. J. and P. L. KIRK, Application of microchemical Techniques: Identity of soil samples, *J. of Crim. Law, Criminol. and Police Sci.*, 38(1947) 267.

HARRY, R. G., *Modern Cosmeticology*, London, 1946, p. 115.

JEVONS, R. H., Differential Thermal Analysis: Its Application to the Study of Mineral Evidence in Scientific Crime Detection, *J. of For. Sci.*, 1(1956) 25.

KIRK, P. L., *Crime Investigation*, New York, 1953.

KLUG, F., O. SCHUBERT and L. L. VAGNINA, A Microchemical Procedure for Paint Chip Comparisons, *J. of For. Sci.*, 4(1959) 91.

LESZCZYNSKI, CH., Farbspuren und Lacksplitter, *Kriminalistik*, 9(1955) 96.

LOCARD, E., *Manuel de Technique Policière*, Paris, 1948, p. 117.

LONGIA, H. S., A convenient and rapid method for the comparison of soils, *J. of Crim. Law, Criminol. and Police Sci.*, 55(1964) 165.

LUCAS, A., *Forensic Chemistry and Scientific Criminal Investigation*, London, 1945, p.50.

LUCAS, D. M. and G. EIJGELAAR, An evaluation of a technique for the examination of lipstick stains, *J. of For. Sci.*, 6(1961) 354.

MEIGANT, J. J., The identification of sand, *Police J.*, 14(1941) 209.

PIRK. G. W., Metallurgical examinations in criminal cases, *Police J.*, 13(1940) 435; 14(1941) 84.

RHODES, H. T. F., *Forensic Chemistry*, London, 1946, p. 54.

SMITH, S., Conviction by fibres, hair and soil, *Police J.*, 12(1939) 369.

TIPPETT, C. F., The Identification of Make, Model and Year of Manufacture of a Car by an Examination of Its Paint Flakes, *Med. Sci. and Law*, 4(1964) 22.

TSUJIMOTO, Y. and S. NAGAKAMA, Identification of paint, I, *Kagaku Keisatsu Kenkyusho Hokoku*, 13(1960) 57.

VERBURGT, J. W., Nur die vollständige Auswertung aller Bodenspuren ermöglicht einen Erfolg, *Tijdschrift voor de Politie*, 49(1963).

Anon., Use of safe insulation as evidence, *FBI Law Enf. Bull.*, 19, no. 2 (1950) 5.

Anon., Soil Evidence in Hit and Run Cases, *FBI Law Enf. Bull.*, 25(1956) 18.

Anon., Analysis of Soil, *FBI Law Enf. Bull.*, 30, no. 3(1961) 14.

Anon., Paint Examination – Techniques Utilized in FBI Laboratory, *FBI Law Enf. Bull.*, 30, no. 9(1961) 12.

Fragments of textiles, textile fibers, etc.

BARNES, H. C., The identification of cloth in criminal investigation, *Police J.*, 4(1931) 44.

BERG, S., Evidentiary Value of Textile Fibers, *Arch. f. Kriminol.*, 127(1961) 97.

BERGH, A. K., Some aspects relative to the identification of synthetic fibres, *Intern. Crim. Pol. Rev.*, 10 (1955) 246.

FREI–SULZER, M., Die Methoden des Faservergleichs in der Kriminalistik, *Kriminalistik*, 17(1963) 197.

GROSS, H. and R. L. JACKSON, *Criminal Investigation*, 5th Ed., 1962, p. 112.

HEPNER, W., Examen des points de rupture de fils de tissage, *Rev. Criminol. Pol. Techn.*, 3(1949) 55.

JONES, W. R., Scientific evidence as a sequel to a black-out accident, *Police J.* 13(1940) 424.

KIRK, P. L., *Crime Investigation*, New York, 1952, p. 126, 632.

KIRK, P. L. and D. Q. BURD, Clothing fibres as evidence, *J. of Crim. Law, Criminol. and Police Sci.*, 32(1941) 353.

KUFFERATH, A., Die schnelle Ermittlung des Werkstoffcharakters von Fäden, Geweben, Leder und lederähnlichen Erzeugnissen, *Kriminalistik*, 15(1941) 126.

LONGHETTI, A. and G. W. ROCHE, Microscopic Identification of Man-Made Fibers from the Criminalistics Point of View, *J. of For. Sci.*, 3(1958) 303.

LUCAS, A., *Forensic Chemistry and Scientific Criminal Investigation*, London, 1945, p. 155.

MARTIN, O., Criminalistic Investigation of Textiles, *Kriminalistik*, 9(1955) 457.

MATTHEWS, J. M. and H. R. MAUERSBERGER, *Textile Fibres*, New York, 1947.

MITCHELL, C. A., Circumstantial evidence from hairs and fibres, *Am. J. Police Sci.*, 1(1930) 594.

O'NEILL, M. E., Police Microanalyses. II. Textile fibres, *J. of Crim. Law, Criminol. and Police Sci.*, 25(1935) 835.

PLAA, G. L., D. C. BARRON and P. L. KIRK, Evaluation of Textile Fibers as Evidence, *J. of Crim. Law, Criminol. and Police Sci.*, 43(1952) 382.

SIMPSON, C. K., Murder at the John Barleycorn, Portsmouth, *Police J.*, 20(1947) 18.

SMITH, S., Conviction by fibres, hair and soil, *Police J.*, 12(1939) 369.

SMITH, S. S., Identification of unknown synthetic fibers, *Am. Dyestuff Reporter*, 47 (1958) 141.

STOVES, J. L., Identification of animal fibres in medico-legal cases, *Med. Leg. J.*, 11 (1943) 185.

TURNER, R. F., *Forensic Science and Laboratory Technics*, Springfield, 1949, p. 48, 120.

Anon., Fibre and fabric analyses, *FBI Law Enf. Bull.*, 22(1953) p. 12.

Tobacco varieties, matches

ENDSJØ, A., Fyrstikkasker som bevis, *Nord. Krim. Tids.*, 11(1941) 35.

HILARIO VEIGA DE CARVALHO, Indicios que os cigaros podem fornecer a policia tecnica, *Arq. Med. Leg. e Ident.*, no. 2(1931) 43.

KIRK, P. L., *Crime Investigation*, New York, 1952, p. 283.

LUCAS, A., *Forensic Chemistry and Scientific Criminal Investigation*, London, 1945, p. 328.

RHODES, H. T. F., *Forensic Chemistry*, London, 1946, p. 41.
SÖDERMAN, H., *Minnesbok för kriminalpolismän*, Stockholm, 1943, p. 71.
TÜRKEL, S., Die von Raucher hinterlassenen Spuren, *Beitr. z. krim. Sympt. u. Tecknik.*, (1931) p. 32.

Writing on burned paper

BENDIKSON, L., Charred documents, *Library J.*, 58(1933) 243.
BLACK, D. A., Decipherment of charred documents, *J. of Crim. Law, Criminol. and Police Sci.*, 38(1948) 542.
BRUFF, CH., Rekonstruksjon av forkullede dokumenter, *Nord. Krim. Tids.*, 13(1943) 97.
CONWAY, J. V. P., *Evidential Documents*, Springfield, 1959, p. 197.
DAVIS, R., Action of charred paper on the photographic plate and a method of deciphering charred records, *FBI Law Enf. Bull.*, Jan., 1933.
DOUD, D., Report on the Reconstruction of Two Time Payment Ledgers Damaged by Fire and Water, *J. Crim. Law, Criminol. and Police Sci.*, 50(1959) 291.
GRANT, J., *Science for the Prosecution*, London, 1941, p. 97, 221.
GRANT, J., Deciphering charred documents: Some recent work and a new method, *The Analyst*, 67(1942) 42.
GROSS, H. and R. L. JACKSON, *Criminal Investigation*, London, 5th Ed., 1962, p. 409.
HARRISON, W. R., The Deciphering of Charred Documents, in *Suspect Documents, Their Scientific Examination*, New York, 1958, p. 110.
HILTON, O., *Scientific Examination of Questioned Documents*, Chicago, 1956, p. 261.
JONES, G. A., Decipherment of charred documents, *Nature*, 147(1941) 676.
KIRK, P. L., *Crime Investigation*, New York, 1953, p. 459.
LANGENBRUCH, H., Ein neues Verfahren zur Wiederlesbarmachung verbrannter Tintenschriften, *Arch. f. Kriminol.*, 114(1944) 1.
LOCARD, E., *Manuel de Technique Policière*, Paris, 1948, p. 242.
LUCAS, A., *Forensic Chemistry and Scientific Criminal Investigation*, London, 1945, p. 126.
MITCHELL, C. A., The deciphering of scorched documents, *Discovery*, 5(1924) 336.
MITCHELL, C. A., The examination of charred documents, *The Analyst*, 50(1925) 174.
MURRAY, H. D., Examination of burnt documents, *Nature*, 148(1941) 199.
O'HARA, CH. E. and J. W. OSTERBURG, *An Introduction to Criminalistics*, New York, 1949, p. 506.
O'NEILL, E., The decipherment of writing on charred documents, *J. of Crim. Law, Criminol. and Police Sci.*, 32(1941) 257.
RADLEY, J. A., *Photography in Crime Detection*, London, 1948, p. 74, 162.
RHODES, H. T. F., *Forensic Chemistry*, London, 1946, p. 118.
SÖDERMAN, H., *Minnesbok för kriminalpolismän*, Stockholm, 1943, p. 160.
SÖDERMAN, H. and J. J. O'CONNELL, *Modern Criminal Investigation*, 5th Ed., 1962, p. 433.
TAYLOR, W. D. and H. J. WALLS, A new method for the decipherment of charred documents, *Nature*, 147(1941) 417.
TYRRELL, J. F., The decipherment of charred documents, *J. of Crim. Law, Criminol. and Police Sci.*, 30(1939) 236.

WALKER, J. T. and P. A. GLASS, Visualization of writing on charred paper, *J. of Crim. Law, Criminol. and Police Sci.*, 42(1951) 112.

Anon., Charred documents important evidence in case involving theft of government property, *FBI Law Enf. Bull*, 7, no. 8(1938) 12.

Anon., Charred Documents, *FBI Law Enf. Bull.*, 30, no. (1961) 12.

Wood

GROSS, H. and R. L. JACKSON, *Criminal Investigation*, 5th Ed., London, 1962, p. 113.

HRABOWSKI, H., Die Bedeutung botanischer Hilfsindizien für die Aufklärung von Tatbeständen, *Arch. f. Kriminol.*, 122(1958) 179.

KIRK, P. L., *Crime Investigation*, New York, 1953, p. 279.

KOEHLER, I. A., Technique used in tracing the Lindbergh kidnapping ladder, *J. of Crim. Law, Criminol. and Police Sci.*, 27(1937) 712.

KISSER, J., Methodik der Herstellung pflanzlicher Aschenbilder und Kieselskelette sowie von Anthrakogrammen, ABDERHALDEN: *Handbuch der Biologischen Arbeitsmethoden*, *Vol. XI*: 4, Berlin–Wien, 1931, p. 193.

KISSER, J. and L. W. SEKYRA, Die mikroskopische Diagnose heimischer Holzarten in zerkleinertem und pulverisiertem Zustand, *Arch. f. Kriminol.*, 103(1938) 19.

KISSER, J. and L. W. SEKYRA, Die diagnostische Wert des mikroskopischen Aschenbildes der wichtigsten heimischen Hölzer, *Mikrochemie*, 15(1938) 158.

KUKACHKA, B. F., Wood Identification: Limitations and Potentialities, *J. of For. Sci.*, 6(1961) 98.

NEUREITER, PIETRUSKY and SCHÜTT, *Handwörterbuch der gerichtlichen Medizin und naturwissenschaftlichen Kriminalistik*, Berlin, 1940, p. 353.

NICKOLLS, L. C., Identification of Traces of Biological Material, Chapter 5, *The Scientific Investigation of Crime*, London, 1956, p. 76.

PENTLAND, A., Wood and associated materials in crime detection, *Police J.*, 12(1939) 242.

RANE, G., Träidentifiering, *Nord. Krim. Tids.*, 28(1958) 161.

SANDOVAL SMART, L., La madera en criminalistica. Determinación de la edad de un árbol, *Rev. Crim. Pol. Cie. IX*, no. 128, p. 11; no. 129, p. 19; no. 130, p. 19(1950).

SÖDERMAN, H. and J. J. O'CONNELL, *Modern Criminal Investigation*, New York, 5th Ed., 1962, p. 259.

VEHSTEDT, R., Holz als kriminalistisches Leitelement, *Kriminalistik*, 4(1950) 154.

Anon., Wood Specimens, *FBI Law Enf. Bull.*, 20(1951) 15.

Broken glass

BAUERNFEIND, X., Schuss oder Steinwurf, *Arch. f. Kriminol.*, 95(1934) 130.

BAUERNFEIND, X., Glasscheibenbrüche, *Arch. f. Kriminol.*, 101(1937) 193.

CLEVE, S., Egendomliga skador på butiksglasruta, *Nord. Krim. Tids.*, 13(1943) 149.

DONOVAN, W., Identification of glass splinters, *The Analyst*, 59(1934) 347.

ENDSJØ, A., Vinduesruten avslørte brannstifteren, *Nord. Krim. Tids.*, 11(1941) 94.

ÉTIENNE–MARTIN and SEIF EL NASR, Étude expérimentale des perforations des vitres 'Triplex' et 'Securit' par les différents projectiles d'armes à feu. Les Blessures qui peuvent en résulter pour les occupants d'une voiture automobile, *Ann. Méd. Lég. etc.*, 19(1939) 3.

FOURCADE, M. J., Étude expérimentale du tir à travers les vitres et les glaces, *Acta Med. Leg. et Soc.*, 1(1948) 353

FREI, M. and J. MEIER, Une Nouvelle Méthode de Bris Silencieux de Vitrine, *Rev. Criminol. Pol. Techn.*, 15(1961) 223.

GAMBLE, L. H., D. Q. BURD and P. L. KIRK, Glass fragments as evidence, *J. of Crim. Law, Criminol. and Police Sci.*, 33(1943) 416.

GRABAR, D. G. and A. H. PRINCIPE, Identification of Glass Fragments by Measurement of Refractive Index and Dispersion, *J. of For. Sci.*, 8(1963) 54.

GROSS, H. and R. L. JACKSON, *Criminal Investigation*, 5th Ed., London, 1962, p. 118.

GRÖN, K. F., Drapforsøk eller uforsiktig omgang med skytevåpen?, *Nord. Krim. Tids.*, 18(1948) 13.

HARPER, W. W., The behavior of bullets fired through glass, *J. of Crim. Law, Criminol. and Police Sci.*, 29(1939) 718.

KIRK, P. L., *Crime Investigation*, New York, 1953, p. 232.

KIRK, P. L. and G. W. ROCHE, Differentiation of similar glass fragments by physical properties, *J. of Crim. Law, Criminol. and Police Sci.*, 38(1947) 168.

LECHNER, M., Einschuss oder Steinschlag, *Kriminalistik*, 16(1962) 216.

LUCAS, A., *Forensic Chemistry and Scientific Criminal Investigation*, London, 1945, p. 137.

MARRIS, N. A., Identification of glass splinters, *The Analyst*, 59(1934) 686.

MATWEJEFF, S. N., Criminal investigation of broken window panes, *Am. J. Police Sci.*, 2(1931) 148.

MATWEJEFF, S. N., Zur Untersuchung zerbrochener und durchgeschossener Fensterscheiben, *Arch. f. Kriminol.*, 89(1931) 129.

MORREN, W. B. R., The photographic and fingerprint department: Its aid in crime detection. A case involving fracture of glass, *Police J.*, 16(1943) 30.

NELSON, D. F., Illustrating the Fit of Glass Fragments, *J. of Crim. Law, Criminol. and Police Sci.*, 50(1959) 312.

NICKENIG, A., Kreisrunde Glasbrüche, *Arch. f. Kriminol.*, 126(1960) 99.

NICKOLLS, L. C., Identification of Traces of Inorganic Material, Chapter 4, *The Scientific Investigation of Crime*, London, 1956, p. 58.

O'HARA, CH. E. and J. W. OSTERBURG, *An Introduction to Criminalistics*, New York, 1949, p. 239, 298.

PIÉDELIÈVRE, R., H. DESOILLE and HÉRISSET, Perforation par les balles des substances dures (crânes, etc.); leur mécanisme, *Ann. Méd. Lég. etc.*, 19(1939) 218.

SCHOENTAG, A., Einschuss oder Steinschlag, *Arch. f. Kriminol.*, 122(1958) 69.

SPENCE, W., A glass case, *Police J.*, 22(1949) 293.

SVEEN, R., Skudd gjennom glassruter, *Nord. Krim. Tids.*, 10(1940) 112.

SVEEN, R., Kriminaltekniske og retsmedisinske undersøkelser angående skudd gjennom en vinduesrute med dødelig utfall, *Nord. Krim. Tids.*, 15(1945) 105.

SÖDERMAN, H., *Minnesbok för Kriminalpolismän*, Stockholm, 1943, p. 82.

SÖDERMAN, H. and J. J. O'CONNELL, *Modern Criminal Investigation*, New York, 5th Ed., 1962, p. 230.

TRYHORN, F. G., The examination of glass, *Police J.*, 12 (1939) 301; *J. of Crim. Law, Criminol. and Police Sci.*, 30(1939) 404.

TRYHORN, F. G., Broken window panes, *FBI Law Enf. Bull.*, 5, no. 10(1936) 2.
TRYHORN, F. G., Identification of glass fragments, *FBI Law Enf. Bull.*, 5, no. 10(1936) 3.
TURNER, R. F., *Forensic Science and Laboratory Technics*, Springfield, 1949, p. 193.
WOLFF, S., Sprengning av glasruter, *Nord. Krim. Tids.*, 18(1948) 90.
Anon., Glass fracture examination, *FBI Law Enf. Bull.*, Sept. (1947) 10.
Anon., Glass fracture examinations aid the investigator, *FBI Law Enf. Bull.*, 21, no. 1(1952) 13.
Anon., Examination of Glass Fragments, *RCMP Gazette*, 23(1961) 11.

Traces on the suspect
ANDERSEN, A. C., Om spor etter pengeskabstyverier, *Nord. Krim. Tids.*, 21(1951) 65.
BREAZEALE, E. L. and J. C. J. KNOTT, The Gonzales test for powder residues, *Police*, 6(1962) 65.
BRÜNING, A. and Prof. WIELAND, Statements against the paraffin test, *Arch. f. Kriminol.*, 118(1956) 107.
CASTELLANOS, I., Dermo-nitrate test in Cuba, *J. of Crim. Law, Criminol. and Police Sci.*, 33(1943) 482.
CASTELLANOS, I., *La Prueba de la Parafina*, Havanna, 1948.
CASTELLANOS, I. and R. PLASENCIA, The paraffin gauntlet: A new technique for the dermo-nitrate test, *J. of Crim. Law, Criminol. and Police Sci.*, 32(1941) 465.
FINNEY, D. J., Police duties at crime scenes, *J. of Crim. Law, Criminol. and Police Sci.*, 27(1936) 435.
GONZALES, T. A., M. VANCE, M. HELPERN and C. J. UMBERGER, *Legal Medicine, Pathology and Toxicology*, 2nd Ed., New York, 1954.
GROSS, H. and SEELIG, *Handbuch der Kriminalistik*, vol. II :2, Berlin, 1951, p. 275.
HANSON, A., Mikroskopisk och mikrokemisk undersökning av skottskador, *Nord. Krim. Tids.*, 15(1945) 37, 63.
HARRISON, H. C. and R. GILROY, Firearms Discharge Residues, *J. of For. Sci.*, 4(1959) 184.
HATHERILL, G., Personal communication, London, 1952.
HEINDL, R., Spuren an der Schiesshand nach Schuss mit Faustfeuerwaffen, *Arch. f. Kriminol.*, 114(1944) 75.
KING, D. P., The dermal nitrate test; useful or not?, *Police*, 7(1963) 60.
KIRK, P. L., *Crime Investigation*, New York, 1953, p. 356.
KOCKEL, H., Über den Wert der Untersuchung von Fingernagelschmutz, *Arch. f. Kriminol.*, 82(1928) 209.
LUCAS, A., *Forensic Chemistry and Scientific Criminal Investigation*, London, 1945, p. 139.
MARSHALL, J. J., A 'visiting card' left: The value of scientific evidence, *Police J.*, 24(1951) 28.
MATHEWS, J. H., The paraffin test, *The American Rifleman*, 102(1954) 20.
MUELLER, B., Untersuchungen über die Befunde an der Schusshand nach Abgabe von Schüssen mit Trommelrevolvern, *Dtsch. Z. ger. Med.*, 27(1937) 149.
O'HARA, CH. E. and J. W. OSTERBURG, *An Introduction to Criminalistics*, New York, 1949, p. 384, 386.

SNYDER, LEM., *Homicide Investigation*, Springfield, 1950, p. 133, 330, 331.

TERÖRDE, F., Hat ein positiver Blutbefund im Fingernagelschmutz eine praktische kriminalistische Bedeutung?, *Arch. f. Kriminol.*, 105(1939) 105.

TURNER, R. F., *Forensic Science and Laboratory Technics*, Springfield, 1949, p. 98.

ZWINGLI, M., Über Spuren an der Schiesshand nach Schuss mit Faustfeuerwaffen, *Arch. f. Kriminol.*, 108(1941) 1.

Anon., The diphenylamine test for gunpowder, *FBI Law Enf. Bull.*, 4, no. 10, (1935) p. 5.

Anon., Use of safe insulation as evidence, *FBI Law Enf. Bull.*, 19, no. 2 (1950) p. 5.

Objects left at the scene

ABBOTT, J. R. and A. C. GERMANN, *Footwear Evidence*, Springfield, 1964.

BESSEMANS, J. F. A., Identifizierung von Streichholzresten, die an einer Brandstelle gefunden wurden, *Arch. f. Kriminol.*, 126(1960) 70.

DAUBNEY, C. G., The scientific examination of a case of arson, *Police J.*, 17(1944) 110.

ENKLAAR, F., A New Burglary Tool and Proof by the Metal Chips, *Kriminalistik*, 10(1956) 452.

JONES, L. V., *Scientific Investigation and Physical Evidence*, Springfield, 1962, p. 17.

RONAYNE, J. A., Investigation of Explosions, *Police*, 4(1960) 64.

WALENSKY, W., Zwei Fälle der Identifizierung von Nägeln, *Arch. f. Kriminol.*, 104(1939) 76.

Bibliography to Chapter 9

Weapons

BALLEISEN, CH. E., *Principles of firearms*, New York–London, 1945.

BELLEMORE, W. M., Ammunition: Manufacturing vs. Identification, *J. of For. Sci.*, 5(1960) 148.

BERG, S., Veranderungen der Textiloberfläche bei Nahschüssen, *Arch. f. Kriminol.*, 124 (1959) 5.

BIASOTTI, A., A Statistical Study of the Individual Characteristics of Fired Bullets, *J. of For. Sci.*, 4(1959) 34.

BIGLER, E. G., A Water Tank System of Bullet Recovery, *Police*, 6(1961) 72.

BRÜNING, A., Raubmordversuch ausschliesslich durch Waffengutachten aufgeklärt; Pistolengeschoss in Scheibenbüchse, *Arch. f. Kriminol.*, 106(1940) 108.

BRÜNING, A., Finkalibriga vapen och deras kriminalistiska betydelse, *Nord. Krim. Tids.*, 21(1951) 97.

BRÜNING, A. and WIETHOLD, Die Untersuchung und Beurteilung von Selbstmörderschusswaffen, *Dtsch. Z. ger. Med.*, 23(1934) 71.

BURRARD, G., *The Identification of Firearms and Forensic Ballistics*, London, 1951.

BURRARD, G., *The Modern Shotgun, Vol. I–III*, London, 1947–1950.

CHURCHILL, R., *Firearms in Crime and its Detection, Vol. I*, London, 1934, p. 193.

DATTA, B. K., The chemical examination of firearms and explosives, *J. Proc. Inst. Chemists (India)*, 32(1960) 211.

DAVIS, J. E., *An Introduction to Tool Marks, Firearms and the Striagraph*, Springfield, 1958.

DAVIS, J. E., Firearms Evidence – Replicas of Fired Bullets, *J. of Crim. Law, Criminol. and Police Sci.*, 51(1961) 666.

FLEISCHMANN, R., Murder, Suicide and Negligent Homicide with 'Harmless Flobert Firearms', *Arch. f. Kriminol.*, 111(1942) 139.

FONTAINE, R., Identification of shells, *J. of Crim. Law, Criminol. and Police Sci.*, 23 (1932) 397.

FORMAGGIO, T., Contributo all'identificazione delle armi da fuoco mediante l'eseme dei bossoli, *Arch. d' Anthropol. Crim.*, 68(1948) 179.

FORMAGGIO, T., Contribution à l'identification des armes à feu par l'examen des douilles, *Rev. Criminol. Pol. Techn.*, 3(1949) 276.

FREI, M., Microscopic Investigation of Projectiles, *Kriminalistik*, 11(1957) 287.

GODDARD, C., Scientific identification of firearms and bullets, *J. of Crim. Law, Criminol. and Police Sci.*, 17(1926) 254.

GODDARD, C., The Valentine day massacre: A study in ammunition tracing, *Am. J. Police Sci.*, 1(1930) 60.

GODDARD, C., Proof tests and proof marks, *Army Ordnance*, 14(1933) 140; 225, 293, 354(1934); 15(1934) 32.

GODDARD, C., The unexpected in firearm identification, *J. of For. Sci.*, 1(1956) 57.

GROSS, H. and R. L. JACKSON, *Criminal Investigation*, 5th Ed., London, 1962, p. 208.

GUNTHER, J. D. and CH. O. GUNTHER, *The Identification of Firearms*, New York, 1935.

HADERSDORFER, Zur Klärung von Schussdelikten: Welcher Schlagbolzeneinschlag an einer Hülse mit mehreren Einschläger löste die Zündung aus?, *Arch. f. Kriminol.*, 120(1957) 104.

HART, A. B., Ramification, Tool Marks in Firearms Identification, *BCI Bull. N.Y. State Police*, 25, no. 4(1960) 10.

HATCHER, J. S., F. J. JURY and J. WELLER, *Firearms Investigation, Identification and Evidence*, Harrisburg, 1957.

HATCHER, J. S., *Hatchers Notebook*, Harrisburg, 1948.

HEPNER, W., Kann aus einer Pistole 7,62 mm. eine 9 mm. Patrone verfeuert werden, *Kriminalistik*, 12(1958) 101.

HEPNER, W. and W. MARESCH, Une arme de suicide peu commune, *Rev. Criminol. Pol. Techn.*, 6(1952) 350.

HUELKE, H. H., Aufklärung von Unfällen durch Schrotschüsse, *Kriminalistik*, 10(1956) 308.

IYENGAR, N. K., Two bullets in the same hole, *The Indian Police J.*, 6(1959) 14.

JOHNSON, M. M. JR. and CH. T. HAVEN, *Automatic Weapons of the World*, New York, 1945.

KIRK, P. L., *Crime Investigation*, New York, 1953, p. 328.

KIRWAN, W. E. and A. B. HART, Water Tank – Bullet Recovery, *BCI Bull. N.Y. State Police*, 21(1956) 3; *Police*, 1(1957) 9.

KOSYRA, H., Aufklärung eines Mordversuches durch ein Pistolenmagasin, *Kriminalistik*, 5(1951) 147.

KRCMA, V., The Identification of Pistols by Serial Numbers and Other Markings, *J. of For. Sci.*, 6(1961) 479.

LOGAN, H. C., Grip Marks on American Handguns, *The American Rifleman*, 110(1962) 55.

LUCAS, A., *Forensic Chemistry and Scientific Criminal Investigation*, London, 1945, p. 179.

MATHEWS, J. H., A measurement of land impressions on fired bullets, *J. of Crim. Law, Criminol. and Police Sci.*, 44(1954) 799.

MATHEWS, J. H., *Firearms Identification*, Madison, 1962.

MEZGER, O., W. HEESS and F. HASSLACHER, Determination of the type of pistol employed from an examination of fired bullets and shells, *Am. J. Police Sci.*, 2(1931) 473; 3(1932) 124.

MICHON, R., The speed of bullets, air-guns, *Intern. Crim. Pol. Rev.*, no. 119(1958) 188.

MUNHALL, B. D., Firearms identification problems pertaining to supplemental chambers, auxiliary cartridges, insert barrels and conversion units, *J. of For. Sci.*, 5(1960) 319.

MUNHALL, B. D., Fundamental ballistics pertaining to investigations involving firearms, *J. of For. Sci.*, 6(1961) 215.

NICKOLLS, L. C., Firearms and Cartridges, Chapter 13, *The Scientific Investigation of Crime*, London, 1956, p. 256.

PRICE, G., Laboratory investigations in firearms cases, *The Criminal Law Rev.*, 1946.

RHODES, H. T. F., *Forensic Chemistry*, London, 1946, p. 59.

RIFE, D. W., The recovery of bullets from high speed ammunition, *Police J.*, 13(1940)73.

ROCHE, G. F., The use of photographs in forensic firearms identification, *Identification News*, 3, no. 6(1953) 3.

SANDOVAL SMART, L., Cartuchos para armas de fuego, *Rev. Crim. Pol. Cie.*, VIII, no. 105(1948) 15.

SANDOVAL SMART, L., Proyectiles para armas de fuego, *Rev. Crim. Pol. Cie.*, VIII, no. 106(1948) 17.

SCHILDT, H., Verschiessen von Geschossen aus Gas- und Schreckschusspistolen, *Kriminalistik*, 11(1957) 430.

SCHÖNTAG, A. and K. HADERSDOFER, Einschuss oder Werkzeugschlag, *Arch. f. Kriminol.*, 122(1958) 174.

SCHÖNTAG, A. and J. ROTH, Zwei neue Verfahren: Bestimmung des Schussalters bei Schrotpatronen. I and II, *Arch. f. Kriminol.*, 121(1958) 8; 121(1958) 123.

SHARMA, B. R., The importance of firing pin impressions in the identification of firearms, *J. of Crim. Law, Criminol. and Police Sci.*, 54(1963) 378.

SIMPSON, C. K., Identification of a firearm in murder without the weapon, *Intern. Crim. Pol. Rev.*, no. 23(1948) 4; *Police J.*, 22(1949) 32.

SMITH, J. E., Foreign military small arms, *The American Rifleman*, 109(1961) 23.

SMITH, L. L., Unusual handguns, *J. of For. Sci.*, 6(1961) 501.

SMITH, L. L., Zip guns, *Police*, 7(1963) 10.

SMITH, W. H. B., *Small arms of the World*, Harrisburg, 1948.

SMITH, W. H. B., *Pistols & Revolvers*, Harrisburg, 1946.

SMITH, W. H. B., *Rifles*, Harrisburg, 1948.

SMITH, S. and J. GLAISTER, *Recent advances in forensic medicine*, London, 1939, p. 27, 67, 80.

SOJAT, J. G. and J. C. STAUFFER, A study of class characteristics of autoloading weapons, *J. of For. Sci.*, 3(1958) 444.

SUTHERLAND, W. W. and V. KRCMA, Test bullet recovery, *J. of For. Sci.*, 7(1962) 493.

SVENSSON, A., Gevärssprängningar, *Nord. Krim. Tids.*, 18(1948) 121.

SVENSSON, A., Självmord eller olyckshändelse, *Nord. Krim. Tids.*, 20(1950) 49.

SVENSSON, A., Skrämskott eller mordförsök, *Nord. Krim. Tids*, 20(1950) 85.

SÖDERMAN, H. and J. J. O'CONNELL, *Modern Criminal Investigation*, 5th Ed., New York, 1962, p. 196.

SÖDERMAN, H., *Minnesbok för kriminalpolismän*, Stockholm, 1949.

TAKKO, O., Der Mord im Österbotten. Über die Bedeutung des Mezger-Heess-Hasslacherschen Pistolenatlasses, *Arch. f. Kriminol.*, 112(1943) 17.

TAKKO, O., Om sällsynta undersökningar av skjutvapen och förnödenheter, *Nord. Krim. Tids.*, 21(1951) 13.

TAKKO, O., Tillvaratagande av skjutvapen såsom bevismaterial, *Nord. Krim. Tids.*, 14(1944) 49.

TURNER, R. F., *Forensic Science and Laboratory Technics*, Springfield, 1949, p. 42, 70.

WESSEL, T. E., How pneumatic arms work, *The American Rifleman*, 110(1962) 52.

WHITE, H. P. and B. D. MUNHALL, *Center Fire Metric Pistol and Revolver Cartridges*, Washington, 1948.

WHITE, H. P. and B. D. MUNHALL, *Center Fire American and British Pistol and Revolver Cartridges*, Washington, 1950.

WILSON, CH. M., The preservation and transportation of firearms evidence, in LeMoyne Snyder; *Homicide Investigation*, Springfield, 1950, p. 145.

WILSON, R. A., Firearms Identification, in *Institute on Homicide Investigation Techniques*, Springfield, 1961, p. 61.

Anon., *The Firearms Directory*, Ed.: S. BRAVERMAN, New York, 1951.

Anon., How far will a gun shoot?, *The American Rifleman*, 109(1961) 22.

Anon., Handling firearms evidence at the scene of a crime, *FBI Law Enf. Bull.*, 19, no. 12(1950) 13.

Anon., Task of field and laboratory in firearms identification, *FBI Law Enf. Bull.*, 27, no. 5(1958) 13.

Explosives

BEBIE, J., Manual of Explosives, *Military Pyrotechnics and Chemical Warfare Agents*, New York, 1943.

CROWTHERS, E. H., Suggestive action upon the receipt of bomb reports, *Penna. Chiefs of Pol. Assoc. Bull.*, 20(1959) 15.

DAVIS, T. L., *The Chemistry of Powder and Explosives*, New York, 1943.

DULLNIG, H., Der Sprengstoffmörder, *Illustrierte Rundschau der Gendarmerie*, 13(1960) 22.

HARRIS, R. I., Explosion, Chapter 30, *Outline of Death Investigation*, Springfield, 1962, p. 197.

HATCHER, J. S., F. J. JURY and J. WELLER, *Firearms Investigation, Identification and Evidence*, Harrisburg, 1957, p. 163.

KOLL, M., J. WIMMER and K. FISCHER, Zum Nachweis von Sprengstoffspuren im Schmauch, *Arch. f. Kriminol.*, 130(1962) 1.

KERN, C. V., Bombing, a Case Study, *FBI Law Enf. Bull.*, 30(1961) 24.

Love, R. C., Planning for Bomb Incidents, *Law and Order*, 8(1960) 52.

Luoao, A., *Forensic Chemistry and Scientific Criminal Investigation*, London, 1945, p. 145.

Meyer, M., *The Science of Explosives*, New York, 1943.

Moran, T. L., Dealing with Bombs and Explosives, *The Fire and Arson Investigator*, 12(1962) 37.

Muehlberger, C. W., The investigation of bombs and explosions, *J. of Crim. Law, Criminol. and Police Sci.*, 28(1937) 406, 581.

Nauckhoff, S., Synpunkter, som böra beaktas vid polisundersökningar efter sprängningsolyckor, *Nord. Krim. Tids.*, 16(1946) 49.

Olsen, A. L. and J. W. Greene, *Laboratory Manual of Explosive Chemistry*, New York–London, 1943.

Pyke, J. A., Some notes on the handling of suspected bombs and the investigation of explosives, *J. of Crim. Law, Criminol. and Police Sci.*, 32(1942) 668.

Rhodes, H. T. F., *Forensic Chemistry*, London, 1946, p. 67.

Robinson, C. S., *Explosions. Their Anatomy and Destructiveness*, New York, 1944.

Ronayne, J. A., Investigating crimes involving explosions, *Police*, 4(1960) no. 3, p. 64; no. 4, p. 11.

Sandoval Smart, L., Pirotecnia Forense, *Rev. Crim. Pol. Cie*, VIII, no. 109, p. 39; no. 110, p. 11 (1948).

Sax, N. I., M. L. O'Herin and W. W. Schultz, *Handbook of Dangerous Materials*, New York, 1951, p. 411.

Smart, R. C., *The Technology of Industrial Fire and Explosions Hazards*, Vol. II, London, 1947, p. 50.

Stettbacher, A., *Spreng- und Schiesstoffe*, Zürich, 1948.

Stoffel, J. F., Explosives and the Police Officer, *Police*, 7, no. 1(1962) 6.

Stoffel, J. F., *Explosives and Homemade Bombs*, Springfield, 1962.

Anon., Handling of Explosives, *FBI Law Enf. Bull.*, 22(1953) 7.

Anon., Safety Precautions for the Handling of Homemade Bombs, *FBI Law Enf. Bull.*, 26, no. 9(1957) 16.

Anon., Law Enforcement and the Handling of Bombing Cases, *FBI Law Enf. Bull.*, 28, no. 9, p. 16; no. 10, p. 14(1959).

Bibliography to Chapter 10

Fahlander, N., *Kriminalpolistjänst*, Karlshamn, 1950, p. 203.

Finney, D. J., Police duties at crime scenes, *J. of Crim. Law, Criminol. and Police Sci.*, 27(1936) 412.

Gross, H. and R. L. Jackson, *Criminal Investigation*, 5th Ed., London, 1962, p. 329.

Kirk, P. L., *Crime Investigation*, New York, 1953, p. 83.

Lane, M. G., Some aspects of burglary investigations, *FBI Law Enf. Bull.*, 19, no. 6(1950) 5.

Nickolls, L. C., *The Scientific Investigation of Crime*, London, 1956, p. 29.

O'Hara, Ch. E., *Fundamentals of Criminal Investigation*, Springfield, 1956, p. 299.

SÖDERMAN, H. and J. J. O'CONNELL, *Modern Criminal Investigation*, 5th Ed., New York, 1962, p. 330.

WERNER, E., Technique and psychology of the burglar, Das *Polizeiblatt für das Land Baden–Württemberg*, 22(1959) 19.

Anon., Science and diligent search solve robbery, *FBI Law Enf. Bull.*, 20, no. 2(1951) 16.

Anon., Case of Safebreaking at Premises of Midland Bank Limited, *Intern. Crim. Pol. Rev.*, no. 128(1959) 146.

Entry through windows, doors, etc.

FABICH, M., Die Straftaten der Gebrüder Sass, *Kriminalistik*, 14(1940) 37, 85; 15(1941) 14, 64, 123.

GROSS, H. and R. L. JACKSON, *Criminal Investigation*, 5th Ed., London, 1962, p. 329.

LOUWAGE, F. E., A curious apparatus for opening locks, *Intern. Crim. Pol. Rev.*, 7(1952) 57.

Anon., Unusual Breaking Implements, *The Australian Police J.*, 17(1963) 72.

The detailed examination of the scene

FINNEY, D. J., Police duties at crime scenes, *J. of Crim. Law, Criminol. and Police Sci.*, 27(1936) 412.

GROSS, H. and R. L. JACKSON, *Criminal Investigation*, 5th Ed., London, 1962, p. 78.

SÖDERMAN, H. and J. J. O'CONNELL, *Modern Criminal Investigation*, 5th Ed., New York, 1962, p. 332.

Safe burglary

BROWN, L. F., A case of safe breaking, *Police J.*, 17(1944) 185.

ENKLAAR, F., Een inbraak . . ., een vierkante millimeter metaal . . ., en twee maal vier jaren gevangenisstraf!, *Algemeen Politieblad*, 105(1956) 243.

FABICH, M., Die Straftaten der Gebrüder Sass, *Kriminalistik*, 14(1940) 37, 85; 15(1941) 14, 64, 123.

FABICH, M., Geldschrankeinbrecher, *Kriminalistik*, 17(1943) 61.

FRANSSEN, F., An Ingenious Case of Safe-Breaking, *Intern. Crim. Pol. Rev.*, no. 118 (1958) 136.

GROSS, H. and R. L. JACKSON, *Criminal Investigation*, 5th Ed., London, 1962, p. 348.

HEPNER, W., Un nouvel engin pour forcer les coffres-forts, *Rev. Criminol. Pol. Techn.*, 5(1951) 215.

HEPNER, W., Un nouvel engin pour percer les coffres-forts, *Rev. Criminol. Pol. Techn.*, 6(1952) 274.

HOLDEN, H. S. and C. H. EDLIN, The laboratory and the police officer, *Police J.*, 14(1941) 61.

JOHNSON, J. P., Safe Burglary, *FBI Law Enf. Bull.*, 21, no. 12(1952) 4.

KADLEC, J., The construction of safes and bank strong rooms, *Intern. Crim. Pol. Rev.*, no. 37(1950) 101; no. 38(1950) 130.

McLELLAN, J. K., Safes and safe-breaking, *Police J.*, 24(1951) 114.

O'HARA, CH. E., *Fundamentals of Criminal Investigation*, Springfield, 1956, p. 303.

SÖDERMAN, H. and J. J. O'CONNELL, *Modern Criminal Investigation*, 5th Ed., New York, 1962, p. 335.
Anon., Use of safe insulation as evidence, *FBI Law Enf. Bull.*, 19, no. 2(1950) 5.

Bibliography to Chapter 11

ALLAN. A. L., Identification of hit-and-run auto by paint flakes, *Police J.*, 19(1946) 299.
BEDDOE, H. L., Hit-Run Murders: Examination of the Body, *J. of Crim. Law, Criminol. and Police Sci.*, 49(1958) 280.
BLAIR, J. G., Photographic Mapping of Accident Sites, *Police J.*, 36(1963) 307.
BROWN, L. F., Unusual findings in a motor accident case, *Police J.*, 16(1943) 199.
CHAVIGNY, P., Identification of glass in motor-car headlights, *Police J.*, 13(1940) 110.
DAVIS, CH. A., Notes on Physical Evidence in Pedestrian Hit and Run Accidents, *J. Crim. Law, Criminol. and Police Sci.*, 50(1959) 302.
ECKERT, W. G., W. T. KEMMERER and N. J. CHETTA, The Traumatic Pathology of Traffic Accidents, *J. of For. Sci.*, 4(1959) 309.
FINNEY, D. J., A modern accident investigation, *J. of Crim. Law, Criminol. and Police Sci.*, 27(1937) 725.
FONG, W., M. FLOHR and G. W. ROCHE, Identification of parking and turn signal lenses, *J. of Crim. Law, Criminol. and Police Sci.*, 51(1960) 99.
FORD, R. and A. L. MOSELEY, Motor vehicular suicides, *J. of Crim. Law, Criminol. and Police Sci.*, 54(1963) 357.
FROENTJES, W., Examination of Traces in Collisions, *Algemeen politieblad van het Koninkrijk der Nederlanden*, 101(1952) 75.
GREENE, R. S. and D. Q. BURD, Headlight glass as evidence, *J. of Crim. Law, Criminol. and Police Sci.*, 40(1949) 85.
GROSS, H. and R. L. JACKSON, *Criminal Investigation*, 5th Ed., London, 1962, p. 167, 419.
HARRIS, R. I., *Outline of Death Investigation*, Springfield, 1962, p. 156.
HESSELINK, W. F., The Examination of Tires in Cases of Collision, *Intern. Crim. Pol. Rev.*, no. 79(1954) 171.
HOLTZ, J. and E. ANGST, Luftreifenspuren in der Kriminalistik, *Kriminalistik*, 14(1960) 198, 245, 316.
JACKSON, R. L., Unusual Result of Vehicle Examination, *Intern. Crim. Pol. Rev.*, no. 145 (1961) 34.
JONES, W. R., Scientific evidence as a sequel to a black-out accident, *Police J.*, 13(1940) 424.
KREMMLING, S. and A. SCHOENTAG, Examination of Headlights in Automobile Accidents, *Arch. f. Kriminol.*, 128(1961) 1.
MORELAND, J. D. and M. M. MILLER, Photographic Mapping of Accident Sites, *Police J.*, 36(1963) 57.
MUEHLBERGER, C. W., 'The investigation of deaths due to highway accidents' in *Homicide Investigation*, LeM. SNYDER, Springfield, 1950, p. 295.
NEILSON, R. A., A case for the Coroner, *Traffic Safety*, 61(1962) 10.

O'Hara, Ch. E. and J. W. Osterburg, *An Introduction to Criminalistics*, New York, 1949, p. 289, 298.

Prokop, O., W. Dürwald and W. Reimann, Die Feststellung von Aufahren bzw. Überfahren durch PKW und LKW mittels Staubuntersuchung unter zuhilfenahme der Stereolupe, *Arch. f. Kriminol.*, 130(1962) 134.

Schaub, G., Fehler in der Ursachenermittlung bei Verkehrsunfällen, *Z. f. Verkehrssicherheit*, 6(1960) 55.

Schöntag, A. and E. Mätzler, Zur Beweiskraft der Abdruckspuren von Zwillingreifen, *Arch. f. Kriminol.*, 126(1960) 50.

Smith, H. W., Physical Evidence in the Investigation of Traffic Accidents, *J. of Crim. Law, Criminol. and Police Sci.*, 48(1957) 93.

Smith, S., Studies in identification and reconstruction, *Police J.*, 17(1944) 25.

Thiele, R., The Examination of Car Lights After a Road Accident, *Intern. Crim. Pol. Rev.*, 13(1958) 78.

Tryhorn, F. G., Scientific evidence in cases of motor accident, *Police J.*, 13(1940) 288.

Williams, J. F., Physical Evidence in Hit-Run Traffic Deaths, *J. of Crim. Law, Criminol. and Police Sci.*, 50(1959) 80.

Willmirth, M. A., Car Identification by Wheelbase and Tread Width File, *FBI Law Enf. Bull.*, 25, no. 12(1956) 18.

Anon., Hairs and Fibers Prove Valuable in Hit-Run Cases, *FBI Law Enf. Bull.*, 30, no. 1(1961) 15.

Anon., Soil Evidence in Hit and Run Cases, *FBI Law Enf. Bul.*, 25, no. 4(1956) 18.

Investigation of Fatal Road Accidents, A Symposium, *J. of For. Sci.*, 1(1960) 28.

Bibliography to Chapter 12

Bartmann, F., *Dubiose Fälle*, Lübeck, 1954.

Dieckmann, Sr., E. A., Is It Natural Death, Suicide, or Murder?, Chapter 7, *Practical Homicide Investigation*, Springfield, 1961, p. 42.

Doyle, F. T., Marshalling of proofs in homicide cases, *J. of Crim. Law, Criminol. and Police Sci.*, 36(1946) 473.

Ducloux, L., A curious case of homicide by misadventure, *Intern. Crim. Pol. Rev.*, no. 32(1949) 27.

Fahlander, N., *Kriminalpolistjänst*, Karlshamn, 1956, p. 243, 306.

Finney, D. J., Police duties at Crime Scenes, *J. of Crim. Law, Criminol. and Police Sci.*, 27(1936) 239.

Ford, R., Death by Hanging of Adolescent and Young Adult Males, *J. of For. Sci.*, 2(1957) 171.

Gonzales, T. A., M. Vance, M. Helpern and C. J. Umberger, *Legal Medicine, Pathology and Toxicology*, 2nd Ed., New York, 1954.

Harlan, H., Five hundred homicides, *J. of Crim. Law, Criminol. and Police Sci.*, 40(1950) 736.

Harris, R. I., Unexpected 'Natural' Deaths, Chapter 19, *Outline of Death Investigation*, Springfield, 1962, p. 117.

HEINDL, R., Mord als Eisenbahnunfall maskiert, *Arch. f. Kriminol.*, 114(1944) 34.

HELPERN, M., The postmortem examination in cases of suspected homicide, *J. of Crim, Law, Criminol. and Police Sci.*, 36(1946) 485.

HIRTH, L., Ein weiterer Fall von Stromtod bei autoerotischer Betätigung, *Dtsch. Z. ger. Med.*, 49(1959) 109.

KOSYRA, H., Tödlicher Unglücksfall auf sexueller Grundlage durch Elektrizität, *Kriminalistik*, 11(1957) 437.

LOCARD, E., *Traité de Criminalistique*, *Vol. VII*, Lyon, 1940.

MANN, G. T., Accidental Strangulation during Perverse Sexual Activity, *J. of For. Sci.*, 5(1960) 169.

PERKINS, R. M., The law of homicide, *J. of Crim. Law, Criminol. and Police Sci.*, 36(1946) 391.

POIROT, H., La momia del cauce, *Rev. Crim. Pol. Cie.*, VIII, no. 110, (1948) 69.

RYAN, E., Investigation of homicide, *FBI Law Enf. Bull.*, 19, no. 3(1950) 6.

SIMPSON, K., Strangling: Murder or Suicide, *Intern. Crim. Pol. Rev.*, no. 138(1960) 137.

SNYDER, LeM., *Homicide Investigation*, Springfield, 1950.

SÖDERMAN, H. and J. J. O'CONNELL, *Modern Criminal Investigation*, New York, 1962, p. 263.

The autopsy

GLAISTER, J., *Medical Jurisprudence and Toxicology*, 11th Ed., Edinburgh, 1962, p. 30.

GONZALES, T. A., M. VANCE, M. HELPERN and C. J. UMBERGER, *Legal Medicine, Pathology and Toxicology*, 2nd Ed., New York, 1954, p. 83.

GRADWOHL, R. B. H., *Legal Medicine*, St. Louis, 1954, p. 20.

HARBITZ, F., *Laerebok i Rettsmedisin*, Oslo, 1950, p. 36.

HELPERN, M., The postmortem examination in cases of suspected homicide, *J. of Crim. Law, Criminol. and Police Sci.*, 36(1946) 485.

POLLAK, O. J., Postmortem examination in cases of suspected rape, *Am. J. Clin. Path.*, 13(1943) 309.

PROKOP, O., *Lehrbuch der gerichtlichen Medizin*, Berlin, 1960, p. 5.

SIMONIN, C., *Médecine Légale Judiciaire*, Paris, 1947, p. 682.

SIMPSON, C., *Forensic Medicine*, London, 1951, p. 203.

SJÖVALL, E., *Rättsmedicin*, Stockholm, 1946.

SMITH, S., *Forensic Medicine*, London, 1945, p. 50.

SNYDER, LeM., *Homicide Investigation*.

Examination of outdoor scenes

ARNET, HANS, Die Verwendung von Metallsuchgeräten im Polizeidienst, *Kriminalistik*, 11(1957) 466.

FINNEY, D. J., Police duties at crime scenes, *J. of Crim. Law, Criminol. and Police Sci.*, 27(1936) 239.

GROSS, H. and R. L. JACKSON, *Criminal Investigation*, 5th Ed., London, 1962, p. 78.

LANDMANN, H., Spezial-Suchhunde finden vergrabene Mordleichen nach 17 Monaten, *Kriminalistik*, 16(1962) 260.

O'HARA, CH. E., *Fundamentals of Criminal Investigation*, Springfield, 1956, p. 41.

Signs and time of death

BALLHAUSE, W. and F. DASSOW, Wann geschah die Tat?, *Kriminalistik*, 16(1962) 84.

BERG, S. P., Nervensystem und Totenstarre, *Dtsch. Z. ger. Med.*, 39(1949) 429.

BREAZEALE, E. L. and E. F. SUAREZ, Estimating the Time of Death, *Police*, 6, no. 2(1961) 49.

CAMPS, F. E., Establishment of the Time of Death, A Critical Assessment, *J. For. Sci.*, 4(1959) 73.

DE SARAM, G. S. W., Estimation of the Time of Death by Medical Criteria, *J. For. Med.*, 4(1957) 47.

DIECKMANN, SR., E. A., The Time Element, Chapter 2, *Practical Homicide Investigation*, Springfield, 1961, p. 8.

DOMENICI, F., Sull'umificazione del cadavere, *Arch. Antrop. Crim.*, 64–65 (1944–45) 91.

DOMENICI, F., État actuel des recherches sur l'humification du cadavre, *Ann. Méd. Lég. etc.*, 27(1947) 179.

FIDDES, F. S. and T. D. PATTEN, A Percentage Method for Representing the Fall in Body Temperature after Death, *J. For. Med.*, 5(1958) 2.

FORD, R., Critical Times in Murder Investigation, *J. of Crim. Law, Criminol. and Police Sci.*, 43(1953) 672.

GLAISTER, J., *Medical Jurisprudence and Toxicology*, Edinburgh, 1950, p. 127.

GONZALES, T. A., M. VANCE, M. HELPERN and C. J. UMBERGER, The Signs of Death, Chapter 4, *Legal Medicine, Pathology and Toxicology*, 2nd Ed., New York, 1954, p. 48.

GRADWOHL, R. B. H., Forensic Thanatology, Chapter 5, *Legal Medicine*, St. Louis, 1954, p. 120.

HARBITZ, F., *Laerebok i Rettsmedisin*, Oslo, 1950, p. 58.

HARRIS, R. I., Post-Mortem Changes, Chapter 18, *Outline of Death Investigation*, Springfield, 1962, p. 97.

JAFFE, F. A., Chemical Post-Mortem Changes in the Intra-Ocular Fluid, *J. of For. Sci.*, 7(1962) 231.

KERR, D. J. A., *Forensic Medicine*, London, 1946, p. 54.

KEVORKIAN, J., The Fundus Oculi as a 'Post-Mortem Clock', *J. of For. Sci.*, 6(1961) 261.

KREJCI, J. and J. HRADIL, Ein Fall beträchtlich vorgeschrittener Leichenzersetzung innerhalb von 12 Stunden, *Soudni lékarství*, (1962) 10.

LAVES, W., Über die Totenstarre, *Dtsch. Z. ger. Med.*, 39(1948) 186.

LUCAS, A., *Forensic Chemistry and Scientific Criminal Investigation*, London, 1945, p. 313.

LUSHBAUGH, C. C., J. ROSE and D. WILSON, A Practical Means for Routine Approximation of the Time of Recent Death, *Police*, 5(1960) 10.

LYLE, H. P. and F. P. CLEVELAND, Determination of the Time of Death by Body Heat Loss, *J. of For. Sci.*, 1(1956) 11.

LYLE, H. P., K. L. STEMMER and F. P. CLEVELAND, Determination of Time of Death, *J. of For. Sci.*, 4(1959) 167.

MANN, G. T., Problems in Estimating Post-Mortem Interval, *J. of For. Sci.*, 5(1960)346.

MAJOSKA, A. V., The Determination of Time of Death in a Case of Suspected Infanticide, *J. of For. Sci.*, 5(1960) 33.

MARSHALL, T. K., Estimating the Time of Death – The Use of the Cooling Formula in the Study of Postmortem Body Cooling, *J. of For. Sci.*, 7(1962) 189.

MARSHALL, T. K. and F. E. HOARE, The Rectal Cooling After Death and Mathematical Expression, *J. of For. Sci.*, 7(1962) 56.

MERKELEY, D. K., The Signs of Death, Chapter 4, *The Investigation of Death*, Springfield, 1957, p. 27.

MUELLER, B., Untersuchungen über die Histologie der Totenflecke, *Dtsch. Z. ger. Med.*, 40(1951) 499.

PONSOLD, A., *Lehrbuch der gerichtlichen Medizin*, Stuttgart, 1950, p. 17.

RACE, F. J. and W. M. NICKEG, Jr., Identification of Bodies Including Skeletal Remains and Determination of the Time of Death, *Police*, 6(1962) 6.

SCHOURUP, K., Determination of time of death, *Intern. Crim. Pol. Rev.*, 6(1951) 279.

SCHWARZ, F. and H. HEIDENWOLF, Post Mortem Cooling and its relation to the time of death, *Intern. Crim. Pol. Rev.*, 8(1953) 339.

SCHWARZFISCHER, F., Chemische Vorgänge bei der Lösung der Totenstarre, *Dtsch. Z. ger. Med.*, 39(1949) 421.

SIMONIN, C., *Médecine Légale Judiciaire*, Paris, 1947, p. 632, 640, 643.

SIMPSON, C. K., *Forensic Medicine*, London, 1951, p. 3,6.

SJÖVALL, E., *Rättsmedicin*, Stockholm, 1946, p. 27.

SJÖVALL, Hj., En ny metod för bestämning av tidpunkten för döden, *Nord. Krim. Tids.*, 21(1951) 1.

SMITH, S., *Forensic Medicine*, London, 1945, p. 17, 34, 37, 39, 276.

SNYDER, LeM., *Homicide Investigation*, Springfield, 1950, p. 29.

SÖDERMAN, H. and J. J. O'CONNELL, *Modern Criminal Investigation*, 5th Ed., New York, 1962, p. 285.

Action of insects and other animals

BEQUAERT, J., Some observations on the fauna of putrefaction and its potential value in establishing the time of death, *The New England J. of Medicine*, 227(1942) 856.

FORBES, G., The brown house moth as an agent in the destruction of mummified human remains, *Police J.*, 15(1942) 141.

GLAISTER, J., *Medical Jurisprudence and Toxicology*, 11th Ed., Edinburgh, 1962, p. 121.

GONZALES, T. A., M. VANCE, M. HELPERN and C. J. UMBERGER, *Legal Medicine, Pathology and Toxicology*, 2nd Ed., New York, 1954, p. 68.

LECLERCQ, M., Entomologie et médecine légale, *Acta Med. Leg. et Soc.*, 2(1949) 179.

LECLERCQ, M. and L. QUINET, Quelques cas d'application de l'entomologie à la détermination de l'époque de la mort, *Ann. Méd. Lég. etc.*, 29(1949) 324.

LECLERCQ, J. and M. LECLERCQ, Données bionomiques pour Calliphora erythrocephala Meigen et cas d'application à la médecine légale, *Bull. Soc. entom. France*, LIII (1948) 101.

LEIM, W., Verdächtiger Leichenfund, *Kriminalistik*, 18(1944) 21.

PESSOA, S. P. and F. LANE, Coleopteros necrophagos de interesse medico-legal, *Arq. Zool. Sao Paulo*, (1941) 389.

PONSOLD, A., *Lehrbuch der gerichtlichen Medizin*, Stuttgart, 1950, p. 129.

PROKOP, O., *Lehrbuch der gerichtlichen Medizin*, Berlin, 1960, p. 51.

SIMONIN, C., *Médecine Légale Judiciaire*, Paris, 1947, p. 645.

SMITH, S., *Forensic Medicine*, London, 1945, p. 38.

SMITH, S. and J. GLAISTER, *Recent Advances in Forensic Medicine*, London, 1939, p.250.

SPECHT, W., Tier-Bissverletzungen an Leichen, *Arch. f. Kriminol.*, 119(1957) 35.

Injuries from external mechanical violence and gunshot injuries

BAIRD, A. J., Injury Caused by Single Shotgun Pellet, *The Australian Police Journal*, 13(1959) 345.

BEDDOE, H. L., Deaths from Cutting and Stabbing, *Police*, 3(1958) 24.

BISCHOFF, J. A., L'examen des vêtements dans les affaires d'homicide, *Rev. Criminol. Pol. Techn.*, 4(1950) 216.

BURGESS, W. A., Comparison Standards – Effective Homicide Investigations Aid San Diego Police, *FBI Law Enf. Bull.*, 32, no. 2(1963) 3.

BUSATTO, S., Ricerche sperimentali sulle ferite del cuoio capelluto da colpi di martello, *Arch. Antrop. Crim.*, 69(1949) 302.

CHABAT, C. G., Détermination du calibre des projectiles se trouvant dans le corps humain, *Rev. Criminol. Pol. Techn.*, 4(1950) 280.

CHABAT, C. G., Calibration of projectiles lodged in the interior of the human body, *Identification News*, 2, no. 6(1952) 4.

DÉROBERT, L., Intérêt de l'étude des orifices d'entrée et de sortie des projectiles dans les côtes pour préciser la direction du tir, *Ann. Méd. Lég. etc.*, 26(1946) 37.

DRAKE, V., Shotgun Ballistics – 2, *The For. Sci. Soc. J.*, 3(1962) 22.

DUTRA, F. R., Progress in medico-legal investigation of gunshot injuries, *J. of Crim. Law, Criminol. and Police Sci.*, 39(1948)524.

ELBEL, H. and K. NAAB, Untersuchungen über den Pulverschmauch, *Beitr. z. gerichtl. Med.*, 16(1942) 14.

ELO, O., Samarbetet mellan rättsläkaren och kriminalpolisen, *Nord. Krim. Tids.*, 11(1941) 29.

ERHARDT, K., Der Kupfernachweis in Schussfeld und seine Bedeutung für die Schussentfernungsbestimmung, *Dtsch. Z. ger. Med.*, 30(1938) 235.

FATTOVICH, G., Tentativo di suicidio in una depressa per mezzo di infissione di un ago nella cavita addominale, *Arch. Antrop. Crim.*, 66(1946) 127.

FOURCADE, J., D. SCHNEIDER and F. LÉVY, Le suicide à la hache. Curieuse tentative avec mise en scène d'agression chez une schizophrène, *Ann. Méd. Lég. etc.*, 30 (1950) 133.

FRITZ, E., Merkwürdiger Befund nach Tötung eines Menschen mittels eines Bolzenschuss-Tiertötungsapparates, *Arch. f. Kriminol.*, 111(1942) 27.

GERKE, TH., Morde und Selbstmorde mit Viehschussmasken, *Arch. f. Kriminol.*, 111 (1942) 19.

GLAISTER, J., *Medical Jurisprudence and Toxicology*, Edinburgh, 1950, p. 236.

GONZALES, T.A., M. VANCE, M. HELPERN and C. J. UMBERGER, *Legal Medicine, Pathology*, 2nd Ed., New York, 1954, p. 157, 187, 323, 381.

GRADWOHL, R. B. H., *Legal Medicine*, St. Louis, 1954, p. 220.

GUERIN, P. F., Shotgun Wounds, *J. of For. Sci.*, 5(1960) 294.

HANSON, A., Mikroskopisk och mikrokemisk undersökning av skottskador, *Nord. Krim. Tids*, 15(1945) 37, 63

HARBITZ, F., Kan man av utsendet av en lesjon trekke slutninger om det anvendte våpen eller redskap?, *Nord. Krim. Tids.*, 6(1944) 61.

HARBITZ, F., *Laerebok i Rettsmedisin*, Oslo, 1950, p. 73.

HARRIS, R. I., Gunshot Wounds, Chapter 31, *Outline of Death Investigation*, Springfield, 1962, p. 200.

HAUSBRANDT, F., Zur Frage der Verspritzung von Organgewebe als Nahschusszeichen, *Dtsch. Z. ger. Med.*, 38(1944) 157.

HEINDL, R., Spuren an der Schiesshand nach Schuss mit Faustfeuerwaffen, *Arch. f. Kriminol.*, 114(1944) 75.

HELPERN, M., Unusual fatal stab wounds of head and neck, *Am. J. of Surgery*, 26(1934) 53.

HEPNER, W. and W. MARESCH, Une arme de suicide peu commune, *Rev. Criminol. Pol. Techn.*, 6(1952) 350.

HEPNER, W. and H. MAURER, Selbstmord einer Frau mittels zweir Pistolen mit beinahe gegenläufiger geschossdeformation, *Kriminalistik*, 16(1962) 558.

HOLZER, F. J., Zur Erkennung des verletzenden Werkzeuger aus Wunden, *Dtsch. Z. ger. Med.*, 39(1948) 35.

KERR, D. J. A., *Forensic Medicine*, London, 1946, p. 72, 108, 112, 122, 139.

KIRK, P. L., *Crime Investigation*, New York, 1953, p. 709.

KLEIN, F., Selbstmord durch Nackenabschneiden, *Schwiez. med. Wschr.*, 11(1942) 1044.

LESZCZYNSKI, CH., Die Bestimmung der Schussentfernung, *Kriminalistik*, 13(1959) 377.

LEIBEGOTT, G., Zur entstehung der Schürfungs- und Stanzverletzungen, *Dtsch. Z. ger. Med.*, 39(1949) 356.

LIPMAN, J. and H. W. TURKEL, Unreliability of Dermal Nitrate Test for Gun Powder, *J. of Crim. Law, Criminol. and Police Sci.*, 46(1955) 281.

LOWBEER, L., An Unusual Gunshot Wound of the Head, *J. of For. Sci.*, 6(1961) 88.

LYLE, H. P., Gunshot Wounds, *J. of For. Sci.*, 6(1961) 255.

MAYER, F. X. and N. WÖLKART, Neue Methode zur Untersuchung von Nahschussspuren, *Arch. f. Kriminol.*, 116(1955) 73.

MENESINI, G., Un caso singolare di suicidio, *Arch. Antrop. Crim.*, 66(1946) 83.

McLAUGHLIN, G. H. and C. H. BEARDSLEY, JR., Distance Determinations in Cases of Gunshot Through Glass, *J. of For. Sci.*, 1(1956) 43.

MERKELEY, D. K., Blunt Force Injuries, Chapter 5, p. 38; Gunshot Wounds, Chapter 7, p. 73; Stab Wounds and Cutting Wounds, Chapter 8, *The Investigation of Death*, Springfield, 1957.

MOLINA, J. F., The Strange Case of One Entrance Wound for Three Bullets, *Finger print Mag.*, 35(1954) 3.

MUELLER, B., Untersuchungen über Schrägschüsse und über das Verhalten der Basophilie in der Umgebung von Schussöffnungen, *Dtsch. Z. ger. Med.*, 36(1942) 53.

MUNBALL, B. D., Fundamental Ballistics Pertaining to Investigations Involving Firearms, *J. of For. Sci.*, 6(1961) 215.

OLBRYCHT, J., Observations critiques et casuistiques sur l'aspect de la plaie en rapport avec l'instrument employé, *Acta Med. Leg. et Soc.*, 4(1951) 15.

OLLIVIER, H. and F. ROBERT, The difficulties of observation of gun shot entry wounds, *Ann. Méd. Lég. etc.*, 38(1958) 378.

POKKE, J., Schartenspuren, durch Werkzeuge veranlasst, *Dtsch. Z. ger. Med.*, 37(1934) 273; *Kriminalistik*, 17(1943) 23.

PONSOLD, A., *Lehrbuch der gerichtlichen Medizin*, Stuttgart, 1950, p. 138.

POZZATO, R., The long firearm with flash eliminator. Typical aspect of the orifice of entry of the projectile, *Intern. Crim. Pol. Rev.*, 6(1951) 201; *Arch. Antrop. Crim.*, 70(1950) 74.

PROKOP, O., Ein Beitrag zur Frage der Form der Platzwunde beim absoluten Nahschuss, *Arch. f. Kriminol.*, 125(1960) 81; 126(1960) 15.

ROMANO, C., Una tecnica microchimica per l'identificazione dei forami d'entrata nei colpi di arma da fuoco, *Arch. Antrop. Crim.*, 69(1949) 326.

SCHÖNTAG, A., Vorschlag einer neuen Methode: Bestimmung der Schussentfernung mittels des 'Schmauchringes', *Arch. f. Kriminol.*, 120(1951) 62.

SCHÖNTAG, A. and F. Baumgärtner, Erweiterung des Messbereiches auf 3m. bei der Bestimmung der Schussentfernung durch Auswendung der Aktivierunganalysis, *Arch. f. Kriminol.*, 131(1963) 1.

SHAPERO, H. A., J. GLUCKMAN and I. GORDON, The Significance of Finger Nail Abrasions of the Skin, *J. For. Med.*, 9(1962) 17.

SIMONIN, C., *Médecine Légale Judiciaire*, Paris, 1947, p. 66, 91, 101, 125, 672.

SIMPSON, C. K., *Forensic Medicine*, London, 1951, p. 46, 67, 101, 288.

SJÖVALL, E., *Rättsmedicin*, Stockholm, 1946, p. 74.

SMITH, S., *Forensic Medicine*, London, 1945, p. 106, 134, 169, 175.

SMITH, S., Wounds from high velocity projectiles, *Police J.*, 15(1942) 104, 264; 16(1943) 23.

SNYDER, LeM., *Homicide Investigation*, Springfield, 1950, p. 97, 177, 277, 291.

SÖDERMAN, H. and J. J. O'CONNELL, *Modern Criminal Investigation*, 5th Ed., New York, p. 221.

THOMAS, F. and G. GALLET, Homicide by blows to the head by means of an axe and identification of the weapon, *Intern. Crim. Pol. Rev.*, no. 10(1947) 13.

TOVO, S., Lo scannamento osservazioni su 39 casi di suicidio e 22 di omicidio, *Arch. Antrop. Crim.*, 66(1946) 159.

TURNER, R. F., *Forensic Science and Laboratory Technics*, Springfield, 1949, p. 101, 103, 105.

WALKER, J. T., Bullet holes and chemical residues in shooting cases, *J. of Crim. Law, Criminol. and Police Sci.*, 31(1940) 497.

WEIMANN, W., Über Stichverletzungen des Kopfes, *Dtsch. Z. ger. Med.*, 10(1927) 360.

WILSON, R. A., Death by Pseudo-Traumatic Injuries, Outside Causes that could be confused with Traumatic Injuries, *Institute on Homicide Investigation Techniques*, Springfield, 1961, p. 84.

Anon., Ein nicht alltäglicher Selbstmord, *Kriminalistik*, 16(1962) 226.

Anon., Felo-de-se, *RCMP Quart.*, April, 1945.

Death by suffocation

GLAISTER, J., *Medical Jurisprudence and Toxicology*, Edinburgh, 1950, p. 168.

GONZALES, T. A., M. VANCE, M. HELPERN and C. J. UMBERGER, *Legal Medicine, Pathology and Toxicology*, and Ed., New York, 1954, p. 454, 475.

GRADWOHL, R. B. H., *Legal Medicine*, St. Louis, 1954, p. 260.

HARBITZ, F., *Laerebok i Rettsmedisin*, Oslo, 1950, p. 196.

HARRIS, R. I., *Outline of Death Investigation*, Springfield, 1962, p. 131, 188.

HOLZER, F. J., Über eigenartige Selbstmorde durch Ertrinken und die Bedeutung des Augenscheins für die Feststellung des Selbstmordes, *Dtsch. Z. ger. Med.*, 39(1948) 46.

KERR, D. J. A., *Forensic Medicine*, London, 1946, p. 152.

KURZMEYER, W., Uncontrovertible evidence, *Intern. Crim. Pol. Rev.*, 6(1951) 348.

MARCHTALER, VON, A., Selbstmord durch Bolus, *Dtsch. Z. ger. Med.*, 39(1949) 487.

MERKELEY, D. K., *The Investigation of Death*, Springfield, 1957, p. 54.

POLSON, C., Strangulation – Manslaughter or Murder, *Med. Leg. J.*, 25(1957) 101–110.

PONSOLD, A., *Lehrbuch der gerichtlichen Medizin*, Stuttgart, 1950, p. 209, 219, 229.

SCHRADES, G., Vortäuschung von Selbstmord durch Erhängen, *Arch. f. Kriminol.*, 113 (1943) 65.

SIMONIN, C., *Médecine Légale Judiciaire*, Paris, 1947, p. 166, 171, 174, 181, 189.

SIMPSON, K., Strangling: Murder or Suicide, *Intern. Crim. Pol. Rev.*, no. 138(1960) 137.

SJÖVALL, E., *Rättsmedicin*, Stockholm, 1946, p. 132.

SMITH, S., *Forensic Medicine*, London, 1945, p. 250.

SNYDER, LeM., *Homicide Investigation*, Springfield, 1950, p. 191, 230.

THOMAS, F., W. VAN HECKE and J. TIMPERMAN, The Medicolegal Diagnosis of Death by Drowning, *J. of For. Sci.*, 8(1963) 1.

Carbon monoxide poisoning

CAMPS, F. E., Carbon monoxide poisoning. Accident, suicide and murder, *Med. Leg. J.*, 18(1950) 75.

GLAISTER, J., *Medical Jurisprudence and Toxicology*, Edinburgh, 1950, p. 581.

GONZALES, T. A., M. VANCE, M. HELPERN and C. J. UMBERGER, *Legal Medicine, Pathology and Toxicology*, 2nd Ed., New York, 1954, p. 496.

GRADWOHL, R. B. H., *Legal Medicine*, St. Louis, 1954, p. 286.

HANNIG, Nachweis einer Kohlenoxydvergiftung bei brennender Gasflamme, *Kriminalistik*, 16(1942) 96.

HESSELINK, W. F., Leuchtgasvergifting, Selbstmord oder Unfall?, *Arch. f. Kriminol.*, 114(1944) 4.

HEYDECK, Ein eigenartiger Unglücksfall, *Kriminalistik*, 15(1941) 77.

HULST, J. P. L., A curious case of suicide, *Intern. Crim. Pol. Rev.*, no. 24(1949) 13.

KERR, D. J. A., *Forensic Medicine*, London, 1946, p. 317.

NICKOLLS, L. C., *The Scientific Investigation of Crime*, London, 1956, p. 353.

PONSOLD, A., *Lehrbuch der gerichtlichen Medizin*, Stuttgart, 1951, p. 200.

SCHWARZ, F., Familienvergiftung mit Leuchtgas, Verbrechen oder Zufall, *Arch. f. Kriminol.*, 111(1942) 11.

SIMONIN, C., *Médecine Légale Judiciaire*, Paris, 1947, p. 460.

SIMPSON, C. K., *Forensic Medicine*, London, 1951, p. 298.

SIMPSON, C. K., The danger of accidental carbon monoxide poisoning. A review of 100 cases, *Brit. Med. J. Okt.*, 1954, p. 774.

SMITH, S., *Forensic Medicine*, London, 1945, p. 280.

SNYDER, LEM., *Homicide Investigation*, Springfield, 1950, p. 232.

STEYAERT, A. and VAN HECKE, W., Calcul de la durée de survie dans l'intoxication par le gaz d'éclairage, *Acta. Med. Leg. et Soc.*, 4(1951) 41.

SÖDERMAN, H. and J. J. O'CONNELL, *Modern Criminal Investigation*, 5th Ed., New York, p. 309.

Sexual murder and rape

BARTMANN, F., Notsucht mit Todesfolge, *Kriminalistik*, 18(1944) 9.

FAHLANDER, N., *Kriminalpolistjänst*, Karlshamn, 1956, p. 312.

FORBES, G., A study of a series of cases of sexual crime, *Police J.*, 14(1941) 163.

FORD, R., Death by Hanging of Adolescent and Young Adult Males, *J. of For. Sci.*, 2(1957) 171.

GLAISTER, J., *Medical Jurisprudence and Toxicology*, Edinburgh, 1950, p. 422.

GODWIN, G., *Peter Kürten. A study in Sadism*, London, 1945.

GONZALES, T. A., M. VANCE, M. HELPERN and C. J. UMBERGER, *Legal Medicine, Pathology and Toxicology*, 2nd Ed., New York, 1954, p. 603.

GROSS, H. and R. L. JACKSON, *Criminal Investigation*, 5th Ed., London, 1962, p. 121.

HARBITZ, F., *Laerebok i Rettsmedisin*, Oslo, 1950, p. 446.

HARRIS, R. I., *Outline of Death Investigation*, Springfield, 1962, p. 241.

HIRTH, L., Ein weiterer Fall von Stromtod bei autoerotischer Betätigung, *Dtsch. Z. ges. Med.*, 49(1959) 109.

HOLDEN, H. S., The Laboratory aspects of sexual crime, *British J. of Venereal Diseases*, 24(1946) 190.

KERR, D. J. A., *Forensic Medicine*, London, 1946, p. 190.

KIRK, P. L., *Crime Investigation*, New York, 1953, p. 206.

KOSYRA, H., Tödlicher Unglücksfall auf sexueller Grundlage durch Elektrizität, *Kriminalistik*, 11(1957) 437.

MANN, G. T., Accidental Strangulation during Perverse Sexual Activity, *J. of For. Sci.*, 5(1960) 169.

MATZKE, Verkennung eines Sexualmordes infolge ungenügender Tatort- und Leichenbeschau, *Kriminalistik*, 17(1943) 18.

MEIXNER, F., *Kriminalität und Sexualität*, Heidelberg, 1951, p. 58.

MERKELEY, D. K., *The Investigation of Death*, Springfield, 1957, p. 105.

NICKOLLS, L. C., *The Scientific Investigation of Crime*, London, 1956, p. 196.

O'HARA, CH. E., *Fundamentals of Criminal Investigation*, Springfield, 1956, p. 249.

POLLAK, O. J., Postmortem examination in cases of suspected rape, *Am. J. Clin. Path.*, 13(1943) 309.

PONSOLD, A., *Lehrbuch der gerichtlichen Medizin*, Stuttgart, 1950, p. 445.

PROKOP, O., *Lehrbuch der gerichtlichen Medizin*, Berlin, 1960.

RIFE, D. W., Scientific evidence in rape cases, *J. of Crim. Law, Criminol. and Police Sci.*, 31(1940) 232.

DE RIVER, P. J., *The Sexual Criminal*, Springfield, 1951, p. 42, 52, 121.

SIMONIN, C., *Médecine Légale Judiciaire*, Paris, 1947, p. 335, 359.

SIMPSON, C. K., *Forensic Medicine*, London, 1951, p. 176.

SIMPSON, C. K., The Heath case, *Police J.*, 20(1947) 266.

SMITH, S., *Forensic Medicine*, London, 1945, p. 295.

SNYDER, LEM., *Homicide Investigation*, Springfield, 1950, p. 327.

WILSON, R. A., *Institute on Homicide Investigation Techniques*, Springfield, 1961, p. 94.

Anon., Hair and fibers help to solve sex crimes, *FBI Law Enf. Bull.*, 19, no. 5(1950) 7.

Death in connection with sexual perversion

BEROUD, G. Pendaison accidentelle d'un masochiste, *Rev. Criminol. Pol. Techn.*, 2(1948) 287.

BOBST, M., A victim of auto-eroticism, *Intern. Crim. Pol. Rev.*, 9(1954) 242.

FORD, R., Death by Hanging of Adolescent and Young Adult Males, *J. of For. Sci.*, 2(1957) 171.

HIRTH, L., Ein weiterer Fall von Stromtod bei autoerotischer Betätigung, *Dtsch. Z. ger. Med.*, 49(1959) 109.

KNAPP, H., Aufschlussreicher tödlicher Unglücksfall bei einem sexuell abartigen Menschen, *Kriminalistik*, 6(1952) 84.

KOOPMANN, Unfall bei abwegiger sexueller Betätigung oder Selbstmord?, *Arch. f. Kriminol.*, 110(1942) 60.

KOOPMANN, Unbeabsichtigte tödliche Zwischenfälle bei abwegiger sexueller Betätigung, *Arch. f. Kriminol.*, 111(1942) 43.

KOSYRA, H., Tödlicher Unglücksfall auf sexueller Grundlage durch Elektrizität, *Kriminalistik*, 11(1957) 437.

MANN, G. T., Accidental Strangulation during Perverse Sexual Activity, *J. of For. Sci.*, 5(1960) 169.

MEIXNER, F., *Kriminalität und Sexualität*, Heidelberg, 1951, p. 19.

MERKELEY, D. K., *The Investigation of Death*, Springfield, 1957, p. 105.

PROKOP, O., *Lehrbuch der gerichtlichen Medizin*, Berlin, 1960.

SCHILLING, K., Lust und Freude am Schmerz. Bericht über den ungewöhnlichen Berlauf einer masochistischen Neigung, *Polizei-Praxis*, 9(1955) 51.

SCHWARZ, F., *Probleme des Selbstmordes*, Bern, 1946, p. 77.

SIMPSON, C. K., *Forensic Medicine*, London, 1951, p. 99.

SMETANA, Seltsamer Todesfall bei Selbstbefriedigung, *Kriminalistik*, 16(1942) 122.

WEIMANN, W., Ein Fall zufälliger Erhängung aus sexuellen Motiven, *Arch. f. Kriminol.*, 97(1935) 62.

ZIEMKE, E., Über zufällige Erhängung und seine Beziehungen zu sexuellen Perversitäten, *Dtsch. Z. ger. Med.*, 5(1925) 103.

Death in connection with criminal abortion

BRINDEAU, A., La folliculine et ses dérivés sont-ils abortifs, *Ann. Méd. Lég. etc.*, 22 (1942) 210.

DAVIS, A., 2,665 cases of abortion. A clinical survey, *Brit. Med. J.*, 2(1950) 123.

DÉROBERT, L. and L. TRUFFERT, L'importance de la recherche toxicologique des substances abortives, *Ann. Méd. Lég. etc.*, 25(1945) 61.

DUTRA, F. R., F. P. CLEVELAND and H. P. LYLE, Criminal abortions induced by intrauterine pastes, *J. Am. Med. Assoc.*, 143(1950) 865.

FISHER, R. S., Criminal abortion, *J. of Crim. Law, Criminol. and Police Sci.*, 42(1951) 242.
FOURCADE, M. J., L'embolie gazeuse massive avec mort subite ou rapide dans l'avortement criminel, *Ann. Méd. Lég. etc.*, 31(1951) 160.
GLAISTER, J., *Medical Jurisprudence and Toxicology*, Edinburgh, 1950, p. 80, 381.
GONZALES, T. A., M. VANCE, M. HELPERN and C. J. UMBERGER, *Legal Medicine, Pathology and Toxicology*, 2nd Ed., New York, 1954, p. 564.
GRADWOHL, R. B. H., *Legal Medicine*, St. Louis, 1954, p. 804.
HALL, W. E. B., Some signs, findings, and interpretations of criminal abortion, *J. of Crim. Law, Criminol. and Police Sci.*, 41(1950) 235.
HARBITZ, F., *Laerebok i Rettsmedisin*, Oslo, 1950, p. 431.
HARRIS, R. I., *Outline of Death Investigation*, Springfield, 1962, p. 124.
HERRMANN, R., Les avortements par injection intra-utérine d'eau de savon, *Rev. Criminol. Pol. Techn.*, 4(1950) 52.
HUBER, O., Anklage wegen Abtreibung mit Safran bei vorgetäuschter Schwangerschaft, *Kriminalistik*, 16(1962) 219.
KERR, D. J. A., *Forensic Medicine*, London, 1946, p. 174.
KULKA, W., Deaths following use of abortifacient paste, *Am. J. Clin. Path.*, 17(1947) 723.
MULLER and MARCHAND–ALPHAND, Contribution à l'étude de mécanisme des avortements provoqués, *Ann. Méd. Lég. etc.*, 24(1944) 45.
NICKOLLS, L. C., *The Scientific Investigation of Crime*, London, 1956, p. 214.
OBERSTEG, J. I., Die Luftembolie bei kriminellem Abort, *Dtsch. Z. ger. Med.*, 39(1949) 646.
O'HARA, CH. E., *Fundamentals of Criminal Investigation*, Springfield, 1956, p. 477.
PARRY, L. A., *Criminal Abortion*, London, 1932.
PONSOLD, A., *Lehrbuch der gerichtlichen Medizin*, Stuttgart, 1950, p. 273.
PROKOP, O., *Lehrbuch der gerichtlichen Medizin*, Berlin, 1960.
QUENNELL, W. K., Abortion, *RCMP Gazette*, 24(1962) 3.
RHODES, H. T. F., *Forensic Chemistry*, London, 1946, p. 146.
SCHWERD, W., Medico-legal proof of abortion by use of soapy water and soap poisoning, *Dtsch. Z. ger. Med.*, 48(1959) 202.
SIMONIN, C., *Médecine Légale Judiciaire*, Paris, 1947, p. 371.
SIMONIN, C., Mort rapide par embolie gazeuse au cours d'un self-avortement, *Ann. Méd. Lég. etc.*, 28(1948) 135.
SIMONIN, C., Embolies gazeuses mortelles consécutives aux manoeuvres abortives (formes médico-légales), *Ann. Méd. Lég. etc.*, 28(1948) 133.
SIMPSON, C. K., *Forensic Medicine*, London, 1951, p. 161, 291.
SIMPSON, C. K., Dangers of criminal instrumental abortion, *Lancet*, 1(1949) 47.
SMITH, S., *Forensic Medicine*, London, 1945, p. 331.
SNYDER, LEM., *Homicide Investigation*, Springfield, 1950, p. 319.
TARSITANO, F., Considerazioni medico-legali sul tetano post-abortivo, *Arch. Antrop. Crim.*, 68(1948) 241.
TEARE, R. D., Air-embolism in criminal abortion, *Lancet*, 2(1944) 242.
TEARE, R. D., The medico-legal significance of death following abortion, *Med. Leg. J.*, 19(1951) 81.

TRILLOT, J., Mort subite ou rapide au cours des tentatives d'avortement, *Ann. Méd. Lég. etc.*, 26(1946) 81.

TRILLOT, J., Un curieux instrument abortif, *Ann. Méd. Lég. etc.*, 27(1947) 85.

WILSON, R. A., *Institute on Homicide Investigation Techniques*, Springfield, 1961, p. 116.

Infanticide

ADELSON, L., Some Medicolegal Observations on Infanticide, *J. of For. Sci.*, 4(1959) 60.

BUHTZ, G., Tötung von drei neugeborenen Kindern durch die eigene eheliche Mutter, *Arch. f. Kriminol.*, 110(1942) 14.

CAMPS, F. E., Lésions de la tête par coups de marteau et érosions et ecchymoses par coups d'ongles à travers les vêtements chez une enfant, *Ann. Méd. Lég. etc.*, 30 (1950) 299.

FOURCADE, J., L. FRUHLING and A. OZTUREL, Sur un cas d'étouffement criminel du nouveau-né sans marques extérieures de violences, *Ann. Méd. Lég. etc.*, 31(1951) 108.

GLAISTER, J., *Medical Jurisprudence and Toxicology*, Edinburgh, 1950, p. 80, 397.

GONZALES, T. A., M. VANCE, M. HELPERN and C. J. UMBERGER, *Legal Medicine, Pathology and Toxicology*, 2nd Ed., New York, 1954, p. 593.

GRADWOHL, R. B. H., *Legal Medicine*, St. Louis, 1954, p. 822.

HARBITZ, F., *Laerebok i Rettsmedisin*, Oslo, 1950, p. 353.

HARRIS, R. I., *Outline of Death Investigation*, Springfield, 1962, p. 223.

KERR, D. J. A., *Forensic Medicine*, London, 1946, p. 180.

MILOSLAVICH, E. L., Uncommon criminal methods of infanticide, *J. of Crim. Law, Criminol. and Police Sci.*, 42(1951) 414.

O'HARA, CH. E., *Fundamentals of Criminal Investigation*, Springfield, 1956, p. 461.

PAUL, C., R. PIÉDELIÈVRE and L. DÉROBERT, Infanticide sadique, *Ann. Méd. Lég. etc.*, 22(1942) 173.

PONSOLD, A., *Lehrbuch der gerichtlichen Medizin*, Stuttgart, 1950, p. 298.

DE RIVER, J. P., *The Sexual Criminal*, Springfield, 1951, p. 168.

SIMONIN, C., *Médecine Légale Judiciaire*, Paris, 1947, p. 201.

SIMPSON, C. K., *Forensic Medicine*, London, 1951, p. 149.

SMITH, S., *Forensic Medicine*, London, 1945, p. 347.

Death from electric current

BORNSTEIN, F. P., Homicide by Electrocution, *J. of For. Sci.*, 7(1962) 516.

GLAISTER, J., *Medical Jurisprudence and Toxicology*, Edinburgh, 1962, p. 186.

GONZALES, T. A., M. VANCE, M. HELPERN and C. J. UMBERGER, *Legal Medicine, Pathology and Toxicology*, 2nd Ed., New York, 1954, p. 534.

GRADWOHL, R. B. H., *Legal Medicine*, St. Louis, 1954, p. 199.

HARBITZ, F., *Laerebok i Rettsmedisin*, Oslo, 1950, p. 255.

HARRIS, R. I., *Outline of Death Investigation*, Springfield, 1962, p. 194.

HOLZHAUSEN, G. and H. HUNGER, Stromtod eines Kleiderfetischisten bei autoerotischer Betätigung, *Arch. f. Kriminol.*, 131(1963) 166.

KERR, D. J. A., *Forensic Medicine*, London, 1946, p. 135.

KOSYRA, H., Mord durch Elektrizität, *Kriminalistik*, 10(1956) 360.

LESSING, K.H., Ein raffinierter Mordversuch, *Polizei-Praxis*, 9(1955) 22.

MULLER, VIELLEDENT and MARCHAND, Lésions histologiques dans un cas de mort tardive par électrocution par courant 220 volts, *Ann. Méd. Lég. etc.*, 20(1940) 159.

PONSOLD, A., *Lehrbuch der gerichtlichen Medizin*, Stuttgart, 1950, p. 306.

PROKOP, O., *Lehrbuch der gerichtlichen Medizin*, Berlin, 1960, p. 127.

REUTER and KASTIRKE, Tödlicher Unfall durch fehlerhaftes Elektrogerät, *Kriminalistik*, 18(1944) 70.

SCHWERD, W. and L. LAUTENBACH, Mord mit elektrischem Strom in der Badewanne, *Arch. f. Kriminol.*, 126(1960) 33.

SIMONIN, C., *Médecine Légale Judiciaire*, Paris, 1947, p. 155.

SIMPSON, C. K., *Forensic Medicine*, London, 1951, p. 127.

SMITH, S., *Forensic Medicine*, London, 1945, p. 241.

SNYDER, LeM., *Homicide Investigation*, Springfield, 1950, p. 286.

VITERBO, B. and E. FORNASARI, Polarographic determination of metals in the portals of entry of electric current, *Minerva Medicolegale*, 78(1958) 254.

Violent death in fires

DÉROBERT, L. and GASCOIN, Chute en gant des téguments de la main après brulure, *Ann. Méd. Lég. etc.*, 30(1950) 255.

DUTRA, F. R., Medicolegal aspects of conflagrations, *J. of Crim. Law, Criminol. and Police Sci.*, 39(1949) 771.

GLAISTER, J., *Medical Jurisprudence and Toxicology*, 11th Ed., Edinburgh, 1962, p. 194.

GONZALES, T. A., M. VANCE, M. HELPERN and C. J. UMBERGER, *Legal Medicine, Pathology and Toxicology*, 2nd Ed., New York, 1954, p. 523.

GRADWOHL, R. B. H., *Legal Medicine*, St. Louis, 1954, p. 205.

HARBITZ, F., *Laerebok i Rettsmedisin*, Oslo, 1950, p. 245.

KENNEDY, J., *Fire and Arson Investigation*, Chicago, 1962, p. 336.

KERR, D. J. A., *Forensic Medicine*, London, 1946, p. 131.

PONSOLD, A., *Lehrbuch der gerichtlichen Medizin*, Stuttgart, 1950, p. 315.

PROKOP, O., *Lehrbuch der gerichtlichen Medizin*, Berlin, 1960, p. 115.

SIMONIN, C., *Médecine Légale Judiciaire*, Paris, 1947, p. 141.

SIMPSON, C. K., *Forensic Medicine*, London, 1951, p. 121.

SJÖVALL, E., *Rättsmedicin*, Stockholm, 1946, p. 109.

SMITH, S., *Forensic Medicine*, London, 1945, p. 232.

SNYDER, LeM., *Homicide Investigation*, Springfield, 1950.

SVENSSON, A., Ett egendomligt självmord, *Nord. Krim. Tids.*, 19(1949) 73.

WILLAS, Meuchelmord durch Verbrennen des Opfers, *Kriminalistik*, 16(1942) 131.

WINTER, R., Anatomische Befunde bei einer Brandleiche, *Kriminalistik*, 15(1941) 43.

Anon., Die 'Fechterstellung' der Brandleichen, *Arch. f. Kriminol.*, 112(1943) 141.

Anon., *BCI Bull. N.Y. State Police*, 12(1947) 8.

Death by freezing

GLAISTER, J., *Medical Jurisprudence and Toxicology*, 11th Ed., Edinburgh, 1962, p. 210.

GONZALES, T. A., M. VANCE, M. HELPERN and C. J. UMBERGER, *Legal Medicine, Pathology and Toxicology*, 2nd Ed., New York, 1954, p. 523.

GRADWOHL, R. B. H., *Legal Medicine*, St. Louis, 1954, p. 196.

HARBITZ, F., *Laerebok i Rettsmedisin*, Oslo, 1950, p. 253.

KERR, D. J. A., *Forensic Medicine*, London, 1946, p. 146.

PROKOP, O., *Lehrbuch der gerichtlichen Medizin*, Berlin, 1960, p. 115.

SIMPSON, S. K., *Forensic Medicine*, London, 1951, p. 121.

SJÖVALL, E., *Rättsmedicin*, Stockholm, 1946, p. 115.

SMITH, S., *Forensic Medicine*, London, 1945, p. 247.

VEJLENS, G., Känslan av hetta vid förfrysning, *Nord. Krim. Tids.*, 22(1952) 141.

Death by poisoning

ANDEREGGEN, P., A propos de 273 tentatives de suicide par empoisonnement; Remarques statistiques et thérapeutiques, *Rev. Méd. Suisse. Rom.*, 68(1948) 257.

BROOKES, V. J. and H. N. ALYEA, *Poisons. Their Properties, Chemical Identification, Symptoms and Emergency Treatments*, New York, 1946.

FABRE, D. R., Modern toxicology and forensic medicine, *Intern. Crim. Pol. Rev.*, 6(1951) 42.

FRANKE, E., Vergiftung mit Thallium, *Kriminalistik*, 17(1943) 91.

GLAISTER, J., *Medical Jurisprudence and Toxicology*, Edinburgh, 1950.

GONZALES, T. A., M. VANCE, M. HELPERN and C. J. UMBERGER, *Legal Medicine, Pathology and Toxicology*, 2nd Ed., New York, 1954, p. 690.

GRADWOHL, R. B. H., *Legal Medicine*, St. Louis, 1954, p. 285.

GRIFFON, H., Emploi du laudanum en injection hypodermique par les toxicomanes, *Ann. Méd. Lég. etc.*, 24(1944) 11.

HERMANN, B., Morfina, *Rev. Crim. Pol. Cie.*, XI, no. 145(1951) 35.

KERR, D. J. A., *Forensic Medicine*, London, 1946.

KIRK, P. L., *Crime Investigation*, New York, 1953, p. 727.

LOCARD, E., Evolution in the psychology of poisoners, *Intern. Crim. Pol. Rev.*, no. 10 (1947) 11.

NICKOLLS, L. C., *The Scientific Investigation of Crime*, London, 1956, p. 348.

O'HARA, CH. E., *Fundamentals of Criminal Investigation*, Springfield, 1956, p. 429.

O'HARA, CH. E. and J. W. OSTERBURG, *An Introduction to Criminalistics*, New York, 1949, p. 432.

RHODES, H. T. F., *Forensic Chemistry*, London, 1946, p. 135.

SCHNEIDER, PH., En serie mord och mordförsök med tallium, *Nord. Krim. Tids.*, 20 (1950) 37; *Intern. Crim. Pol. Rev.*, 6(1951) 352.

SIMPSON, C. K., *Forensic Medicine*, London, 1951.

SIMPSON, C. K. and J. R. MOLONY, The Seconal Capsule Murder, *Med. Leg. J.*, 25(1957) 53.

SMITH, S., *Forensic Medicine*, London, 1945.

SNYDER, LEM., *Homicide Investigation*, Springfield, 1950, p. 231.

SÖDERMAN, H. and J. J. O'CONNELL, *Modern Criminal Investigation*, 5th Ed., New York, 1962, p. 284.

TASCHEN, B., Über Blausäurevergiftungen, *Kriminalistik*, 4(1950) 156.

Trunk murder, dismemberment of the body

CAMPS, F. E. and H. S. HOLDEN, The case of Stanley Setty, *Med. Leg. J.*, 19(1951) 2.

DOSI, G., She made soap with the bodies of her victims, *Intern. Crim. Pol. Rev.*, no. 37(1950) 113.

GLAISTER, J. and J. C. BRASH, *Medico-Legal Aspects of the Ruxton Case*, Edinburgh, 1937.

GONZALES, T. A., M. VANCE, M. HELPERN and C. J. UMBERGER, *Legal Medicine, Pathology and Toxicology*, 2nd Ed., New York, 1954, p. 29.

HABERDA, A., Kriminelle Leichenzerstückelung, *Dtsch. Z. ger. Med.*, 10(1927) 242.

PIETRUSKY, F., Über kriminelle Leichenzerstückelung. Fall Denke, *Dtsch. Z. ger. Med.*, 8(1926) 703.

POLKE, J., Leichenzerstückelung mittels Papierschneidemaschine, *Kriminalistik*, 13(1939) 14.

SIMPSON, C. K., Studies in reconstruction, III. The Luton sack murder, *Intern. Crim. Pol. Rev.*, no. 2(1946) 6.

Suicide investigation

ANDEREGGEN, P., A propos de 273 tentatives de suicide par empoisonnement; Remarques statistiques et thérapeutiques, *Rév. Méd. Suisse Rom.*, 68(1948) 257.

BISCHOFF, M. A., Un cas curieux de suicide avec mise en scène de meurtre, *Ann. Méd. Lég. etc.*, 28(1948) 140.

BLENCH, T. H., An unusual case of suicide, *Acta. Med. Leg. et Soc.*, 1(1948).

BRANDENBURG, F., Selbstmord als vorgetäuschter Mord, *Kriminalistik*, 18(1944) 85.

BREBECK, Tödlicher Nackenschuss und doch Selbstmord, *Kriminalistik*, 16(1942) 124.

BRUNELLI, A. M., Crimenes y suicidios, *Rev. Crim. Pol. Cie.*, IX, no. 117(1949) 55.

DESBORDES, J. and J. LAURENT, Suicide chez un persécuté halluciné, *Ann. Méd. Lég. etc.*, 22(1942) 213.

DIECKMANN, SR., E. A., Is It Natural Death, Suicide of Murder?, Chapter 7, *Practical Homicide Investigation*, Springfield, 1961, p. 42.

GONZALES, T. A., M. VANCE, M. HELPERN and C. J. UMBERGER, *Legal Medicine, Pat hology and Toxicology*, 2nd Ed., New York, 1954.

GRADWOHL, R. B. H., *Legal Medicine*, St. Louis, 1954, p. 245.

HARRIS, R. I., *Outline of Death Investigation*, Springfield, 1962, p. 260.

KERR, D. J. A., *Forensic Medicine*, London, 1946, p. 103.

KERR, D. J. A., Forensic Medicine, III, Suicide, *Police J.*, 12(1939) 78.

LUDWIG, H., Vorgetäuschter Selbstmord, *Arch. f. Kriminol.*, 113(1943) 125.

MARTIN, F. W., Suicide, *Police J.*, 13(1940) 303.

SCHWARZ, F., *Probleme des Selbstmordes*, Bern, 1946.

SIMONIN, C., *Médecine Légale Judiciaire*, Paris, 1947, p. 794.

SÖDERMAN, H. and J. J. O'CONNELL, *Modern Criminal Investigation*, 5th Ed., New York, 1962, p. 274.

Bibliography to Chapter 13

BEDDOE, H. L., Problems of Identifying a Body, *Police*, 3(1959) 11.

BRUES, A. M., Identification of Skeletal Remains, *J. of Crim. Law, Criminol. and Police Sci.*, 48(1957) 551.

FAHLANDER, N., *Kriminalpolistjänst*, Karlshamn, 1950, p. 180.

GLAISTER, J., *Medical Jurisprudence and Toxicology*, 11th Ed., Edinburgh, 1962, p. 56.

GONZALES, T. A., M. VANCE, M. HELPERN and C. J. UMBERGER, *Legal Medicine, Pathology and Toxicology*, 2nd Ed., New York, 1954, p. 17.

GRADWOHL, R. B. H., *Legal Medicine*, St. Louis, 1954, p. 407.

HARRIS, R. I., *Outline of Death Investigation*, Springfield, 1962, p. 67.

KERR, D. J. A., *Forensic Medicine*, London, 1946, p. 41.

KROGMAN, W., *The Human Skeleton in Forensic Medicine*, Springfield, 1962.

LUCAS, A., *Forensic Chemistry and Scientific Criminal Investigation*, London, 1945, p. 313.

PONSOLD, A., *Lehrbuch der gerichtlichen Medizin*, Stuttgart, 1950, p. 130.

SASSOUNI, V., Cephalometric Identification – A Proposed Method of Identification of War-Dead by Means of Roentgenographic Cephalometry, *J. of For. Sci.*, 4(1959) 1.

SIMONIN, C., *Médecine Légale Judiciaire*, Paris, 1947, p. 727.

SIMPSON, C. K., *Forensic Medicine*, London, 1951, p. 6, 17.

SMITH, S., *Forensic Medicine*, London, 1945, p. 34, 37, 60.

SNYDER, LeM., *Homicide Investigation*, Springfield, 1950, p. 51.

Taking of finger prints

BUGGE, J. N., Ein interessanter Fall der Identifizierung einer Wasserleiche, *Kriminalistik*, 14(1940) 13.

BERANEK, S., Neue Fingerabdruck-Methode, *Kriminalistik*, 16(1962) 323.

BRIDGES, B. C., *Practical Fingerprinting*, New York, 1962.

CORR, J., Post Mortem Printing Under Difficult Conditions, *Finger Print Mag.*, 41, no. 8(1960) 4.

COWAN, M. E., Preparation of Fingers for Post Mortem Printing Following Extreme Deterioration, *Finger Print Mag.*, 41, no. 1(1959) 16.

CHERRILL, F., A new method of taking the finger prints of cadavers, *Intern. Crim. Pol. Rev.*, 6(1951) 205.

DAVIS, CH. A., A Method of Obtaining Finger Prints for Identification by Histologic Section, *J. of Crim. Law, Criminol. and Police Sci.*, 48(1957) 468.

ERIKSSON, S. A. and O. RISPLING, *Identifieringslärans grunder*, Stockholm, 1959, p. 80, 119.

FRITZ, E., Ein einfaches Verfahren zur Herstellung von Fingerabdrücken bei Mumifikation, *Dtsch. Z. ger. Med.*, 29(1938) 426.

HAMMOND, B. J., Fingerprints and the Ruxton Murder, *J. of Crim. Law, Criminol. and Police Sci.*, 43(1953) 803.

KOBABE, A., Fingerabdrucknahme bei unbekannten Wasserleichen mit vortgeschrittener Waschhautbildung, *Kriminalistik*, 10(1956) 364.

LIEBENBERG, I. J., Obtaining a print from a mummified finger, *Rev. Criminol. Pol. Techn.*, 3(1949) 293.

MERCER, J. T., Tanning of Murder Victim's Fingers Results in His Identification, *Finger Print Mag.*, 42(1961) 3.

O'HARA, CH. E. and J. W. OSTERBURG, *An Introduction to Criminalistics*, New York, 1949, p. 90.

PADRON, F., Necrodactylography, *Finger Print Mag.*, 45(1963) 3.

RISPLING, O., Avgjutning av plastiska fingeravtryck, *Nord. Krim. Tids.*, 25(1955) 144.

RISPLING, O., Säkring av fingerblommemönster från lik, *Nord. Krim. Tids.*, 26(1956) 11.

SCHLEYER, F., Zur Histologie der Waschhaut, *Dtsch. Z. ger. Med.*, 40(1951) 680.

SCOTT, W. R., *Fingerprint Mechanics*, Springfield, 1951, p. 167.

SIMONIN, C., *Médecine Légale Judiciaire*, Paris, 1947, p. 193.

Anon., Fingerprinting dead bodies, *Police J.*, 21(1948) 57.

Anon., Legible fingerprints obtained from mummified fingers, *FBI Law Enf. Bull.*, p. 18, Dec. 1946.

Anon., Problems and practices in fingerprinting the dead, *FBI Law Enf. Bull.*, p. 2, April 1949.

Photographing

CLAUSEN, L. S., Overhead photography in confined spaces, *Police J.*, 25(1952) 29.

FREI–SULZER, M., Photographie und Kriminalistik, *Kriminalistik*, 16(1962) 446.

MURPHY, B., *Police and Crime Photography*, New York, 1960.

RADLEY, J. A., *Photography in Crime Detection*, London, 1948, p. 40, 171.

SCOTT, C. C., Photography in criminal investigation, *J. of Crim. Law, Criminol. and Police Sci.*, 29(1938) 383.

TUTTLE, H. B., Color Photography in Police Science, *Law and Order*, 8(1960) 6.

Anon., *Photography in Law Enforcement*, Rochester, 1959.

Marks of trades or occupations

EULER, H., Tannlaegevitenskapelig medvirken i kriminalistikken, *Nord. Krim. Tids.*, 7(1947) 124.

FORBES, G., Some observations on occupational markings, *Police J.*, 19(1946) 266; *J. of Crim. Law, Criminol. and Police Sci.*, 38(1947) 423.

RONCHESE, F., *Occupational Marks*, New York, 1948.

SIMONIN, C., *Médecine Légale Judiciaire*, Paris, 1947, p. 716, 761.

SMITH. S., *Forensic Medicine*, London, 1945, p. 85.

SÖDERMAN, H., *Minnesbok för Kriminalpolismän*, Stockholm, 1943, p. 7.

Laundry marks

HAMILTON, D., A registry of laundry marks, *Police J.*, 25(1952) 190.

KIRWAN, W. E. and D. HARDY, Laundry and Dry Cleaner Marks, *BCI Bull. N.Y. State Police*, 21, no. 2(1956) 3.

MAISE, C. R., Organization of A Laundry Mark and Dry Cleaner's File, *J. of Crim. Law, Criminol. and Police Sci.*, 44(1954) 671.

O'HARA, CH. E., *Fundamentals of Criminal Investigation*, Springfield, 1956, p. 566.

RADLEY, J. A., *Photography in Crime Detection*, London, 1948, p. 90.

RADLEY, J. A., Fluorescent laundry marks, *Police J.*, 24(1951) 263.

YULCH, A., Modern methods of identification by laundry and cleaner's marks, *J. of Crim. Law, Criminol. and Police Sci.*, 37(1946) 105.

Anon., Connecticut to require laundry and cleaner mark registration, *Finger Print Mag.*, 33, no. 2(1951) 31.

Anon., Baltimore, Md. Police Department laundry mark file, *FBI Law Enf. Bull.*, 20, no. 11(1951) 2.

Watchmakers marks and jewelry

FEISTLE, H., Die Taschenuhr als Fahndungsmittel, *Krim. Monatsh.*, 10(1936) 34.

HAGANS, O. R., Watch Mark File is Useful Aid to the Investigator, *FBI Law Enf. Bull.*, 28, no. 7(1959) 6.

SÖDERMAN, H., *Minnesbok för kriminalpolismän*, Stockholm, 1943, p. 115.

WEBSTER, R., Jewellery and the Expert Witness, *Med. Sci. and Law*, 3(1963) 228.

Anon., Jewelry Scratch Mark File Maintained by Police, *FBI Law Enf. Bull.*, 32, no. 12(1963) 20.

Teeth

BASAURI, C., Forensic Odontology and Identification, *Intern. Crim. Pol. Rev.*, no. 145 (1961) 45.

DALITZ, G. D., Age Determination of Adult Human Remains by Teeth Examination, *For. Sci. Soc. J.*, 3(1962) 11.

DE CAŞTROVERDE, Y. and J. A. CABRERA, Forensic odontology and the identostomagram, *Intern. Crim. Pol. Rev.*, 7, no. 54(1952) 14.

ECHEVERRI, A., Odontological classification, *Intern. Crim. Pol. Rev.*, 10(1955) 139.

ERIKSSON, S. A. and O. RISPLING, *Identifieringslärans grunder*, Stockholm, 1959, p. 171.

GLAISTER, J., *Medical Jurisprudence and Toxicology*, 11th Ed., Edinburgh, 1962, p. 64.

GONZALES, T. A., M. VANCE, M. HELPERN and C. J. UMBERGER, *Legal Medicine, Pathology and Toxicology*, 2nd Ed., New York, 1954, p. 46.

GRADWOHL, R. B. H., *Legal Medicine*, St. Louis, 1954, p. 451.

GRANT, E. A., W. K. PRENDERGAST and E. A. WHITE, Dental identification in the Noronic disaster, *J. Can. Dent. Ass.*, 18(1952) 3.

HARRIS, R. I., *Outline of Death Investigation*, Springfield, 1962, p. 91.

LINDBOE, NORDTÖMME, H. and F. STRÖM, Exhumation and identification of the bodies of 183 persons executed by the Germans at Trandum (Norway), *Intern. Crim. Pol. Rev.*, no. 3(1946) 7.

PEDOUSSAUT, A., Identification in air accidents, *Intern. Crim. Pol. Rev.*, 7, no. 54(1952) 3.

PONSOLD, A., *Lehrbuch der gerichtlichen Medizin*, Stuttgart, 1950, p. 501.

RYAN, E. J., Identification through dental records, *J. of Crim. Law, Criminol. and Police Sci.*, 28(1937) 253.

SIMONIN, C., *Médecine Légale Judiciaire*, Paris, 1947, p. 749.

SIMPSON, C. K., *Forensic Medicine*, London, 1951, p. 24.

SMITH, S., *Forensic Medicine*, London, 1945, p. 74.

SNYDER, LeM., *Homicide Investigation*, Springfield, 1950, p. 53.

STEVENS, P. J. and S. W. TARLTON, Identification of Mass Casualties: Experience in Four Civil Air Disasters, *Med. Sci. and Law*, 3(1963) 154.

Sveen, R., Odontologisk identifikasjon av forulykkede, *Nord. Krim. Tids.*, 10(1940) 24; 11(1941) 122.

Symposium, The Human Dentition in Forensic Medicine, *J. of For. Sci.*, 2(1957) 377, 388, 401, 420, 428.

Anon., Identifizierung einer Leiche durch zahntechnische Überprüfung, *Kriminalistik*, 17(1943) 107.

Anon., Dental Chart Clue, *FBI Law Enf. Bull.*, 20, no. 2(1951) 18.

Taking a death mask

Clarke, C. D., The technic of molding and casting for medical science, *J. of Crim. Law, Criminol. and Police Sci.*, 26(1936) 928.

Clarke, C. D., *Molding and Casting*, Baltimore, 1938.

Gross, H. and R. L. Jackson, *Criminal Investigation*, 5th Ed., London, 1962, p. 282.

Kirk, P. L., *Crime Investigation*, New York, 1953, p. 290.

Nickolls, L. C., *The Scientific Investigation of Crime*, London, 1956, p. 112.

O'Hara, Ch. E. and J. W. Osterburg, *An Introduction to Criminalistics*, New York, 1949, p. 134.

Söderman, H. and J. J. O'Connell, *Modern Criminal Investigation*, 5th Ed., New York, 1962, p. 482.

Anon., Plaster Masks Give Police 3-D Views of Wanted Criminals, *Popular Mechanics*, 116(1961) 105.

Anon., Silicone – A New Material for Identification Work, *Finger Print Mag.*, 41(1960) 7.

Identification of a greatly altered body or skeleton

Büsing, C. W., Die Identifizierung einer 12 Monate alten Wasserleiche durch nachgewiesene Schwangerschaft im 5 Monat, *Dtsch. Z. ger. Med.*, 39(1949) 455.

Carmine, Antonio Vox, Un metodo segnaletico della sagoma cranio-facciale, *Minerva Medicolegale*, 73(1953) 197.

Chase, D. A. L., The case of the headless corpse. R. v. Vincent Silvera, *Police J.*, 27(1954) 205.

Clark, G., Urn-fields and vital statistics, *Antiquity*, no. 89, March 1949.

Clavelin, P., Considérations sur l'ostéometrie anthropo-médico-légale, *Ann. Méd. Lég. etc.*, 27(1947) 157.

Clavelin, P. and L. Dérobert, *Ostéométrie Anthropo-Médico-Légale*, Paris, 1946.

Clavelin, P. and L. Dérobert, L'Identification raciale déduite de l'étude ostéologique des membres inférieurs, *Ann. Méd. Lég. etc.*, 29(1949) 75.

Culbert and Law, Identification by comparison of roentgenograms of nasal accessory sinuses and mastoid processes, *J. Am. Med. Assoc.*, 88(1927) 1634.

Dechaume, M. and L. Dérobert, Les racines dentiares au cours de la carbonisation des cadavres, *Ann. Méd. Lég. etc.*, 27(1947) 81.

Euler, H., Über das Altern des menschlichen Zahnsystems, *Dtsch. Zahnärztl. Wochenschr.*, 43(1940) 393.

Forbes, G., The effects of heat on the histological structure of bone, *Police J.*, 14(1941) 50.

FÖRSTER, A. and H. J. GOLDBACH, Die histologische Differenzierung von Femurdia-
physen Neugeborener, Kleinkinder und kleiner Haustiere, *Dtsch. Z. ger. Med.*,
43(1954) 273.

GLAISTER, J., *Medical Jurisprudence and Toxicology*, Edinburgh, 1962, p. 66.

GLAISTER, J. and J. C. BRASH, *Medico-Legal Aspects of the Ruxton Case*, Edinburgh,
1937.

GONZALES, T.A., M. VANCE, M. HELPERN and C. J. UMBERGER, *Legal Medicine,
Pathology and Toxicology*, New York, 1954, p. 38.

GRADWOHL, R. B. H., *Legal Medicine*, St Louis, 1954, p. 407.

GUSTAFSSON, G., Betydelsen av enstaka tandfynd för identifiering vid olyckor och brott,
Nord. Krim. Tids., 16(1946) 89.

GUSTAFSSON, G., Åldersbestämning på tänder, *Nord. Krim. Tids.*, 17(1947) 73.

GUSTAFSSON, G., Microscopic examination of the teeth as a means of identification in
forensic medicine, *J. Am. Dent. Assoc.*, 35(1947) 720.

GUSTAFSSON, G., Age determinations on teeth, *J. Am. Dent. Assoc.*, 41(1950) 45.

HOLDEN, H. S. and F. E. CAMPS, Some notes on the examination of a human skeleton
found off the Essex coast, *Police J.*, 24(1951).

HOLDEN, H. S. and F. E. CAMPS, The investigation of some human remains found at
Fingringhoe, *Police J.*, 25(1952) 173.

HRDLICKA, A. and T. D. STEWART, *Practical Anthropometry*, Philadelphia, 1947.

KERR, D. J. A., *Forensic Medicine*, London, 1946, p. 41.

KREFFT, S., Zur Frage der postmortalen Farbveränderunger der Haare, *Dtsch. Z. ger.
Med.*, 44(1955) 231.

KROGMAN, W. M., Role of the physical anthropologist in the identification of human
skeletal remains, *FBI Law Enf. Bull.*, 12, no. 7; and no 8(1943).

KROGMAN, W. M., A problem in human skeletal remains, *FBI Law Enf. Bull.*, 17. no.
6(1948).

KROGMAN, W. M., *The Human Skeleton in Forensic Medicine*, Springfield, 1962.

LINDBOE, NORDTÖMME, H. and F. STRÖM, Exhumation and identification of the bodies of
183 persons executed by the Germans at Trandum (Norway), *Intern. Crim. Pol.
Rev.*, no. 3(1946) 7.

LUCAS, A., *Forensic Chemistry and Scientific Criminal Investigation*, London, 1945,
p. 314.

NOUSIAINEN, H., The discovery of a corpse at Valkeakoski, *Intern. Crim. Pol. Rev.*, no.
39(1950) 178.

ORELLI, VON W., A peculiar medico-legal expert examination. A corpse torn into pieces
by elephants, *Intern. Crim. Pol. Rev.*, no. 13(1947) 14.

PONSOLD, A., *Lehrbuch der gerichtlichen Medizin*, Stuttgart, 1950, p. 499.

PRINSLOO, I., The identification of skeletal remains, *J. For. Med.*, 1(1953) 11.

RÄMSH, R. and B. ZERNDT, Vergleichende Untersuchungen der Haverischen Kanäle
zwischen Menschen und Haustieren, *Arch. f. Kriminol.*, 131(1963) 74.

SAETTELE, R., Körpergrössenbestimmung menschlicher Früchte an Hand der Längern-
masse einzelner Skeletteile oder deren Diaphysen, *Dtsch. Z. ger. Med.*, 40(1951)
567.

SCHMIDT, G., Arsenbefunde in Leichenaschen, *Dtsch. Z. ger. Med.*, 43(1954) 245.

SCHOURUP, K., Expérience sur l'exhumation de cadavres vieux de 2 à 4 ans, *Acta Med. Leg. et Soc.*, 2(1949) 211.

SCHOURUP, K., Exhumation et identification des cadavres de prisonniers danois morts dans les camps de concentration allemands, *Acta Med. Leg. et Soc.*, 3(1951) 41.

SIMONIN, C., *Médecine Légale Judiciaire*, Paris, 1947, p. 728.

SIMONIN, C., Identification des corps des soldats américains inconnus, *Acta Med. Leg. et Soc.*, 1(1948) 382.

SIMPSON, C. K., *Forensic Medicine*, London, 1947, p. 19.

SIMPSON, C. K., Studies in Reconstruction, 1. The Baptist Church Cellar Murder, *Guy's Hosp. Reps.*, 92(1943) 74; *Med. Leg. J.*, 11(1943) 132; *Police J.*, 16(1943) 270.

SIMPSON, C. K., Studies in Reconstruction, 2. The Godalming 'Wigwam' Murder. Rex. v. Sangret, *Guy's Hosp. Reps.*, 93(1944) 67; *Police J.*, 17(1944) 212.

SIMPSON, C. K., Rex. v. John George Haigh. ('The acid-bath murder'), *Med. Leg. J.*, 18(1950) 38.

SMITH, S., *Forensic Medicine*, London, 1945, p. 60.

SMITH, S., Studies in identification and reconstruction, *Police J.*, 13(1940) 23; 14(1941) 368; 15(1942) 32.

SNYDER, LeM., *Homicide Investigation*, Springfield, 1950, p. 59.

STEWART, T. D., What the bones tell, *FBI Law Enf. Bull.*, 20, no. 2(1951) 2.

STEWART, T. D., Medico-legal aspects of the skeleton. I. Age, sex, race and stature, *The Laboratory Digest*, 15(1951) 2.

SVENSSON, A., Identifiering av ett skelettfynd, *Nord. Krim. Tids.*, 17(1947) 97.

SVENSSON, A., Ett skelettfynd, *Nord. Krim. Tids.*, 28(1958) 145–151.

THOMAS, F. and W. VAN HECKE, Autopsy of 65 persons shot by the Germans, *Intern. Crim. Pol. Rev.*, no. 25(1949) 16.

WASHBURN, S. L., Sex difference in the pubic bone, *Am. J. Phys. Anthrop.*, 6(1948) 199.

WASHBURN, S. L., Determination of the Sex of Skeleton Remains, *Proceedings of the American Academy of Forensic Sciences*, 1(1951) 40.

Anon., Skeletal remains provide means of identification, *FBI Law Enf. Bull.*, 20, no. 4(1951) 14.

Identification in catastrophes

BROWN, T. C., Medical identification in the Noronic disaster, *Finger Print Mag.*, 32, no. 6(1950) 3; *Proc. of the American Academy of Forensic Sciences*, 2(1952) 109.

CORR, J. J. JR., Post Mortem Printing Under Difficult Conditions, *Finger Print Mag.*, 41(1960) 4.

COWAN, M. E., Preparation of Fingers for Post Mortem Printing Following Extreme Deterioration, *Finger Print Mag.*, 41(1959) 3.

COWAN, M. E. and S. R. GERBER, Associated Evidence as a Means of Identification in Mass Disaster, *J. of Crim. Law, Criminol. and Police Sci.*, 44 (1953) 393.

GARRISON, H., Identification in disasters, *Pacific Coast Intern. Law Enf. News*, 15(1948) 5; *J. of Crim. Law, Criminol. and Police Sci.*, 40(1949) 246.

GERBER, S. R., Identification in Mass Disasters by Analysis and Correlation of Medical Findings, *Proc. of the American Academy of Forensic Sciences*, 2(1952) 82.

GONZALES, T. A., M. VANCE, M. HELPERN and C. J. UMBERGER, *Legal Medicine, Pathology and Toxicology*, 2nd Ed., New York, 1954, p. 17.

HARRIS, R. I., *Outline of Death Investigation*, Springfield, 1962, p. 263.

HOLMES, R. H., Identification of Battlefield Killed-in-Action, *Proc. of American Academy of Forensic Sciences*, 2(1952) 99.

PEDOUSSANT, A., Identification in air accidents, *Intern. Crim. Pol. Rev.*, 7, no. 54(1952) 3.

PIÉDELIÈVRE, R., L. DÉROBERT and SILVAIN, Organisation de la reconnaissance et de l'identification des corps des victimes d'accidents et de catastrophes lointains à l'institut médico-légal de Paris, *Ann. Méd. Lég. etc.*, 30(1950) 296.

SNYDER, LEM., *Homicide Investigation*, Springfield, 1950, p. 67.

STEVENS, P. J. and S. W. TARLTON, Identification of Mass Casualties: Experience in Four Civil Air Disasters, *Med. Sci. and Law*, 3(1963) 154.

STRÖM, F., Om fremgangsmåten ved identifikasjon av dödsofrene etter bombeangrep, *Nord. Krim. Tids.*, 13(1943) 153.

TEAUBEAUT, J. R., II, Problems of Identification in Military-Civilian Catastrophies, *Proc. of the American Academy of Forensic Sciences*, 2(1952) 105.

WAALER, E. and T. KRAMER, Om identifiseringen av individer som er omkommet ved bombe- og eksplosjonsulykker, *Nord. Krim. Tids.*, 15(1945) 73.

VOLLMER, R. M., Identification in the Cubana air disaster, *Finger Print Mag.*, 33, no. 10(1952) 15.

Anon., FBI Disaster Squad Stands Ever Ready To Give Assistance, *FBI Law Enf. Bull.*, 30, no. 4(1961) 17.

Bibliography to Appendix

ANDERSEN, A. C., Kriminalteknisk udrustning ved almindelige gerningsstedsundersøgelser, *Nord. Krim. Tids.*, 21(1951) 81.

ASCHER J., Magnetic Metals Detector Used in Crime Detection, *FBI Law Enf. Bull.*, 27(1958) 22.

BATSON, W. C., Thames Division, The London river police, *Intern. Crim. Pol. Rev.*, 6, no. 74(1954) 3.

CHERRILL, F., A new method of taking the finger prints of cadavers, *Intern. Crim. Pol. Rev.*, 6, no. 49(1951) 205.

DUBOWSKI, K., Organization of Forensic Chemical Laboratories in Non-Metropolitan Areas, *J. of Crim. Law, Criminol. and Police Sci.*, 51(1961) 575.

FAHLANDER, N., Kriminalteknisk utrustning, *Nord. Krim. Tids.*, 29(1959) 1, 25, 313.

FERRARI, M. J., Camden Police Mobile Crime Unit, *Police*, 7(1962) 72.

GROSS, H. and R. L. JACKSON, *Criminal Investigation*, 5th Ed., London, 1962, p. 91.

KELLY, J. J., Equipping and using a mobile crime laboratory, *FBI Law Enf. Bull.*, 24 (1955) 12.

KIRWAN, W. E., Underwater Activity, *BCI Bull. N.Y. State Police*, 26(1961) 1.

NICKOLLS, L. C., *The Scientific Investigation of Crime*, London, 1956, p. 1.

O'HARA, CH. E. and J. W. OSTERBURG, *An Introduction to Criminalistics*, New York, 1949, p. 21, 30.

OSTLER, R. D., A Scientific Scenes of Crime Kit, *Police J.*, 36(1963) 222.

PATTERSON, CH. E., Valuable use of portable police investigation kit, *FBI Law Enf. Bull.*, 25(1956) 22.

SCOTT, W. R., *Fingerprint Mechanics*, Springfield, 1951, p. 87, 91.

SKOUSEN, W. C., What About A Mobile Crime Lab?, *Law and Order*, 10(1962) 22.

WILSON, C. M. and M. E. O'NEILL, A homicide investigation kit, *J. of Crim. Law, Criminol. and Police Sci.*, 31(1940) 357.

WRIGHT, D. J., New Innovation for Using Police Dog – To Discover If Crime Had Been Committed, *RCMP Quart.*, 28(1962) 127.

ZMUDA, CH.W., Permanent magnet, *J. of Crim. Law, Criminol. and Police Sci.*, 41(1950) 113.

Anon., Field investigation kit, *BCI Bull. N.Y. State Police*, March 1942, p. 3. Dec.,

Anon., Equipment for developing latent fingerprints at crime scene, *FBI Law Enf. Bull.*, 1947, p. 19.

Anon., Keep evidence kits available for instant use, *FBI Law Enf. Bull.*, 21, no. 1(1952) 23.

General Bibliography

ANDRESEN, P. H., *The Human Blood Groups*, Springfield, 1952.

ANUSCHAT, E., *Waffenkunde für Kriminalisten und Polizeibeamte*, Berlin.

ASHLEY, C., *The Ashley Book of Knots*, New York, 1944.

BALLEISEN, CH. E., *Principles of Firearms*, New York, 1945.

BALTHAZARD, V., *Précis de Police Scientifique, Vol. I–III*, Paris, 1934–1936.

BALTHAZARD, V., *Précis de Médecine Légale*, Paris, 1944.

BATTLEY, H., *Single Finger Prints*, New Haven, 1931

BEBIE, J., *Manual of Explosives, Military Pyrotechnics and Chemical Warfare Agents*, New York, 1943.

BERGEN, W. and W. VON KRAUSS, *Textile Fiber Atlas. A collection of Photomicrographs of Old and New Textile Fibers*, New York, 1945.

BISCHOFF, M. A., *La Police Scientifique*, Paris, 1938.

BRAVERMAN, S., *The Firearms Directory*, New York, 1951.

BREND, W. A., *A Handbook of Medical Jurisprudence and Toxicology*, London, 1941.

BRIDGES, B. C., *Practical Fingerprinting*, New York, 1942.

BROOKES, V. J. and H. N. ALYEA, *Poisons. Their Properties, Chemical Identification, Symptoms and Emergency Treatments*, New York, 1946.

BROWNE, D. G. and A. BROCK, *Fingerprints. Fifty Years of Scientific Crime Detection*, London, 1953.

BURRARD, G., *The Identification of Firearms and Forensic Ballistics*, 3rd Edition, London, 1962.

BURRARD, G., *The Modern Shotgun, Vol. I–III*, London, 1947–1950.

CASTELLANOS, I., *Identifications Problems – Criminal and Civil*, New York, 1939.

CHAPEL, CH. E., *Fingerprinting. A Manual of Identification*, New York, 1941.

CLARKE, C. D., *Molding and Casting*, Baltimore, 1938.

CLAVELIN, P. and L. DÉROBERT, *Ostéométrie Anthropo-Médico-Légale*, Paris, 1946.

DAVIS, J. E., *An Introduction to Tool Marks, Firearms and the Striagraph*, Springfield, 1958.

DAVIS, T. L., *The Chemistry of Powder and Explosives*, New York, 1943.

DAY, C. L., *The Art of Knotting and Splicing*, Binghamton, 1947.

DETTLING, SCHÖNBERG and SCHWARTZ, *Lehrbuch der gerichtlichen Medizin*, Basel, 1951.

DIECKMANN, SR., E. A., *Practical Homicide Investigation*, Springfield, 1961.

DIENSTEIN, W., *Technics for the Crime Investigator*, Springfield, 1952.

DUNCAN, J. H., *An Introduction to Fingerprints*, London, 1942.

E. I. Du Pont de Nemours & Co., *Blaster's Handbook*, 14th Edition, 1958.

ELSE, W. M. and H. LINGEMANN, *Handwörterbuch der Kriminologie, Vol. I–II*, Berlin.

ERIKSSON, S. A. and O. RISPLING, *Identifieringslärans grunder*, Stockholm, 1959.

FAHLANDER, N., *Kriminalpolistjänst*, Karlshamn, 1956.

FARBER, S., *The Post-mortem Examination*, Baltimore, 1938.

F. B. I., *Classification of Fingerprints*, Washington, 1963.

FELSTEAD, S. TH., *Shades of Scotland Yard*, London, 1951.

FISHER, J., *The Art of Detection*, New Jersey, 1948.

FITZGERALD, M. J., *Handbook of Criminal Investigation*, New York, 1952.

FLOHERTY, J. J., *Inside the F.B.I.*, Philadelphia, 1943.

FRICKE, CH. W., *Criminal Investigation*, Los Angeles, 1945.

GLAISTER, J., *Hairs of Mammalia from the Medico-Legal Aspect*, Cairo, 1931.

GLAISTER, J., *Medical Jurisprudence and Toxicology*, Edinburgh, 1950.

GLAISTER, J. and J. C. BRASH, *Medico-Legal Aspects of the Ruxton Case*, Edinburgh, 1937.

GODDARD, C., *A History of Firearm Identification*, Chicago, 1936.

GODWIN, G., *Peter Kürten. A Study in Sadism*, London, 1945.

GONZALES, T. A., M. VANCE, M. HELPERN and C. J. UMBERGER, *Legal Medicine, Pathology and Toxicology*, 2nd Edition, New York, 1954.

GRADWOHL, R. B. H., Ed., *Legal Medicine*, St. Louis, 1954.

GRANT, J., *Science for the Prosecution*, London, 1941.

GRANT, J. J., *Single-Shot Rifles*, New York, 1947.

GROSS, H. and R. L. JACKSON, *Criminal Investigation*, 5th Edition, London, 1962.

GUNTHER, J. D. and CH. O. GUNTHER, *The Identification of Firearms*, New York, 1935.

HARLEY, D., *Medico-Legal Blood Group Determination*, London, 1944.

HARRIS, R. I., *Outline of Death Investigation*, Springfield, 1962.

HARRY, R. G., *Modern Cosmeticology*, London, 1946.

HATCHER, J. S., F. J. JURY and J. WELLER, *Firearms Investigation, Identification and Evidence*, Harrisburg, 1957.

HATCHER, J. S., *Hatchers Notebook*, Harrisburg, 1948.

HEFFRON, F. N., *Evidence for the Patrolman*, Springfield, 1958.

HRDLICKA, A. and T. D. STEWART, *Practical Anthropometry*, Philadelphia, 1947.

JOHNSON, M. M. JR. and CH. T. HAVEN, *Automatic Weapons of the World*, New York, 1945.

JOHNSON, M. M. JR. and CH. T. HAVEN, *Ammunition. Its History, Development and Use*, New York, 1943.

KERR, D. J. A., *Forensic Medicine*, London, 1946.

KIRK, P. L., *Crime Investigation*, New York, 1953.

KUHNE, F., *The Fingerprint Instructor*, New York, 1943.

LARSON, J. A., *Single Finger Print System*, New York and London, 1924.
LEIBIG, C., *Kriminaltechnik*, München–Berlin, 1937.
LIEHEM, A., *Die Kriminalpolizei*, Graz, 1935.
LITTLEJOHN, H., *Forensic Medicine*, London, 1925.
LOCARD, E., *La Police et les Méthodes Scientifiques*, Paris, 1934.
LOCARD, E., *La Criminalistique*, Lyons, 1937.
LOCARD, E., *Traité de Criminalistique, Vol. I–VII*, Lyon, 1930–1940.
LOCARD, E., *Manuel de Technique Policière*, Paris, 1948.
LOCHTE, TH., *Atlas der menschlichen und tierischen Haare*, Leipzig, 1938.
LOCHTE, TH., *Grundriss der Entwicklung des menschlichen Haares*, (Vol. 5 of ʻ*Beiträge zur Haut-, Haar- und Fellkunden*ʼ), Frankfurt, 1951.
LOUWAGE, F. E., *Cours de Police Technique et de Tactique de Police Criminelle*, Belgium, 1939.
LUCAS, A., *Forensic Chemistry and Scientific Criminal Investigation*, London, 1945.
MATHEWS, J. H., *Firearms Identification*, Madison, 1962.
MATTHEWS, J. M. and H. R. MAUERSBERGER, *Textile Fibers*, New York, 1947.
McHENRY, R. C. and W. F. ROPER, *Smith & Wesson Hand Guns*, Huntington, 1945.
MEIXNER, F., *Kriminalität und Sexualität*, Heidelberg, 1951.
MERKEL, H. and K. WALCHER, *Gerichtärztliche Diagnostik und Technik*, Leipzig, 1936.
MERKELEY, D. K., *The Investigation of Death*, Springfield, 1957.
MEYER, M., *The Science of Explosives*, New York, 1943.
MITCHELL, C. H., *The Scientific Detective and the Expert Witness*, London, 1931.
MORITZ, A. R., *The Pathology of Trauma*, Philadelphia, 1942.
MORLAND, N., *An Outline of Scientific Criminology*, Norwich, 1950.
MORRISH, R., *The Police and Crime Detection To-day*, London, 1946.
NEUREITER, PIETRUSKY and SCHÜTT, *Handwörterbuch der gerichtlichen Medizin und naturwissenschaftlichen Kriminalistik*, Berlin, 1940.
NICEFORO, A. and H. LINDENAU, *Die Kriminalpolizei und ihre Hilfswissenschaften*.
NICKOLLS, L. C., *The Scientific Investigation of Crime*, London, 1956.
Nitroglycerin AB, Gyttorp, *Synpunkter, som böra beaktas vid polisundersökningar efter sprängningsolyckor*, Nora, 1939.
O'HARA, CH. E., *Fundamentals of Criminal Investigation*, Springfield, 1956.
O'HARA, CH. E. and J. W. OSTERBURG, *An Introduction to Criminalistics*, New York, 1949.
OLSEN, A. L. and J. W. GREENE, *Laboratory Manual of Explosive Chemistry*, New York and London, 1943.
PARRY, L. A., *Criminal Abortion*, London, 1932.
PERKINS, F. M., *Elements of Police Science*, Chicago, 1942.
PIÉDELIÈVRE, R., L. DÉROBERT and G. HAUSSER, *Abrégé de Médecine Légale*, Paris, 1947.
POLSON, C. J., R. P. BRITTAIN and T. K. MARSHALL, *The Disposal of the Dead*, London, 1953.
POLZER, W., *Der Sachbeweis in der Kriminalistik*, München, 1938.
POLZER, W., *Leitfaden für kriminalistische Tatbestands-Aufnahme*, Graz–Wien, 1947.
PONSOLD, A., *Lehrbuch der gerichtlichen Medizin*, Stuttgart, 1950.
PROKOP, O., *Lehrbuch der gerichtlichen Medizin*, Berlin, 1960.

RADLEY, J. A., *Photography in Crime Detection*, London, 1948.

RADLEY, J. A. and J. GRANT, *Fluorescence Analysis in Ultraviolet light*, London, 1943.

RAMSEYER, A., *Schiess- und Waffenkenntnis für Polizeibeamte*, Basel.

RAWLING, S. O., *Infra-Red Photography*, London, 1943.

REIK, TH., *The Unknown Murder*, New York, 1945.

RHODES, H. T. F., *Forensic Chemistry*, London, 1946.

RHODES, H. T. F., *Science and the Police Officer*, London, 1933.

RHODES, W. F., I. GORDON and R. TURNER, *Medical Jurisprudence*, Capetown, 1945.

RIBEIRO, L., *Policia Scientifica*, Rio de Janeiro, 1934.

DE RIVER, P. J., *The Sexual Criminal*, Springfield, 1951.

ROBINSON, C. S., *Explosions. Their Anatomy and Destructiveness*, New York and London, 1944.

RODRIGUEZ, S., *La Idendificatión Humana*, La Plata, 1944.

RONCHESE, F., *Occuptional Marks*, New York, 1948.

RYFFEL, J. H., *Aids to Forensic Medicine and Toxicology*, London, 1943.

SANNIÉ, CH. and D. GUÉRIN, *Éléments de Police Scientifique, Vol. I–IV*, Paris, 1938–1940.

SAX, N. I., M. J. O'HERIN and W. W. SCHULTZ, *Handbook of Dangerous Materials*, New York, 1951.

SCHIFF, F. and W. E. BOYD, *Blood Grouping Technic*, New York, 1942.

SCHNEICKERT, H., *Der Beweis durch Fingerabdrücke*, Berlin, 1943.

SCHNEICKERT, H., *Kriminalistische Spurensicherung*, Berlin, 1944.

SCHWARZ, F., *Probleme des Selbstmordes*, Bern, 1946.

SCOTT, CH. C., *Photographic Evidence*, Kansas City, 1947.

SCOTT, W. R., *Fingerprint Mechanics*, Springfield, 1951.

SHARPE, P. B., *The Rifle in America*, New York, 1947.

SIMONIN, C., *Médecine Légale Judiciaire*, Paris, 1947.

SIMPSON, C. K., *Forensic Medicine*, London, 1951.

SIMPSON, C. K., *Modern Trends in Forensic Medicine*, London, 1953.

SJÖVALL, E., *Kompendium i rättsmedicin*, Lund, 1938.

SJÖVALL, E., *Rättsmedicin*, Stockholm, 1946.

SMART, R. C., *The Technology of Industrial Fire and Explosions Hazards*, London, 1947.

SMITH, S., *Forensic Medicine*, London, 1945.

SMITH, S. and J. GLAISTER, *Recent Advances in Forensic Medicine*, London, 1939.

SMITH, S. and W. G. H. COOK, *Taylor's Principles and Practice of Medical Jurisprudence*, Vol. I–II, London, 1948–1949.

SMITH, W. H. B., *Pistols and Revolvers*, Harrisburg, 1946.

SMITH, W. H. B., *Small Arms of the World*, Harrisburg, 1948.

SMITH, W. H. B., *Walther Pistols*, Harrisburg, 1946.

SMITH, W. H. B., *Mauser Rifles and Pistols*, Harrisburg, 1946.

SMITH, W. H. B., *Mannlicher Rifles and Pistols*, Harrisburg, 1948.

SMITH, W. H. B., *Rifles*, Harrisburg, 1948.

SMITH, W. H. B., *Gas, Air and Spring Guns of the World*, Harrisburg, 1957.

SNYDER, LE MOYNE, *Homicide Investigation*, Springfield, 1950.

STETTBACHER, A., *Spreng- und Schiesstoffe*, Zürich, 1948.

STOFFEL, J. F., *Explosives and Homemade Bombs*, Springfield, 1962.

SÖDERMAN, H. and J. J. O'CONNELL, *Modern Criminal Investigation*, 5th Edition, New York, 1962.
TEIGNMOUTH SHORE, W., *Crime and its Detection, Vol. I–II*, London, 1934.
THÉLIN, M.H., *Précis de Médecine Légale*, Lausanne, 1948.
TURNER, R. F., *Forensic Science and Laboratory Technics*, Springfield, 1949.
UNDERHILL, F. P. and T. KOPPANYI, *Toxicology*, Philadelphia, 1936.
WALCHER, K., *Gerichtlich-medizinische und kriminalistische Blutuntersuchung*, Berlin, 1939.
WEBSTER, R. W., *Legal Medicine and Toxicology*, Philadelphia, 1930.
WENTWORTH, B. and H. H. WILDER, *Personal Identification*, Chicago, 1932.
WHELEN, T., *Small Arms Design and Ballistics, Vol. I–II*, Plantersville, 1945–1946.
WHITE, H. P. and B. D. MUNHALL, *Center Fire Metric Pistol and Revolver Cartridges*, Washington, 1948.
WHITE, H. P. and B. D. MUNHALL, *Center Fire American and British Pistol and Revolver Cartridges*, Washington, 1950.
WHITE, H. P. and B. D. MUNHALL, *Cartridge Headstamp Guide*, Bel Air, Md., 1963.
WIENER, A. S., *Blood Groups and Transfusion*, Springfield, 1945.
WIETHOLD and HOLTER, *Leitfaden durch die Praxis der gerichtlichen Medizin*, Berlin.
WILSON, R. A., *Institute on Homicide Investigation Techniques*, Springfield, 1961.
WILSON, R. K., *Textbook of Automatic Pistols*, Plantersville, 1943.
VIVAS, J. R., *Dactiloscopia*, Caracas, 1943.

Periodicals

Acta Criminologiae et Medicinae Legalis Japonica, Japan.
Acta Medicinae Legalis et Socialis (*Acta Med. Leg. et Soc.*), Belgium.
Acta Pathologica et Microbiologica Scandinavica (*Acta Pathologica*), Denmark.
American Journal of Clinical Pathology (*Am. J. Clin. Path.*), USA.
American Journal of Medical Jurisprudence (*Am. J. Med. Juris.*), USA.
American Journal of Physical Anthropology (*Am. J. Phys. Anthrop.*), USA.
Annales de Médecine Légale, de Criminologie et de Police Scientifique (*Ann. Méd. Lég. etc.*), France.
Archiv für Kriminologie (*Arch. f. Kriminol.*), Germany.
Archive d'Anthropologie Criminelle (*Arch. d'Anthropol. Crim.*), France.
Archives of Pathology (*Arch. of Path.*), USA.
Archivio di Antropologia Criminale, Psichiatria e Medicina Legale (*Arch. Antrop. Crim.*), Italy.
Archivos de Sociedade de Medicina Legal e Criminologia de S. Paulo, Brasil.
Archivos de Insituto de Medicina Legal de Lisboa, Portugal.
Arquivos de Medicina Legal e Identificação (*Arq. Med. Leg. e Ident.*), Brasil.
Beiträge zur gerichtliche Medizin (*Beitr. z. gerichtl. Med.*), Germany.
Beiträge zur kriminalistischen Symptomatologie und Technik (*Beitr. z. krim. Sympt. u Technik.*), Austria.
British Medical Journal (*Brit. Med. J.*), England.

Bulletin, Bureau of Criminal Identification, New York State Police (*BCI Bull. N. Y. State Police*), USA.

Criminal Law Quarterly, England.

Deutsche Zeitschrift für die gesamte gerichtliche Medizin (*Dtsch. Z. ger. Med.*), Germany.

Die Neue Polizei, Germany.

Excerpta Criminologica, USA.

Federal Bureau of Investigation Law Enforcement Bulletin (*FBI Law Enf. Bull.*), USA.

Finger Print and Identification Magazine (*Finger Print Mag.*), USA.

Identification News, USA.

International Criminal Police Review (*Intern. Crim. Pol. Rev.*), France.

Journal of Forensic Medicine (*J. For. Med.*), Union of South Africa.

Journal of Forensic Sciences (*J. of For. Sci.*), USA.

Journal of The American Medical Association (*J. Am. Med. Assoc.*), USA.

Journal of Criminal Law, Criminology and Police Science, formerly Journal of Criminal Law and Criminology including the American Journal of Police Science (*J. of Crim. Law, Criminol. and Police Sci.*), USA.

Kriminalistik, Germany.

Kriminalistische Monatshefte (*Krim. Monatsh.*), Germany.

Kriminalistische Rundschau (*Krim. Rundschau*), Germany.

Law and Order, USA.

Medicine, Science and the Law (*Med. Sci. and Law*), England.

Minerva Medicolegale. Archivio di Antropologia Criminale Psichiatria e Medicina Legale (*Minerva Medicolegale*), Italy.

Nordisk Kriminalteknisk Tidskrift (*Nord. Krim. Tids.*), Norway.

Police, USA.

Polizei-Praxis, Germany.

Revista de Criminologia y Policia Cientifica (*Rev. Crim. Pol. Cie.*), Chile.

Revue de Criminologie et de Police Technique (*Rev. Criminol. Pol. Techn.*), Switzerland.

Revue Internationale de Criminalistique (*Rev. Intern. Criminal.*), France.

Royal Canadian Mounted Police Gazette (*RCMP Gazette*), Canada.

Royal Canadian Mounted Police Quarterly Review (*RCMP Quart.*), Canada.

The American Rifleman, USA.

The Analyst, England.

The Australian Police Journal, Australia.

The Gun Digest, USA.

The Fire and Arson Investigator, USA.

The Medico-Legal Journal (*Med. Leg. J.*), England.

The Forensic Science Society, Journal, England.

The Police Journal (*Police J.*), England.

The Scientific Police Institute Reports, Japan.

Subject index